Demand for and supply of periodic financial reports

Statement of comprehensive
Chapter 4: Revenue and exp

Balance sheet – assets
Chapter 5: Cash and receivables
Chapter 6: Inventories
Chapter 7: Financial assets
Chapter 8: Property, plant, and equipment
Chapter 9: Intangible assets, goodwill, mineral
              resources, and agriculture
Chapter 10: Applications of fair value

Balance sheet – liabilities
Chapter 11: Current liabilities and contingencies
Chapter 12: Non-current financial liabilities

Balance sheet – equity
Statement of equity
Chapter 13: Equities

Special topics
Chapter 14: Complex financial instruments
Chapter 15: Earnings per share
Chapter 16: Accounting for income taxes
Chapter 17: Pensions and other employee
              future benefits
Chapter18: Accounting for leases

Cash flow statement
Chapter 19: Statement of cash flows

Volume II

INTERMEDIATE ACCOUNTING

KIN LO | GEORGE FISHER

University of British Columbia   Douglas College

INTERMEDIATE ACCOUNTING

VOLUME 2

Pearson Canada
Toronto

Library and Archives Canada Cataloguing in Publication

Lo, Kin, 1970–
Intermediate accounting / Kin Lo, George Fisher.

Includes index.
Contents: v. 1. Chapters 1–10 — v. 2. Chapters 11–19.
ISBN 978-0-13-701337-1 (v. 1).— ISBN 978-0-13-701336-4 (v. 2)

1. Accounting. I. Fisher, George, 1957– II. Title.

HF5636.L6 2011   657'.044   C2010-907258-8

ISBN: 978-0-13-701336-4

Vice-President, Editorial Director: Gary Bennett
Editor-in-Chief: Nicole Lukach
Acquisitions Editor: Megan Farrell
Senior Developmental Editor: John Polanszky
Developmental Editor: Joanne Sutherland
Executive Marketing Manager: Cas Shields
Lead Project Manager: Avinash Chandra
Production Editor: Susan Bindernagel
Copy Editor: Kelli Howey
Proofreader: Susan Bindernagel
Compositor: MPS Limited, a Macmillan Company
Photo Researcher: Dawn du Quesnay
Permissions Researcher: Dawn du Quesnay
Art Director: Julia Hall
Cover and Interior Designer: Anthony Leung
Cover Image: Shutterstock

For permission to reproduce copyrighted material, the publisher gratefully
acknowledges the copyright holders listed here and throughout the
text, which are considered an extension of this copyright page.

Photo credits: page 392, Terasen Gas Inc.; page 437, THE CANADIAN PRESS/Ryan
Remiorz; page 474, CP PHOTO/Don Denton; page 509, Luis Garcia; p. 537, MARK
BLINCH/Reuters/Landov; p. 576, The Canadian Press Images/Francis Vachon; p. 613,
Adrian Wyld/TCPI/The Canadian Press; p. 651, Thinkstock; p. 689, THE CANADIAN
PRESS/Nathan Denette. Credits for exhibits, tables, and other material are gratefully
acknowledged within the text.

Excerpts from Financial Accounting: Assets [FA2 Exams] or Financial Accounting Liabilities
and Equities [FA3 Exams] published by the Certified General Accountants Association of
Canada © (2008, 2009 or 2010) CGA Canada, reproduced with permission.

Excerpts from the IFRS Framework and Standards are copyright © 2010
IFRS Foundation. All rights reserved. No permission granted to reproduce
or distribute.

1 2 3 4 5   15 14 13 12 11
Printed and bound in the United States of America.

*In memory of my mother, who did not have the benefit of schooling,
but gave me the freedom to question, unconditional support of my pursuits,
and the humility to know that there is always more to learn.*

Kin Lo

*My passion for teaching has been richly rewarded by many opportunities
including the privilege of co-authoring this text. I dedicate this book to my
family, friends, colleagues, and students who have
encouraged me along the way.*

George Fisher

ABOUT THE AUTHORS

Kin Lo, PhD, CA is an Associate Professor at the Sauder School of Business at the University of British Columbia. He holds the CA Professorship in Accounting established by the Institute of Chartered Accountants of British Columbia (ICABC). After receiving a Bachelor of Commerce from the University of Calgary, he articled at PricewaterhouseCoopers and subsequently earned his doctorate from the Kellogg School of Management at Northwestern University in Chicago in 1999. His research has been published in the most important accounting journals, including *Journal of Accounting Research* and *Journal of Accounting and Economics*, and he has served as an Associate Editor at the latter journal since 2003.

Since joining UBC in 1999, Professor Lo has taught extensively in intermediate-level financial accounting for undergraduates, as well as master and doctoral-level courses. He has coached numerous winning teams in regional, national, and global case competitions. His outstanding teaching has been recognized by the Killam Teaching Prize. Kin has also been a visiting professor at MIT Sloan School of Management and the Paul Merage School of Business at the University of California, Irvine.

Aside from research and teaching, Kin is also active in the professional accounting community, serving on provincial and national committees and contributing as a columnist to the ICABC's magazine *Beyond Numbers*. Professor Lo is currently a member of the Board of Evaluators for the Chartered Accountants' national Uniform Final Evaluation (UFE) and a member of the Academic Advisory Council for the Accounting Standards Board of Canada.

George Fisher, MBA, CGA is a faculty member at Douglas College, where he teaches financial accounting in the College's Bachelor of Business Administration program. He currently holds the additional title of International Coordinator. George has been associated with the Certified General of Accountants of BC and the Certified General Accountants of Canada for the past 10 years in a number of roles including authoring numerous courses and developing case questions for the Professional Applications 2 comprehensive examination. His publications include *Model Financial Statements*, *Corporate Finance Fundamentals (FN1)*, *Financial Accounting Assets (FA2)*, and *Financial Accounting: Consolidations and Advanced Issues (FA4)* for CGA-Canada.

BRIEF CONTENTS

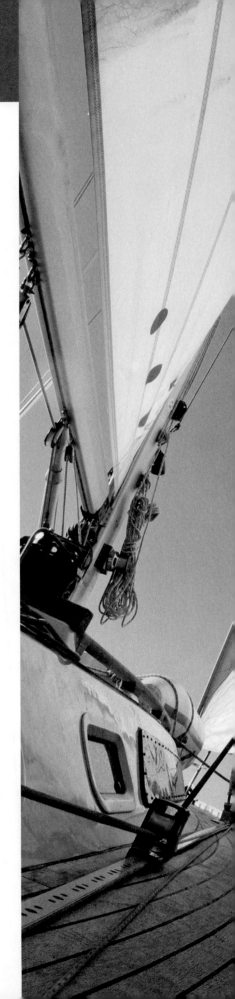

CONTENTS

PREFACE

"There is too much material to learn!" is a complaint commonly heard among both students and instructors of intermediate-level financial accounting. The current environment in Canada involving multiple accounting standards certainly adds to the problem. However, this sentiment was prevalent even before the splintering of Canadian generally accepted accounting principles (GAAP) in 2011. So what is the source of the problem, and how do we best resolve it?

Regardless of one's perspective—as an instructor of intermediate accounting, as a student, or as a researcher reading and writing papers—often *the problem of too much content is an illusion*. Instead, the issue is really one of *flow*, not just of words, but *of ideas*. Why does a class, research paper, or presentation appear to cover too much, and why is it difficult to understand? Most often, it is because the ideas being presented did not flow—they were not coherent internally within the class, paper, or presentation, or not well connected with the recipients' prior knowledge and experiences.

Connecting new ideas to a person's existing knowledge and efficiently structuring those new ideas are not just reasonable notions. Modern neuroscience tells us that in order for ideas to be retained they need to be logically structured to each other and presented in ways that connect with a person's prior knowledge and experiences.

OUR APPROACH

How can we better establish the flow of ideas in intermediate accounting? One way is to apply more accounting theory to help explain the "why" behind accounting standards and practices. Inherently, humans are inquisitive beings who want to know not just how things work, but also why things work a particular way. When students understand "why," they are better able to find connections between different ideas and internalize those ideas with the rest of their accumulated knowledge and experiences.

This approach contrasts with that found in existing intermediate accounting textbooks, which present accounting topics in a fragmented way, not only between chapters but within chapters. For example, how is the conceptual framework connected with other ideas outside of accounting? How do the components such as qualitative characteristics relate to the elements of financial statements? Fragmented ideas are difficult to integrate into the brain, which forces students to rely on memorization tricks that work only for the short term.

Also different from alternative textbooks, we do not aim to be encyclopedic—who wants to read an encyclopedia? This textbook is designed as a learning tool for students at the intermediate level, rather than as a comprehensive reference source they might use many years in the future. Being comprehensive burdens students with details that are not meaningful to them. At the rate at which standards are changing, books become outdated rapidly, and students should learn to refer to official sources of accounting standards such as the *CICA Handbook*.

ARE INTERMEDIATE ACCOUNTING STUDENTS READY FOR ACCOUNTING THEORY?

Most programs that offer an accounting theory course do so in the final year with good reason: concepts in accounting theory are difficult. Thorough exploration of these concepts requires a solid grounding in accounting standards and practices and higher-level thinking skills. However, not exposing students to these concepts earlier is a mistake.

Other management (and non-management) disciplines are able to integrate theory with technical applications. For example, when finance students study investments and diversification, the capital asset pricing model is an integral component. Finance students also learn about firms' capital structure choices in the context of Modigliani and Miller's propositions, the pecking order theory, and so on. Students in operations management learn linear programming as an application of optimization theory. Relegating theory to the end of a program is an exception rather than the rule.

Accounting theory is too important to remain untouched until the end of an accounting program. This text exposes students to the fundamentals of accounting theory in the first chapter, which lays the foundation for a number of *threshold concepts* (see Meyer and Land, 2003[1]).

THRESHOLD CONCEPTS

While by no means perfect, this textbook aims to better establish the flow of ideas throughout the book by covering several threshold concepts in the first three chapters. Threshold concepts in this case are the portals that connect accounting standards and practices with students' prior knowledge and experiences. As Meyer and Land suggest, these threshold concepts will help to *transform* how students think about accounting, help students to *integrate* ideas within and between chapters, and *irreversibly improve* their understanding of accounting. Introducing these concepts is not without cost, because threshold concepts will often be troublesome due to their difficulty and the potential conflict between students' existing knowledge and these new concepts.

The inside front cover identifies the threshold concepts and the layout of the chapters in both volumes of this text. Crucially, the first chapter in Volume 1 begins with the threshold concepts of *uncertainty* and *information asymmetry*. The need to make decisions under uncertainty and the presence of information asymmetries results in *economic consequences of accounting choice*. These concepts open up the notion of *supply and demand for accounting information*, which forms the basis of the conceptual frameworks for financial reporting (Chapter 2). Decision making under uncertainty leads to the issues surrounding the *timing of recognition* under accrual accounting (Chapter 3), which in turn lead to the concept of *articulation* between financial statements. The presence of information asymmetries leads to considerations of the *quality of earnings* (Chapter 3).

---

1. Meyer, J.H.F., and R. Land. 2003. "Threshold Concepts and Troublesome Knowledge 1: Linkages to Ways of Thinking and Practicing." In *Improving Student Learning: Ten Years On*, C. Rust (Ed.), Oxford, UK: Oxford Centre for Staff and Learning Development.

These concepts then resurface at different points in the remaining 16 chapters. For example, the concept of information asymmetry is fundamental to understanding the reasons that companies issue complex financial instruments (Chapter 14). Another example is the important role of the moral hazard form of information asymmetry in explaining why accounting standards do not permit the recognition of gains and losses from equity transactions through net income. A third example is the influence of uncertainty and executives' risk aversion on the accounting standards for pension plans, which allow the smoothing of income through the deferral and amortization of gains and losses. A fourth example is the application of information asymmetry to the accounting for leases (Chapter 18).

ACCOUNTING STANDARDS AND PRACTICES

Along with the unique approach of introducing and integrating theory through the use of threshold concepts, this text also provides thorough coverage of accounting standards and practices typically expected of an intermediate accounting course.

Following an overview of the four financial statements in Chapter 3 in Volume 1, Chapter 4 explores revenue and expense recognition to highlight the connection financial reporting has to enterprises' value creation activities. Chapters 5 to 10 in this book then examine, in detail, issues involving the asset side of the balance sheet.

The second volume begins with coverage of the right-hand side of the balance sheet in Chapters 11 to 13. Coverage in Chapters 14 to 18 then turns to special topics that cut across different parts of the balance sheet and income statement: complex financial instruments, earnings per share, pension costs, income taxes, and leases, respectively. Finally, Chapter 19 examines the cash flow statement, which integrates the various topics covered in Chapters 4 through 18.

Integration of IFRS

This is the first Canadian text written with International Financial Reporting Standards (IFRS) in mind throughout the development process, rather than as an afterthought. For example, we devote a separate chapter (Chapter 10) to explore issues surrounding asset revaluation and impairment because these issues cut across different asset categories under IFRS. The complete integration of standards in the development process adds to the smooth flow of ideas in and between chapters. Another example is Chapter 9's coverage of agriculture activities, a topic covered by IFRS but not by past Canadian standards.

Coverage of ASPE

While this text puts emphasis on IFRS, we do not neglect Accounting Standards for Private Enterprises (ASPE). Near the end of each chapter is a table that identifies differences between IFRS and ASPE. In contrast to other textbooks, we identify only substantive differences rather than every detail. In addition to the summary table, we carefully choose to discuss certain important differences in the main body of the chapters to create opportunities for understanding the subjective nature of accounting standards and the advantages and disadvantages of different

IFRS	ASPE Section
IAS 1—Presentation of Financial Statements	1400—General Standards of Financial Statement Presentation
	1520—Income Statement
IAS 33—Earnings per Share	No equivalent guidance

standards. For example, Chapter 8 discusses the different treatments of interest capitalization under IFRS and ASPE.

REFERENCE TO ACCOUNTING STANDARDS

Consistent with the threshold concepts described above, this textbook avoids treating accounting standards in a matter-of-fact manner. Ultimately, it is people who make accounting standards and it is important to analyze and evaluate the choices that standard setters make in order to understand the rationale behind the standards. Where appropriate, the chapters provide specific quotations from authoritative standards so that students begin to develop their ability to interpret the standards themselves rather than rely on the interpretations of a third party.

CHAPTER FEATURES

This text contains a number of features that augment the core text. We are mindful that too many "bells and whistles" serve only to distract students, so we have been selective to include only features that reinforce student learning. The result is an uncluttered page layout in comparison to competing textbooks. We firmly believe that clean design supports clear thinking.

Opening vignettes

Each chapter opens with a short vignette of a real world example that students will easily recognize and to which they will relate. These examples range from household names such as Bank of Montreal, Blackberry, and Telus, to car shopping and Christopher Columbus. As mentioned earlier, this connection to existing knowledge and experiences is crucial to learning new concepts. Each vignette serves to motivate interesting accounting questions that are later addressed in the chapter.

INTEGRATION OF LEARNING OBJECTIVES

To enhance the flow of material, each chapter fully integrates learning objectives from beginning to end. Each chapter enumerates four to six learning objectives that the chapter covers. The end of each chapter summarizes the main points relating to each of these learning objectives. We have also organized the problems at the end of each chapter to match the order of these learning objectives.

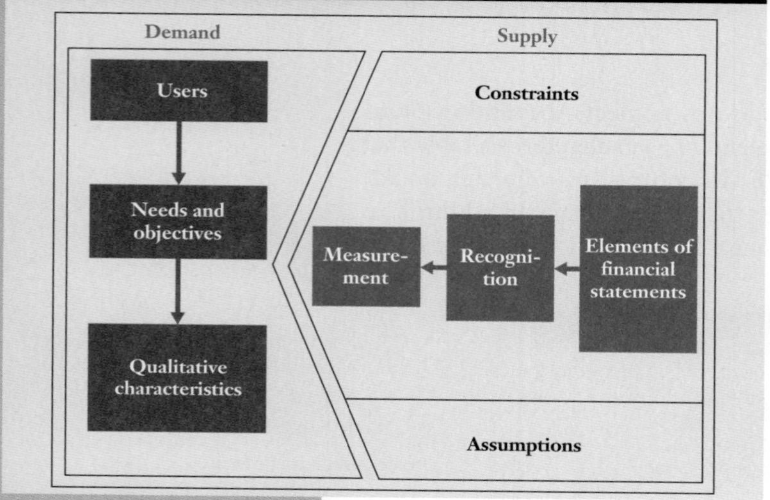

Charts and diagrams

We have chosen to use graphics sparingly but deliberately. These graphics always serve to augment ideas in a logical way rather than to serve as memory "gimmicks" that lack meaning. For instance, it has been popular to use a triangle to organize the conceptual framework for financial reporting. We eschew the use of this triangle because that shape has

Exhibit 2-2 Outline of a conceptual framework for financial reporting

no logical foundation or connection with the conceptual framework. Instead, we develop the conceptual framework from fundamental forces of supply and demand, so we provide a diagram that illustrates the interaction of those forces.

Feature boxes

When warranted, we provide more in-depth discussions to reinforce the core message in the main body of the chapters. These discussions often take the form of alternative viewpoints or surprising research results that serve to broaden students' perspectives on the issues. Compass icons identify these feature boxes to denote the different perspectives on various issues.

 TERMINOLOGY FOR TAX ASSETS AND LIABILITIES

Canadian GAAP prior to 2000 also used the term "deferred tax liability," because the term is consistent with the deferral method. The change to the accrual method in 2000, which has a balance sheet focus, resulted in a change in terminology to "future income tax" to de-emphasize the idea of deferral, which is an income statement concept. However, IFRS continues to use the terms "deferred tax liability" and "deferred tax asset." Given the different terminology used in different standards and during different time periods, accountants tend to use the two sets of terms interchangeably. In this text, we will use "deferred tax" asset or liability.

End-of-chapter problems

The end of each chapter contains many questions for students to hone their skills. We choose to use a single label—"Problems"—for all questions. This choice follows from our focus on learning objectives. We organized the Problems in the order of the learning objectives, and within each learning objective, according to the Problem's level of difficulty (easy, medium, and difficult). This approach allows students to work on each learning objective progressively, starting with easier questions and then mastering more difficult questions on the same learning objective. This approach is preferable to having students jump around from "exercises" to "discussion questions" to "assignments," and so on. Problems in the textbook that are coloured red are also available on MyAccountingLab. Students have endless opportunities to practise many of these questions with new data and values every time they use MyAccountingLab.

Go to MyAccountingLab at **www.myaccountinglab.com**. You can practise the indicated exercises as often as you want, and guided solutions will help you find answers step by step. You'll find a personalized study plan available to you too!

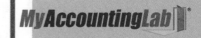

Cases

We have included mini-cases that are based on, or mimic, real business scenarios. The distinguishing feature of these cases is their focus on decision-making. While they are technically no more challenging than Problems, cases bring in additional real world subjective considerations that require students to apply professional judgment.

TECHNOLOGY RESOURCES

MyAccountingLab

Intermediate accounting demands both technical proficiency and the development of professional judgment. Instructors have found that *MyAccountingLab* reduces the amount of class time necessary to develop technical proficiency because students can hone their skills on their own time. Valuable class time then becomes more available for the discussion of cases and complex issues involving judgment and critical reasoning skills.

Features include:

- Personalized Study Plan: Pre- and Post-Tests with remediation to the eText help you understand and apply the concepts with which you need the most help.
- MyAccountingLab and textbook integration: The online content matches many of the end-of-chapter Problems to provide a consistent teaching approach.
- Interactive elements: Many hands-on activities and exercises let you experience and learn firsthand, whether it's with the Pearson eText in which you can search for specific keywords or page numbers, highlight specific sections, enter notes right on the eText page, and print reading assignments with notes for later review, or with other materials such as videos, glossary flashcards, and the interactive Accounting Cycle Tutorial.

CourseSmart for Instructors

CourseSmart goes beyond traditional expectations—providing instant online access to the textbooks and course materials you need at a lower cost for students. And even as students save money, you can save time and hassle with a digital eTextbook that allows you to search for the most relevant content at the very moment you need it. Whether it's evaluating textbooks or creating lecture notes to help students with difficult concepts, CourseSmart can make life a little easier. See how when you visit www.coursesmart.com/instructors.

CourseSmart for Students

CourseSmart goes beyond traditional expectations-providing instant, online access to the textbooks and course materials you need at an average savings of 60%. With instant access from any computer and the ability to search your text, you'll find the content you need quickly, no matter where you are. And with online tools like highlighting and note-taking, you can save time and study efficiently. See all the benefits at www.coursesmart.com/students.

Technology Specialists

Pearson's Technology Specialists work with faculty and campus course designers to ensure that Pearson technology products, assessment tools, and online course materials are tailored to meet your specific needs. This highly qualified team is dedicated to helping schools take full advantage of a wide range of educational resources, by assisting in the integration of a variety of instructional materials and media formats. Your local Pearson Education sales representative can provide you with more details on this service program.

SUPPLEMENTS

Instructor resources are password protected and available for download via http://vig.pearsoned.ca. For your convenience, many of these resources are also available on the **Instructor's Resource CD-ROM** (ISBN 978-0-13-237420-0).

- **Instructor's Solutions Manual.** Created by Kin Lo and George Fisher, this resource provides complete, detailed, worked-out solutions for all the Problems in the textbook.
- **Instructor's Resource Manual.** Written by Kin Lo and George Fisher, the Instructor's Resource Manual features additional resources and recommendations to help you get the most out of this textbook for your course.
- **TestGen and Test Item File.** For your convenience, our testbank is available in two formats. TestGen is a computerized testbank containing a broad variety of multiple choice, short answer, and more complex problem questions. Questions can be searched and identified by question type, learning objective, level of difficulty, and skill type (computational or conceptual). All Multiple Choice questions have also been written to conform to CGA specifications. Each question has been checked for accuracy and all are available in the latest version of TestGen software. This software package allows instructors to custom design, save, and generate classroom tests. The test program permits instructors to edit, add, or delete questions from the test bank; edit existing graphics and create new ones; analyze test results; and organize a database of tests and student results. This software allows for greater flexibility and ease of use. It provides many options for organizing and displaying tests, along with search and sort features. The same questions can also be found in a Test Item File available in Word format.
- **PowerPoint® Presentations.** Approximately 30-40 PowerPoint® slides, organized by Learning Objective, accompany each chapter of the textbook.
- **Image Library (on IRCD only).** The Image Library provides access to many of the images, figures, and tables in the textbook.

ACKNOWLEDGMENTS

During the development of this book, we obtained many helpful and invaluable suggestions and comments from colleagues from across the country. We sincerely thank the following instructors who either provided written reviews or participated in our focus group:

Anne Bigelow, University of Western Ontario
Walt Burton, Okanagan College
Robert Collier, University of Ottawa
Sandra Daga, University of Toronto, Scarborough
Pauline Downer, Memorial University of Newfoundland
Robert G. Ducharme, University of Waterloo
Allan Foerster, Wilfrid Laurier University
Gordon Hoyler, Vancouver Island University
Sepand Jazzi, Kwantlen Polytechnic University
Lesley Johnson, Sheridan College
Stuart H. Jones, University of Calgary
Glenn Leonard, University of New Brunswick
Raymond Leung, University of Fraser Valley
Robert Madden, St. Francis Xavier University
Marie Madill-Payne, George Brown College
Douglas Mann, Georgian College
Bruce McConomy, Wilfrid Laurier University
Fiaz Merani, Southern Alberta Institute of Technology
Joe Pidutti, Durham College
James Reimer, Lethbridge College
Doug Ringrose, Grant MacEwan University
Wendy Roscoe, Concordia University
David Sale, Kwantlen Technical University
Ramesh Saxena, Humber College and University of Guelph-Humber
Eckhard Schumann, McMaster University
Catherine Seguin, University of Toronto
Zvi Singer, McGill University
Dragon Stojanovic, University of Toronto
Desmond Tsang, McGill University

We would also like to acknowledge the assistance of the many members of the team at Pearson Canada who were involved throughout the writing and production process: Nicole Lukach, Editor in Chief, Business and Economics; Megan Farrell, Acquisitions Editor; John Polanszky, Senior Developmental Editor; Joanne Sutherland, Developmental Editor; Avinash Chandra, Lead Project Manager; Susan Bindernagel, Production Editor; Kelli Howey, Copy Editor; Victoria Naik, Media Content Developer; and Cas Shields, Executive Marketing Manager.

Finally, we are particularly grateful to Johan de Rooy for his contributions to the end of chapter Problems.

Kin Lo
George Fisher

INTERMEDIATE ACCOUNTING

CHAPTER 11

Current Liabilities and Contingencies

© 2009 Terasen Gas Inc.

LEARNING OBJECTIVES

After studying this chapter, you should be able to:

L.O. 11-1. Describe the nature of liabilities and differentiate between financial and non-financial liabilities.

L.O. 11-2. Describe the nature of current liabilities and account for common current liabilities including provisions.

L.O. 11-3. Describe the nature of contingent assets and liabilities and account for these items.

L.O. 11-4. Describe the nature of commitments and guarantees and apply accrual accounting to them.

In 2000, Terasen Gas Inc. (www.terasengas.com) built a natural-gas pipeline through the interior of British Columbia. To facilitate the construction, Terasen purchased millions of dollars in equipment. Terasen carefully structured its affairs to avoid paying the 7% provincial sales tax (PST) on the equipment purchase. Avoidance techniques included reselling the equipment to a trust it created for this purpose and leasing the equipment back.

In 2006, the BC government reassessed Terasen and ordered the company to pay an additional $37.1 million in PST, which through negotiation was reduced to $7.0 million including interest. In 2009, the BC Supreme Court found in favour of Terasen, setting aside the BC government's reassessment.

How do companies such as Terasen determine the amount to report as liabilities at the end of a fiscal year? What is required when the amount originally estimated is subsequently found to be incorrect? What do they do when the amount owed depends upon the outcome of a future event?

CONTENTS

A. INTRODUCTION

In simple terms, liabilities are obligations to provide cash, other assets, or services to external parties.[1] However, this perspective suffices for only simple transactions and balances. For anything other than rudimentary transactions and balances, we must look to the framework and specific standards in IFRS (International Financial Reporting Standards). As alluded to in the opening vignette

---

1. For example, Horngren et al., *Accounting*, volume 1, Canadian seventh edition, p. 12, provides the definition "liabilities are debts that are payable to outsiders."

regarding Terasen, substantive challenges can exist in determining the amount that must ultimately be paid, because a number of different factors can affect the value of the indebtedness. These factors include whether:

- the obligation is a financial liability or a non-financial liability;
- the market rate of interest is different from that recorded in the loan documentation;
- the market rate of interest has changed since the liability was incurred;
- there is uncertainty about the amount owed;
- the amount owed depends upon the outcome of a future event; or
- the obligation is payable in a foreign currency.

In this chapter and the next, we will examine how these (and a few other) factors affect the value of the indebtedness reported on the balance sheet.

The amount reported for liabilities is important to creditors, investors, suppliers, and other interested parties. Information on how much the company owes, to whom, and when the amounts are due is useful to stakeholders in their decisions to lend to the firm, to invest in the company, or to extend trade credit.

B. DEFINITION, CLASSIFICATION, AND MEASUREMENT OF LIABILITIES

L.O. 11-1. Describe the nature of liabilities and differentiate between financial and non-financial liabilities.

Financial statements convey information. For any communication to be effective, the receiver must understand the sender's message. Imagine that you are travelling in Italy and ask, in English, for directions from a passerby. If that person speaks English, he/she will comprehend your request and will probably assist you. However, a person who speaks only Italian will not understand you and will not be able to help. This example extends to communicating information of a technical nature, like accounting, even when a language barrier does not exist. For instance, if a physicist summarizes Einstein's theory of relatively as "$E = mc^2$; energy and mass are equivalent and transmutable," you will have little chance of understanding what the scientist is trying to communicate unless you know that E stands for energy; m for mass; and c for the speed of light. To enhance the quality of communication between preparers and users of financial statements, IFRS defines key terms in each of its standards. We will now discuss some of these definitions pertaining to liabilities.

1. Liabilities defined

Paragraph 49 of the IFRS Framework for the Preparation and Presentation of Financial Statements defines a liability as follows:

liability A present obligation of the entity arising from past events, the settlement of which is expected to result in an outflow of resources.

¶49. A *liability* is a present obligation of the entity arising from past events, the settlement of which is expected to result in an outflow from the entity of resources embodying economic benefits.

This definition includes three key elements as elaborated on in IFRS Framework paragraphs 60–63:

1. present obligation;
2. arising from a past event; and
3. expected to result in an outflow of economic benefits.

This is an "and" situation, as all three criteria must be satisfied. Present obligations are normally legally enforceable but can also be constructive in nature (i.e., obligations that arise from recurring practice). For example, a company that regularly repairs products after the warranty period to maintain good customer relations would report a liability for the amounts that are expected to be expended both in the warranty period and in the period afterward.

The past event criterion is fairly straightforward: present obligations normally arise from past events rather than a decision to do something in the future. For example, if you borrowed money from a bank last week—a past event—you incurred a liability and have a present obligation. If, however, last week you simply resolved to borrow money from the bank next week—a decision to do something in the future—you have not yet incurred a liability.

The expectation of an outflow of economic benefits is also relatively uncomplicated. For a liability to exist, you must have an expectation that you are going to give up something in the future to satisfy the creditor's claim. That "something" could be cash, other assets, or services.

2. Recognition

The definition of a liability set out above does not require that we know the precise amount of the obligation. Just as for assets, recognition on the financial statements requires a liability to be measured reliably (IAS 37 paragraph 14). However, IAS 37 suggests that it would be rare that a reliable estimate cannot be obtained. This presumption differs from the treatment of assets, which may or may not be measured reliably (e.g., research and development).

The fact that there is uncertainty over the amount or timing of payments does not imply that a liability cannot be reliably measured. For example, payments for warranty costs are uncertain in terms of both amount and timing, yet we would still record a liability for the estimated cost of fulfilling warranties. To identify liabilities that are uncertain in amount or timing, we use the label **provisions.**

> **provision** A liability in which there is some uncertainty as to the timing or amount of payment.

3. Financial and non-financial liabilities

In the introduction we suggested that whether an obligation is a financial or non-financial liability may impact how the debt is valued. A **financial liability** is a contractual obligation to deliver cash or other financial assets to another party. For example, a loan from the bank is a financial liability of the company that borrowed the money. Non-financial liabilities are obligations that meet the criteria for a liability, but are not financial liabilities. Non-financial obligations are typically settled through the delivery of goods or provision of services. For instance, magazines routinely sell subscriptions for one or more years. The publisher's obligation to the subscribers is to provide the magazine for the agreed-upon period. This is a non-financial liability as it will be settled by delivering the periodical, rather than paying cash or providing a financial asset. Warranties are another example of non-financial liabilities. Lastly, liabilities established by legislation such as income taxes payable and provincial sales tax payable are also non-financial liabilities as they are not contractual in nature. For example, if Terasen had lost the court challenge, its resultant PST payable would have been non-financial in nature.

> **financial liability** A contractual obligation to deliver cash or other financial assets to another party.

From an accounting perspective, it is important to distinguish between financial and non-financial liabilities as IFRS requires that some financial liabilities must be measured at their fair value rather than amortized cost.[2]

4. Current versus non-current liabilities

Current liabilities, the primary focus of this chapter, are obligations that are expected to be settled within one year of the balance sheet date or the business' normal operating cycle, whichever is longer. As most businesses' operating

> **current liabilities** Obligations that are expected to be settled within one year of the balance sheet date or the business' normal operating cycle, whichever is longer. Also includes held-for-trading liabilities.

---

2. Amortized cost is discussed in Chapter 12.

cycles are one year or less we will simply refer to current liabilities as those due in the following year. IAS 1 paragraph 60 normally requires that current liabilities be presented separately from non-current liabilities in the balance sheet.[3]

In addition to the length of time until maturity, certain financial liabilities classified as "held for trading" would also be reported as current liabilities.[4] In practice, relatively few companies elect to report financial liabilities as held for trading.

5. Measurement

The process of measuring a liability, both initially and subsequently, is determined to some degree by the nature of the obligation. Broadly speaking, we have three categories of indebtedness:

fair value The amount for which an asset could be exchanged, or a liability settled, between knowledgeable, willing parties in an arm's-length transaction.

a. *Financial liabilities held for trading* should be initially and subsequently measured at fair value. (Recall that **fair value** is the amount for which an asset could be exchanged, or a liability settled, between knowledgeable, willing parties in an arm's-length transaction.)

b. *Other financial liabilities* (i.e., not held for trading) should be initially measured at fair value minus the transaction costs directly associated with incurring the obligation, so this is no different from recording assets at their acquisition cost. However, subsequent to the date of acquisition, financial liabilities not held for trading are measured at amortized cost using the effective rate method.[5]

Determining the fair value of longer-term debt obligations is usually fairly straightforward. In many cases fair (market) values are readily available, as in the case for bonds issued in public markets. Determining the fair value of shorter-term liabilities can be more difficult, though, as normally these types of obligations are not actively traded (e.g., a trade payable to a supplier). Moreover, the time to maturity may be uncertain. Recognizing the inherent difficulties in accurately determining the fair value of short-term obligations, and given that the time value of money is usually immaterial in the short term, accounting standards permit many current obligations to be recognized at their maturing face value.

c. *Non-financial liabilities:* The measurement of non-financial liabilities depends on their nature. For instance, warranties are recorded at management's best estimate of the future cost of meeting the entity's contractual obligations.[6] In comparison, the liability for prepaid magazine subscription costs are valued at the consideration initially received less the amount earned to date through performance. For example, a publisher that received $75 in advance for a three-year subscription and has delivered the magazine for one year would report an obligation of $50 ($75 – $25).

---

3. The standard does provide that liabilities may be presented in order of liquidity when this style will result in more reliable and relevant information. Financial institutions typically use the liquidity style of presentation.

4. There are certain exceptions to this as set out in IAS 1 paragraph 71. Discussion of these exclusions is beyond the scope of this text.

5. The effective rate method is discussed in Chapters 7 and 12.

6. Part C of Guidance on Implementing IAS 37 establishes that "best estimate" refers to the present value of the obligation when the time value of money effect is material.

C. CURRENT LIABILITIES

This chapter includes a wide-ranging discussion of accounting for current liabilities (in this section), contingencies (Section D), and guarantees (Section E). Long-term liabilities will be the focus of the next chapter (Chapter 12). Before getting into the specifics, it may be helpful to think of these obligations in terms of the "big picture," specifically:

L.O. 11-2.   Describe the nature of current liabilities and account for common current liabilities including provisions.

- Current liabilities arise from past events: the amount to be paid is known or can be reasonably estimated.
- Contingencies arise from past events: the amount to be paid is determined by future events.
- Financial guarantees arise from contracts previously entered into: the amount to be paid is determined by future events.

The focus of this section is current liabilities, of which there are several that are common across almost all entities and a few that are relatively unique. Some of the more universal obligations include trade payables, notes payable, revolving credit facilities, taxes payable, provision for warranties, and deferred revenues. An entity generally uses its **current assets** such as cash to pay its current liabilities when due.

current assets   Assets that are expected to be consumed or sold within one year of the balance sheet date or the business' normal operating cycle, whichever is longer. Also includes assets held primarily for trading purposes.

Distinguishing liabilities that are current from those that are long-term is important because financial statement users often use this information. For instance, financial analysts often use the relationship between a company's current assets and current liabilities in the form of the current ratio (current ratio = current assets/current liabilities) or working capital (working capital = current assets − current liabilities).

The following discussion examines the pertinent features of current liabilities commonly encountered.

1. Trade payables

Trade payables and accruals are obligations to pay for goods received or services used. Trade payables are also commonly called accounts payable or trade accounts payable. Due to processing delays, not all invoices for trade payables will have been received at the end of a year (or another reporting period). In such instances, an enterprise needs to record an "accrued liability" for invoices not yet received but for which the enterprise owes an obligation. Trade payables and accrued liabilities are typically reported as one total on the balance sheet.

trade payables   Obligations to pay for goods received or services used.

As the amount owing is usually known with a high degree of certainty, there are few concerns that arise in accounting for trade payables. There are two issues that must be considered, however:

1. *Cut-off:* Caution must be exercised near the end of a reporting period to ensure that the obligation is properly reported in the period to which it pertains.
2. *Gross versus net:* Some suppliers offer discounts to encourage early payment by purchasers; for example, they may sell on terms of 2/10 net 30. These trade terms mean that buyers have 30 days to pay the face amount of the invoice (n/30), but they will be entitled to a 2% discount if they pay within 10 days (2/10). The question is, should a buyer report an obligation for the full value of a $100,000 invoice (for example), or the net amount of $98,000?

The answer is not clear-cut, and both methods are seen in practice. From a theoretical perspective the net method should be used, as $98,000 is the cost of the goods and $2,000 is the cost of financing the purchase for 20 days (from days 11 to 30). This approach is supported by IAS 2 Inventories, which indicates that the cost of inventory should exclude trade discounts. From a practical perspective, though, it is much easier to record invoices at their face value. Moreover, when the net method is employed and discounts are not availed of, entities must report a finance expense for "purchase discounts lost." Managers are loath to do this, as forgoing available discounts is usually considered a poor business practice.[7] Given these considerations, it is not surprising that businesses predominantly use the gross method, which can usually be justified on the basis of cost-benefit and materiality factors. Exhibit 11-1 contrasts the journal entries for the two methods using a hypothetical invoice of $100,000, assuming that the entity uses a perpetual inventory system.

Exhibit 11-1	Supporting journal entries for the gross and net methods for a $100,000 trade payable with terms of 2/10 net 30			
	Gross Method		**Net Method**	
Purchase date				
Dr. Inventory	100,000		98,000	
Cr. Trade payables		100,000		98,000
If discount taken				
Dr. Trade payables	100,000		98,000	
Cr. Cash		98,000		98,000
Cr. Inventory		2,000		
If discount not taken				
Dr. Trade payables	100,000		98,000	
Dr. Purchase discounts lost (an expense)			2,000	
Cr. Cash		100,000		100,000

2. Notes payable

Trade payables arise in the normal course of business. While a legally enforceable obligation, trade payables are not supported by a written promise to pay. In some instances, suppliers who provide credit terms over an extended period require the purchaser to sign a promissory note. Loans from banks and finance companies are invariably supported by a note payable as well. The note will normally detail the amount owed, the interest rate, the payment due date(s), and the security provided. The classification of notes payable as current, non-current, or a combination thereof is based on the payment due date(s). Notes payable can be interest bearing or non-interest bearing.

In the absence of transaction costs, interest bearing notes are recognized at the fair value of the consideration received, which is normally the transaction price.[8] Thus, if an enterprise issues a note to a supplier in exchange for $200,000 in inventory, a liability of $200,000 is recognized as set out in Exhibit 11-2.

Exhibit 11-2	Journal entry to record the issue of an interest bearing note at the market rate of interest	
Dr. Inventory	200,000	
Cr. Note payable		200,000

The fair value of non-interest bearing notes is normally estimated using other valuation techniques, the most common of which is discounted cash flow analysis.

---

7. While trade terms vary considerably, 2/10 net 30 is relatively common. The effective cost of not taking this discount on an annualized basis is 44.59% $\{[(1 + 2/98)^{365/20} - 1] \approx 44.59\%\}$.

8. This assumes that the interest rate stated in the note approximates the market rate of interest for similar transactions. If otherwise, the value of the note would be determined using the present value techniques similar to that discussed in conjunction with valuing non-interest bearing notes.

For example, if an enterprise issues an $80,000, one-year, non-interest bearing note in exchange for a luxury automobile of uncertain worth, you must determine the note's present value before recording the transaction. Assuming a market rate of interest of 5% for similar transactions, the enterprise would recognize an obligation as follows:

Exhibit 11-3	Journal entry to record the issuance of a non-interest bearing note for $80,000 due in one year	
Dr. Automobile	76,190	
Cr. Note payable ($80,000/1.05)		76,190

The Application Guidance (AG) accompanying IAS 39 provides for an exception to the requirement to use the fair value:

> ¶AG79. Short-term receivables and payables with no stated interest rate may be measured at the original invoice amount if the effect of discounting is immaterial.

A rule of thumb enterprises often employ is to use the face value for notes payable with duration of 90 days or less, and discount notes payable for a longer period. The aspect of materiality, though, remains a matter of professional judgment and must be applied on a case-by-case basis.

Having established the fundamentals, we will now illustrate accounting for a variety of notes payable from inception to liquidation in Exhibit 11-4.

Exhibit 11-4	Accounting for the issuance and retirement of notes payable[9]		
	Scenario 1	**Scenario 2**	**Scenario 3**
Face amount of note issued	$100,000	$100,000	$100,000
Date issued	May 1, 2010	May 1, 2010	May 1, 2010
Due date	June 30, 2010	May 1, 2011	May 1, 2011
Interest rate in the note	0%	0%	6% (payable at maturity)
Market rate of interest	6%	6%	6%
Consideration received	Inventory	Equipment	Cash
Company year-end	Dec. 31	Dec. 31	Dec. 31
Scenario 1 Journal entries			
Note issuance: Dr. Inventory	100,000		
Cr. Note payable		100,000	
Payment: Dr. Note payable	100,000		
Cr. Cash		100,000	
Comment: The obligation has been recorded at face value as the effect of discounting is immaterial.			
Scenario 2 Journal entries			
Issuance: Dr. Equipment	94,340		
Cr. Note payable ($100,000/1.06)		94,340	
At year-end: Dr. Interest expense ($94,340 × 6% × 245/365 = $3,799)	3,799		
Cr. Note payable		3,799	
Payment: Dr. Interest expense ($94,340 × 6% × 120/365 = $1,861)	1,861		
Cr. Note payable		1,861	
Dr. Note payable	100,000		
Cr. Cash		100,000	

(Continued)

9. For ease of illustration, assume that the company does not prepare interim financial statements.

Exhibit 11-4	Continued		
Scenario 3 Journal entries			
Issuance	Dr. Cash	100,000	
	Cr. Note payable		100,000
At year-end	Dr. Interest expense ($100,000 × 6% × 245/365 = $4,027)	4,027	
	Cr. Accrued interest payable		4,027
Payment	Dr. Interest expense ($100,000 × 6% × 120/365 = $1,973)	1,973	
	Dr. Accrued interest payable	4,027	
	Dr. Note payable	100,000	
	Cr. Cash		106,000

3. Credit (loan) facilities

Companies frequently arrange to borrow money on an ongoing basis by way of a line of credit with their financial institution to fund their day-to-day operations. The revolving line of credit can take many forms; a very common one is an overdraft facility in which the company can borrow up to an agreed-upon limit and pay interest only on the amount actually borrowed. Lines of credit are particularly useful for seasonal businesses that require financing that varies through the year according to the levels of sales and purchasing activity. The terms of a credit facility, including collateral (security pledged), interest rate and fees, financial covenants (promises), and other conditions, are formally documented in a credit agreement. Most revolving credit facilities are payable on demand, meaning that the company must repay the indebtedness if the bank issues a demand for repayment.

Outstanding lines of credit are a financial liability governed by the various standards covering accounting for financial instruments including IFRS 7 Financial Instruments: Disclosures, IAS 32 Financial Instruments: Presentation, and IAS 39 Financial Instruments: Recognition and Measurement. Due to the demand feature discussed above, the outstanding amount of the line of credit is reported as a current liability. These standards require that the terms and conditions of the credit facilities be disclosed. Exhibit 11-5 reproduces select disclosures made by Hyder Consulting PLC in its 2009 Financial Statements pertaining to its credit facilities.[10]

Exhibit 11-5	Excerpts from 2009 financial statements of Hyder Consulting PLC

Note 14 Financial Instruments

Liquidity risk

The Group has a policy of maintaining a blend of short and long term committed facilities designed to ensure there are sufficient funds available for operations. To manage working capital and funding requirements the Group has two principal revolving credit facilities in the UK, with HSBC (£20m) and Barclays (£18m) which expire in April 2012 and February 2013 respectively, a £1.5m overdraft with HSBC in the UK and other working capital facilities through local relationship banks in the countries that we operate in. In order to fund special contributions to the AGPS and incentive payments to members, who accepted the offer to transfer their liabilities out of the AGPS, the Group has 15 year term facilities totalling £9.1m with HSBC in the UK. All of the above facilities are unsecured. Total committed facilities amount to £47.6m.

(Continued)

10. Note that these disclosures pertain to Hyder's credit facilities, which include both current and non-current obligations.

Exhibit 11-5	Continued

Collateral

Contained within borrowings is a loan of £0.5m (2008: £0.8m), secured on property with a net book value of £3.1m (2008: £2.7m).

Available borrowing facilities

The Group has £35.1m of undrawn committed borrowing facilities, as at 31 March 2009. Of this amount £23.9m relates to the undrawn parts of two revolving credit facilities in the UK of £20m and £18m, which expire in April 2012 and February 2013 respectively. These facilities are unsecured. £6.9m relates to annual facilities in various jurisdictions and are subject to review within 12 months. A further loan balance of £3m can be utilised for special contributions and incentive payments to members of the AGPS and can be drawn down before 31 May 2009.

Source: Hyder Consulting PLC Annual Report 2009, *pages 71–73.*

4. Taxes payable

As set out in the opening vignette, Terasen was ultimately successful in avoiding having to pay provincial sales tax on the equipment in question. The company accomplished this by strictly complying with tax laws. Most entities are not so fortunate, however. Indeed, Benjamin Franklin (1706–1790) uttered these famous words, "In this world nothing can be said to be certain, except death and taxes," highlighting the difficulty in avoiding taxes. In Canada, we have many different forms of taxation, but by far the most common are sales taxes and income taxes.

Federal and provincial statutes require people and corporations to pay taxes on various activities such as the purchase of goods and services or earning income. As the obligations to pay are legislative in nature, rather than contractual, they do not fit the definition of a financial liability set out in IAS 32 paragraph 11 and hence are non-financial liabilities. A brief overview of the nature of these obligations follows.

a. Sales taxes

Depending on the province or territory they sell in and the nature of the good or service sold, vendors may be required to collect provincial sales tax (PST), goods and services tax (GST), or harmonized sales tax (HST). The vendor is required by law to charge the appropriate amount of tax on the transaction and remit the funds to the government at a later date.

Historically, the provincial governments levied PST and the federal government charged the GST. The result was that in many jurisdictions, businesses were required to collect two separate taxes on most sales. Subsequently, the government entered into agreements with some provinces to impose only one tax— the HST—and to split the proceeds on a predetermined basis. As at January 1, 2011 the rates applicable in the provinces and territories were:

	PST	**GST**	**HST**
British Columbia	—	—	12%
Alberta	—	5%	—
Saskatchewan	5%	5%	—
Manitoba	7%	5%	—
Ontario	—	—	13%
Quebec*	8.5%	5%	—
New Brunswick	—	—	13%
Nova Scotia	—	—	15%

(Continued)

	PST	GST	HST
Prince Edward Island**	10%	5%	—
Newfoundland	—	—	13%
Nunavut	—	5%	—
Yukon	—	5%	—

Notes:

* The Quebec Sales Tax (QST) is in substance harmonized with the GST but is collected separately. The QST is charged on the total of the sales price plus GST.

** In Prince Edward Island, PST is charged on the total of the sales price plus GST.

The concept of sales tax is fairly straightforward: the business charges and collects taxes on its sales and remits the tax portion to the government(s). However, the application is not as simple, for a number of reasons:

- Taxes are not uniformly applied to all sales. Some products are exempt from PST and others are exempt from GST.
- The regulations and rates in each province differ somewhat, including which products are exempt.
- Businesses are generally permitted to deduct the GST and HST paid on their purchases from the GST and HST collected and to remit the net amount owing to the federal government. (In the case of PST, goods purchased for resale are exempt from PST, but businesses generally cannot recover PST paid on other purchases.)

With the foregoing in mind, we have provided only a general overview here. Exhibit 11-6 illustrates the accounting for the collection and subsequent remittance of PST.

Exhibit 11-6	Journal entries to record the collection and payment of PST related to the sale of goods

Facts: Company A, which employs a perpetual inventory system, sells goods on account for $5,000 in Manitoba, which has a 7% PST. The cost of the goods was $3,000. The company subsequently remits the sales taxes collected to the government.

Note: The obligation to collect GST has been purposefully ignored.

Sale of goods		
Dr. Accounts receivable	5,350	
Cr. Sales		5,000
Cr. PST payable ($5,000 × 7%)		350
Dr. Cost of goods sold	3,000	
Cr. Inventory		3,000
Settlement of sales tax obligation		
Dr. PST payable	350	
Cr. Cash		350

With respect to GST and HST, businesses generally establish two general ledger accounts: GST or HST recoverable, and GST or HST payable. Assuming that the company is doing business in an HST jurisdiction, it debits the asset account HST recoverable for HST paid on purchases and credits the liability account HST payable for HST charged on sales. Typically, the HST collected exceeds the amount paid (because revenues usually exceed expenses), resulting in a current liability for the net amount, payable to the Canada Revenue Agency (CRA). It is possible that the recoverable amount exceeds the payable amount, for example when a company has paid HST on a large purchase of capital assets.

In these circumstances, the net amount would be reported as a current asset for the HST refund due from the CRA. Unlike the general prohibition against the netting of assets and liabilities under IFRS, netting out of the tax receivables and payables is acceptable because the relevant tax laws permit this offsetting.

In the foregoing example, for expository purposes we ignored the GST that the vendor would have had to collect. Exhibit 11-7 below is based on the same facts except that the vendor now also charges and remits the GST.

Exhibit 11-7	Journal entries to record the collection and payment of PST and GST related to the sale of goods

Facts: Company A, which employs a perpetual inventory system, sells goods on account for $5,000 in Manitoba, which has a 7% PST, and the GST rate is 5%. The cost of the goods was $3,000. The company subsequently remits the sales taxes and GST collected to the government.

Sale of goods		
Dr. Accounts receivable	5,600	
Cr. Sales		5,000
Cr. GST payable ($5,000 × 5%)		250
Cr. PST payable ($5,000 × 7%)		350
Dr. Cost of goods sold	3,000	
Cr. Inventory		3,000
Settlement of tax obligations		
Dr. GST payable	250	
Dr. PST payable	350	
Cr. Cash		600

A growing number of jurisdictions now charge HST rather than PST and GST separately; British Columbia and Ontario both adopted the HST on July 1, 2010. Exhibit 11-8 demonstrates the payment, collection, and remittance of the net amount of HST payable.

Exhibit 11-8	Journal entries to record the payment and collection of HST and the remittance of the net HST payable

Facts: Company B, located in Ontario, purchases $40,000 inventory on account. It subsequently sells goods that cost $30,000 on account for $50,000. Lastly, the company remits the net HST owing to the CRA. The HST rate in Ontario is 13%. The company uses a perpetual inventory system.

Purchase of goods		
Dr. Inventory	40,000	
Dr. GST recoverable ($40,000 × 13%)	5,200	
Cr. Accounts payable		45,200
Sale of goods		
Dr. Accounts receivable	56,500	
Cr. Sales		50,000
Cr. HST payable ($50,000 × 13%)		6,500
Dr. Cost of goods sold	30,000	
Cr. Inventory		30,000
Settlement of sales tax obligation		
Dr. HST payable	6,500	
Cr. HST recoverable		5,200
Cr. Cash		1,300

b. Income taxes

The federal government and all of the provinces require businesses to pay tax on the taxable income they earn. The amount of income tax owing is normally recorded as a current liability. However, there are additional amounts to be recorded in addition to the amount currently due. Chapter 16 discusses the accounting for income taxes in detail.

5. Warranties

There are two common forms of warranties: those provided by the manufacturer included in the sales price of the product and those sold separately, either by the manufacturer itself or by another party. Warranties sold separately are accounted for in accordance with IAS 18 *Revenue*, which was discussed in Chapter 4 and therefore is not repeated here. The following discussion focuses on manufacturers' warranties.

warranty A guarantee that a product will be free from defects for a specified period.

To facilitate the sale of their merchandise, manufacturers often include a guarantee that products will be free from defects for a specified period, agreeing to fix or replace them if they are faulty. This obligation, known as a **warranty,** is accounted for as a provision in accordance with IAS 37. Recall from above that a provision is an obligation that is uncertain in either amount or timing. Subsequent claims are charged against the provision, rather than expensed.

expected value The value determined by weighting possible outcomes by their associated probabilities.

We estimate warranty provisions using **expected value** techniques, which weight possible outcomes by their associated probabilities. The computations are similar to those used in the accounting for bad debts under the aging method. While neither the exact amount of the obligation nor the customers that will require warranty work are known with certainty, the provision represents a reasonable estimate of the amount that will ultimately be provided in goods and/or services.

Although we discuss warranties as part of current liabilities, warranties can often extend beyond one year. For example, manufacturers' warranties on automobiles often provide coverage for three, five, or even ten years. The expected obligation for the year following the balance sheet date is reported as a current liability, and the remainder would be classified as a non-current provision. The following exhibit illustrates the accounting for warranties.

Exhibit 11-9	Example of accounting for warranty provisions, accrual basis

Facts

- In 2010 Vanderhoof Automobile Manufacturing Inc. manufactured and sold $100,000,000 of specialty cars
- Vanderhoof provides a three-year warranty on each new car it sells
- Using expected-value techniques, Vanderhoof estimates that the cost of the warranty obligation will be 1% of sales in each of the first two years following the year of sale and 2% of sales in the third year following the sale
- In 2011, the cost to Vanderhoof of meeting its warranty obligations was $900,000 ($500,000 for parts and $400,000 for labour)

To recognize the provision in 2010

Dr. Warranty expense	4,000,000	
Cr. Provision for warranty payable		4,000,000
$100,000,000 \times (1\% + 1\% + 2\%)$		

To recognize partial satisfaction of the warranty obligation in 2011

Dr. Provision for warranty payable	900,000	
Cr. Parts inventory		500,000
Cr. Wage expense		400,000

(Continued)

Exhibit 11-9	Continued

Comments

- The expected value of all warranty costs is provided for in the year of sale in accordance with the matching principle
- At the end of 2010 Vanderhoof will report provisions for warranties on its balance sheet totalling $4,000,000 ((1% + 1% + 2%) × $100,000,000). $1,000,000 would be reported as a current liability and $3,000,000 as a non-current liability

If management's estimate subsequently proves to be incorrect, the change in estimate should be adjusted prospectively in the manner discussed in Chapter 3.

If warranty obligations are immaterial, the costs can be expensed as the enterprise incurs them. This is often referred to as the cash basis of accounting for warranties. The process is fairly straightforward, as illustrated in Exhibit 11-10.

Exhibit 11-10	Example of accounting for warranties, cash basis

Facts

- In 2010 Zander Lynn Inc. manufactured and sold $10,000,000 of steel shelving
- Zander Lynn provides a one-year unconditional warranty on all shelving it sells
- Due to the nature of the product, few clients have occasion to claim under the warranty and the amount of the claims are immaterial. Accordingly, Zander Lynn accounts for its warranty expenses using the cash basis
- During the year, the costs of Zander Lynn meeting its warranty obligations for replacement shelving totalled $10,000

To recognize partial satisfaction of the warranty obligation in 2010

Dr. Warranty expense	10,000	
Cr. Shelving inventory		10,000

6. Deferred revenues

Deferred revenue is a non-financial obligation arising from the collection of assets that have not yet been earned.[11] Many companies require a partial or full payment prior to delivery of the agreed-upon good or service. For instance, if you order a new car from the dealership, you have to make a down payment (deposit) before they will procure the car from the manufacturer. Similarly, when you book a cruise or flight, the travel agent collects the full fare from you before departure. Companies' reasons for requiring full or partial prepayment are many, but include encouraging performance on the purchaser's part and cash flow considerations. Whatever the motive, the accounting outcome is the same: the company has incurred a non-financial obligation referred to as deferred revenue, unearned revenue, or deposits.

Deferred revenues also arise from customer loyalty programs. This topic is discussed in the section that follows, because the nature of this obligation warrants independent coverage.

Like warranties, deferred revenues may have both a current and a non-current portion. For example, a publisher that sold a three-year subscription would report its obligation to provide the magazines in the year following the balance sheet date as a current obligation and the remainder of the commitment as a non-current liability.

When the good is delivered or the service provided, the seller recognizes revenue in the normal manner as per Exhibit 11-11.

deferred revenue A non-financial obligation arising from the collection of revenue that has not yet been earned.

---

11. See for example IAS 18 paragraph 14, which establishes that revenue is recognized when the goods are delivered.

Exhibit 11-11	**Accounting for deferred revenues**	
Facts		

- In December 2010 Kamlona Airlines Co. sold a $3,000 one-way ticket for a flight from Vancouver, BC to Repulse Bay, Nunavut for passage in January 2011 and a $3,500 ticket from Toronto, Ontario to Kugluktuk, Nunavut for passage in February 2011
- Kamlona does not maintain a customer loyalty program
- The passengers fly at the scheduled time

Journal entries		
To record the receipt of cash in December 2010		
Dr. Cash	6,500	
Cr. Deferred revenue		6,500
To recognize partial satisfaction of the obligation in January 2011		
Dr. Deferred revenue	3,000	
Cr. Revenue		3,000
To recognize satisfaction of the remaining obligation in February 2011		
Dr. Deferred revenue	3,500	
Cr. Revenue		3,500

7. Customer loyalty programs

Many businesses offer reward programs to encourage consumers to purchase their products on a regular basis. Examples include grocery stores and pharmacies that award points for purchases that can be saved up and redeemed for merchandise, and airline frequent flyer plans that award miles that can be exchanged for subsequent flights or other products.

Loyalty programs have become increasingly fashionable over the years. As their popularity has increased, many businesses have aligned themselves with reward programs offered by other parties. There are now three primary methods of offering awards:

1. Companies offer rewards that they supply themselves. This is fairly common in the airline and hotel industry but is not always the case.
2. Businesses offer rewards that are supplied by a third party. For example, Air Canada offers Aeroplan miles to its customers. Aeroplan, Canada's largest loyalty marketing program, is now owned and operated by an independent firm, Groupe Aeroplan Inc.
3. Firms offer customers the choice of receiving rewards from their own programs or those of a third party. For example, guests staying at Marriott hotel properties have the choice of receiving Marriott points or frequent flyer points on their favourite airline.

These programs give rise to future costs when plan members redeem their points. Enterprises need to record a liability for these future costs in accordance with IAS 18 paragraph 13 and IFRIC 13 *Customer Loyalty Programmes*. IFRIC 13 states the following:

> ¶5. An entity shall apply paragraph 13 of IAS 18 and account for award credits as a separately identifiable component of the sales transaction(s) in which they are granted (the 'initial sale'). The fair value of the consideration received or receivable in respect of the initial sale shall be allocated between the award credits and the other components of the sale.

Paragraph 6 additionally requires that award credits be measured at their fair value with the supporting Application Guidance (AG) providing specific direction on how the fair value may be determined. In many cases the fair value estimate should factor in the points that are not expected to be redeemed.

The accounting differs depending on whether a third party or the reporting entity itself supplies the rewards for the loyalty program.

- *Third-party rewards:* Accounting for third-party rewards does not pose any special challenges. The enterprise can record the full revenue for the sale that generates the reward points. The enterprise would also recognize an expense for the points awarded, and this expense is readily determinable based on how much it costs to purchase the points from the third party.[12] The rationale here is that the reporting entity has no further obligation to its customer after the sale.
- *Rewards supplied by the entity:* Using the frequent flyer point program as an example, when the airline sells a ticket it has two distinct components. The first is the customer's right to fly the specified route; the second is the customer's entitlement to miles that will be accumulated and used for future travel. From an accounting standpoint, these two sources of revenue must be accounted for separately, as the airline will earn the component parts at different points in time. We call these separate revenue events "multiple deliverables." Initially, the entire sales price of the ticket is unearned. The airline first earns the flight portion when the passenger takes the scheduled trip, and later earns the reward segment when the customer redeems the miles. Exhibit 11-12 illustrates accounting for rewards supplied by a hotel.

Exhibit 11-12	Accounting for customer loyalty programs, own rewards

Facts

- Frank's hotel maintains a customer loyalty program that grants members points for each hotel stay. Members can redeem these points, which do not expire, for future hotel stays.
- In 2010 the hotel received $5,000,000 in room-related revenue and awarded 50,000 points. The fair value of the points is estimated to be $50,000. Management expects that 80% of these points will be redeemed.
- In 2011, customers redeem 30,000 of these points.
- In 2012, customers redeem 10,000 of these points.

To recognize the room-related revenue in 2010

Dr. Cash	5,000,000	
Cr. Room revenue		4,950,000
Cr. Unearned revenue (award points)		50,000

To recognize award point revenue in 2011

Dr. Unearned revenue (award points)	37,500	
Cr. Award revenue		37,500

To recognize award point revenue in 2012

Dr. Unearned revenue (award points)	12,500	
Cr. Award revenue		12,500

Supporting computations

- To obtain the amount of reward revenue to recognize, the denominator is the number of points expected to be converted rather than the number awarded. The hotel expects 40,000 points to be redeemed (50,000 × 80% = 40,000), so the value per point is $50,000/40,000 points = $1.25/point.
- In 2011, 30,000 points redeemed × $1.25/point = $37,500
- In 2012, 10,000 points redeemed × $1.25/point = $12,500

---

12. A determination must be made as to whether the selling firm is acting as an agent for the third party or as a principal. A full discussion of this aspect is beyond the scope of this text.

Management's estimate as to the redemption rate may subsequently prove to be incorrect. If so, the change in estimate must be adjusted prospectively in the manner discussed in Chapter 3.

8. Other current liabilities

There are many other types of current liabilities, including certain obligations to employees. Rather than attempt to compile an extended list of other current liabilities, we shall discuss some liabilities that warrant special consideration given their unique characteristics.

a. Obligations denominated in foreign currencies

Accounting for obligations denominated in foreign currency, both current and non-current, is fairly straightforward and governed by IAS 21 *The Effects of Changes in Foreign Exchange Rates*. The standard requires:

1. translation of the foreign currency debt into the functional currency at the exchange rate evident on the transaction date;[13]
2. revaluation of the foreign currency obligation at the end of a period using the exchange rate at that time; and
3. recognition of the gain or loss from revaluation in the income statement.

Exhibit 11-13 illustrates the accounting for a foreign currency obligation.

Exhibit 11-13	Accounting for a foreign denominated liability	
Facts		
■ Langleed Corp. purchases inventory from a U.S.-based company on December 20, 2010. The invoice is for US$80,000. The spot exchange rate at the transaction date was C$1.00 = US$0.92.		
■ Langleed's year-end is December 31. The spot exchange rate at December 31, 2010 was C$1.00 = US$0.91.		
■ Langleed paid the obligation in full on January 20, 2011 when the spot exchange rate was C$1.00 = US$0.93.		
To recognize the purchase of inventory		
Dr. Inventory	86,957	
Cr. Trade account payable		86,957
US$80,000 × C$1.00/US$0.92 = C$86,957		
To revalue the obligation at period-end		
Dr. Foreign exchange loss	955	
Cr. Trade account payable		955
US$80,000 × C$1.00/US$0.91 = C$87,912; $87,912 – $86,957 = $955 (a loss)		
To revalue the obligation at payment date and recognize payment of the payable		
Dr. Trade account payable	1,890	
Cr. Foreign exchange gain		1,890
Dr. Trade account payable	86,022	
Cr. Cash		86,022
US$80,000 × C$1.00/US$0.93 = C$86,022; $86,022 – $87,912 = –$1,890 (a gain)		

---

13. The functional currency is that used by the company when it prepares its financial statements. For Canadian companies it is usually the Canadian dollar.

b. Maturing debt to be refinanced

Term loans by their nature have a maturity date. At maturity, the company must either repay the indebtedness or make arrangement with the lender to refinance the obligation. If a company does not reach an agreement to refinance the maturing debt before the balance sheet date, then the obligation is classified as a current liability irrespective of whether arrangements are made to refinance before the financial statements are authorized for issue. In the latter case, the fact that arrangements had been made to refinance the obligation subsequent to the balance sheet date should be disclosed as a non-adjusting event.

c. Non-current debt in default

If the borrower defaults on the terms of a non-current liability before the balance sheet date and as a result the loan becomes payable on demand (which is very common), then the obligation is classified as a current liability. If the lender agrees before the end of the reporting period to provide a grace period extending at least twelve months after the balance sheet date, then the loan can be classified as non-current. If agreement is reached after the statement date but before the statements are issued, the liability must be presented as a current obligation with the details of the grace period disclosed (IAS 1 paragraphs74–76). Exhibit 11-14 summarizes the treatment of maturing debt and loans in default.

Exhibit 11-14	Classification of maturing debt and loans in default

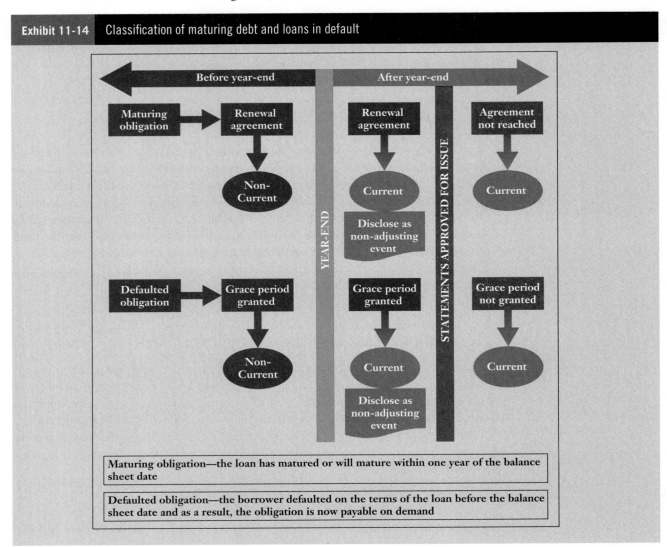

D. CONTINGENCIES

L.O. 11-3. Describe the nature of contingent assets and liabilities and account for these items.

contingency An existing condition that depends on the outcome of one or more future events.

probable The probability of occurrence is greater than 50%.

possible A probability of 50% or less.

In this section we address one of the questions posed in the opening Terasen vignette: what should companies do if the amount owed depends upon the outcome of a future event? The short answer is that they report a contingency. The word "contingent" simply means "depends upon," and a **contingency** is an existing condition that depends on the outcome of one or more future events. A contingency can involve either a potential future inflow or outflow of resources.

The nature of a contingency is that it involves one or more uncertain future outcomes. Thus, the probability of those future outcomes is crucial. IFRS refers to three ranges of probabilities that are important for accounting purposes.

- **Probable:** the probability of occurrence is greater than 50% (IAS 37 paragraph 23).
- **Remote:** is not numerically defined in IAS 37, but rather uses the common meaning of the word. This is a matter of professional judgment, with each case being decided on its own merits. The upper bound of remote would normally fall between 5% and 10%.
- **Possible:** This term is also not explicitly defined in IAS 37. However, given that IAS 37 defines "probable" as being greater than 50%, "possible" is 50% or less, but more than remote.[14]

Exhibit 11-15	The probability continuum		
Remote	**Possible**		**Probable**
0% 5–10%		50%	>50%

The fact that a contingency depends on a future outcome raises a second issue: are the amounts of the potential future inflows or outflows measurable with sufficient reliability? Amounts that cannot be reliably quantified pose obvious problems for accounting. However, IAS 37 paragraphs 25–26 assert that only in extremely rare cases will the entity be unable to determine a range of possible outcomes by which to estimate the extent of the obligation. The combination of measurability and probability of the future inflows or outflows jointly determines the accounting treatment for the contingency. We first address potential outflows followed by inflows.

1. Contingencies involving potential outflows

Contingent outflows can result in one of three accounting treatments: recognition of a liability through a provision, disclosure of a contingent liability, or no action. (We defer the definition of a contingent liability, as it can only be appreciated after the following discussion.) The following exhibit summarizes these three possible accounting treatments and the conditions that would lead to those treatments. The cells in the table have been labelled 1 through 6 for ease of reference below.

---

14. These are mutually exclusive categories for accounting purposes. In ordinary language, "possible" means anything that has non-zero probability, which includes both remote and probable events.

Exhibit 11-16	Accounting for contingent outflows			

		Likelihood		
		Remote	**Possible**	**Probable**
Measurability	Obligation can be reliably measured	No action required ⟨3⟩	Disclose contingent liability in the notes to the financial statements ⟨2⟩	Recognize provision for the obligation using expected value techniques ⟨1⟩
	Obligation cannot be reliably measured (rare)	No action required ⟨6⟩	Disclose contingent liability in the notes to the financial statements ⟨5⟩	Disclose contingent liability in the notes to the financial statements ⟨4⟩

a. Recognition of a provision

Refer to cell 1 in the top right corner of Exhibit 11-16. When the future outflow is probable and measurable, the enterprise should record a provision for the obligation. For example, a manufacturer that includes a warranty with its products would normally fall into this scenario. The reason is not that there is a greater than 50% probability that any single unit is defective, but that the probability that at least some of the products have a defect is likely to be greater than 50%; the company would also likely have sufficient information to estimate the cost of fulfilling the warranty. Thus, companies generally need to record provisions for warranties, as previously discussed in Section B.

If there is a range of potential outcomes, IFRS requires the use of expected value techniques to estimate the amount of the provision. In other words, the amount of the provision equals the weighted average of the potential outcomes. For example, suppose a company is facing a lawsuit, and its legal counsel believes that a loss is probable. Counsel estimates that there is a 70% probability that the courts will award $500,000 and a 30% probability that they will award $300,000. In this case, the company will record a $440,000 provision for the expected value of the loss (($500,000 × 70%) + ($300,000 × 30%) = $440,000).

b. Disclose as a contingent liability

When the probability of the contingent outflow is only possible but not probable, then the enterprise would not be required to recognize a liability. Instead, it would just disclose the fact that it has a contingent liability. This situation includes cells 2 and 5 in Exhibit 11-16. In addition, even in situations when the future outflows are probable but cannot be measured reliably, then the standard criterion for recognition fails; therefore such situations also result in the disclosure of a contingent liability. This is cell 4 in Exhibit 11-16.

While somewhat obtuse, IFRS defines a contingent liability as those contingent outflows that require disclosure. Specifically, IAS 37 states the following (with bracket references to Exhibit 11-16 added):

¶10. A **contingent liability** is

(a) a possible obligation that arises from past events and whose existence will be confirmed only by the occurrence or non-occurrence of one or more uncertain future events not wholly within the control of the entity; [i.e., cells 2 and 5] or

contingent liability Is (a) a possible obligation that arises from past events and whose existence depends on one or more future events; or (b) a present obligation that arises from past events that is not recognized as a liability because: (i) it is not probable that an outflow of economic resources will be required to settle the obligation; or (ii) the amount of the obligation cannot be measured with sufficient reliability.

(b) a present obligation that arises from past events that is not recognized because:

    (i) it is not probable that an outflow of resources embodying economic benefits will be required to settle the obligation; [i.e., cells 2 and 5] or

    (ii) the amount of the obligation cannot be measured with sufficient reliability. [i.e., cell 4]

It should be noted that this use of "contingent liability" in IFRS is narrower than a plain English interpretation of the two words, which is how Canadian standards have traditionally used the term.

c. No action required

When the probability of the contingent outflow is remote, then neither recognition nor disclosure is warranted. This outcome is reflected in cells 3 and 6.

Exhibit 11-17 sets out various situations that serve to illustrate how to apply the information just discussed and summarized in Exhibit 11-16.

Exhibit 11-17	Illustrations of accounting for contingencies

Scenario 1

Frieda Hengemolen slips on a wet floor in Fred Geotechnical's office, falls, and breaks her arm. Frieda sues Fred Geotechnical for $2 million in damages alleging negligence. Fred's law firm advises that the company is indeed liable and that the courts will likely award damages to the litigant. The lawyers suggest that it is very unlikely the courts will award the full $2 million sought as the normal settlement for this type of injury is $100,000 to $200,000. In their opinion, all payouts within this range are equally likely.

Required accounting: In this instance Fred Geotechnical provides for a $150,000 liability (the midpoint of the range) as payout is probable and can be reasonably estimated.

Scenario 2

Zulu Geothermal sues Roxanne Geothermal for patent infringement seeking $10 million in damages. The matter is a highly technical one that hinges upon the judge's understanding of the testimony of a number of scientists. Roxanne's lawyers are unsure as to the outcome but estimate the plaintiff's probability of success to be about 25%.

Required accounting: In these circumstances, Roxanne Geothermal discloses the details of the contingent liability in the notes to its financial statements but does not make provision for a liability as payout is estimated to be possible, but not probable.

Scenario 3

Angel Smith, who lives close to the ZMEX radio station, sues for $100 million in damages. Smith alleges that the radio waves broadcast by ZMEX caused his wife's brain cancer and ultimately led to her death. ZMEX's law firm advises the company that this is a nuisance lawsuit that is unlikely to succeed. They are confident that the courts will dismiss the case as being without merit.

Required accounting: Given these circumstances, ZMEX does not provide for a liability nor does it disclose the lawsuit in the notes to its financial statements. No action is required as the litigant's probability of success is remote.

In the context of contingent liabilities, think back to the opening vignette. The purpose of this anecdote was to illustrate the inherent uncertainty and imprecision in valuing obligations, particularly those for which the amount owing is determined by future events. During the period discussed, Terasen prepared its financial statements in accordance with Canadian GAAP, which differed from IFRS with respect to accounting for contingencies. Nevertheless, it is instructive to look at how Terasen accounted for this contingent liability during the still incomplete process. A synopsis follows:

- 2000–2005: Terasen believed that they owed nothing, a view subsequently upheld by the courts. Moreover, they had not yet been reassessed. As such, they neither provided for a liability nor disclosed a contingency.
- 2006: Terasen was reassessed and ordered to pay $37.1 million in PST and interest. Terasen disclosed a contingent liability in its notes to the financial statements stating that the amount had not been provided for as they did not believe that they were liable and as the company was appealing the settlement. The reduction in the assessment to $7.0 million in March 2007 was disclosed as a subsequent event.
- 2007–2008: Terasen disclosed a contingent liability of $7 million.
- 2009: Terasen was successful in its appeal to the Supreme Court of BC. They continued to disclose a contingency, however, as the Province of BC has been granted leave to appeal the decision to the BC Court of Appeal.

Throughout the continuing period of uncertainty, Terasen's note disclosure provides its readers with information to alert them to the possibility that the company may have to expense the reassessed amount at a later date. Note that if Terasen had been ultimately unsuccessful in its appeal, it would have to record an expense as an error requiring retrospective restatement or as a change in estimate, as discussed in Chapter 3.[15]

2. Contingencies involving potential inflows

The treatment of contingent inflows does not mirror the treatment of outflows just described. As discussed in Chapters 1 and 2, management has a tendency to overstate assets and income, so the principle of prudence (conservatism) requires stronger evidence before contingent inflows are recognized.

a. Recognition as an asset

Only in circumstances in which the future outcome is virtually certain will an enterprise be permitted to recognize a contingent inflow. IAS 37 does not define "virtual certainty," but in practice this is generally believed to fall in the range of 95% to 100% probable.[16] In contrast, a contingent outflow would be recognized as a provision if it is simply probable (i.e., greater than 50% likelihood).

b. Disclose as a contingent asset

When the contingent inflow is probable (>50%), IFRS recommends disclosing a contingent asset, which IAS 37 defines as follows:

> ¶10. A ***contingent asset*** is a possible asset that arises from past events and whose existence will be confirmed only by the occurrence or non-occurrence of one or more uncertain future events not wholly within the control of the entity.

> **contingent asset**   A possible asset that arises from past events and whose existence will be confirmed only by the occurrence or non-occurrence of one or more future events.

c. No action required

When the contingent inflow is not probable, the enterprise should neither recognize nor disclose such potential inflows.

---

15. It is difficult to be definitive as to whether this loss on appeal would result in an error or a change in estimate, because we do not have access to all the facts in the lawsuit. IFRS and the then-current CICA standards both provide that errors include misinterpretation of facts. Based on what we know, if Terasen ultimately lost, it could be because they misinterpreted the facts of the case (an error) or the court had a different interpretation of the law than the company's lawyers (a difference of opinion).

16. Page 1482, International GAAP 2009, published by John Wiley & Sons, Ltd., ISBN 978-0-470-74400-0.

To visualize a situation involving virtual certainty, consider the example of Zedco, in which Zedco is awarded damages by the courts and the judgment is no longer subject to appeal. This constitutes virtual certainty, as Zedco has a legally enforceable right to collect the monies due after the appeal process has been exhausted. Assuming that Zedco was awarded $1,000,000, the company would report a pre-tax gain on the settlement of lawsuit of $1,000,000.

When realization is probable, the contingency should be disclosed in the notes to the financial statements. Probable has the same meaning as that described above for the contingent liabilities subsection (i.e., a probability in excess of 50%).

To illustrate the disclosures pertaining to contingencies, Exhibit 11-18 sets out select disclosures made by British Airways PLC in its 2009 financial statements.

Exhibit 11-18	Excerpts from 2009 financial statements of British Airways PLC

British Airways 2008/09 Annual Report and Accounts, page 130

Note 37 Contingent liabilities

There were contingent liabilities at March 31, 2009, in respect of guarantees and indemnities entered into as part of the ordinary course of the Group's business. No material losses are likely to arise from such contingent liabilities. A number of other lawsuits and regulatory proceedings are pending, the outcome of which in the aggregate is not expected to have a material effect on the Group's financial position or results of operations.

The Group and the Company have guaranteed certain borrowings, liabilities and commitments, which at March 31, 2009, amounted to £185 million (2008: £173 million) and £498 million (2008: £448 million) respectively. For the Company these included guarantees given in respect of the fixed perpetual preferred securities issued by subsidiary undertakings.

The Group is involved in certain claims and litigation related to its operations. In the opinion of management, liabilities, if any, arising from these claims and litigation will not have a material adverse effect on the Group's consolidated financial position or results of operations. The Group files income tax returns in many jurisdictions throughout the world. Various tax authorities are currently examining the Group's income tax returns. Tax returns contain matters that could be subject to differing interpretations of applicable tax laws and regulations and the resolution of tax positions through negotiations with relevant tax authorities, or through litigation, can take several years to complete. While it is difficult to predict the ultimate outcome in some cases, the Group does not anticipate that there will be any material impact on the Group's financial position or results of operations.

3. Treatment of contingencies under ASPE

Similar to IFRS, ASPE treats contingent inflows differently from contingent outflows. However, ASPE (Section 3290) uses a different range of probabilities for future events. Instead of "probable" ASPE uses the word "likely," which is often interpreted as a probability around 70%. Another difference relates to the terms used to describe contingent inflows and outflows. Whereas IFRS uses terms focused on the balance sheet (contingent assets and liabilities), ASPE focuses on the income statement (contingent gains and losses).

For example, if an enterprise determines that there is an 80% chance of losing a lawsuit, ASPE would require recognition of this contingent loss in the financial statements. If the probability is only 60%, the enterprise would disclose that contingent loss. In this latter case, IFRS would require recognition of a provision because 60% is within the meaning of probable.

A third difference relates to instances when the enterprise is required to recognize a contingent loss and there is a range of estimates for the dollar amount of contingent outflows. Within this range, if there is one estimate that is most probable, the enterprise would use that estimate. However, when no one estimate is better than any other in the range, the enterprise would only need to recognize a contingent loss for the minimum in the range and disclose the remainder. In contrast, IFRS would require using the expected value in the range as discussed previously.

E. COMMITMENTS AND GUARANTEES

1. Commitments

Companies enter into legally binding contracts, both oral and written, on an ongoing basis. Many of these are mutually unexecuted contracts in that neither party has yet completed any part of the agreement. You may recall from your introductory financial accounting course that we do not report the assets and liabilities that will eventually arise from mutually unexecuted contracts until they meet the IFRS criteria for these items (either assets or liabilities). However, this does not mean that enterprises can ignore mutually unexecuted contracts for accounting purposes. Since commitments require companies to do certain things in the future, users of financial statements should be made aware of these future obligations. Consistent with this demand for information, accounting standards require companies to disclose certain commitments in the notes to the financial statements and to explicitly recognize other commitments on the balance sheet.

> **L.O. 11-4.** Describe the nature of commitments and guarantees and apply accrual accounting to them.

If an enterprise commits to buy property, plant, and equipment, it must disclose this fact (IAS 16 paragraph 74). This requirement applies equally to mutually unexecuted and partially executed contracts.

IAS 37 paragraphs 66–69 require companies to recognize the cost of onerous contracts on the balance sheet. Briefly, an **onerous contract** is one in which the unavoidable costs of fulfilling the contract exceed the benefits expected to be received. Note that the comparison uses the expected future benefits to be received from the goods or services acquired in the contract rather than the current market value of the item. Accordingly, a contract to buy assets for more than the current market price is not necessarily onerous, because the future benefit could be higher.

> **onerous contract** A contract in which the unavoidable costs of fulfilling it exceed the benefits expected to be received.

Exhibit 11-19 illustrates how a drop in the market price may or may not lead to an onerous contract, and whether a liability needs to be recognized in the financial statements.

Exhibit 11-19	Example of onerous contracts

Facts:

- Zeppy Distributors Inc. entered into a non-cancellable contract to buy 100,000 litres of paint for $4 per litre from the manufacturers for resale to retail outlets. Zeppy intends to resell the paint at $5 per litre as it typically charges a 25% mark-up.

- Subsequent to the contract being entered into, and before delivery is taken, the manufacturer reduces the price to $3 per litre due to weak demand.

- In situation 1, Zeppy must reduce the resale price to $3.75 per litre (the current market price plus the 25% mark-up) in order to remain competitive.

- In situation 2, Zeppy is able to maintain the resale price at $5.00 per litre as it is the sole distributor of the product.

(Continued)

Exhibit 11-19	Continued	
	Situation 1	**Situation 2**
Expected economic benefit	100,000 × $3.75 = $375,000	100,000 × $5.00 = $500,000
Unavoidable costs	100,000 × $4.00 = $400,000	100,000 × $4.00 = $400,000
Profit/(loss)	$(25,000)	$100,000
Result	Onerous contract for which the expected loss must be provided	Non-onerous contract

Situation 1 would require the following journal entry:

Dr. Loss on onerous contract	25,000	
Cr. Provision for loss on onerous contract (a liability)		25,000

2. Guarantees

IFRS includes guidance with respect to the measurement and disclosure of guarantees. Guarantees come in many forms, including financial guarantees, performance guarantees, indemnities, and letters of credit. An extended discussion of the various types of indemnities and how to account for each is beyond the scope of this text. However, the following provides a brief discussion of accounting for financial guarantee contracts, and Chapter 14 considers guarantees that meet the definition of a derivative financial instrument.

financial guarantee contract A contract that requires the issuer to make specified payments to reimburse the holder for a loss it incurs because a specified debtor fails to make payment when due.

IAS 39 defines a **financial guarantee contract** as:

> ¶9. . . . a contract that requires the issuer to make specified payments to reimburse the holder for a loss it incurs because a specified debtor fails to make payment when due in accordance with the original or modified terms of a debt instrument.

A very common form of guarantee, particularly for two companies under common control, involves one entity (company A) guaranteeing the bank loans of another entity (company B). The essence of the commitment is that if company B defaults upon the loan, company A will pay the creditor the principal and interest due. For accounting purposes, the guarantor (company A) must initially recognize a liability for the fair value of the guarantee of company B's indebtedness (IAS 39 paragraph 48).[17] Company A must also disclose details of the guarantee in accordance with IFRS 7:

> ¶B10(c) [An entity shall disclose] the maximum exposure to credit risk [from granting financial guarantees, which] is the maximum amount the entity could have to pay if the guarantee is called on, which may be significantly greater than the amount recognized as a liability.

To illustrate the accounting for guarantees, Exhibit 11-20 includes selected disclosures made by BT Group PLC in its 2009 financial statements.

Exhibit 11-20	Excerpts from the 2009 financial statements of BT Group PLC

Financial guarantees

Financial guarantees are recognized initially at fair value plus transaction costs and subsequently measured at the higher of the amount determined in accordance with the accounting policy relating to provisions and the amount initially determined less, when appropriate, cumulative amortization. (p. 84)

(Continued)

---

17. Subsequently, the guarantee is measured at the higher of the best estimate to settle and the remaining provision recorded in the financial statements. Discussion of this point is beyond the scope of this text.

Exhibit 11-20	Continued

The group has cross undertaking guarantee facilities across certain bank accounts which allow a legally enforceable right of set off of the relevant cash and overdraft balances on bank accounts included within each scheme. Included within overdrafts at 31 March 2009 were balances of £160m (2008: £256m) which had a legally enforceable right of set off against cash balances of £96m (2008: £112m). These balances have not been netted above as settlement is not intended to take place simultaneously or on a net basis. (p. 102)

BT Group PLC Annual Report and Form 20-F

F. PRESENTATION AND DISCLOSURE

Throughout the chapter we have discussed some of the more important presentation and disclosure requirements for current liabilities. The disclosure requirements for liabilities, particularly financial liabilities, are quite complex. Indeed, these wide-ranging requirements are one of the main reasons why the notes to the financial statements of publicly accountable enterprises (PAEs) are so extensive, often in excess of 100 pages!

Disclosure standards that must be observed include the following:

- IAS 1 Presentation of Financial Statements;
- IAS 32 Financial Instruments: Presentation;
- IAS 37 Provisions, Contingent Liabilities and Contingent Assets;
- IAS 39 Financial Instruments: Recognition and Measurement; and
- IFRS 7 Financial Instruments: Disclosures.

As many of these requirements apply to both current and non-current obligations, we will defer further discussion of the particulars until Chapter 12.

The Accounting Standards Board (AcSB) of the CICA has long recognized that such extensive disclosure requirements, while perhaps appropriate for PAEs, are difficult and overly costly for many private companies relative to the benefits to users. Recognizing the different environments of PAEs and private enterprises, the disclosure requirements in the ASPE standards are substantively reduced.

G. SUBSTANTIVE DIFFERENCES BETWEEN RELEVANT IFRS AND ASPE

ISSUE	IFRS	ASPE
Contingencies—focus on balance sheet or income statement	Standard refers to contingent assets or liabilities.	Classified as contingent gains or losses.
Contingencies—terminology	Contingent assets and contingent liabilities refer to contingencies that are not recognized as provisions.	Contingent gains and contingent losses refer to the potential for gains or losses that depend on future events, irrespective of accounting treatment.
Contingencies—range of estimates for recognition of contingent loss	Recognize the expected value of the range as a provision.	Use the amount for the most probable outcome in the range. If no estimate in the range is more likely than another, recognize the minimum value in the range as a contingent loss and disclose remainder.

(Continued)

ISSUE	IFRS	ASPE
Customer loyalty programs	IFRIC 13 requires sales transactions to be segregated into components: earned revenue arising from the sale of goods or service; and unearned revenue for the obligation to provide an award credit at a later date.	ASPE does not specifically address accounting for customer loyalty programs.
Disclosures for liabilities	Disclosure requirements are complex. Relevant standards that must be observed include IAS 37, IAS 39, and IFRS 7.	Disclosure requirements are much less demanding because users have the ability to obtain additional details from the reporting enterprise.

H. STANDARDS IN TRANSITION

The International Accounting Standards Board (IASB) is planning to replace IAS 37 Provisions, Contingent Liabilities and Contingent Assets with a new IFRS. The objectives of this project include:

- improving the guidance on identifying liabilities;
- reducing the differences between IAS 37 and US GAAP;
- aligning the recognition requirements for those liabilities covered in the scope of IAS 37 to be consistent with those of other liabilities; and
- clarifying the requirements for measuring liabilities.

At time of writing, the IASB was planning to issue the new IFRS in late 2010 but the effective date had not yet been determined.

The IASB is also in the midst of replacing IAS 39 Financial Instruments: Recognition and Measurement with IFRS 9 Financial Instruments. The goal of this project is to replace IAS 39 in its entirety by mid-2011. The planned mandatory adoption date is for annual periods beginning on or after January 1, 2013. The multi-phase process will replace portions of IAS 39 with new chapters in IFRS 9. Brief details of the status of the project as at June 30, 2010 are as follows:

- Phase Ia: Classification and measurement of financial assets. The portion of IFRS 9 dealing with financial assets has been approved.
- Phase Ib: Classification and measurement of financial liabilities. An exposure draft (ED), Fair Value Option for Financial Liabilities, was issued in May 2010.
- Phase II: Impairment methodology. An ED, Amortized Cost and Impairment, was issued in November 2009.
- Phase III: Hedge accounting. The board planned to issue an exposure draft in sufficient time to allow for finalization of the standard by mid-2011.

I. SUMMARY

L.O. 11-1. Describe the nature of liabilities and differentiate between financial and non-financial liabilities.

- Liabilities are present obligations of the entity arising from past events that are expected to result in an outflow of resources.
- Financial liabilities are contractual obligations that will be settled in cash or by transferring another financial asset to the creditor.
- A non-financial liability is an obligation that meets the definition of a liability but is not a financial liability. Non-financial liabilities are often settled through the provision of goods or delivery of services.

L.O. 11-2. Describe the nature of current liabilities and account for common current liabilities including provisions.

- Current liabilities are obligations that are expected to be settled within one year of the balance sheet date or the business's normal operating cycle, whichever is longer.
- Current liabilities are reported separately from non-current liabilities in the balance sheet unless they are presented in order of liquidity to provide more reliable and relevant information.

L.O. 11-3. Describe the nature of contingent assets and liabilities and account for these items.

- A contingent liability is:
  - a possible obligation whose existence can be confirmed only by future events that are not wholly controlled by the entity; or
  - it is possible (≤50%) but not probable that the obligation will have to be paid; or
  - the obligation cannot be measured with sufficient reliability.
- Contingencies that are probable (>50%) are reported as provisions.
- Contingencies that are possible are disclosed in the notes to the financial statements.
- A contingent asset is a possible asset whose existence can be confirmed only by future events that are not wholly controlled by the entity.
- Contingent assets are not recognized in the financial statements.

L.O. 11-4. Describe the nature of commitments and guarantees and apply accrual accounting to them.

- Contractual commitments pertaining to the acquisition of property, plant, and equipment must be disclosed.
- Enterprises shall record provisions for onerous contracts.
- Enterprises shall record provisions for financial guarantee contracts and disclose such guarantees.

J. References

Authoritative standards:

IFRS	ASPE Section
IAS 1—Presentation of Financial Statements	1400—General Standards of Financial Statement Presentation
	1505—Disclosure of Accounting Policies
	1521—Balance Sheet
IAS 18—Revenue	3400—Revenue
IFRIC 13—Customer Loyalty Programmes	No equivalent guidance
IAS 21—The Effects of Changes in Foreign Exchange Rates	1651—Foreign Currency Translation
IAS 32—Financial Instruments: Presentation	3856—Financial Instruments
IAS 39—Financial Instruments: Recognition and Measurement	
IFRS 7—Financial Instruments: Disclosures	
IAS 37—Provisions, Contingent Liabilities and Contingent Assets	3290—Contingencies

Other references:

Ernst & Young (Editor), *International GAAP 2009: Generally Accepted Accounting Practice under International Financial Reporting Standards (IFRS)*, John Wiley & Sons 2009.

K. Glossary

contingency: An existing condition that depends on the outcome of one or more future events.

contingent asset: A possible asset that arises from past events and whose existence will be confirmed only by the occurrence or non-occurrence of one or more future events.

contingent liability: Is (a) a possible obligation that arises from past events and whose existence depends on one or more future events; or (b) a present obligation that arises from past events that is not recognized as a liability because: (i) it is not probable that an outflow of economic resources will be required to settle the obligation; or (ii) the amount of the obligation cannot be measured with sufficient reliability.

current assets: Assets that are expected to be consumed or sold within one year of the balance sheet date or the business' normal operating cycle, whichever is longer. Also includes assets held primarily for trading purposes.

current liabilities: Obligations that are expected to be settled within one year of the balance sheet date or the business' normal operating cycle, whichever is longer. Also includes held-for-trading liabilities.

deferred revenue: A non-financial obligation arising from the collection of revenue that has not yet been earned.

expected value: The value determined by weighting possible outcomes by their associated probabilities.

fair value: The amount for which an asset could be exchanged, or a liability settled, between knowledgeable, willing parties in an arm's-length transaction.

financial guarantee contract: A contract that requires the issuer to make specified payments to reimburse the holder for a loss it incurs because a specified debtor fails to make payment when due.

financial liability: A contractual obligation to deliver cash or other financial assets to another party.

liability: A present obligation of the entity arising from past events, the settlement of which is expected to result in an outflow of resources.

onerous contract: A contract in which the unavoidable costs of fulfilling it exceed the benefits expected to be received.

possible: A probability of 50% or less.

probable: The probability of occurrence is greater than 50%.

provision: A liability in which there is some uncertainty as to the timing or amount of payment.

trade payables: Obligations to pay for goods received or services used.

warranty: A guarantee that a product will be free from defects for a specified period.

L. PROBLEMS

 Go to MyAccountingLab at **www.myaccountinglab.com**. You can practise the indicated exercises as often as you want, and guided solutions will help you find answers step by step. You'll find a personalized study plan available to you too!

P11-1. Financial and non-financial liabilities   (**L.O.** 11-1) (Easy – 10 minutes)

A list of liabilities follows. For each item, indicate by using the letter F that it is a financial liability or N that it is a non-financial liability. For obligations that are non-financial in nature, briefly explain why they do not meet the criteria of a financial liability.

Item Liability	Financial or non-financial obligation?	Explanation
1. Accounts payable		
2. Warranties payable		
3. USD bank loan		
4. Bank overdraft		
5. Sales tax payable		
6. Notes payable		
7. Unearned revenue		
8. Finance lease obligation		
9. HST payable		
10. Bank loan		
11. Bonds payable		
12. Obligation under customer loyalty plan		
13. Income taxes payable		

P11-2. Financial and non-financial liabilities (**L.O.** 11-1) (Medium – 15 minutes)

A list of liabilities follows. For each item, indicate by using the letter C that it will be reported as a current liability, N that it will be reported as a non-current liability, or B that it potentially can be reported as either or both a current and non-current liability. For obligations that you determine to be N or B, briefly explain why this is the case.

Item Liability	Current or non-current liability, or potentially both?	Explanation
1. Accounts payable		
2. Warranties payable		
3. Deposits		
4. Bank overdraft		
5. Sales tax payable		
6. Bank loan maturing in five years was in default during the year; before year-end, the lender grants a grace period that extends 12 months after the balance sheet date.		
7. Five-year term loan, amortized payments are payable annually		
8. Unearned revenue		
9. Finance lease obligation		
10. HST payable		
11. 90-day bank loan		
12. Bond payable that matures in two years		
13. Obligation under customer loyalty plan		
14. Income taxes payable		
15. Bank loan that matures in five years that is currently in default		
16. Three-year bank loan that matures six months after the balance sheet date		

P11-3. Accounting for taxes payable   (**L.O.** 11-2) (Easy – 15 minutes)

Select transactions and other information pertaining to the Best City in the World Inc. (BCW) are detailed below.

Facts:

a. BCW is domiciled in Vancouver, British Columbia and all purchases and sales are made in BC.
b. The HST rate in British Columbia is 12%.
c. The balances in BCW's HST recoverable account and HST payable account as at March 31, 2012 were $8,000 and $12,000, respectively.
d. BCW uses a perpetual inventory system.
e. Inventory is sold at a 100% mark-up on cost. (Cost of goods sold is 50% of the sales price.)

Select transactions in April 2012:

1. BCW purchased inventory on account at a cost of $10,000 plus HST.
2. BCW purchased equipment on account at a cost of $20,000 plus HST. It paid an additional $500 plus HST for shipping.
3. Cash sales—BCW sold inventory for $15,000 plus HST.
4. Sales on account—BCW sold inventory for $20,000 plus HST.
5. BCW paid the supplier in full for the equipment previously purchased on account.
6. At the end of the month, BCW remitted the net amount of HST owing to the Canada Revenue Agency.

Required:

Prepare summary journal entries to record the transactions detailed above.

P11-4. Accounting for taxes payable   (**L.O.** 11-2) (Easy – 10 minutes)

Select transactions and other information pertaining to Anne Greene Ltd. (AGL) are detailed below.

Facts:

a. AGL is domiciled in Charlottetown, Prince Edward Island and all purchases and sales are made in PEI.
b. The PST rate in PEI is 10%. The GST rate is 5%. Remember that, in PEI, PST is charged on the total of the sales price and the GST.
c. The balances in AGL's GST recoverable, GST payable, and PST payable accounts as at June 30, 2015 were $21,000, $20,000, and $22,000, respectively.
d. AGL uses a perpetual inventory system.
e. Inventory is sold at a 50% mark-up on cost. (Cost of goods sold is two-thirds of the sales price).

Select transactions in July 2015:

1. AGL purchased inventory on account at a cost of $40,000 plus applicable taxes.
2. Cash sales—AGL sold inventory for $30,000 plus applicable taxes.
3. Sales on account—AGL sold inventory for $60,000 plus applicable taxes.
4. At the end of the month, AGL remitted the net amount of GST owing to the Canada Revenue Agency and the PST payable to the Province of PEI.

Required:

Prepare summary journal entries to record the transactions detailed above. Remember that the purchase of inventory for resale is PST exempt.

P11-5. Measurement   (**L.O.** 11-1) (Medium – 10 minutes)

a. Identify the three broad categories of liabilities.
b. Explain how each of these three classes of liabilities is initially measured.
c. Explain how each of these three classes of liabilities is subsequently measured.

P11-6. Accounting for deferred revenues   (**L.O.** 11-2) (Easy – 5 minutes)

Build a Deck Inc. (BaD) enters into a contract to construct six decks adjacent to a commercial building. The purchaser has agreed to pay $5,000 for each deck (total $30,000). The terms of the contract call for a 40% deposit ($2,000 per deck) at time of contract signing and payment of the balance ($3,000 per deck) as each deck is completed. The contract is signed on October 1, 2014. Two decks are completed in 2014 and the balance in 2015. BaD has a December 31 year-end. The cost to BaD of constructing each deck is $2,300, which it pays in cash.

Required:

a. Prepare summary journal entries for 2014 and 2015.
b. What is the balance in the deferred revenue account as at December 31, 2014?

P11-7. Liabilities defined—the nature of liabilities   (**L.O.** 11-1) (Easy – 10 minutes)

What are the three criteria of a liability? Describe how trade accounts payable meet each of the criteria.

P11-8. Liabilities defined—provisions, and financial and non-financial liabilities
                                            (**L.O.** 11-1) (Easy – 10 minutes)

a. Explain what provisions are.
b. Explain what financial liabilities are and how they differ from non-financial liabilities.
c. Provide three examples of financial liabilities and three examples of non-financial liabilities.

P11-9. Accounting for warranties   (**L.O.** 11-2) (Easy – 5 minutes)

In 2017, Surinder's Cycles Inc. sold 2,500 mountain bikes. For the first time, Surinder offered an in-store, no-charge, two-year warranty on each bike sold. Company management estimates that the average cost of providing the warranty is $5 per unit in the first year of coverage and $7 per unit in the second year.

   Surinder's warranty-related expenditures totalled $6,000 for labour costs during 2017.

Required:

a. Prepare the summary journal entry to recognize Surinder's warranty expense in 2017.
b. Prepare the summary journal entry to recognize the warranty service provided in 2017.
c. Determine the total provision for warranty obligations that will be reported on the company's balance sheet at year-end. Assuming that all sales transactions and warranty service took place on the last day of the year, how much of the warranty obligation will be classified as a current liability? As a non-current liability?

P11-10. Accounting for obligations denominated in foreign currencies
                                            (**L.O.** 11-2) (Easy – 5 minutes)

On May 1, 2016, St. John's Brew Supplies Inc. borrowed US$140,000 from its bank. St. John's year-end is December 31, 2016. Exchange rates were as follows:

May 1, 2016	US$1.00 = C$1.02
December 31, 2016	US$1.00 = C$1.04
Average rate May 1–Dec. 31, 2016	US$1.00 = C$1.03

Required:

Prepare the required journal entries to record receipt of the loan proceeds and for any adjustments required at year-end.

P11-11. Customer loyalty plans   (**L.O.** 11-2) (Easy – 5 minutes)

The text identified three primary methods of offering awards under customer loyalty programs:
1. The company offers rewards that it supplies itself
2. The business offers rewards supplied by an outside party
3. The firm offers its customers a choice of receiving awards from its own program or those of a third party

Required:

a. When is revenue recognized for the award portion of sales under the first two methods?
b. How is the price charged for the good or service in the underlying transaction apportioned between sales revenue and awards revenue?

P11-12. Accounting for notes payable   (**L.O.** 11-2) (Easy – 10 minutes)

On January 1, 2014, GFF Transmission Services Co. issued a $20,000, non-interest bearing note, due on January 1, 2015, in exchange for a custom-built computer system. The fair value of the computer system is not easily determinable. The market rate of interest for similar transactions is 4%. GFF's year-end is December 31.

Required:

a. Prepare the journal entry to record the issuance of the note payable.
b. Prepare the journal entry to record the accrual of interest at December 31, 2014, assuming that GFF prepares adjusting entries only at year-end.
c. Prepare the journal entry to record the retirement of the note payable on January 1, 2015.

P11-13. Accounting for notes payable and trade payables

      (**L.O.** 11-2) (Medium – 25 minutes)

North Vancouver Laundry (NVL) recently hired Fred as its payable clerk, a position that has been vacant for two months. While the other accounting staff have taken care of the "must do's," there are a number of transactions that have not yet been recorded.

    Nov. 15, 2017—NVL purchases $5,000 supplies inventory on account. The terms offered are 2/10, net 30.

    Nov. 22, 2017—NVL purchases 10 washing machines. NVL issues an $8,000 non-interest bearing note payable due on 01/15/18.

    Nov. 28, 2017—NVL borrows $20,000 from the bank. NVL signs a demand note for this amount and authorizes the bank to take the interest payments from its bank account. Interest is payable monthly at 4% per annum.

    Dec. 18, 2017—NVL purchases $4,000 supplies inventory on account. The terms offered are 2/10, net 30.

    Dec. 21, 2017—NVL purchases 15 dryers. NVL issues a $10,000 non-interest bearing note payable due on Dec. 21, 2018.

    Dec. 22, 2017—Fred pays the Nov. 15, 2017 and Dec. 18, 2017 invoices.

    Dec. 31, 2017—Fred processes the payroll for the month. The gross payroll is $20,000; $1,400 is withheld for the employees' Canada Pension Plan and Employment Insurance premiums.[18]

Other information

- NVL uses the net method to record accounts payable.
- NVL's year-end is Dec. 31 and interim statements are normally prepared on a monthly basis.

---

18. While accounting for payroll withholding taxes has not been dealt with explicitly in this chapter, it is assumed that students were introduced to this topic in their introductory accounting course(s).

- Due to the vacancy in the accounting department, NVL's latest interim statements are for the period ended Oct. 31, 2017. The necessary accruals were made at that time.
- The market rate of interest for NVL's short-term borrowings is 4%.

Required:

a. Prepare journal entries to record the documented events and the necessary accruals for the months of November and December. Compute interest accruals based on the number of days, rather than months.

b. Contrast the gross and net methods of accounting for trade payables.

P11-14. Current versus non-current liabilities—balance sheet classification of maturing liabilities (**L.O.** 11-2) (Medium – 5 minutes)

Explain how a long-term loan maturing within one year of the balance sheet date is reported in the financial statements, assuming that the company intends to renew the liability for a further five years.

P11-15. Balance sheet classification of non-current obligations in default (**L.O.** 11-2) (Medium – 5 minutes)

Explain how a non-current obligation in default is reported in the financial statements.

P11-16. Accounting for deferred revenues (**L.O.** 11-2) (Medium – 10 minutes)

HF Magazines Corp. sells three-year magazine subscriptions for $180 cash each. The cost of producing and delivering each magazine is $2.00 paid in cash at the time of delivery. HF's sales activity for the year follows:

- On January 1, 2017, HF sells 10,000 subscriptions.
- On April 1, 2017, HF sells 5,000 subscriptions.
- On November 1, 2017, HF sells 12,000 subscriptions

HF delivers the magazines at the end of the month. HF's year-end is December 31.

Required:

a. Prepare journal entries to record the subscription sales during the year.
b. Prepare summary journal entries to record the revenue earned during the year and the related expense.

P11-17. Accounting for warranties (**L.O.** 11-2) (Medium – 10 minutes)

SST Jetski Corp. has sold motorized watercraft for a number of years. SST includes a three-year warranty on each watercraft they sell. Management estimates that the cost of providing the warranty coverage is 1% of sales in the first year and 2% of sales in each of years two and three. Other facts follow:

- SST reported a $260,000 provision for warranty payable on its December 31, 2012 balance sheet.
- SST's sales for 2013 totalled $4,800,000 spread evenly through the year.
- The cost to SST of meeting their warranty claims in 2013 was $240,000: $150,000 for parts and $90,000 for labour.
- SST's sales for 2014 totalled $5,400,000 spread evenly through the year.
- The cost to SST of meeting their warranty claims in 2014 was $300,000: $180,000 for parts and $120,000 for labour. Based on recent claims history, SST revises their 2014 warranty provision to 7% of sales.

Required:

a. Prepare summary journal entries to record warranty expense and warranty claims in 2013 and 2014.
b. Determine the provision for warranty payable that SST will report as a liability on December 31, 2014.

P11-18. Accounting for warranties   (**L.O.** 11-2) (Medium – 15 minutes)

Stanger Educational Services Corp. sells multimedia presentation systems. In its first year of operations in 2011, the company sold 1,000 units for $5,000 cash each representing a 25% mark-up over cost. Stanger provides a one-year parts and labour warranty on each system they sell; the estimated cost of providing the warranty coverage is $400 per unit.

The cost to Stanger of meeting their warranty claims in 2011 was $170,000: $50,000 for parts and $120,000 for labour.

For part a, assume that Stanger properly provides for the warranties on an accrual basis. For part b, assume that Stanger erroneously concludes that the warranty costs are immaterial and elects to account for the warranty obligations on a cash basis.

Required:

a. Prepare journal entries to record the foregoing events on an accrual basis.
b. Prepare journal entries to record the foregoing events on a cash basis.
c. Discuss why the cash basis cannot normally be used to account for warranty expenses.
d. Warranty claims in 2012 related to 2011 sales were $300,000, raising the total cost to $470,000. How should Stanger account for the $70,000 claimed in excess of that previously provided for?

P11-19. Accounting for deferred revenue   (**L.O.** 11-2) (Difficult – 20 minutes)

GHF Computer Systems Inc. maintains office equipment under contract. The contracts are for labour only; customers must reimburse GHF for parts. GHF's rate schedule follows:

	One year	Two years	Three years
Photocopiers	$240	$420	$600
Fax machines	$180	$320	$450

GHF's 2018 sales of maintenance agreements is set out below:

	One year	Two years	Three years
Photocopiers	24	12	36
Fax machines	24	24	36

Required:

Assuming that sales occurred evenly through the year:
a. What amount of revenue will GHF recognize for the year ended December 31, 2018?
b. What amount of deferred revenue will GHF report as a current liability on December 31, 2018?
c. What amount of deferred revenue will GHF report as a non-current liability on December 31, 2018?

P11-20. Accounting for deferred revenue   (**L.O.** 11-2) (Difficult – 25 minutes)

Muscles Gym Corp. offers a variety of fitness packages to its members. Options include:

■ a pay-as-you-go membership for the use of the fitness facilities costing $40 per month
■ a one-year, non-cancellable membership costing $420 per year
■ a two-year, non-cancellable membership costing $720 ($360 per year)
■ a personal trainer package (PTP) of ten coupons for one-hour sessions costing $750

The matrix that follows summarizes Muscles' membership numbers and relevant financial information at December 31, 2016.

	# of Customers	Liability	Current Liability	Non-Current Liability
Pay as you go	220	$ 0	$ 0	$ 0
One year	180	40,950	40,950	0
Two year	120	45,000	33,300	11,700
Unused personal training sessions	352	26,400	26,400	0
		$112,350	$100,650	$11,700

Other information:

- All fees are payable in advance. One- and two-year memberships are effective the first of the month following sale.
- Fifteen one-year memberships were sold every month in 2016.
- Five two-year memberships were sold every month in 2015 and 2016.
- Historically, all personal trainer session coupons are redeemed within one year of purchase.
- To simplify their accounting somewhat, and as the amounts are not material, Muscles recognizes the pay-as-you-go membership fees as revenue in the month charged even if they are purchased during the month.

Transactions during January 2017:

- Thirty-four pay-as-you-go members cancelled their memberships before paying for January.
- Muscles attracted 45 new pay-as-you-go members.
- Muscles sold 20 new one-year memberships.
- Muscles sold 10 new two-year memberships.
- 112 coupons for personal training sessions were redeemed.
- Ten new personal trainer packages were sold.

Required:

a. Prepare journal entries to recognize the receipt of cash and recognize revenue in January.
b. What is the total deferred revenue that Muscles will report as a liability as at January 31? How much of this will be reported as a current liability? [*Hint:* it is easier to determine the non-current portion and subtract this from the total obligation to determine the current portion.]

P11-21. Accounting for customer loyalty programs   (L.O. 11-2) (Difficult – 15 minutes)

Halifax Air Shuttle Inc. offers a customer loyalty program that grants members reward miles for each flight taken. Members can redeem the miles, which expire five years after issuance, for future flights. Members must redeem 15,000 miles and pay a $100 service charge to obtain a flight under the reward program. Other facts follow:

- In 2014, Halifax Air received $10,000,000 cash in flight-related revenue for flights taken in 2014.
- Halifax Air expects that 80% of the 9,375,000 miles awarded in 2014 will be redeemed before they expire.
- The fair value of the miles awarded is estimated to be $75,000.
- Management anticipates that 40% of the forecast reward flights will be taken in 2015; 30% will be taken in 2016; and the remainder will be taken evenly during 2017–2019.
- During 2015, 200 reward flights were claimed.
- During 2016, 150 reward flights were claimed.

Required:

a. Prepare a summary journal entry to record the flight-related revenue in 2014.
b. Prepare summary journal entries to recognize award revenue in 2015 and 2016.
c. Determine the amount of unearned award miles revenue that Halifax Air will report as a **current** liability on December 31, 2016.

P11-22. Accounting for contingencies and customer loyalty programs
(L.O. 11-2, L.O. 11-3) (Medium – 10 minutes)

It is early in February 2017 and you are conducting the audit of Adventuresome Airlines Ltd.'s 2016 financial statements. Through discussion with Adventuresome's Chief Financial Officer you learn of matters that have not yet been incorporated into the 2016 financial statements:

■ In July 2016, 57 passengers on board Adventuresome Airlines Flight 007 were seriously injured when the plane missed the runway on final approach. In January 2017, the injured passengers launched a class action lawsuit against Adventuresome seeking damages of $10 million. Adventuresome's internal investigation of the incident determined that the pilot was intoxicated during the flight. The company's solicitors suggest that if the matter goes to court, Adventuresome will be found liable and ordered to pay the $10 million.

   In an attempt to reduce its loss, Adventuresome's solicitors made a settlement offer of $8 million to the plaintiffs. The litigants' attorney has not provided a formal response but has indicated that the offer is being seriously considered. Adventuresome's lawyers estimate that there is an 80% probability the plaintiffs will accept the offer.

■ During 2016, Adventuresome began a customer loyalty program. For each aeronautical mile that a passenger travels on a paid flight, the passenger accrues one flight mile. Passengers can redeem accrued flight miles for free air travel. Earned miles do not expire.

   Adventuresome's analysis of its competitors' programs suggests an average redemption rate of 80%. In 2016, Adventuresome awarded 30,000,000 flight miles, 4,800,000 of which were redeemed. Management estimates the fair value of the flight miles is $720,000.

Required:

Prepare the journal entries to record the required adjustments for the above events.

P11-23. Describe the nature of contingent assets and liabilities
(L.O. 11-3) (Medium – 10 minutes)

a. Explain what contingencies are.
b. Describe how to account for contingent liabilities.
c. Describe how to account for contingent assets.

P11-24. Accounting for contingencies   **(L.O. 11-3)** (Medium – 10 minutes)

Discuss the terms "probable," "possible," and "remote" in relation to contingencies. In what circumstances are contingencies provided for in the financial statements, and when are they simply disclosed?

P11-25. Accounting for contingencies   **(L.O. 11-3)** (Medium – 15 minutes)

The following are six independent situations. The underlined entity is the reporting entity.

1. The Supreme Court of Canada ordered a supplier to pay Pangay Strobes Inc. $100,000 for breach of contract.
2. Ynot Pharmaceuticals Inc. sued Xbot Agencies Ltd. for $20 million alleging patent infringement. While there may be some substance to Ynot's assertion, Xbot's legal counsel estimates that Ynot's likelihood of success is about 20%.
3. Environment Canada sued Canless Isotopes Ltd. for $10 million seeking to recover the costs of cleaning up Canless's accidental discharge of radioactive

materials. Canless acknowledges liability but is disputing the amount, claiming that the actual costs are in the range of $5 million to $6 million. Canless's $10 million environmental insurance policy includes a $1 million deductible clause.

4. Calfed Cattle Inc. sued <u>Toropost Feed Ltd.</u> for $2 million alleging breach of contract. Toropost's legal counsel estimates that Calfed's likelihood of success is about 70%. Based on its experience with cases of this nature, the law firm estimates that, if successful, the litigants will be awarded $1,000,000 to $1,200,000, with all payouts in this range being equally likely.

5. Helen Threlfall broke her leg when she tripped on an uneven floor surface in Montpearson Co.'s office. On the advice of legal counsel, Montpearson has offered Threlfall $100,000 to settle her $300,000 lawsuit. It is unknown whether Threlfall will accept the settlement offer. <u>Montpearson's</u> legal counsel estimates that Threlfall has a 90% probability of success, and that if successful, she will be awarded $200,000.

6. The courts ordered a competitor to pay $500,000 to <u>Winfland Boxes Corp.</u> for patent infringement. The competitor's legal counsel indicated that the company will probably appeal the amount of the award.

Required:

a. For each of the six situations described above, indicate whether the appropriate accounting treatment is to:
   A. Recognize an asset or liability.
   B. Disclose the details of the contingency in the notes to the financial statements.
   C. Neither provide for the item nor disclose the circumstances in the notes to the financial statements.
b. For each situation that requires the recognition of an asset or liability, record the journal entry.

P11-26. Accounting for guarantees   (**L.O.** 11-4) (Easy – 5 minutes)

ZSK Interiors Ltd. guarantees SIL Exterior Co.'s $150,000 bank loan. Describe how ZSK will initially account for the guarantee and discuss the nature of the required disclosure.

P11-27. Accounting for commitments   (**L.O.** 11-4) (Easy – 5 minutes)

Explain what onerous contracts are and how are they accounted for.

P11-28. Accounting for commitments   (**L.O.** 11-4) (Medium – 10 minutes)

Kitchener Distributors Inc. entered into a non-cancellable contract to buy 10,000 litres of linseed oil for $3 per litre for resale purposes. Kitchener intends to resell the oil to retail paint outlets for $4 per litre. The contract was entered into on October 31, 2016 for delivery on January 15, 2017. Kitchener's year-end is December 31.

On December 12, 2016, Kitchener's supplier reduces the price to $2.00 per litre due to adverse market conditions.

Required:

a. Outline the required accounting treatment assuming that Kitchener expects it can sell the oil for $3.20 per litre.
b. Outline the required accounting treatment assuming that Kitchener expects it can sell the oil for $2.75 per litre.

P11-29. Accounting for various situations

        (**L.O.** 11-2, **L.O.** 11-3, **L.O.** 11-4) (Difficult – 20 minutes)

A number of independent situations are set out below.

1. A former employee of Moncton Minimarket Inc. sued the company for $500,000, alleging that the company owner sexually harassed her. Moncton's lawyers suggest that the lawsuit has a 20–30% probability of success and that, if successful, the plaintiff will be awarded between $100,000 and $200,000.

2. Calgary Pyrotechnics Ltd. received a $5,000 fee to guarantee the $500,000 bank indebtedness of Edmonton Fireworks Inc. The fair value of the guarantee is initially estimated to be $5,000.

3. Humboldt Syringes Co. sued a competitor for $300,000, alleging corporate espionage. Humboldt's legal counsel believes that the company will be successful and will be awarded somewhere in the range of $250,000 to $300,000.

4. A customer sued Cache Creek Tractor Corp. for $100,000 for breach of contract. Cache Creek's solicitors advise that they will almost certainly be found liable. Based on previous results, counsel estimates that there is a 50% probability that the courts will award the $100,000 being sought; a 30% probability that $90,000 will be conferred; and a 20% probability that the judgment will be $80,000.

5. Saskatoon Conveyor and Clutch Ltd. are in the midst of preparing their financial statements for the year ended December 31, 2018. Saskatoon has been in ongoing discussions with its bankers about renewing its $5,000,000 loan maturing on June 30, 2019. While nothing had been finalized by year-end, the bank did agree to extend the maturity by five years on January 15, 2019.

Required:

For each of the above situations, describe how the event should be dealt with in the financial statements and explain why. Prepare all required journal entries.

P11-30. Accounting for various situations (**L.O.** 11-2, **L.O.** 11-4) (Difficult – 20 minutes)

A number of independent situations are set out below.

1. Montreal Pool and Skeet Corp.'s debt to equity ratio is 1.6:1 based on its draft financial statements for the year ended December 31, 2016. This leverage ratio exceeds the 1.5:1 maximum stipulated in Montreal's loan agreement pertaining to a $1,000,000 loan maturing on March 15, 2019. The loan agreement stipulates that the loan becomes payable on demand upon breach of any of the loan covenants. Montreal's creditors agreed on December 15, 2016 to waive their right to demand payment until December 31, 2017 for reason only that the firm's leverage ratio exceeds the stipulated maximum.

2. Bathurst Piano Storage Inc. issued a $20,000, 30-day, non-interest bearing note to Len's Crating for storage bins. The market rate of interest for similar transactions is 2%.

3. On November 30, 2014, Port Mellon Fertilizer Ltd. entered into a non-cancellable agreement to buy 10 tonnes of phosphorus for $1,000 per tonne for delivery on February 28, 2015. Phosphorus is a key component of the custom fertilizer that Port Mellon produces. The market price of phosphorus is extremely volatile, as evident by the $700 per tonne that it could be acquired for on December 31, 2014. Notwithstanding the premium price paid for the phosphorus, the company expects that fertilizer sales will remain profitable. Port Mellon's year-end is December 31, 2014.

4. Gander Airport Parking Ltd. awards customers 250 reward miles per stay, in a well-known airline mileage program. Gander pays the airline $0.02 for each mile. Gander, which is not an agent for the airline, estimates that the fair value of the miles is the same as the price paid—$0.02. Parking revenues on May 24, 2017 were $25,000. Gander awarded 50,000 airline points to its customers.

5. On October 15, 2013, Charlottetown Windows and Sash properly recorded the issue of a $20,000, 6% note due April 15, 2014. Charlottetown is preparing its financial statements for the year ended December 31, 2013. Charlottetown does not make adjusting entries during the year.

Required:

For each of the situations described above, prepare the required journal entry for the underlined entity. If a journal entry is not required, explain why.

M. MINI-CASES

CASE 1

Cool Look Limited
(40 minutes)[19]

Cool Look Limited (CLL) is a high-end clothing design and manufacturing company that has been in business in Canada since 1964. CLL started as an owner-managed enterprise created and run by Hector Gauthier. Its ownership has stayed within the family and is now in its third generation of management by the Gauthier/Roy family. Martin Roy, Hector's grandson, is the newly appointed President, Chief Executive Officer, and Chairman of the Board of CLL, and wants to modernize the company.

You, CA, are the audit senior on the CLL audit for its fiscal year ended November 30, 2015. Today is December 9, 2015, and you are reviewing correspondence from CLL's bank. You come upon a letter dated November 1, 2015, from the bank credit manager, that causes you some concern (Exhibit I). After you finish reviewing the letter, you recall the other issues that are causing you concern in the audit (Exhibit II). You pull out your notes from your review of Board minutes (Exhibit III) and the November 30, 2015, management-prepared draft financial statements (Exhibit IV) to clarify your thoughts further.

As you contemplate the work to be completed, you decide to write a memorandum to the file that discusses the outstanding accounting issues that are currently facing CLL, the audit procedures that are required to gain adequate assurance over those issues, and other areas of concern you want to raise with your partner.

Required:

Prepare a memo that i) discusses the going-concern assumption as it relates to this case; and ii) identifies and discusses the accounting issues that need to be resolved before the financial statements can be finalized.

Exhibit I	Letter to CLL from bank

November 1, 2015

Dear Sir:

We have reviewed CLL's internal third-quarter financial statements, dated August 31, 2015. As a result of this review, we have determined that your financial ratios continue to decline and that you are in default of the covenants in our agreement for the second consecutive quarter.

However, since the bank and CLL have a long history, and because CLL continues to make required debt payments on time, we are willing to extend the $6,000,000 secured operating line of credit until the end of February 2016.

Based on CLL's February 29, 2016, internal financial statements, we will expect CLL to meet the following financial ratios. If this is not done, we reserve the right to call the loan at that time.

Ratios:

Current ratio no less than 1:1

Maximum debt-to-equity ratio (Debt / Debt + Equity) of 80%; debt is defined as total liabilities.

We thank you for your business.

Yours truly,
Mr. Vuiton Burbery
Credit Manager

---

19. Adapted with permission from The Canadian Institute of Chartered Accountants, Toronto, Canada. Any changes to the original material are the sole responsibility of the author and have not been reviewed or endorsed by the CICA.

Exhibit II	Excerpts from audit file regarding outstanding issues

Capital Assets

At a physical inspection of the CLL factory, audit staff noted that only about one-half of the equipment at the factory was being used, even though it was 2 o'clock on a Wednesday afternoon. The rest was covered by tarps. The plant manager explained that the equipment covered by tarps was outdated and unable to manufacture products in its current condition. Senior management is investigating whether it can be refitted with updated technology to make it usable. This refitting would cost approximately $1.5 million and would take three to six months to complete. The equipment covered by tarps cost $2.9 million and has a current net book value of $1.3 million.

Maintenance expenses are currently about 25% of last year's amount. The plant manager indicated that some of the functioning equipment is not running at full efficiency due to the need to perform maintenance soon. He stated that, while there would normally be some safety issues when maintenance is reduced, his staff consists of well-trained, seasoned employees, and he is not concerned.

Inventory Transaction

Finished goods inventory at a cost of $565,000 was shipped by CLL to Big Bargain Clothing (BBC), a national retail clothing outlet store, on November 29, 2015. The shipment was recorded as sales revenue of $1,000,000, generating a gross profit of $435,000. CLL and BBC signed a special agreement stating that BBC can return unsold goods to CLL at any time after February 1, 2016.

Long-Term Debt

CLL's long-term debt includes the $6,000,000 secured operating line of credit. The line of credit is a revolving loan callable on three months' notice by the bank if certain financial covenants are not met. It had been classified as long-term debt in 2014 because the bank waived its right to call the loan before December 1, 2015.

Exhibit III	Excerpts from notes taken during review of Board minutes

August 7, 2015—Management presented a document discussing the temporary cash crunch at CLL. Management presented options to conserve cash until the Christmas buying season, when a new large contract with a U.S. chain of stores begins. One alternative was to discontinue making required contributions to the CLL pension plan. Another alternative was to delay remitting GST and employee withholdings. The Board passed a resolution to temporarily delay remitting GST and employee withholdings until cash flows improved.

September 5, 2015—The Board received information from management regarding an incident at the factory. Some dirty rags had caught fire in a metal garbage can. The fire was put out quickly and no damage was done. Management and the Board were quite relieved that the fire had not spread, because CLL has not renewed its fire and theft insurance this year due to the need to conserve cash. For the same reason, CLL has not renewed the directors' liability insurance. The Board decided that the renewals would be done immediately after cash flow improved.

November 10, 2015—The Board passed a motion to allow Martin Roy to postpone repayment of his interest-free shareholder loan by another six months to May 31, 2016. He owes CLL $500,000. The Board also received a report from management on the November 1, 2015 letter from the bank.

The Board is concerned that, even with its efforts to conserve cash, CLL may be unable to meet the ratio requirements. The Board is curious to know whether CLL's efforts thus far have produced results.

Exhibit IV

CLL
Extracts from the draft balance sheet
As at November 30
(in thousands of dollars)

	2015 (unaudited)	2014 (audited)
Current assets		
Cash	$ 1,094	$ 1,376
Accounts receivable	1,148	736
Inventory	2,241	2,358
Prepaid expenses	184	134
Due from shareholder	500	500
	5,167	5,104
Property, plant, and equipment (net)	9,392	9,719
	$ 14,559	$ 14,823
Current liabilities		
Accounts payable	$ 2,315	$ 995
Current portion of long-term debt	821	803
	3,136	1,798
Pension benefit liability	208	236
Long-term debt	9,149	9,234
	9,357	9,470
Share capital	10,386	10,386
Deficit	(8,320)	(6,831)
	2,066	3,555
	$ 14,559	$ 14,823

CLL
Extracts from the draft income statement
For the year ended November 30
(in thousands of dollars)

	2015 (unaudited)	2014 (audited)
Operating revenues	$ 16,620	$ 16,285
Cost of sales	9,321	8,995
Gross profit	7,299	7,290
Selling and administrative expenses	6,580	5,900
Depreciation and amortization	1,310	1,485
Operating loss	(591)	(95)
Interest expense	898	902
Net loss	$ (1,489)	$ (997)

CASE 2

Earth Movers Ltd.

(60 minutes)[20]

Earth Movers Ltd. (EML) is in the business of supplying heavy equipment and work crews for landfill operations, road construction, and gravel pit operations. Kevin Donnelly started the company 28 years ago with a small inheritance. EML has contracts with several municipalities in two provinces and recently obtained a contract in a third province. In addition, EML owns and operates two landfill sites.

Kevin owns 50% of EML's shares; his wife, Leslie, owns 25% of the shares; and his daughter, Brenda, owns the other 25% of the shares. Brenda, who graduated with a business administration degree four years ago, joined the company in February 2014 after leaving her job as a buyer for a department store chain. Her current responsibilities as assistant controller include payroll administration and supervision of the billing clerk. It is anticipated she will move into the controller's role when the controller, Betty Wylie, retires in two years.

EML has recently appointed White & Bean, Chartered Accountants, (WB), as auditors for the year ended June 30, 2014. Fred Spot, CA, a good friend of Kevin Donnelly, was the auditor for the past several years. Mr. Spot has advised WB that he is not aware of any reason why they should not accept the appointment of auditor.

In early June, the company had been served notice by its bank, the Dominion Royal, that the interest rate charged on its loan will be increased from prime + 1% to prime + 3%. Interest is payable monthly and principal is repayable over 10 years. Kevin has approached several banks in order to obtain new financing and only one, S&L Bank, has offered a lower rate. It will supply financing at prime + 1% pending receipt of audited financial statements. The amount of financing provided, some of which will be long term and some short term, will depend on certain asset balances and financial ratios (see Exhibit I). Kevin would like EML to repay the loan he made to the company and has asked WB to determine how much financing EML can expect to obtain. Kevin wants to be fully informed of any accounting concerns WB may have in determining the financing available.

Terry Mitchell, the engagement partner, has asked you, CA, to prepare a report that provides the information requested by Kevin including all necessary explanations and assumptions.

It is now July 2, 2014, and you are back in your office after attending the spare parts inventory count and verifying the existence of fixed assets. Your notes from this visit are attached (see Exhibit II). You have reviewed and discussed the draft financial statements with Betty Wylie and made some notes (attached as Exhibit III).

Required:

Prepare the report to the client.

Exhibit I	S&L Bank financing offer

1. No financing is available if the working capital ratio is below 1.00. Calculation of the working capital ratio excludes any financing from S&L Bank.
2. Subject to 1 above, S&L Bank will provide financing to EML based on the following formulae:

Formula 1

If the working capital ratio is 1.0 to 1.25, S&L Bank will advance funds equal to (70% × accounts receivable) + (30% × inventory) due on demand, and (50% × land, building, and equipment, net) as long-term debt.

Formula 2

If the working capital ratio is greater than 1.25, S&L Bank will advance funds equal to (80% × accounts receivable) + (40% × inventory) due on demand, and (70% × land, building, and equipment, net) as long-term debt.

3. EML will supply S&L Bank with monthly unaudited financial statements, accompanied by comments from management.
4. Credit limits and long-term debt renewal will be based on the annual audited financial statements.
5. Interest on the loans will be payable monthly.

---

20. Adapted with permission from The Canadian Institute of Chartered Accountants, Toronto, Canada. Any changes to the original material are the sole responsibility of the author and have not been reviewed or endorsed by the CICA.

Exhibit II	Notes from inventory count and asset existence test

1. One of the trucks in the sample was not on the client's premises. Betty explained that it was at a repair shop because there had been a fire in the cab. Kevin has not decided whether it is worthwhile to repair the truck but is expecting to receive $90,000 from the insurance company. At his insistence, Betty recorded $90,000 as a current receivable and as a gain on asset disposition.
2. Spare parts inventory includes the spare metal wheels for the earth mover vehicles, as follows:

| Size 250H | 7 wheels | $570,000 |
| Size 350H | 5 wheels | $150,000 |

The metal wheels are used until the tracks wear down. Each earth mover has three wheels that must be replaced approximately every five years. The old wheels are removed and rebuilt, so the number of wheels in inventory is fairly constant. EML's fleet includes two old earth movers that use size 250H wheels. The other 19 earth movers use size 350H wheels.

Two earth movers were scrapped in fiscal 2014. Six size 250H wheels were transferred to spare parts inventory at the book value of the scrapped vehicles, which was $550,000. No entry has been recorded for the remaining parts from the scrapped vehicles, which will be sold to a scrap metal dealer for about $60,000.

Kevin said that he plans to change the method of depreciation for all heavy equipment. In the past, the declining balance method was used. He has decided to use the straight-line method, as he had heard that one of his main competitors has been using this method for years. He suggests adding a note to the financial statements explaining the straight-line method and the average useful life of the equipment.

Exhibit III	

Earth Movers Ltd.
Balance sheet
As at June 30, 2014
(unaudited, in thousands of dollars)

Assets

Cash	$ 84
Accounts receivable	585
Spare parts inventory	907
Land, building, and equipment (net)	2,759
Landfill sites	415
	$4,750

Liabilities

Accounts payable	$ 347
Current portion of long-term debt	89
Income taxes payable	53
Long-term debt	2,428
Due to Kevin Donnelly	300
Deferred taxes	47
	3,264

Shareholders' Equity

Common shares	1
Retained earnings	1,485
	$4,750

CA's notes from review of the financial statements

1. EML owns and operates two landfill sites. The Banbury site has an estimated remaining life of nine years and a book value of $290,000. The Eckleforth site has a remaining life of two years and a book value of $125,000. Kevin plans to offer the Eckleforth site to the City of Eckleforth for use as a recreational area in exchange for the city taking the responsibility for cleaning up the site. In this way he is hoping to avoid spending $250,000 to $350,000 in cleanup costs.

2. Income taxes payable relate to Kevin and Leslie's personal taxes. The amount is large, as they recently lost an appeal regarding the tax treatment of some personal property. Fred Spot, CA, has prepared the Donnellys' tax returns for a nominal fee for several years.

3. During the winter, several staff painted and generally cleaned up the interior of EML's office and shop building. Kevin says the place looks "as good as new" and therefore told Betty to record the $9,700 cost of their labour as an addition to land, building, and equipment.

4. Repairs and maintenance expense includes $15,800 worth of parts and labour for the overhaul of a 350H earth mover. Kevin bought the machine at an auction this year for the low price of $95,000 since he knew that Mack Jacobs, the shop foreman, would enjoy the challenge of making it operational. The machine is now in use at the Banbury site.

5. Accounts receivable include $85,000 in disputed invoices relating to the operation of a gravel pit. Kevin has not been pressing for collection because the contract to operate the gravel pit is up for renewal and he feels he can use the receivable as a bargaining tool.

6. Accounts payable include $146,000 due to Fred Spot, CA, for consulting services and for the annual audits for the fiscal years 2011 to 2013.

CASE 3
Lisa's Insurance Services Ltd.
(20 minutes)

Lisa Ramage, who owns a number of businesses, opened an insurance agency called Lisa's Insurance Services Ltd. [LISL] at the beginning of the year. Year-end (December 31, 2013) is fast approaching and Lisa has asked you, the company accountant, to prepare a report outlining how the following items should be reported in LISL's financial statements. LISL has various obligations, including a $500,000 overdraft facility and a $2,000,000 three-year term loan with its bank GFF Financial Inc.

1. On July 1, 2013, LISL took advantage of a vendor-provided financing offer to acquire computer equipment. LISL signed a $20,000 note, payable in full on July 1, 2016. Interest is payable annually at a rate of 2% per annum. LISL's bank previously advised that it would charge an interest rate of 8% per annum for a loan on similar terms.

2. LISL has been sued by S. Berg Ltd. (SBL), a client, for unspecified damages. The lawsuit alleges negligence and contends that LISL sold SBL an insurance policy that was inadequate for its needs. When SBL's premises were destroyed by fire, the insurance proceeds were $1 million less than that required to reconstruct the facilities. LISL's legal counsel believes that the courts may possibly find in favour of SBL, and if they do so the range of the award will likely be between $600,000 and $800,000 with no one estimate better than the rest.

3. LISL has guaranteed $100,000 of the indebtedness of Kaitlyn's Studios Inc. (KSI), a related corporation. KSI has a long record of profitability and the probability of default is thought to be remote.

4. LISL's loan agreement with GFF Financial Inc. includes a covenant that the company will maintain its current ratio of no less than 1.30:1. If LISL fails to meet this or any of the other covenants at year-end, all loan facilities become immediately due and payable. As it appears that LISL's current ratio at year-end will be slightly less than this, LISL obtained a letter from GFF dated December 15, 2013 agreeing to provide until December 31, 2014 for LISL to remedy this defect.

Required:

Prepare the report to Lisa.

CHAPTER 12 Non-current Financial Liabilities

I n June 2007, BCE Inc. (www.bce.ca), a telecommunications company listed on the Toronto Stock Exchange (ticker: BCE), announced that it was going private, with all shares being sold to a consortium headed up by the Ontario Teachers' Pension Plan (OTPP). The buyers intended to borrow heavily against BCE's assets to finance the $35 billion required to complete the purchase; the leveraged buyout would increase BCE's debt load by approximately $32 billion.[1]

Shareholders were virtually unanimous in approving the deal, which would have seen them receiving $42.75 per common share—a premium of 40% above the average share price of around $30 in the first quarter of 2007. Bondholders were not so ecstatic, however, and petitioned the courts to block the transaction. They argued that the agreement was prejudicial to their interests due to the increased risks associated with the proposed extent of financial leverage.

The Supreme Court of Canada refused to nullify the contract. The Court's underlying reasoning was that BCE's responsibility to the bondholders was limited to complying with the terms of the various bond indentures, terms which did not restrict BCE's ability to borrow.

The privatization agreement between BCE and the OTPP included a number of conditions that had to be met before the arrangement would be finalized. One of the terms required KPMG to deliver an opinion that BCE would meet the stipulated post-transaction solvency tests. The accord was terminated when KPMG advised that the firm could not provide a positive solvency opinion based on market conditions prevailing at the time. The cancellation of the agreement was good news for BCE bondholders as it alleviated their concerns about the proposed leverage—and bad news for BCE shareholders, who saw the market value of their shares plummet to $23, or 46% less than the previously negotiated sale price.

Long-term debt is a very important source of financing for companies. For companies such as BCE, what is a "safe" level of debt? Why do companies borrow money and lever up their balance sheets? What are the advantages and disadvantages of financial leverage? What are the key issues that accountants should be aware of in relation to debt financing?

LEARNING OBJECTIVES

After studying this chapter, you should be able to:

L.O. 12-1. Describe financial leverage and its impact on profitability.

L.O. 12-2. Describe the categories and types of non-current liabilities.

L.O. 12-3. Describe the initial and subsequent measurement of non-current financial liabilities and account for these obligations.

L.O. 12-4. Apply accrual accounting to the derecognition of financial liabilities.

L.O. 12-5. Describe how non-current liabilities are presented and disclosed.

---

1. The transaction was valued at $52 billion, including $17 billion in debt, preferred equity, and non-controlling interests. OTTP already owned 6.8% of the common shares before the privatization bid. The consortium required $35 billion in cash to purchase the remaining common shares and to redeem the preferred shares. $32 billion of the $35 billion required was to be borrowed by BCE.

CONTENTS

A. INTRODUCTION

1. Overview

L.O. 12-1. Describe financial leverage and its impact on profitability.

non-current liabilities Obligations that are expected to be settled more than one year after the balance sheet date or the business' normal operating cycle, whichever is longer.

Non-current liabilities are obligations expected to be settled more than one year after the balance sheet date or the business' normal operating cycle, whichever is longer. As discussed in Chapter 11, many current liabilities arise from financing the firm's day-to-day operating activities. Borrowing comprises the major portion of non-current liabilities, although other significant liabilities do exist, as we will see in other chapters.

There are two key reasons why companies borrow to acquire assets: (i) they have insufficient cash available to pay for the acquisition, or (ii) they expect to profit by investing in assets that will generate income in excess of borrowing costs.

It is helpful to think of these motives in personal terms. People routinely take out loans to buy new cars or mortgages to purchase real estate when they do not have enough of their own cash. Similarly, individuals borrow money to buy stocks or other investments expecting that the return generated will exceed the cost of borrowing.

2. Financial leverage

Whatever the underlying reason, when a business borrows money its total debt level increases, and so too does its financial leverage. **Financial leverage** is one measure of solvency. While there are different ways to calculate financial leverage, in simple terms it quantifies the relationship between the relative level of a firm's debt and its equity base. Financial leverage offers shareholders an opportunity to increase their return on equity (ROE) when the business performs well but exposes them to an increased risk of loss as well. For this reason leverage is often referred to as a double-edged sword. Moreover, increased financial leverage also amplifies the risk of bankruptcy as the company has additional payments (interest and principal) that must be made on an ongoing basis. See Exhibit 12-1 for an illustration of how financial leverage affects the return to the shareholders.

financial leverage Quantifies the relationship between the relative level of a firm's debt and its equity base.

Exhibit 12-1	An illustration of financial leverage's impact on profitability

Facts: Vernon Hydroponics Services Inc. is a new company. Its only asset is $100,000 of cash raised by issuing common shares.[2]

	Scenario 1 (unlevered)		Scenario 2 (levered)	
	Vernon invests the **$100,000** in a venture that will pay out either **$75,000** or **$130,000** at the end of one year depending on the success of the venture.		Vernon borrows $200,000 at 6% interest and invests **$300,000** in the same project outlined in scenario 1. The payout will be **$225,000** ($75,000 × 3) or **$390,000** ($130,000 × 3) because it invests three times as much.	
	Unsuccessful	**Successful**	**Unsuccessful**	**Successful**
Opening equity	$100,000	$100,000	$100,000	$100,000
Loan proceeds	—	—	200,000	200,000
Investment	$100,000	$100,000	$300,000	$300,000
Payout expected	$ 75,000	$130,000	$225,000	$390,000
Repay loan	—	—	(200,000)	(200,000)
Pay loan interest	—	—	(12,000)	(12,000)
Closing equity	$ 75,000	$130,000	$ 13,000	$178,000
Opening equity	$100,000	$100,000	$100,000	$100,000
Profit/(loss)	$ (25,000)	$ 30,000	$ (87,000)	$ 78,000
Return on opening equity (ROE)	–25%	30%	–87%	78%

Commentary: This example demonstrates how leverage can increase investors' returns while concurrently exposing them to large losses.

---

2. IFRS uses "ordinary" shares to refer to common shares.

Exhibit 12-1	Continued

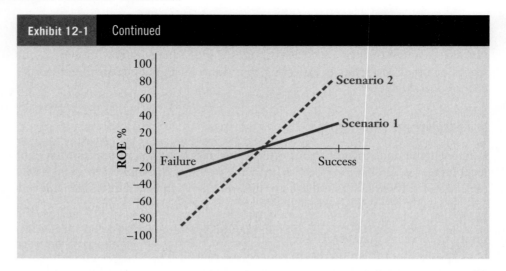

In the BCE opening vignette, one question posed was, "What is a safe level of debt?" This is a very difficult question to answer as opinions vary widely.[3] Indeed, it is quite clear that the purchasing consortium and bondholders had markedly different views as to what was an acceptable degree of financial leverage for BCE. Ultimately, the deal collapsed because, in KPMG's opinion, the attempted **leveraged buyout** of BCE was too risky from a solvency perspective. A leveraged buyout is a purchase where a significant part of the purchase price is raised by borrowing against the acquired assets.

leveraged buyout A purchase where a significant part of the purchase price is raised by borrowing against the acquired assets.

3. Debt rating agencies

Debt rating agencies such as DBRS and Moody's Investors Service evaluate the financial strength of governments and companies that issue publicly traded debt and preferred shares. The credit rating conferred is the agency's assessment of the borrower's ability to pay the obligation when due. The higher the ranking awarded, the lower the perceived probability of default. For example DBRS's bond ratings range from AAA to D. The Province of Alberta's debt is rated AAA. This seldom-conferred rating signifies that there is virtually no chance of default; in contrast, a company awarded a D has announced its intent to default on its obligations—or has defaulted already.

Rating companies provide investors with an independent evaluation of the riskiness of debt securities to assist them (the investors) in making informed investment decisions. A major evaluative criterion used by the rating companies is that of financial leverage. Due to concerns about excessive debt levels, rating agencies downgraded BCE's bonds when the privatization deal was first announced. In an October 2007 press release DBRS supported its downgrade with the comment:

> Today's action concludes DBRS's review, which consisted of a comprehensive evaluation of the privatization, the business risk profile of BCE and its operating subsidiaries, the financing involved to fund the privatization and the resulting financial risk profile, which, when completed, will have increased and consist of a *significant amount of leverage*. (emphasis added)[4]

3. A full discussion of this issue is beyond the scope of this text. Considerations in the choice of leverage include the nature of the industry, degree of operating leverage, stability of cash flows, competitive factors, and economic outlook.

4. All information is correct as of date of press release.

B. COMMON NON-CURRENT FINANCIAL LIABILITIES

Chapter 11 outlined how liabilities are either financial or non-financial in nature. There are two categories of financial liabilities: held-for-trading financial liabilities and other financial liabilities. The previous chapter has already considered held-for-trading financial liabilities, which are classified as current, and many of the more common non-financial liabilities including warranty obligations and deferred revenue. This chapter will focus on non-current financial liabilities including notes payable and bonds such as those proposed by the consortium that intended to take BCE private. Recall that **financial liabilities** are contractual obligations to deliver cash or other financial assets to another party at a future date.

L.O. 12-2. Describe the categories and types of non-current liabilities.

financial liability   A contractual obligation to deliver cash or other financial assets to another party.

Exhibit 12-2	Topical coverage	
	Financial	**Non-financial**
Current	Chapter 11	Chapter 11
Non-current	Chapter 12	Chapter 11

There are additional non-current, non-financial liabilities, such as deferred income taxes, pension liabilities, and lease obligations. These topics are addressed respectively in Chapters 16, 17, and 18.

1. Notes payable

The remaining time to maturity differentiates non-current and current notes payable. For most privately owned companies, notes are issued to a bank or supplier and are not publicly traded. A mortgage is a special type of note payable specifically secured by a charge over real estate. Many large, well-known companies such as Ford Credit Canada issue (sell) notes directly to the investment community, who then trade these notes on recognized exchanges and over-the-counter (OTC) markets.

Banks and other institutions are financial intermediaries using deposits by some customers to make loans to other clients. At the risk of oversimplifying a complex business model, banks make money by charging a "spread"—an interest rate on loans that is higher than the rate they pay on deposits. One reason why companies sell notes directly to investors is to lower interest costs by reducing or eliminating the spread. For example assume that Bank A is paying 1% interest on one-year deposits and charging 3% on one-year loans. Borrower B and depositor C are both better off if they are able to bypass the bank and deal with each other directly, with B paying C 2% for the use of its money.

Exhibit 12-3	Reducing the spread

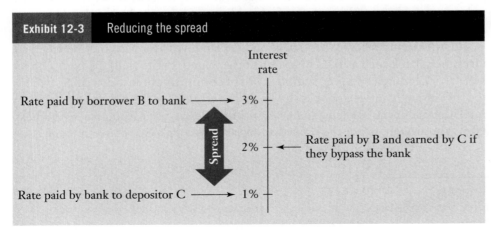

Of course, banks do not earn a spread without good reason—the spread is compensation for value-added services. Banks are able to offer a low rate on deposits because they offer a safe place for depositors to put their funds, whereas someone buying a note from a company faces significant information asymmetry about the company. On the lending side, banks have developed specialized processes to evaluate the creditworthiness of borrowers.

2. Bonds

a. Overview

Governments and publicly traded companies issue (sell) bonds directly to investors to raise large amounts of long-term funds. Bonds are a very common form of long-term debt. For these reasons, much of this chapter is devoted to accounting for bonds. Many of the ideas will also be applicable to other kinds of long-term debt.

covenant   The borrower's promise to restrict certain activities.

Lending money to a company entails moral hazard, since the company's management has control of the funds lent by the creditors (see Chapter 1). To reduce this moral hazard, bonds include **covenants**, which are restrictions on the borrower's activities. Covenants can be positive or negative, respectively requiring or forbidding certain actions. An example of a positive covenant is the borrower pledging to maintain its current ratio in excess of 1.5:1; a negative covenant is agreeing not to pay dividends in excess of $1,000,000 per year.

bond indenture   Contract that outlines the terms of the bond, including the maturity date; rate of interest and interest payment dates; security pledged; and financial covenants.

A **bond indenture** is the contract that outlines the terms of the bond, including the maturity date, rate of interest and interest payment dates, security pledged, and financial covenants. As evidenced in the opening vignette, providing that the borrower strictly complies with the covenants, lenders cannot otherwise restrict its activities. Recall that the Supreme Court of Canada refused to nullify the proposed sale of BCE despite the negative effect on its bondholders, as BCE's responsibility was limited to honouring the terms of the contract.

By convention, the coupon return on bonds is quoted as a nominal annual rate while interest payments are usually paid semi-annually. For example, 6% bonds pay interest of 3% every six months, resulting in an actual annual return of 6.09%.[5]

Reasons for issuing bonds (instead of using a bank loan, for example) include reducing the cost of borrowing and accessing large amounts of capital. Due to transaction costs, the minimum deal size for a bond issue is about $100 million— and is often much larger. For example, in August 2009 the Government of Canada announced its intent to issue US$3 billion in five-year bonds. It is very difficult or impossible for entities to borrow amounts this substantial from a single party because lenders want to avoid concentrated exposures to risk. Lenders such as banks would rather have diversified holdings of loans such that the default of any single borrower will not entail severe consequences for the lender.

firm commitment underwriting   Occurs where the investment bank guarantees the borrower a price for the bonds.

best efforts approach   Occurs where the broker simply agrees to try to sell as much of the (debt) issue as possible to investors.

Corporations seldom sell the bonds themselves. Rather, they engage an investment bank such as BMO Nesbitt Burns to underwrite (sell) the bonds on its behalf.[6] The more common method is a **firm commitment underwriting**, where the investment bank guarantees the borrower a price for the bonds, expecting to resell them to its investment clients at a profit. A lesser-used arrangement is a **best efforts approach**, where the broker simply agrees to try to sell as much of the issue as possible to investors.

---

5. $(1 + 0.03)^2 - 1 = 0.0609 = 6.09\%$

6. It is very common for the lead investment bank to form a syndicate with other investment banks to help sell the bonds to institutional and private investors.

b. Types of bonds

Once a corporation decides to raise capital by issuing bonds, it must determine the characteristics (features) of the indebtedness, such as the maturity date. While the company's investment bank will advise the firm in this respect, the business must consider a number of factors including investor preferences, projected cash flows, desired capital structure, and minimizing its cost of capital. Reflecting these various considerations, there are many different types of bonds to satisfy these diverse needs. Some of the more common features are described below.

- **Secured bonds** are bonds backed by specific collateral such as a mortgage on real estate.
- **Debentures** are unsecured bonds.
- **Stripped (zero-coupon) bonds** are bonds that do not pay interest. Stripped bonds are sold at a discount and mature at face value.
- **Serial bonds** are a set of bonds issued at the same time but that mature at regular scheduled dates rather than all on the same date.
- **Callable bonds** permit the issuing company to "call" for the bonds to be redeemed before maturity. A **call premium** is the excess over par value paid to the bondholders when the security is called.
- **Convertible bonds** allow the holder to exchange or "convert" the bond into other securities in the corporation, usually common shares. Convertible bonds are an example of compound financial instruments discussed in Chapter 14.
- **Inflation-linked** or **real-return bonds** protect investors against inflation. While the mechanics differ slightly across issues, the basic premise is that the cash flows are indexed to inflation. Inflation-linked bonds are seldom issued in Canada, although their popularity is increasing.
- **Perpetual bonds** are bonds that never mature. Perpetual bonds are seldom issued in Canada.

secured bonds Bonds backed by specific collateral such as a mortgage on real estate.

debentures Unsecured bonds.

stripped (zero-coupon) bonds Bonds that do not pay interest; stripped bonds are sold at a discount and mature at face value.

serial bonds A set of bonds issued at the same time but that mature at regularly scheduled dates rather than all on the same date.

callable bonds Bonds that permit the issuing company to "call" for the bonds to be redeemed before maturity.

call premium The excess over par value paid to the bondholders when the security is called.

convertible bonds Bonds that allow the holder to exchange or "convert" the bond into other securities in the corporation, usually common shares.

inflation-linked (real-return) bonds A bond that provides protection against inflation.

perpetual bonds Bonds that never mature.

C. INITIAL MEASUREMENT

Non-current financial liabilities, like all financial statement elements, must be assigned a value when they are first recognized on the balance sheet. In general, enterprises should initially record financial liabilities at fair value minus debt issue costs (IAS 39 paragraph 43). Examples of transaction costs include fees charged by investment banks and regulatory agencies; legal and accounting fees; and outlays for promotion. For example, if an enterprise issues a bond for gross proceeds and fair value of $100 million and incurs $2 million of bond-issue costs, it would record the bond at the amount of the net proceeds of $98 million.

L.O. 12-3. Describe the initial and subsequent measurement of non-current financial liabilities and account for these obligations.

The one exception to the inclusion of transaction costs is held-for-trading financial liabilities. Enterprises should initially recognize these liabilities at fair value only, with all transaction costs expensed. This exception to the general rule makes sense to the extent that held-for-trading financial instruments must be measured at fair value at each balance sheet date, so any transaction costs included in the initially recognized amount would be expensed when the item is re-measured at fair value. For instance, using the example just given, if the bond is classified as held for trading, the company would record $100 million for the liability and expense the $2 million. If at year-end the bond still has a fair value of $100 million, no additional income or expense would be recorded. However, if the bond had initially been recorded at the amount of net proceeds ($98 million), then the $100 million fair value at year-end would result in a $2 million increase in liability and a corresponding $2 million expense. The outcome is the same: both treatments result in $2 million of expense.

In many cases, the fair value of the debt is easily determinable. For example, if a company issues a standard bond at par value for cash, and the timing matches the interest payment date, then the fair value of the note equals the cash received. Not all situations are this straightforward, however. Some common departures include receiving non-cash assets, bonds issued at premium or discount, issuance of hybrid financial instruments, and debt issuance dates that differ from the interest payment dates. We discuss these issues below.

1. Debt exchanged for non-cash assets

Notes or other debt instruments exchanged for assets are recognized at fair value. This treatment is supported by IAS 16 *Property, Plant and Equipment*, which reads in part:

> ¶6. *Cost* is the amount of cash or cash equivalents paid or the fair value of the other consideration given to acquire an asset at the time of its acquisition . . .

Paragraphs 48–49 of IAS 39, supported by the application guidance in AG69–AG82 of IAS 39, provide considerable guidance on techniques for determining fair value, including in order of preference: using active market values; referencing recent similar transactions; and employing discounted cash flow analysis.

2. Debt issued at non-market rates of interest

If the liability is non-interest bearing or the stated rate of interest is different from the market rate of interest, the fair value of the debt will differ from the face (maturity) value. This includes bonds issued at a premium or discount discussed later in this chapter. If the note is issued for consideration other than cash, the fair value must be estimated in accordance with paragraphs 48–49 of IAS 39. In the absence of similar market transactions, discounted cash flow analysis would normally be used to determine the liability to be recognized.

Exhibit 12-4 illustrates accounting for the issuance of debt in exchange for cash or non-cash assets, and a third scenario involving debt issued at a non-market interest rate.

Exhibit 12-4	Accounting for the issuance of debt		
	Scenario 1	**Scenario 2**	**Scenario 3**
Face amount of note issued	$150,000	$150,000	$150,000
Date issued	Jan 1, 2010	Jan 1, 2010	Jan 1, 2010
Due date	Jan 1, 2012	Jan 1, 2012	Jan 1, 2012
Interest rate in the note	4%	0%	4% (payable annually)
Market rate of interest	4%	Unknown	6%
Consideration received	Cash	Equipment	Land
Value of similar transaction	not applicable	$140,000	not applicable
Fair value determination	Cash received	Similar transactions, per IAS 39 par.48A	Discounted cash flow analysis
Journal entry on issuance (NP = Note payable)	Dr. Cash 150,000 Cr. NP 150,000	Dr. Equipment 140,000 Cr. NP 140,000	Dr. Land 144,500 Cr. NP 144,500

Comment—Scenario 3

The note payable consists of two types of cash flows: an ordinary annuity for the periodic coupon payments and a single sum due at maturity for the principal. The value of the note is the sum of the present value (PV) of the two parts. PVFA is the present value factor for an annuity.

- PV of coupons = $6,000 × PVFA (6%, 2) = $6,000 × 1.8334 = $11,000
- PV of principal = $150,000/1.06^2 = $133,500
- PV of the note = $11,000 + $133,500 = $144,500

3. Compound financial instruments

A compound financial instrument is one with both debt and equity features. For example, a bond that can be exchanged for common shares in the issuing company has elements of both debt (the bond), and equity (the right to exchange the bond for shares). The issue (sales) price of the instrument must be separated into its component parts when it is initially recognized, as detailed in Chapter 14.

4. Issuing bonds at par, premium, or a discount

The **coupon** or stated rate of interest on a bond is the interest rate specified in the bond indenture.[7] This rate is expressed as a percentage of the bond's face value. The **yield** or **market rate** of interest is the rate of return (on a bond) actually earned by the investor at a particular time. The yield at the date of a bond's issuance is the **effective interest rate** for that bond. For a given amount of coupon and maturity value, the more that the borrower is able to sell the bond for, the lower the effective rate of interest that will be paid. The inverse relationship between bond price and the effective interest rate is demonstrated in Exhibit 12-5.

coupon (stated) rate The interest rate specified in the bond indenture.

yield or **market rate** The rate of return (on a bond) actually earned by the investor at a particular time.

effective interest rate The yield on the date of issuance of a debt security.

Exhibit 12-5	Illustration of inverse relationship between bond prices and the effective interest rate		

Facts
A $100,000, 10-year, 6% bond that pays interest annually dated January 1, 2011 is offered for sale on January 1, 2011.

	Scenario 1 $100,000 in bonds are sold for **$99,000**	**Scenario 2** $100,000 in bonds are sold for **$100,000**	**Scenario 3** $100,000 in bonds are sold for **$101,000**
Inputs			
Maturity value	$100,000	$100,000	$100,000
Interest payments	$ 6,000	$ 6,000	$ 6,000
Number of payments	10	10	10
Price paid for the bond	$ 99,000	$100,000	$101,000
Solve for Effective rate	6.14%	6.00%	5.86%

Note that solving for the effective rate when the number of periods is two or more requires a financial calculator or a computer spreadsheet.
Commentary
The cost to the company (the effective cost of borrowing) decreases as the price received for the bond increases.

From Exhibit 12-5 we can conclude that:

- Bonds will sell at a discount (less than par value) when the coupon rate is less than the market rate (Scenario 1).
- Bonds will sell at **par value** (the amount to be repaid to the investor at maturity) when the coupon rate equals the market rate (Scenario 2).
- Bonds will sell at a premium (more than par value) when the coupon rate is greater than the market rate (Scenario 3).

par value The amount to be repaid to the investor at maturity.

Companies normally aim to issue the bonds at par by setting the coupon rate to equal the prevailing market rate of interest. Due to the issuer having to obtain regulatory approval for the bond sale and other factors, there is inevitably a time lag between when the company determines the coupon rate and the time of sale. Changes in the market rate in the intervening period cause the actual sale price

7. Coupon is a historical term from when bonds were printed and issued to the purchaser. The bond was comprised of the body, which had to be surrendered at maturity, and a coupon for each interest payment—hence the name. On the interest due date, the investor would detach the coupon and submit it to the borrower for payment. Today, bond certificates are seldom printed; most interest payments are electronically credited to the investor's account.

to change so as to provide investors with the required market rate of return. Such price changes result in the bond selling at a discount or premium.

5. Determining the sales price of a bond when the yield is given

Much of the discussion in this chapter focuses on determining the effective rate of interest from the sales price and other information such as the coupon rate and term. Nevertheless, it is sometimes useful to determine the sales price of a bond from a given yield. The reason is that investors normally demand a certain yield—and their requirements drive the price, not the other way around. Having received the price that the investors agreed to pay, the company then uses this information to determine the effective rate of interest that they are paying.

Determining the sales price of a bond when the yield is known involves two calculations using the formula approach, which may be combined when using a financial calculator or computer spreadsheet. The first step is to compute the present value of the coupons, and the second step is to compute the present value of the maturity amount. The sum of these two amounts is the sales price of the bond, as demonstrated in Exhibit 12-6 below.

Exhibit 12-6	Determining the sales price of a bond when the yield is known

Facts: A $100,000, 5-year, 6% bond that pays interest annually dated January 1, 2011 is offered for sale on January 1, 2011. The bond is sold to yield a 7% return to the investors.

Required: Determine the selling price of the bonds.

Maturity value	$100,000
Interest payments	$6,000
Number of payments	5
Effective rate (yield)	7%
Price paid for the bond	$95,900 as per the computations below

Calculation of sales price when the effective rate of interest is known

We need to determine the value of the bond, which has two types of cash flows: an ordinary annuity for the periodic coupon payments and a single sum due at maturity for the principal.

- PV of coupons = $6,000 × PVAF (7%, 5) = $6,000 × 4.1002 = $24,601
- PV of principal = $100,000/$1.07^5$ = $71,299
- PV of the note = $24,601 + $71,299 = $95,900

6. Timing of bond issuance

a. Selling bonds on the issue date specified in the indenture

Exhibit 12-7 illustrates the journal entries the issuing company would make in each of the three situations detailed in Exhibit 12-5. We also include a fourth scenario, in which the company paid $3,000 to obtain regulatory approval.

Exhibit 12-7	Accounting for the issuance of bonds, using facts established in Exhibit 12-5			
	Scenario 1	**Scenario 2**	**Scenario 3**	**Scenario 4**
Maturity value	$100,000	$100,000	$100,000	$100,000
Sales price	$ 99,000	$100,000	$101,000	$101,000
Transaction costs	$ 0	$ 0	$ 0	$ 3,000
Journal entry on issuance (BP denotes bonds payable)	Dr. Cash 99,000 Cr. BP 99,000	Dr. Cash 100,000 Cr. BP 100,000	Dr. Cash 101,000 Cr. BP 101,000	Dr. Cash 101,000 Cr. Cash 3,000 Cr. BP 98,000

Comment—Scenario 4

The obligation is measured at the net of the fair value ($101,000) and transaction costs as required by paragraph 43 of IAS 39.

b. Selling bonds after the specified issue date

The preceding examples assume that the bonds were sold on their issue date. On occasion, though, due to adverse market conditions or regulatory delays, a company may not sell its bonds until after the issue date. Consider a $1,000 five-year, 6% bond, dated January 1, 2011, that pays interest on June 30 and December 31 and is sold at par on March 1, 2011. The bond indenture assumed that the bonds would sell on the issue date and provided that the purchaser receive $30 ($1,000 × 6% × 6/12), representing six months of interest on June 30, 2011. The problem is that the investors are only entitled to $20 ($1,000 × 6% × 4/12), as they have owned the bonds for only four months.

By convention, when bonds are sold between interest payment dates, the purchaser pays the seller the agreed-upon price for the bond plus interest that has accrued since the last payment date. In the example above this would be $10 ($1,000 × 6% × 2/12), bringing the total consideration received to $1,010 accounted for as set out in Exhibit 12-8.

Exhibit 12-8	Accounting for the issuance of bonds between interest payment dates		
On date of sale			
Dr. Cash		1,010	
Cr. Bonds payable			1,000
Cr. Accrued interest on bond payable (balance sheet)[8]			10
On date of first interest payment			
Dr. Accrued interest on bond payable		10	
Dr. Interest expense		20	
Cr. Cash			30

Due to the delay in sale of the bonds, any premiums or discounts must be amortized over a reduced length of time from the actual sale date to the maturity date. In the example just given, the two-month delay would reduce the amortization period from 60 months (five years) to 58 months.

D. SUBSEQUENT MEASUREMENT

After initial recognition, all financial liabilities excepting those held for trading are measured and reported at **amortized cost,** which is the amount initially recognized for the debt adjusted by subsequent amortization of premium or discount. There are two essential steps that must be taken to determine the amortized cost of a financial liability:

amortized cost (of debt) The amount initially recognized for the debt adjusted by subsequent amortization of premium or discount.

1. establish the effective interest rate; and
2. amortize the premium or discount using the effective interest method.

The following discussion explores these two steps in more detail.

1. Effective interest rate

In IFRS, the effective interest method must be used to determine amortized cost. Applying this method requires the **effective interest rate**, which is the yield of

---

8. Alternatively, the company may credit interest expense on date of sale in which case the debit to interest expense on the date of the first payment would be $30. This is a bookkeeping matter much like the payment for insurance policies that can be debited to prepaid insurance or insurance expense. The key is that the company should adopt a policy, apply it consistently, and make appropriate adjusting entries at period end.

the debt on the date of issuance.[9] Exhibit 12-5 demonstrated the procedure for calculating the effective interest rate.

2. Amortization using the effective interest method

After determining the effective interest rate, the process of applying the effective method is shown in Exhibit 12-9.

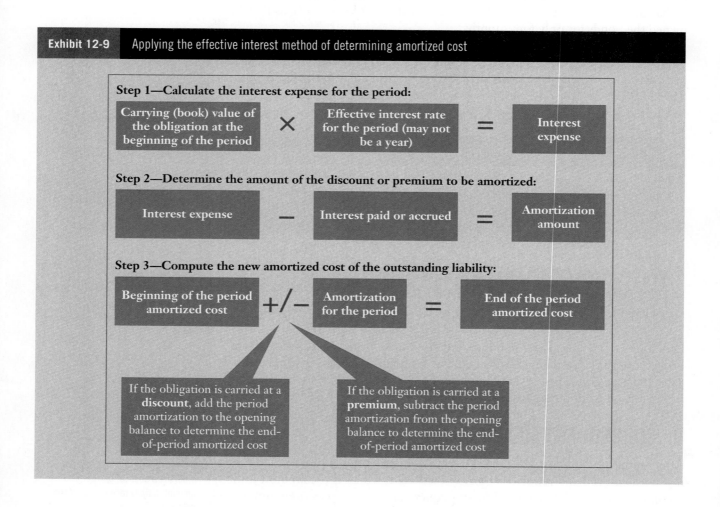

Exhibit 12-9   Applying the effective interest method of determining amortized cost

Step 1—Calculate the interest expense for the period:

Carrying (book) value of the obligation at the beginning of the period ✕ Effective interest rate for the period (may not be a year) = Interest expense

Step 2—Determine the amount of the discount or premium to be amortized:

Interest expense − Interest paid or accrued = Amortization amount

Step 3—Compute the new amortized cost of the outstanding liability:

Beginning of the period amortized cost +/− Amortization for the period = End of the period amortized cost

If the obligation is carried at a **discount**, add the period amortization to the opening balance to determine the end-of-period amortized cost

If the obligation is carried at a **premium**, subtract the period amortization from the opening balance to determine the end-of-period amortized cost

Companies frequently use spreadsheets to compute interest expense and determine the amortized cost of bonds to be reported at each balance sheet date. Exhibits 12-10 and 12-11 demonstrate the process outlined above and include select journal entries to record the issuance of the bonds and subsequent payment and accrual of interest. In both examples, the fiscal year-end is December 31.

While working through the two examples that follow, you should observe the following:

■ At maturity, the amortized cost of the bond (the carrying value or net book value) equals the maturity (face) value of the bond.

---

9. IAS 39 paragraph 9 technically defines the effective interest rate as the rate that exactly discounts estimated future cash payments or receipts through the expected life of the financial instrument.

- The original discount or premium is charged to interest expense over the life of the bond. Amortizing bond discounts increases interest expense relative to the coupon payment; premiums decrease interest expense.
- For bonds sold at a discount, the interest expense per period increases each period. This is because the amortized cost of the bond increases each period and interest expense is a function of the bond's book value. Conversely, for bonds sold at a premium, the interest expense decreases each period.

Exhibit 12-10	Schedule for determining the interest expense and amortized cost of a discount bond

Facts:

- Port Bay Inc. sells $1,000,000 of 3-year bonds on January 1, 2011 for **$981,000**
- The coupon rate on the bonds is 6% payable on July 1 and January 1
- Transaction costs directly attributable to issuing the bonds total $15,000

First, determine the effective interest rate using a financial calculator or spreadsheet.

- The net proceeds (PV) to Port Bay are $981,000 − $15,000 = $966,000
- The maturity value (FV) of the bonds is $1,000,000
- N = 3 years × 2 payments/year = 6
- PMT = $1,000,000 × 6%/2 = $30,000
→ Effective semi-annual rate = 3.6410%

Date	Interest expense @3.6410%	Interest paid	Discount amortized	Amortized cost
2011 Jan 01				$ 966,000 (a)
2011 Jul 01	$ 35,172 (b)	$ 30,000 (c)	$ 5,172 (d)	971,172 (e)
2012 Jan 01	35,361	30,000	5,361	976,533
2012 Jul 01	35,556	30,000	5,556	982,089
2013 Jan 01	35,758	30,000	5,758	987,847
2013 Jul 01	35,968	30,000	5,968	993,815
2014 Jan 01	36,185	30,000	6,185	1,000,000
	$ 214,000	$ 180,000	$34,000	

Calculations:

(a) $981,000 − $15,000 = $966,000 (initial proceeds net of issuance cost)
(b) $966,000 × 3.6410% = $35,172
(c) $1,000,000 × 6%/2 = $30,000
(d) $35,172 − $30,000 = $5,172
(e) $966,000 + $5,172 = $971,172

Journal entries		
Issuance	Dr. Cash (Sales proceeds)	981,000	
2011 Jan 01	Cr. Cash (Transaction costs)		15,000
	Cr. Bonds payable ($981,000 – $15,000)		966,000
Interest payment	Dr. Interest expense	35,172	
2011 Jul 01	Cr. Cash		30,000
	Cr. Bonds payable ($35,172 – $30,000)		5,172
Year-end	Dr. Interest expense	35,361	
2011 Dec 31	Cr. Interest payable		30,000
	Cr. Bonds payable ($35,361 – $30,000)		5,361
Interest payment	Dr. Interest payable	30,000	
2012 Jan 01	Cr. Cash		30,000

| Exhibit 12-11 | Schedule for determining the interest expense and amortized cost of a premium bond |

Facts:

- Port Bay Inc. sells $1,000,000 of 3-year bonds on January 1, 2011 for **$1,025,000**
- The coupon rate on the bonds is 6% payable on July 1 and January 1
- Transaction costs directly attributable to issuing the bonds total $15,000

First, determine the effective interest rate using a financial calculator or spreadsheet.

- The net proceeds (PV) to Port Bay are $1,025,000 − $15,000 = $1,010,000
- The maturity value (FV) of the bonds is $1,000,000
- N = 3 years × 2 payments/year = 6
- PMT = $1,000,000 × 6%/2 = $30,000
- → Effective semi-annual rate = 2.8165%

Date	Interest expense @2.8165%	Interest paid	Premium amortized	Amortized cost
2011 Jan 01				$1,010,000 (a)
2011 Jul 01	$ 28,447 (b)	$ 30,000 (c)	$ 1,553 (d)	1,008,447 (e)
2012 Jan 01	28,403	30,000	1,597	1,006,850
2012 Jul 01	28,358	30,000	1,642	1,005,208
2013 Jan 01	28,312	30,000	1,688	1,003,520
2013 Jul 01	28,264	30,000	1,736	1,001,785
2014 Jan 01	28,215	30,000	1,785	1,000,000
	$170,000	$180,000	$10,000	

Calculations:

Small differences in spreadsheet due to rounding
(a) $1,025,000 − $15,000 = $1,010,000
(b) $1,010,000 × 2.8165% = $28,447
(c) $1,000,000 × 6%/2 = $30,000
(d) $28,447 − $30,000 = $1,553
(e) $1,010,000 − $1,553 = $1,008,447

Journal entries			
Issuance	Dr. Cash (Sales proceeds)	1,025,000	
2011 Jan 01	Cr. Cash (Transaction costs)		15,000
	Cr. Bonds payable ($1,025,000 – $15,000)		1,010,000
Interest payment	Dr. Interest expense	28,447	
2011 Jul 01	Dr. Bonds payable ($30,000 – $28,447)	1,553	
	Cr. Cash		30,000
Year-end	Dr. Interest expense	28,403	
2011 Dec 31	Dr. Bonds payable ($30,000 – $28,403)	1,597	
	Cr. Interest payable		30,000
Interest payment	Dr. Interest payable	30,000	
2012 Jan 01	Cr. Cash		30,000

3. Amortization using the straight-line method

IFRS unambiguously requires that amortized cost be determined using the effective interest method. Canadian standards, however, permit use of the straight-line method by some companies. A brief history follows:

- Prior to the adoption of S. 3855, Financial Instruments—Recognition and Measurement, Canadian GAAP permitted all companies to amortize debt discounts and premiums using either the effective interest or straight-line method.

- The Accounting Standards Board (AcSB) issued S. 3855 effective for fiscal years beginning on or after October 1, 2006. Like IFRS, this standard mandated the use of the effective interest method to determine amortized cost. Adoption of this section was mandatory for publicly accountable enterprises but optional for private companies.
- The AcSB issued Accounting Standards for Private Enterprises (ASPE) effective for fiscal periods beginning on or after January 1, 2011. These standards include S. 3856 Financial Instruments, which does not specify the method for determining amortized cost, so this standard implicitly permits straight-line amortization of premiums and discounts.

The straight-line method of determining amortized cost continues to be widely used by private enterprises in Canada. Advocates of the straight-line method assert that it is simple to use and note that the results do not usually differ materially from those obtained under the effective interest method. We have included an illustration of the application of the straight-line method in Exhibit 12-12, contrasting it to the effective interest method.

Exhibit 12-12	Comparing the straight-line and effective interest methods of amortizing a bond discount

Facts:

- Sointula Educational Services Ltd. sells $1,000,000 of 3-year bonds on January 1, 2011 for $973,357.
- The coupon rate on the bonds is 6% per year, payable on July 1 and January 1; the bonds yield 7% per year, or 3.5% per period.
- Sointula Educational Services' year-end is December 31.

The process for the straight-line method:

- Determine the amount of discount (or premium as the case may be), which is $1,000,000 − $973,357 = $26,643.
- To determine the amount to be amortized each period, divide this discount by the number of periods until maturity: $26,643/6 = $4,441 (rounded).
- Interest expense for each period is the sum of interest paid or accrued and the discount amortized: $30,000 + $4,441 = $34,441.

	Straight-line method				Effective interest method			
Date	Interest expense	Interest paid	Discount amortized	Amortized cost	Interest expense	Interest paid	Discount amortized	Amortized cost
2011 Jan 01				$ 973,357				$ 973,357
2011 Jul 01	$ 34,441 (a)	$ 30,000 (b)	$4,441 (c)	977,798 (d)	$ 34,068	$ 30,000	$4,068	977,425
2012 Jan 01	34,441	30,000	4,441	982,239	34,210	30,000	4,210	981,635
2012 Jul 01	34,441	30,000	4,441	986,680	34,357	30,000	4,357	985,992
2013 Jan 01	34,441	30,000	4,441	991,121	34,510	30,000	4,510	990,502
2013 Jul 01	34,441	30,000	4,441	995,562	34,668	30,000	4,668	995,170
2014 Jan 01	34,438	30,000	4,438 (e)	1,000,000	34,831	30,000	4,831	1,000,000
	$206,643	$180,000	$26,643		$206,643	$180,000	$26,643	

Notes

(a) $30,000 + $4,441 = $34,441
(b) $1,000,000 × 6%/2 = $30,000
(c) $1,000,000 − $973,357 = $26,643; $26,643/6 = $4,441 (rounded)
(d) $973,357 + $4,441 = $977,798
(e) small difference due to rounding

Commentary:

- Under the straight-line method, interest expense remains constant each period.
- Total interest expense over the life of the bond is the same under both the straight-line and effective interest methods.

E. DERECOGNITION

To derecognize a financial liability is to remove it from the entity's balance sheet. For the most part, firms can derecognize liabilities when they extinguish the obligations. IAS 39 paragraph 39 provides that an obligation is extinguished when the underlying contract is discharged, cancelled, or expires. Paragraph AG57 of IAS 39 clarifies that extinguishment occurs when the entity pays off the debt or when it legally no longer has primary responsibility for the liability. Obviously, the most common way to extinguish an obligation is by paying the creditor cash or providing goods and services as specified in the contract. We look at this typical method as well as other transactions that would lead to derecognition.

1. Derecognition at maturity

The customary way to extinguish obligations is to settle them when due. For example, a $100,000 bank loan maturing on June 22, 2012 will be extinguished when you pay the bank $100,000 plus interest on the due date. Accounting for the derecognition of a matured obligation does not provide any special challenges as there will not be a gain or loss on retirement; amortized cost equals the principal amount due.

Refer back to the bond obligation introduced in the spreadsheet in Exhibit 12-11. The journal entry required derecognizing the obligation on January 1, 2014 is shown in Exhibit 12-13.

Exhibit 12-13	Journal entry to record the derecognition of a maturing obligation		
2014 Jan 01	Dr. Bonds payable	1,000,000	
	Dr. Interest payable	30,000	
	Cr. Cash		1,030,000

2. Derecognition prior to maturity

Companies sometimes pay off their obligations prior to maturity. For example, a company may use surplus cash to purchase its own bonds in the financial markets or exercise a call provision that requires the bondholders to tender their bonds for redemption. The process to extinguish the liability is the same in both cases and is analogous to recording the disposition of a depreciable asset. Derecognition of a financial liability should follow these steps:

i. The company updates its records to account for interim interest expense, including the amortization of discounts or premiums up to the derecognition date.
ii. The entity records the outflow of assets expended to extinguish the obligation.
iii. The entity records a gain or loss on debt retirement equal to the difference between the amount paid and the book value of the liability derecognized. Exhibit 12-14 demonstrates this process.

If the entity retires only a portion of a liability, the obligation is derecognized on a pro rata basis. For example, if a company retires 40% of a bond, it would derecognize 40% of the book value including 40% of the unamortized premium or discount.

Exhibit 12-14	Derecognition prior to maturity

Facts:

- On October 1, 2012, Port Bay Inc. repurchases the bonds issued in Exhibit 12-10. For ease of reference, excerpts of the amortization worksheet are reproduced below.
- In scenario 1 Port Bay repurchases the bonds on the open market for total consideration of $980,000 cash.
- In scenario 2 Port Bay calls the bonds and pay each holder the face amount of the bonds, plus accrued interest ($15,000), together with a 2% call premium ($20,000). The total consideration paid is $1,035,000

Date	Interest expense @3.6410%	Interest paid	Discount amortized	Amortized cost
2011 Jan 01				$966,000
2011 Jul 01	$35,172	$30,000	$5,172	971,172
2012 Jan 01	35,361	30,000	5,361	976,533
2012 Jul 01	35,556	30,000	5,556	982,089
2012 Oct 01	**17,879** (a)	**15,000**	**2,879**	**984,968** (b)

(a) Interest for three months: $982,089 \times 3.6410\% \times 3/6 = \$17,879$

(b) This line records the effects of Port Bay updating its records on 2012 Oct 01

Commentary:

Prior to the repurchase, the bond discount was last amortized on 2012 Jul 01. The journal entry required to update Port Bay's amortization of the discount from July to October is the same for both scenarios irrespective of the consideration paid. Thus, we need only show it once.

Scenarios 1 and 2—Journal entry to update Port Bay's records (2012 Oct 01)

Dr. Interest expense	17,879	
Cr. Interest payable ($30,000 / 2)		15,000
Cr. Bonds payable ($17,879 − $15,000)		2,879

Scenario 1—Journal entry to record extinguishment (2012 Oct 01)

Dr. Interest payable (given)	15,000	
Dr. Bonds payable (from schedule)	984,968	
Cr. Cash (given)		980,000
Cr. Gain on bond redemption		19,968

Scenario 2—Journal entry to record extinguishment (2012 Oct 01)

Dr. Interest payable (given)	15,000	
Dr. Bonds payable (from schedule)	984,968	
Dr. Loss on bond redemption	35,032	
Cr. Cash ($1,000,000 + $15,000 + $20,000)		1,035,000

In practice, the outstanding bond balance ($984,968 in this example) can be quickly determined by referring to the general ledger. In a classroom setting, the net book value can be determined in a number of ways.

1. Manually compute the bond amortization on a period-by-period basis. This is a time-consuming task and very prone to error especially if the number of payment periods is large.

2. Construct a spreadsheet. While not difficult to do, many students do not have access to a spreadsheet program in the classroom and even fewer can use one in an examination.

3. The most feasible method is to directly calculate the amortized cost by using present value methods. We explain this method more fully here.

   - The necessary starting point for preparing the journal entries is the bond liability balance at the interest payment date prior to the redemption (2012 Jul 01 in this example).

(Continued)

Exhibit 12-14 Continued

- When originally sold, there were six periods until the bonds mature. On 2012 Jul 01, the bonds have been outstanding for three periods and accordingly there are now only three periods left until maturity. (2012 Jul 01 is 18 months or three periods before the maturity date of 2014 Jan 01.)
- Using the effective interest rate for this bond (3.6410% per period), compute the present value of the remaining three coupon payments and the principal payment due upon maturity.
- PV of coupons = $30,000 \times$ PVFA (3.6410%, 3) = $30,000 \times 2.7941$ = $83,823.
- PV of principal = $1,000,000/1.03641^3$ = $898,266.
- Total PV = $83,823 + 898,266$ = $982,089. Note how this amount exactly corresponds with the amount derived using the spreadsheet method.

3. Derecognition through offsetting and in-substance defeasance

a. Offsetting

Offsetting is the practice of showing the net amount of related assets and liabilities on the balance sheet, rather than showing each of the components separately. For example, company A has a receivable of $10,000 owing from company B as well as a payable of $7,000 owing to the same company. If offset against each other, Company A would report a net asset of $3,000 as opposed to an asset of $10,000 and a liability of $7,000. Offsetting usually improves key financial ratios, making it easier to meet lenders' restrictive covenants. Moreover, it may also free up borrowing capacity as loan agreements typically limit the maximum debt a company can carry. In the simple receivable/payable example above, offsetting may permit company A to borrow an additional $7,000.

IFRS asserts that separately reporting assets and liabilities generally conveys more information than reporting the net amount, and that offsetting compromises the user's ability to correctly interpret the financial results. Consequently, paragraph 32 of IAS 1 prohibits offsetting generally, unless specifically allowed by another standard. One such exception is paragraph 42 of IAS 32:

> ¶42. A financial asset and a financial liability shall be offset and the net amount presented in the statement of financial position when, and only when, an entity:
> (a) currently has a legally enforceable right to set off the recognized amounts; and
> (b) intends either to settle on a net basis, or to realize the asset and settle the liability simultaneously.

In other words, the reporting entity must be both willing and legally able to offset the amounts against each other.

An example of when these tests would normally be met occurs when an entity has two chequing accounts with the same bank, one of which is overdrawn. Offsetting is appropriate in this instance because it better reflects the economic substance of the situation.

b. In-substance defeasance

Companies may want to satisfy a liability before the maturity date but are precluded from doing so by restrictions in the loan agreement or onerous prepayment penalties. In an effort to avoid reporting the liability, firms may indirectly extinguish their debt. **In-substance defeasance** is an arrangement where funds sufficient to satisfy a liability are placed in trust with a third party to pay the creditors directly. (See Chapter 1 for a case study on this issue.) While popular for a period of time in the 1990s, current accounting standards make this type of arrangement ineffective. In particular, IAS 39 specifies the following in its Application Guidance (AG) paragraph 59:

in-substance defeasance An arrangement where funds sufficient to satisfy a liability are placed in trust with a third party to pay directly to the creditor at maturity.

¶AG59   Payment to a third party, including a trust (sometimes called 'in-substance defeasance'), does not, by itself, relieve the debtor of its primary obligation to the creditor, in the absence of legal release.

The essence of this guidance is that the borrower cannot usually derecognize the obligation through in-substance defeasance, which is a unilateral arrangement put in place by the debtor. The defeasance would result in derecognition of the liability only if the creditor also formally confirms that the entity is no longer liable for the indebtedness.

F. PUTTING IT ALL TOGETHER—A COMPREHENSIVE BOND EXAMPLE

Creative Conundrums Ltd. (CCL) raised $9,500,000 by selling $10,000,000 of five-year, 5% bonds dated January 1, 2011. CCL used part of the proceeds to pay its investment bank's fee of $200,000 and related legal and accounting fees of $300,000. Interest is payable on June 30 and December 31 each year. CCL can call the bonds on January 1, 2013 at 102 ("102" means 102% of the face value, so for each $1,000 bond outstanding CCL will pay the holder $1,020 plus accrued interest). The company exercises this privilege, redeeming 60% of the bonds on the call date. The company's year-end is December 31.

Required:

Prepare journal entries to record:

a. the issuance of the bonds on January 1, 2011.
b. payment of interest and related amortization on June 30, 2011.
c. payment of interest and related amortization on December 31, 2012.
d. repurchase of the bonds on January 1, 2013.
e. retirement of the remaining bonds on December 31, 2015 assuming that the final interest payment has already been recorded in the company's books.

Note: you will need to use a financial calculator or a computer spreadsheet to determine the effective rate. The suggested solution is based on the use of a financial calculator to determine the effective rate and the use of a spreadsheet to determine interest expense, discount amortization, and the amortized cost of the bonds.

Solution:

Exhibit 12-15	Solution to comprehensive problem

Determining the effective interest rate for the period using a BAII Plus financial calculator:

The net proceeds (PV) are $9,500,000 − $200,000 − $300,000 = $9,000,000;

N = 10 (5 × 2);

PMT = ($10,000,000 × 5% × 6/12) = $250,000

Key in: 10N, 9000000 +/− PV, 10000000 FV, 250000 PMT, CPT I/Y

Output: I/Y = 3.7155% (rounded)

(Continued)

Exhibit 12-15	Continued

Spreadsheet

Effective rate per period: 3.7155%

Date	Interest expense	Interest paid	Discount amortized	Amortized cost
01/01/2011				$9,000,000 (a)
06/30/2011	$334,396	$250,000 (b)	$84,396 (c)	9,084,396 (d)
12/31/2011	337,532	250,000	87,532	9,171,928
06/30/2012	340,784	250,000	90,784	9,262,712
12/31/2012	344,157	250,000	94,157	9,356,869
01/01/2013	Redeem and derecognize 60% of the outstanding bonds			(5,614,121)
				3,742,747
06/30/2013	139,062	100,000 (e)	39,062	3,781,810
12/31/2013	140,514	100,000	40,514	3,822,323
06/30/2014	142,019	100,000	42,019	3,864,342
12/31/2014	143,580	100,000	43,580	3,907,922
06/30/2015	145,199	100,000	45,199	3,953,121
12/31/2015	146,879	100,000	46,879	4,000,000

Minor differences in the spreadsheet are due to rounding.

(a) The net sale proceeds of the bonds ($9,500,000 − $200,000 − $300,000 = $9,000,000)
(b) $10,000,000 × 5%/2 = $250,000
(c) $334,396 − $250,000 = $84,396
(d) $9,000,000 + $84,396 = $9,084,396
(e) $250,000 × (1 − 60%) = $100,000 or
$10,000,000 (1 − 60%) × 5%/2 = $4,000,000 × 5%/2 = $100,000

a. Journal entry on issuance (2011 Jan 1)

Dr. Cash (Sales proceeds – transaction costs)	9,000,000	
Cr. Bonds payable ($9,500,000 − $200,000 − $300,000)		9,000,000

b. Journal entry on interest payment date (2011 Jun 30)

Dr. Interest expense (from spreadsheet)	334,396	
Cr. Cash		250,000
Cr. Bonds payable		84,396

c. Journal entry on interest payment date (2012 Dec 31)

Dr. Interest expense (from spreadsheet)	344,157	
Cr. Cash		250,000
Cr. Bonds payable		94,157

d. Journal entry on reacquisition of the bonds (2013 Jan 1)

Dr. Loss on bond redemption ($6,120,000 − $5,614,121)	505,879	
Dr. Bonds payable (from spreadsheet)	5,614,121	
Cr. Cash ($6,000,000 × 102%)		6,120,000

e. Journal entry on retirement of the bonds (2015 Dec 31)

Dr. Bonds payable	4,000,000	
Cr. Cash		4,000,000

G. OTHER ISSUES

1. Decommissioning costs

Chapter 8 includes a discussion and worked-through example of accounting for the costs of dismantling equipment and site restoration at the end of an asset's useful life. Decommissioning costs required to meet an entity's legal obligations are provided for in accordance with IAS 37. The provision must be recognized for estimated future obligations discounted by an appropriate interest rate that reflects the risk of the obligation (IAS 37 paragraph 47). ASPE standards (Section 3110) are essentially the same as those in IAS 37, although Section 3110 refers to these decommissioning responsibilities as asset retirement obligations (AROs).

2. Off-balance-sheet obligations

We previously suggested that a company may be motivated to keep debts off its balance sheet so as to improve key financial ratios and free up borrowing capacity. These incentives may also encourage management to structure its affairs in a manner that ensures certain obligations need not be recognized.

The IASB appreciates that the true extent of an entity's debt is very relevant to financial statement users. Over the years the IASB has developed increasingly stringent requirements governing the recognition of obligations, with its goal being to ensure that entities recognize all of their liabilities on the balance sheet. Obligations that were previously left off-balance-sheet but now have to be recognized include those emanating from derivative contracts; special purpose entities (SPEs); decommissioning costs; and finance leases. An example of an off-balance-sheet financing technique that remains available to companies is operating leases.

The nature of the obligations arising from derivatives, decommissioning costs, and leases and how to account for each are discussed in other chapters; accounting for SPEs, other than the brief discussion below, is beyond the scope of this text.

Special purpose entities gained notoriety in the Enron debacle in 2001. Enron, a U.S.-based energy company (once named "America's Most Innovative Company" for six consecutive years by *Fortune* magazine), used non-consolidated SPEs to hide debt and inflate reported earnings. As a direct result of the Enron scandal, both the Accounting Standards Board of the CICA and the U.S. Financial Accounting Standards Board introduced stringent standards mandating the consolidation of nearly all SPEs.

Briefly, SPEs are entities that are created to perform a specific function such as undertaking research and development activities. The reasons for creating SPEs are many, and include tax considerations and isolating the backer from financial risk. A distinguishing feature of SPEs is that control is usually achieved by the sponsoring firm through a beneficial interest rather than owning more than 50% of the voting shares. SIC Interpretation 12, Consolidation—Special Purpose Entities, requires the consolidation of most SPEs.

H. PRESENTATION AND DISCLOSURE

As suggested in Chapter 11, IFRS requires extensive disclosure as to the nature of an entity's liabilities. The company is required to disclose information that enables users to evaluate the significance of financial liabilities on its financial position and performance. Standards that must be considered include the presentation and disclosure requirements in:

L.O. 12-5. Describe how non-current liabilities are presented and disclosed.

- IAS 1 Presentation of Financial Statements
- IAS 32 Financial Instruments: Presentation
- IAS 37 Provisions, Contingent Liabilities and Contingent Assets
- IAS 39 Financial Instruments: Recognition and Measurement
- IFRS 7 Financial Instruments: Disclosures

We will not reproduce the complete list of the requirements here, but the disclosures should cover the following essential aspects:

- the nature of contingent liabilities;
- a summary of the accounting policies used to determine the measurement basis of valuing liabilities—for example, amortized cost;
- pertinent details of the indebtedness including collateral pledged and call or conversion privileges;
- the fair value of each class of financial liability and how this was determined—for example, discounted cash flow analysis; this information need not be provided for financial instruments whose carrying value reasonably approximates their fair value—for example, trade payables;
- total interest expense on liabilities other than those valued at fair value through profit and loss;
- a schedule that details the contractual maturity dates of financial liabilities;
- the nature and extent of risks arising from financial liabilities, including credit risk, liquidity risk, and market risk; and
- details of any obligations in default, including the carrying amount of loans in default at statement date and whether the default was remedied before the financial statements were issued.

The format and extent of disclosure differs between companies. To gain some insight into the level of detail provided, please refer to select disclosures made by British Airways PLC in its 2009 financial statements. Exhibit 12-16 sets out specific areas to review.

Exhibit 12-16   Excerpts from 2009 financial statements of British Airways PLC

Note	Title	Page number	Pertinent disclosure
9	Finance costs and income	93	Finance costs including interest
26	Trade and other payables	108	Composition of payables
27	Other long-term liabilities	108	Composition of other long-term liabilities
28	Long-term borrowings	109–110	Composition of borrowings including segregation into current and non-current components; maturity analysis; interest rate disclosure; and collateral pledged
30	Provisions for liabilities and charges	112–113	Composition of provisions including segregation into current and non-current components, and a reconciliation of changes during the year
31	Financial risk management objectives and policies	113–117	Qualification and quantification of the various financial risks faced by the company together with an explanation as to how they manage these risks
32	Financial instruments	118–120	Composition of financial liabilities including segregation into current and non-current components; schedule contrasting the carrying value and fair value of financial liabilities; and details of liabilities arising from hedging activities
37	Contingent liabilities	130	Quantification of guarantees provided, and general disclosure with respect to ongoing litigation against the company

I. SUBSTANTIVE DIFFERENCES BETWEEN RELEVANT IFRS AND ASPE

Issue	IFRS	ASPE
Amortization of premiums and discounts on financial liabilities	Enterprises must use the effective interest method.	Enterprises may use either the effective interest method or the straight-line method because ASPE does not specify a method of amortization.

J. SUMMARY

L.O. 12-1. Describe financial leverage and its impact on profitability.

- Financial leverage quantifies the relationship between the relative level of a firm's debt and its equity base.
- Financial leverage offers shareholders an opportunity to increase their return on equity (ROE) when things go well but exposes them to an increased risk of loss as well.

L.O. 12-2. Describe the categories and types of non-current liabilities.

- Non-current liabilities are expected to be settled more than one year after the balance sheet date.
- Non-current liabilities are either financial or non-financial in nature. Examples of financial liabilities include bonds and notes payable. Examples of non-financial liabilities include deferred revenue and warranty payables.

L.O. 12-3. Describe the initial and subsequent measurement of non-current financial liabilities and account for these obligations.

- Financial liabilities are initially recognized at fair value less costs directly attributable to issuing the debt.
- Financial liabilities are subsequently measured at amortized cost, excepting those held for trading, which are measured at fair value.

L.O. 12-4. Apply accrual accounting to the derecognition of financial liabilities.

- Liabilities are derecognized when they are settled or when the debtor is legally released from primary responsibility for the liability.
- Retiring an obligation prior to maturity may lead to a gain or loss on retirement which flows through income.

L.O. 12-5. Describe how non-current liabilities are presented and disclosed.

- IFRS requires extensive disclosure as to the nature of an entity's liabilities.
- Standards that need to be complied with in respect to presentation and disclosure include IAS 1, IAS 32, IAS 37, IAS 39, and IFRS 7.
- Required disclosure includes detailing the essential aspects of contingent liabilities; a summary of accounting policies pertaining to the measurement basis of valuing liabilities; pertinent details of the indebtedness; the fair value of each class of financial liability; and details of obligations in default.

K. References
Authoritative standards:

IFRS	ASPE Section
IAS 1—Presentation of Financial Statements	1400—General Standards of Financial Statement Presentation
	1505—Disclosure of Accounting Policies
	1521—Balance Sheet
IAS 16—Property, Plant and Equipment	3061—Property, Plant and Equipment
IAS 32—Financial Instruments: Presentation	3856—Financial Instruments
IAS 39—Financial Instruments: Recognition and Measurement	
IAS 37—Provisions, Contingent Liabilities and Contingent Assets	3110—Asset Retirement Obligations
SIC Interpretation 12—Consolidation—Special Purpose Entities	AcG 15—Consolidation of Variable Interest Entities

L. Glossary

amortized cost (of debt): The amount initially recognized for the debt adjusted by subsequent amortization of premium or discount.

best efforts approach: Occurs where the broker simply agrees to try to sell as much of the (debt) issue as possible to investors.

bond indenture: Contract that outlines the terms of the bond, including the maturity date; rate of interest and interest payment dates; security pledged; and financial covenants.

call premium: The excess over par value paid to the bondholders when the security is called.

callable bonds: Bonds that permit the issuing company to "call" for the bonds to be redeemed before maturity.

convertible bonds: Bonds that allow the holder to exchange or "convert" the bond into other securities in the corporation, usually common shares.

coupon (stated) rate: The interest rate specified in the bond indenture.

covenant: The borrower's promise to restrict certain activities.

debentures: Unsecured bonds.

effective interest rate: The **yield** on the date of issuance of a debt security.

financial leverage: Quantifies the relationship between the relative level of a firm's debt and its equity base.

financial liability: A contractual obligation to deliver cash or other financial assets to another party.

firm commitment underwriting: Occurs where the investment bank guarantees the borrower a price for the bonds.

inflation-linked (real-return) bonds: A bond that provides protection against inflation.

in-substance defeasance: An arrangement where funds sufficient to satisfy a liability are placed in trust with a third party to pay directly to the creditor at maturity.

leveraged buyout: A purchase where a significant part of the purchase price is raised by borrowing against the acquired assets.

market rate: See yield.

non-current liabilities: Obligations that are expected to be settled more than one year after the balance sheet date or the business' normal operating cycle, whichever is longer.

par value: The amount to be repaid to the investor at maturity.

perpetual bonds: Bonds that never mature.

secured bonds: Bonds backed by specific collateral such as a mortgage on real estate.

serial bonds: A set of bonds issued at the same time but that mature at regularly scheduled dates rather than all on the same date.

stripped (zero-coupon) bonds: Bonds that do not pay interest; stripped bonds are sold at a discount and mature at face value.

yield: The rate of return (on a bond) actually earned by the investor at a particular time.

M. PROBLEMS

Go to MyAccountingLab at **www.myaccountinglab.com**. You can practise the indicated exercises as often as you want, and guided solutions will help you find answers step by step. You'll find a personalized study plan available to you too!

P12-1.   Financial leverage and other aspects of borrowing
(L.O. 12-1, L.O. 12-2) (Easy – 5 minutes)

a. Describe financial leverage and outline the principal benefit and drawbacks of borrowing funds to finance the acquisition of assets.
b. What is the function of debt rating agencies like DBRS and Moody's Investors Service?
c. What are financial liabilities?
d. What is the primary advantage to corporations of selling notes directly to the investing public, rather than borrowing from a financial institution?

P12-2.   Off-balance-sheet obligations
(L.O. 12-1) (Easy – 5 minutes)

a. Provide two reasons why companies may be motivated to keep debt off the balance sheet.
b. Give three examples of obligations that IFRS now requires to be reported on the balance sheet when this was previously not the case.

P12-3.   Financial leverage
(L.O. 12-1) (Medium – 15 minutes)

I Love Debt Inc. is in the process of acquiring another business. In light of the acquisition, shareholders are currently re-evaluating the appropriateness of the firm's capital structure (the types of and relative levels of debt and equity). The two proposals being contemplated are detailed below:

	Proposal one	Proposal two
Estimated EBIT*	$300,000	$300,000
Long-term debt	$2,000,000	$3,000,000
Market value of equity	$2,000,000	$1,000,000
Interest rate on long-term debt	4%	4%
Tax rate	30%	30%

*Earnings before interest and taxes

Required:

a. Calculate the estimated return on equity   (ROE) under the two proposals. (ROE = net income after taxes / market value of equity; net income after taxes = (EBIT − interest on long-term debt) × (1 − tax rate).)
b. Which proposal will generate the higher estimated ROE?
c. What is the primary benefit of adopting the capital structure that generates the higher estimated ROE? What are two drawbacks to this approach?

P12-4. Bonds (**L.O.** 12-2) (Easy – 10 minutes)

a. What is a bond indenture?
b. What are covenants? What are the two general categories of covenants?
c. Why do companies issue bonds instead of borrowing from a bank?
d. How do companies normally sell a new bond issue to the investing public?

P12-5. Types of bonds (**L.O.** 12-2) (Medium – 10 minutes)

Briefly describe the distinguishing characteristic of the bonds listed below:

- Callable bonds
- Convertible bonds
- Debentures
- Real-return bonds
- Perpetual bonds
- Secured bonds
- Serial bonds
- Stripped (zero-coupon) bonds

P12-6. Measurement of non-current financial liabilities

(**L.O.** 12-3) (Easy – 10 minutes)

Discuss how non-current financial liabilities are initially and subsequently valued.

P12-7. Accounting for notes payable (**L.O.** 12-3) (Easy – 5 minutes)

On May 1, 2012, Ripley Ltd. purchases a new automobile for $36,000 from the dealer who provides the financing. The three-year, interest-free loan is repayable at $1,000 per month. The market rate of interest for similar transactions is 0.5% per month.

Required:

Prepare journal entries to record:

a. the purchase of the automobile.
b. the accrual of interest and the loan payment at the end of May 2012.

P12-8. Accounting for notes payable (**L.O.** 12-3) (Easy – 5 minutes)

Patrice Wall Accounting Inc. takes advantage of a well-known office furnishings store's low-interest-rate financing. Patrice buys furniture on the first day of its fiscal year, signing a $10,000, three-year note. The note is payable in full at maturity. Interest is payable annually at 2%. The market rate of interest for similar transactions is 4%.

Required:

Prepare journal entries to record:

a. The purchase of the office furniture.
b. The payment of interest and related amortization of the discount at the end of year 1.

P12-9. Accounting for notes payable (**L.O.** 12-3) (Medium – 20 minutes)

You are the accountant for Simply the Best Fireworks. The company has been negotiating with various car dealers in an attempt to get the best deal on a new Vroom Vroom XKY. The purchasing manager provides you with a summary of three offers and asks you to analyze them to determine the best arrangement. The options available are to:

i. Pay $40,000 cash.
ii. Issue an interest-free note for $43,200 repayable in 36 equal monthly installments.
iii. Issue a 9% note for $38,000 repayable in 36 equal monthly installments.

For a car loan, Simply's bank will charge the company a nominal rate of 6% per annum, payable monthly.

Required:

a. Analyze the offers in terms of the cost of the purchase expressed in present value terms.
b. Independent of requirement (a), prepare the journal entry to record i) the purchase of the automobile assuming that Simply issued the $38,000 note, and ii) the first payment on the loan.

P12-10.   Issuance of bonds (various)   (**L.O.** 12-3) (Easy – 15 minutes)

Golf for Life Inc. issues three series of $1,000,000 six-year bonds dated January 1, 2011 on the issue date. Interest is payable on June 30 and December 31 each year. Series A has a coupon rate of 5%; series B is 6%; and series C is 7%. The market rate of interest at time of issue is 6%.

Required:

a. Prior to making any numerical calculations, comment on whether:
   i. Series A will sell at a discount, par, or premium and briefly explain why.
   ii. Series B will sell at a discount, par, or premium and briefly explain why.
   iii. Series C will sell at a discount, par, or premium and briefly explain why.
b. Prepare journal entries to record the issuance of:
   i. The series A bonds.
   ii. The series B bonds.
   iii. The series C bonds.

P12-11.   Selling par bonds after the specified issue date

(**L.O.** 12-3) (Easy – 10 minutes)

On the River Co. (OTRC) sells $1,000,000 of 10-year, 4% bonds at par plus accrued interest. The bonds are dated January 1, 2012 but due to market conditions are not issued until May 1, 2012. Interest is payable on June 30 and December 31 each year.

Required:

Prepare journal entries to record:

a. The issuance of the bonds on May 1, 2012. Assume that OTRC has adopted a policy of crediting accrued interest payable for the accrued interest on the date of sale.
b. Payment of interest on June 30, 2012.
c. Payment of interest on December 31, 2012.

P12-12.   Issuing bonds at a discount   (**L.O.** 12-3) (Medium – 10 minutes)

Escape to Egypt Travel Inc. issues $4,000,000 of five-year, 4% bonds dated January 1, 2012. Interest is payable on January 1 and July 1 each year. The proceeds realized from the issue were the $3,900,000 sales price less the $40,000 fee charged by Escape's investment bank. Escape's year-end is December 31.

Required:

Prepare journal entries to record:

a. The issuance of the bonds.
b. Payment of interest and related amortization on July 1, 2012.
c. Accrual of interest and related amortization on December 31, 2012.

P12-13.   Issuing bonds at a premium   (**L.O.** 12-3) (Medium – 10 minutes)

Australian Balloon Rides Ltd. issues $4,000,000 of five-year, 4% bonds dated January 1, 2011. Interest is payable on January 1 and July 1 each year. The proceeds realized from the issue were the $4,200,000 sales price less the $20,000 fee charged by Balloon's lawyers. Balloon's year-end is December 31.

Required:

Prepare journal entries to record:
 a. The issuance of the bonds.
 b. Payment of interest and related amortization on July 1, 2011.
 c. Accrual of interest and related amortization on December 31, 2011.

P12-14. Issuing bonds at a discount
(**L.O.** 12-3) (Medium – 10 minutes)

Really Really Cheap Vacations Ltd. issues $2,000,000 of five-year, 5% bonds dated January 1, 2012. Interest is payable on January 1 and July 1 each year. The proceeds realized from the issue were the $1,900,000 sales price less the $10,000 fee charged by Really's investment bank. Really's year-end is December 31.

Required:

Prepare journal entries to record:
 a. The issuance of the bonds.
 b. Payment of interest and related amortization on July 1, 2012.
 c. Accrual of interest and related amortization on December 31, 2012.

P12-15. Issuing bonds at a premium
(**L.O.** 12-3) (Medium – 10 minutes)

Outstanding Accountants Co. sells $1,000,000 of 10-year, 4% bonds priced to yield 3.9%. The bonds are dated and issued on January 1, 2011. Interest is payable on January 1 and July 1 each year. Outstanding's year end is June 30.

Required:

Prepare journal entries to record:
 a. The issuance of the bonds.
 b. Accrual of interest and related amortization on June 30, 2011.
 c. Payment of interest on July 1, 2011.
 d. Payment of interest and related amortization on January 1, 2012.

P12-16. Amortizing a premium using the effective interest method and the straight-line method
(**L.O.** 12-3) (Medium – 15 minutes)

Golf Is Great Corp. sells bonds to friends and families to finance the acquisition of a driving range. On January 1, 2011, Golf Is Great sells $3,000,000 in four-year, 5% bonds priced to yield 4% for $3,109,882. Interest is payable on June 30 and December 31 each year. The corporate year-end is December 31.

 Golf Is Great is a private corporation and the bonds are not publicly traded. As such, Golf Is Great may elect to use either the straight-line or effective interest method to amortize the premium.

Required:

 a. Complete a bond amortization spreadsheet that contrasts the use of the straight-line method and the effective interest method. Use the format that follows as employed in Exhibit 12-12.[10]

Straight-line method				Effective interest method				
Date	Interest expense	Interest paid	Premium amortized	Amortized cost	Date	Interest expense	Interest paid	Premium amortized	Amortized cost

 b. Review your results tabulated in part (a). Does the choice of methods affect:
   i. cash flow for each of the periods, and if so how?
   ii. the total interest expense over the life of the bond, and if so how?
   iii. reported profitability on a year-to-year basis, and if so how?

---

10. Exhibit 12-12 illustrates the amortization of a discount. This question requires you to amortize a premium and the spreadsheet computations must be adjusted accordingly.

P12-17. Amortizing a discount using the effective interest method and the straight-line method   (**L.O.** 12-3) (Difficult – 25 minutes)

Buy Low Sell High Corp. issues bonds to finance the acquisition of marketable securities. On January 1, 2015, Buy Low sells $1,000,000 in three-year, 5% bonds for $970,000. Interest is payable on June 30 and December 31 each year. The corporate year-end is December 31.

    Buy Low's junior accountant, Bob Blades, has been asked to prepare a bond discount amortization spreadsheet. Bob is not sure whether he should use the straight-line or effective interest method to amortize the discount so he prepares both.

Required:

a. Complete a bond amortization spreadsheet that contrasts the use of the straight-line method and the effective interest method. Use the format that follows as employed in Exhibit 12-12.

Straight-line method					Effective interest method				
Date	Interest expense	Interest paid	Discount amortized	Amortized cost	Date	Interest expense	Interest paid	Discount amortized	Amortized cost

Prepare journal entries to record:

b. The issuance of the bonds on January 1, 2015.
c. Payment of interest and related amortization on June 30, 2015 under the straight-line method.
d. Payment of interest and related amortization on June 30, 2015 under the effective interest method.
e. Retirement of the bonds on December 31, 2017 assuming that the final interest payment has already been recorded in the company's books.
f. Compare and contrast the two methods. Interest expense in the first period is higher under which method for bonds sold at a discount? For bonds sold at a premium? Why does IFRS require public companies to use the effective interest method? Why do the Accounting Standards for Private Enterprises allow companies to use the straight-line method?

P12-18. Offsetting and in-substance defeasance   (**L.O.** 12-4) (Easy – 5 minutes)

a. What is offsetting? When is it allowed? What are some benefits to the company of offsetting?
b. What is in-substance defeasance? When do defeasance arrangements qualify for offsetting?

P12-19. Derecognition prior to and at maturity   (**L.O.** 12-4) (Easy – 10 minutes)

Mississauga Wheels Ltd. (MW) sold $5,000,000 of five-year, 6% bonds at par on January 1, 2012. Interest is payable on June 30 and December 31 each year. The bonds can be called at any time at 101 plus accrued interest. On April 1, 2013, MW bought back $1,000,000 of bonds on the open market for $984,736 including accrued interest and retired them. On August 1, 2014, MW called $500,000 of bonds and retired them. MW prepares accrual entries only at year-end.

Required:

Prepare journal entries to record:

a. The open market purchase of the bonds on April 1, 2013.
b. The calling of the bonds on August 1, 2014.
c. Retirement of the remaining bonds on December 31, 2016, assuming that the final interest payment has already been recorded in the company's books.

P12-20. Derecognition prior to maturity—refinancing a bond issue

(**L.O.** 12-3, **L.O.** 12-4) (Medium – 10 minutes)

Adler Corp issued $4,000,000, 4.5% 10-year bonds on January 1, 2011 at par. Interest is due annually on December 31. The market rate of interest has since increased dramatically to 8%. As such, Adler can repurchase its bonds on the open market for $3,441,000. They decided to take advantage of this situation, and on January 1, 2016 issued a new series of bonds in the amount of $3,441,000 [five-year bonds, 8% interest payable annually]. The bonds were sold at par and the proceeds were used to retire the 4.5% bonds.

Journal entry for the sale of the new bonds		
Dr. Cash	3,441,000	
Cr. Bonds payable		3,441,000
Journal entry to retire the old bonds		
Dr. Bonds payable	4,000,000	
Cr. Cash		3,441,000
Cr. Gain on bond redemption		559,000

Adler has recorded a gain on the retirement which increases its net income for the year. Ignoring transaction costs and taxation effects, is Adler any better off? Discuss.

P12-21. Selling bonds after the specified issue date; derecognition prior to maturity (**L.O.** 12-3, **L.O.** 12-4) (Medium – 10 minutes)

Legally Yours, a law firm, sells $5,000,000 of four-year, 6% bonds priced to yield 4.2%. The bonds are dated January 1, 2011, but due to some regulatory hurdles are not issued until March 1, 2011. Interest is payable on January 1 and July 1 each year. The bonds sell for $5,315,703 plus accrued interest.

In mid-June, Legally Yours earns an unusually large fee of $7,000,000 for one of its cases. They use part of the proceeds to buy back the bonds in the open market on July 1, 2011 after the interest payment has been made. Legally Yours pays a total of $5,400,000 to reacquire the bonds and retires them.

Required:

Prepare journal entries to record:

a. The issuance of the bonds—assume that Legally Yours has adopted a policy of crediting interest expense for the accrued interest on the date of sale.
b. Payment of interest and related amortization on July 1, 2011.
c. Reacquisition and retirement of the bonds.

P12-22. Issuing bonds at a discount; derecognition prior to and at maturity (**L.O.** 12-3, **L.O.** 12-4) (Difficult – 20 minutes)

Fredericton Aerospace Inc. raised $10,500,000 by selling $10,000,000 of six-year, 4% bonds dated January 1, 2013. Fredericton used part of the proceeds to pay its investment bank's fee of $400,000 and related legal and accounting fees of $200,000.

Interest is payable on June 30 and December 31 each year. Fredericton can call the bonds on January 1, 2016 at 101. The company exercises this privilege, redeeming 40% of the bonds on the call date and retiring them. The company year ends on December 31.

Required:

Prepare journal entries to record:

a. The issuance of the bonds on January 1, 2013.
b. Payment of interest and related amortization on December 31, 2015.
c. Repurchase of the bonds on January 1, 2016.
d. Retirement of the remaining bonds on December 31, 2018, assuming that the final interest payment has already been recorded in the company's books.

P12-23. Issuing bonds (various); derecognition prior to maturity
(**L.O.** 12-3, **L.O.** 12-4) (Medium – 25 minutes)

There are three independent situations summarized below. In all three cases the bonds are sold on January 1, 2011 and the issuing company has a December 31 year-end. In situation three, the bonds were all repurchased at par on January 1, 2015.

	Situation 1	Situation 2	Situation 3
Face value	$10,000,000	$20,000,000	$40,000,000
Coupon rate	14%	10%	12%
Coupon dates(s)	6/30; 12/31	12/31	12/31
Market rate	12%	12%	14%
Time to maturity	6 years	12 years	8 years

Required:

Prepare journal entries to record:

a. The issuance of the three bonds.
b. Payment of interest and related amortization on December 31, 2011.
c. Retirement of the situation 3 bond on January 1, 2015.

P12-24. Selling bonds after the specified issue date; derecognition prior to maturity   (**L.O.** 12-3, **L.O.** 12-4) (Difficult – 30 minutes)

Avoiding Faux Pas (AFP), a leading international school of etiquette, sells $3,000,000 of six-year, 6% bonds priced to yield 7.2%. The bonds are dated July 1, 2016, but due to some regulatory hurdles are not issued until December 1, 2016. Interest is payable annually on June 30 each year. AFP can call the bonds on July 1, 2020 at 102. The bonds sell for $2,838,944 plus accrued interest.

AFP sells shares to the public for the first time in early 2019. They use part of the IPO (initial public offering) proceeds to buy back $1,000,000 (face value) of the bonds in the open market on July 1, 2019. AFP pays a total of $950,000 to reacquire the bonds and retires them.

On July 1, 2020, AFP calls the remaining bonds and retires them. The company's year-end is June 30.

Required:

a. Complete a bond amortization spreadsheet using the format that follows, the use of which was illustrated in Exhibit 12-10. Include the partial redemption of bonds on July 1, 2019.

Date	Interest expense	Interest paid	Discount amortized	Amortized cost

Prepare journal entries to record:

b. The issuance of the bonds on December 1, 2016, assuming that AFP has adopted a policy of crediting interest expense for the accrued interest on the date of sale.
c. Payment of interest and related amortization on June 30, 2017.
d. Payment of interest and related amortization on June 30, 2019.
e. Repurchase of the bonds on July 1, 2019.
f. Payment of interest and related amortization on June 30, 2020.
g. Repurchase of the bonds on July 1, 2020.

P12-25. Issuance and derecognition of bonds
(**L.O.** 12-3, **L.O.** 12-4) (Medium – 20 minutes)

On July 1, 2014, Inuvialuit Golf Corp. issued $5,000,000 of five-year, 6%, semi-annual bonds for $5,040,000. At time of issue, Inuvialuit paid its investment bank a $40,000 sales commission. On July 31, 2017, Inuvialuit calls $3,000,000 of the bonds, paying 102 plus accrued interest, and retires them. On March 31, 2018, Inuvialuit purchases the remaining bonds on the open market for $1,980,000 including accrued interest and retires them. Inuvialuit's year-end is August 31. The company does not use reversing entries.

Required:

a. Prepare journal entries to record:
   i. The issuance of the bonds on July 1, 2014.
   ii. Repurchase of the bonds on July 31, 2017.
   iii. Payment of interest on December 31, 2017.
   iv. Retirement of the remaining bonds on March 31, 2018.
b. Provide a brief explanation as to the most likely reasons that Inuvialuit was able to repurchase its bonds at a discount.

P12-26.   Accounting for bonds; various scenarios

(**L.O.** 12-3, **L.O.** 12-4) (Difficult – 30 minutes)

Three independent situations follow:

1. I'm Alive Ltd. (IAL) issued $5,000,000 in stripped (zero-coupon) bonds that mature in 10 years. The market rate of interest for bonds of a similar nature is 3.6% compounded monthly. 5½ years after issue, when the market rate was 4.8%, IAL repurchased $2,000,000 of the bonds on the open market. IAL accrues interest monthly. Bonds are carried at amortized cost.
2. Creative Accountants sold $2,000,000 of five-year bonds that pay the market rate of interest of 6% annually on December 31. The bonds are dated January 1, 2014, but were not issued until February 1, 2014. Creative's year-end is December 31. Creative does not accrue interest throughout the year and has adopted a policy of crediting interest expense for the interest accrued up to the date of sale.
3. On January 1, 2016, Able Minded Professors Corp. (AMPC) sold $3,000,000 of three-year, 5% bonds priced to yield 4.5%. Interest is payable on June 30 and December 31 each year.

Required:

a. Prepare journal entries to record:
   i. The sale and retirement of the bonds in scenario 1.
   ii. The sale of the bonds in scenario 2 and payment of interest on December 31, 2014.
   iii. The sale of the bonds in scenario 3.
b. Prepare a schedule of interest expense and bond amortization during the life of the bond in scenario 3.

P12-27.   Accounting for bonds; various topics

(**L.O.** 12-3, **L.O.** 12-4) (Difficult – 20 minutes)

On March 15, 2014, Candoit Inc. sold $10,000,000 of five-year, 3% bonds for $9,972,469. From the proceeds, Candoit paid its investment bank a $200,000 sales commission. Interest is payable semi-annually on March 15 and September 15. On March 16, 2018, Candoit buys back $2,000,000 of bonds on the open market for their face value.

Required:

a. What are the nominal and effective rates of interest that Candoit is paying on the bonds expressed as an annual percentage rate?
b. Assuming that Candoit records the bond liability at amortized cost, what is the net book value of the bonds outstanding on March 16, 2016? On September 16, 2016? Use your financial calculator to determine these amounts and then verify them by constructing a schedule of interest expense and bond amortization during the life of the bond.
c. On the date of the open market purchase, had market interest rates increased or decreased since the bonds were issued? Explain.
d. Did the repurchase result in an *economic* gain or loss for either Candoit or the investor? Explain.

P12-28. Issuance of bonds (various); derecognition prior to maturity

(**L.O.** 12-3, **L.O.** 12-4) (Difficult – 20 minutes)

Two independent situations follow:

1. On January 1, 2011, Cute Koalas Inc. issued $4,000,000 of 7%, 12-year, callable bonds priced to yield 6%. The bonds may be called at 102* on or after December 31, 2016. Interest is payable on June 30 and December 31. Cute Koalas calls the bonds on January 1, 2018.
2. On January 1, 2014, Cuddly Kangaroos Ltd. issued $6,000,000 of 5%, eight-year bonds priced to yield 6.5%. Interest is payable on June 30 and December 31. Cuddly repurchases the outstanding bonds on July 1, 2017, at which time the market rate of interest is 6%.

Required:

Prepare journal entries to record:

a. The sale and retirement of the bonds in scenario 1.
b. The sale and retirement of the bonds in scenario 2.

P12-29. Disclosure

(**L.O.** 12-5) (Easy – 5 minutes)

List five types of disclosures made regarding companies' indebtedness.

P12-30. Accounting for notes payable and disclosure

(**L.O.** 12-3, **L.O.** 12-5) (Medium – 25 minutes)

Sarah Braun is the owner of Sarah's Shameless Boutique Corp. (SSBC), a newly incorporated company. Sarah believes that she has a great concept but does not have a lot of money to start the business. Sarah is fairly resourceful, though, and has been able to arrange the following:

1. On July 1, 2014, SSBC provides a vendor with a $10,500 non-interest-bearing note due on July 1, 2015 in exchange for furniture with a list price of $10,000. Sarah Braun guarantees the debt.
2. On August 1, 2014, SSBC buys a photocopier listed for $3,400. The office supply store agrees to accept a $500 down payment and a $3,000, three-year note payable at $1,040 per year including interest at 2% with the first payment due on August 1, 2015. The loan is secured by a lien on the photocopier.
3. On September 1, 2014, SSBC borrows $10,000 from its bank for working capital purposes. The loan, plus interest at 6% per annum, is due on June 30, 2015. SSBC grants the bank a security interest in its accounts receivables and inventory.

Unfortunately, SSBC's target audience is a bit more prudish than she anticipated and sales have been slow. While the company was able to retire the bank loan on the due date, it had insufficient cash to pay off the furniture loan. The vendor agrees to accept 1,000 common shares in SSBC in settlement of the obligation. Sarah believed that the shares are worth $15 each, but as this was the first time that SSBC had issued shares to anyone other than Sarah, a fair market price was not yet established.

SSBC's year-end is June 30. The company's banker has suggested that an appropriate market rate for SSBC is 6% per annum for loans that mature in one year or less and 8% for loans with longer maturities.

Required:

a. Prepare journal entries to record:
    i.   The purchase of the office furniture.
    ii. The acquisition of the photocopier.
    iii. The receipt of the loan proceeds.
    iv. Payments and accruals on June 30, 2015.
    v.   The retirement of the office furnishings loan on July 1, 2015.
b. Briefly describe the note disclosure that would be required with respect to the foregoing liabilities.

⚓ N. MINI-CASES

CASE 1
Jackson Capital Inc.
(45 minutes)[11]

Jackson Capital Inc. (JCI) is a new private investment company that provides capital to business ventures. JCI's business mission is to support companies to allow them to compete successfully in domestic and international markets. JCI aims to increase the value of its investments, thereby creating wealth for its shareholders.

Funds to finance the investments were obtained through a private offering of share capital, conventional long-term loans payable, and a bond issue that is indexed to the TSX Composite. Annual operating expenses are expected to be $1 million before bonuses, interest, and taxes.

Over the past year, JCI has accumulated a diversified investment portfolio. Depending on the needs of the borrower, JCI provides capital in many different forms, including demand loans, short-term equity investments, fixed-term loans, and loans convertible into share capital. JCI also purchases preferred and common shares in new business ventures where JCI management anticipates a significant return. Any excess funds not committed to a particular investment are held temporarily in money market funds.

JCI has hired three investment managers to review financing applications. These managers visit the applicants' premises to meet with management and review the operations and business plans. They then prepare a report stating their reasons for supporting or rejecting the application. JCI's senior executives review these reports at their monthly meetings and decide whether to invest and what types of investments to make.

Once the investments are made, the investment managers are expected to monitor the investments and review detailed monthly financial reports submitted by the investees. The investment managers' performance bonuses are based on the returns generated by the investments they have recommended.

It is August 1, 2012. JCI's first fiscal year ended on June 30, 2012. JCI's draft balance sheet and other financial information are provided in Exhibit I. An annual audit of the financial statements is required under the terms of the bond issue. Potter & Cook, Chartered Accountants, has been appointed auditor of JCI. The partner on the engagement is Richard Potter. You, CA, are the in-charge accountant on this engagement. Mr. Potter has asked you to prepare a memo discussing the significant accounting issues, audit risks, and related audit procedures for this engagement.

Required:

Prepare the memo requested by Mr. Potter pertaining to issues with respect to the company's debt, equity, and cash flow.

Exhibit I	Draft balance sheet and other financial information
Jackson Capital Inc.	
Draft balance sheet	
As at June 30, 2012	
(in thousands of dollars)	
Assets	
Cash and marketable securities	$ 1,670
Investments (at cost)	21,300
Interest receivable	60
Furniture and fixtures (net of accumulated depreciation of $2)	50
	$ 23,080

(Continued)

11. Adapted with permission from The Canadian Institute of Chartered Accountants, Toronto, Canada. Any changes to the original material are the sole responsibility of the author and have not been reviewed or endorsed by the CICA.

Liabilities

Accounts payable and accrued liabilities	$ 20
Accrued interest payable	180
Loans payable	12,000
	12,200

Shareholders' equity

Share capital	12,000
Deficit	(1,120)
	10,880
	$23,080

Jackson Capital Inc.
Summary of investment portfolio
As at June 30, 2012

Investments	Cost of investment
15% common share interest in Fairex Resource Inc., a company listed on the TSX Venture Exchange. Management intends to monitor the performance of this mining company over the next six months and to make a hold/sell decision based on reported reserves and production costs.	$3.8 million
25% interest in common shares of Hellon Ltd., a private Canadian real estate company, plus 7.5% convertible debentures with a face value of $2 million, acquired at 98% of maturity value. The debentures are convertible into common shares at the option of the holder.	$6.2 million
5-year loan denominated in Brazilian currency (reals) to Ipanema Ltd., a Brazilian company formed to build a power generating station. Interest at 7% per annum is due semi-annually. 75% of the loan balance is secured by the power generating station under construction. The balance is unsecured.	$8.0 million
50% interest in Western Gas, a jointly owned gas exploration project operating in western Canada. One of JCI's investment managers sits on the three-member board of directors.	$2.0 million
50,000 stock warrants in Tornado Hydrocarbons Ltd., expiring March 22, 2014. The underlying common shares trade publicly.	$1.3 million

Jackson Capital Inc.
Capital structure
As at June 30, 2012

Loans payable

The Company has $2 million in demand loans payable with floating interest rates, and $4 million in loans due September 1, 2016, with fixed interest rates.

In addition, the Company has long-term 5% stock indexed bonds payable. Interest at the stated rate is to be paid semi-annually, commencing September 1, 2012. The principal repayment on March 1, 2017, is indexed to changes in the TSX Composite as follows: the $6 million original balance of the bonds at the issue date of March 1, 2012, is to be multiplied by the stock index at March 1, 2017, and then divided by the stock index as at March 1, 2012. The stock-indexed bonds are secured by the Company's investments.

Share capital

Issued share capital consists of:

1 million 8% Class A (non-voting) preference shares redeemable at the holder's option on or after August 10, 2016	$7 million $5 million
10,000 common shares	

CASE 2
Total Protection Limited
(30 minutes)[12]

Total Protection Limited (TPL) was recently incorporated by five home-builders in central Canada to provide warranty protection for new-home buyers. While most home-builders provide one-year warranties, TPL offers ten-year warranties and includes protection for a number of items not usually covered. For example, if a problem arose as a result of faulty construction or construction materials, TPL would protect its customers against any resulting decline in the market value of their property and would provide for the costs of restoring the property. TPL does not, however, cover general declines in market value.

The five shareholders believe TPL will increase their home sales and at the same time minimize their individual risks. The idea for TPL originated with Safe-Way Builders and, therefore, this shareholder will receive a royalty payment of 5% of income before income taxes. The shareholders have engaged your firm to prepare a report that will assist them in managing TPL in order to maximize its long-term profitability. In addition, as a separate report, the shareholders would like your firm to recommend appropriate financial accounting policies for TPL.

You, CA, and the partner on the engagement, meet with Gus Filmore, president of Safe-Way Builders. Gus is currently operating TPL from the offices of Safe-Way Builders, for which TPL will be charged rent. Gus provides you with the following information on TPL's operations.

TPL's revenues consist of an initial fee paid at the time of purchase of the warranty and an annual maintenance fee paid over the term of the warranty. Currently, the initial fee and annual maintenance fee depend on a number of factors, including the cost of the home, reputation of the builder, construction design of the home (e.g., brick versus aluminum siding), and the home's location. The warranties are sold through each builder, who can adjust the initial fee and annual maintenance fee if an adjustment is considered necessary to make the sale. The builder receives a commission of 10% of the total warranty revenue, which should ensure that the builder will try to maximize the initial fee and annual maintenance fee. Typically, a buyer of a brick house worth $250,000 that was constructed by a good quality builder should expect to pay an initial fee of $2,000 plus an annual maintenance fee of $250.

To date, TPL has been doing very well, primarily as a result of two factors, (1) Central Canada has been experiencing a boom in the residential construction industry, and (2) TPL has expanded to offer coverage for homes built by builders other than the shareholders'. "Quite frankly," explains Gus, "an increasing share of our business is from these outside builders, many of which have entered the industry just to try to capitalize on the demand. We don't think that permitting these home-builders to sell coverage will hurt our home sales since most of these builders are in the low-price segment of the market, keeping costs down by employing new, less expensive construction methods and materials. We require that their initial fee must be at least $1,500 per home to ensure that they don't lower the price just to make a sale."

"Our real problem is keeping up with the paperwork," continues Gus. "I have my own business to run and cannot devote much time to TPL. We haven't even had time to get organized or set up any system for TPL. Lately, I must admit that I've lost track of what's going on. All I know is that we're making money. In just 11 months, TPL has collected about $1.6 million while paying out only $224,000 in repair costs. Keep in mind, however, that I've been able to keep these repair costs down by having Safe-Way Builders do the repairs. Business will only get better since we plan to expand within the next month to offer coverage in western Canada and the southwestern United States. We don't know what to do with all this cash. We're considering investing it all in real estate for future development. After all, that's what we're good at! On the other hand, some shareholders are looking forward to receiving the cash themselves."

Just before you leave the client's premises, you manage to collect some additional information on the operations of TPL (see Exhibit I).

When you return to the office, the partner asks you to prepare the reports requested by the shareholders.

---

12. Adapted with permission from The Canadian Institute of Chartered Accountants, Toronto, Canada. Any changes to the original material are the sole responsibility of the author and have not been reviewed or endorsed by the CICA.

Exhibit I   Information Gathered from Client Records

	Larkview Estates	Towne Homes	Granite Homes	Kings Road	Safe-Way Builders	Other Builders	Total
			TPL Shareholders				
Number of warranties sold	50	85	190	250	175	465	1,215
Warranty revenue ($000's)	$120	$165	$395	$90	$160	$705	$1,635
Repair costs incurred ($000's)	$ 6	$ 9	$ 21	$42	$ 39	$107	$ 224

Required:

Prepare a report recommending appropriate financial accounting policies for TPL.

Kaitlyn's Cats Inc. (KCI) is a chain of pet stores that specializes in the sale and veterinary care of *felis catus*, more commonly known as cats. On October 1, 2011, KCI raised a net of $523,973 by issuing $500,000 in 10-year, 6% bonds that pay interest on April 1 and October 1. The market rate of interest at time of issue was 5%. Transaction costs directly attributable to the debt issue totalled $15,000. KCI elected not to designate the liability as held for trading.

Kaitlyn Reid, owner of KCI, is contemplating how to present the bond indebtedness on KCI's balance sheet at issue date. She has set out her initial thoughts as to some possibilities below in advance of her meeting with the company accountant to discuss this matter.

CASE 3
Kaitlyn's Cats Inc.
(20 minutes)

Possibility	
1. Bonds payable	$ 523,973
2. Bond issue costs (report as a non-current asset)	$ 15,000
Bonds payable	$ 500,000
Premium on bonds payable	$ 38,973
3. Bond issue costs (expensed)	$ 15,000
Bonds payable	$ 538,973

Required:

a. Discuss the advantages and disadvantages of each of the three methods being considered. Which of the three options complies with the requirements of IAS 39?
b. What is the effective rate of interest on this obligation? Why is this rate used to determine interest expense, rather than the stated coupon rate?
c. Why were investors willing to pay $538,973 for a debt instrument with a maturity value of $500,000?
d. Assume that KCI designated the liability as held for trading. Would your answer to part (a) change? If so, how would it change?

NADIAN TIRE

LA SOCIÉTÉ CANADIAN TIRE LIMITÉE

CASH BONUS ▪ BILLET ▪ BONI

CANADIAN TIRE CORPORATION, LIMITED

CP PHOTO/Don Denton

LEARNING OBJECTIVES

After studying this chapter, you should be able to:

L.O. 13-1. Describe the characteristics of different types of share equity and identify the characteristics that are relevant for accounting purposes.

L.O. 13-2. Identify the different components of equity for accounting purposes that apply to a transaction and analyze the effect of the transaction on those equity components.

L.O. 13-3. Apply the accounting standards and procedures for transactions relating to contributed capital.

L.O. 13-4. Apply the accounting standards and procedures for transactions relating to the distribution of retained earnings.

Canadian Tire (www.canadiantire.ca; Toronto Stock Exchange tickers CTC and CTC-A), the iconic retailer known for having Canada's unofficial second currency (Canadian Tire "dollars"), has grown from its first store in 1925 to more than 400 locations today. The company has two classes of shares: Common and Class A. In its 2008 annual report, the company reported the following information regarding its share capital:

($ in millions)		2008	2007
Authorized			
3,423,366	Common Shares		
100,000,000	Class A Non-Voting Shares		
Issued and outstanding			
3,423,366	Common Shares	$ 0.2	$ 0.2
78,178,066	Class A Non-Voting Shares	715.2	700.5
		$715.4	$700.7

Why do companies such as Canadian Tire have different classes of shares, and how do we account for them? What are the distinctions among "authorized," "issued," and "outstanding"? How do we account for differences between shares authorized and shares issued, or between the number issued and the number outstanding?

The company also disclosed that it issued and repurchased Class A shares. How do we account for such equity transactions?

CONTENTS

A. INTRODUCTION

Equity refers to the ownership interest in the assets of an entity after deducting its liabilities. In other words, equity is a residual amount that is determined by assets and liabilities through the balance sheet equation: equity = assets − liabilities. Indeed, if the balance sheet equation is to hold, equity must be a residual amount rather than defined independently, since the conceptual framework already defines assets and liabilities. The residual nature of equity, however, does not mean that we can be cavalier about it—it is still necessary to provide information useful to financial statement readers. The questions are, then, who uses information about equity, and what information about equity would be useful?

First, equity has legal **priority** below that of liabilities in general, meaning that available funds go toward paying off liabilities prior to paying equity claims should the enterprise be liquidated. As a result, debtors have little interest in the specifics of what happens with equity beyond the overall amount of equity to assess solvency of the enterprise. In contrast, equity holders are concerned about both liabilities and equity accounts. Thus, information about equity is primarily geared toward equity holders themselves.

priority The rank of a liability or equity claim when a company liquidates, where higher priority confers preferential payout before other claimants of lower priority.

Second, equity holders who do have residual claims on the enterprise are concerned about the size of their claims, and they need to be aware of changes to their share of profits. Consequently, accounting reports need to provide detailed information about the composition of equity and changes in equity that can result in the dilution of owners' stakes in the business. This information asymmetry between management and owners is particularly high, and the information need is particularly strong, when there are multiple types of equity and when there are many equity holders such as for public companies.

Third, equity holders are interested in distinguishing (i) changes in equity due to direct contributions or withdrawals of capital from (ii) changes in equity derived from return on equity capital (i.e., income). This categorization is natural because it separates capital transactions with *owners* from the entity's income-generating transactions with *non-owners* such as customers, employees, and suppliers.[1] This chapter follows this categorization by first discussing contributed capital followed by two equity accounts that accumulate income: retained earnings and accumulated other comprehensive income (AOCI). We then discuss the effect of various transactions on equity: stock issuances, stock splits, stock re-acquisitions, dividend payments, and transfers to reserves.

From this point forward in this chapter, we will focus on the incorporated form of business, so we will refer to shareholders rather than the more generic "equity holder." However, the material is equally applicable and therefore transferable to other forms of organizations such as proprietorships, partnerships, and trusts.

B. COMPONENTS OF EQUITY FOR ACCOUNTING PURPOSES

As noted in the introduction, accounting separates equity into three components: contributed capital, retained earnings, and AOCI. Within each of these three components are sub-components that differ from each other in a variety of ways.

1. Contributed capital

L.O. 13-1. Describe the characteristics of different types of share equity and identify the characteristics that are relevant for accounting purposes.

L.O. 13-2. Identify the different components of equity for accounting purposes that apply to a transaction and analyze the effect of the transaction on those equity components.

Contributed capital refers to amounts received by the reporting entity from transactions with shareholders, net of any repayments from capital (rather than accumulated income). In a simple case where a company issues 10,000 shares for $20 each, and later repurchases 1,000 of these shares at the same price, the contributed capital would equal 10,000 shares × $20/share − 1,000 shares × $20/share = $180,000. (Section C will consider other cases when the share price changes from issuance to repurchase.)

Shares have a number of characteristics, including whether they have residual claims, par value, cumulative dividends, or voting rights, and whether they are authorized, issued, or outstanding. We discuss these characteristics below and any accounting implications involved.

contributed capital　The component of equity that reflects amounts received by the reporting entity from transactions with its owners, net of any repayments from capital.

common share　An equity interest that has the lowest priority and represents the residual ownership interest in the company.

ordinary share　See **common share**.

a. Common shares (or ordinary shares)

In Canada, the shares that represent the ultimate residual interest in a company are usually called **common shares**. The equivalent term for common shares in IFRS is **ordinary shares**. These are the shares that have lowest priority, but claims to all residual profits after the entity satisfies all other debt or equity claims. These

---

1. In some cases, an owner can also engage in transactions with the reporting entity as someone other than an owner (e.g., a customer). For instance, many shareholders of large financial institutions such as the Bank of Montreal or the Royal Bank of Canada will also have deposits or loans with these banks. In such cases, we need to identify whether these individuals are acting as owners or non-owners.

shares have the most upside potential should the enterprise be successful, but also the most downside should the business fail. Because common shares represent the ownership interest, every corporation must have a class of common shares.

b. Preferred shares

While every corporation must have a class of common shares, some corporations also have additional classes of shares. Any share that does not represent the residual interest in the company is called a **preferred share**. For example, a company may have, in addition to a class of common shares, "Class A shares" and "Class B preferred shares." For accounting purposes, these other classes are all considered to be preferred shares to reflect their economic substance, whether the company literally labels them as "preferred" or not. Preferred shares, as the name suggests, have priority ahead of common shares.

preferred shares Any shares that are not common shares.

c. Par value vs. shares with no par value

The **par value** of a share is a legal term referring to the nominal value of a share, in contrast to the actual share price. The Canada Business Corporations Act (CBCA) does not permit companies to issue shares with par value.[2] However, provincial laws such as those in Ontario and British Columbia permit the use of par value for companies incorporated under those laws.[3]

For preferred shares, par value is important for the determination of dividends. For example, a preferred share with par value of \$20/share could either specify a dividend rate of \$1/share or 5%; that 5% is expressed relative to the par value, so that \$20/share × 5% = \$1/share. This use of par value is similar to that for bonds discussed in Chapter 12. For common shares, par value has no particular economic significance because common shares do not have a pre-specified dividend rate. For this reason, most companies do not specify a par value for common shares. For both common and preferred shares, the par value has no bearing on the price at which shareholders buy or sell the shares. Actual prices can be higher or lower than par value.

For accounting purposes, when a company does issue shares with par value, we identify the amount from the par value separately from the amount received above par.[4] We denote the component of contributed capital other than par as **contributed surplus**. An example of transactions with shares with and without par value will follow in Section C.

par value shares Shares with a dollar value stated in the articles of incorporation; for preferred shares, the dividend rate may be stated as a percentage of the par value.

contributed surplus The component of contributed capital other than par value.

d. Cumulative vs. non-cumulative dividends

Regardless of whether a share is a common or preferred share, dividends are always discretionary payments. A corporation need only pay dividends when it declares them to be payable. This discretion applies even if there is a stated dividend rate on the shares. As an added measure of protection, many preferred shares will require *cumulative dividends*, meaning that the company must pay for any past dividend payments that it missed (i.e., those scheduled but not declared) prior to paying any dividends on common shares. In other words, a company can defer but not avoid a cumulative dividend on preferred shares if it is to pay dividends on common shares. However, there is no interest to compensate for the time value of money lost on the deferral. Shares with non-cumulative dividends do not have any rights to missed dividend payments.

2. Canada Business Corporations Act (R.S.C. 1985, c. C-44) Section 24 Paragraph (1).

3. Ontario Corporations Act (RSO 1990 c. 38) Section 25 Paragraph 1 and British Columbia Business Corporations Act (SBC 2002, c. 57) Section 52 Paragraph 1.

4. We do not consider instances where issue price is below par because this rarely occurs in practice.

In either case, companies are loath to miss dividend payments even though dividends are discretionary. A dividend schedule is a commitment to disburse cash to shareholders on a regular basis, and breaking that commitment is a sure sign of trouble.

e. Voting rights

A corporation may assign voting rights in a variety of ways according to its articles of incorporation. The vast majority of large, publicly traded enterprises will have one vote per common share, so that decision rights match economic ownership (in terms of rights to future cash flows). A small minority of public companies deviate from this practice. However, private companies use shares with a variety of voting rights to suit their needs.

The opening vignette outlined the contributed capital for Canadian Tire, which has two classes of shares: 3,423,366 Common Shares and 78,178,066 Class A Non-Voting Shares. It turns out that, while the voting rights differ between these two classes, they are both common shares and they are practically identical to each other economically. Specifically, the 2008 Financial Statements (Footnote 10) indicates the following:

> In the event of the liquidation, dissolution or winding-up of the Company, all of the property of the Company available for distribution to the holders of the Class A Non-Voting Shares and the Common Shares shall be paid or distributed equally share for share, to the holders of the Class A Non-Voting Shares and to the holders of the Common Shares without preference or distinction.

The common shares, which have the voting rights, are closely held by the Billes family, who founded the company in 1925. Holding the two classes of shares is the family's way of maintaining voting control of the company while allowing them to secure additional capital from the stock market.

f. Number of shares authorized, issued, or outstanding

shares authorized The number of shares that are allowed to be issued by a company's articles of incorporation.

shares issued The number of shares issued by the corporation, whether held by outsiders or by the corporation itself.

shares outstanding Those shares held by outsiders.

treasury shares Shares issued but held by the issuing corporation; treasury shares are not outstanding.

There are three figures that refer to the number of shares, two of which are important for accounting purposes. The number of **shares authorized** is the number of shares that the corporation is permitted to issue as specified in the articles of incorporation. This is a legal detail that has no practical significance. Indeed, many companies specify an unlimited number of authorized shares.

The two important figures are the number of shares issued and outstanding. **Shares issued** has the intuitive meaning—the number of shares issued by the corporation. However, some issued shares may not be outstanding. **Shares outstanding** are those shares held by outsiders. In other words, a corporation may hold some of its issued shares in treasury; these shares are **treasury shares**.

Based on this discussion, the following relationships always hold:

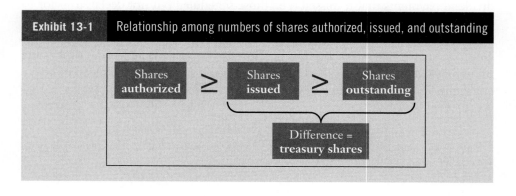

Exhibit 13-1   Relationship among numbers of shares authorized, issued, and outstanding

2. Retained earnings

Recall from introductory accounting that **retained earnings** reflect the cumulative net income (profit or loss) minus dividends paid. Some companies allocate a portion of retained earnings as reserves to identify amounts in equity that they do not intend to pay out as dividends. In some instances, the reserves are required by laws or regulations. **Appropriation** is the term for the process that allocates a portion of retained earnings to an appropriated reserve. For example, most universities have a portion of their net assets[5] set aside as reserves for the endowments that they have received from donors, when the donors specify that the university should spend only the income and not the capital from those donations. The use of an endowment reserve account ensures that the university does not spend the donated capital. Another common example is the appropriation of retained earnings for the purpose of repaying a long-term bond that requires the bond issuer to maintain a "sinking fund." Suppose a company issues a $50 million bond due in 10 years, and the bond indenture specifies that the company must set aside $5 million per year in a sinking fund so that the company will have funds to repay the bondholders at the end of 10 years. Assuming that the company complies with the contractual requirements, the journal entry would be as follows for each of the 10 years:

retained earnings A component of equity that reflects the cumulative net income (profit or loss) minus dividends paid.

appropriation The process that allocates a portion of retained earnings to a reserve.

Exhibit 13-2	Journal entries for the annual appropriation of retained earnings of $5 million for a sinking fund reserve	
Dr. Retained earnings	5,000,000	
Cr. Sinking fund reserve (or appropriated retained earnings)		5,000,000
Dr. Restricted cash	5,000,000	
Cr. Cash		5,000,000

Notice that two journal entries are required. The first one appropriates the retained earnings, while the second one shows the actual cash being set aside.

3. Accumulated other comprehensive income (AOCI)

As discussed in Chapters 3, 7, and 10, accounting recognizes other comprehensive income (OCI) on some unrealized transactions, such as the increase in fair value of available-for-sale investments. This component of equity accumulates OCI from all prior periods similar to the accumulation of realized profits and losses in retained earnings.

It is important to note that AOCI needs to be distinguished by source. For example, a company needs to distinguish AOCI arising from available-for-sale investments separately from amounts arising from revaluation.[6]

---

5. "Net assets" for a not-for-profit organization has the same meaning as "equity" for a for-profit entity.

6. In practice, accumulated OCI needs to be even more specifically identified. For example, we would specify "Accumulated OCI from the revaluation of Land at 333 Yonge Street, Toronto, ON" due to the need to track the revaluation reserve according to the item (or group of items) being revalued.

4. Summary

The following diagram summarizes the accounting classification of the different components and sub-components of equity.

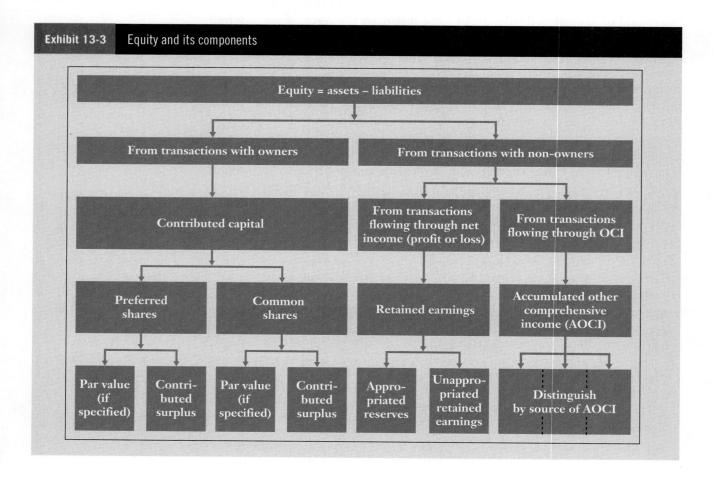

Exhibit 13-3 Equity and its components

The next two sections will examine the accounting for transactions relating to contributed capital and retained earnings. We do not consider issues relating to AOCI further because other chapters address the specific transactions or events that give rise to AOCI.

C. EQUITY TRANSACTIONS RELATING TO CONTRIBUTED CAPITAL

L.O. 13-3. Apply the accounting standards and procedures for transactions relating to contributed capital.

This section discusses the accounting for transactions affecting primarily contributed capital, although in some transactions there will also be ancillary effects on retained earnings.

1. Issuance of shares

The accounting for the issuance of shares is fairly straightforward. For example, suppose Naples Inc. and Parksville Company are both incorporated in 2010 and they both issue 10,000 common shares and receive $20/share from investors. Naples' shares have no par value, while Parksville's have a par value of $1. The journal entry to record this share issuance is as follows:

| Exhibit 13-4 | Journal entries for the issuance of common shares with or without par value |

Naples Inc.—with no par value		Parksville Company—with par value of $1/share		
Dr. Cash	200,000	Dr. Cash	200,000	
Cr. Common shares	200,000	Cr. Common shares—par value		10,000
		Cr. Contributed surplus		190,000

As noted previously, the par value in this case has no economic significance. Therefore, we should consider the effect of the above two journal entries to be the same. In other words, we should think of the amount from the par value ($10,000) and the contributed surplus ($190,000) for Parksville Company together as a single amount of $200,000 for contributed capital. This aspect will be important for understanding the reacquisition of shares discussed below.

2. Stock splits

A **stock split** is an increase in the number of shares issued without the issuing company receiving any consideration in return. For instance, a company can double the number of shares issued by undergoing a 2-for-1 stock split. The economic positions for the company as well as every single shareholder remain the same. It is no different from having, say, either five $20 bills or ten $10 bills—the total value is still $100. Because there are no changes in economic substance, there is no journal entry required, other than a memo entry to note that the number of shares has changed.

Companies engage in stock splits typically to bring their share price to a desired range. Typical trading rules on exchanges require multiples (called "lots") of 100 shares, so a share price of $200 per share is often considered too high because trades would involve a minimum value of $20,000. A more modest price of $20 per share would lower the minimum trading value to $2,000, which can increase trading volume and improve liquidity in the market for the company's shares.

Companies can also engage in reverse stock splits to reduce the number of shares issued and increase the stock price correspondingly. Reverse stock splits are also called share consolidations.

stock split An increase in the number of shares issued without the issuing company receiving any consideration in return.

3. Reacquisition of shares

Companies buy back their own shares for a number of reasons. First, share repurchases are a tax-efficient alternative to dividend payments to return cash to shareholders. The tax advantage arises from the fact that companies choosing to pay dividends must pay them equally to each share in a class, whereas in a share buyback shareholders can choose whether (and when) to sell their shares back to the company. Investors' ability to choose when to sell allows for better tax planning.

Second, buying back shares alleviates information asymmetry by providing a credible positive signal to the market similar to the positive signal from the announcement of dividend increases. (See Chapter 1 for a discussion of signalling.) The signal is credible because it is costly for the company to expend cash to buy back its own shares. From the buyback, we infer that corporate executives believe their company's shares to be undervalued.

Third, many companies offer stock compensation to executives and other employees. To make these shares available, the company can either issue new shares or buy back existing shares that had been previously issued. The latter is often administratively less cumbersome.

Finally, share buybacks decrease the number of shares outstanding, which lowers the denominator in the calculation of earnings per share (EPS). Depending on the cost of the shares at the time of repurchase and the amount of profits, it is possible to increase reported EPS. (See Chapter 15 for details of calculating EPS.)

There are other reasons for buying back shares, but the above discussion suffices to show that companies have many reasons for engaging in these transactions, and therefore we expect these transactions to be fairly common. As the opening vignette notes, Canadian Tire in 2008 did in fact repurchase some of its Class A Non-Voting Shares.

The accounting for share repurchases can be complex, and depends on whether the shares are cancelled after repurchase or held in treasury. We discuss these two situations separately below. Note that the following discussion is based on ASPE; IFRS provides little guidance in this area because international standards are unable to deal with the wide variety of country-specific laws that affect business ownership.

a. Cancellation of reacquired shares

A business that is incorporated under the Canada Business Corporations Act is not permitted to hold its own shares.[7] Therefore, any repurchased shares must be retired. To illustrate the accounting for share repurchases, we continue the example of Naples Inc. and Parksville Company from page 481 (Exhibit 13-4). Recall that each company issued 10,000 shares for $20/share. Naples' shares have no par value, while Parksville's shares have a $1 par value.

Now suppose that each company repurchases 1,000 of its own shares at $18 in 2011, and cancels them immediately. How would we account for this repurchase?

First, note that the amounts for contributed capital before the repurchase are as follows:

Exhibit 13-5	Contributed capital for Naples Inc. and Parksville Company before share repurchases		
Naples Inc.—with no par value		**Parksville Company—with par value of $1/share**	
Common shares (10,000 shares)	$200,000	Common shares (10,000 shares)	
		Par value ($1/share)	$ 10,000
		Contributed surplus	190,000
		Total contributed capital	$200,000

Observe that both companies' accounts reflect the original share issue price of $20/share ($200,000/10,000 shares). Also observe that the repurchase price of $18 is below the issue price. In other circumstances, we would consider this to be a "gain" because the sale price exceeds the purchase cost by $2/share. However, accounting standards do not allow this "gain" to flow through the income statement like other gains. Instead of a gain, we record the $2/share difference as a credit to increase contributed surplus.

---

7. Canada Business Corporations Act (R.S.C. 1985, c. C-44) Section 30 Paragraph (1).

WHEN A GAIN IS NOT A GAIN

A commonly given reason for why accounting does not recognize gains on share repurchase transactions is that it involves a company buying its own shares from its shareholders rather than a transaction with an external party. However, this is not a satisfying explanation because the (former) shareholders who sold the shares on the other side of the transaction would have recorded losses had they purchased at the issue price of $20/share and sold back to the company at $18/share. Instead, there are two other explanations that are more compelling. First, a drop in a company's share price is hardly good news for shareholders, so recording a gain in this situation would be inconsistent with the underlying economics. Second, permitting the recognition of gains creates a moral hazard (see Chapter 1). Since management has superior information relative to shareholders, management could record gains by judiciously timing share issuances and repurchases to the detriment of shareholders if accounting standards permitted the recognition of such gains.

Exhibit 13-6	Journal entries for the repurchase and cancellation of 1,000 shares at $18/share

Naples Inc.—no par value shares		Parksville Company—par value of $1/share		
Dr. Common shares	20,000	Dr. Common shares—par value	1,000	
(1,000 sh × $20/sh)		Dr. Contributed surplus	19,000	
Cr. Cash (1,000 sh × $18/sh)	18,000	Cr. Cash		18,000
Cr. Contributed surplus—from repurchase of shares	2,000	Cr. Contributed surplus—from repurchase of shares		2,000

Notice that in both cases, a total of $20,000 is removed (i.e., debited) from contributed capital, amounting to $20/share. In addition, it is important to note that the $2,000 credited to contributed surplus needs to be identified as arising from share repurchases and, for Parksville Company, separated from the contributed surplus that previously arose from share issuance. The $19,000 debit and $2,000 credit to contributed surplus have not been and *cannot be netted out* because they relate to two different types of contributed surplus. There is also a third type of contributed surplus that can be created by other transactions. We can summarize these three types of contributed surplus as follows and identify each type by a letter for ease of reference later.[8]

Exhibit 13-7	Types of contributed surplus

Type	Description
A	Created by the issuance of shares, being the amount in excess of par; this amount would have been recorded in common shares had there been no par value.
B	Created by repurchase and resale of previously issued shares.
C	Created by any transactions other than the above (e.g., issuance of stock options).

Distinguishing the different types of contributed surplus is especially important for instances when the cost of share repurchase is higher than the amount

---

8. The labelling of contributed surplus as Types A, B, and C matches the references used in ASPE 3240.11 shown below.

previously received. ASPE Section 3240 provides the following guidance (italics in original):

¶11. *When a company redeems its own shares, or cancels its own shares that it has acquired, and the cost of such shares is equal to or greater than their par, stated or assigned value, the cost shall be allocated as follows:*

(a) *to share capital, in an amount equal to the par, stated or assigned value of the shares (see paragraph 3240.14 for computation of assigned value);*

(b) *any excess, to contributed surplus to the extent that contributed surplus was created by a net excess of proceeds over cost on cancellation or resale of shares of the same class;*

(c) *any excess, to contributed surplus in an amount equal to the pro rata share of the portion of contributed surplus that arose from transactions, other than those in (b) above, in the same class of shares; and*

(d) *any excess, to retained earnings.*[9]

In this paragraph, the reference to "assigned value" in (a) refers to the amount generated from the issuance of shares. If the shares have no par value, that amount is the amount recorded to common stock. If the shares do have a par value, that amount is comprised of two parts: the par value and Type A contributed surplus. The "pro rata" reference in (c) means in proportion to the number of shares involved, relative to the number of shares outstanding prior to the transactions. In essence, we withdraw Type C contributed surplus in the same manner as Type A:

> reduction in Type A contributed surplus
> = number of shares repurchased × Type A contributed surplus per share

> reduction in Type C contributed surplus
> = number of shares repurchased × Type C contributed surplus per share

In contrast, we withdraw as much Type B contributed surplus as necessary and available in the account.

To illustrate a repurchase that affects all types of contributed surplus, let us continue with the example of Naples and Parksville. Suppose each company issues some stock options in the year 2012, which creates Type C contributed surplus in the amount of $27,000, which is $3/share ($27,000/9,000 shares outstanding). Subsequently, in 2013, Naples and Parksville each repurchase another 2,000 shares at $30/share. The journal entry to record the repurchase would be as follows:

Exhibit 13-8 — Journal entries for the repurchase and cancellation of 2,000 shares at $30/share

Naples Inc.—no par value shares		Parksville Company—par value of $1/share	
Dr. Common shares (2,000 sh × $20/sh)	40,000	Dr. Common shares—par value (2,000 sh × $1/sh)	2,000
		Dr. Contributed surplus—excess over par (Type A) (2,000 sh × $19/sh)	38,000
Dr. Contributed surplus—from repurchase of shares (Type B)*	2,000	Dr. Contributed surplus—from repurchase of shares (Type B)*	2,000
Dr. Contributed surplus (Type C) (2,000 sh × $3/sh)	6,000	Dr. Contributed surplus (Type C) (2,000 sh × $3/sh)	6,000
Dr. Retained earnings	12,000	Dr. Retained earnings	12,000
Cr. Cash (2,000 sh × $30/sh)	60,000	Cr. Cash	60,000

*From Exhibit 13-6, the previous repurchase and cancellation of 1,000 shares in 2011 created $2,000cr of Type B contributed surplus.

9. Reproduced with permission of The Canadian Institute of Chartered Accountants.

The $60,000 cost of repurchase needs to be allocated first to common shares at $20/share, or $40,000 total. We then allocate $2,000 to Type B contributed surplus because this is the total amount available from the previous repurchase transaction in 2011. For Type C contributed surplus, while there is a total of $27,000 available, we use only $6,000 because this is the pro rata amount, being calculated as either:

2,000 shares repurchased × $3/share of Type C contributed surplus = $6,000

---

or

$$\frac{2,000 \text{ shares repurchased}}{9,000 \text{ shares outstanding}} \times \$27,000 \text{ of Type C contributed surplus} = \$6,000$$

The remainder of $12,000 must be debited from retained earnings according to ASPE 3240.11.

These different treatments of contributed surplus can seem arbitrary and bewildering. We can explain the reason for the differences as follows. Type A contributed surplus arises from the issuance of shares, and only when the shares have par value. In substance, this is part of the share price received, so it makes sense that we only withdraw Type A contributed surplus in amounts equal to their recorded per-share amounts (e.g., $19/share for Parksville Company). In contrast, Type B contributed surplus arises from share repurchase and resale transactions that generate "gains" (that are not recorded as such). As a result, it is logical that "losses" (again, not recorded as such) should go to offset prior "gains" to the extent that there are such "gains" accumulated because they are similar transactions. Finally, Type C contributed surplus arises from transactions that are not share repurchases or resales. This type of contributed surplus is attributable to every share outstanding, and therefore we withdraw Type C contributed surplus at a rate equal to their recorded per-share amounts.

To summarize the accounting for share repurchases and cancellations, when the repurchase price ($18) is less than the average share value ($20), the "gain" is recorded in contributed surplus, increasing equity. When the repurchase price ($30) is higher than the average common stock value ($20), the "loss" goes to reduce contributed surplus and retained earnings.

b. Holding reacquired shares in treasury

While a company incorporated under the Canada Business Corporations Act is generally not permitted to hold its own shares, companies incorporated in other jurisdictions may be allowed to do so. For example, the British Columbia Business Corporations Act allows companies to hold repurchased shares.[10] Shares in treasury are issued but not outstanding. Treasury shares have no voting rights and receive no dividends.

There are two methods that can be used to account for treasury shares: the single-transaction method and the two-transaction method. The single-transaction method treats the reacquisition of shares and the subsequent selling off of shares as two parts of the same transaction. The two-transaction method

---

10. British Columbia Business Corporations Act (SBC 2002 c. 57) Section 82 Paragraph 1.

treats the two parts as components of two transactions: the repurchase is the close of a transaction that began with the initial issuance of the shares; and the subsequent resale is the beginning of the next sale-repurchase pair.

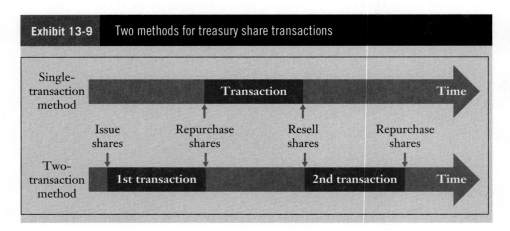

Exhibit 13-9 Two methods for treasury share transactions

Accounting standards indicate a preference for the single-transaction method over the two-transaction method, although both methods are acceptable (see ASPE 3240.06).

To illustrate the accounting for treasury stock transactions, suppose Smithers Company reacquired 3,000 no par shares at $8 per share and subsequently sold 1,000 of these shares at $12. Assume that the average price of shares outstanding is $10 and there is no contributed surplus before this transaction. The journal entries would be as follows under each method:

Exhibit 13-10 Journal entries for the repurchase of 3,000 shares and later resale of 1,000 shares at $12/share

Single-transaction method			Two-transaction method		
Repurchase 3,000 shares @ $8/share					
Dr. Treasury stock	24,000		Dr. Common shares (3,000 sh × $10/sh)	30,000	
Cr. Cash (3,000 sh × $8/sh)		24,000	Cr. Cash		24,000
			Cr. Contributed surplus		6,000
Resell 1,000 shares @ $12/share					
Dr. Cash (1,000 sh × $12/sh)	12,000		Dr. Cash	12,000	
Cr. Treasury stock (1,000 sh × $8/sh)		8,000	Cr. Common shares		12,000
Cr. Contributed surplus—from repurchase or resale of shares (Type B)		4,000			

As this example shows, the two methods have different effects on contributed surplus both in terms of amount and timing. In the single transaction method, we increase contributed surplus when the repurchased shares are later resold (i.e., when the single transaction cycle is complete). In the two transactions method, we increase contributed surplus at the time of repurchase.

For the single transaction method, we have a separate treasury stock account. The amount recorded in treasury stock is a contra account in equity until these shares are sold off.

In instances when companies resell treasury shares for less than the repurchase cost (akin to a loss), the difference first comes out of Type B contributed surplus to the extent available and then out of retained earnings. We do not involve Type C contributed surplus because shares in treasury are issued but not outstanding, so none of the Type C contributed surplus can be attributed to these non-outstanding shares. ASPE Section 3240 indicates the following (italics in original):

> ¶16. *When a company resells shares that it has acquired, any excess of the proceeds over cost shall be credited to contributed surplus; any deficiency shall be charged to contributed surplus to the extent that a previous net excess from resale or cancellation of shares of the same class is included therein, otherwise to retained earnings.*[11]

To illustrate this accounting, suppose Smithers Company from above resells the other 2,000 shares that it previously repurchased. The resale price is only $5/share. Prior to these transactions, the relevant balances in Smithers' accounts are as follows under the single transaction method:

Exhibit 13-11	Smithers' account balances prior to the second treasury stock transaction
Treasury shares	16,000 Dr
Contributed surplus—from repurchase or resale of shares (Type B)	4,000 Cr

The journal entry for the resale would be as follows:

Exhibit 13-12	Journal entry to record Smithers' second resale of 2,000 shares of treasury stock @ $5/share		
Dr. Cash		10,000	
Dr. Contributed surplus—from repurchase or resale of shares (Type B)		4,000	
Dr. Retained earnings		2,000	
Cr. Treasury shares			16,000

In this repurchase and resale, the cost of $8/share exceeds the sale price of $5/share. The difference of $3/share on 2,000 shares totals $6,000. We first allocate this amount to Type B contributed surplus to the extent that it is available ($4,000). The remainder of $2,000 goes to reduce retained earnings.

D. EQUITY TRANSACTIONS RELATING TO RETAINED EARNINGS

In this section, we discuss transactions that result in the distribution of retained earnings. We do not discuss accumulations of retained earnings, which have been dealt with in other chapters (such as Chapter 4, which dealt with recognition of revenues and expenses).

L.O. 13-4. Apply the accounting standards and procedures for transactions relating to the distribution of retained earnings.

Very few companies would pay all of their retained earnings as dividends, as there are cash flow implications, uncertainty as to the future performance of the business, contractual restrictions, and signalling effects. However, the amount of retained earnings does serve as a ceiling as to how much in dividends can be paid. On the other hand, it is commonly misunderstood that retained earnings represent funds available—that is not the case! Retained earnings may have been spent on equipment, for example, and not be available as cash. *Retained earnings is not cash.* To pay cash dividends, cash must be available.

1. Cash dividends

Cash dividends are by far the most common kind of dividends. These require attention to some relevant dates.

---

11. Reproduced with permission of The Canadian Institute of Chartered Accountants.

a. Declaration date

Dividends are discretionary payments, even for preferred shares that have cumulative provisions. Prior to declaration, a company has no obligation to pay, and therefore it records no liabilities for dividends. However, once the board of directors declares a dividend, the company then has an obligation to pay and should record a dividend payable.

b. Ex-dividend date and date of record

These two dates are closely related. The date of record is when the company compiles the list of shareholders to determine who should be paid how much in dividends. This date is specified at the time of dividend declaration. For shares that are publicly traded, the ex-dividend date will be several days before the record date. For the Toronto Stock Exchange, the ex-dividend date is currently two business days prior to the date of record. The ex-dividend date is the date on which a share trades without the right to receive a dividend that has been declared. Prior to ex-dividend, an investor who holds the share would be entitled to receive the previously declared dividend. For example, a dividend record date falling on a Monday would have an ex-dividend date on the previous Thursday (in a regular five-day work week). Investors who buy and hold the shares on Wednesday would be entitled to the dividends, whereas those who buy on Thursday would not receive the dividend.

c. Payment date

This is the date when the funds for the dividend are transferred to shareholders.

d. Summary

For accounting purposes, only the declaration date and payment date are relevant. The ex-dividend date is important to investors who need to know whether they should pay a price that includes the dividend or not. The date of record is a matter of administrative necessity to identify whom the company should pay.

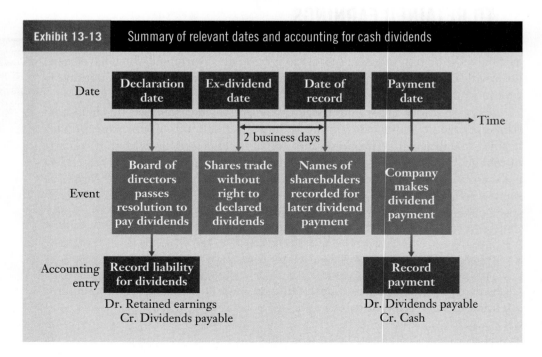

Exhibit 13-13 Summary of relevant dates and accounting for cash dividends

2. Stock dividends

Companies can issue stock dividends instead of paying out a cash dividend. However, doing so simply increases the number of shares issued and there is no cash outflow. Each shareholder owns the same fraction of the company as before the stock dividend. For example, suppose Trail Company has 800,000 no par shares outstanding and it declares a 5% stock dividend. Before the stock dividend, the shares traded at $11.55. If you were a shareholder who owned 8,000 shares (1%) of Trail before the dividend, you would own 8,400 shares afterward, again 1% of 840,000 shares outstanding. Economically, stock dividends have the same effect as stock splits: both increase the number of shares without any change to the company's resources. The value of the company's shares before the stock dividend was $9,240,000 (= 800,000 shares × $11.55). We would expect no significant change in the company's value due to the dividend, so we would expect the ex-dividend stock price to be $9,240,000/840,000 shares = $11.00.

As noted above in Section C, we make no journal entries for stock splits. However, we do record a journal entry for stock dividends. The difference in accounting treatment between stock splits and stock dividends is largely a result of legal and tax requirements. For tax purposes, stock dividends are treated as income to the shareholders just like cash dividends, but no tax consequences arise in stock splits. Stock dividends also result in an adjustment to the shares' tax basis (technically called paid up capital), which is relevant in the windup of a company.

Assuming that the stock price ex-dividend is $11.00 as expected, we would record the following journal entry:

Exhibit 13-14	Journal entry to record a stock dividend of 40,000 shares at $11/share for Trail Company	
Dr. Retained earnings	440,000	
Cr. Common shares (40,000 shares × $11/share)		440,000

This transfer from retained earnings to the contributed capital (common share) account explains why stock dividends are sometimes called "capitalization of retained earnings."

In general, the ex-dividend price of $11 is the appropriate price to use. To see why, consider a simpler but more extreme scenario where the stock dividend is 100%, so that the number of shares doubles. Suppose the market value of the shares outstanding is $100 and there is only one share pre-dividend. The share price should therefore be $100/share before the stock dividend, and $50/share afterward. This ex-dividend price equals the $50 of value transferred from the first share to the second share.[12]

For companies with shares that are not publicly traded, the stock dividend can be recorded using book value per share. Since the result of a stock dividend is just a transfer of retained earnings into the contributed capital account, the company can choose whichever dividend rate will result in the desired amount of transfer.

3. Property dividends (dividends in kind)

Instead of cash, companies can also pay dividends using non-cash assets rather than cash. This method of distributing value to shareholders is uncommon because different investors will value the distributed property differently, and

---

12. For Trail Company, the 40,000 shares distributed will be part of the 840,000 shares outstanding after the dividend, or 40/840 = 1/21 = 4.762% of shares outstanding. The value of these 40,000 shares at the ex-dividend price of $11 is $440,000, which is equal to 1/21 of the market value of equity (1/21 × $9,240,000 = $440,000). In contrast, the pre-dividend price of $11.55 would result in a dividend value that is too high (40,000 shares × $11.55/share = $462,000).

some may not appreciate it at all. For example, a cookie manufacturer could send its shareholders boxes of cookies, which could be a problem if a shareholder owned many shares. More practically, a property dividend could be used to transfer assets from a subsidiary to a parent company.

Since the assets being distributed are non-monetary, it is necessary to estimate the fair value of those assets for purposes of recording the value of the dividend.

E. PRESENTATION AND DISCLOSURE

As noted in the introduction, the information relating to equity is primarily to serve the needs of the shareholders (rather than creditors or other parties). Consequently, the presentation and disclosure rules are geared toward enabling shareholders to understand the different equity claims and categories, and changes in them.

Companies should prepare a statement of changes in equity that includes the following items (see IAS 1 ¶106).

■ For each component of equity (e.g., contributed capital, unappropriated retained earnings, reserves, AOCI), a reconciliation of the opening and closing balances.
■ The total comprehensive income for the period.
■ The effect of retrospective changes in accounting policies.

To illustrate the presentation of these items, the following exhibit shows the 2008 Statement of Changes in Equity for Canadian Tire.

Exhibit 13-15	Canadian Tire's 2008 Statement of Changes in Equity	
For the years ended ($ in millions)	**January 3, 2009**	**December 29, 2007**
Share capital		(Restated – Note 1)
Balance, beginning of year	$ 700.7	$ 702.7
Transactions, net (Note 10)	14.7	(2.0)
Balance, end of year	$ 715.4	$ 700.7
Contributed surplus		
Balance, beginning of year	$ 2.3	$ 0.1
Transactions, net	(2.3)	2.2
Balance, end of year	$ –	$ 2.3
Retained earnings		
Balance, beginning of year as previously reported	$ 2,440.9	$ 2,083.7
Transitional adjustment on adoption of new accounting policies (Note 1)	14.2	20.1
Balance, beginning of year as restated	2,455.1	2,103.8
Net earnings for the year	374.2	411.7
Dividends	(68.4)	(60.4)
Repurchase of Class A Non-Voting Shares	(5.4)	–
Balance, end of year	$ 2,755.5	$ 2,455.1
Accumulated other comprehensive income (loss)		
Balance, beginning of year	$ (50.0)	$ 8.6
Other comprehensive income (loss) for the year	147.2	(58.6)
Balance, end of year	$ 97.2	$ (50.0)
Retained earnings and accumulated other comprehensive income	$ 2,852.7	$ 2,405.1

Notice that Canadian Tire has shown the opening and closing balances of each component of equity, and the transactions that explain the changes in these balances. In addition, the reporting entity should also disclose, either in a formal financial statement or in the notes (see IAS 1 paragraphs 79 and 107):

- Equity disaggregated into its components (par value, contributed surplus, retained earnings, by class of shares, etc.).
- The number of shares authorized, issued, and outstanding for each class of shares; a reconciliation of shares outstanding at the beginning and end of the year; whether the shares have par value; and any rights, preferences, or restrictions on the shares.
- A description of the nature and purpose for each reserve.
- The amount of dividends declared.

As an example, Canadian Tire presents this information in Note 10 of its 2008 financial statements:

Exhibit 13-16	Canadian Tire's note disclosure for its equity

10. SHARE CAPITAL

($ in millions)		2008	2007
Authorized			
3,423,366	Common Shares		
100,000,000	Class A Non-Voting Shares		
Issued			
3,423,366	Common Shares (2007 – 3,423,366)	**$ 0.2**	$ 0.2
78,178,066	Class A Non-Voting Shares (2007 – 78,048,062)	**715.2**	700.5
		$715.4	$700.7

During 2008 and 2007, the Company issued and repurchased Class A Non-Voting Shares. The net excess of the issue price over the repurchase price results in contributed surplus. The net excess of the repurchase price over the issue price is allocated first to contributed surplus, to the extent of any previous net excess from the issue of shares, with any remainder allocated to retained earnings.

The following transactions occurred with respect to Class A Non-Voting Shares during 2008 and 2007:

($ in millions)	2008 Number	2008 $	2007 Number	2007 $
Shares outstanding at the beginning of the year	78,048,062	$ 700.5	78,047,456	$ 702.5
Issued				
Dividend reinvestment plan	58,579	3.2	30,459	2.3
Stock option plan	500	–	4,600	0.3
Employee Stock Purchase Plan	477,661	26.6	338,236	25.9
Employee Profit Sharing Plan	60,348	4.0	46,140	3.6
Associate Dealer profit sharing plans	52,716	3.1	38,171	3.0
Repurchased	(519,800)	(29.9)	(457,000)	(34.9)
Excess of repurchase price over issue price (issue price over repurchase price)	–	7.7	–	(2.2)
Shares outstanding at the end of the year	78,178,066	$ 715.2	78,048,062	$ 700.5

Due to Canadian Tire's unusual dual-class common share structure, Note 10 continues with further disclosures regarding the two classes of common shares:

Exhibit 13-17	Further disclosures on Canadian Tire's equity

Conditions of Class A Non-Voting Shares and Common Shares   The holders of Class A Non-Voting Shares are entitled to receive a preferential cumulative dividend at the rate of $0.01 per share per annum. After payment of preferential cumulative dividents at the rate of $0.01 per share per annum on each of the Class A Non-Voting Shares in respect of the current year and each preceding year and payment of a non-cumulative dividend on each of the Common Shares in respect of the current year at the same rate, the holders of the Class A Non-Voting Shares and the Common Shares are entitled to further dividends declared and paid in equal amounts per share without preference or distinction.

In the event of the liquidation, dissolution or winding-up of the Company, all of the property of the Company available for distribution to the holders of the Class A Non-Voting Shares and the Common Shares shall be paid or distributed equally share for share, to the holders of the Class A Non-Voting Shares and to the holders of the Common Shares without preference or distinction.

The holders of Class A Non-Voting Shares are entitled to receive notice of and to attend all meetings of the shareholders but, except as provided by the Business Corporations Act (Ontario) and as hereinafter noted, are not entitled to vote thereat. Holders of Class A Non-Voting Shares, voting separately as a class are entitled to elect the greater of (i) three Directors or (ii) one-fifth of the total number of the Company's Directors.

The holders of Common Shares are entitled to receive notice of, to attend and to have one vote for each Common Share held at all meetings of holders of Common Shares, subject only to the restriction on the right to elect directors as set out above.

Common Shares can be converted, at any time and at the option of each holder of Common Shares, into Class A Non-Voting Shares on a share-for-share basis. The authorized number of shares of either class cannot be increased without the approval of the holders of the other class. Neither the Class A Non-Voting Shares nor the Common Shares can be changed by way of subdivision, consolidation, reclassification, exchange or otherwise unless at the same time the other class of shares is also changed in the same manner and in the same proportion.

Should an offer to purchase Common Shares be made to all or substantially all of the holders of Common Shares (other than an offer to purchase both Class A Non-Voting Shares and Common Shares at the same price and on the same terms and conditions) and should a majority of the Common Shares then issued and outstanding be tendered and taken up pursuant to such offer, the Class A Non-Voting Shares shall thereupon be entitled to one vote per share at all meetings of the shareholders.

The foregoing is a summary of certain of the conditions attached to the Class A Non-Voting Shares of the Company and reference should be made to the Company's articles for a full statement of such conditions.

As at January 3, 2009, the Company had dividends payable to holders of Class A Non-Voting Shares and Common Shares of $17.1 million (2007 – $15.1 million).

Notice that the required disclosure regarding $17.1 million in dividends declared but not yet paid at year-end appears at the end of this note.

F. COMPREHENSIVE ILLUSTRATION OF EQUITY TRANSACTIONS

This section provides a comprehensive example that illustrates most of the equity transactions discussed in this chapter. Suppose Flatrock Kitchen Decor Ltd. was incorporated on January 1, 2011. The incorporation documents authorized an unlimited number of common shares and 100,000 preferred shares. During the following fiscal year, the company engaged in the following transactions relating to its equity.

a. On January 1, the company issued 10,000 no par value common shares at $10 per share. On the same day, it issued 500 preferred shares for proceeds of $120 per share. These preferred shares have a par value of $100 per share and cumulative dividends of 8% per year.

b. On March 15, the company issued an additional 10,000 common shares at $20 per share.

c. On April 20, Flatrock repurchased and cancelled 2,000 common shares at a cost of $12 per share.

d. On September 1, the company issued stock options to its executives. These stock options entitle the executives to purchase up to 10,000 common shares at a price of $25 per share over the next five years. The board of directors intended the options to compensate for management's services for the eight months from January 1 to August 31, 2011. Compensation consultants have estimated the value of these options to be $18,000.

e. On September 2, the company repurchased and cancelled 2,000 shares at $20 per share.

f. For the fiscal year ended December 31, 2011, the company had net income of $30,000 and zero other comprehensive income. The board of directors declared the 8% dividends payable to preferred shareholders and $15,000 of dividends for the common shareholders.

To analyze these transactions, it is often useful to use a spreadsheet. Similar to inventory accounting, it is necessary to keep track of both the dollar amounts and the number of units (shares). In addition, it is necessary to separate the equity components among common and preferred shares, any contributed surplus for each class of shares, as well as retained earnings. The following table shows such a spreadsheet for Flatrock's transactions in 2011:

Exhibit 13-18	Analysis of Flatrock's equity transactions

	Common shares						Preferred shares					Retained earnings
	Common stock			Type B CS	Type C CS			Par value		Type A CS		
Trx	# sh	$	$/sh	$	$	$/sh	# sh	$	$/sh	$	$/sh	$
a.	10,000	$100,000	$10				500	$50,000	$100	$10,000	$20	
b.	10,000	200,000	$20									
	20,000	$300,000	$15									
c.	−2,000	− 30,000	$15	6,000								
	18,000	$270,000	$15	$6,000								
d.	–	–	$ –	–	18,000	$1						
	18,000	$270,000	$15	$6,000	$18,000	$1						
e.	−2,000	− 30,000	$15	−6,000	− 2,000	$1						− 2,000
	16,000	$240,000	$15	$ –	$16,000	$1						
f.	Net income											30,000
	Preferred dividends (8% × $50,000)											− 4,000
	Common dividends											−15,000
												$ 9,000

Callouts:
- Repurchase at $12/share. Withdraw at average carrying value of $15/share. Difference ("gain") of $3/share goes to Type B contributed surplus.
- $18,000/18,000 shares = $1/share.
- Repurchase at $20/share. Withdraw at average carrying value of $15/share. Difference ("loss") of $5/share or $10,000 total first comes out of Type B CS as much as is available. $1 per share comes out of Type C CS. Remainder comes from retained earnings.

Note: CS = contributed surplus

The journal entries that accompany these transactions would be as follows:

Exhibit 13-19	Journal entries for Flatrock's equity transactions		
a. Jan. 1	Dr. Cash	100,000	
	Cr. Common stock (10,000 sh × $10/sh)		100,000
	Dr. Cash (500 sh × $120/sh)	60,000	
	Cr. Preferred stock—par value (500 sh × $100/sh)		50,000
	Cr. Contributed surplus on preferred shares (Type A) (500 sh × $20/sh)		10,000
b. Mar. 15	Dr. Cash	200,000	
	Cr. Common stock (10,000 sh × $20/sh)		200,000
c. Apr. 20	Dr. Common stock (2,000 sh × $15/sh)	30,000	
	Cr. Cash (2,000 sh × $12/sh)		24,000
	Cr. Contributed surplus on common shares (Type B) (2,000 sh × $3/sh)		6,000
d. Sep. 1	Dr. Compensation expense (amount given)	18,000	
	Cr. Contributed surplus on common shares—from issuance of employee stock options (Type C)		18,000
e. Sep. 2	Dr. Common stock (2,000 sh × $15/sh)	30,000	
	Dr. Contributed surplus on common shares (Type B) (amount as needed)	6,000	
	Dr. Contributed surplus on common shares (Type C) (2,000 sh × $1/sh)	2,000	
	Dr. Retained earnings (remainder)	2,000	
	Cr. Cash (2,000 sh × $20/sh)		40,000
f. Dec. 31	Net income—not explicitly journalized; results from the net of revenues, expenses, gains, and losses.		
	Dr. Retained earnings	19,000	
	Cr. Preferred dividends payable		4,000
	Cr. Common dividends payable		15,000

As this example shows, it is very important to maintain clear records of each class of shares and the different components associated with each class. It is not acceptable to intermingle different types of contributed surplus and amounts for different classes of shares.

G. SUBSTANTIVE DIFFERENCES BETWEEN RELEVANT IFRS AND ASPE

As indicated earlier in the chapter, IFRS does not provide specific recognition and measurement standards for items of equity. Therefore, preparers of financial reports for public enterprises need to consult guidance outside of IFRS. In Canada, the most relevant guidance is contained in ASPE (Part II of the *CICA Handbook*).

ISSUE	IFRS	ASPE
Accounting for repurchase and resale of shares	No specific guidance.	ASPE prescribes the allocation of repurchase costs and proceeds from resale of shares.
Accounting for treasury shares	No specific guidance.	ASPE permits the use of the single-transaction or the two-transaction method, although the former is preferred.
Accumulated other comprehensive income (AOCI)	AOCI is a component of equity.	There is no concept of "other comprehensive income" in ASPE, and therefore no AOCI.
Presentation	A statement of changes in equity presents balances and transactions for all equity components.	A statement of retained earnings presents balances and transactions for retained earnings. Information relating to other equity components should be disclosed.

H. SUMMARY

L.O. 13-1. Describe the characteristics of different types of share equity and identify the characteristics that are relevant for accounting purposes.

- Shares can have a variety of characteristics involving par value, preference for dividends, the accumulation of dividends, and voting rights.
- For accounting purposes, par value affects how we record the proceeds received from the issuance of shares. Different classes of shares need to be separately recorded.

L.O. 13-2. Identify the different components of equity for accounting purposes that apply to a transaction and analyze the effect of the transaction on those equity components.

- We can divide equity into two broad components: contributed capital and accumulated income.
- Contributed capital consists of amounts received from the issuance of shares. In the case of par value shares, contributed capital has two components: par value and contributed surplus.
- Accumulated income consists of the accumulation of comprehensive income less dividends paid. The retained earnings portion derives from profit or loss, while amounts from other comprehensive income accumulate separately as accumulated other comprehensive income (AOCI). Certain amounts of retained earnings may be set aside as reserves.

L.O. 13-3. Apply the accounting standards and procedures for transactions relating to contributed capital.

- Proceeds from the issuance of shares affect contributed capital and, in some instances, retained earnings.
- For accounting purposes, contributed surplus needs to be identified by source, which in this chapter we labelled as Types A, B, and C. Type A arises from the issuance of

shares with par value, Type B from the repurchase and resale of shares, and Type C from all other transactions.

L.O. 13-4. Apply the accounting standards and procedures for transactions relating to the distribution of retained earnings.

■ Dividends reduce retained earnings when they are declared.
■ Stock dividends require a transfer from retained earnings to contributed capital, in contrast to stock splits, which require no journal entry. Generally, the ex-dividend price provides a fair measure of the value of the dividend.

I. References

Authoritative standards:

IFRS	ASPE Section
Framework for the Preparation and Presentation of Financial Statements	1000—Financial Statement Concepts
IAS 1—Presentation of Financial Statements	1400—General Standards of Financial Statement Presentation
IAS 32—Financial Instruments: Presentation	3240—Share Capital
	3251—Equity
	3260—Reserves

J. Glossary

appropriation: The process that allocates a portion of retained earnings to a reserve.

common share: An equity interest that has the lowest priority and represents the residual ownership interest in the company.

contributed capital: The component of equity that reflects amounts received by the reporting entity from transactions with its owners, net of any repayments from capital.

contributed surplus: The component of contributed capital other than par value.

ordinary share: See **common share**.

par value shares: Shares with a dollar value stated in the articles of incorporation; for preferred shares, the dividend rate may be stated as a percentage of the par value.

preferred shares: Any shares that are not common shares.

priority: The rank of a liability or equity claim when a company liquidates, where higher priority confers preferential payout before other claimants of lower priority.

retained earnings: A component of equity that reflects the cumulative net income (profit or loss) minus dividends paid.

shares authorized: The number of shares that are allowed to be issued by a company's articles of incorporation.

shares issued: The number of shares issued by the corporation, whether held by outsiders or by the corporation itself.

shares outstanding: Those shares held by outsiders.

stock split: An increase in the number of shares issued without the issuing company receiving any consideration in return.

treasury shares: Shares issued but held by the issuing corporation; treasury shares are not outstanding.

K. PROBLEMS

Go to MyAccountingLab at **www.myaccountinglab.com**. You can practise the indicated exercises as often as you want, and guided solutions will help you find answers step by step. You'll find a personalized study plan available to you too!

P13-1.   Types of share equity and their characteristics (**L.O.** 13-1) (Easy – 5 minutes)

Identify whether the following statements are true or false.

Statement	T/F
a. Common (ordinary) shares have priority over preferred shares.	
b. A share with cumulative dividends must be a preferred share.	
c. Investors favour purchasing preferred shares.	
d. Common shares always have voting rights.	

P13-2.   Types of share equity and their characteristics (**L.O.** 13-1) (Easy – 5 minutes)

Identify whether the following statements are true or false.

Statement	T/F
a. The number of shares issued > number outstanding > number authorized.	
b. A share with a fixed dividend rate (i.e., a preferred share) is more valuable than one without (i.e., a common share).	
c. All issued shares are eligible to vote for the board of directors.	
d. All outstanding shares are eligible to vote for the board of directors.	

P13-3.   Types of share equity and their characteristics (**L.O.** 13-1) (Easy – 10 minutes)[13]

Canada and many other countries discourage and even prohibit the use of "par value" for common shares because it could be a misleading label.

Required:

Why is the term "par value" for *common* shares a misleading idea for many investors?

P13-4.   Types of share equity and their characteristics (**L.O.** 13-1) (Easy – 10 minutes)

Having a cumulative dividend is a common feature of preferred shares.

Required:

a. What does it mean to have a cumulative dividend feature?
b. Why do preferred shares commonly have this feature?
c. Can common shares have a cumulative dividend feature? Explain briefly.

P13-5.   Accounting standards for share equity (**L.O.** 13-1) (Medium – 15 minutes)

Preferred shares are defined as being a form of equity by the Canada Business Corporations Act (CBCA). Preferred shares generally have a specified dividend rate and in the event of bankruptcy or liquidation have priority over common shares. However, preferred shares do not have a residual interest in the entity.

Required:

a. Why is residual interest central to the value of common shares?
b. Identify qualities of preferred shares that make them similar to debt financing; identify qualities that make them similar to equity financing.
c. Discuss three reasons why management would want to use preferred shares as a source of financing.

---

13. © 2009 CGA-Canada. Reproduced with permission.

P13-6. Accounting standards for share equity   (**L.O.** 13-1) (Medium – 10 minutes)

A major objective of IFRS is to harmonize accounting rules and procedures around the world. Yet for the details and specifics of accounting for equity accounts (e.g., repurchase of the company's own shares), there are no international rules; rather, countries like Canada are defining the accounting standards for equity accounting and reporting.

Required:

  a. Why are there no specific IFRS standards relating to equity accounts?
  b. Is it a problem that there are not uniform standards for equity accounting and reporting?

P13-7. Share equity characteristics relevant for accounting

(**L.O.** 13-1) (Medium – 10 minutes)

For accounting purposes, of the following characteristics, which distinguish a common share from a preferred share? Explain your answer briefly.

- The share has no par value.
- The share has voting rights.
- The share has a residual claim.
- The share does not have cumulative dividends.
- The share is issued and outstanding.

P13-8. Components of equity   (**L.O.** 13-2) (Easy – 5 minutes)

Financial reporting distinguishes equity into two broad components: contributed capital and accumulated income; the latter is further separated into retained earnings and accumulated other comprehensive income (AOCI).

Required:

Briefly explain why equity needs to be separated into these categories.

P13-9. Components of equity   (**L.O.** 13-2) (Easy – 5 minutes)[14]

Which of the following are accounts reported in the equity section of the balance sheet?

Account	Equity section	Asset or liability
Preferred shares		
Investment in Company A common shares		
Treasury shares		
Accumulated other comprehensive income		
Bonds payable		
Donated assets		
Appropriated reserves		
Provision for warranties		

P13-10. Components of equity   (**L.O.** 13-2) (Easy – 5 minutes)

Which of the following are accounts reported in the contributed capital section of equity?

---

14. Adapted from CGA-Canada FA3 examination, June 2010.

Account	Contributed capital	Not contributed capital
Common shares		
Retained earnings		
Preferred shares		
Accumulated other comprehensive income		
Appropriated reserves		
Equity in associate		
Contributed surplus—common shares		
Treasury shares		

P13-11. Components of equity

(L.O. 13-2) (Easy – 5 minutes)

Which of the following transactions have the potential to directly affect the retained earnings portion of equity? Exclude indirect effects such as the transfer of income into retained earnings at the end of a year.

Account	Has potential to directly affect retained earnings	No direct effect on retained earnings
Declaration of a cash dividend		
Issuance of common shares		
Issuance of preferred shares		
Appropriation for a reserve		
Stock split		
Declaration of a stock dividend		
Omission of a cumulative dividend on preferred shares		

P13-12. Accounting for contributed capital

(L.O. 13-3) (Easy – 5 minutes)

When shares are repurchased at more than their original issue price, then held in treasury or cancelled, the journal entry potentially includes which of the following components?

Account	Transaction potentially affects this account in the manner indicated (Yes / No)
Debit to share capital	
Debit to contributed surplus	
Debit to treasury stock	
Debit to loss on share retirement	
Debit to retained earnings	
Debit to accumulated other comprehensive income (AOCI)	

P13-13. Accounting for contributed capital

(L.O. 13-3) (Easy – 5 minutes)[15]

When shares are repurchased and cancelled at more than their original issue price, the journal entry to record the retirement potentially includes which of the following components?

---

15. Adapted from CGA-Canada FA3 examination, June 2009.

Account	Transaction potentially affects this account in the manner indicated (Yes/No)
Debit to cash	
Debit to retained earnings	
Credit to share capital	
Debit to loss on share retirement	
Debit to contributed surplus	
Debit to treasury stock	

P13-14. Accounting for contributed capital   (**L.O.** 13-3) (Easy – 5 minutes)

When shares are repurchased and held in treasury, and the purchase is at more than the original issue price, the journal entry to record the repurchase potentially includes which of the following components under the single-transaction method?

Account	Transaction potentially affects this account in the manner indicated (Yes / No)
Debit to share capital	
Debit to contributed surplus	
Debit to retained earnings	
Debit to treasury stock	
Debit to accumulated other comprehensive income (AOCI)	
Credit to share capital	

P13-15. Accounting for contributed capital   (**L.O.** 13-3) (Medium – 10 minutes)

Accounting standards do not permit the recognition of capital transactions (those involving owners acting as owners) to flow through net income. Explain why accounting standards prohibit the recognition of gains or losses on capital transactions on the income statement.

P13-16. Accounting for contributed capital   (**L.O.** 13-3) (Medium – 20 minutes)

When a corporation engages in a capital transaction (those relating to its contributed capital), the journal entry may involve either a debit or a credit to contributed surplus. While not permitted by accounting standards, *if these debits or credits were to be recognized through income*, a debit would be called a "loss" and a credit would be called a "gain."
     Consider the following sequence of transactions:

Jan. 1, 2007: Company issues 10,000,000 no par common shares at $10 each.
Jan. 1, 2013: Company reacquires 100,000 common shares in the open market at $8 each, and cancels them immediately.

There were no other capital transactions and the company had not paid any dividends.

Required:

a. Prepare the journal entries for the two transactions.
b. Review the journal entry for January 1, 2013. How much was credited other than cash? Does this credit reflect good or bad management? As a shareholder, would you be happy or unhappy about this credit entry?
c. What would have been the journal entry for January 1, 2013 had the repurchase price been $30?
d. In the journal entry for part (c), explain why the debit goes to reduce retained earnings. How would a shareholder interpret the reduction in retained earnings?

P13-17. Accounting for contributed capital   (**L.O.** 13-3) (Medium – 15 minutes)

Cambridge Corp. has a single class of shares. As at its year ended December 31, 2012, the company had 2,500,000 shares issued and outstanding. On the stock exchange, these shares were trading at around $10. In the company's accounts, these shares had a value of $30,000,000. The equity accounts also show $450,000 of contributed surplus from previous repurchases of shares.

   On January 15, 2013, Cambridge repurchased and cancelled 100,000 shares at a cost of $10 per share. Later in the year, on August 20, the company repurchased and cancelled a further 300,000 shares at a cost of $15 per share.

Required:

Record the journal entries for the two share transactions in 2013.

P13-18. Accounting for contributed capital   (**L.O.** 13-3) (Medium – 15 minutes)

Drayton Inc. was incorporated under provincial legislation with a December 31 year-end. The company has a single class of shares. As at December 31, 2011, it had 200,000 shares issued and outstanding. These shares had a book value of $5,000,000 on the balance sheet.

   During 2012, Drayton repurchased 10% of the issued shares from one of the minority shareholders at a cost of $30 per share. The company held these in treasury and later found a buyer for half of these shares at $35. The other half were sold at $28 to another investor.

Required:

Record the share transactions using the single-transaction method for treasury stock, which is the preferred accounting method.

P13-19. Accounting for contributed capital   (**L.O.** 13-3) (Medium – 15 minutes)

Refer to the facts for Drayton Inc. presented in the previous question.

Required:

Record the share transactions using the alternative two-transaction method for treasury stock.

P13-20. Accounting for contributed capital   (**L.O.** 13-3) (Medium – 15 minutes)

Elgin Company had the following shareholders' equity account balances on December 31, 2011:

Common stock, no par, 40,000 authorized, 30,000 issued	$720,000
Contributed surplus on repurchases and resales	25,000
Treasury shares, 5,000 shares	(165,000)
Retained earnings	350,000
Total shareholders' equity	$930,000

   During 2012, the following transactions occurred:

   i. May 1: Elgin resold 800 of the treasury shares at $48 per share.
   ii. Dec. 30: The board of directors declared cash dividends of $2 per share.
   iii. Dec. 31: Net income for the year ended December 31, 2012 was $120,000.

Elgin uses the single transaction method for treasury shares.

Required:

a. Record the journal entries for the transactions in 2012 and make all the necessary year-end entries relating to shareholders' equity accounts.
b. Prepare the presentation of the shareholders' equity section of Elgin's balance sheet as at December 31, 2012.

P13-21. Accounting for retained earnings (**L.O.** 13-3, **L.O.** 13-4) (Medium – 20 minutes)[16]

Great-West Lifeco Inc. announced the following share issuances:

November 1, 2008

8,000,000 6% non-cumulative five-year rate reset first preferred shares (series J) for par value of $25 each. After five years the dividend rate will be reset to the five-year Canada bond rate plus 3.07%. Dividends are payable as declared by the board of directors.

December 9, 2008

28,920,000 common shares for $20.75 per share. This represents approximately 3.2% of Lifeco's total outstanding common shares.

The CEO of the company stated the following regarding these share issuances:

For many years, Great-West Life and its subsidiaries have pursued a risk-averse strategy with respect to both liabilities and assets. Consequently, today the company's balance sheet is one of the strongest in its industry. With this issue, the company will move forward with an enhanced capability to take advantage of market opportunities.

Required:

a. Prepare the journal entries to record the share issuances.
b. Explain how the share issuances result in a "risk-averse strategy with respect to both liabilities and assets," and how this results in a strong balance sheet that allows the company to take advantage of market opportunities, such as profitable investments.
c. Assume the board of directors declares dividends on December 31, 2008 in the amount of $10,000,000. Calculate the amount of dividends to be paid to preferred shareholders and common shareholders (assume the company only has the above stated series of preferred shares outstanding).

P13-22. Accounting for retained earnings (**L.O.** 13-4) (Easy – 5 minutes)[17]

Mark Corporation declared and distributed a 5% stock dividend. Mark had 400,000 common shares outstanding and 1,000,000 common shares authorized before the stock dividend. The board of directors determined the appropriate market value per share as $7.

Required:

How much should be recorded for the stock dividend? Record the journal entry (if any) for the shares distributed.

P13-23. Accounting for retained earnings (**L.O.** 13-4) (Easy – 10 minutes)

Acton Company has two classes of shares that were both issued on January 1, 2010:

- Class A, $100 par value, 5% preferred shares, 100,000 shares issued and outstanding;
- Class B, no par value common shares issued at $50/share, 1,000,000 shares issued and outstanding.

Due to challenging start-up problems in 2010 and 2011 there were no dividends paid; in 2012, dividends of $6,000,000 were paid. For 2013, dividends paid totalled $17,000,000, and for 2014 total dividends paid were $15,000,000.

Required:

How much was the amount of dividends paid to preferred and common shares in 2010 to 2014? First assume that the preferred shares are non-cumulative, then assume that they are cumulative. Use the following table for your answer.

---

16. Adapted from CGA-Canada FA3 examination, December 2009. CEO quotation is from "Great-West Lifeco Inc. Announces $1 Billion Offering of Common Shares", Press Release December 9, 2008, retrieved from www.greatwestlifeco.com/web5/groups/common/@public/documents/web_content/s5_011778.pdf.

17. © 2010 CGA-Canada. Reproduced with permission.

($000's)	2010	2011	2012	2013	2014
Total dividends	0	0	$6,000	$17,000	$15,000
Non-cumulative preferred dividends					
Common dividends					
Total dividends	0	0	$6,000	$17,000	$15,000
Cumulative preferred dividends					
Common dividends					

P13-24. Accounting for retained earnings (L.O. 13-4) (Medium – 10 minutes)

Belmont Corporation has a December 31 year-end. On December 15, 2011, the board of directors declared a cash dividend of $0.50 per common share, payable on January 30, 2012. The date of record for this dividend is January 14, and the ex-dividend date is January 12, 2012. Additional information relating to the shares follows:

	No. of common shares at end of day	
Date	Issued	Outstanding
2011 Dec 15	4,000,000	4,000,000
2012 Jan 11	4,000,000	3,800,000
2012 Jan 14	4,000,000	3,600,000
2012 Jan 30	3,600,000	3,600,000

Required:

a. Determine the dollar amount of dividends to be paid as a result of the dividend declaration on December 15, 2011.
b. Record all the journal entries related to this dividend in 2011 and 2012.

P13-25. Accounting for retained earnings (L.O. 13-4) (Medium – 20 minutes)

Cardiff Corporation is a public company traded on a major exchange. Cardiff's common shares are currently trading at $20 per share. The board of directors is debating whether to issue a 25% stock dividend or a five-for-four stock split (i.e., a shareholder who holds four shares would receive a fifth share). The board is wondering how shareholders' equity would be affected, and whether the value of the typical shareholder's investment will change.

Details of Cardiff's equity section of the balance sheet is as follows:

Common shares, no par, 10,000,000 shares issued and outstanding	$ 56,500,000
Retained earnings	170,000,000
Total shareholders' equity	$226,500,000

Required:

a. At what price would you expect the shares to trade after either transaction? Explain with calculations.
b. Show what the equity section of the balance sheet for Cardiff would look like after the stock dividend or stock split.
c. Assume that an investor has 4,000 common shares before the stock dividend or stock split. What would be the value of the investor's holdings before and after the stock dividend or stock split?
d. What is your recommendation to the board of directors?

P13-26. Accounting for retained earnings   (**L.O.** 13-4) (Medium – 15 minutes)

Below are details relating to balances for the equity accounts of Barrie Company, and changes to those balances. Note that AOCI is accumulated other comprehensive income.

Balances or changes	Amount (000's)
Common stock, 2011 Jan 1	$20,000
Unappropriated retained earnings, 2011 Jan 1	11,000
Appropriated retained earnings for sinking fund reserve, 2011 Jan 1	2,000
AOCI from revaluations, 2011 Jan 1	1,000
Net income for 2011	3,000
Retained earnings appropriated for sinking fund reserve during 2011	1,300
AOCI from revaluations in 2011	500
Dividends declared during 2011	1,000
Net income for 2012	4,000
Retained earnings appropriated for sinking fund reserve during 2012	400
AOCI from revaluations in 2012	(200)
Dividends declared during 2012	1,200

Required:

Prepare a statement of changes in equity for the years ended December 31, 2011 and 2012. The following format will be helpful for preparing this statement for each of the two years.

Common stock	Retained earnings	Appropriated retained earnings	AOCI	Total
Changes during year 20XX:				
⋮				
Balance Jan. 1, 20XX				
Balance Dec. 31, 20XX				

P13-27. Accounting for contributed capital and retained earnings

(**L.O.** 13-3, **L.O.** 13-4) (Medium – 20 minutes)

As of January 1, 2014, the equity section of BC Marine Co.'s balance sheet contained the following:

Common stock, 10,000,000 authorized, 2,000,000 issued and outstanding	$5,000,000
Contributed surplus—from repurchase and cancellation of common shares	150,000
Contributed surplus—expired options on common shares	200,000
Preferred stock, $2 cumulative dividend, 5,000,000 authorized, 50,000 issued and outstanding	1,050,000
Retained earnings	2,400,000
Total shareholders' equity	$8,800,000

On May 1, 2014, the company spent $500,000 to repurchase 100,000 common shares. These shares were cancelled immediately.

On July 15, 2014, the company repurchased and cancelled 1,000 preferred shares at $20/share.

On November 1, 2014, the company declared and paid the annual cash dividends on the preferred shares. On the same day, the company issued a 10% stock dividend on common shares. BC Marine's stock traded at $6/share after the dividend.

Required:

Record the journal entries for the above transactions occurring in 2014.

P13-28. Accounting for contributed capital and retained earnings
(**L.O.** 13-3, **L.O.** 13-4) (Difficult – 20 minutes)

The following is an extract from the balance sheet of Devlin Ltd. as at December 31, 2011.

Shareholders' equity	
Preferred shares, $1 per share non-cumulative dividend, redeemable at $12 per share, 500,000 authorized, 50,000 issued and outstanding	$ 500,000
Contributed surplus—preferred shares, from share repurchases and resales	150,000
Common shares, 10,000,000 authorized, 1,000,000 issued and outstanding	2,637,489
Retained earnings	12,649,187
Total shareholders' equity	$15,936,676

The company did not declare dividends on preferred shares in 2011. Transactions in 2012 include the following:

i. March 15: Devlin purchased 10,000 preferred shares on the stock exchange for $11.50 per share and held these in treasury.
ii. March 28: The company redeemed 15,000 preferred shares directly from shareholders.
iii. July 1: The market price of common shares shot up to $45 per share, so Devlin decided to split the common shares four to one.
iv. August 1: Devlin cancelled 8,000 preferred shares that were held in treasury.
v. December 31: The company declared dividends of $0.10 per common share.

Required:

Prepare the journal entries to record the above transactions. The company uses the single-transaction method to account for treasury shares.

P13-29. Accounting for contributed capital and retained earnings
(**L.O.** 13-3, **L.O.** 13-4) (Difficult – 30 minutes)

Fenwick Ltd. began operations in 2008. The fiscal year-end is December 31. Components of the condensed balance sheet as at December 31, 2010 are as follows:

Current liabilities	$ 400,000
Bonds payable—7%, mature 2014	8,000,000
Total liabilities	$8,400,000
Common shares—500,000 authorized, 300,000 issued and outstanding	$6,000,000
Contributed surplus—common shares, from share repurchases and resales	400,000
Retained earnings (deficit)	(200,000)
Total shareholders' equity	$6,200,000

During 2011, Fenwick had the following activities:

    i. Jan. 1: Issued 40,000 preferred shares with cumulative dividends of $1.25 per share. Proceeds were $480,000, or $12 per share.
    ii. July 1: Repurchased and cancelled 50,000 common shares at a cost of $18 per share.
    iii. Net income for the year was $1,700,000.

During 2012, the company had the following activities:

    i. July 1: Repurchased and cancelled 60,000 common shares at a cost of $30 each.
    ii. Dec. 31: Fenwick declared dividends totalling $400,000.
    iii. Net income for the year was $800,000.

Required:

  a. Prepare the journal entries required for 2011.
  b. Prepare the equity section of the balance sheet as at December 31, 2011, including any notes that would be required.
  c. Prepare the journal entries required for 2012.
  d. Prepare the equity section of the balance sheet as at December 31, 2012, including any notes that would be required.

P13-30. Accounting for contributed capital and retained earnings

(**L.O.** 13-3, **L.O.** 13-4) (Difficult –30 minutes)

Hamilton Holdings had the following balances in shareholders' equity as at December 31, 2011:

Preferred shares, $1 cumulative dividend, 1,000,000 authorized, 700,000 issued and outstanding	$17,500,000
Common shares, no par, unlimited number authorized, 1,200,000 issued	9,600,000
Contributed surplus—common shares, from share repurchases and resales	120,000
Treasury shares, 320,000 common shares	(1,920,000)
Retained earnings	23,450,000
Total shareholders' equity	$48,750,000

In addition, the financial statement notes on this date indicated that two years of preferred share dividends were in arrears, totalling $1,400,000.
The following transactions occurred during 2012:

    i. Jan. 31: Hamilton resold half of the shares held in treasury for proceeds of $7.50 each.
    ii. Mar. 30: The company repurchased and immediately cancelled 200,000 common shares at a cost of $1,620,000.
    iii. June 1: The company repurchased and retired 175,000 preferred shares at a price of $30 each. Note that repurchased shares lose any rights to dividends.
    iv. July 13: The company issued 250,000 common shares in exchange for some heavy machinery. The market price of the shares was $9 on this day.
    v. Aug. 1: The remaining shares held in treasury were cancelled. The share price was $9.50.
    vi. Sept. 30: The board of directors declared and issued a 10% stock dividend on common shares. The shares were trading at $11 per share on this day. On the ex-dividend date of October 31, the share price was $10. In order to issue this stock dividend, the board also declared dividends on preferred shares for the current year and the two years in arrears.

Required:

Prepare the journal entries to reflect Hamilton's equity transactions in 2012. It may be helpful to use a tabular schedule similar to Exhibit 13-18 to track the number of shares and dollar amounts.

L. MINI-CASES

Peterborough Printers specializes in high-volume reproduction of advertising leaflets, such as those distributed by direct mail or inserted in newspapers. Located in Scarborough and founded by Peter Pang over 40 years ago, the company has been publicly traded for the past 20 years. Through its history, the company has successfully attracted and retained a solid and stable base of business clients largely as a result of Peter's savvy salesmanship.

Peterborough has two classes of shares, common and preferred. The common shares are listed on the Toronto Stock Exchange, and Peter still holds 20% of these shares. The preferred shares are privately held by five individuals, and they pay cumulative dividends.

You are the CFO of Peterborough Printers. You recently met with Peter to discuss financial matters. The following is an excerpt from that conversation.

PETER: This recession is a lot deeper and lasting a lot longer than I and many others had anticipated. Our sales are way down and I'm becoming more and more worried.

YOU: There's no doubt about it. We'll need to be on our toes to come out of this in one piece.

PETER: On top of the recession, there has been a gradual but noticeable drop in our printing volume over the past decade.

YOU: I think it has a lot to do with companies relying less on print media and switching to online advertising.

PETER: That's probably right. I am working on adjusting our production capabilities in light of this long-term trend.

YOU: That's good to hear.

PETER: So, the reason we're meeting today is to see what we might do on the financial side of things to help us cope with the current economic pressures. In hindsight, we have been very fortunate, having built up a substantial cushion of cash and short-term investments during the good years. We are still in good shape now, but I expect another one or two lean years will take us to the breaking point.

As you know, Peterborough has been able to consistently maintain and increase dividends to our common shareholders over the past 20 years. Under the circumstances, we need to seriously think about whether we can continue with this policy. I wonder if there is anything we can do to maintain our financial health while not disappointing our shareholders. I've heard that some companies pay stock dividends. I'm not exactly sure how they work, but I've been told that paying these dividends doesn't cost us any cash.

YOU: What are your thoughts on the dividends on the preferred shares?

PETER: I'm not as concerned about maintaining those dividends. As it is, the dividends are cumulative, so these shareholders will get their money sooner or later, even if we have to miss paying them this year or next year.

YOU: Well, let me think about these dividend issues and get back to you tomorrow.

Required:

Draft a short report discussing the dividend policy alternatives and your recommendations.

CASE 1
Peterborough Printers
(30 minutes)

A relaxing bath represents a busy day's more enjoyable moments for many people. For over a hundred years, Thamesford Tubs has been fulfilling this need, manufacturing bathtubs of all shapes and sizes and in all quality ranges. The company enjoyed decades of success along with North America's burgeoning population, which created great demand for new homes and new bathtubs. At the company's peak, production reached 500,000 tubs a year.

In more recent years, however, demand for the company's products has decreased significantly due to a confluence of many factors. Consumer tastes have evolved toward a preference for showers over baths for several reasons: people have become more aware of the lower water consumption of showers compared to baths; increasing numbers of people live in condominiums/apartments in which space is at a premium

CASE 2
Thamesford Tubs
(45 minutes)

compared to detached homes; fewer consumers value distinctive and high-quality tubs; and there was a bursting of the housing bubble which dramatically lowered the rate of new home construction. Due to the significant drop in sales, Thamesford has experienced three consecutive years of losses, and management expects a net loss of around $2 million this year before business recovers to profitability.

It is mid-September, almost three-quarters of the way to Thamesford's fiscal year-end of December 31. The company has a $20 million bank loan coming due next March 30. Given recent years' operating results, the company's financial resources have been stretched, and there is little available to repay this loan in seven months' time.

In addition to this $20 million loan, Thamesford has another long-term loan outstanding for $16 million, which is due in five years, bearing interest at 8%. This loan requires Thamesford to maintain a current ratio of at least 1.0 and a debt-to-equity ratio less than 3:1 at each fiscal year-end. Violating these covenants would make the loan immediately due and payable. As of the previous fiscal year-end, the company was in compliance with these covenants. Other liabilities, which consist primarily of accounts payable, stood at $14 million, so liabilities totalled $50 million. These figures resulted in a current ratio of 1.5 and a debt-to-equity ratio of 2.5:1.

Top management is considering the options available to the company. The bank that lent the $20 million due next March is willing to refinance the loan for another three years, but at a considerably higher interest rate of 15% plus a pledge of the company manufacturing facilities as collateral. Alternatively, the company could issue preferred shares with a cumulative dividend rate of 12%. The investment firm proposing this option also suggested that the dividend rate could be lowered to 10% if Thamesford added a provision to give the preferred shareholders the right to retract the shares at the issuance price (i.e., the company must redeem the shares if a shareholder demanded it). A third alternative is to issue common shares, although Thamesford's share price is understandably depressed under the circumstances.

Required:

Play the role of Thamesford's chief financial officer and analyze the three financing alternatives. Provide a recommendation to your CEO and board of directors.

Detail of the monument to Columbus
at the Plaza de Colón, Madrid.
Photograph by Luis Garcia

As every school-aged child knows (or should know), Christopher Columbus "discovered" the Americas in 1492 while searching for a westerly route from Europe to Asia. Venturing across the oceans at the time was dangerous at best, and unimaginably more treacherous when done over territory that was literally uncharted. Such voyages were also expensive. If you were Columbus asking Queen Isabella of Spain to finance this expedition, what would you propose? If you were the Queen, what proposal would you accept?

In this scenario, there are immense information problems. How far would the ships have to travel westward to reach any type of land? Columbus had some crude estimates and the Queen and her counsel knew even less. How large should the ships be; how many ships should be sent; and what quantity of supplies should be provided? These all factor into the financing required, and there was no assurance that the Queen would recover any of these funds. More funds increases the chances of success to some extent, but what if the Queen advanced too much to Columbus—would that just increase her losses? Would Columbus misspend the funds or perhaps even run off with the bounty to some unknown land? These questions suggest that the problems of adverse selection and moral hazard are pervasive in this situation.

While the voyage of Christopher Columbus is unique in many respects, the financing problem is not. Consider a company mining for gold. Funds are required for geological tests to determine whether there are gold deposits at a particular site. If the results are promising, the company will require further funds to drill ore samples to determine whether the ore concentration is high enough. The final stages of ore extraction and refinement also require a lot of equipment and financing. How much should investors advance to a gold mining company? Too much financing and the funds could be wasted on unpromising projects. Too little financing and a good project may never be completed.

One solution is to provide financing in stages—supplying an initial amount but committing to provide further funds if the project is successful (or at least looks increasingly promising). Such staged financing can be accomplished by the use of compound financial instruments, such as convertible debt and stock warrants issued along with shares. How do we account for such compound financial instruments? How do we account for financial instruments other than a simple liability or equity instrument?

LEARNING OBJECTIVES

After studying this chapter,
you should be able to:

L.O. 14-1. Describe the nature of standard financial instruments, derivatives, and compound financial instruments, and identify when transactions involve such instruments.

L.O. 14-2. Apply the accounting standards for derivatives.

L.O. 14-3. Apply the accounting standards for compound financial instruments from the perspective of the issuer.

L.O. 14-4. Apply the accounting standards for employee stock options from the perspective of the issuer.

L.O. 14-5. Describe the nature of hedges and identify situations in which hedge accounting may be appropriate.

CONTENTS

A. INTRODUCTION

Accounting for financial instruments is a complex area. The accounting standards for financial instruments have been almost continuously deliberated and re-deliberated for over two decades, with frequent revisions during that time. The frequent modifications reflect the rapid changes in the field of finance, which seems to find no bounds to the creation of new financial instruments. Many of these new financial instruments are innovative and meet the needs of financial market participants. However, not all such financial innovations are beneficial, as amply demonstrated in the financial crisis of 2008 (see Chapter 1 for a discussion of this crisis). In particular, some financial innovations are designed to circumvent accounting standards to achieve desired results for accounting purposes. For this reason, it is important to understand the economic substance of each financial instrument so that the reported results ultimately reflect the transactions' substance rather than their form.

This chapter will first look at the economic characteristics of different financial instruments before turning to the accounting for these instruments. We will focus on the fundamental ideas in the accounting standards for financial instruments. These fundamentals will be applicable for enterprises applying IFRS or ASPE. More advanced study is required for a full appreciation of all the requirements in IFRS, which are contained in IAS 39 (recognition and measurement), IAS 32 (presentation), and IFRS 7 (disclosures).

B. TYPES OF FINANCIAL INSTRUMENTS

This section identifies and distinguishes the different types of financial instruments. First, we review the relatively basic financial assets, financial liabilities, and equity instruments. We then discuss derivatives. Finally, we look at compound financial instruments, which comprise more than one basic financial instrument or derivative in some combination.

> **L.O.** 14-1. Describe the nature of standard financial instruments, derivatives, and compound financial instruments, and identify when transactions involve such instruments.

1. Basic financial assets, financial liabilities, and equity instruments

Various previous chapters in this text discussed the three basic types of financial instruments:

- Chapter 7 discussed financial assets;
- Chapters 11 and 12 discussed financial liabilities; and
- Chapter 13 discussed equity instruments.

As Chapter 7 notes, a holder of a financial asset has a counterparty that has either a financial liability or an equity instrument. An investor holding a bond has a financial asset, while the bond issuer has a financial liability. An investor holding a share has a financial asset, while the company that issued the share has an equity instrument outstanding. As discussed in those chapters, we can summarize the accounting for these financial instruments as follows:

Exhibit 14-1	Summary of accounting for simple financial assets, financial liabilities, and equity instruments	
Financial assets can be accounted for using	*Financial liabilities* can be accounted for using	*Equity instruments* can be accounted for using
■ consolidation for controlled subsidiaries	■ amortized cost for held-to-maturity debt (most financial liabilities for non-financial companies)	■ historical cost
■ proportionate consolidation for joint ventures	■ fair value through profit or loss for held-for-trading liabilities	
■ equity method for associates	■ fair value through OCI for available-for-sale liabilities	
■ fair value through profit or loss for held-for-trading investments		
■ fair value through OCI* for available-for-sale investments		
■ amortized cost for held-to-maturity investments and loans/receivables		

*OCI = other comprehensive income

Since other chapters have dealt with these basic financial instruments in some depth, there is no need to repeat that material here. Instead, we will proceed with other types of financial instruments.

derivative A financial instrument that is derived from some other underlying quantity.

2. Derivative financial instruments

A **derivative** is a financial instrument that is derived from some other underlying quantity. That **underlying quantity** can be the value of an asset, an index

underlying quantity or **underlying** The value of an asset, an index value, or an event that helps determine the value of a derivative.

value, or an event. (In technical jargon, finance and accounting professionals will often use the expedient but grammatically incorrect term "**underlying**," which omits the required noun.) For example, a derivative can be based on the price of a share, the value of the Toronto Stock Exchange Index, or the exchange rate between Canadian and U.S. dollars.

The underlying quantity need not be financial in nature. For example, a derivative can be based on the minimum temperature in Florida in January. Such a derivative can be useful to orange producers, who face large losses when temperatures drop below freezing. If orange growers are able to buy derivatives that pay them when the temperature drops below zero degrees Celsius, they would be able to reduce their losses under those circumstances. For a reasonable price, there will be other people willing to take on the other side of that derivative contract. Thus, even though there is little we can do about the weather, financial innovation allows for risk sharing through the use of derivatives.

Below, we discuss the nature of five types of common derivatives.

a. Options

An **option** contract gives the holder the right, but not the obligation, to buy or sell something at a specified price. The most common type of option is a **call option**, which gives the holder the *right to acquire* an underlying instrument at a pre-specified price within a defined period of time. The pre-specified price is called the *exercise price* or *strike price*. A **put option** has the opposite characteristic, giving the holder the *right to sell* at a specified price. Other more exotic options are possible. We focus our discussion on the call option because it is the most frequently encountered. For concreteness, we will assume that the underlying instrument is a share of common stock.

The option holder's decision to exercise an option is dependent on the difference between the exercise price, which is fixed, and the market price of the underlying instrument. For a call option on a share, if the market price of the share (S) is less than the exercise price (K), the option is "**out-of-the-money**" and, of course, the holder of the option would not exercise the option. On the other hand, if the market price exceeds the strike price ($S > K$), the call option is "**in-the-money**" and the option holder may choose to exercise the option, but need not do so.

The value of an option (V) can be decomposed into two parts: its intrinsic value and its time value. The **intrinsic value** of a call option is the greater of zero and ($S - K$), the difference between the market price and the strike price. When $S = K$, the intrinsic value is exactly zero. Graphically, the value of call and put options prior to expiration can be depicted as follows in Exhibit 14-2.

As the graph for a call option shows, above the strike price K, the intrinsic value of the option increases 1:1 with the share price S. The **time value** of an option reflects the probability that the future market price of the underlying instrument will exceed the strike price. The time value increases with the length of time to expiration and the volatility of the underlying instrument (such as the stock price). The time value is always positive until the option expires, so the total value of an unexpired option is always greater than the intrinsic value. At expiration, there is no longer any time value left, so total value equals the intrinsic value.

In contrast to a call, the put option's intrinsic value increases when the underlying share price declines below the strike price because a put allows the holder to sell at the strike price. For example, if the strike price is K = $10 and the underlying share price is S = $6, then a holder of a put can buy a share for $6 and exercise the put option to sell the share at $10, for a profit of $4.

---

option A derivative contract that gives the holder the right, but not the obligation, to buy or sell an underlying financial instrument at a specified price. A call option gives the right to buy, whereas a put option provides the right to sell.

call option See option.

put option See option.

out-of-the-money When the value of the underlying instrument in an option contract is unfavourable to the holder exercising the option compared with letting the option expire. In the case of a call option, this is when the underlying price is lower than the strike price; for a put option, it is when the underlying price is higher than the strike price.

in-the-money When the value of the underlying instrument in an option contract is favourable to the holder exercising the option compared with letting the option expire. In the case of a call option, this occurs when the underlying price exceeds the strike price; for a put option, it is when the underlying price is below the strike price.

intrinsic value of an option In a call option, the greater of zero and (S − K), the difference between the market price and the strike price.

time value of an option The portion of an option's value that reflects the probability that the future market price of the underlying instrument will exceed the strike price.

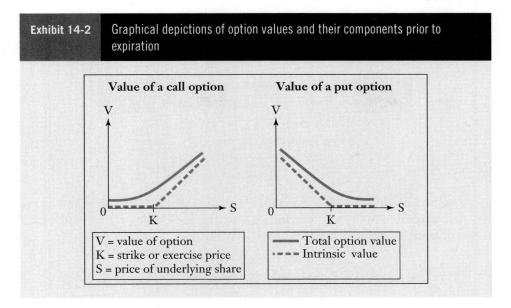

Exhibit 14-2 Graphical depictions of option values and their components prior to expiration

An important type of call option is an **employee stock option**, which a company issues to its employees, giving them the right to buy shares in their employer at a pre-specified price. Companies often use employee stock options to compensate employees to substitute for other forms of compensation and to reduce the moral hazard inherent in an employer–employee relationship. (See Chapter 1 on moral hazard.)

More generally, options on a company's shares can be issued not only by the company itself, but also by others outside the company. For larger public companies, there are many call and put options written on their share prices. For example, in mid-January 2010, when Royal Bank of Canada common shares were trading for around $55, there were more than 150 different call or put options with maturity ranging from February 2010 to January 2012 and strike prices ranging from $22 to $70.

employee stock option An option a company issues to its employees, giving them the right to buy shares in their employer at a pre-specified price.

b. Warrants

Warrants provide the holder the right, but not the obligation, to buy a company's shares at a specified price over a specified period of time. Thus, warrants are similar to call options. The main differences are that warrants are issued only by the company whose shares are the underlying instrument. Warrants also tend to have longer time to maturity (typically 3 to 10 years) compared with options, and they tend to be issued in combination with other financial instruments such as bonds, preferred shares, and common shares.

warrant A right but not the obligation to buy a share at a specified price over a specified period of time. Can be considered a type of *call option.*

c. Forwards

In a **forward** contract, one party to the contract commits to buy something at a specified price at a specified future date. A forward differs from an option because a party to a forward contract does not have a choice in the purchase or sale in the future. For example, suppose on December 15, 2011, Axel Inc. agrees to buy US$1 million for C$1.05 million in 90 days from Bluebird Corp. The underlying quantity is the USD:CAD exchange rate. Axel Inc. enters into this forward because it expects the U.S. dollar to appreciate in value; hence, it wants to make sure that for each U.S. dollar it pays only C$1.05 and no more. For Bluebird Corp., the expectation is the opposite: it is concerned that the U.S. dollar might have a value less than C$1.05. Forwards are possible only if the two parties to the agreement have different expectations or risk tolerances regarding future price changes.

forward A contract in which one party commits upfront to buy or sell something at a defined price at a defined future date.

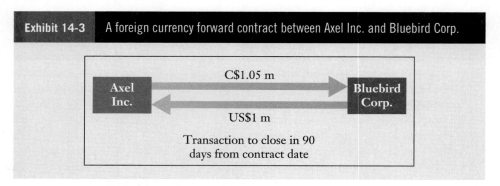

Exhibit 14-3 A foreign currency forward contract between Axel Inc. and Bluebird Corp.

The two parties to a forward contract can specify any price and any maturity date agreeable to both. Thus, forwards are quite flexible in their contractual terms in contrast to futures, which we discuss next.

d. Futures

future Similar to a forward but contract is written in more standardized terms (e.g., prices, maturity dates) and involves commonly traded items (e.g., commodities, currencies).

A **future** is similar to a forward, except that a future contract is written in more standardized terms (e.g., prices, maturity dates) and they involve commonly traded items (e.g., commodities, currencies). The reason for the standardized terms is that futures are tradable in organized markets, and standardization increases liquidity since more investors are trading the same contracts. For example, a commodities futures contract on gold could specify a price of $1,050 per ounce to be settled in June 2012.[1] In contrast, a forward contract can be more specific, such as $1,051.22 per ounce to be settled on June 3, 2012.

e. Swaps

swap A derivative contract in which two parties agree to exchange cash flows.

A **swap** is a derivative contract in which two parties agree to exchange cash flows. For example, if Beowulf Company has $100 million in debt that has a floating rate of prime + 2% it could arrange a swap with another company (such as an investment bank) to fix the interest rate at 6%. The ability to complete a swap

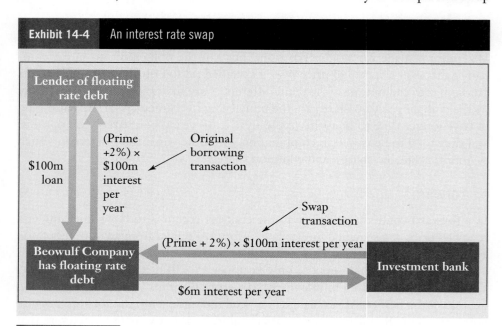

Exhibit 14-4 An interest rate swap

---

1. Although the futures contract specifies simply June 2012, it refers to one specific date in the month, depending on the exchange. On North American exchanges, that day is the third Friday of the month. Also, many futures contracts use only one expiration per quarterly period (i.e., March, June, September, and December) to further concentrate trading and liquidity.

of course depends on whether one party desires to have the cash flow stream of the other party.

3. Compound financial instruments

As introduced in the opening vignette about the voyages of Columbus, sometimes companies require financial instruments that are more than just debt or just equity. There are situations when it is beneficial to commit to staged financing, and this can often be accomplished with **compound financial instruments**—those that have more than one financial instrument component.

For instance, a frequently used compound financial instrument is a convertible bond. Typically, these bonds allow the holder to convert the bond into shares at a specific conversion rate. For example, a convertible bond might specify that the holder can convert each $1,000 bond (where $1,000 refers to the face value) into 50 common shares. Another common compound financial instrument is the issuance of warrants attached to shares or bonds. For example, a common share may be issued for $20/share and include a warrant to purchase another share within five years at $30 per share.

The conversion feature and the warrants are commonly referred to as "sweeteners" that enhance the attractiveness of an offering of bonds or shares. However, that description is not an adequate explanation for why companies use these compound financial instruments. If these additions "sweeten" an offer, why don't all companies issue bonds and shares with these additional features?

A more compelling explanation is that these compound financial instruments solve problems of information asymmetry. A company that issues common shares sends a negative signal to investors because the share issuance indicates a lack of confidence in the future prospects of the company. If management were more confident, it would instead use internally generated cash flow, issue debt, or perhaps issue preferred shares. Indeed, announcements of common share issuances are usually greeted with significant declines in the share price. As a result, companies issue shares as a last resort. Adverse selection poses a significant cost to issuing equity.

A compound financial instrument such as a convertible bond alleviates this adverse selection problem. With such a bond, the company is initially issuing debt, which does not send the negative signal that share issuances do. Investors who hold these bonds will exercise the conversion option only when it is beneficial to them; that is, when converting into common shares becomes more valuable than holding the debt. Thus, conversion would occur when the firm performs well. The conversion decreases debt and increases equity, thereby decreasing leverage and increasing debt capacity. Should the company wish to bring in additional financing at this point, it can do so by issuing additional debt. Through this entire process, the company did not have to directly issue shares, which would have sent a negative signal. Instead, it issued shares indirectly via the conversion of bonds into shares.

A similar thought process can explain the usefulness of a debt or equity instrument with warrants attached. Holders of the warrants would exercise the warrants only if the warrants are in-the-money, which is when the company is doing well. Upon exercise, the warrant holders contribute to the firm an amount of cash equal to the exercise price. Just as for convertible bonds, the company increases equity not by issuing shares directly, but by issuing shares indirectly via investors exercising their warrants to purchase shares.

Another useful function of these compound financial instruments is that they provide the company with funds in more than one stage, which is helpful at alleviating moral hazard. Investors do not want to give too much money to

compound financial instruments Those financial instruments with more than one financial instrument component.

management when outcomes are highly uncertain because management may misspend the funds. At the same time, the conversion option and warrants are a commitment from investors to provide additional funding—but only if the company performs well. If the company performs poorly, the conversion option or warrant will be out-of-the-money, and investors will choose to not exercise these rights.

Compound financial instruments are suitable and therefore commonly used when operational uncertainty is relatively high, such as for early-stage companies and mining companies. In fact, some 200 companies have tradable warrants listed on the Canadian Venture Exchange, which specializes in early-stage public companies and those in the mining sector.

C. ACCOUNTING FOR COMPLEX FINANCIAL INSTRUMENTS

The previous section has discussed the nature of complex financial instruments. Now we turn to how we treat these instruments for accounting purposes. These complex financial instruments often involve one or more equity components. As noted in Chapter 13, IFRS is not specific regarding which equity account should be used. Thus, the following discussion uses the more specific terminology available in ASPE for equity accounts, as described in Chapter 13.

1. Derivatives

L.O. 14-2. Apply the accounting standards for derivatives.

As discussed in Chapter 7 on financial assets, we generally classify derivative investments as held for trading and measure them at fair value, with changes in fair value recorded through income. This general rule applies to both sides of a derivative transaction. There are two exceptions to this general rule. The first is for derivatives that are part of hedging transactions, which we discuss in the next section. The second exception is for derivatives that relate to the reporting entity's own equity, which should be recorded at historical cost. Warrants on common shares and employee stock options are examples of derivatives on the company's own equity.

To illustrate the general treatment of derivatives, recall the example of the forward contract above involving Axel Inc. and Bluebird Corp. Axel agrees to buy US$1 million for C$1.05 million from Bluebird. The contract was made on December 15, 2011 and closes 90 days later. At inception, neither company records the forward, because nothing changes hands at this date.

At the companies' year-end of December 31, 2011, the exchange rate is US$1 to C$0.98. This exchange rate means that US$1,000,000 is worth only C$980,000. However, Axel has committed to pay C$1,050,000 to buy this US$1,000,000, so it has a mark-to-market loss of C$70,000 (= $1,050,000 − $980,000). Correspondingly, Bluebird would record a gain of C$70,000.

Exhibit 14-5	Journal entries to record fair value changes in the currency forward contract between Axel and Bluebird

Axel Inc.		Bluebird Corp.	
Dr. Loss on currency derivative	70,000	Dr. Foreign currency derivative	70,000
Cr. Foreign currency derivative	70,000	Cr. Gain on currency derivative	70,000

This example illustrates a derivative involving no transfers on the contract initiation, so neither party records a journal entry at that time. Other derivatives do require entries upon initiation. For example, suppose that, instead of a forward, Axel had bought a futures contract that entitles the company to buy US$1 million at a cost of C$1.05 million on March 15, 2011. Axel would have incurred a cost to buy this futures contract. Supposing that cost is $10,000, the company would record the following entry for the purchase:

Exhibit 14-6	Journal entry to record Axel's purchase of a foreign currency futures contract	
Dr. Foreign currency derivative (classified as held-for-trading financial asset)	10,000	
Cr. Cash		10,000

The value of this futures contract becomes more valuable if the U.S. dollar appreciates, and less valuable when the U.S. dollar depreciates. In fact, if the U.S. dollar depreciates enough, the value of Axel's currency futures contract will have negative value (i.e., it becomes a liability). Consider two scenarios in which the exchange rates increase or decrease by C$0.03 to either US$1:C$1.08 or US$1:C$1.02 on December 31, 2011, which causes the futures contract price to increase or decrease to either $40,000 or –$20,000.[2] In these scenarios, Axel would record one of the following journal entries:

Exhibit 14-7	Two scenarios and journal entries to account for changes in value in Axel's U.S. dollar foreign currency futures contract			
Scenario	Resulting exchange rate Dec. 31, 2011	Value of futures contract	Journal entry	
USD appreciates by C$0.03	US$1:C$1.08	$40,000	Dr. Foreign currency derivative	30,000
			Cr. Gain on currency derivative	30,000
USD depreciates by C$0.03	US$1:C$1.02	–$20,000	Dr. Loss on foreign currency derivative	30,000
			Cr. Foreign currency derivative	30,000

In the second scenario, notice that the $30,000cr adjustment to the "Foreign currency derivative" combined with the original balance of $10,000dr results in a net credit of $20,000, so Axel would report this amount as a liability on its December 31, 2011 financial statements.

2. Compound financial instruments

a. Issuance

Enterprises must separate the components of a compound financial instrument and account for each separately. For example, a convertible bond would need to be separated into its debt component and the conversion option. In such situations, the question arises as to how one should allocate amounts to each of the two or more components. There are three reasonable methods:

L.O. 14-3. Apply the accounting standards for compound financial instruments from the perspective of the issuer.

i. *Proportional method:* Estimate the fair value of all components and allocate proportionally to all components. This approach is similar to that used to allocate the cost of bundled purchases of property, plant, and equipment discussed in Chapter 8.

2. Actual prices of futures contracts do not move in lockstep with exchange rates. We assume these figures for simplicity.

ii. *Incremental method:* Estimate the fair value of components and allocate amounts to these components in descending order according to the reliability of each component's fair value (i.e., most reliable first). The component relating to common shares is always considered the least reliably measured and it is allocated the residual amount after allocations have been made to all other components. For example, for a convertible bond, the issuing entity would record a liability for the estimated value of the bond without the conversion feature. The remainder would be recorded as contributed surplus in equity for the option to convert into common shares.

iii. *Zero common equity method:* Assign zero value to the common equity component. For a convertible bond, all of the bond value would be counted as a liability.

IFRS recommends method (ii). ASPE permits both methods (ii) and (iii).[3]

b. Measurement at the balance sheet date

Once a compound financial instrument has been separated into its components, the accounting for each component follows the standards applicable to that component. Enterprises would report a financial liability for a convertible bond at amortized cost; it would report the contributed surplus for the conversion option in equity at historical cost.

c. Accounting for an exercise of options or warrants

The accounting for this type of transaction is fairly straightforward. The exercise of an option or warrant extinguishes that financial instrument in exchange for the issuance of common shares. For instance, suppose Callisto Company had issued 500,000 warrants in 2011 along with some shares. The company estimated the value of the warrants to be $0.20 each, for a total of $100,000, which the company credited to contributed surplus. Each warrant allows an investor to buy a common share in the company at $15. In 2013, Callisto's share price increased to $18. Investors exercised 200,000 warrants. The journal entry to record this exercise of warrants would be as follows:

Exhibit 14-8	Journal entry to record the exercise of warrants for Callisto Company	
Dr. Cash (200,000 warrants × 1 share/warrant × $15/share)	3,000,000	
Dr. Contributed surplus − warrants (200,000/500,000 × $100,000 or 200,000 warrants × $0.20/warrant)	40,000	
Cr. Common stock		3,040,000

The amount recorded in common stock is just the sum of the cash received and the amount removed from contributed surplus.

d. Accounting for conversions of bonds or preferred shares

There are two methods to record the conversion of bonds or preferred shares into an equity instrument (most often common shares). These are called the book value and market value methods. IFRS recommends using the book value method. In particular, IAS 32 indicates the following in its Application Guidance:

¶AG32 On conversion of a convertible instrument at maturity, the entity derecognizes the liability component and recognizes it as equity. The original equity component remains as equity (although it may be transferred from one line item within equity to another). There is no gain or loss on conversion at maturity.

---

3. U.S. GAAP requires method (iii).

In this paragraph, the word "maturity" should be interpreted to include the date of exercise, which could be before the expiry date of the conversion option. That is, the act of conversion by the investor causes the instrument to mature.

In contrast, ASPE recommends the market value method. Section 3856 states the following (italics in original):

> ¶28.   *The difference between the carrying amount of a financial liability (or part of a financial liability) extinguished or transferred to another party and the fair value of the consideration paid, including any non-cash assets transferred, liabilities assumed or equity instruments issued, shall be recognized in net income for the period.*[4]

To see the differences in these two methods, suppose Dante Corp. issued convertible bonds with a face value of $10 million in 2011, and the share price at this time was $15. Each $1,000 bond can be converted into 50 shares. In 2015, the company's stock price increased significantly to $25, such that investors found it attractive to convert all of the bonds to shares. (The 50 shares converted from each $1,000 bond would be worth $50 \times \$25 = \$1,250$.) At the time of conversion, we assume Dante's account balances to be as follows:

Exhibit 14-9	Accounts prior to bond conversion for Dante Corp. ($000's)
Bond payable face value	$10,000 Cr
Bond discount[5]	1,000 Dr
Bond payable net of bond discount	9,000 Cr
Contributed surplus—convertible bond	2,000 Cr
Total book value of convertible bond	$11,000 Cr

The conversion would be recorded in one of two ways, as follows:

Exhibit 14-10	Book value and market value methods for bond conversion of Dante Corp. ($000's)			
Book value method (IFRS)			**Market value method (ASPE)**	
Dr. Bonds payable	9,000		Dr. Bonds payable	9,000
Dr. Contributed surplus—conv. bond	2,000		Dr. Contributed surplus—conv. bond	2,000
Cr. Common stock		11,000	Cr. Common stock*	12,500
			Dr. Loss on conversion (plug)	1,500

*(10,000 bonds × 50 shares/bond × $25/share) = $12,500,000

The book value method takes the amounts already recorded for the convertible bond and transfers them to the common stock account. In contrast, the market value method looks at the value of the shares issued upon conversion and determines any loss that flows from the conversion.[6]

There is an argument for the market value method in that the issuance of common shares at below market prices is a loss to existing shareholders. However, this method is inconsistent with the treatment of warrant exercises shown

---

4. Reproduced with permission of The Canadian Institute of Chartered Accountants.

5. Note that there would normally be a discount on a convertible bond. The coupon rate is typically lower than the market rate of interest at the date of issuance; the addition of the conversion option adds value to the convertible bond, allowing the issuing company to lower the coupon rate.

6. There is unlikely to be a gain in such instances. Investors exercise their conversion rights only when it is to their own benefit, meaning that the market price of shares must be high relative to the bond value for the conversion to occur.

above. For warrants, there is no loss recognition even though the warrant exercise price is below the current market price for shares (which should always be the case for an exercise to occur). More importantly, the market value method does not acknowledge the compound nature of the convertible bond and the reason for its issuance in the first place. The issuance of shares at a below market price for the conversion is not a loss, per se, but rather the consequence of successful operations that have driven up the market price of common shares.

3. Stock compensation plans

How should a company account for stock options it issues to employees? There are three items that need to be addressed. First, how should we value the stock options for financial reporting purposes? Second, over what period of time should the cost be allocated? Third, how do we account for the exercise or expiration of the options?

a. Value of stock options

Both IFRS and ASPE require the use of the stock options' fair value, which includes both the intrinsic value and the time value of options (as discussed in Section B, subsection 2 on page 511).[7] Employee stock options are not traded like other options, so their fair value needs to be estimated using models such as the Black-Scholes or binomial pricing models.

b. Period of expense recognition

Once the enterprise has determined the value of the stock options granted, it needs to determine the period over which to recognize that value as an expense. While some companies issue stock options to employees every year for that year's service, others will issue them for more than one year of service. The period covered can include past as well as future years.

c. Accounting for option exercise or expiration

Stock options give the holder the right but not the obligation to buy the company's shares, so employees can choose to exercise their options or let them expire. If employees exercise their options, they pay the company the exercise price, surrender the options, and receive the shares. The accounting for the company reflects these three components by recording:

- a cash receipt for the exercise price;
- a reduction of contributed surplus relating to the stock options; and
- an increase to the common share account for the balance.

On the other hand, if employees choose to let the options expire, then the company only needs to record a housekeeping journal entry to remove the contributed surplus relating to the stock options and transfer the amount to "contributed surplus—expired stock options."

To illustrate the above, suppose Enchanted Forest grants 10,000 options to its employees at the beginning of 2012, giving them the right to buy shares at $60 each. The grant is intended for two years of service (fiscal years 2012 and 2013). The fair value estimate for these options is $220,000 on the date of grant, which

---

7. Prior to 2003, it was acceptable to use the intrinsic value method, which records only the intrinsic value of an option at the date the company grants the options. Most often, this intrinsic value is zero.

is $22/option. In this case, the following journal entry would be recorded at the fiscal year-ends of 2012 and 2013:

Exhibit 14-11	Journal entries to record employee stock option grants for Enchanted Forest	
Dr. Compensation expense (10,000 options × $22/option ÷ 2 years)	110,000	
Cr. Contributed surplus – stock options		110,000

If the stock options were for either past service or for 2012 only, then the entire $220,000 would be recorded as an expense in the year of grant (2012).

If employees exercise 20% of the options (i.e., 2,000 options) in 2014, the employees will need to pay the exercise price of $60 per share. The journal entry would be:

Exhibit 14-12	Journal entries to record employee stock option exercises for Enchanted Forest	
Dr. Cash (2,000 options – 1 share/option × $60/share)	120,000	
Dr. Contributed surplus – stock options (2,000 options × $22/option)	44,000	
Cr. Common stock (balance)		164,000

If the remaining 8,000 options expire unexercised, the following entry would be recorded to transfer the contributed surplus:

Exhibit 14-13	Journal entries to record employee stock option exercises for Enchanted Forest	
Dr. Contributed surplus – stock options ($220,000 – $44,000)	176,000	
Cr. Contributed surplus – expired stock options		176,000

This transfer of contributed surplus is cosmetic and does not change total equity. All of the amounts increasing and decreasing contributed surplus for the employee stock options are Type C contributed surplus discussed in Chapter 13 (i.e., they are neither related to proceeds from stock issuance in excess of par, nor are they from the repurchase/cancellation/resale of shares). However, the entry is necessary to clean up the amount of contributed surplus that relates to unexpired options.

D. ACCOUNTING FOR HEDGES

Enterprises often use financial instruments to reduce risk. For example, a company could enter into a forward contract to buy U.S. dollars not for the purpose of speculation, but in anticipation of a liability that needs to be settled in U.S. dollars. In the Axel-Bluebird example given in Section B2, Axel's purchase of a forward for US$1 million in exchange for C$1.05 million would reduce Axel's risk if it also had a U.S.-dollar obligation due in 90 days, such as an account payable to a U.S. supplier. Buying the forward ensures that the company pays exactly C$1.05 million. In other words, the forward hedges the exchange-rate risk arising from the U.S.-dollar obligation. However, if Axel didn't have such a U.S.-dollar obligation, then the purchase of the forward would be simply a

L.O. 14-5. Describe the nature of hedges and identify situations in which hedge accounting may be appropriate.

speculative investment that bets on the direction of currency movements, which increases the company's risk.

Generally speaking, one item hedges another if their values tend to move in opposite directions. For accounting purposes, a hedge can be either a fair value hedge or a cash flow hedge.[8] A **fair value hedge** reduces the exposure to changes in fair value of a recognized asset or liability. The Axel-Bluebird example just given is an example of a fair value hedge, since Axel's purchase of the forward contract limits its exposure to changes in the value of its U.S.-dollar accounts payable. A **cash flow hedge** reduces the exposure to changes in future cash flows. An example of a cash flow hedge is an interest-rate swap.

To qualify for hedge accounting, enterprises need to take three steps: (i) identify the risk exposure (i.e., the item that needs to be hedged); (ii) designate the hedging instrument; and (iii) demonstrate that the hedge will likely be effective.

A natural question to ask is, Why do we need hedge accounting? If the hedging instrument and the hedged item experience changes in opposite directions, wouldn't other accounting procedures result in the desired outcome of no (or little) net change? The reason is that in the absence of hedge accounting, in some circumstances, a hedging instrument and the hedged item would be recorded differently from each other. For instance, an available-for-sale financial asset would be marked-to-market, with fair value changes flowing through other comprehensive income (OCI); a derivative that offsets those fair value changes would have its gains and losses flowing through net income (as is required for all derivatives). Hedge accounting allows the hedged item and the hedging instrument to be treated in the same way so that the effects offset, at least partially. (A perfect hedge would have completely offsetting effects, but hedges need not be 100% perfect.)

For fair value hedges, the changes in fair value for both the hedged item and the hedging instrument flow through income. For cash flow hedges, the changes in cash flow pass through OCI.

Application of hedge accounting is relatively complex, and additional considerations are beyond the scope of this text.

E. SUBSTANTIVE DIFFERENCES BETWEEN RELEVANT IFRS AND ASPE

ISSUE	IFRS	ASPE
Initial recognition of compound financial instruments	Use residual value method, allocating amounts first to the component(s) that are more reliably measured; any common equity component receives the residual allocation of the transaction value.	Use either the residual value method or the zero value method. The latter assigns zero value to the common equity component.
Accounting for conversions of convertible securities	Apply book value method; no gains or losses arise.	Apply market value method: record gain or loss for difference between the carrying amount of extinguished instrument and the market value of instrument issued upon conversion.

8. There is a third category, hedge of a net investment in a foreign operation. As this category relates to foreign operations, it is a topic for advanced financial accounting and not addressed in this text.

F. SUMMARY

L.O. 14-1. Describe the nature of standard financial instruments, derivatives, and compound financial instruments, and identify when transactions involve such instruments.

- Standard financial instruments are financial liabilities and equity instruments.
- Derivatives are financial instruments whose values derive from other financial instruments.
- Compound financial instruments have more than one component financial instrument. Use of such instruments in the right context can help alleviate information asymmetries.

L.O. 14-2. Apply the accounting standards for derivatives.

- Enterprises should generally report derivatives at fair value, with changes in fair value reported through net income.

L.O. 14-3. Apply the accounting standards for compound financial instruments from the perspective of the issuer.

- Enterprises need to separately account for the component parts of compound financial instruments. Under IFRS, the common equity component should be allocated the residual value after allocation to all other components.

L.O. 14-4. Apply the accounting standards for employee stock options from the perspective of the issuer.

- When an enterprise grants stock options to employees, it needs to estimate the fair value of those options and allocate that amount over the period of service expected from those employees.

L.O. 14-5. Describe the nature of hedges and identify situations in which hedge accounting may be appropriate.

- Hedges reduce an enterprise's exposure to risk.
- Enterprises can identify specific transactions and items as hedges, but must demonstrate that the hedge is effective.

G. References
Authoritative standards:

IFRS	ASPE Section
IAS 39—Financial Instruments: Recognition and Measurement	3856—Financial Instruments (includes recognition, measurement, presentation, and disclosure)
IAS 32—Financial Instruments: Presentation	
IFRS 7—Financial Instruments: Disclosures	
IFRS 2—Share-based Payment	3870—Stock-based Compensation and Other Stock-based Payments

H. Glossary

call option: See **option**.

cash flow hedge: A financial instrument that reduces the exposure to changes in future cash flows.

compound financial instruments: Those financial instruments with more than one financial instrument component.

derivative: A financial instrument that is derived from some other underlying quantity.

employee stock option: An option a company issues to its employees, giving them the right to buy shares in their employer at a pre-specified price.

fair value hedge: Reduces the exposure to changes in fair value.

forward: A contract in which one party commits upfront to buy or sell something at a defined price at a defined future date.

future: Similar to a forward but contract is written in more standardized terms (e.g., prices, maturity dates) and involves commonly traded items (e.g., commodities, currencies).

in-the-money: When the value of the underlying instrument in an option contract is favourable to the holder exercising the option compared with letting the option expire. In the case of a call option, this occurs when the underlying price exceeds the strike price; for a put option, it is when the underlying price is below the strike price.

intrinsic value of an option: In a call option, the greater of zero and $(S - K)$, the difference between the market price and the strike price.

option: A derivative contract that gives the holder the right, but not the obligation, to buy or sell an underlying financial instrument at a specified price. A call option gives the right to buy, whereas a put option provides the right to sell.

out-of-the-money: When the value of the underlying instrument in an option contract is unfavourable to the holder exercising the option compared with letting the option expire. In the case of a call option, this is when the underlying price is lower than the strike price; for a put option, it is when the underlying price is higher than the strike price.

put option: See **option**.

swap: A derivative contract in which two parties agree to exchange cash flows.

time value of an option: The portion of an option's value that reflects the probability that the future market price of the underlying instrument will exceed the strike price.

underlying quantity or underlying: The value of an asset, an index value, or an event that helps determine the value of a derivative.

warrant: A right but not the obligation to buy a share at a specified price over a specified period of time. Can be considered a type of **call option**.

I. PROBLEMS

MyAccountingLab® Go to MyAccountingLab at www.myaccountinglab.com. You can practise the indicated exercises as often as you want, and guided solutions will help you find answers step by step. You'll find a personalized study plan available to you too!

P14-1. Nature and identification of financial instruments

(**L.O.** 14-1) (Easy – 5 minutes)

Identify whether each of the following is a financial instrument.

a. Account payable
b. Note payable
c. Warranty provision
d. Long-term debt
e. Common share

P14-2. Nature and identification of financial instruments

(**L.O.** 14-1) (Easy – 5 minutes)

Identify whether each of the following is a financial liability.

a. Account payable
b. Note payable
c. Warranty provision
d. Long-term debt
e. Deferred tax liability

P14-3. Nature and identification of financial instruments

(**L.O.** 14-1) (Easy – 5 minutes)

Identify whether the following financial instruments are (i) a basic financial asset, financial liability, or equity instrument; (ii) a derivative; or (iii) a compound financial instrument.

Item	Basic financial asset, financial liability, or equity instrument	Derivative	Compound financial instrument
a. 10-year bond payable			
b. Convertible debenture			
c. Preferred shares			
d. Convertible preferred shares			
e. Stock warrants			
f. Interest rate swap			

P14-4. Identifying financial instruments (**L.O.** 14-1) (Easy – 5 minutes)

Identify whether the following financial instruments are (i) a basic financial asset, financial liability, or equity instrument; (ii) a derivative; or (iii) a compound financial instrument.

Item	Basic financial asset, financial liability, or equity instrument	Derivative	Compound financial instrument
a. Employee stock option			
b. Shares with warrants			
c. Bank loan			
d. Convertible bond			
e. Currency forward			

P14-5. Identifying financial instruments (**L.O.** 14-1) (Easy – 10 minutes)

In relation to stock options, identify whether each of the following statements is true or false.

Item	True/False
a. A stock option provides a right to buy but not a right to sell a share.	
b. An option's fair value is at least as high as its intrinsic value.	
c. A stock option's fair value increases with the volatility of the underlying stock.	

(Continued)

Item	True / False
d. A stock option's exercise price is the price of the share at the time of exercise.	
e. An option's intrinsic value cannot be negative.	
f. An option's intrinsic value increases with the length of time until the option matures.	
g. An in-the-money option is one in which the exercise price is higher than the market price.	

P14-6. Nature and identification of financial instruments (**L.O.** 14-1) (Medium – 10 minutes)

In the table below, choose the derivative instrument on the left side that best matches the example on the right side. There is one example for each instrument.

Type of derivative	Example
Option	A company contracts to sell 10,000 oz of gold at $1,100/oz on March 15, 2012 on the Chicago Mercantile Exchange.
Warrant	A company contracts with an investment bank to pay the bank 5% interest on $25 million of debt in exchange for receiving LIBOR + 1% from the bank. (LIBOR is the London Interbank Offered Rate, similar to the Prime Rate.)
Forward	A company purchases the right but not the obligation to purchase U.S. dollars for C$1.02/US$ within a 90-day period.
Future	Company X contracts to buy 10,000 oz of gold at $1,100/oz on March 15, 2012 from Company Y.
Swap	A company purchases the right but not the obligation to purchase 500,000 shares in another company at $12 each over a 10-year period.

P14-7. Accounting for derivatives (**L.O.** 14-2) (Easy – 5 minutes)

On December 15, a company enters into a foreign currency forward to buy €200,000 at C$1.32 per euro in 30 days. The exchange rate on the day of the company's year-end of December 31 was C$1.30: €1.

Required:

Record the journal entries related to this forward contract.

P14-8. Accounting for derivatives (**L.O.** 14-2) (Easy – 5 minutes)

A company pays $8,000 to purchase futures contracts to buy 200 oz of gold at $1,200/oz. At the company's year-end, the price of gold was $1,230 and the value of the company's futures contracts increased to $12,000.

Required:

Record the journal entries related to these futures.

P14-9. Accounting for derivatives (**L.O.** 14-2) (Medium – 10 minutes)

On August 15, 2011, Jarvis Company issued 50,000 options on the shares of RBC (Royal Bank Corporation). Each option gives the option holder the right to buy one share of RBC at $60 per share until March 16, 2012. Jarvis received $150,000 for issuing these options. At the company's year-end of December 31, 2011, the options contracts traded on the Montreal Exchange at $2.50 per contract. On March 16, 2012, RBC shares closed at $58 per share, so none of the options was exercised.

Required:

Record the journal entries related to these call options.

P14-10. Accounting for derivatives (**L.O.** 14-2) (Medium – 15 minutes)

Kearney Corporation issued call options on 20,000 shares of BCE Inc. on October 21, 2012. These options give the holder the right to buy BCE shares at $33 per share until May 17, 2013. For issuing these options, Kearney received $30,000. On December 31, 2012 (Kearney's fiscal year-end), the options traded on the Montreal Exchange for $3.50 per option. On May 17, 2013, BCE's share price increased to $37 and the option holders exercised their options. Kearney had no holdings of BCE shares.

Required:

For Kearney Corporation, record the journal entries related to these call options.

P14-11. Accounting for compound financial instruments (**L.O.** 14-3) (Easy – 5 minutes)

A company issues convertible bonds with face value of $6,000,000 and receives proceeds of $6,540,000. Each $1,000 bond can be converted, at the option of the holder, into 40 common shares. The underwriter estimated the market value of the bonds alone, excluding the conversion rights, to be approximately $6,200,000.

Required:

Record the journal entry for the issuance of these bonds.

P14-12. Accounting for compound financial instruments (**L.O.** 14-3) (Easy – 5 minutes)

A company issued 100,000 preferred shares and received proceeds of $6,540,000. These shares have a par value of $60 per share and pay cumulative dividends of 8%. Buyers of the preferred shares also received a detachable warrant with each share purchased. Each warrant gives the holder the right to buy one common share at $30 per share within 10 years. The underwriter estimated that the market value of the preferred shares alone, excluding the conversion rights, is approximately $62 per share. Shortly after the issuance of the preferred shares, the detachable warrants traded at $2 each.

Required:

Record the journal entry for the issuance of these shares and warrants.

P14-13. Accounting for compound financial instruments (**L.O.** 14-3) (Easy – 5 minutes)[9]

A company had a debt-to-equity ratio of 1.52 before issuing convertible bonds. This ratio included $400,000 in equity. The company issued convertible bonds. The value reported for the bonds on the balance sheet is $254,000 and the conversion rights are valued at $21,000. After the issuance of the convertible bonds, what is the value of the debt-to-equity ratio?

P14-14. Accounting for compound financial instruments (**L.O.** 14-3) (Medium – 10 minutes)[10]

Complete the following table by indicating whether the listed transactions would improve, worsen, or have no effect on the financial ratios listed below. Consider each transaction independently. The answer for the first transaction is presented as an example.

---

9. © 2009 CGA-Canada. Reproduced with permission.

10. © 2010 CGA-Canada. Reproduced with permission.

Ratio	Return on common shareholders' equity	Current ratio	Operating margin
Ratio definition	(Net income – preferred dividends) / common equity	Current assets/ current liabilities	Operating profit/ revenue
Ratio without transaction	16%	1.25	10%
Repayment of a bond on the first day of the fiscal year	No effect	Worsen	No effect
Conversion of a bond with a 10% stated rate into common shares			
Sale of 2,000 common shares for cash			
Sale of $5,000 of inventory on credit for $6,000 revenue			

P14-15. Accounting for compound financial instruments (**L.O.** 14-3) (Medium – 15 minutes)[11]

JKD Company reported the following amounts on its balance sheet at July 31, 2013:

Liabilities	
Convertible bonds payable, $4,000,000 face value 10%, due July 31, 2014	$3,859,649
Equity	
Contributed surplus—common stock conversion rights	345,000
Preferred shares, no par, 3,100,000 shares authorized, 20,000 outstanding	2,000,000
Common shares, no par, 1,000,000 shares authorized, 120,000 outstanding	6,000,000
Additional information	
1. The bonds pay interest each July 31. Each $1,000 bond is convertible into 15 common shares. The bonds were originally issued to yield 14%. On July 31, 2014, all the bonds were converted after the final interest payment was made. JKD uses the book value method to record bond conversions as recommended under IFRS.	
2. No other share or bond transactions occurred during the year.	

Required:

a. Prepare the journal entry to record the bond interest payment on July 31, 2014.
b. Calculate the total number of common shares outstanding after the bonds' conversion on July 31, 2014.
c. Prepare the journal entry to record the bond conversion.

P14-16. Accounting for compound financial instruments (**L.O.** 14-3) (Medium – 20 minutes)

On September 30, 2011, Niagara Co. issued a $2 million, 8%, 10-year convertible bond maturing on September 30, 2021 with semi-annual coupon payments on March 31 and September 30. Each $1,000 bond can be converted into 80 no par value common shares. In addition, each bond included 20 detachable common stock warrants with an exercise

---

11. © 2009 CGA-Canada. Reproduced with permission.

price of $20 each. Immediately after issuance, the warrants traded at $4 each on the open market. Gross proceeds on issuance were $2.6 million (including accrued interest). From these proceeds, the company paid underwriting fees of $45,000. Without the warrants and conversion features the bond would be expected to yield 6% annually. Niagara's year-end is December 31.

On February 22, 2014, warrant holders exercised one-half of the warrants. The shares of Niagara traded at $44 each on this day.

Required:

  a. Determine how Niagara should allocate the $2,600,000 proceeds into its components.
  b. Prepare all the journal entries for fiscal year 2011.
  c. Record the journal entry for the exercise of stock warrants on February 22, 2014.

P14-17. Accounting for compound financial instruments (**L.O.** 14-3) (Medium – 20 minutes)

On January 1, 2013, Portside Co. issued a $10 million, 8%, 9-year convertible bond with annual coupon payments. Each $1,000 bond was convertible into 25 shares of Portside's common shares. Starboard Investments purchased the entire bond issue for $10.2 million on January 1, 2013. Starboard estimated that without the conversion feature, the bonds would have sold for $9,400,475 (to yield 9%).

On January 1, 2015, Starboard converted bonds with a par value of $4 million. At the time of conversion, the shares were selling at $45 each.

Required:

  a. Prepare the journal entry to record the issuance of convertible bonds.
  b. Prepare the journal entry to record the conversion according to IFRS (book value method).
  c. Prepare the journal entry to record the conversion according ASPE (market value method).

P14-18. Accounting for compound financial instruments
(**L.O.** 14-3) (Difficult – 25 minutes)[12]

On August 1, 2010, LOL Corporation issued 15-year, $5,000,000, 8%, convertible bonds for proceeds of $5,325,000. The bonds pay interest annually each July 31. Each $1,000 bond is convertible into 50 common shares at the investor's option. If the bond had been sold without the conversion feature, it would have sold for $4,240,000, reflecting a market interest rate of 10%.

LOL's controller recorded the bond issuance on August 1 as follows:

Dr. Cash	5,325,000	
Cr. Bonds payable		5,325,000

The controller did not make any other journal entries related to the bonds as of the company's year-end, December 31.

LOL closed its general ledger accounts and is now preparing its December 31, 2010 financial statements. Upon reviewing the long-term liabilities, you come across the convertible bond journal entry shown above. You know LOL has debt covenants that specify its debt-to-equity ratio cannot exceed 1.20. The preliminary financial statements show total liabilities to be $25,000,000 and total equity of $20,000,000.

Required:

  a. Prepare the correcting journal entry or entries related to the issuance of the convertible bonds.
  b. Prepare the correcting journal entry or entries for the interest on the convertible bonds. Ignore any tax implications. (Remember that the general ledger accounts have been closed for the year.)

---

12. © 2010 CGA-Canada. Reproduced with permission.

c. Discuss the effect of any corrections to the bond recording on the debt-to-equity ratio. However, you do not need to recalculate the ratio.

P14-19. Accounting for employee stock options (**L.O.** 14-4) (Easy – 10 minutes)

Oshawa Motor Parts issued 100,000 stock options to its employees. The company granted the stock options at-the-money, when the share price was $30. These options have no vesting conditions. By year-end, the share price had increased to $32. Oshawa's management estimates the value of these options at the grant date to be $1.50 each.

Required:

Record the issuance of the stock options.

P14-20. Accounting for employee stock options (**L.O.** 14-4) (Easy – 5 minutes)

Pelham Farms granted 200,000 stock options to its employees. The options expire 10 years after the grant date of January 1, 2011, when the share price was $25. Employees still employed by Pelham five years after the grant date may exercise the option to purchase shares at $50 each; that is, the options vest to the employees after five years. A consultant estimated the value of each option at the date of grant to be $1.00 each.

Required:

Record the journal entries relating to the issuance of stock options.

P14-21. Accounting for employee stock options (**L.O.** 14-4) (Easy – 10 minutes)

Rainy Lake Lodge issued 30,000 at-the-money stock options to its management on January 1, 2012. These options vest on January 1, 2015. Rainy Lake's share price was $12 on the grant date and $18 on the vesting date. Estimates of the fair value of the options showed that they were worth $2 on the grant date and $7 on the vesting date. On the vesting date, management exercised all 30,000 options. Rainy Lake has a December 31 year-end.

Required:

Record all of the journal entries relating to the stock options.

P14-22. Accounting for employee stock options (**L.O.** 14-4) (Easy – 15 minutes)[13]

[*Note:* this question also applies material covered in Chapter 13.]
The following is an excerpt from Manitoba Telecom Services Ltd.'s 2007 audited financial statements.

Share capital (in part, dollar amounts in millions)				
	2007		**2006**	
	Number	**Value**	**Number**	**Value**
Common shares issued				
Opening balance	66,817,707	$1,305.1	67,739,257	$1,315.0
Issued pursuant to stock options	191,460	6.9	442,050	16.8
Purchased for cancellation	(2,377,500)	(46.5)	(1,363,600)	(26.7)
Ending balance	64,631,667	$1,265.5	66,817,707	$1,305.1

(Continued)

---

13. © 2010 CGA-Canada. Reproduced with permission.

Contributed surplus		
Opening balance	$ 16.9	$ 18.2
Stock option expense	1.8	0.4
Exercise of stock options	(1.0)	(1.7)
Ending balance	$ 17.7	$ 16.9

During 2007, 191,460 stock options were exercised (2006 – 442,050 stock options) for cash consideration of $5.9 million (2006 – $15.1 million), of which $6.9 million was credited to share capital (2006 – $16.8 million) and $1.0 million was charged to contributed surplus (2006 – $1.7 million).

During 2007, the company purchased 2,377,500 common shares for cancellation (2006 – 1,363,600 common shares) for cash consideration of $111.0 million, pursuant to its normal course issuer bid (2006 – $61.9 million). The excess of the purchase price over the stated capital in the amount of $64.5 million was charged to retained earnings (2006 – $35.2 million).

Required:

a. Prepare the journal entries for MTS to record stock option expense and the exercise of stock options for 2007.
b. Prepare the journal entry for MTS to record the cancellation of the shares repurchased in 2007.

P14-23. Accounting for employee stock options (**L.O.** 14-4) (Medium – 15 minutes)

On January 1, 2011, Thomasburg Inc. granted stock options to officers and key employees for the purchase of 200,000 of the company's no par value common shares at $25 each. The options were exercisable within a five-year period beginning January 1, 2013 by grantees still in the employ of the company, and they expire December 31, 2017. The market price of Thomasburg's common share was $20 per share at the date of grant. Using the Black-Scholes option pricing model, the company estimated the value of each option on January 1, 2011 to be $3.00.

On March 31, 2013, 120,000 options were exercised when the market value of common stock was $40 per share. The remainder of the options expired unexercised. The company has a December 31 year-end.

Required:

Record the journal entries for Thomasburg's stock options.

P14-24. Accounting for compound financial instruments and employee stock options (**L.O.** 14-3, **L.O.** 14-4) (Medium – 15 minutes)[14]

On July 1, 2008, Ameri-Can Limited issued $3,000,000 of convertible bonds. The bonds pay annual interest of 10% on June 30. Each $1,000 bond is convertible into 75 common shares, at the investor's option, between July 1, 2013 and July 1, 2018, at which time the bonds mature. The financial instrument was issued for total proceeds of $3,402,605, yielding 8%. The bonds without the conversion feature were valued at $2,660,987, yielding 12%.

Ameri-Can also has a stock option plan. During the year, the company issued 5,000 options to employees to buy common shares at $20 per share. An option pricing model valued these options at $50,000. The vesting period is five years. At the end of the year, $5,000 worth of options that had been granted in previous years expired unexercised.

Ameri-Can has a December 31 year-end.

Required:

a. Prepare the journal entry to record the issuance of the bonds on July 1, 2008.
b. Prepare the journal entries to record the issuance and expiration of stock options.

---

14. © 2009 CGA-Canada. Reproduced with permission.

P14-25. Accounting for equity transactions, complex financial instruments, and employee stock options (L.O. 14-3, L.O. 14-4) (Difficult – 60 minutes)

[*Note:* this question also applies material covered in Chapter 13.]

Corus Manufacturing Ltd., a sailboat manufacturer, is preparing its financial statements for the year ended August 31, 2011. It is September 15 and your CFO presents you (the controller) with a list of issues that require additional attention.

i. The company repurchased 100,000 common shares at $17/share on March 31, 2011. Of these, 70,000 were put into treasury, and the remainder were cancelled.

ii. Corus has a stock option plan for its management team. At the beginning of fiscal year 2011, the company had outstanding 200,000 stock options with an exercise price of $12; the value of these options at the grant date was $1.50 per option. On April 30, 2011, 150,000 of these options were exercised, and 50,000 expired. The company used treasury shares to supply the shares for the stock option exercises.

iii. On May 1, 2011, the company granted to management employees another 50,000 stock options for services to be rendered from the grant date until April 30, 2013. These options had an exercise price of $18, vest with the employees on April 30, 2015, and expire on April 30, 2020. These options had estimated fair value of $2.40 per option on the grant date.

iv. Corus had a 2-for-1 stock split on May 31, 2011. Relevant conditions of convertible securities and stock options were adjusted for this split.

v. The company issued long-term bonds to a group of private investors. The bonds were issued on June 30, 2011, had maturity value of $20 million on June 30, 2021, and pay semi-annual interest at a rate of 7% per year. Each $1,000 bond is convertible into 50 common shares. Proceeds of the issuance were $21.5 million. Without the conversion feature, the bond would have been priced to yield 8%/a, resulting in proceeds of $18,640,967.

The company had net income of $10.5 million for fiscal 2011, a tax rate of 30%, and $16 average stock price.

The equity section of the company's balance sheet on August 31, 2010 (end of the prior fiscal year) showed the following:

Preferred stock ($200 par, 6% cumulative, 50 million authorized, 100,000 issued and outstanding)	$ 20,000,000
Common stock (no par, unlimited number authorized, 9.5 million issued, 9.42 million outstanding)	57,000,000
Treasury stock (80,000 common shares)	–1,200,000
Contributed surplus—issuance of preferred stock	800,000
Contributed surplus—repurchases/resales of common stock	300,000
Contributed surplus—stock options	475,000
Contributed surplus—expired stock options	285,000
Contributed surplus—conversion rights*	950,000
Retained earnings	34,500,000
Total shareholders' equity	$113,110,000

* The bonds with these conversion rights were issued in fiscal 2005, had face value of $5 million and coupon payments of 8%/a payable semi-annually, yielded 6%, and mature on September 30, 2015. Each $100 bond is convertible into 10 common shares. On April 1, 2011, all of these bonds were converted into common shares.

Required:

a. Record the repurchase of 100,000 shares on March 31, 2011. Use the number of shares issued (rather than outstanding) to compute any per share amounts of contributed surplus. [*Hint:* you need two separate journal entries.]

b. Compute the April 1, 2011 carrying value of the debt portion of the convertible bond issued in fiscal 2005.

c. Record the conversion of the $5 million of bonds into common shares on April 1, 2011. Use the book value method.
d. Record the exercise of stock options and the related sale of treasury shares on April 30, 2011.
e. Record the entry to reflect stock option expiration on April 30, 2011.
f. Record the issuance of stock options on May 1, 2011.
g. Record the $20 million security issuance of bonds on June 30, 2011.
h. Show in good form the equity section of the balance sheet for Corus as at August 31, 2011.

P14-26. Nature of hedges   (**L.O.** 14-5) (Easy – 5 minutes)

Identify whether each of the following derivatives provides a fair value hedge or a cash flow hedge if it is used as a hedging instrument.

Item	Fair value hedge or cash flow hedge?
a. A forward contract to buy US$1 million for C$1.05 million.	
b. A swap of investment with a variable interest rate with one providing a fixed return.	
c. A swap of a U.S.-dollar denominated bond payable for one denominated in Canadian dollars.	
d. A futures contract to sell 10,000 oz of gold at US$1,150/oz.	

P14-27. Nature of hedges   (**L.O.** 14-5) (Medium – 10 minutes)

A company located in Canada spends $6,000 to purchase a foreign currency futures contract to buy US$500,000 at C$1.02:US$1.00. The contract matures 90 days later. Under which of the following circumstances could the company consider this future contract to be a fair value hedge for accounting purposes?

Circumstance	Futures contract to buy USD can be considered as a fair value hedge?
a. The company has an account receivable of US$500,000 due in 90 days.	
b. The company has an account payable of US$500,000 due in 90 days.	
c. The company has an investment in shares traded on a U.S. stock exchange and plans to sell these shares in 90 days.	
d. The company intends to buy US$500,000 of inventories for which it must pay 90 days later.	

P14-28. Nature of hedges   (**L.O.** 14-5) (Medium – 10 minutes)

The following is selected balance sheet information for Taylor Company, which has operations located primarily in Canada. Amounts are in Canadian dollars unless otherwise indicated.

Assets	Amount	Liabilities and equity	Amount
Cash	$ 30,000	Accounts payable	$ 350,000
Cash (US$)	200,000	Accounts payable (US$)	300,000
Accounts receivable	500,000	Long-term debt, 6% interest	1,000,000
Property, plant, and equipment	1,200,000	Common stock	600,000
Goodwill	400,000	Retained earnings	250,000

Required:

Taking into account the above information, first identify whether Taylor Company could potentially identify the following items as hedging instruments for accounting purposes. If it is a potential hedging instrument, identify the item being hedged. If not, explain why not.

Item	Potential hedging instrument?	Item being hedged or explanation
a. A forward contract to sell US$200,000.		
b. A forward contract to sell US$100,000.		
c. A forward contract to buy US$100,000.		
d. An interest rate swap involving future payments of 6% interest and receipts of prime + 2% on $1,000,000 principal.		

J. MINI-CASES

Ultramart is a chain of large discount supermarkets with 30 locations primarily in southern Ontario. The company was founded about 40 years ago. Although the company is now publicly traded, the founding family still has 30% of the 50 million common shares outstanding, which are trading around $40 per share. The second generation of the family holds the important posts in management.

The CEO, Theodor (Ted) Chamberlain has bold plans to expand Ultramart beyond the Ontario border. Recently, he attended a conference on finance and strategy where there was much discussion about less conventional types of financial instruments. After the conference, he comes to you, the CFO of Ultramart, to talk about some of what he heard and saw.

TED: The investment bankers went over quite a few financial instruments. In keeping with the theme of the conference, they didn't spend much time on traditional stocks and bonds. Instead, they talked a lot about options, swaps, and so on. I didn't find much of it relevant, but one thing that did catch my eye was the idea of hybrids. They said that hybrids, or compound financial instruments, are a combination of different instruments, such as a bond that is convertible into shares. I know that hybrid cars are very popular these days, and it seems that the trend is catching on in finance as well.

YOU: Yes, I have heard of hybrid instruments before.

TED: As you know, we are going to ramp up our expansion plans. To do that, we need to bring in a lot more financing, probably $500 million or so. I am wondering whether these hybrids are a good alternative. We could go the traditional way and issue more shares or bonds to the public. The speakers at the conference talked about convertible bonds benefitting from lower interest rates of 3%–4% because of the sweeteners in the deal. If this works, we could save quite a bit of money. What do you think? Could you write me a memo explaining these hybrids and whether we should go with some sort of hybrid or more traditional financing sources?

Required:

Prepare the memo requested by the CEO.

Stephanie Baker is an audit senior with the public accounting firm of Wilson & Lang. It is February 2014 and the audit of Canadian Development Limited (CDL) for the year ended December 31, 2013, is proceeding. Stephanie has identified several transactions that occurred in the 2013 fiscal year that have major accounting implications. The engagement partner has asked Stephanie to draft a memo to him addressing the accounting implications of these transactions.

CDL is an important player in many sectors of the economy. The company has both debt and equity securities that trade on a Canadian stock exchange. Except for a controlling interest (53%) owned by the Robichaud family, CDL's shares are widely held. The company has interests in the natural resources, commercial and residential real estate, construction, transportation, and technology development sectors, among others.

Changes in capital structure

During 2013, CDL's underwriters recommended some changes to the company's capital structure. As a result, the company raised $250 million by issuing one million convertible, redeemable debentures at $250 each. Each debenture is convertible into one common share at any time. A sizeable block of the one million debentures issued was acquired by CDL's controlling shareholders; the remainder were taken up by a few large institutional investors such as pension funds.

CASE 1
Ultramart
(30 minutes)

CASE 2
Canadian Development Limited
(30 minutes)[14]

---

14. Adapted with permission from the Uniform Final Examination (1989), The Canadian Institute of Chartered Accountants, Toronto, Canada. Any changes to the original material are the sole responsibility of the author and have not been reviewed or endorsed by the CICA.

The company proposes to partition the balance sheet in a manner that will include a section entitled "Shareholders' Equity and Convertible Debentures." The company views this classification as appropriate because the convertible debt, being much more akin to equity than debt, represents a part of the company's permanent capital. Maurice Richard, the controller of CDL, has emphasized that the interest rate on the debentures is considerably lower than on normal convertible issues and that it is expected that the majority of investors will exercise their conversion privilege. The company has the option of repaying the debt at maturity in 20 years' time through the issuance of common shares. The company's intention is to raise additional permanent capital, and convertible debt was chosen because of the attractive tax savings from the deductibility of interest payments.

The debentures are redeemable at the option of the holder at $250 from January 1, 2019 to January 1, 2022.

At the same time as the company issued the convertible debentures, 2 million common shares were converted into 2 million preferred, redeemable shares. The net book value of the 2 million common shares was $20 million. The preferred shares do not bear dividends and are mandatorily redeemable in five years at $15 per share. They have been recorded at their redemption value of $30 million; the difference between this redemption value and the net book value of the common shares (a difference of $10 million) has been charged against retained earnings.

Required:

Take the role of Stephanie Baker and prepare the memo for the partner.

Earnings per Share

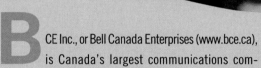

CE Inc., or Bell Canada Enterprises (www.bce.ca), is Canada's largest communications company. Its product lines include high-speed Internet access for businesses and individuals, and local, long distance, and wireless phone services.

For the year ended December 31, 2008, BCE reported basic earnings per share (EPS) of $1.02 and diluted EPS of $1.01. These results were down sharply from the $4.88 basic EPS and the $4.87 diluted EPS reported the previous year.

Why does BCE report EPS in its financial statements? Why does it report both basic and diluted EPS? What is the difference between basic and diluted EPS, and how is each calculated?

LEARNING OBJECTIVES

After studying this chapter, you should be able to:

L.O. 15-1. Describe the reasons for reporting basic and diluted earnings per share.

L.O. 15-2. Calculate basic earnings per share.

L.O. 15-3. Differentiate between dilutive and antidilutive potential ordinary shares.

L.O. 15-4. Calculate diluted earnings per share.

CONTENTS

A. INTRODUCTION TO BASIC AND DILUTED EARNINGS PER SHARE

L.O. 15-1. Describe the reasons for reporting basic and diluted earnings per share.

earnings per share (EPS)
Measures each ordinary share's interest in a company's earnings.

For the year ended October 31, 2009, the Royal Bank of Canada (RBC) earned a profit of $3.858 billion. If you owned an RBC common share, a natural question to ask when you read this information would be, "How much of the profit belongs to me?" As one among many thousands of shareholders, the total amount RBC earns is not as meaningful to you as your share of profit. In this case, each share in RBC earned $2.59, which is RBC's **earnings per share (EPS)**. EPS measures each common share's interest in a company's earnings. (IFRS uses the term "ordinary share" to refer to what traditionally have been known as common shares in Canada. This chapter will use the IFRS terminology.)

The EPS figure is frequently quoted by the financial press. It is used by investors and analysts to assess company performance, to predict future earnings, and to estimate the value of the firm's shares. (Section C of Appendix A to this text describes some basic approaches for valuing a company.) There are two EPS statistics: basic and diluted.

- Basic EPS communicates "ownership" of earnings based on the average number of ordinary shares *actually* outstanding during the period.
- Diluted EPS is more abstract in nature as it conveys the *hypothetical* worst-case scenario that considers the effect of potentially dilutive securities—securities that could lead to the issuance of additional ordinary shares. Examples of securities that are potentially dilutive include convertible securities and stock options, discussed in Chapter 14.

Capital structures that do not include potentially diluted securities are commonly referred to as **simple capital structures;** those that have such securities are known as **complex capital structures**. All publicly accountable entities must report basic EPS information in their financial statements. Moreover, companies with a complex financial structure must also report diluted EPS. The IASB's reasons for requiring disclosure of EPS information are set out in IAS 33, Earnings Per Share.

simple capital structure   A capital structure that does not include potentially dilutive securities. Contrast with **complex capital structure**.

complex capital structure   A capital structure that includes potentially dilutive securities. Contrast with **simple capital structure**.

¶1.   The objective of this Standard is to prescribe principles for the determination and presentation of earnings per share, so as to improve performance comparisons between different entities in the same reporting period and between different reporting periods for the same entity.

¶11.   The objective of basic earnings per share information is to provide a measure of the interests of each ordinary share of [an] entity in the performance of the entity over the reporting period.

¶32.   The objective of diluted earnings per share is consistent with that of basic earnings per share—to provide a measure of the interest of each ordinary share in the performance of an entity—while giving effect to all dilutive potential ordinary shares outstanding during the period.

The need for basic EPS is simply to increase the understandability and comparability of the earnings number. The need for diluted EPS is to prevent moral hazard, which was discussed in Chapter 1. In the absence of diluted EPS, it would be easier for management to mislead shareholders regarding the profitability of the company by issuing securities such as convertible bonds and stock options that do not entail the issuance of ordinary shares immediately, but which could lead to share issuances in the future.

Accounting Standards for Private Enterprises (ASPE) in Canada do not require companies to report EPS information in their financial statements because the owners of such private enterprises normally have substantial ownerships such that per share amounts are no more informative than the aggregate earnings.[1] For private companies that choose to apply international standards, IFRS also does not require such private companies to disclose EPS information unless they are in the process of going public (paragraph 2 of IAS 33).

basic EPS   An indicator of profitability that measures how much of the company's earnings are attributable (belong) to each ordinary share.

B. CALCULATING BASIC EPS

L.O. 15-2. Calculate basic earnings per share.

Basic EPS is an indicator of profitability that measures how much of the company's earnings are attributable (belong) to each ordinary share. Recall from the

---

1. Recall that a private enterprise is a profit-oriented entity that is neither a publicly accountable enterprise nor an entity in the public sector.

opening vignette that BCE's basic EPS for 2008 was $1.02. The equation for basic EPS is simply the following ratio:

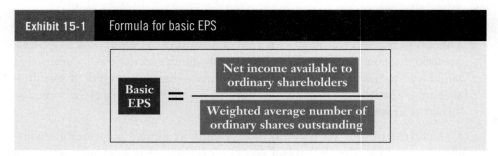

| Exhibit 15-1 | Formula for basic EPS |

$$\text{Basic EPS} = \frac{\text{Net income available to ordinary shareholders}}{\text{Weighted average number of ordinary shares outstanding}}$$

The ratio that is basic EPS is certainly intuitive. However, the components of the ratio require some more exploration, as detailed below.

1. Numerator: Net income available to ordinary shareholders

For purposes of earnings per share, the measure of earnings is not net income but a slightly different measure called **net income available to ordinary shareholders**, which is net income less dividends on preferred shares. There are two important points regarding the numerator. First, it is important to note that we exclude other comprehensive income (OCI) from the numerator because EPS is intended to measure performance (see IAS 33 paragraph 1 above); items in OCI are deemed not to be a part of current period performance. For example, OCI contains unrealized gains or losses on available-for-sale securities (Chapter 7), which are classified as such because management does not intend to actively trade those securities.

Second, we need to adjust for dividends on preferred shares. There are two groups that have claims on a company's profit: ordinary shareholders and preferred shareholders. While dividend payments made to the preferred shareholders do not flow through the income statement, these monies are not available to ordinary shareholders and must be deducted for EPS purposes. The amount subtracted reflects either the stated dividend rate or actual dividends, depending on whether the preferred shares are cumulative or non-cumulative.

- For cumulative preferred shares, deduct the preferred shareholders' entitlement to dividends according to the stated dividend rate regardless of whether they were declared or paid. If there are dividends in arrears, only the current period's dividend rate should be considered.
- For non-cumulative preferred shares, deduct the dividends declared (whether paid or not) without considering the stated entitlement.

The logic underlying these requirements is rooted in the matching concept.

i. The obligation to pay dividends on cumulative preferred shares arises from the passage of time. The responsibility cannot be avoided, as the preferred shareholders must receive all dividends due before any monies are distributed to ordinary shareholders. As such, it is appropriate to deduct the dividend entitlement from net income for the corresponding period even if they have not been declared.

ii. The company is not required to pay non-cumulative preferred dividends unless the board of directors declares them. Accordingly, it is proper to deduct dividends from net income only if they have been declared.

iii. EPS is based on profit or loss for the period, rather than cash flow; accordingly, we deduct dividends in the period to which they relate rather than when they are paid.

net income available to ordinary shareholders The company's net income less dividends on preferred shares.

Exhibit 15-2 illustrates how to determine net income available to ordinary shareholders.

Exhibit 15-2	Example for computing net income available to ordinary shareholders (basic EPS numerator)

Facts:

■ For the year ended December 31, 2011, Stewart Hyder Co. earned $5,000,000.

■ Stewart Hyder had $1,000,000 in cumulative preferred shares outstanding the entire year. The dividend rate is 4% (i.e., $40,000 per year).

■ The dividends on the cumulative preferred shares were not declared in 2010.

■ Stewart Hyder had $2,000,000 in non-cumulative preferred shares outstanding for the entire year. The dividend rate is 5% (i.e., $100,000 per year)

■ Dividend declaration and payment dates are noted are as follows:

	Scenario 1	Scenario 2	Scenario 3
Cumulative preferred shares			
Amount declared in 2011	$ 80,000[a]	$ 40,000[b]	$ 0
Amount paid	$ 60,000	$ 0	$ 0
Dividend payment date	2012 Jan 15	2011 Oct 15	NA
Non-cumulative preferred shares			
Amount declared in 2011	$ 100,000	$ 100,000	$ 0
Amount paid	$ 100,000	$ 30,000	$ 0
Dividend payment date	2012 Jan 15	2011 Oct 15	NA

Notes:

(a) Scenario 1: The $80,000 declaration includes $40,000 for 2010 and $40,000 for 2011.

(b) Scenario 2: The dividends declared on the cumulative preferred shares pertain to 2010.

Computation of net income available to ordinary shareholders			
Net income	$ 5,000,000	$ 5,000,000	$ 5,000,000
Less: Cumulative preferred dividends	40,000	40,000	40,000
Less: Non-cumulative preferred dividends	100,000	100,000	0
Net income available to ordinary shareholders	**$4,860,000**	**$4,860,000**	**$4,960,000**

Comments:

■ The *annual* entitlement to cumulative preferred dividends must be deducted from net income in all three scenarios. Whether the dividends were declared and the amount and date paid are irrelevant.

■ The amount of non-cumulative preferred dividends declared in 2011 are deducted from net income in scenarios 1 and 2. A deduction is not made in scenario 3 as non-cumulative dividends were not declared during the year. The stated entitlement and the amount and date they were paid are of no consequence.

2. Denominator: Weighted average number of ordinary shares outstanding

The denominator in the EPS formula is the weighted average number of ordinary shares outstanding (WASO). We need to determine a weighted average rather than the number at the year-end because the number of ordinary shares outstanding may change significantly during the year. Reasons for the change in the number of shares are many. For example, a company issues new shares to raise capital, to meet its commitment under employee share purchase agreements, or for a stock split or stock dividend. Sometime, companies will repurchase shares on the open market.

Subject to some special rules discussed below, computing WASO is no different from computing any other weighted average. In the case of WASO, the weights are the number of days a particular share has been outstanding during the fiscal year. A share that has been outstanding for 12 months has 12 times the weight of a share that was outstanding for one month. To reduce computational complexity the examples use monthly figures. In practice, though, the number of ordinary shares outstanding is based on a daily average.

Exhibit 15-3 illustrates how to compute WASO in the absence of complicating factors.

Exhibit 15-3	Computing weighted average ordinary shares outstanding (WASO)

Facts:

- Stewart Hyder Co. had 120,000 ordinary shares outstanding on January 1, 2011.
- On March 1, 2011, Stewart Hyder issued an additional 60,000 ordinary shares.
- On June 1, 2011, Stewart Hyder repurchased 30,000 ordinary shares and cancelled them.
- On November 1, 2011, Stewart Hyder issued an additional 90,000 ordinary shares.

Date (2011)	Activity	Shares outstanding (A)	Fraction of year (B)	Contribution to WASO (A × B)
Jan 1–Feb 28	Opening balance	120,000	2/12	20,000
Mar 1	Issue 60,000 shares	+60,000		
Mar 1–May 31	Balance	180,000	3/12	45,000
Jun 1	Repurchase 30,000 shares	−30,000		
Jun 1–Oct 31	Balance	150,000	5/12	62,500
Nov 1	Issue 90,000 shares	+90,000		
Nov 1–Dec 31	Balance	240,000	2/12	40,000
			12/12	
Weighted average number of ordinary shares outstanding (WASO)				167,500

Thus, the computation multiplies each balance by the amount of time for which that balance is valid (e.g., 120,000 shares × 2/12). The sum of these products is the weighted average number of ordinary shares outstanding, which amounts to 167,500 in this example. Note in the above table that the fractions of the year must sum up to one. And as with any type of average, the weighted average must be between the lowest and highest balances (120,000 and 240,000 in this example).

A graphical depiction of the shares outstanding may help understanding. In the following bar chart, each bar represents the number of shares outstanding for that month. The weighted average is the average height of the 12 bars. That average height is equal to the height of a rectangle with the same width as the 12 bars covering the same amount of area as the 12 bars combined.[2]

---

2. There is an alternate but equivalent method to compute WASO. The one already described uses the *balances* in the number of shares after each transaction. The alternative is to start with the beginning-of-year amount and adjust for all of the *transactions* during the year. Graphically, the one already discussed determines the area covered by the bars by summing vertical strips. The alternative computes the same area by summing (and sometimes subtracting in cases of share repurchases) horizontal strips.

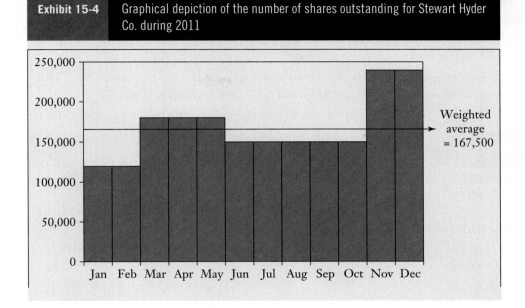

Exhibit 15-4 Graphical depiction of the number of shares outstanding for Stewart Hyder Co. during 2011

3. Complicating factors

There are two factors that complicate the computation of WASO: (a) treasury shares, and (b) stock splits and stock dividends.

a. Treasury shares

As discussed in Chapter 13, while the Canada Business Corporations Act no longer allows companies to hold treasury shares, some provincial jurisdictions still permit them. Shares in treasury are issued but not outstanding, so they are not included in the weighted average number of ordinary shares *outstanding*.

Exhibit 15-5 illustrates the computation of WASO when treasury shares are involved.

b. Stock splits and stock dividends

Stock splits and stock dividends affect EPS as they increase the number of shares outstanding.[3] Note that neither stock splits nor stock dividends bring about any changes in company resources and obligations. These types of changes are different from the changes in shares discussed earlier, such as share issuances, because those transactions increase the EPS denominator number of shares as well as contribute resources to the enterprise, which should increase the earnings in the numerator. The only change from stock splits and stock dividends is the number of shares, which is an entirely cosmetic change. Having one share that is at some point split into two is not any different from changing a single $20 bill into two $10 bills.

Unlike share issuances or repurchases, the actual date of the stock split or dividend is not considered for computing WASO. Instead, we convert all shares to end-of-year equivalents. For example, if a company has 100 shares at the

---

3. We do not explicitly discuss instances where companies engage in reverse stock splits (also called share consolidations) that reduce the number of shares outstanding. The effect is similar but of course opposite to what we discuss here.

Exhibit 15-5	Computing WASO when there are treasury share transactions

Facts:

- Stewart Hyder Co. had 120,000 ordinary shares outstanding on January 1, 2011.
- On March 1, 2011, Stewart Hyder issued an additional 60,000 ordinary shares.
- On June 1, 2011, Stewart Hyder repurchased 30,000 ordinary shares **and held them as treasury shares.**
- On November 1, 2011, Stewart Hyder sold 90,000 ordinary shares including the 30,000 shares held in treasury.

Date (2011)	Activity	Shares outstanding (A)	Fraction of year (B)	Contribution to WASO (A × B)
Jan 1–Feb 28	Opening balance	120,000	2/12	20,000
Mar 1	Issue 60,000 shares	+60,000		
Mar 1–May 31	Balance	180,000	3/12	45,000
Jun 1	Repurchase 30,000 shares	−30,000		
Jun 1–Oct 31	Balance	150,000	5/12	62,500
Nov 1	Issue 90,000 shares	+90,000		
Nov 1–Dec 31	Balance	240,000	2/12	40,000
			12/12	
Weighted average number of ordinary shares outstanding (WASO)				167,500

Comments:

- When the shares are repurchased and held as treasury shares, they are issued but not outstanding and are disregarded for WASO purposes
- Note that the only difference between Exhibit 15-3 and this one is whether the repurchased shares were cancelled or held in treasury. The resulting WASOs are the same in both scenarios (167,500) as treasury shares are ignored in the calculations.

beginning of the year and there is a 2-for-1 stock split on July 1, each of the 100 shares outstanding from January 1 to June 30 would be considered to be two shares, while each of the 200 shares outstanding from July 1 to December 31 would be just one share. Thus, it is as if the company for the whole year had 200 shares outstanding in terms of end-of-year shares. It is of course possible to state the number of shares as beginning-of-year equivalents (100 shares in this example). However, using end-of-year equivalents makes more sense because financial statement readers are evaluating EPS after the end of the year, so the share basis closest to the end of the year is the most relevant to them.

The reasons for standardizing the adjustment date for splits and dividends are to preclude possible manipulation of EPS through discretionary timing; to ensure that EPS is prepared on a consistent basis by all companies; and to enhance comparability. Exhibit 15-6 illustrates the effect of stock splits and stock dividends.

Exhibit 15-6	Computing WASO when there are stock splits or stock dividends

Facts:

- Stewart Hyder Co. had 120,000 ordinary shares outstanding on January 1, 2011.
- On March 1, 2011, Stewart Hyder issued an additional 60,000 ordinary shares.
- **On April 1, 2011, Stewart Hyder declared and issued a 2:1 stock split.**
- On June 1, 2011, Stewart Hyder repurchased 60,000 ordinary shares.
- On November 1, 2011, Stewart Hyder sold 180,000 ordinary shares.
- On December 1, 2011, Stewart Hyder declared and issued a 10% stock dividend.

(Continued)

| Exhibit 15-6 | Continued | | | | |

Date (2011)	Activity	Shares outstanding (A)	Share adjustment factor (B)	Fraction of year (C)	Contribution to WASO (A × B × C)
Jan 1–Feb 28	Opening balance	120,000	2 × 1.1[a]	2/12	44,000
Mar 1	Issue 60,000 shares	+60,000			
Mar 1–Mar 31	Balance	180,000	2 × 1.1[a]	1/12	33,000
Apr 1	**2:1 stock split**	× 2			
Apr 1–May 30	Balance	360,000	1.1[b]	2/12	66,000
Jun 1	Repurchase 60,000 sh.	−60,000			
Jun 1–Oct 31	Balance	300,000	1.1[b]	5/12	137,500
Nov 1	Issue 180,000 shares	+180,000			
Nov 1–Nov 30	Balance	480,000	1.1[b]	1/12	44,000
Dec 1	**10% stock dividend**	× 1.1			
Dec 1–Dec 31	Balance	528,000	1[c]	1/12	44,000
				12/12	
Weighted average number of ordinary shares outstanding (WASO)					**368,500[d]**

Supporting comments and computations:

(a) For WASO purposes we assume that the stock split and stock dividend both took place at the beginning of the year. We adjust for this by multiplying the actual number of shares outstanding by 2 (2:1 stock split) and then again by 1.1 (1 + 10% stock dividend).

(b) As the actual number of shares already includes those issued in the stock split, we need only adjust it for the stock dividend.

(c) As the outstanding number of shares includes those issued in the stock split and stock dividend, we need not make any further adjustments.

(d) Notice that the WASO of 368,500 is exactly 2.2 times 167,500, the result obtained in Exhibit 15-3. This is expected because all the transactions are the same in the two examples except for the stock split and the stock dividend.

4. Basic EPS

Having demonstrated how to calculate the numerator (the net income available to ordinary shareholders) and the denominator (the weighted average number of ordinary shares outstanding), we use this information to compute EPS. Select information from Exhibits 15-2 and 15-6 is reproduced below and used to calculate EPS.

Exhibit 15-7	Computing basic EPS for Stewart Hyder Co.*	
Numerator information from Exhibit 15-2 (Scenario 1)		
Net income		$5,000,000
Less: Cumulative preferred dividends		$ 40,000
Less: Non-cumulative preferred dividends		$ 100,000
Net income available to ordinary shareholders		$4,860,000
Denominator information from Exhibit 15-6		
Weighted average number of ordinary shares outstanding		368,500
Basic EPS ($4,860,000/368,500 shares)		$ 13.19/sh

*In Canada, EPS is always rounded to the nearest whole cent and expressed in dollars and cents ($X.xx).

C. CALCULATING DILUTED EPS

Diluted EPS measures the amount of the company's earnings attributable to each ordinary shareholder in a hypothetical scenario in which all dilutive securities are converted to ordinary shares. It is a conservative metric that reports the lowest possible EPS. The procedures for calculating diluted EPS ensure that it will always be less than or equal to basic EPS. Recall from the opening vignette that BCE's diluted EPS for 2008 was $1.01, which was less than its basic EPS of $1.02. The formula for diluted EPS is as follows:

diluted EPS Measures the amount of the company's earnings attributable to each ordinary shareholder in a hypothetical scenario in which all dilutive securities are converted to ordinary shares.

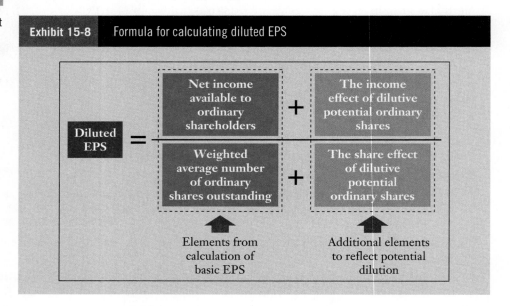

Exhibit 15-8 Formula for calculating diluted EPS

As shown in this formula, the calculation of diluted EPS begins with the numerator and denominator of basic EPS. We then adjust each of these two elements for the effect of "dilutive potential ordinary shares," which is the technical term IFRS uses to describe potentially dilutive securities. **Potential ordinary shares (POS)** are "financial instrument[s] or other contract[s] that may entitle its holder to ordinary shares" (IAS 33 paragraph 5).

potential ordinary share A financial instrument or other contract that may entitle its holder to ordinary shares.

Not all POS are dilutive; some are antidilutive. Thus, **dilutive potential ordinary shares** are those POS that decrease EPS or increase the loss per share from continuing operations. Since the objective of reporting diluted EPS is to provide the lowest possible EPS figure, we include all dilutive POS but exclude any antidilutive POS. If there is a combination of many (or even just a handful of) potentially dilutive factors, it could be quite laborious to determine which combination would produce the lowest EPS. Fortunately, there is an algorithm that guarantees that we are able to determine the lowest EPS. There are four steps in the process to separate dilutive from antidilutive POS and to calculate diluted EPS, as follows.

dilutive potential ordinary shares Potential ordinary shares whose conversion to ordinary shares would decrease EPS or increase loss per share from continuing operations.

1. Identify all potential ordinary shares.
2. Compute "incremental EPS" for each category of potential ordinary shares.
3. Rank order incremental EPS on potential ordinary shares from the lowest (the most dilutive) to the highest (least dilutive).
4. Sequentially compare incremental EPS to "provisional EPS"[4] to determine diluted EPS.

We now examine each of these four steps in more detail.

---

4. "Provisional EPS" is not a defined term in IFRS nor is it reported in the financial statements. Rather, it is used to establish whether a given POS is dilutive or antidilutive.

1. Identify all potential ordinary shares

This step is fairly straightforward. Go through the company records to identify financial instruments or other contracts that entitle the holder to obtain ordinary shares at a later date on predefined terms. The shares that the company may have to issue under these agreements are referred to as potential ordinary shares. Financial instruments that give rise to POS include the following:

- convertible bonds that can be exchanged for ordinary shares;
- convertible preferred shares that can be exchanged for ordinary shares; and
- stock options and warrants that permit the holder to buy ordinary shares from the company at a predetermined price.

The terms of conversion or purchase are specified in the original financial instrument. These terms include:

- the date or range of dates when the exchange may take place;
- the rate of substitution (e.g., one $1,000 bond can be traded for 60 ordinary shares); or
- the price to be paid (e.g., an ordinary share can be purchased for $17).

When the holder exchanges convertible securities for ordinary shares, the company's obligations under the original instrument are extinguished, and the firm is no longer required to pay interest or dividends on those securities.

2. Compute incremental EPS for all potential ordinary shares

Incremental EPS is used to rank order the securities in terms of their dilutiveness. As we will show, this information is needed to identify dilutive and antidilutive POS and ensure that we obtain the lowest diluted EPS. Computing incremental EPS involves taking the ratio of the income effect to the share effect arising from dilutive potential ordinary shares. The following exhibit shows this formula:

incremental EPS Quantifies the relationship between the income effect and the share effect for each class of potential ordinary share.

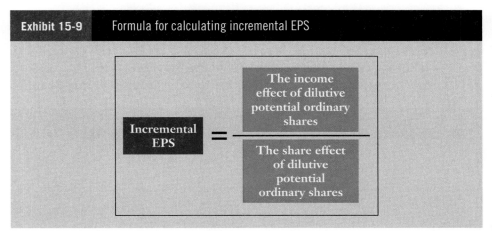

Exhibit 15-9 Formula for calculating incremental EPS

$$\text{Incremental EPS} = \frac{\text{The income effect of dilutive potential ordinary shares}}{\text{The share effect of dilutive potential ordinary shares}}$$

Income effect: In this formula, the **income effect** indicates the incremental after-tax income available to ordinary shareholders if a category of potential ordinary shares had been converted into ordinary shares. There is a different income effect for each class of POS.

Share effect: The **share effect** indicates the incremental number of ordinary shares outstanding if a category of potential ordinary shares had been converted into ordinary shares. There is a different share effect for each class of POS. In addition, it is necessary to treat convertible securities differently from options/warrants because of the different nature of the two types of securities.

income effect Indicates the incremental after-tax income available to ordinary shareholders if a category of potential ordinary shares had been converted into ordinary shares.

share effect Indicates the incremental number of ordinary shares outstanding if a category of potential ordinary shares had been converted into ordinary shares.

a. Convertible bonds and preferred shares: The if-converted method

if-converted method Assumes: i) that the security was converted into ordinary shares at the beginning of the period; and ii) interest and/or dividends were not paid on the security during the year.

We calculate incremental EPS on convertible bonds and preferred shares using the if-converted method. The **if-converted method** assumes: i) that the security had been converted into ordinary shares at the beginning of the period; and ii) that the company had not paid interest or preferred dividends on the security during the year because the security had already been converted. The purpose is to determine what the effect would be had the securities been converted. This is accomplished by isolating the after-tax increase in income that would accrue to ordinary shareholders had the POS been converted, and then dividing this amount by the additional number of ordinary shares that would be issued upon conversion.

Interest on bonds payable is usually a tax-deductible expense, while dividends on preferred shares are not. For convertible securities, we are interested in the after-tax effect on income, calculated as follows:

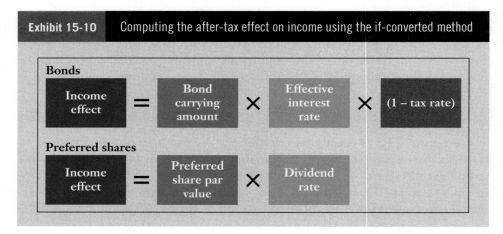

Exhibit 15-10	Computing the after-tax effect on income using the if-converted method

Bonds

Income effect = Bond carrying amount × Effective interest rate × (1 − tax rate)

Preferred shares

Income effect = Preferred share par value × Dividend rate

When preferred shares do not have a par value, then the dividend rate would be stated in dollar terms and that dollar amount would be the income effect of the preferred shares.

The following provides two examples showing the calculation of incremental EPS, one for convertible bonds and the other for convertible preferred shares.

Exhibit 15-11	Example for computing incremental EPS for convertible bonds

Facts:

- Smithers Rupert Co. has $1,000,000 in 6% bonds outstanding.
- The bonds' carrying amount equals their face value; therefore the yield equals the coupon rate.
- The bonds were issued on January 1, 2010 and mature on January 1, 2018.
- Each $1,000 bond is convertible into 20 ordinary shares.
- The company's income tax rate is 30%.

Required:

Determine the incremental EPS of the bond issue for the year ended December 31, 2011.

Income effect	= Carrying amount × yield × (1 − tax rate) = $1,000,000 × 6% × (1 − 30%)	$42,000
Share effect	= ($1,000,000/$1,000) bonds × 20 shares/bond	20,000
Incremental EPS	Income effect/share effect	$ 2.10

Exhibit 15-12	Example for computing incremental EPS for convertible preferred shares

Facts:

- Smithers Rupert Co. has 10,000 preferred shares outstanding with face value of $1,000,000 and dividend rate of 5%.
- The preferred shares were issued on January 1, 2010 and do not mature.
- Each $100 preferred share is convertible into three ordinary shares.
- Smithers Rupert's income tax rate is 30%.

Required:

Determine the incremental EPS of the preferred share issue for the year ended December 31, 2011.

Analysis:

Income effect	Par value × dividend rate = $1,000,000 × 5%	$50,000
Share effect	10,000 pfd × 3 ordinary/pfd	30,000
Incremental EPS	Income effect/share effect	$ 1.67

b. Options and warrants: The treasury stock method

Similar to the treatment of convertible securities, we assume that options or warrants are exercised at the beginning of the period (or date of issue, if it occurs during the period). However, whereas convertible debt has a clear amount of interest that would be saved if it had been converted, it is not clear what the corresponding adjustment would be for options and warrants. How much income would have been earned from funds received from the exercise of options or warrants? To avoid making such subjective adjustments to the numerator, which could be subject to manipulation, the required approach completely reflects the dilution in the denominator using the **treasury stock method**.

However, for purposes of computing diluted EPS, we consider only call options and warrants that are **in-the-money**, which is when the market price of the underlying security exceeds the exercise price (also called the strike price). They are said to be in-the-money as the holder could pay the agreed-upon exercise price (say $20) and immediately resell the security for the market price (say $22) and earn a profit. Conversely, call options and warrants are **out-of-the-money** when the market price of the security is less than the exercise price. They are said to be out-of-the-money because the holder would have to pay more for the security (say $24) than he/she could simultaneously sell it for in the market (say $22), and as such would generate a loss if this sub-optimal strategy were pursued. Options and warrants are **at-the-money** when the market price of the security is equal to the exercise price. For purposes of diluted EPS, the determination of whether an option is in the money uses the *average* market price for the reporting period.

In this method, the proceeds from the assumed option exercise are used to purchase common shares from the market. However, since the exercise price of an in-the-money call option or warrant is below the average market price in the year, the number of shares that could be repurchased using the proceeds from the option exercise must be less than the number of shares issued for the options. The difference between the number of shares needed for full exercise and the number of shares that could be repurchased represents the incremental shares that the company would have had to issue to cover the exercise. It is the incremental shares needed that is added to the weighted average

treasury stock method The process used to determine the share effect for call options and warrants.

in-the-money (options or warrants) Describes the condition of an option when the market price is favourable for exercising the option; a call option or warrant is in-the-money if the market price of the share exceeds the exercise price. Contrast with **out-of-the-money**.

out-of-the-money (options or warrants) The condition of an option when the market price is unfavourable for exercising the option; a call option or warrant is out-of-the-money if the market price of the share is less than the exercise price. Contrast with **in-the-money**.

at-the-money An option is at the money if the market price of the share equals the exercise price. Compare with **in-the-money** and **out-of-the-money**.

number of shares outstanding in the denominator.[5] Out-of-the-money options are ignored since holders of these options would not have exercised their options.

As set out in the opening vignette, BCE's basic and diluted EPS for 2008 were $1.02 and $1.01, respectively. While not evident from the information provided, the difference is due entirely to the dilutive effect of in-the-money stock options. BCE's weighted average number of shares outstanding for basic EPS purposes was 805.8 million common (ordinary) shares, which was diluted (i.e., increased) by 1.4 million shares from the share effect of the stock options.

The application of the treasury stock method is summarized below in Exhibit 15-13.

| Exhibit 15-13 | Computing incremental shares from options (or warrants) |

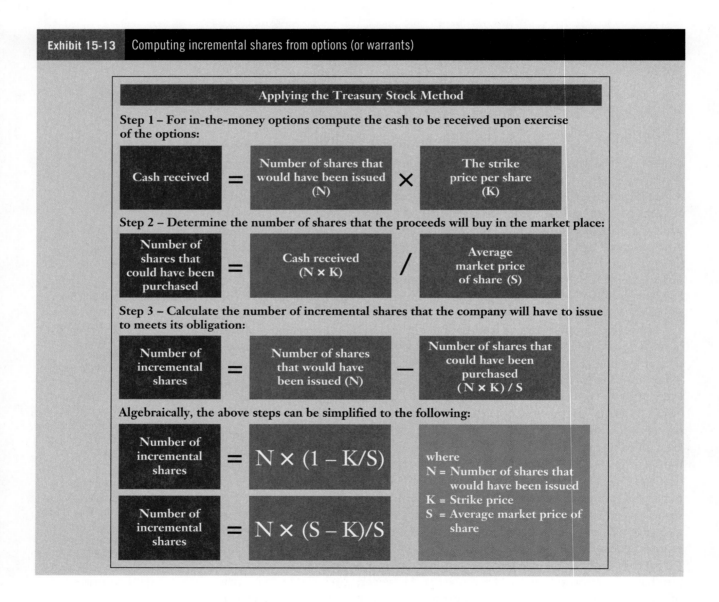

Applying the Treasury Stock Method

Step 1 – For in-the-money options compute the cash to be received upon exercise of the options:

$$\text{Cash received} = \text{Number of shares that would have been issued (N)} \times \text{The strike price per share (K)}$$

Step 2 – Determine the number of shares that the proceeds will buy in the market place:

$$\text{Number of shares that could have been purchased} = \text{Cash received } (N \times K) \, / \, \text{Average market price of share (S)}$$

Step 3 – Calculate the number of incremental shares that the company will have to issue to meets its obligation:

$$\text{Number of incremental shares} = \text{Number of shares that would have been issued (N)} - \text{Number of shares that could have been purchased } (N \times K) / S$$

Algebraically, the above steps can be simplified to the following:

$$\text{Number of incremental shares} = N \times (1 - K/S)$$

$$\text{Number of incremental shares} = N \times (S - K)/S$$

where
N = Number of shares that would have been issued
K = Strike price
S = Average market price of share

The following exhibit provides an example to demonstrate the calculation of incremental EPS for options and warrants.

---

5. The dilutive effect of company-issued put options is calculated using the reverse treasury stock method. Discussion of this process is beyond the scope of this text.

Exhibit 15-14	Example showing the calculation of incremental EPS for options and warrants

Facts:

- Smithers Rupert Co. has options outstanding that entitle the holders to purchase 10,000 ordinary shares for $42 each.
- The options were issued on January 1, 2010 and expire on January 1, 2016.
- The average market price of Smith Rupert's ordinary shares during 2011 was $48.
- The company's income tax rate is 30%.

Required:

- Determine the incremental number of shares that may be issued for diluted EPS purposes.
- Determine the incremental EPS for the year ended December 31, 2011.

Analysis:

Were options in the money?	Average market price ($48) > option price ($42)	Options are in the money
# of shares that would have been issued		10,000
# of shares that could have been purchased	Proceeds = 10,000 × $42 = $420,000 # shares purchased = $420,000/$48 = 8,750	8,750
Incremental shares	10,000 − 8,750	1,250*
Incremental EPS	Income effect/share effect = $0/1,250	$0.00

*We can compute this figure directly by formula: N(1 − K/S) = 10,000 × (1 − $42/$48) = 1,250

3. Rank order incremental EPS

The third step is to rank order incremental EPS on potential ordinary shares from the lowest (the most dilutive) to the highest (the least dilutive). This step is easy to perform, as demonstrated in the following table. Note that in-the-money stock options and warrants are always the most dilutive because they have incremental EPS of zero. If there is more than one in-the-money option or warrant, the options and warrants may be ranked in any order.

Exhibit 15-15	Rank ordering incremental EPS computed in Exhibits 15-11, 15-12, and 15-13

Potential ordinary shares	Income effect	Share effect	Incremental EPS	Rank order
Convertible bonds	$42,000	20,000	$2.10	3rd
Convertible preferred shares	$50,000	30,000	$1.67	2nd
Stock options	$ 0	1,250	$0.00	1st

4. Sequentially compare incremental EPS to provisional EPS to determine diluted EPS

As stated previously, when calculating diluted EPS the goal is to identify the scenario that maximizes dilution. Using the rankings just obtained in Step 3 above, compare incremental EPS of the most dilutive POS to basic EPS. If incremental EPS is lower than basic EPS, include the POS in the diluted EPS computation to obtain provisional EPS. Repeat with the next rank-ordered item and compare incremental EPS to provisional EPS. Continue the process until all dilutive POS have been considered or until incremental EPS exceeds provisional EPS. At this point, no further calculations are required because the last recorded provisional EPS equals diluted EPS.

Exhibit 15-16 combines the above four steps to calculate diluted EPS.

Exhibit 15-16	Sequentially computing EPS by adding dilutive factors			
From Exhibit 15-7				
Net income available to ordinary shareholders				$4,860,000
Weighted average number of ordinary shares outstanding				368,500
Basic EPS				$ 13.19
From Exhibit 15-15				
Potential ordinary shares	**Income effect**	**Share effect**	**Incremental EPS**	**Rank order**
Convertible bonds	$ 42,000	20,000	$2.10	3rd
Convertible preferred shares	$ 50,000	30,000	$1.67	2nd
Stock options	$ 0	1,250	$0.00	1st

Required: Calculate diluted EPS

	Income	**Shares**	**Incremental EPS**	**EPS**
Basic EPS	$4,860,000	368,500		$13.19
Rank 1: Stock options	0	1,250	$0.00	
Provisional EPS	$4,860,000	369,750		$13.14
Rank 2: Convertible preferred shares	50,000	30,000	$1.67	
Provisional EPS	$4,910,000	399,750		$12.28
Rank 3: Convertible bonds	42,000	20,000	$2.10	
Diluted earnings per share	$4,952,000	419,750		**$11.80**

1. After rank ordering the incremental EPS, we sequentially add dilutive factors and recalculate EPS. Including in-the-money stock options is always dilutive, and doing so reduces EPS from $13.19 to $13.14.

2. Convertible preferred shares are dilutive since the incremental EPS of $1.67 is less than the EPS just computed. Adding in the convertible preferred shares using the if-converted method results in an EPS of $12.28.

3. Likewise, the incremental EPS on convertible bonds of $2.10 is lower than the EPS just computed. Adding in the effect of convertible bonds reduces the EPS to $11.80.

4. There are no more dilutive securities, so diluted EPS is $11.80.

In the preceding example, all potential ordinary shares were dilutive. While this will not always be the case, the process used remains the same, as illustrated in Exhibit 15-16. The following example illustrates the importance of the sequential inclusion of dilutive factors according to the ranking of incremental EPS.

Exhibit 15-17	Illustration of the importance of sequential inclusion of dilutive factors

Facts:

Bob Beanery Ltd.'s net income for the year ended December 31, 2008	$500,000
Weighted average number of ordinary shares outstanding	390,000
Average market price of ordinary shares in 2008	$ 25
Fiscal 2008 year-end market price of ordinary shares	$ 28
Bob Beanery Ltd.'s income tax rate for 2008	30%

Potential Ordinary Shares

- 10% convertible bonds: $100,000 convertible bonds were sold at par on January 1, 2002, maturing January 1, 2015. Each $1,000 bond is convertible into 60 ordinary shares at the option of the holder at any time after January 1, 2010.

- 8% cumulative convertible preferred stock: $200,000 convertible preferred shares were sold at par on July 1, 2001. Each $100 preferred shares is convertible into 20 ordinary shares at the option of the holder at any time after issuance. Dividends were not declared in 2008.

- Stock options A: Option to purchase 20,000 shares for $20 per share, expiring December 31, 2014. The options may be exercised at any time prior to expiry.

- Stock options B: Option to purchase 10,000 shares for $30 per share, expiring June 30, 2009. The options may be exercised at any time prior to expiry.

Required: Compute Bob's basic and diluted earnings per share for 2008.

Basic EPS

Net income available to ordinary shareholders = net income − dividends = $500,000 − ($200,000 × 0.08) (Note 1)	$484,000
Basic EPS = net income available to ordinary shareholders/weighted average number of ordinary shares outstanding = $484,000/390,000	$ 1.24

Diluted EPS

Step 1. Identify all potential ordinary shares—there are four potential ordinary shares as set out in the fact section above ("Facts")

Step 2. Compute the incremental EPS for all potential ordinary shares

Convertible bonds (Note 2)

Income effect	Face amount of bonds × coupon rate × (1 − income tax rate) = $100,000 × 10% × (1 − 30%)	$ 7,000
Share effect	Conversion factor = ($100,000/$1,000) × 60	6,000
Incremental EPS	Income effect/share effect = $7,000/6,000	$ 1.17

Convertible preferred shares

Income effect	Par value × dividends = $200,000 × 8%	$ 16,000
Share effect	Conversion factor = ($200,000/$100) × 20	40,000
Incremental EPS	Income effect/share effect = $16,000/40,000	$ 0.40

Stock Options A (Note 3)

Dilutive or antidilutive?	Average market price ($25) > option price ($20)	Options are dilutive
Incremental shares	N(1 − K/S) = 20,000 × (1 − $20/$25) = 4,000	4,000

Stock Options B

Dilutive or antidilutive?	Average market price ($25) < option price ($30)	Options are antidilutive

(Continued)

Exhibit 15-17 (Continued)

Step 3. Rank order the incremental EPS on potential ordinary shares from the lowest (the most dilutive) to the highest (least dilutive)

Potential ordinary shares	Incremental EPS	Rank order
Convertible bonds	$1.17	3rd
Convertible preferred shares	$0.40	2nd
Stock options A	$0.00	1st
Stock options B	antidilutive	—

Step 4. Sequentially compare the incremental EPS to the provisional EPS to determine diluted EPS

Diluted earnings per share	Income	Shares	Incremental EPS	Diluted EPS
Basic EPS	$484,000	390,000		$1.24
Stock options A	0	4,000	$0.00	
Provisional EPS	$484,000	394,000		$1.23
Convertible preferred shares	16,000	40,000	$0.40	
Provisional EPS	$500,000	434,000		$1.15
Convertible bonds—antidilutive (Note 4)	0	0	$1.17 > $1.15	
Diluted earnings per share	$500,000	434,000		$1.15

Notes:

1. The preferred shares are cumulative, thus we deduct the dividend entitlement even though they were not declared.
2. We include the convertible bonds in the 2008 dilution calculations even though the earliest that it can be converted is January 1, 2010.
3. For stock options, we use the average price throughout the year, not the year-end price.
4. The bonds are antidilutive as the incremental EPS of $1.17 > provisional EPS of $1.15. To determine whether POS are dilutive, we compare their incremental EPS to provisional EPS, rather than basic EPS.

This example demonstrates why it is imperative to check POS for dilution potential in the prescribed manner. Had we first compared the bond's incremental EPS of $1.17 to the basic EPS of $1.24, we would have incorrectly concluded that the bonds were dilutive.

5. Effect of discontinued operations

Profit or loss has potentially two distinct components when a company reports discontinued operations in a period. IFRS requires EPS to be separately calculated and reported for continuing operations and for discontinued operations. For computing diluted EPS, net income or loss available to ordinary shareholders from continuing operations (which excludes the effect of discontinued operations) is used as the control number (starting point) for determining the dilutiveness of potential ordinary shares. This requirement is set out in paragraph 41 of IAS 33, which reads:

> ¶41. Potential ordinary shares shall be treated as dilutive when, and only when, their conversion to ordinary shares would decrease earnings per share or increase loss per share from continuing operations.

6. Diluted EPS when basic EPS is negative

When a company loses money during the year, or preferred dividends exceed income, basic EPS would be negative, meaning that there is a loss per ordinary share. When basic EPS is less than zero, POS that would otherwise be dilutive are antidilutive, as illustrated in the example in Exhibit 15-18. For this reason, when basic EPS from continuing operations is negative, all potential ordinary shares are deemed to be antidilutive.

Exhibit 15-18	Illustration of diluted EPS when basic EPS is negative

Facts:

- There is a single ordinary share outstanding
- There is one bond outstanding that can be converted into one ordinary share. The after-tax income effect is $2.00
- In scenario 1, the firm earns a profit of $3.00
- In scenario 2, the firm suffers a loss of $3.00

	Scenario 1			Scenario 2		
	Income	Shares	EPS	Income	Shares	EPS
Basic EPS	$3.00	1	$3.00	$(3.00)	1	$(3.00)
Convertible bond	$2.00	1		$ 2.00	1	
Diluted EPS if bond included	$5.00	2	$2.50	$(1.00)	2	$(0.50)
Observation	Bond is dilutive: EPS decreases from $3.00 to $2.50			Bond is antidilutive: loss per share decreases from $(3.00) to $(0.50)		

There are situations where a company can report a loss from continuing operations and still be profitable overall in terms of net income. For example, a company may report net income of $50,000, consisting of a $100,000 loss from continuing operations and a $150,000 gain from discontinued operations. In these circumstances, all POS are antidilutive as there is a loss from continuing operations. As noted above, it is income available to ordinary shareholders from continuing operations that determines the dilutiveness of POS.

7. Other considerations

a. Convertible securities issued, redeemed, or exchanged during the year

The preceding examples assumed that the securities giving rise to potential ordinary shares were outstanding the entire year. This may not always be the case. During the year, dilutive securities may have been issued, redeemed, or converted into ordinary shares; or, the right of exchange may have lapsed. How should we reflect these events in the computation of diluted EPS?

- *Issued during the year:* If convertible securities are issued during the year, both the income and share effect are pro-rated to reflect the date of issuance. For example, if the preferred shares in Exhibit 15-17 had been issued on April 1, 2008, the income effect would be $16,000 × 9/12 = $12,000 and the share effect 40,000 shares × 9/12 = 30,000 shares. The incremental EPS remains unchanged at $0.40/share ($12,000/30,000 shares).
- *Redeemed or lapsed during the year:* If a convertible security is redeemed or the right to convert expires during the year, the income and share effects are pro-rated to include only the portion of the year for which the security was outstanding.

■ *Converted during the year*: If a convertible security is exchanged during the year, the income effect is the after-tax amount expensed during the period the security was outstanding.[6] The potential ordinary shares are included until the date of conversion. The shares issued for the conversion would have already been included in the basic EPS calculation.

Thus, the general idea is to reflect the amount of time during the year for which the convertible securities were available to be converted into ordinary shares.

b. Convertible securities with more than one conversion option

Some securities have multiple conversion options. For example, a convertible bond might permit the holder to exchange it for five ordinary shares on December 31, 2011 or four ordinary shares on December 31, 2013. For EPS purposes, we use the most dilutive alternative—in this case, the five ordinary shares (IAS 33 paragraph 39).

c. Potential ordinary shares that are not yet eligible to be converted/exercised

Many POS can be exchanged or exercised only at specific times or after a specific date. For example, a convertible bond may allow for conversion into 50 ordinary shares three years after the issue date but not before. For diluted EPS purposes, we include the POS in the computation of diluted EPS regardless of when the conversion option becomes effective. This approach is entirely consistent with the treatment of "convertible securities with more than one conversion option" discussed above. Specifically, we can think of the conversion privilege of the bond as currently zero but increasing to 50 ordinary shares three years after the issue date. Accordingly, we use the most dilutive alternative (the 50 ordinary shares) for EPS purposes.

d. Bonds sold at a discount or premium

When a bond's carrying amount and its face value differ, the effective interest rate differs from the coupon rate. Since it is the effective interest rate—rather than the coupon rate—that determines the amount of interest expense, we use the effective interest rate to determine the income effect of the bond.

e. Purchased options versus written options

To date, the discussion of options concentrated on call options granted (written) by the company, which may be dilutive or antidilutive. If the company is on the other side of the transaction, buying call options on its own shares from an outside party, then its role is reversed from that discussed previously. Whereas issued options are potentially dilutive, purchased options are always antidilutive (see IAS 33 paragraph 62).

---

6. Because bonds can be issued at a discount or premium, the income effect reflects the after-tax amount of interest expensed, rather than paid.

8. Putting it all together: A comprehensive example

In this chapter we have set out the steps to compute both basic and diluted EPS. You now have an opportunity to work through a comprehensive example to confirm your knowledge of the topic. When complete, compare your answer to the solution that follows.

Exhibit 15-19	Comprehensive example*

Scenario

■ Zero Tolerance Accounting Inc.'s (ZTA) ordinary shares are actively traded on the Toronto Stock Exchange.

■ The company accountant has been asked to calculate ZTA's basic and diluted EPS for the year ended December 31, 2012.

Facts

■ There were 75,000 ordinary shares outstanding at January 1, 2012. An additional 150,000 shares were issued on July 1, 2012.

■ A 2-for-1 stock split was declared and distributed on October 1, 2012.*

■ On January 1, 2011, ZTA issued at par $300,000 in 8% bonds that mature on January 1, 2019. Each $1,000 bond is convertible into 55 common shares. Ignore the equity component arising from the issuance of convertible bonds and assume that the effective interest rate is 8%.

■ There are 15,000 outstanding cumulative preferred shares that are each entitled to an annual dividend of $0.30. Dividends were not declared or paid during 2012. Each preferred share is convertible into two ordinary shares.

■ ZTA previously granted its employees options to acquire 5,000 ordinary shares at an exercise price of $25.00 each. These options expire on June 30, 2017.

■ ZTA previously granted its executives options to acquire 1,800 ordinary shares at an exercise price of $20.00 each. These options expire on August 31, 2018.

■ ZTA's net income for the year ended December 31, 2012 was $183,000. Its income tax rate is 30%. The average market price of its shares during 2012 was $24.00.

*Convertible securities and options normally include a clause that adjusts the conversion rate or exercise price to counteract the effect of stock splits and stock dividends. While a full discussion of this point is beyond the scope of this text, for purposes of this exercise assume that the conversion rates and the exercise prices set out in the facts section have already been adjusted for the stock split.

Solution:

Zero Tolerance Accounting Inc.'s basic and diluted EPS are $0.60 and $0.55, respectively. These amounts were determined using the procedures discussed earlier in the chapter and shown in the following exhibit.

Exhibit 15-20	Computations supporting the solution to comprehensive example	
Calculation of Basic EPS		
Calculation of numerator		
Net income		$ 183,000
Less: Preferred dividends (cumulative)	(15,000 × $0.30)	$ (4,500)
Net income to ordinary shareholders		**$178,500**

(Continued)

Exhibit 15-20 Continued

Calculation of denominator

Date (2012)	Activity	Shares O/S	Adjustment factor	Fraction of year	WASO
Jan 1–Jun 30	Opening balance	75,000	2.0	6/12	75,000
Jul 1	Issue 150,000 sh.	150,000			
Jul 1–Sep 30	Balance	225,000	2.0	3/12	112,500
Oct 1	2:1 stock split	225,000			
Oct 1–Dec 31	Balance	450,000	1.0	3/12	112,500
Weighted average number of ordinary shares outstanding					**300,000**
Basic EPS	= $178,500/300,000				**$0.60**

Calculation of Diluted EPS

Computation of incremental EPS and ranking of dilutiveness

Potential ordinary shares	Income effect	Share effect	Incremental EPS	Rank order
Convertible bonds	($300,000 × .08) × (1 − 30%) = $16,800	($300,000 / $1,000) × 55 = 16,500	$1.02	3rd
Convertible preferred shares	15,000 × $0.30 = $4,500	15,000 × 2 = 30,000	$0.15	2nd
Stock options – employees	Exercise price ($25.00) > average market price ($24.00), therefore *antidilutive*		—	—
Stock options – executives	N(1 − K/S) = 1,800 × (1 − $20/$24) = 300		$0.00	1st

Sequentially compare the incremental EPS to the provisional EPS to determine diluted EPS

	Income	Shares	Incremental EPS	Diluted EPS
Basic EPS	$178,500	300,000		$0.60
Stock options – executives	0	300	$0.00	
Provisional EPS	$178,500	300,300		$0.59
Convertible preferred shares	4,500	30,000	$0.15	
Provisional EPS	$183,000	330,300		$0.55
Convertible bonds – anti-dilutive	0	0	$1.02 > $0.55	
Diluted earnings per share	**$183,000**	**330,300**		**$0.55**

D. PRESENTATION AND DISCLOSURE

The following summarizes the requirements for presenting and disclosing EPS information according to IAS 33 paragraphs 66–73A.

1. Presentation

Information to be presented on the face of the income statement[7] includes:

■ basic EPS;
■ diluted EPS if the company has any potential ordinary shares, even if it is the same as basic EPS; and

- basic and diluted EPS arising from operations, continuing operations, and discontinued operations if the company has discontinued operations. Alternatively, EPS from discontinued operations may be disclosed in the notes to the financial statements.

2. Disclosure

Particulars that must be included in the notes to the financial statements include the following items:

- the income available to ordinary shareholders used to calculate both basic and diluted EPS;
- the weighted average number of ordinary shares used to calculate both basic and diluted EPS;
- particulars of potential ordinary shares that were not included in the diluted EPS calculations as they were antidilutive for the period;
- details of post-balance sheet date transactions that significantly change either the number of ordinary shares outstanding or the number of potential ordinary shares; and
- information regarding stock splits or dividends that occur after year-end but before the statements are authorized for issue. Note that basic and diluted EPS for the year is based on the new number of outstanding shares.

As an example, the EPS information disclosed in British Airways PLC's 2009 financial statements is reproduced in Exhibit 15-21.

Exhibit 15-21	Excerpts from British Airways PLC's 2009 Financial Statements[8]		
Group consolidated income statement For the year ended March 31, 2009 £ million	Notes		
(Loss)/profit after tax from continuing operations		**(358)**	*728*
Loss from discontinued operations (after tax)	5	**—**	*(2)*
(Loss)/profit after tax		**(358)**	*726*
Attributable to:			
Equity holders of the parent		**(375)**	*712*
Minority interest		**17**	*14*
		(358)	*726*
Earnings/(loss) per share Continuing operations:			
Basic	13	**(32.6)p**	*62.1p*
Diluted	13	**(32.6)p**	*61.6p*
Discontinued operations:			
Basic	13		*(0.2)p*
Diluted	13		*(0.2)p*
Total:			
Basic	13	**(32.6)p**	*61.9p*
Diluted	13	**(32.6)p**	*61.4p*

(Continued)

7. Companies can present income in an income statement or as part of a single statement of comprehensive income. In this section, the term "on the face of the income statement" encompasses "on the face of the single statement of comprehensive income."

8. Courtesy of British Airways.

Exhibit 15-21	Continued

13 Earnings per share

	Profit		Earnings per share	
	2009 **£ million**	*2008* *£ million* *Restated*	**2009** **Pence**	*2008* *Pence* *Restated*
(Loss)/profit for the year attributable to shareholders and basic earnings per share	**(375)**	*712*	**(32.6)**	*61.9*
Represented by:				
Continuing operations	**(375)**	*714*	**(32.6)**	*62.1*
Discontinued operations		*(2)*		*(0.2)*
Diluted (loss)/profit for the year attributable to shareholders and diluted earnings per share	**(375)**	*712*	**(32.6)**	*61.4*
Represented by:				
Continuing operations	**(375)**	*714*	**(32.6)**	*61.6*
Discontinued operations		*(2)*		*(0.2)*
Weighted average number of shares for basic EPS ('000)			**1,151,230**	*1,150,537*
Dilutive potential ordinary shares:				
Employee share options ('000)			**2,702**	*8,093*
Weighted average number of shares for diluted EPS ('000)			**1,153,932**	*1,158,630*

Basic earnings per share are calculated on a weighted average number of ordinary shares in issue after deducting shares held for the purposes of Employee Share Ownership Plans including the Long Term Incentive Plan.

The Group has granted additional options over shares to employees that were not dilutive during the year but which may be dilutive in the future. Details of the Group's share options can be found in note 34.

E. SUBSTANTIVE DIFFERENCES BETWEEN RELEVANT IFRS AND ASPE

ISSUE	IFRS	ASPE
Requirement to present EPS information	IFRS requires publicly accountable enterprises or private entities in the process of going public to present EPS information in accordance with IAS 33.	ASPE does not require entities to present earnings per share information.

F. SUMMARY

L.O. 15-1. Describe the reasons for reporting basic and diluted earnings per share.

- EPS provides information about how much of the reported earnings belongs to each ordinary shareholder
- EPS facilitates comparison of an entity's performance to that of other companies and to the entity's accomplishments in other reporting periods

L.O. 15-2. Calculate basic earnings per share.

- Basic EPS = net income available to ordinary shareholders / weighted average number of ordinary shares outstanding

L.O. 15-3. Differentiate between dilutive and antidilutive potential ordinary shares.

- Dilutive potential ordinary shares, if converted, will decrease EPS or increase the loss per share from continuing operations
- Antidilutive potential ordinary shares, if converted, will increase EPS or decrease the loss per share from continuing operations

L.O. 15-4. Calculate diluted earnings per share.

- Diluted EPS = (net income available to ordinary shareholders + the income effect of dilutive potential ordinary shares) / (weighted average number of ordinary shares outstanding + the share effect of dilutive potential ordinary shares)

G. References

Authoritative standards:

IFRS	ASPE Section
IAS 1—Presentation of Financial Statements	1400—General Standards of Financial Statement Presentation
	1520—Income Statement
IAS 33—Earnings per Share	No equivalent guidance

H. Glossary

at-the-money: An option is at the money if the market price of the share equals the exercise price. Compare with **in-the-money** and **out-of-the-money**.

basic EPS: An indicator of profitability that measures how much of the company's earnings are attributable (belong) to each ordinary share.

complex capital structure: A capital structure that includes potentially dilutive securities. Contrast with **simple capital structure**.

diluted EPS: Measures the amount of the company's earnings attributable to each ordinary shareholder in a hypothetical scenario in which all dilutive securities are converted to ordinary shares.

dilutive potential ordinary shares: Potential ordinary shares whose conversion to ordinary shares would decrease EPS or increase loss per share from continuing operations.

earnings per share (EPS): Measures each ordinary share's interest in a company's earnings.

if-converted method: Assumes: i) that the security was converted into ordinary shares at the beginning of the period; and ii) interest and/or dividends were not paid on the security during the year.

in-the-money (options or warrants): Describes the condition of an option when the market price is favourable for exercising the option; a call option or warrant is in-the-money if the market price of the share exceeds the exercise price. Contrast with **out-of-the-money**.

income effect: Indicates the incremental after-tax income available to ordinary shareholders if a category of potential ordinary shares had been converted into ordinary shares.

incremental EPS: Quantifies the relationship between the income effect and the share effect for each class of potential ordinary share.

net income available to ordinary shareholders: The company's net income less dividends on preferred shares.

out-of-the-money (options or warrants): The condition of an option when the market price is unfavourable for exercising the option; a call option or warrant is out-of-the-money if the market price of the share is less than the exercise price. Contrast with **in-the-money**.

potential ordinary share: A financial instrument or other contract that may entitle its holder to ordinary shares.

share effect: Indicates the incremental number of ordinary shares outstanding if a category of potential ordinary shares had been converted into ordinary shares.

simple capital structure: A capital structure that does not include potentially dilutive securities. Contrast with **complex capital structure**.

treasury stock method: The process used to determine the share effect for call options and warrants.

I. PROBLEMS

MyAccountingLab ° Go to MyAccountingLab at www.myaccountinglab.com. You can practise the indicated exercises as often as you want, and guided solutions will help you find answers step by step. You'll find a personalized study plan available to you too!

P15-1. Earnings per share (EPS) concepts   (**L.O.** 15-1) (Easy – 5 minutes)

a. What information does EPS communicate to investors?
b. Describe the difference between basic and diluted EPS.
c. What are potential ordinary shares?
d. Provide three examples of potential ordinary shares.

P15-2. Basic EPS concepts   (**L.O.** 15-2) (Easy – 5 minutes)

a. What is the formula for basic EPS?
b. How is net income available to ordinary shareholders determined?
c. How does other comprehensive income affect the calculation of EPS?

P15-3. Net income available to ordinary shareholders

(**L.O.** 15-2) (Medium – 10 minutes)

a. Discuss how declared and undeclared dividends on cumulative preferred shares and on non-cumulative preferred shares affect the computation of net income available to ordinary shareholders.
b. Explain the underlying logic for these requirements.

P15-4. Net income available to ordinary shareholders   (**L.O.** 15-2) (Easy – 5 minutes)

For the year ended December 31, 2011, Ghostly Productions Inc. earned $5,000,000. Outstanding preferred shares included $1,000,000 in 3% cumulative preferred shares issued on January 1, 2010 and $2,000,000 in 6% non-cumulative preferred shares issued on January 1, 2011. Dividends on the cumulative preferred shares were not declared in 2010.

The following are three independent situations.

a. On December 15, 2011, Ghostly declared and paid $60,000 in dividends on the 3% cumulative shares including the arrears. Ghostly also declared and paid the $120,000 dividends on the non-cumulative shares.
b. Ghostly did not declare any dividends during 2011.
c. On December 15, 2011, Ghostly declared $120,000 in dividends on the non-cumulative preferred shares, payable on January 15, 2012. Dividends on the cumulative preferred shares are neither declared nor paid.

Required:

For each of these three independent situations, determine the net income available to ordinary shareholders for the year ended December 31, 2011.

P15-5. Net income available to ordinary shareholders (**L.O.** 15-2) (Easy – 5 minutes)

For the year ended December 31, 2015, Mixed Up Productions Inc. earned $10,000,000. Outstanding preferred shares included $2,000,000 in 4% cumulative preferred shares issued on January 1, 2012 and 30,000 $100 non-cumulative preferred shares issued on January 1, 2014 that are each entitled to dividends of $6.00 per annum. Dividends were neither declared nor paid on either class of the preferred shares in 2013 or 2014.

The following are three independent situations.

a. On December 15, 2015, Mixed Up declared and paid the $160,000 dividends in arrears on the 4% cumulative preferred shares. Mixed Up also declared and paid $180,000 dividends on the non-cumulative preferred shares.
b. On December 15, 2015, Mixed Up declared and paid $140,000 of the dividends in arrears on the 4% cumulative preferred shares.
c. On December 15, 2015, Mixed Up declared $150,000 dividends on the 4% cumulative preferred shares and $120,000 in dividends on the non-cumulative preferred shares, both payable on January 15, 2016.

Required:

For each of these three independent situations, determine the net income available to ordinary shareholders for the year ended December 31, 2015.

P15-6. Weighted average number of shares outstanding (**L.O.** 15-2) (Easy – 5 minutes)

a. Describe how each of the following affects the determination of the weighted average number of shares outstanding (WASO):
   i. Treasury shares (ordinary)
   ii. Stock splits
   iii. Stock dividends
b. Provide three reasons why IFRS requires a standardized adjustment date for stock splits and stock dividends.

P15-7. Weighted average number of ordinary shares outstanding (**L.O.** 15-2) (Easy – 10 minutes)

Potatohead Corporation had 150,000 ordinary shares outstanding on January 1, 2011. On April 1, 2011, Potatohead issued an additional 80,000 shares. On July 1, 2011, Potatohead repurchased 60,000 ordinary shares and cancelled them. On October 1, 2011, Potatohead issued an additional 20,000 ordinary shares.

a. What was the weighted average number of ordinary shares outstanding in 2011?
b. Assume that on July 1, 2011 Potatohead repurchased the shares and held them as treasury shares. Will the weighted average number of ordinary shares outstanding in 2011 change from the amount in part a? Why or why not?

P15-8. Weighted average number of shares outstanding (**L.O.** 15-2) (Easy – 10 minutes)

Eggplant Solutions Inc. had 150,000 ordinary shares outstanding on January 1, 2011. On April 1, 2011, Eggplant issued an additional 80,000 shares. On June 1, 2011, the company declared and issued a 2-for-1 stock split. On July 1, 2011, Eggplant repurchased 60,000 ordinary shares and cancelled them. On October 1, 2011, Eggplant issued an additional 20,000 ordinary shares. On November 1, 2011, Eggplant declared and issued a 10% stock dividend.

Required:

What was the weighted average number of ordinary shares outstanding in 2011?

P15-9. Calculating basic EPS (**L.O.** 15-2) (Easy – 10 minutes)

Trust Me Renovations Corp. (TMRC) was incorporated on January 1, 2014. At that time it issued 100,000 ordinary shares; 10,000, $100, 4% preferred shares "A"; and 20,000, $100, 5% preferred shares "B." Net income for the year ended December 31, 2014 was $400,000. TMRC declares and pays a total of $200,000 in dividends.

The following are three independent situations.

i. Both the preferred shares series A and B are cumulative in nature. Series A must be fully paid their current entitlement as well as any arrears before any monies are paid to the Series B shareholders.
ii. The series A preferred shares are cumulative and the series B preferred shares are non-cumulative. Series A must be fully paid their current entitlement before any monies are paid to the Series B shareholders.
iii. Both the preferred shares series A and B are non-cumulative in nature. Series A must be fully paid their current entitlement before any monies are paid to the Series B shareholders.

Required:

For each of these three independent situations, compute basic EPS.

P15-10. Calculating basic EPS   (**L.O.** 15-2) (Easy – 10 minutes)

Balloons Aloft Inc. (BAI) was incorporated on January 1, 2014. At that time it issued 100,000 ordinary shares; 10,000, $100, 4% preferred shares "A"; and 20,000, $100, 5% preferred shares "B." Net income for the year ended December 31, 2014 was $300,000. BAI declares and pays a total of $100,000 in dividends.

The following are three independent situations.

i. Both the preferred shares series A and B are cumulative in nature. Series A must be fully paid their current entitlement as well as any arrears before any monies are paid to the Series B shareholders.
ii. The series A preferred shares are cumulative and the series B preferred shares are non-cumulative. Series A must be fully paid their current entitlement before any monies are paid to the Series B shareholders.
iii. Both the preferred shares series A and B are non-cumulative in nature. Series A must be fully paid their current entitlement before any monies are paid to the Series B shareholders.

Required:

For each of these three independent situations, compute basic EPS.

P15-11. Calculating basic EPS   (**L.O.** 15-2) (Easy – 10 minutes)

Umbrellas Unlimited Ltd. (UUL) was incorporated on January 1, 2014. At that time, it issued 100,000 ordinary shares; 10,000, $100, 4% preferred shares "A"; and 20,000, $100, 5% preferred shares "B." Net income for the year ended December 31, 2014 was $200,000. UUL neither declares nor pays dividends during the year.

The following are three independent situations.

i. Both the preferred shares series A and B are cumulative in nature. Series A must be fully paid their current entitlement as well as any arrears before any monies are paid to the Series B shareholders.
ii. The series A preferred shares are cumulative and the series B preferred shares are non-cumulative. Series A must be fully paid their current entitlement before any monies are paid to the Series B shareholders.
iii. Both the preferred shares series A and B are non-cumulative in nature. Series A must be fully paid their current entitlement before any monies are paid to the Series B shareholders.

Required:

For each of these three independent situations, compute basic EPS.

P15-12. Calculating basic EPS   (**L.O.** 15-2) (Medium – 15 minutes)

Burlington Bathrooms Inc. (BBI) had 100,000 ordinary shares outstanding on January 1, 2015. Transactions throughout 2015 affecting its shareholdings follow.

- February 1: BBI issued 10,000, $100, cumulative 5% preferred shares.
- March 1: BBI issued 30,000 ordinary shares.
- April 1: BBI declared and issued a 10% stock dividend on the ordinary shares.

- July 1: BBI repurchased and cancelled 20,000 ordinary shares.
- October 1: BBI declared and issued a 3-for-1 stock split on the ordinary shares.
- December 31: BBI declared and paid $50,000 in dividends on the ordinary shares.
- BBI's net income for the year ended December 31, 2015 was $250,000. Its tax rate was 40%.

Required:

a. What was BBI's weighted average number of ordinary shares outstanding in 2015?
b. What was BBI's basic EPS in 2015?
c. If the preferred shares issued on February 1, 2015 were non-cumulative, what would BBI's basic EPS for 2015 have been?

P15-13. Calculating basic EPS   (**L.O.** 15-2) (Medium – 20 minutes)

Princess and Frog Corp. was formed on January 1, 2013. At that time it issued 50,000 ordinary shares and 50,000, $100, cumulative 4% preferred shares. Subsequent transactions affecting its shareholdings follow.

2013

- September 1: Princess issued 20,000, $100, non-cumulative 6% preferred shares.
- December 1: Princess issued 10,000 ordinary shares.
- Dividends were not declared in 2013.

2014

- February 1: Princess issued 15,000 ordinary shares.
- June 1: Princess repurchased 20,000 shares and held them as treasury shares.
- July 1: Princess declared and paid $300,000 in dividends on the cumulative preferred shares, $60,000 on the non-cumulative preferred shares, and $50,000 on the ordinary shares.
- September 1: Princess reissued (sold) the 20,000 shares held in treasury.
- October 1: Princess declared and issued a 2-for-1 stock split on the ordinary shares.
- December 1: Princess declared and paid $100,000 in dividends on the cumulative preferred shares, $60,000 on the non-cumulative preferred shares, and $50,000 on the ordinary shares.
- Princess's net income for the year ended December 31, 2014 was $500,000. Its tax rate was 30%.

Required:

a. What was Princess's weighted average number of ordinary shares outstanding in **2014**?
b. What was Princess's basic EPS in **2014**?

P15-14. Calculating basic EPS   (**L.O.** 15-2) (Difficult – 30 minutes)

The ordinary-share transactions of Caltown Financing Inc. and net income for its latest three years are summarized below:

	2012	2013	2014
Net income	$300,000	$250,000	$350,000
Ordinary shares			
Outstanding January 1	100,000	125,000	103,500
Issued April 1, 2012	25,000		
Repurchased February 1, 2013		(35,000)	
15% stock dividend May 1, 2013		13,500	
Issued April 1, 2014			46,500
1.5-for-1 stock split October 1, 2014			75,000
Outstanding December 31	125,000	103,500	225,000

Caltown does not have any preferred shares outstanding.

Required:

a. Calculate the weighted average number of ordinary shares outstanding in each of 2012, 2013, and 2014.
b. Calculate basic EPS for each of 2012, 2013, and 2014.
c. Assume that Caltown includes three years of financial statement data in its annual report. Calculate the weighted average number of ordinary shares that would be used to calculate basic EPS in 2012, 2013, and 2014 as reported in Caltown's annual report for the year ended December 31, 2014.
d. Calculate basic EPS for each of 2012, 2013, and 2014 based on the weighted average number of ordinary shares outstanding that you determined in requirement c.
e. Your answers to part b and part d represent two sets of EPS statistics for the same company. Does the unadjusted or adjusted set of EPS statistics provide investors with better information for decision-making purposes? Why?

P15-15. Definitions relating to potential dilution (**L.O.** 15-3) (Easy – 5 minutes)

a. Define a simple capital structure.
b. Define a complex capital structure.
c. Define in-the-money call options.
d. Define at-the-money call options.
e. Define out-of-the-money call options.

P15-16. Differentiating between dilutive and antidilutive potential ordinary shares
(**L.O.** 15-3) (Easy – 10 minutes)

Four different companies have many similarities, including the following:

■ They all earned net income of $2,000,000 for the year ended December 31, 2017;
■ They are all subject to a 30% tax rate;
■ The average price of all four companies' ordinary shares during the year was $35; and
■ Each company had 1,000,000 ordinary shares outstanding during the year.

They do have slightly different complex capital structures, however. Specifically:

■ Company A had stock options outstanding the entire year that allowed employees to buy 10,000 ordinary shares for $32 each until December 31, 2019.
■ Company B had stock options outstanding the entire year that allowed employees to buy 5,000 ordinary shares for $30 each between January 1, 2018 and December 31, 2019.
■ Company C had $1,000,000 in 4% non-cumulative preferred shares outstanding the entire year. Each $100 share is convertible into three ordinary shares. Dividends were not declared in 2017.
■ Company D had $2,000,000 in 5% bonds maturing on December 31, 2019 that were outstanding the entire year. Each $1,000 bond is convertible into 15 ordinary shares anytime before expiry.

Required:

a. Calculate the basic EPS of the four companies.
b. Prepare a schedule that sets out the income effect, share effect, and incremental EPS for each company's security that is convertible into ordinary shares.
c. Consider each company's POS and determine whether it is dilutive or antidilutive. For company D assume that the effective rate of interest on the bonds equals the coupon rate and ignore the equity component of the conversion option.

P15-17. Diluted EPS concepts (**L.O.** 15-3, **L.O.** 15-4) (Medium – 15 minutes)

a. What is the formula for diluted EPS?
b. What are dilutive potential ordinary shares? Antidilutive potential ordinary shares? How do they each impact on the computation of diluted EPS?
c. Describe the procedure for identifying dilutive and antidilutive potential ordinary shares and calculating diluted EPS.

P15-18. **If-converted method and diluted EPS**

(**L.O.** 15-3, **L.O.** 15-4) (Medium – 20 minutes)

The net income for Rip's Curling Corp. for the year ended December 31, 2015 was $700,000. Rip had 50,000 ordinary shares outstanding at the beginning of the year. Rip declared and distributed a 3-for-1 stock split on May 1, 2015 and issued (sold) 30,000 ordinary shares on November 1, 2015. Select details of Rip's liabilities and equities follow:

- Bonds A—$1,000,000, 6%, 10-year, semi-annual bonds issued on July 1, 2015. At the option of the holder, each $1,000 bond can be converted into 14 ordinary shares at any time before expiry.
- Bonds B—$1,000,000, 5%, semi-annual bonds maturing September 30, 2019. The owners of the bonds elect to convert them into 12,000 ordinary shares on December 1, 2015.
- 100,000 cumulative preferred shares that are each entitled to dividends of $2.00 per annum. Dividends are not declared in 2015.

Rip's corporate tax rate was 40%. The recorded conversion factor for the convertible bonds has already been adjusted for the stock split.

Required:

Assuming that the effective rate of interest on the bonds equals the coupon rate:

a. Calculate Rip's basic earnings per share for 2015.
b. Prepare a schedule that sets out the income effect, share effect, and incremental EPS for each security that is convertible into ordinary shares. Rank the potential ordinary shares by their dilutiveness.
c. Calculate Rip's diluted earnings per share for 2015.

P15-19. **Treasury stock method**   (**L.O.** 15-4) (Easy – 10 minutes)

a. What is the treasury stock method and when is it used?
b. Briefly describe the application of the treasury stock method.
c. What does the treasury stock method assume about the exercise date? What is the exception to the rule with respect to the assumed exercise date? What alternative procedure is employed in this instance?

P15-20. **Treasury stock method**   (**L.O.** 15-4) (Easy – 10 minutes)

During 2015, Fun with Numbers Inc. (FWNI) had four series of employee stock options outstanding, the details of which follow:

1. Options A entitle employees to purchase 10,000 ordinary shares for $19.00 each. This series of options was granted on February 1, 2013 and expires on December 31, 2017.
2. Options B entitle employees to purchase 15,000 ordinary shares for $20.00 each. This series of options was granted on June 1, 2012 and expires on December 31, 2016.
3. Options C entitle employees to purchase 20,000 ordinary shares for $21.00 each. This series of options was granted on April 1, 2014 and expires on December 31, 2018.
4. Options D entitle employees to purchase 20,000 ordinary shares for $18.00 each. This series of options was granted on April 1, 2015 and expires on December 31, 2018.

The average market price of FWNI's ordinary shares for the year ended December 31, 2015 was $20.00.

Required:

a. For each of the options series, indicate whether they are dilutive or antidilutive in nature in 2015 and provide the reason why.
b. For each of the options series that are dilutive, determine the number of incremental shares to be notionally issued.
c. For each of the options series determine the incremental EPS.

P15-21. Treasury stock method   (**L.O.** 15-3, **L.O.** 15-4) (Medium – 10 minutes)

I Am Free Corp. has three stock option plans outstanding on December 31, 2015. They provide the holders with the following entitlements:

i. Stock option A—The holders may purchase 30,000 ordinary shares at any time on or before December 31, 2019 for $20 each.
ii. Stock option B—The holders may purchase 6,000 ordinary shares at any time on or before December 31, 2016 for $22 each. From January 1, 2017 to December 31, 2019 the holders may purchase 10,000 ordinary shares for $25 each.
iii. Stock option C—The holders may purchase 5,000 ordinary shares at any time on or before December 31, 2017 for $26 each.

The average price of ordinary shares in 2015 was $24. I Am Free's basic EPS from continuing operations for the year was $1.22.

Required:

a. Which of the stock options are dilutive and which are antidilutive in 2015? What is the rule in this respect?
b. Assuming that all three option plans have been in place the entire year, for each plan, determine the incremental number of shares, if any, that need to be considered for diluted EPS purposes.
c. Assume that stock option A was issued on April 1, 2015. Does this change your answer to part b? If so, what is the revised number of incremental shares for option A that need to be considered for diluted EPS purposes?

P15-22. Treasury stock method   (**L.O.** 15-3, **L.O.** 15-4) (Medium – 10 minutes)

During 2015, Fuzzy Pandas Inc. (FPI) had three series of employee stock options outstanding, details of which follow:

1. Options A entitle employees to purchase 10,000 ordinary shares for $22.00 each. This series of options was granted on February 1, 2013 and expires on June 30, 2015.
2. Options B entitle employees to purchase 15,000 ordinary shares for $26.00 each until December 31, 2016 and $23.00 thereafter. This series of options was granted on June 1, 2012 and expires on December 31, 2019.
3. Options C entitle employees to purchase 20,000 ordinary shares for $21.00 each. This series of options was granted on April 1, 2015 and expires on December 31, 2018.

The average market price of FPI's ordinary shares for the year ended December 31, 2015 was $25.00.

Required:

a. For each of the options series, indicate whether they are dilutive or antidilutive in nature in 2015 and provide the reason why.
b. For each of the options series that are dilutive, determine the number of incremental shares to be notionally issued.

P15-23. Treasury stock method   (**L.O.** 15-3, **L.O.** 15-4) (Medium – 15 minutes)

In 2014, TC Ash Inc.'s net income was $150,000. Ash had 100,000 ordinary shares outstanding at year-end. There were two ordinary share transactions during the year: i) Ash declared and distributed a 2-for-1 stock split on March 1, 2014; and ii) Option C was exercised on April 1, 2014. Details of Ash's stock option plans follow:

- Option A entitles employees to purchase 10,000 ordinary shares for $15.00 each. This option was granted during 2013 and expires in 2016.
- Option B entitles employees to purchase 10,000 ordinary shares for $25.00 each. This option was granted on July 1, 2014 and expires in 2017.
- Option C entitles employees to purchase 10,000 ordinary shares for $18.00 each. This option was granted during 2012 and was exercised on April 1, 2014.
- Option D entitles employees to purchase 10,000 ordinary shares for $16.00 each. This option was granted on September 1, 2014 and expires in 2017.

The average market price of Ash's ordinary shares for the year is $20.00. Ash does not have any preferred shares or convertible bonds outstanding. The recorded exercise prices and number of shares that can be acquired under the stock option plans have already been adjusted for the stock split.

Required:

a. Calculate Ash's basic earnings per share for the year ended December 31, 2014.
b. Calculate Ash's diluted earnings per share for the year ended December 31, 2014.

P15-24. Calculating diluted EPS   (**L.O.** 15-4) (Medium – 10 minutes)

Broken Man Inc. had 100,000 ordinary shares outstanding in all of 2013. On January 1, 2011, Broken issued at par $500,000 in 7% bonds maturing on January 1, 2019. Each $1,000 bond is convertible into 30 ordinary shares. Assume that the effective interest rate is 7%.

There are 10,000 outstanding cumulative preferred shares that are each entitled to an annual dividend of $0.32. Dividends were not declared or paid during 2013. Each preferred share is convertible into two ordinary shares.

Broken's net income for the year ended December 31, 2013 was $150,000. Its income tax rate was 25%.

Required:

a. Calculate Broken's basic EPS for 2013.
b. Are the convertible bonds dilutive or antidilutive in nature? The convertible preferred shares?
c. Calculate Broken's diluted EPS for 2013.

P15-25. Calculating basic and diluted EPS
(**L.O.** 15-2, **L.O.** 15-3, **L.O.** 15-4) (Medium – 15 minutes)

Select information for George's Dive Adventures Corp. (GDAC) follows.

- GDAC earned net income of $4,000,000 for the year ended December 31, 2016.
- GDAC was subject to a 30% tax rate.
- GDAC had 2,000,000 ordinary shares outstanding during the entire year; their average market price was $17.
- GDAC had $1,000,000 in 5% non-cumulative preferred shares outstanding during the entire year. Each $100 share is convertible into two ordinary shares.
- GDAC declared and paid the stated dividend on the preferred shares as well as $400,000 of dividends on the ordinary shares.
- GDAC had series A stock options outstanding the entire year that allowed employees to buy 5,000 ordinary shares for $15 each until December 31, 2019.
- GDAC had series B stock options outstanding the entire year that allowed employees to buy 10,000 ordinary shares for $20 each until December 31, 2019.
- GDAC had $5,000,000 in 7% bonds maturing on December 31, 2019 that were outstanding the entire year. Each $1,000 bond is convertible into 40 ordinary shares anytime before expiry.

Assume that the effective rate of interest on the bonds equals the coupon rate, and ignore the equity component of the conversion option.

Required:

a. Calculate GDAC's basic EPS for the year ended December 31, 2016.
b. Prepare a schedule that sets out the income effect, share effect, and incremental EPS for each security that is convertible into ordinary shares. Rank order the shares by their dilutiveness.
c. Calculate GDAC's diluted EPS for the year ended December 31, 2016.

P15-26. Calculating basic and diluted EPS

(**L.O.** 15-2, **L.O.** 15-3, **L.O.** 15-4) (Medium – 20 minutes)

The following information is available for Jill's Emporium Ltd., which reports its financial results in accordance with IFRS:

Net income for 2018	$ 800,000
Income tax rate during 2018	32%
Liabilities and equity outstanding as at December 31, 2018	
8% bonds	$1,000,000
7% convertible bonds—each $1,000 bond is convertible into 7.5 ordinary shares	$ 850,000
5% non-cumulative preferred shares	$ 500,000
4% cumulative preferred shares—each $100 preferred share is convertible into four ordinary shares	$ 400,000
Ordinary shares	$1,000,000

The bonds and preferred shares were outstanding for the entire year.

Dividends were not declared on either series of the preferred shares in 2018.

	Activity	Ordinary shares outstanding
January 1, 2018	Opening balance	50,000
March 1, 2018	20% stock dividend	60,000
June 1, 2018	2-for-1 stock split	120,000
December 1, 2018	Repurchased 30,000 shares	90,000

Required:
a. Compute Jill's basic EPS for the year ended December 31, 2018.
b. Prepare a schedule that sets out the income effect, share effect, and incremental EPS for each security that is convertible into ordinary shares. Rank the potential ordinary shares by their dilutiveness.
c. Compute Jill's diluted EPS for the year ended December 31, 2018.

P15-27. Calculating basic and diluted EPS

(**L.O.** 15-2, **L.O.** 15-3, **L.O.** 15-4) (Medium – 20 minutes)

The following information is available for Bobby's Baubles Corp. that reports its financial results in accordance with IFRS.

Net income for 2016	$500,000
Income tax rate during 2016	35%
Liabilities and equity outstanding as at December 31, 2016	
6% convertible bonds—each $1,000 bond is convertible into 8 ordinary shares	$500,000
5% convertible bonds—each $1,000 bond is convertible into 6 ordinary shares	$700,000
4% cumulative preferred shares—each $100 preferred share is convertible into 5 ordinary shares	$200,000
Ordinary shares	$500,000

The bonds and preferred shares were outstanding for the entire year

Dividends were not declared on the preferred shares in 2015

$16,000 dividends were declared and paid on the preferred shares in 2016

	Activity	Ordinary shares outstanding
January 1, 2016	Opening balance	50,000
April 1, 2016	Sold 20,000 shares	70,000
May 1, 2016	Repurchased 10,000 shares	60,000
December 1, 2016	Sold 20,000 shares	80,000

Required:

a. Compute Bobby's basic EPS for the year ended December 31, 2016.
b. Prepare a schedule that sets out the income effect, share effect, and incremental EPS for each security that is convertible into ordinary shares. Rank the potential ordinary shares by their dilutiveness.
c. Compute Bobby's diluted EPS for the year ended December 31, 2016.
d. Show the required presentation of the EPS data on the income statement.

P15-28. Calculating basic and diluted EPS (comprehensive)
(**L.O.** 15-2, **L.O.** 15-3, **L.O.** 15-4) (Difficult – 30 minutes)

Select details of Kingston Objects Inc.'s capital structure as at January 1, 2014 follow:

- 200,000 ordinary shares issued and outstanding
- 100,000 cumulative preferred shares "A" that are each entitled to dividends of $4.00 per annum
- 50,000, $100 non-cumulative shares "B" with a stated dividend rate of 3% per annum. At the option of the holder, each preferred share can be converted into two ordinary shares on December 31, 2019
- Bonds A—$1,000,000, 6%, semi-annual bonds maturing December 31, 2018
- Bonds B—$2,000,000, 5%, semi-annual bonds maturing June 30, 2024. At the option of the holder, each $1,000 bond can be converted into 10 ordinary shares at any time between January 1, 2019 and December 31, 2019
- Bonds C—$500,000, 3%, semi-annual bonds maturing December 31, 2019. At the option of the holder, each $1,000 bond can be converted into 8 ordinary shares
- Option A—grants the holder the right to purchase 10,000 ordinary shares at any time before December 31, 2017 for $20 per share
- Option B—grants the holder the right to purchase 5,000 ordinary shares for $12 per share. The option expires on December 31, 2015

During the year Kingston issued ordinary shares as follows:

- March 1, 2014—issued (sold) 20,000 ordinary shares
- October 1, 2014—issued (sold) 10,000 ordinary shares
- December 1, 2014—declared and distributed a 20% stock dividend

Kingston was subject to a 30% tax rate. Its net income for the year ended December 31, 2014 totalled $1,339,000. During the year, Kingston declared and paid the stated dividends on both classes of preferred shares as well as $200,000 of dividends on its ordinary shares. The average market rate in 2014 for Kingston's ordinary shares was $15.

The recorded exercise prices and number of shares under the stock options plans that can be acquired have already been adjusted for the stock dividend. Similarly, the recorded conversion factor for the convertible bonds and preferred shares have already been adjusted for the stock dividend.

Assume that the effective rate of interest on the bonds equals the coupon rate and ignore the equity component of the conversion option.

Required:

a. Calculate Kingston's basic EPS for the year ended December 31, 2014.
b. Prepare a schedule that sets out the income effect, share effect, and incremental EPS for each security that is convertible into ordinary shares. Rank the potential ordinary shares by their dilutiveness.
c. Calculate Kingston's diluted EPS for the year ended December 31, 2014.

P15-29. EPS when there are discontinued operations

(**L.O.** 15-2, **L.O.** 15-3, **L.O.** 15-4) (Difficult – 30 minutes)

Four independent situations follow:

	Situation 1	Situation 2	Situation 3	Situation 4
Earnings (loss) from continuing operations	$500,000	$(500,000)	$ (50,000)	$ 50,000
Earnings (loss) from discontinued operations	$100,000	$ 100,000	$100,000	$(100,000)
Net income (loss)	$600,000	$(400,000)	$ 50,000	$ (50,000)
Weighted average number of ordinary shares outstanding	100,000	100,000	100,000	100,000
Preference shares	None outstanding	None outstanding	None outstanding	None outstanding
Potential ordinary shares	10,000 options on ordinary shares—exercise price $20, average market price $25	10,000 options on ordinary shares—exercise price $20, average market price $25	10,000 options on ordinary shares—exercise price $20, average market price $25	10,000 options on ordinary shares—exercise price $20, average market price $25

Required:

a. For each of the four independent situations, compute basic earnings per share and diluted earnings per share from each of continuing operations, discontinued operations, and net income.

b. Summarize IFRS requirements with respect to determining diluted EPS when there is a loss from continuing operations.

c. Summarize IFRS requirements with respect to determining diluted EPS when there is a net loss; however, earnings from continuing operations is positive.

d. Describe the presentation requirement for EPS including permissible alternatives.

P15-30. Calculating basic and diluted EPS (comprehensive)

(**L.O.** 15-2, **L.O.** 15-3, **L.O.** 15-4) (Difficult – 35 minutes)

Select details of Simple Objects Inc.'s capital structure as at January 1, 2011 follow.

■ 300,000 ordinary shares were issued; 250,000 were outstanding

■ Bonds A—$1,000,000, 3%, semi-annual bonds maturing December 31, 2019. At the option of the holder, each $1,000 bond can be converted into seven ordinary shares at any time prior to maturity.

■ Bonds B—$2,000,000, 5%, semi-annual bonds maturing December 31, 2017. At the option of the holder, each $1,000 bond can be converted into six ordinary shares at any time prior to maturity.

■ 10,000 non-cumulative preferred shares "A" that are each entitled to dividends of $3.00 per annum. At the option of the holder, each preferred share can be converted into two ordinary shares.

■ 100,000, $100 non-cumulative shares "B" with a stated dividend rate of 4% per annum. At the option of the holder, each preferred share can be converted into three ordinary shares.

■ Employee stock option—grants the holder the right to purchase 8,000 ordinary shares at any time before December 31, 2015 for $10 per share.

■ Warrant—grants the holder the right to purchase 5,000 ordinary shares for $8 per share. The warrant, which can be exercised at any time, expires on December 31, 2017.

During the year Simple Objects issued and redeemed ordinary shares as follows.

- March 1, 2011—declared and issued a 2-for-1 stock split
- July 1, 2011—sold 20,000 ordinary shares from treasury
- September 1, 2011—repurchased 10,000 ordinary shares and held them as treasury shares
- October 1, 2011—sold 30,000 ordinary shares from treasury

Simple was subject to a 25% tax rate. Its net income for the year ended December 31, 2011 totalled $3,300,000. In 2011 the average market rate for Simple's ordinary shares was $12.

Simple declared dividends totalling $500,000 on December 15, **2010** payable on January 15, **2011**. Of the $500,000, $30,000 pertained to the preferred "A" shares; $400,000 related to the preferred "B" shares; with the balance being allocated to the ordinary shares. Dividends were not declared in 2011.

The recorded exercise prices and number of shares under the stock options plans that can be acquired have already been adjusted for the stock split. Similarly, the recorded conversion factors for the convertible bonds and preferred shares have already been adjusted for the stock split.

Assume that the effective rate of interest on the bonds equals the coupon rate, and ignore the equity component of the conversion option.

Required:

a. Calculate Simple's basic EPS for the year ended December 31, 2011.
b. Prepare a schedule that sets out the income effect, share effect, and incremental EPS for each security that is convertible into ordinary shares. Rank the potential ordinary shares by their dilutiveness.
c. Calculate Simple's diluted EPS for the year ended December 31, 2011.

J. MINI-CASES

CASE 1
XYZ Company
(20 minutes)[9]

XYZ, a public company, is required to disclose earnings per share information in its financial statements for the year ended December 31, 2010. The facts about XYZ's situation are as follows:

- At the beginning of fiscal 2010, 450,000 ordinary shares, issued for $5.75 million, were outstanding. The authorized number of ordinary shares is 1 million. On January 1, 2010, 50,000 10% cumulative preferred shares were also outstanding. They had been issued for $500,000.
- On September 30, 2010, XYZ issued 100,000 ordinary shares for $1.5 million cash.
- On January 15, 2011, XYZ made a private share placement of 25,000 ordinary shares, raising $350,000 cash.
- XYZ reported net income of $2.5 million for the year ended December 31, 2010.
- Managers of XYZ hold options to purchase 20,000 ordinary shares of XYZ at a price of $11.50 per share. The options expire on July 31, 2013.
- At January 1, 2010, XYZ had outstanding $1 million of 8% convertible bonds ($1,000 face value), with interest payable on June 30 and December 31 of each year. Each bond is convertible into 65 ordinary shares at the option of the holder, before December 31, 2015. On June 30, 2010, $400,000 of the bonds were converted.
- XYZ has an effective tax rate of 40% and has an average after-tax rate of return of 10%. The average market rate in 2010 for XYZ's ordinary shares was $13.

Required:

Calculate the basic and diluted earnings per share figures for 2010.

CASE 2
Mom and Dot Reid Inc.
(45 minutes)

Mom and Dot Reid Inc. [MDRI] is a Canadian company listed on the Toronto Stock Exchange that manufactures component parts for automobiles. MDRI, like many public companies, has various stock option plans for its executives and employees. Charlotte Ash, the CEO of MDRI, is scheduled to retire on March 31, 2015. Charlotte is concerned about the recent drop in the company's share price as her various stock options all expire on her retirement date. While Ms. Ash is a brilliant ideas person and has spearheaded the launch of many successful new products, her financial savvy is mediocre at best.

Charlotte has heard that a firm's stock price is affected to some degree by both the reported earnings per share (EPS) and the magnitude of the change from the previous year. It is now September 15, 2014 and Charlotte is contemplating ways of increasing MDRI's reported EPS for the year ending December 31, 2014 so as to improve the company's share price before she retires. In this respect, Charlotte has a number of proposals summarized below and has called you, Terri Fisher, a certified general accountant and the CFO of MDRI, into her office to solicit your input. To prepare for the meeting you have summarized MDRI's currently projected EPS and other pertinent information as set out in Exhibit I below.

Charlotte's proposals

1. MDRI could purchase five million of its own ordinary shares on the open market for $325 million and retire them. While the company would have to borrow to do this, it does have several underutilized credit facilities with its banking consortium and accessing the necessary funds would not be difficult.
2. MDRI has $300 million in 3% bonds outstanding that mature in three years. The bonds were issued several years ago at par when interest rates were at historical lows. Rates have recently risen due to inflationary pressures and as such Charlotte believes that the bonds can be redeemed on the open market for about $276 million. Her

---

9. Adapted with permission from The Canadian Institute of Chartered Accountants, Toronto, Canada. Any changes to the original material are the sole responsibility of the author and have not been reviewed or endorsed by the CICA.

thoughts are that the $24 million gain on redemption will improve earnings and hence EPS. Charlotte suggests that the redemption be financed by issuing a new series of bonds at the current market rate of 6%.

3. MDRI closed and sold one of its plants during the year suffering a pre-tax loss of $20 million. The autonomously run plant was one of three plants located in Windsor, Ontario that produced automobile engines. It was closed due to a prolonged drop in demand due to stagnant new car sales. Charlotte suggests that this loss be classified as arising from discontinued operations so as to remove the loss from "core" EPS.

4. MDRI has an opportunity to sell one of its plants for a pre-tax gain of $50 million providing that they irrevocably agree to lease back the property for a 20-year period. The lease rates would initially be market based and subsequently adjusted every four years to reflect the change in the Consumer Price Index during the intervening period. If MDRI enters into this transaction, it will close on December 31, 2014.

5. MDRI could complete a reverse stock split in which it would issue one new ordinary share for each two old ordinary shares currently outstanding. Charlotte knows that EPS measures income available to the ordinary shareholders divided by the weighted average number of ordinary shares outstanding and expects that reducing the number of outstanding shares will increase the reported EPS.

After the meeting you reflect on the legitimacy of the proposals, which you know have not been discussed with the board of directors.

Required:

Prepare a memo addressed to Charlotte Ash analyzing the effect on EPS for each of her proposals. Discuss any concerns that you may have with respect to the manner in which Charlotte has proposed to increase EPS.

Exhibit I	MDRI Projected Earnings per Share for the year ending December 31, 2014	
	Actual 2013	**Projected 2014 (existing)**
Basic EPS		
Net income		$140,000,000
Preferred dividends		10,000,000
Net income available to ordinary shareholders		$130,000,000
Weighted average number of ordinary shares outstanding (WASO)		40,000,000
Basic EPS	$3.35	$ 3.25
Corporate income tax rate		30%
MDRI stock price 09/15/2014		65.00
Interest rate on the bank consortium credit facilities		5%

Refer to Appendix B for the British Airways PLC financial statements for the year ended March 31, 2009.

Required:

a. Does the British Airways Group have potential ordinary shares in its capital structure? How can you quickly determine this?

b. Identify the type(s) of potential ordinary shares that the British Airways Group has outstanding.

c. British Airways Group's 2009 basic and diluted earnings per share are the same. Explain why this is the case.

CASE 3
British Airways PLC
(20 minutes)

CHAPTER 16

Accounting for Income Taxes

The Canadian Press Images/Francis Vachon

For many decades, Canadian corporations have reported on their balance sheets large amounts of liabilities for "deferred taxes" or "future income taxes." These amounts had surpassed the $100 billion mark by 2006, even counting only those corporations that are publicly traded, and the amount continues to grow.[1] To put this figure in context, total corporate income taxes collected by the federal and provincial governments are about $50 billion per year for all corporations, public and private. From time to time, politicians cite these figures, in aggregate and for specific corporations, to suggest that the government is providing "corporate welfare" to companies by allowing them to defer tax payments that are owing to the government.

Is this interpretation justified? What are deferred taxes and future income taxes that appear on companies' balance sheets? What causes these amounts to arise and build up to such large magnitudes? If companies report these amounts as liabilities on the balance sheet, are they taxes owing to the government and not yet paid?

---

1. Amount computed from Compustat database.

CONTENTS

A. INTRODUCTION

Accounting for income taxes is a complex topic that involves the interaction of financial reporting and tax reporting. The complexity arises because financial reporting rules differ from tax rules, resulting in accounting income that differs from taxable income. While we will not identify every one of these differences, we can say that, as a rule of thumb, tax rules tend to more closely follow cash flows than accrual accounting. The tendency for this difference exists because the fair enforcement of laws in general requires a higher standard of verifiability (reliability) in comparison to the degree of reliability required for financial reporting.

To see the difference in financial and tax reporting, consider Tahsis Company. In each of 2011 and 2012, the company records $100,000 of revenue on long-term contracts using the percentage-of-completion method for financial reporting purposes (see Chapter 4 for this method of revenue recognition). Meanwhile, for tax purposes, the company uses the completed contract method and recorded revenue of $80,000 and $120,000 for 2011 and 2012, respectively. For simplicity of illustration, assume that Tahsis incurs no expenses other than income taxes. If Tahsis faces a tax rate of 40%, it would have a tax payable for the year 2011 of $32,000 (= 40\% \times \$80,000)$. *If one were to account only for the amount of taxes payable,* the journal entry would be as follows:

Exhibit 16-1	Journal entry to record Tahsis Company's income tax payable in 2011	
Dr. Income tax expense	32,000	
Cr. Income tax payable		32,000

taxes payable method A method that records an amount for income tax expense equal to the tax payments for the current period.

We call the method just illustrated the **taxes payable method**, which records an amount for income tax expense equal to the tax payments required for the fiscal year. However, this method has an obvious problem: there is a mismatch of income and income tax expense. We can see this mismatch by looking at the amounts Tahsis would report under this method for 2011 and 2012, assuming no other transactions in either year:

Exhibit 16-2	Reporting outcome using the taxes payable method for Tahsis Company		
	2011	**2012**	**Total**
Income before tax	$100,000	$100,000	$200,000
Income tax expense*	(32,000)	(48,000)	(80,000)
Net income	$ 68,000	$ 52,000	$120,000
Effective tax rate (income tax expense ÷ income before tax)	32%	48%	40%

*40% of taxable income of $80,000 and $120,000 in 2011 and 2012, respectively.

As shown in Exhibit 16-2, even though the amount of income before tax is the same in both years, the taxes payable method results in different amounts of income tax expense, so there is poor matching of tax expense to the revenue recognized in the period. The tax expense is $32,000 for $100,000 of pre-tax income in 2011—representing a rate of only 32%. The next year, the $48,000 of income tax results in an effective tax rate of 48%, since the tax payable is based on $120,000 of taxable income. Only when both years are combined do we see the expected result of 40% for the tax rate.

The difference in timing between (i) the accrual accounting income recognized for financial reporting and (ii) income recognized for tax purposes is the crux of the problem in accounting for income taxes. The next section addresses this issue conceptually. After that, we will discuss the specific approaches permitted by accounting standards.

This chapter addresses only issues related to the accounting for taxes based on income. Other government levies such as sales tax, carbon tax, goods and services tax, and import tax are outside the scope of this chapter.

B. METHODS OF ACCOUNTING FOR INCOME TAXES

L.O. 16-1. Describe the conceptual differences among the three methods of accounting for income taxes and apply the taxes payable method under ASPE.

Conceptually, there are three possible ways to account for income taxes:

i. taxes payable method;
ii. income statement approach (deferral method); and
iii. balance sheet approach (accrual method).

The latter two methods are considered "tax allocation" approaches. We will discuss each of these three methods in more detail below.

1. Taxes payable method

This is the simplest method of accounting for income taxes. The introductory section has already described the essence of this approach, which is to record the income statement expense for income taxes and the corresponding liability according to the amount payable to the tax authorities. In Canada, we have income tax assessed at both the federal and provincial levels, so the amount of income taxes needs to account for both levels of tax.

It is also important to note that the label "taxes payable method" should not be interpreted too literally. If a company makes installment payments on its income taxes during the year, the amount of tax payment due when it files its tax return at the end of a year could be very small or even negative (i.e., the company is entitled to a refund because its installments exceeded the tax due). The amount of tax expense recorded is the sum of the installments and the final payment or refund expected when the enterprise files its tax return.

For example, if Tahsis Company, which has a tax payable of $32,000 for 2011, had paid tax installments totalling $30,000 during 2011, then it would need to pay just the final $2,000 when it files its tax return. The journal entries would be as follows:

Exhibit 16-3	Journal entries to record Tahsis Company's income taxes using the taxes payable method		
During 2011	Dr. Income tax installments (asset)	30,000	
	Cr. Cash		30,000
Dec. 31, 2011	Dr. Income tax expense	32,000	
	Cr. Income tax installments		30,000
	Cr. Income tax payable		2,000

The taxes payable method is simple and the least costly of the three methods. There is no need to make further computations or to keep track of numerous other figures required for the other methods discussed below. However, this method does not satisfy the matching principle, as illustrated in Exhibit 16-2, and it potentially omits significant assets and liabilities for future taxes. The other two methods below will address these problems.

2. Tax allocation methods

As mentioned in the introduction, income for financial reporting purposes (**accounting income**) will generally differ from income for tax purposes (**taxable income**). As a result, the amount of income taxes payable derived from taxable income can be higher or lower than the amount of tax expense attributable to the amount of income reported on the *income statement* for a particular year. On a cumulative basis, the *balance sheet* amount of assets and liabilities will also differ between the tax report and accounting reports.

Conceptually, there are two methods to help account for these temporary differences between accounting income and taxable income. (Section C below will define temporary differences precisely.) The **deferral method** focuses on obtaining the income statement value for income tax expense that best matches the amount of income recognized for the year. In contrast, the **accrual method** focuses on obtaining the balance sheet value for the income tax liability (or asset)

accounting income The amount of income (before subtracting income tax) recognized for financial reporting purposes. Contrast with **taxable income**.

taxable income The amount of income recognized for tax purposes used to compute taxes payable; contrast with **accounting income**.

deferral method (of accounting for income tax) Focuses on obtaining the income statement value for income tax expense that best matches the amount of income recognized for the year.

accrual method (of accounting for income tax) Focuses on obtaining the balance sheet value for the income tax liability (or asset) that best reflects the assets and liabilities recognized on the balance sheet.

that best reflects the assets and liabilities recognized on the balance sheet. Collectively, these two methods are called tax allocation methods because they allocate the tax effects to periods in which the enterprise recognizes the related financial reporting amounts (in contrast to the taxes payable method, which simply records the tax effect in the period the tax is payable).

a. Income statement approach—Deferral method

The deferral method focuses on the income statement in order to best match the income tax expense to the revenues, expenses, gains, and losses recognized in that period, regardless of when the cash flows occur. Take the example of Tahsis Company given in the introduction. Recall that Tahsis recognized $100,000 of accounting income in 2011, but the company reported only $80,000 of taxable income. Since the tax rate is 40%, the income tax expense that best matches this amount of accounting income is $100,000 × 40% = $40,000. However, the tax payable due is 40% × $80,000 = $32,000. The $8,000 difference between the tax expense and tax payable goes to an account for deferred tax (which may be an asset or liability depending on the circumstance).

Exhibit 16-4	Journal entry to record Tahsis Company's income tax expense under the deferral method[2]	
Dr. Income tax expense[2] (40% × $100,000)	40,000	
Cr. Deferred tax liability (balancing figure)		8,000
Cr. Income tax payable (40% × $80,000)		32,000

In the following year, Tahsis also reports $100,000 of accounting income and the $40,000 (= 40% × $100,000) of tax expense. Thus, the result of the deferral method on the income statement is as follows (with taxes payable method also shown for comparison):

Exhibit 16-5	Reporting outcome using the deferral method for Tahsis Company (with taxes payable method also shown for comparison)		
Deferral method	**2011**	**2012**	**Total**
Income before tax	$100,000	$100,000	$200,000
Income tax expense	(40,000)	(40,000)	(80,000)
Net income	$ 60,000	$ 60,000	$120,000
Effective tax rate (income tax expense/income before tax)	40%	40%	40%
Taxes payable method (see Exhibit 16-2)	**2011**	**2012**	**Total**
Income before tax	$100,000	$100,000	$200,000
Income tax expense	(32,000)	(48,000)	(80,000)
Net income	$ 68,000	$ 52,000	$120,000
Effective tax rate (income tax expense/income before tax)	32%	48%	40%

2. At this point, we do not separate this income tax expense into its current and deferred components. We will make that distinction later in this chapter.

Notice that the deferral method produces an effective tax rate that is consistently 40% in both years, which is the rate expected based on the assumed statutory tax rate. In contrast, the taxes payable method results in fluctuating tax rates even though the statutory rate remains constant. Thus, the deferral method better matches the income tax expense to the amount of income recorded because it applies the appropriate current tax rate to the income recognized.

b. Balance sheet approach—Accrual method

As noted before, the accrual method focuses on obtaining the balance sheet value for the tax liability (or asset) that best reflects the assets and liabilities recognized on the balance sheet. When there are no changes in tax rates, the accrual method and the deferral method both produce the same results, although the sequence of logic and computations differ.

To illustrate, again consider Tahsis Company. The company recorded $100,000 of revenue on its construction contracts in 2011 using the percentage of completion method, but only $80,000 worth was completed in the year. Further assume that the company invoices its clients at the end of each contract. The following journal entry summaries the entries that would have been made during 2011:

Exhibit 16-6	Journal entry to record Tahsis Company's construction contracts	
Dr. Cash and accounts receivable	80,000	
Dr. Construction in progress (inventory)	20,000	
Cr. Revenue on long-term contracts		100,000

As a result, $20,000 remains in inventory at year-end. The balance sheet for Tahsis at December 31, 2011 before taking account of tax effects would be as follows:

Exhibit 16-7	Balance sheet for Tahsis Company as at December 31, 2011 before accounting for income tax
Cash and accounts receivable	$ 80,000
Construction in progress	20,000
Total assets	$100,000
Equity (retained earnings)	$100,000
Total liabilities and equity	$100,000

The accrual method computes the amount of taxes that relate to the construction in progress of $20,000. At a tax rate of 40%, this amount is $8,000. Furthermore, this amount is a liability, because when the $20,000 of inventory is later recognized into income in 2012, there will be tax payable of $8,000.

Under the accrual method, Tahsis would record the following journal entry for income taxes:

Exhibit 16-8	Journal entry to record Tahsis Company's income tax expense under the accrual method	
Dr. Income tax expense (balancing figure)	40,000	
Cr. Deferred tax liability (40% × $20,000)		8,000
Cr. Income tax payable (40% × $80,000)		32,000

Notice that this entry looks exactly the same as the one shown in Exhibit 16-4. The only difference is the order in which the figures are computed. The accrual method just described computes the balance sheet amount first (the $8,000 for the deferred tax liability), leaving the income statement expense as the residual "plug" figure; the deferral method calculation goes in the opposite order.

While the results of the deferral and accrual methods are the same for the example just illustrated, the two methods are equal only when tax rates remain constant from year to year. When tax rates change, the two methods will produce different results. The difference in results arises because when there is a change in tax rates:

■ the deferral method focuses on the income statement and applies the new tax rate to the current year's income only and ignores the effect on accumulated balances; whereas

■ the accrual method focuses on the balance sheet and applies the new tax rate to the accumulated tax amounts on the balance sheet as well as any new amounts for the current year.

To illustrate, we take the example of Tahsis Company and modify it slightly. As before, assume the company recorded $100,000 in revenue in 2011 and the tax rate in 2011 was 40%. Now also assume that the company had a deferred tax liability of $35,000 at the end of the prior year (2010). This liability was recorded when the tax rate was 35%. Under the deferral method, the journal entry to record income taxes would be no different from that shown in Exhibit 16-4, which is as follows.

Exhibit 16-9	Journal entry to record Tahsis Company's income tax expense under the deferral method	
Dr. Income tax expense (40% × $100,000)	40,000	
Cr. Deferred tax asset (balancing figure)		8,000
Cr. Income tax payable (40% × $80,000)		32,000

There is no change in the journal entry from that previously recorded because the deferral method does not reflect the effect of the change in tax rate from 35% to 40% on any balances carried forward from 2010 into 2011.

In contrast, under the accrual method, the deferred tax liability of $35,000 needs to be revalued from the original tax rate of 35% to the new tax rate of 40%. At the old tax rate of 35%, the $35,000 deferred tax liability corresponds to a $100,000 taxable temporary difference. At the new tax rate of 40%, this temporary difference translates into a $40,000 liability. Thus, the change in tax rate increases the deferred tax liability by $5,000, from $35,000 to $40,000. (A general formula for computing the effect of tax rate changes will follow in Section D.)

For Tahsis, the journal entry to record its tax expense in 2011, including the effect of the tax rate change, would be as follows:

Exhibit 16-10	Journal entry to record Tahsis Company's income tax expense under the accrual method	
Dr. Income tax expense (balancing figure)	45,000	
Cr. Deferred tax liability (40% × $20,000)		8,000
Cr. Deferred tax liability ($40,000 − $35,000)		5,000
Cr. Income tax payable (40% × $80,000)		32,000

As a result of the increase in deferred tax liability by $5,000, the income tax expense also increases by that amount, going from $40,000 to $45,000. The resulting effective tax rate is then $45,000/$100,000 = 45%, which is higher than the 40% prevailing tax rate for 2011.

It is often useful to separate the above journal entry into two separate entries to reflect the different sources of the income tax expense. The following shows journal entries that separate out the effect of the tax rate change from the effect of the current-year temporary difference:

Exhibit 16-11	Separate journal entries for temporary differences and tax rate change for Tahsis Company	
Dr. Income tax expense	40,000	
Cr. Deferred tax liability (40% × $20,000)		8,000
Cr. Income tax payable (40% × $80,000)		32,000
Dr. Income tax expense	5,000	
Cr. Deferred tax liability ($40,000 − $35,000)		5,000

3. Summary of alternative approaches

These three methods of accounting for income taxes roughly parallel the three methods of accounting for bad debts, as shown in the following table:

Exhibit 16-12	Comparison of accounting methods for income taxes and for bad debts	
Conceptual focus	**Accounting method for income taxes**	**Accounting method for bad debts**
Cash basis	Taxes payable method	Direct write-off
Income statement approach	Deferral method	Percentage of sales
Balance sheet approach	Accrual method	Aging of accounts receivable

The taxes payable method is close to cash basis accounting because the tax effect is recorded in the period in which the tax becomes due/payable.[3] This is similar to recognizing bad debts only when the enterprise determines that the accounts are uncollectible. The deferral method and the percentage of sales method are similar in that they both apply a percentage to an income statement amount to determine an expense (tax rate × income before tax; bad debt percentage × credit sales). The accrual method and aging of accounts receivable are similar because they both use information from the balance sheet to compute the amounts to recognize.

---

3. For the taxes payable method to be strictly cash accounting, the tax effect would be recorded only when the tax is paid, not when it is due/payable.

The following diagram is another way to summarize these three methods of accounting for income taxes.

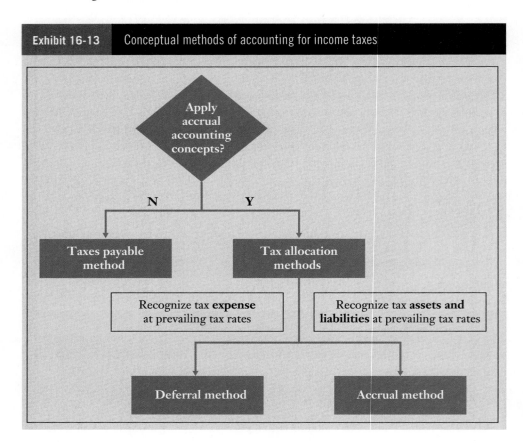

Exhibit 16-13 Conceptual methods of accounting for income taxes

Currently, the *accrual method is the accepted approach* in both IFRS and ASPE. The deferral method had been the accepted approach in the past, but is not currently accepted.[4] However, that method has left a legacy of some terminology that continues to be used, as we will see below. The taxes payable method is an accepted alternative to the accrual method under ASPE.

C. APPLYING THE ACCRUAL METHOD: PERMANENT AND TEMPORARY DIFFERENCES

As the introduction already indicated, the complexity in accounting for income taxes is due to the differences between (i) how we record transactions and events for financial reporting purposes and (ii) how tax rules treat these transactions and events. These differences come in two varieties: permanent and temporary.

1. Permanent differences

A **permanent difference** arises from a transaction or event that affects accounting income but never taxable income, or vice versa. For example, lottery winnings in Canada are not taxable, but are nonetheless income for financial reporting

L.O. 16-2. Analyze the effect of permanent and temporary differences on income tax expense and income tax liabilities under IFRS.

permanent difference Arises from a transaction or event that affects accounting income but never taxable income, or vice versa; contrast with **temporary difference**.

---

4. The deferral method was the accepted approach in Canada until the end of 1999.

purposes. While we do not expect to see this particular item very often in companies, there are some more common examples of permanent differences:

Exhibit 16-14	Common examples of permanent differences		
	Item	**Accounting treatment**	**Tax treatment**
a.	Dividends received by corporations	Include in income	Not taxable
b.	Initiation fees for membership in clubs and associations	Expense	Not deductible
c.	Life insurance premiums for employees	Expense	Not deductible
d.	Capital gains	Include full gain in income	Include half of capital gain in taxable income

Due to the nature of permanent differences, the amount of accounting income and taxable income will never reconcile. As a result, for purposes of accounting for income taxes, we follow the tax treatment to compute the tax expense for financial reporting purposes. In other words, the income tax expense would be the same as the tax payable when there are only permanent differences.

For example, suppose that in 2011 Wynndel Limited buys 500 shares of RBC Financial at $60/share (RBC is also known as Royal Bank). During 2013, Wynndel receives dividend income of $4/share from RBC. At the end of 2013, Wynndel sells all 500 shares at $80/share. For 2013, Wynndel's sales revenue and operating expenses are $500,000 and $420,000, respectively. The combined federal and provincial tax rate is 40%. Note that only one-half of the capital gain on the sale of shares is taxable.

Based on these facts, Wynndel would report the following results:

Exhibit 16-15	Accounting and taxable income for Wynndel Limited	
	Accounting income	**Taxable income**
Sales revenue	$500,000	$500,000
Operating expenses	(420,000)	(420,000)
Dividend income (500 shares × $4/share; non-taxable)	2,000	0
Gain on sale of shares (500 shares @ $20/share; ½ taxable)	10,000	5,000
Income before tax or taxable income	$ 92,000	$ 85,000
Tax rate		× 40%
Income tax payable		$ 34,000
Income tax expense (= income tax payable)	(34,000)	
Net income	$ 58,000	

Since all of the differences between accounting and taxable income are permanent, the $34,000 in taxes payable is the amount of the income tax expense.

In practice, rather than going through all the items in accounting income and taxable income in parallel as just shown, it is more expedient to start with the accounting income number and then make the necessary adjustments for the permanent differences. The following exhibit shows this approach.

Exhibit 16-16	Computation of income tax expense	
Income before tax		$92,000
Less: Non-taxable dividends		(2,000)
Less: Non-taxable portion of capital gains		(5,000)
Income for computing tax expense		$85,000
Tax rate		× 40%
Income tax expense		$34,000

Focusing on the items where there are differences is useful not only for permanent differences, but also temporary differences, which we discuss next.

2. Temporary differences

temporary difference Arises from a transaction or event that affects both accounting income and taxable income but in different reporting periods.

A **temporary difference** is a difference between the carrying amount of an asset or liability in the balance sheet and its tax base (IAS 12 paragraph 5). Most (but not all) temporary differences arise from transactions and events that affect both accounting income and taxable income but *just in different reporting periods.*[5] The different timing of construction revenue recognition for Tahsis Company given in the introduction is an example of a temporary difference. Let's review and explore that example in more depth.

- Accounting income of $100,000 *is more than* taxable income of $80,000 in 2011. The difference of $20,000 is reflected in construction in process inventory on the balance sheet, but this asset has zero value on a tax basis because taxable income includes only the $80,000 of revenue from completed contracts.

deferred tax liability The amount of income tax payable in future periods as a result of taxable temporary differences.

- Since taxable income is $20,000 less in 2011, the amount of tax payable is less than the income tax expense by $8,000 based on a tax rate of 40%. However, this $8,000 will become payable in the future when the $20,000 is recognized in taxable income. In other words, the temporary difference of $20,000 will reverse in the future.

taxable temporary difference A temporary difference that results in future taxable income being higher than accounting income; contrast with **deductible temporary difference**.

- In this example, the temporary difference reverses in 2012, resulting in taxable income of $120,000 exceeding accounting income of $100,000. As a result, tax payable exceeds income tax expense by $8,000. That future tax payment of $8,000 constitutes a liability at the end of 2011. We call this $8,000 a **deferred tax liability** in IFRS and "future income tax liability" in ASPE.

deductible temporary difference A temporary difference that results in *future* taxable income being less than accounting income; contrast with **taxable temporary difference**.

This example illustrates a case when *future* taxable income will be higher than accounting income; thus, we call this a **taxable temporary difference**.

The opposite case involves a **deductible temporary difference**, which occurs when the temporary difference results in future taxable income that will be lower than accounting income. In this case, we should record an asset for the reduction in taxes payable in the future. We call this asset a **deferred tax asset** in IFRS and a "future income tax asset" in ASPE.

deferred tax asset The amount of income tax recoverable in future periods as a result of deductible temporary differences, losses carried forward, or tax credits carried forward.

---

5. There are rare instances of temporary differences that do not involve different timing of income or expense recognition which are beyond the scope of this text.

TERMINOLOGY FOR TAX ASSETS AND LIABILITIES

Canadian GAAP prior to 2000 also used the term "deferred tax liability," because the term is consistent with the deferral method. The change to the accrual method in 2000, which has a balance sheet focus, resulted in a change in terminology to "future income tax" to de-emphasize the idea of deferral, which is an income statement concept. However, IFRS continues to use the terms "deferred tax liability" and "deferred tax asset." Given the different terminology used in different standards and during different time periods, accountants tend to use the two sets of terms interchangeably. In this text, we will use "deferred tax" asset or liability.

Exhibit 16-17 summarizes permanent and temporary differences.

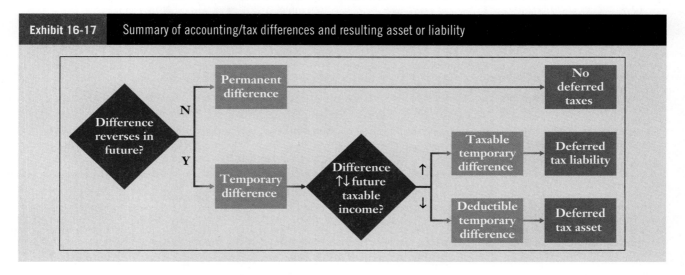

| Exhibit 16-17 | Summary of accounting/tax differences and resulting asset or liability |

a. Common temporary differences

A difference in revenue recognition on long-term contracts is just one example of temporary differences. There are potentially many temporary differences due to the fact that politicians/governments set tax rules with objectives that differ from the objectives of accounting standard setters and financial statement preparers. Some of these temporary differences include the following:

Exhibit 16-18	Common examples of temporary differences		
	Item	**Accounting treatment**	**Tax treatment**
a.	Revenue on construction contracts	Recognize using percentage-of-completion method	Can use completed contract method
b.	Fair value increase on biological assets (e.g., grape vines, cattle, trees)	Recognize fair value gains through income	Recognize income upon disposal of or production from biological assets
c.	Warranty costs	Accrue expense to match revenue recognition	Deduct when actual costs incurred
d.	Depreciation, depletion, and amortization	Record expenses using methods and rates according to company's accounting policy	Deduct capital cost allowance using rates and methods specified in tax rules

For most enterprises, the last item in this table—depreciation—is the largest temporary difference. We examine this temporary difference in more detail next.

b. Temporary differences due to depreciation

capital cost allowance (CCA) Depreciation for tax purposes.

Usually, the amount of depreciation for tax purposes, or **capital cost allowance (CCA)**, exceeds the amount of depreciation for accounting purposes. This tendency is due to governments' desire to encourage investment in capital assets: high capital cost allowance deductions decrease the present value of taxes because less taxes are due in the early periods of the assets' lives. As a result, taxable income tends to be less than accounting income, and companies tend to report significant amounts of deferred tax liabilities. To see this result, consider the following example of Yale Company.

Exhibit 16-19	Yale Company: An example to illustrate temporary differences due to depreciation

Yale Company has a single depreciable asset purchased at a cost of $300,000 at the beginning of 2011. The asset has a useful life of three years and residual value of zero. The capital cost allowance for the asset is $150,000, $100,000, and $50,000 for 2011, 2012, and 2013, respectively.[6] In each of the three years, Yale Company has $500,000 of income before taxes (after subtracting depreciation), and the company uses the straight-line depreciation method for financial reporting purposes. The company faces a 40% tax rate in all years.

Computation of tax expense and taxes payable	2011	2012	2013	Total
Income before taxes	$500,000	$500,000	$500,000	$1,500,000
Add back: non-deductible depreciation	100,000	100,000	100,000	300,000
Subtract: CCA	(150,000)	(100,000)	(50,000)	(300,000)
Taxable income	$450,000	$500,000	$550,000	$1,500,000
Income tax expense (40% × income before taxes)	$200,000	$200,000	$200,000	$600,000
Taxes payable (40% × taxable income)	$180,000	$200,000	$220,000	$600,000

Journal entries	2011 Dr	2011 Cr	2012 Dr	2012 Cr	2013 Dr	2013 Cr
Current income tax expense	180,000		200,000		220,000	
Income tax payable		180,000		200,000		220,000
Deferred income tax expense	20,000					20,000
Deferred tax liability		20,000			20,000	

Balance sheet at Dec. 31	2011	2012	2013
Deferred tax liability	20,000 Cr	20,000 Cr	0

As shown in this example, the fact that CCA exceeds depreciation in 2011 results in a taxable temporary difference of $50,000, which, at a tax rate of 40%, translates into a deferred tax liability of $20,000. In 2012, CCA equals depreciation, so the current-year temporary difference is zero. However, the *cumulative* temporary difference is $50,000, and the balance sheet amount for deferred tax liability is $20,000, which is the amount carried forward from 2011. In 2013, the temporary difference reverses because CCA is less than depreciation, resulting in a drawdown (debit) of the deferred tax liability of $20,000.

6. For ease of illustration, the CCA amounts for this example differ from the typical pattern, which uses a declining balance method. What is important is that CCA tends to be higher in the early years of asset ownership.

This example also illustrates the idea of originating and reversing differences. An **originating difference** is a temporary difference that widens the gap between accounting and tax values of an asset or liability. A **reversing difference** narrows that gap. The $50,000 difference between CCA and accounting depreciation in 2011 is an originating difference. The $50,000 difference in 2013 is a reversing difference.

Note that we distinguish the income tax expense into a current component and a deferred component. The current component is for taxes payable for the year, while the deferred portion relates to taxes in future years. For example, in 2011, the total income tax expense is $200,000, separated into $180,000 for the current tax expense and $20,000 for future tax expense.

In substance, temporary differences for depreciation are distinct from other temporary differences only in their magnitude and duration. In the example of Yale Company, the temporary difference reverses over three years—the useful life of the asset. In reality, depreciable assets can have much longer useful lives— 10, 20, 40 years or even longer. Thus, the reversal of temporary differences due to depreciation can take decades. In fact, temporary differences due to depreciation tend to build up over time because enterprises continually acquire assets to augment those that are aging and to expand capacity for growth. This accumulation of temporary differences explains the large and growing amount of deferred tax liabilities on corporations' balance sheets mentioned in the opening vignette.

originating difference A temporary difference that widens the gap between accounting and tax values of an asset or liability; contrast with **reversing difference**.

reversing difference A temporary difference that narrows that gap between accounting and tax values of an asset or liability; contrast with **originating difference**.

3. Disposals of depreciable assets

A sale or other disposal of a depreciable asset can result in a gain or loss for financial reporting purposes. That gain or loss is equal to the proceeds less the carrying value of the asset. For tax purposes, the amount of gain or loss will tend to differ from the amount for financial reporting purposes because of differences between the depreciation and CCA previously recorded. Furthermore, the tax gain or loss potentially has two components: one relating to regular income and the other relating to capital. The distinction is important because only one-half of capital gains are taxable. As a result, disposals of depreciable assets can involve both temporary and permanent differences. To account for the temporary and permanent differences requires some detailed knowledge of the Income Tax Act that is potentially beyond your knowledge base and the scope of this text. Nevertheless, the following summarizes these issues at a basic level.

a. Disposal of an asset from an asset pool

For tax purposes, depreciable assets are generally put into classes according to their type. For example, aircraft would be put into Class 9, while trucks would be put into Class 10. An important concept in tax depreciation is the **undepreciated capital cost (UCC)**, which is the tax version of carrying amount in financial accounting. In other words, UCC is cost less accumulated CCA. For most asset classes, the UCC is treated as a "pool" such that the costs are not specifically identified with a particular asset. For such assets, disposals simply reduce the balance of UCC of the class, resulting in no gain or loss for tax purposes. However, future CCA will be less due to the reduced UCC. The result of a disposal from a UCC pool is a temporary difference equal to the amount of gain or loss recognized for accounting purposes.[7]

undepreciated capital cost (UCC) The net carrying amount of an asset or asset class for tax purposes.

---

7. For assets treated in a pool, there are special cases such as the disposal of the last asset in the class and when the disposal proceeds exceed the amount of UCC in the class. We do not explicitly address these cases, but their treatment is similar to the following discussion for specifically identified assets.

b. Disposal of specifically identified assets

Tax rules specify that some depreciable assets need to be specifically identified rather than put into a pool. For example, buildings are Class 1 assets for tax purposes, but each building must be treated as a separate class (i.e., specifically identified). This treatment is similar to the specific identification method for inventory accounting, while the asset pools discussed above are comparable to the non-specific methods (weighted average and first-in, first-out). The disposal of a specifically identified asset can result in one of three cases. The different cases arise because of the different tax treatments of regular income and capital gains. Exhibit 16-20 provides an overview of these three cases, after which we will look at each case individually.

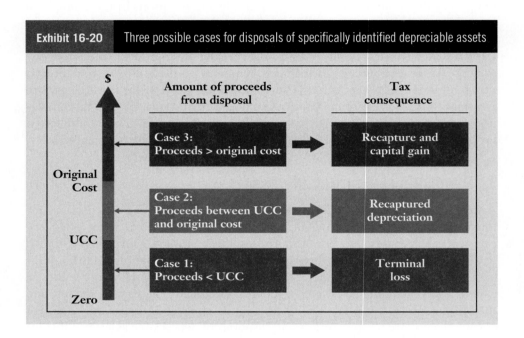

| Exhibit 16-20 | Three possible cases for disposals of specifically identified depreciable assets |

Case 1:   When the proceeds from disposal are less than the UCC of the asset, there is a loss for tax purposes called a **terminal loss**. A terminal loss is deductible against other income in full, in contrast to capital losses, which are only one-half deductible (just as capital gains are one-half taxable). This case results in a temporary difference equal to the difference between the accounting gain or loss and the amount of the terminal loss.

Case 2:   When the proceeds from disposal are more than the UCC of the asset but less than the original cost, the enterprise records income for tax purposes called **recaptured depreciation**, or simply "recapture." This label reflects the fact that the amount of tax depreciation (capital cost allowance) has been too generous, resulting in a UCC that is below the asset's market value at time of disposal. Recapture is fully taxable, just as CCA is fully deductible. The difference between the accounting gain or loss and the amount of recapture is a temporary difference.

Case 3:   When the proceeds from disposal are more than the original cost of the asset, there will be both recapture and capital gains. The amount of recapture equals the difference between the original cost and UCC, while the amount of capital gains equals the difference between the

terminal loss The tax loss arising from the sale of an asset for proceeds below its undepreciated capital cost. Applies to assets separately identified for tax purposes.

recaptured depreciation The taxable income recorded for the reversal of previous capital cost allowance when the sale proceeds of an asset exceed its undepreciated capital cost. Applies to assets separately identified for tax purposes.

sale proceeds and original cost. Recapture is fully taxable, but only one-half of capital gains are included in taxable income. This case results in a permanent difference for the one-half of the capital gains that is non-taxable. There will also be a temporary difference for the difference between the carrying amount and UCC.

The following example illustrates these three cases.

Exhibit 16-21	Illustration of tax effects of disposals of specifically identified depreciable assets, Comox Co.

In 2013, Comox Co. sells a building with a cost of $10 million and undepreciated capital cost (UCC) of $4 million for tax purposes. For financial reporting, the building has carrying amount of $6 million. The sale price of the building is one of three values: $3, $7, or $12 million. Aside from the sale of the building, the company has other income (before taxes) of $5 million. There are no other permanent or temporary differences. The company faces an income tax rate of 30%.

($000's)	Case 1	Case 2	Case 3
Computation of accounting income			
Proceeds from sale of building	3,000	7,000	12,000
Carrying amount	6,000	6,000	6,000
Accounting gain (loss)	(3,000)	1,000	6,000
Other accounting income	5,000	5,000	5,000
Accounting income before tax	2,000	6,000	11,000
Computation of taxable income			
Proceeds from sale	3,000	7,000	12,000
UCC	4,000	4,000	4,000
Tax basis gain (loss)	(1,000)	3,000	8,000
Portion for recapture (terminal loss)	(1,000)	3,000	6,000
Portion for capital gain	0	0	2,000
Recapture (terminal loss)	(1,000)	3,000	6,000
Capital gain	0	0	2,000
Less: non-taxable portion of capital gain	0	0	(1,000)
Taxable income (loss) due to sale	(1,000)	3,000	7,000
Other taxable income	5,000	5,000	5,000
Total taxable income	4,000	8,000	12,000
Accounting vs. tax basis			
Permanent difference	—	—	(1,000)
Temporary difference*	2,000	2,000	2,000
Journal entries			
Dr. Current income tax expense	1,200	2,400	3,600
Cr. Taxes payable[a]	1,200	2,400	3,600
Dr. Deferred tax liability[b]	600	600	600
Cr. Deferred income tax recovery	600	600	600

*Temporary differences can be defined in either direction. For convenience, we define the differences as (taxable income – accounting income) for the particular temporary difference. When defined this way, positive temporary differences correspond to debits and negative temporary differences correspond to credits of deferred taxes.

[a] Taxes payable = taxable income × 30%

[b] Reduction in deferred tax liability = reversing taxable temporary difference × 30%

D. CHANGES IN TAX RATES

The discussion in Section C is valid for transactions and events occurring in each year, using the tax rates appropriate for that year. However, tax amounts on the balance sheet (deferred tax assets and deferred tax liabilities) carry forward from year to year. If tax rates change from one year to another, the values of these balances need to be adjusted.

In fact, tax rates do change from time to time, and sometimes frequently. For instance, the federal corporate tax rate declined from 22.5% to 19.5% as of January 1, 2008, and further by 0.5%, 1%, 1.5%, and 1.5% at the beginning of each of the next four years to reach 15% at the beginning of 2012. These are just the changes at the federal level. Provinces also change their provincial income tax rates. Such changes in tax rates are important when we use the accrual method, as discussed in Section B.

To illustrate the effect of tax rate changes, consider the example of Delta Inc. Assume that, at the beginning of 2012, the company had taxable temporary differences amounting to $400,000 corresponding to $100,000 of deferred tax liabilities at a tax rate of 25%. Also suppose that the government increased the tax rate to 30% at the beginning of 2012. During 2012, Delta had additional temporary differences resulting from taxable income being $100,000 less than accounting income. The following table shows the results of the above assumed facts on Delta's deferred taxes.

Exhibit 16-22	Illustration of change in tax rates, Delta Inc.		
($000's)	Deductible (taxable) temporary differences	× Tax rate =	Deferred tax Dr. (Cr.)
Beginning balance, Jan. 1, 2012	(400)	25%	(100)
Adjustment for change in tax rate	—	+5%	(20)
Adjusted balance	(400)	30%	(120)
Temporary differences during 2012	(100)	30%	(30)
Ending balance, Dec. 31, 2012	(500)	30%	(150)

As this example illustrates, the value of deferred tax assets and liabilities will increase and decrease along with income tax rates. The $100,000 of deferred tax liability at the beginning of the year needs to be adjusted upward due to the 5% increase in tax rates. Given the old tax rate and the new tax rate, we can compute the amount of the adjusted deferred tax balance using either the beginning balance of deferred tax or the balance of temporary differences.

Exhibit 16-23	Formula to calculate adjusted balance of deferred taxes when tax rates change

$$\text{Adjusted deferred tax balance} = \frac{\text{Beginning deferred tax balance}}{\text{Old tax rate}} \times \text{New tax rate}$$

$$= \text{Beginning temporary difference balance} \times \text{New tax rate}$$

For Delta Inc., the calculations are as follows:

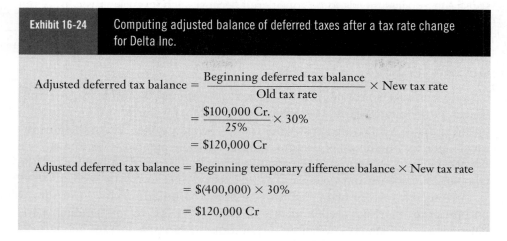

Exhibit 16-24   Computing adjusted balance of deferred taxes after a tax rate change for Delta Inc.

$$\text{Adjusted deferred tax balance} = \frac{\text{Beginning deferred tax balance}}{\text{Old tax rate}} \times \text{New tax rate}$$

$$= \frac{\$100,000 \text{ Cr.}}{25\%} \times 30\%$$

$$= \$120,000 \text{ Cr}$$

$$\text{Adjusted deferred tax balance} = \text{Beginning temporary difference balance} \times \text{New tax rate}$$

$$= \$(400,000) \times 30\%$$

$$= \$120,000 \text{ Cr}$$

Given that the opening deferred tax liability balance is $100,000 Cr., the amount of adjustment is $20,000 Cr., recorded as follows:

Exhibit 16-25   Journal entry to record change in tax rate for Delta Inc.

Dr. Deferred income tax expense	20,000	
Cr. Deferred tax liability		20,000

Based on the above analysis, a somewhat more direct computation of the amount required for the journal entry is as follows:

Exhibit 16-26   Formula to calculate adjustment to deferred tax balance for tax rates change

$$\text{Adjustment} = \text{Beg. deferred tax balance} \times \frac{\text{New tax rate}}{\text{Old tax rate}} - \text{Beg. deferred tax balance}$$

$$= \text{Beg. deferred tax balance} \times \left(\frac{\text{New tax rate}}{\text{Old tax rate}} - 1 \right)$$

$$= \$100,000 \text{ Cr.} \times \left(\frac{30\%}{25\%} - 1 \right)$$

$$= \$100,000 \text{ Cr.} \times (1.2 - 1)$$

$$= \$20,000 \text{ Cr.}$$

Looking at the term in parentheses, we see that the term is positive if the tax rate increases, and negative if the tax rate decreases. Thus, if the deferred tax balance is an asset, that asset becomes more valuable if the tax rate increases and less so if the tax rate decreases. Likewise, if the deferred tax balance is a liability, that liability becomes more costly if the tax rate increases and less costly if the tax rate decreases.

Another issue relating to changes in tax rates is that enterprises should use tax rates that have been "enacted or substantively enacted" (IAS 12 paragraph 46). This means enterprises need to take account of changes in future tax rates if such changes have already been put into legislation. Even legislation that has not yet received royal assent, but which is almost certain to pass through the legislative process, needs to be considered because such legislation is considered "substantively enacted."

E. TAX LOSSES

L.O. 16-4. Analyze the effect of tax losses on past and future income taxes, and evaluate whether and how much of these tax loss benefits can be recognized as assets under IFRS.

When a business is profitable, it pays taxes according to its taxable income multiplied by the tax rate. If the tax system were symmetric for profits and losses, a business that has a loss in a year would receive a tax payment from the government equal to the amount of loss multiplied by the tax rate. However, the income tax system treats income and losses asymmetrically. The government will pay the company sometimes, but not at other times, as we will see shortly.

Income tax laws in many countries permit a corporation with a loss for tax purposes (i.e., negative taxable income) to carry that loss to surrounding years. Currently, Canadian tax laws allow corporations to carry an operating loss backward for 3 years and forward for 20 years, and capital losses backward for 3 years and forward indefinitely.[8] Carrying a loss back to offset taxable income in a prior year produces a tax refund. However, carrying a loss forward has no immediate cash flow benefits; the company realizes the benefit in the future when it earns income.

 WHY DOES THE TAX SYSTEM TREAT PROFITS AND LOSSES ASYMMETRICALLY

On the surface, it may seem unfair for the government to treat profits and losses asymmetrically for tax purposes. Supposing the tax rate were 30%, each dollar of profit would require the payment of 30 cents, so shouldn't the government compensate the corporation 30 cents for each dollar of loss?

The reason for the asymmetric treatment is rooted in the concept of moral hazard discussed in Chapter 1. Moral hazard is relevant because we can think of the government as a silent partner who holds an equity interest in the corporation and moral hazard is a concern for any equity interest holder. The government's equity interest is equal to the tax rate (say 30%) because for each dollar of pre-tax profits, 30 cents goes to the government and 70 cents goes to the non-government owners.

When the business is profitable, the government is happy to receive its 30% share. However, the government is reluctant to contribute its 30% share for losses because it may not have reliable information on the source of that loss. For example, the loss may have been incurred because management has consumed the business resources, and the government does not wish to subsidize consumption. Furthermore, the business may not even be a bona fide business that could be expected to earn a profit. Given the limited liability of corporations, the government would not be able to recover funds that it has contributed toward losses, even if those losses were illegitimate. Consequently, the government is only willing to provide refunds on taxes previously paid for losses carried back, but it is unwilling to pay for losses in the absence of prior profits.

---

8. The carryforward period for operating losses was 10 years for losses incurred prior to 2006 and 7 years prior to March 23, 2004.

1. Carryback of tax losses

When a company incurs a tax loss and also has taxable income in past years, it is eligible to apply the loss to offset income in those prior years. Currently, that carryback period is three years. Technically, the carryback works as follows:

- The company chooses one of the previous three years to apply the loss. Normally, the optimal choice is the earliest of the three years. The loss reduces the taxable income in that prior year, but cannot create or increase a loss in that prior year.
- The company recalculates the tax payable for that prior year using the revised taxable income that includes the effect of the loss carried back. It uses the tax rate in force for that prior tax year.
- The difference between the recalculated tax payable and the tax actually paid previously for that prior year is the amount of refund owing to the company.

For example, suppose Esquimalt Company has taxable income of $10 million in 2011 and pays taxes of $3 million (i.e., its tax rate was 30%). Later, in year 2014, the company incurs an operating tax loss of $8 million when the tax rate is 35%. For financial reporting purposes, Esquimalt's loss before tax is $6 million.

Based on these facts, Esquimalt would be entitled to claim a tax refund of $2.4 million by carrying the $8 million loss back to reduce the taxable income in 2011. The following exhibit summarizes the effect of the loss carryback.

Exhibit 16-27	Effect of losses carried back for Esquimalt Company			
($millions)	Taxable income	× Tax rate	=	Taxes payable
2011 as previously filed	10	30%		3.0
Losses carried back from 2014 to 2011	(8)	30%		(2.4)
2011 after losses carried back	2	30%		0.6

The amount of the refund is determined by the tax rate of 30%, which was the rate in force for 2011. The 35% tax rate in 2014 is not relevant. In other words, the company previously paid $3 million on $10 million of taxable income for 2011. After carrying the 2014 loss of $8 million back to 2011, the taxable income reduces to $2 million, and the tax at 30% is only $0.6 million. The reduction in tax for 2011 from $3 million to $0.6 million is $2.4 million.

Esquimalt would record the following journal entries. Note that "income tax recovery" is an income statement account for a negative income tax expense.

Exhibit 16-28	Journal entries to record tax recovery for Esquimalt Company		
Dr. Income tax receivable ($8,000,000 loss × 30%)	2,400,000	
Cr. Current income tax recovery		2,400,000
Dr. Deferred income tax expense ($2,000,000 × 35%)	700,000	
Cr. Deferred income tax liability		700,000

The second entry reflects temporary differences totalling $2 million, since the accounting loss is $6 million while the tax loss is $8 million.

2. Carryforward of tax losses

Whereas carrying back losses results in a *definite and immediate* cash inflow, carrying losses forward only results in *uncertain future* cash flows because the loss has benefit in the future only if future years have taxable income. Therefore, if a company has taxable income in prior years, it would generally prefer to first carry any losses back rather than forward. Nevertheless, it is frequently the case that a company will need to carry losses forward because it has exhausted its ability to carry losses backward, or it simply did not have prior taxable income. For example, companies in the start-up phase typically incur losses for a number of years before turning a profit.

The fact that losses carried back have benefits that are definite and immediate means there is no issue whether an enterprise should record an asset for the tax refund receivable, such as that shown in Exhibit 16-28. In contrast, losses carried forward have uncertain future benefits, so there is an issue as to whether an enterprise should record an asset for a loss carried forward. IAS 12 paragraph 34 indicates the following:

> ¶ 34.   A deferred tax asset shall be recognized for the carryforward of unused tax losses and unused tax credits to the extent that it is probable that future taxable profit will be available against which the unused tax losses and unused tax credits can be utilized.

This paragraph suggests that whether an enterprise recognizes an asset for the tax loss carryforward depends on a probability assessment, with "probable" usually interpreted to mean "more likely than not" or greater than 50%. This is the same interpretation of "probable" in reference to contingencies discussed in Chapter 11. However, the standard goes on to state the following:

> ¶ 35.   . . . the existence of unused tax losses is strong evidence that future taxable profit may not be available. Therefore, when an entity has a history of recent losses, the entity recognizes a deferred tax asset arising from unused tax losses or tax credits only to the extent that the entity has sufficient taxable temporary differences or there is convincing other evidence that sufficient taxable profit will be available . . .

This paragraph suggests that the very fact that the enterprise needs to carry losses forward creates a presumption that it will not be able to realize the benefits of the losses. Management has the burden of proof to show that it will be profitable enough in the future to use up these losses.

To illustrate the accounting for a loss carryforward, suppose Esquimalt Company, discussed above, did not have prior years with taxable income against which it could use the $8 million tax loss incurred in 2014. As a result, it must carry the loss forward. If Esquimalt's management believes that the loss will be used against taxable income in future years (up to 20 years based on current legislation), then it can record the following entry for its income tax in 2014. (Note that the tax rate in 2014 is 35%.)

Exhibit 16-29	Entries to record taxes when there are probable future benefits of tax losses carried forward	
Dr. Deferred tax asset ($8,000,000 loss × 35%)	2,800,000	
Cr. Deferred income tax recovery		2,800,000
Dr. Deferred income tax expense ($2,000,000 × 35%)	700,000	
Cr. Deferred income tax liability		700,000

Notice that the second journal entry for the temporary difference remains the same as in Exhibit 16-28. The first entry records the deferred tax asset using the current tax rate of 35%. As noted earlier, if future tax rates have been enacted or substantially enacted, the enterprise should use those future rates to determine the value of the deferred tax asset due to the losses carried forward. For instance, if Esquimalt expects to use the tax loss in the year 2018, and legislation indicates that the tax rate applicable to 2018 will be 40%, then the deferred tax asset would be $8,000,000 \times 40\% = \$3,200,000$, instead of $2,800,000 shown in Exhibit 16-29.

If Esquimalt's management believes that that it will *not* be probable that the tax loss will be used in the future, then it would not record the deferred tax asset. The impact on financial results is clearly significant, since the loss before tax is not mitigated by any tax recovery. That is, the full $6 million loss before tax would be the net loss after tax for the year. In comparison, recognizing the tax loss benefit results in a net loss of $3.9 million (= $6,000,000 - $2,800,000 + $700,000).

Finally, probability assessments need to be updated annually. Deteriorating economic conditions may require the write-down or write-off of deferred tax assets previously recognized for tax losses carried forward. Likewise, if circumstances improve, the enterprise could record deferred tax assets for previously unrecognized tax losses.

F. MEASUREMENT: NO DISCOUNTING FOR TIME VALUE OF MONEY

The discussion above has not made mention of the time value of money and computations of present value. The absence of this discussion should be somewhat surprising given that we are dealing with amounts that can vary in timing for many years, such as temporary differences for depreciable assets and tax losses carried forward. However, IAS 12 indicates the following:

¶ 53.   Deferred tax assets and liabilities shall not be discounted.

The rationale for this requirement is based on considerations of costs and benefits as well as comparability among enterprises.

¶ 54.   The reliable determination of deferred tax assets and liabilities on a discounted basis requires detailed scheduling of the timing of the reversal of each temporary difference. In many cases such scheduling is impracticable or highly complex. Therefore, it is inappropriate to require discounting of deferred tax assets and liabilities. To permit, but not to require, discounting would result in deferred tax assets and liabilities which would not be comparable between entities. Therefore, this Standard does not require or permit the discounting of deferred tax assets and liabilities.

G. PRESENTATION AND DISCLOSURE

1. Presentation and disclosure of income tax expense

The amount of tax expense is obviously important to financial statement readers for performance evaluation. Thus, the total income tax expense must be shown on the face of the income statement. In addition to this aggregate amount, enterprises need to explain the composition of this tax expense in the note

L.O. 16-5.   Apply the presentation and disclosure standards for income taxes.

disclosures. In particular, the notes should distinguish the amount for current versus deferred tax:

- current tax expense;
- deferred tax expense due to temporary difference; and
- deferred tax expense due to changes in tax rates.

In addition, a write-down of deferred tax asset or recognition of a previously unrecognized deferred tax asset can significantly increase or decrease the tax expense. Enterprises need to disclose the impact of these changes of deferred tax assets on current and deferred tax expense.

As noted in a number of other chapters, the income tax expense on the income statement relates only to ordinary activities. Taxes on discontinued operations would be presented with those discontinued operations (or netted against those operations with additional note disclosure of the related income tax). Any taxes on items relating to other comprehensive income would be presented in other comprehensive income rather than in profit or loss.

A particularly useful disclosure relates to the difference between (i) the actual tax expense and (ii) the tax expense expected based on the before-tax income multiplied by the statutory tax rate. Essentially, this disclosure identifies all the permanent differences impacting the tax expense for the year. Enterprises have a choice of explaining in terms of either the dollar amounts of taxes involved or the tax rates (i.e., dollar amount of taxes divided by before-tax income).

2. Presentation and disclosure of income tax assets and liabilities

As shown earlier in this chapter, the accounting for income taxes produces a number of different items on the balance sheet: current tax payables or recoveries, deferred tax assets, and deferred tax liabilities. Enterprises must present these items separately (i.e., not offset an asset against a liability). In addition, enterprises face multiple tax jurisdictions, such as the Canadian federal government, provincial governments, and foreign governments. Since each jurisdiction demands compliance with its own tax laws, enterprises cannot offset tax assets for one jurisdiction against liabilities relating to another jurisdiction. Likewise, governments usually assess taxes according to the legal entity, so an enterprise consisting of two or more component entities (e.g., corporations) cannot offset the tax liabilities of one component entity with tax assets of another. In general, then, an enterprise is prohibited from offsetting unless it is legally authorized to offset.

In terms of disclosure, enterprises need to identify deferred tax assets or liabilities according to their sources. For example, a deferred tax asset from warranty costs would be disclosed separately from another deferred tax asset from unearned revenue. Also, enterprises need to disclose the amount of deferred tax assets recognized for tax losses carried forward. Regardless of the source of the deferred tax asset or liability, enterprises must classify them as non-current items when the enterprises use the current/non-current presentation for the balance sheet (IAS 1 paragraph 56).

Under ASPE, Section 3465 indicates less onerous disclosures. Private enterprises using the accrual method need to disclose the following amounts (if not already presented elsewhere):

a. current income tax expense
b. future income tax expense
c. income taxes related to capital transactions
d. unrecognized tax assets arising from unused tax losses or deductible temporary differences.

As noted earlier in the chapter, private enterprises can simplify their accounting for income taxes by choosing to use the taxes payable method. Doing so also removes the disclosures related to future income tax expense, deferred tax assets, and deferred tax liability. On the other hand, an enterprise using the taxes payable method needs to provide a reconciliation of (i) the effective income tax rate corresponding to the income tax expense to (ii) the statutory tax rate. This disclosure would identify the permanent and temporary differences arising in the year. (This reconciliation under the accrual method would not identify temporary differences.)

H. SUBSTANTIVE DIFFERENCES BETWEEN RELEVANT IFRS AND ASPE

ISSUE	IFRS	ASPE
Method of accounting for income taxes	Entities should use the accrual method of accounting.	Entities can use either the accrual method or the taxes payable method.
Presentation and disclosures	Deferred tax assets and liabilities need to be identified by source.	There is no requirement to identify tax assets and liabilities by source. Entities choosing the taxes payable method need to reconcile their effective tax rate to the statutory tax rate.

I. SUMMARY

L.O. 16-1. Describe the conceptual differences among the three methods of accounting for income taxes and apply the taxes payable method under ASPE.

- The taxes payable method records a tax expense equal to the taxes payable for the current period. This method is not conceptually appealing, but is an accepted alternative for private enterprises in Canada due to its simplicity.
- The deferral and accrual methods try to allocate an amount of tax expense to the period in which the relevant event or transaction occurs.
- The deferral method focuses on obtaining the tax expense on the income statement that best matches the income recognized in the period.
- The accrual method focuses on obtaining balance sheet values of tax assets and liabilities that best reflect the amount of tax benefit or obligation ultimately due.
- The accrual method is the only acceptable method in IFRS and is also an accepted alternative for private enterprises in Canada.

L.O. 16-2. Analyze the effect of permanent and temporary differences on income tax expense and income tax liabilities under IFRS.

- Permanent differences relate to events and transactions that impact accounting income but never taxable income, or vice versa.
- Temporary differences reverse in future years.
- Deductible temporary differences are those that result in future taxable income being *lower* than accounting income.
- Taxable temporary differences are those that result in future taxable income being *higher* than accounting income.

L.O. 16-3.   Analyze the effect of changes in tax rates on income tax expenses, assets, and liabilities, and account for these effects under IFRS.

■ Enterprises need to revalue deferred tax assets and liabilities for changes in tax rates. These increases and decreases in assets and liabilities result in a corresponding change in income tax expense.

L.O. 16-4.   Analyze the effect of tax losses on past and future income taxes, and evaluate whether and how much of these tax loss benefits can be recognized as assets under IFRS.

■ Enterprises can carry losses back three years and forward for up to 20 years.
■ Losses carried back result in a definite and immediate cash inflow and are therefore immediately recognized as tax recoveries and receivables.
■ Losses carried forward result in uncertain future reductions in taxes payable, so enterprises should recognize deferred tax assets for these losses only if it will be probable that such losses can be used in future years.

L.O. 16-5.   Apply the presentation and disclosure standards for income taxes.

■ Income taxes pervasively affect business transactions and in different ways. Presentation and disclosure standards try to ensure that users are able to determine the effect of tax laws on the enterprise's operations.

J. References
Authoritative standards:

IFRS	ASPE Section
IAS 12—Income Taxes	3465—Income taxes

K. Glossary

accounting income: The amount of income (before subtracting income tax) recognized for financial reporting purposes. Contrast with **taxable income**.

accrual method (of accounting for income tax): Focuses on obtaining the balance sheet value for the income tax liability (or asset) that best reflects the assets and liabilities recognized on the balance sheet.

capital cost allowance (CCA): Depreciation for tax purposes.

deductible temporary difference: A temporary difference that results in *future* taxable income being less than accounting income; contrast with **taxable temporary difference**.

deferral method (of accounting for income tax): Focuses on obtaining the income statement value for income tax expense that best matches the amount of income recognized for the year.

deferred tax asset: The amount of income tax recoverable in future periods as a result of deductible temporary differences, losses carried forward, or tax credits carried forward.

deferred tax liability: The amount of income tax payable in future periods as a result of taxable temporary differences.

originating difference: A temporary difference that widens the gap between accounting and tax values of an asset or liability; contrast with **reversing difference**.

permanent difference: Arises from a transaction or event that affects accounting income but never taxable income, or vice versa; contrast with **temporary difference**.

recaptured depreciation: The taxable income recorded for the reversal of previous capital cost allowance when the sale proceeds of an asset exceed its undepreciated capital cost. Applies to assets separately identified for tax purposes.

reversing difference: A temporary difference that narrows that gap between accounting and tax values of an asset or liability; contrast with **originating difference**.

taxable income: The amount of income recognized for tax purposes used to compute taxes payable; contrast with **accounting income**.

taxable temporary difference: A temporary difference that results in future taxable income being higher than accounting income; contrast with **deductible temporary difference**.

taxes payable method: A method that records an amount for income tax expense equal to the tax payments for the current period.

temporary difference: Arises from a transaction or event that affects both accounting income and taxable income but in different reporting periods.

terminal loss: The tax loss arising from the sale of an asset for proceeds below its undepreciated capital cost. Applies to assets separately identified for tax purposes.

undepreciated capital cost (UCC): The net carrying amount of an asset or asset class for tax purposes.

L. PROBLEMS

Go to MyAccountingLab at www.myaccountinglab.com. You can practise the indicated exercises as often as you want, and guided solutions will help you find answers step by step. You'll find a personalized study plan available to you too!

P16-1. Methods of accounting for income taxes

(**L.O.** 16-1) (Easy – 3 minutes)

A company earns $300,000 in pre-tax income, while its tax return shows taxable income of $250,000. At a tax rate of 30%, how much is the income tax expense under the taxes payable method permitted under ASPE?

P16-2. Methods of accounting for income taxes

(**L.O.** 16-1) (Easy – 3 minutes)

A company uses the accrual method and reports $600,000 for income tax expense for the year. The company did not have any transactions that would have created permanent differences. Assume that the statutory tax rate is 25% and this rate is constant from year to year. How much was the company's pre-tax income?

P16-3. Methods of accounting for income taxes

(**L.O.** 16-1) (Easy – 5 minutes)

A company facing a 25% tax rate has calculated its taxable income for the year to be $2,400,000. It made installment payments during the year totalling $650,000; this amount has been recorded in an asset account as "income tax installments." Prepare the journal entry to record the adjusting entry for income taxes at the end of the year under the taxes payable method.

P16-4. Methods of accounting for income taxes   (**L.O.** 16-1) (Easy – 5 minutes)[9]

PLC Company reported $400,000 in income tax expense for the year under the accrual method. Its balance sheet reported an overall increase in deferred income tax liability of $10,000 and a decrease in income tax payable of $15,000. How much would PLC report as income tax expense had it used the taxes payable method?

---

9. © 2010 CGA-Canada. Reproduced with permission.

P16-5.   Methods of accounting for income taxes   (**L.O.** 16-1) (Easy – 5 minutes)

For each of the following characteristics, identify which of the three methods of accounting for income tax (taxes payable, deferral, or accrual) best matches that characteristic.

Characteristic	Accounting method
Closest to cash basis accounting	
Focuses on the balance sheet values of deferred tax	
Similar to direct write-off method for bad debts	
Focuses on the income statement tax expense	
Records an income tax expense adjustment when tax rates change	
Analogous to percentage-of-sale method for estimating bad debts	
Analogous to aging of accounts receivable approach for estimating bad debts	
Income tax asset and liability balances reflect the prevailing tax rate	
Income tax expense for the period reflects the prevailing tax rate	

P16-6.   Methods of accounting for income taxes   (**L.O.** 16-1) (Medium – 10 minutes)

Earlton Inc. began operations in 2011. Due to the untimely death of its founder, Earl Davies, the company was wound up in 2013. The following table provides information on Earlton's income over the three years.

	2011	2012	2013
Income before tax	$10,000	$80,000	$50,000
Taxable income	nil	60,000	80,000

The statutory income tax rate remained at 30% throughout the three years.

Required:

a.   For each year and for the three years combined, compute the following:
   – income tax expense under the taxes payable method;
   – the effective tax rate (= tax expense ÷ pre-tax income) under the taxes payable method;
   – income tax expense under the accrual method;
   – effective tax rate under the accrual method.

b.   Briefly comment on any differences between the effective tax rates and the statutory rate of 30%.

P16-7.   Permanent and temporary differences   (**L.O.** 16-2) (Easy – 5 minutes)[10]

Identify whether each of the following items is a permanent or temporary difference.

	Item	Permanent	Temporary
a.	Golf club dues that are not deductible for tax purposes		
b.	Depreciation of property, plant, and equipment versus the tax method of CCA		
c.	Warranty liabilities for which only the actual amount of cash paid is deductible for tax purposes		
d.	Percentage of completion income that is taxable only once the contract is complete		
e.	Dividends received that are not taxable		

P16-8. **Permanent and temporary differences** (**L.O.** 16-2) (Easy – 5 minutes)

Identify whether each of the following items would cause income taxes payable to be higher or lower than income tax expense.

	Item	Higher	Lower	Neither
a.	Rent revenue collected in advance that is taxable in the year received			
b.	CCA that exceeds depreciation expense for property, plant, and equipment			
c.	Membership dues that are not deductible			
d.	Percentage of completion income that is taxable only once the contract is complete			
e.	Dividends received that are not taxable			

P16-9. **Permanent and temporary differences** (**L.O.** 16-2) (Easy – 5 minutes)

Identify whether the following items are related to (i) a deductible temporary difference, (ii) a taxable temporary difference, or (iii) neither.

	Item	Deductible temporary difference	Taxable temporary difference	Neither
a.	Warranty expense accrued but not deductible until actual costs incurred			
b.	CCA that exceeds depreciation expense for property, plant, and equipment			
c.	Dividends received that are not taxable			
d.	A deferred tax asset for rent revenue received in advance and taxed upon receipt			
e.	Equipment that has a carrying value above undepreciated capital cost			

P16-10. **Permanent and temporary differences** (**L.O.** 16-2) (Easy – 3 minutes)

A company has income before tax of $300,000, which includes a permanent difference of $60,000 relating to non-taxable dividend income. There are no other permanent or temporary differences. The income tax rate is 20%.

Required:

Compute the amount of taxes payable and income tax expense.

P16-11. **Permanent and temporary differences** (**L.O.** 16-2) (Easy – 3 minutes)

A company has income before tax of $300,000. The company also has a temporary difference of $60,000 relating to capital cost allowance (CCA) in excess of depreciation expense recorded for the year. There are no other permanent or temporary differences. The income tax rate is 20%.

Required:

Compute the amount of taxes payable and income tax expense.

P16-12. Permanent and temporary differences (**L.O.** 16-2) (Easy – 10 minutes)

The following summarizes information relating to Grafton Corporation's operations for the current year.

Sales revenue	$4,500,000
Dividend income (not taxable)	100,000
Operating expenses other than depreciation	(3,200,000)
Depreciation	(800,000)
Income before tax	$ 600,000
Capital cost allowance claimed	$1,000,000
Income tax rate	25%

Required:

Compute the amount of taxes payable and income tax expense for Grafton Corporation.

P16-13. Permanent and temporary differences (**L.O.** 16-2) (Easy – 10 minutes)

For each of the following differences between the amount of taxable income and income recorded for financial reporting purposes, compute the effect of each difference on deferred taxes balances on the balance sheet. Treat each item independently of the others. Assume a tax rate of 25%.

Item	Amount
Depreciation for financial reporting purposes	$20,000
Depreciation for tax purposes (CCA)	30,000
Non-taxable dividends	40,000
Provision for warranty	60,000
Unearned rent revenue	80,000
CCA in excess of depreciation	10,000

P16-14. Permanent and temporary differences (**L.O.** 16-2) (Medium – 15 minutes)[11]

At the beginning of the current fiscal year, Vation Corporation had a deferred income tax liability balance of $15,000, which relates to depreciable assets.

During the year, Vation reported the following information:

i. Income before income taxes for the year was $550,000 and the tax rate was 30%.
ii. Depreciation expense was $45,000 and CCA was $30,000.
iii. Unearned rent revenue was reported at $40,000. Rent revenue is taxable when the cash is received. There was no opening balance in the unearned rent revenue account at the beginning of the year.
iv. No other items affected deferred tax amounts other than these transactions.

Required:

Prepare the journal entry or entries to record income taxes for the year.

P16-15. Permanent and temporary differences (**L.O.** 16-2) (Medium – 20 minutes)

The following data represent the differences between accounting and tax income for Oriental Imports Inc., whose pre-tax accounting income is $860,000 for the year ended December 31. The company's income tax rate is 40%. Additional information relevant to income taxes includes the following.

---

11. © 2010 CGA-Canada. Reproduced with permission.

a. Capital cost allowance of $202,500 exceeded accounting depreciation expense of $100,000 in the current year.

b. Rents of $5,000, applicable to next year, had been collected in December and deferred for financial statement purposes but are taxable in the year received.

c. In a previous year, the company established a provision for product warranty expense. A summary of the current year's transactions appears below:

Provision for warranties, January 1 balance	$ 96,300
Provision for the year	35,600
Payments made to fulfil product warranties	(26,000)
Provision for warranties, December 31 balance	$105,900

For tax purposes, only actual amounts paid for warranties are deductible.

d. Insurance expense to cover the company's executive officers was $5,200 for the year, and you have determined that this expense is not deductible for tax purposes.

Required:

Prepare the journal entries to record income taxes for Oriental Imports.

P16-16. Permanent and temporary differences with asset impairment

(**L.O.** 16-2) (Difficult – 20 minutes)

The following information relates to the accounting income for Manitoba Press Company (MPC) for the current year ended December 31.

Accounting income before income taxes	$210,000
Dividend income (non-taxable)	30,000
Depreciation expense	100,000
Capital cost allowance claimed	70,000
Impairment loss on land—see additional information below	200,000
Income tax rate	35%

The company had purchased land some years ago for $500,000. Recently, it was discovered that this land is contaminated by industrial pollution. Because of the soil remediation costs required, the value of the land has decreased. For tax purposes, the impairment loss is not currently deductible. In the future when the land is sold, half of any losses is deductible against taxable capital gains (i.e., the other half that is not taxable or deductible is a permanent difference).

The deferred income tax liability account on January 1 had a credit balance of $76,000. This balance is entirely related to property, plant, and equipment.

Required:

Prepare the journal entries to record income taxes for MPC.

P16-17. Permanent and temporary differences with disposal of depreciable asset

(**L.O.** 16-2) (Medium – 15 minutes)

The following information relates to the accounting income for Saskatchewan Uranium Enterprises (SUE) for the current year ended December 31.

Accounting income before income taxes	$840,000
Depreciation and depletion expense	450,000
Capital cost allowance claimed	570,000
Membership initiation fees (not deductible)	5,000
Loss on disposal of equipment—see additional information below	40,000
Income tax rate	30%

During the year, the company sold one of its machines with carrying value of $60,000 for proceeds of $20,000, resulting in an accounting loss of $40,000. This loss has been included in the pre-tax income figure of $840,000 shown above. For tax purposes, the proceeds from the disposal were removed from the undepreciated capital cost (UCC) of Class 8 assets.

The deferred income tax liability account on January 1 had a credit balance of $150,000. This balance is entirely related to property, plant, and equipment.

Required:

Prepare the journal entries to record income taxes for SUE.

P16-18. **Permanent and temporary differences with disposal of specifically identified depreciable asset** **(L.O.** 16-2) (Difficult – 15 minutes)

The following information relates to the accounting income for Alberta Real Estate Company (AREC) for the current year ended December 31.

Accounting income before income taxes	$600,000
Depreciation and depletion expense	300,000
Capital cost allowance (CCA) excluding recapture on building disposal	300,000
Gain on disposal of building—see additional information below	240,000
Income tax rate	25%

During the year, the company sold one of its buildings with carrying value of $720,000 for proceeds of $960,000, resulting in an accounting gain of $240,000. This gain has been included in the pre-tax income figure of $600,000 shown above. For tax purposes, the acquisition cost of the building was $800,000. For purposes of CCA, it is a Class 1 asset, which treats each building as a separate class. The undepreciated capital cost (UCC) on the building at the time of disposal was $600,000.

Required:

Prepare the journal entries to record income taxes for AREC.

P16-19. **Effect of tax rate changes** **(L.O.** 16-3) (Easy – 3 minutes)

A company has a deferred tax liability of $40,000 at the beginning of the fiscal year relating to a taxable temporary difference of $100,000. The tax rate for the year increased from 40% to 45%.

Required:

Provide the journal entry to reflect the tax rate change.

P16-20. **Effect of tax rate changes** **(L.O.** 16-3) (Easy – 5 minutes)

A company has a deferred tax liability of $29,900 at the beginning of the fiscal year. The company's records show that it had taxable temporary differences totalling $115,000 entering the year. In the current fiscal year, the tax rate is 24%.

Required:

Provide the journal entry to reflect the tax rate change (if any).

P16-21.   Effect of tax rate changes

(**L.O.** 16-3) (Medium – 20 minutes)[12]

RCD Company started operations in 2013. The financial statements of RCD reflected the following pre-tax amounts for its December 31 year-end:

	2013	2014
Income statement (summarized)		
Revenues	$200,000	$230,000
Depreciation expense	25,000	25,000
Other operating expenses	110,000	120,000
Pre-tax accounting income	65,000	85,000
Balance sheet (partial)		
Property, plant, and equipment, cost	$250,000	$250,000
Accumulated depreciation	(25,000)	(50,000)
Net	$225,000	$200,000
Unearned rent revenue	—	7,000

RCD has a tax rate of 30% in 2013 and 35% in 2014, enacted in February each year. The unearned rent revenue represents cash received from a tenant that will be moving into the building February 1, 2015. For tax purposes, any cash received for future rent is taxed when the cash is received. RCD claimed CCA for income tax purposes of $12,500 in 2013 and $23,500 in 2014.

Required:

a. Calculate the income taxes payable for 2014.
b. For each year (2013 and 2014), calculate the deferred tax balance on the balance sheet at the end of the year. Indicate whether the amount is an asset or a liability.

P16-22.   Effect of tax rate changes

(**L.O.** 16-3) (Difficult – 20 minutes)[13]

Vanier Corporation reported the following information at the beginning of its current fiscal year:

Deferred income tax asset (warranties)	$ 2,400 Dr
Deferred income tax liability (depreciable assets)	$10,500 Cr

During the year, Vanier reported the following information:

i. Income before income taxes for the year was $850,000 and the tax rate was 32%.
ii. Depreciation expense was $75,000 and CCA was $80,000. The carrying amount of property, plant, and equipment at the end of the year was $420,000 while UCC was $380,000.
iii. Warranty expense was reported at $40,000, while actual cash paid out was $38,000. The warranty liability had a year-end balance of $10,000.
iv. No other items affected deferred tax amounts other than these transactions.

Required:

Prepare the journal entry or entries to record income tax for the year.

P16-23.   Accounting for tax losses

(**L.O.** 16-4) (Easy – 5 minutes)

In the first two years of operations, a company reports taxable income of $100,000 and $150,000, respectively. In the first two years, the company paid $20,000 and $36,000. It is now the end of the third year, and the company has a loss of $220,000 for tax purposes. The company carries losses to the earliest year possible. The tax rate is currently 25%.

Required:

Compute the amount of income tax payable or receivable in the current (third) year.

---

12. © 2009 CGA-Canada. Reproduced with permission.
13. © 2009 CGA-Canada. Reproduced with permission.

P16-24. Accounting for tax losses **L.O.** 16-4) (Easy – 5 minutes)

In the first year of operations, a company reports taxable income of $160,000 and paid $32,000 of income taxes. It is now the end of the second year, and the company has a loss of $300,000 for tax purposes. The company's management believes it is probable the company will be able to use up its tax losses. The tax rate is currently 25%.

Required:

Compute the amounts of income tax receivable and/or deferred income tax asset in the current (second) year.

P16-25. Permanent and temporary differences; losses

L.O. 16-2, **L.O.** 16-4) (Medium – 20 minutes)[14]

During its first year of operations, Kinkle Corporation reported the following information:

  i. Income before income taxes for the year was $450,000 and the tax rate was 30%.
 ii. Depreciation expense was $195,000 and CCA was $97,500. The carrying amount of property, plant, and equipment at the end of the year was $620,000, while UCC was 717,500.
iii. Warranty expense was reported at $160,000, while actual cash paid out was $75,000.
 iv. $45,000 of expenses included in income were not deductible for tax purposes.
  v. No other items affected deferred tax amounts besides these transactions.

Required:

 a. Prepare the journal entries to record income tax expense for the year.
 b. Assume Kinkle reported a loss instead of income in its first year of operations. Explain what accounting policy choices are available to Kinkle to record the tax implications of the loss, and provide a recommendation.

P16-26. Accounting for tax losses with tax rate changes

L.O. 16-3, **L.O.** 16-4) (Difficult – 30 minutes)

West Limited reported the following amounts and information for four years ended on December 31 as follows:

	2011	2012	2013	2014
Accounting income (loss)	$550,000	$(1,400,000)	$200,000	$1,900,000
Add: depreciation	100,000	100,000	100,000	100,000
Less: CCA	(170,000)	(170,000)	(170,000)	(250,000)
Taxable income (loss)	$480,000	$(1,470,000)	$130,000	$1,750,000
Tax rate	40%	45%	50%	55%

Deferred tax relating to property, plant, and equipment (PPE) on December 31, 2010 was $200,000 Cr. This is the only tax account on the balance sheet. It relates to the difference between the UCC of $1,000,000 and net carrying value of $1,400,000 of depreciable assets. The taxable incomes for the two years prior to 2011 were $0. Assume any changes to future tax rates are not enacted until the year of the tax change. West's management is confident that it is probable the company will be able to utilize the losses carried forward.

Required:

Prepare all income tax-related journal entries for the four years 2011 to 2014.

---

14. © 2010 CGA-Canada. Reproduced with permission.

P16-27. Accounting for tax losses and tax rate changes
(**L.O.** 16-3, **L.O.** 16-4, **L.O.** 16-5) (Difficult – 40 minutes)

	2011	2012	2013	2014
Accounting income (loss)	$250,000	$(900,000)	$200,000	$800,000
Add: depreciation	250,000	60,000	50,000	50,000
Less: CCA	(110,000)	0	0	(120,000)
Taxable income (loss)	$390,000	$(840,000)	$250,000	$730,000
Tax rate	40%	45%	45%	45%

Taxable income in the two years prior to 2011 was zero. At the beginning of 2011, the company had a deferred income tax (DIT) liability of $160,000, which relates to property, plant, and equipment (PPE) whose carrying value of $1,500,000 exceeded its undepreciated capital cost (UCC) of $1,100,000.

Required:

a. Case A: Prepare the income tax journal entries for the four years 2011 to 2014 assuming that it is probable the company will realize the benefits of tax losses carried forward.
b. Case B: Prepare the income tax journal entries for the four years 2011 to 2014 assuming that it is **not** probable the company will realize the benefits of tax losses carried forward.
c. For both Cases A and B, prepare income statement excerpts including line items between income before tax and net income.
d. Compute the effective tax rate (total tax expense or recovery ÷ income before tax) for each year for both Case A and B. Comment on any differences or patterns in the effective tax rates.

P16-28. Comprehensive question with temporary differences, tax rate changes, and tax losses   (**L.O.** 16-2, **L.O.** 16-3, **L.O.** 16-4) (Difficult – 30 minutes)

Coastal Forests International began operations in 2011. Selected information relating to the company's operations is shown in the following table. DIT denotes deferred income tax. Amounts other than percentages are $000's.

Fiscal years ending December 31:	2011	2012	2013	2014	2015
Pre-tax accounting income (loss)	200	50	(360)	(200)	320
Temporary differences	(40)	(30)	(20)	50	(20)
Taxable income (loss) before carryforward or –back	160	20	(380)	(150)	300
Cumulative balance of deductible (taxable) temporary differences	(40)	(70)	(90)	(40)	(60)
Statutory tax rate (rate changes not known before the year to which they apply)	35%	30%	30%	30%	30%
End-of-year assessment of the degree of likelihood that the benefit of accumulated tax losses will be realized in the future (each year's likelihood is not known before that year)	N/A	N/A	70%	20%	90%
Tax losses carried back to prior years	—	—			
Beginning balance of tax losses carried forward	—	—			
Current-year tax losses carried forward	—	—			
Use of tax losses carried forward from prior years	—	—			
End-of-year balance of tax losses carried forward	—	—			

Fiscal years ending December 31:	2011	2012	2013	2014	2015
End-of-year DIT asset for losses carried forward	—	—			
End-of-year DIT liability for temporary differences					(18)
Journal entry [Please show credit amounts in (parentheses)]					
Income tax expense (recovery)	70		(116)		
Income tax receivable (payable)	(56)			0	0
DIT asset for losses carried forward	—				
DIT liability for temporary differences	(14)				

Required:

Complete the missing information in the table.

P16-29. Presentation and disclosure   (**L.O.** 16-5) (Medium – 15 minutes)

For the year ended October 31, 2009, BMO Financial Group (Bank of Montreal) reported income before tax of $2,080 million and income tax expense of $217 million, for an effective tax rate of 10.4% ($217m / $2,080m). In the notes to the financial statements, BMO's disclosures included the following information:

Reconciliation of statutory and effective tax rates	Amount ($ millions)	Rate (%)
Combined Canadian federal and provincial income taxes at the statutory tax rate	$ 657	31.6%
Increase (decrease) resulting from:		
Tax-exempt income	(161)	(7.7)
Foreign operations subject to different tax rates	(212)	(10.2)
Change in tax rate for deferred income taxes	5	0.2
Intangible assets not deductible for tax purposes	8	0.4
Recovery of prior years' income taxes	(75)	(3.6)
Other	(5)	(0.2)
Income tax expense and effective tax rate	$ 217	10.5%

(Dollar amounts in millions)	2009	2008
Deferred income tax assets	$1,055	$1,196
Deferred income tax liabilities	872	791

Required:

a. From BMO's disclosures provided above, identify any permanent differences.
b. In which direction did the tax rate change from 2008 to 2009?
c. Refer to the line "Recovery of prior years' income taxes" in the above disclosures. What does this information imply about BMO's treatment of tax losses in prior years?

M. MINI-CASES

Income taxes came into being in Canada in 1917 as a "temporary" measure to finance the costly First World War. Ever since then, as surely as night follows day, complaints about income taxation have been frequent but expected. These complaints come from all directions, varying from cries that tax rates are too high, or that governments waste tax revenues, to certain taxpayers do not pay their fair share of taxes.

The global recession in 2008–2009 threw the budgets of most governments in the world out of balance. Canadian governments were not spared. For example, the federal government's budget swung from a modest surplus of $3 billion in the fiscal year ended March 31, 2008, to a deficit of $54 billion for the year ended March 31, 2010. Under these circumstances, the government sought any means possible to reverse the dramatic deficits.

Your good friend Clark Stevens, a (fictitious) member of parliament, has heeded the call for ideas and is examining ways for the government to obtain higher revenues. Stevens is of course aware that raising the tax rate will help to increase revenues, but higher tax rates will also dampen economic activity, which has already suffered due to the recession. Thus, Stevens is looking for more creative alternatives.

Knowing that you are an expert in financial reporting, Stevens meets with you to discuss his ideas.

STEVENS: I have two ideas to raise more tax revenue, but I don't know if they'll work.

YOU: I'll see if I can help.

STEVENS: Well, for my first idea, I want to close down some of the bigger tax loopholes that are unfairly rewarding some taxpayers, especially large corporations. For example, I was looking at the financial statements of Toronto Dominion Bank (TD), one of Canada's largest financial institutions. The bank seems to pay an amazingly small amount of tax and that's not right!

He hands you the financial statements for the year ended October 31, 2009, with the following excerpt in Note 28 highlighted:

Exhibit 1 Reconciliation to statutory tax rate		
	Amount ($ millions)	**Rate (%)**
Income taxes at Canadian statutory income tax rate	$1,006	31.8%
Increase (decrease) resulting from:		
Dividends received	(333)	(10.5)
Rate differentials on international operations	(448)	(14.1)
Other	16	0.4
Provision for income taxes and effective income tax rate	$ 241	7.6%

STEVENS: Look at that—7.6%. Who do you know pays only 7.6% in taxes?

YOU: Hmm. Interesting.

Stevens: Not only that, but take a look at this.
(He points to the following excerpt.)

Exhibit 2 Deferred income tax liabilities[15]	
	Amount ($ millions)
Intangible assets	$ 898
Deferred income	72
Employee benefits	323
Other	519
Deferred income tax liabilities	$1,812

15. Denoted as "Future income tax liabilities" in original financial statements. Adapted here to match contemporary terminology.

CASE 1
The political economy of income tax reporting
(30 minutes)

STEVENS: Looks like TD has paid only $241 million and owes the government another $1.8 billion that it hasn't paid. I don't know how these guys are getting away with it, but I want to put a stop to it. And I don't think it's just TD—there are probably dozens or even hundreds of other companies in similar situations. If we could get even half of what's owed to us, we could cut the deficit down to size in a hurry.

YOU: Well, it's not quite that straightforward.

STEVENS: Why don't you think about it carefully and then write me a short report so I fully understand the issues? Then I'll know how to approach Cabinet about this.

YOU: All right, I'll do my best.

Required:

Draft the report requested by Clark Stevens.

CASE 2
Whitney Equity Partners
(30 minutes)

Whitney Equity Partners (WEP) is a private equity firm that specializes in buying under-performing firms, installing new management or implementing improved management techniques, and then selling the companies at a higher price.

You are one of the analysts at WEP who specialize in financial analysis. The firm has identified two potential targets. Your colleagues have provided you with the financial reports from these two targets. In particular, they have brought to your attention the note disclosures relating to income taxes; Exhibits 1 and 2 are excerpts from relevant parts of these disclosures.

Exhibit 1 Income tax note excerpt for Nieman Inc.

	%	$000's
Combined federal and provincial income tax at statutory rate	31.0%	$4,510
Increase (decrease) resulting from:		
Tax-exempt dividend income	(4.5)	(655)
Income tax expense	26.5%	$3,855

Exhibit 2 Income tax note excerpt for Marcus Company.

	$000's
Current tax expense	$2,110
Deferred income tax relating to increases in tax rates	610
Income tax expense	$2,720*

*This income tax expense of $2,720,000 represents 40% of Nieman's pre-tax income.

Your colleague Jane, who supports the buyout of Nieman Inc., argues that the company must have a management team that is adept at minimizing tax costs. She argues that the low effective tax rate of 26.5% is proof. "Nieman doesn't fit our typical profile for a buyout, but it would be ideal if we are able to get that tax management talent and apply it to all the companies that we buy," she notes.

Kevin, another of your colleagues who supports the buyout of Marcus Company, argues that Marcus Company fits perfectly with WEP's strategy of buying poorly run companies. He notes that the effective tax rate of 40% is much higher than the current statutory rate of 31%. He argues, "The management of Marcus must not be very savvy at tax planning, which suggests that they are probably not that great at management more generally."

Required:

Prepare a memo to respond to the issues raised by your colleagues.

Pensions and Other Employee Future Benefits

Adrian Wyld/TCPI/The Canadian Press

n 2008, almost six million people in Canada participated in over 19,000 pension plans, covering more than 38% of all workers. In the public sector, this percentage rises to 83%, but even in the private sector it is a significant 25% of the total. Clearly, pension plans are important to a large segment of the population.[1]

Of the six million people covered by pension plans, the vast majority (77%) are in defined benefit plans. What are defined benefit plans? How do they differ from other pension plans?

One prominent company that offers defined benefit pension plans is Air Canada, which as of 2009 employed some 22,000 staff. The company has 10 separate pension plans covering various groups of staff ranging from pilots to machinists to management personnel.

At the end of 2008, the company disclosed that it had $10.7 billion in pension obligations. Subtracting from this amount the $9.7 billion of assets in the pension plan, the net obligation was $1.0 billion. Yet, the company reported only $0.54 billion in pension liabilities on the balance sheet. Why is Air Canada able to report only half a billion in liabilities rather than the full $10.7 billion, or even a net liability of $1.0 billion? Is this outcome unique to Air Canada, or should we expect to see this discrepancy in other companies' financial reports? How does Air Canada derive this information and how should we interpret it?

LEARNING OBJECTIVES

After studying this chapter, you should be able to:

L.O. 17-1. Explain the nature of pension plans and distinguish between defined contribution and defined benefit plans.

L.O. 17-2. Apply the accounting standards for defined contribution pension plans.

L.O. 17-3. Analyze an array of pension plan data to determine the amount of pension expense for defined benefit pension plans.

L.O. 17-4. Integrate pension plan information by preparing the note disclosures including the reconciliation of the pension asset or liability recorded on a company's accounts with the amount recorded by the pension plan.

L.O. 17-5. Analyze the effect of actuarial assumptions on the financial statement assets, liabilities, and income, and evaluate the appropriateness of assumptions used to account for pensions.

---

1. Statistics Canada, *The Daily*, June 8, 2009.

CONTENTS

A. INTRODUCTION

Companies frequently offer benefits to their employees in addition to cash pay. Benefits such as extended health and dental plans, life insurance, counselling services, and so on can comprise a significant portion of employees' total pay package (sometimes up to one-third). There are many reasons for having these benefit arrangements instead of wage payments, but the two most important are risk sharing and tax advantages.

First, different people will require services such as health care at different times. Since people are generally risk-averse, it is efficient for a group of people to pay into a health plan that defrays their costs when they subsequently need health services. Fundamentally, this is the reason for universal health care that is funded by the Canadian federal and provincial governments through taxes. The same logic applies to extended health plans that cover services beyond basic health needs (such as dental services and prescription glasses), as well as to other non-health benefit plans.

Second, many employee benefit plans are tax advantageous relative to cash payments to employees. Cash wages are of course deductible to employers and taxable to employees. However, a number of non-cash benefits are deductible to employers but non-taxable to employees. Extended health benefits, dental plans, and disability insurance are examples of these deductible but non-taxable benefits.

From the employer's perspective, it is fairly straightforward to account for employee benefits that are consumed in the same period in which the employees earn them (such as extended health coverage). That is, the employer records an expense for the amount of benefits employees earn in a year, similar to the recording of compensation expense for wages earned. However, the accounting becomes more complicated when employees *earn* the rights to benefits *now* but *consume* those benefits far into the *future*. Pension benefits are one obvious example, which is the focus of this chapter. Sometimes, employers also commit to provide other types of benefits to their employees, such as health care, even after employees have retired; we address this issue toward the end of this chapter.

B. NATURE OF PENSION PLANS

Pension plans involve three parties: the employer, the employees, and the pension trust. The **pension trust** is the legal entity that holds the investments and discharges the obligations of a pension plan; it is managed by a trustee who is independent of the company. A number of flows occur among these three parties:

L.O. 17-1. Explain the nature of pension plans and distinguish between defined contribution and defined benefit plans.

pension trust The legal entity that holds the investments and discharges the obligations of a pension plan.

i. Employees provide services to their employer. To partially compensate for employees' services, the employer pays wages to them.
ii. As part of the employees' compensation, the employer also pays into a pension plan, which will pay employees in the future when they retire.
iii. In many pension plans, employees must also contribute to the pension plan; in other plans, employees have the option to contribute to the pension plan in order to increase the future benefits that they expect to receive.

The following diagram summarizes the relationship among the parties, along with the flows of services and dollars. The dotted arrows indicate flows that are not of particular interest to our discussion in this chapter.

Exhibit 17-1 Schematic of the parties involved in a pension plan and flows between them

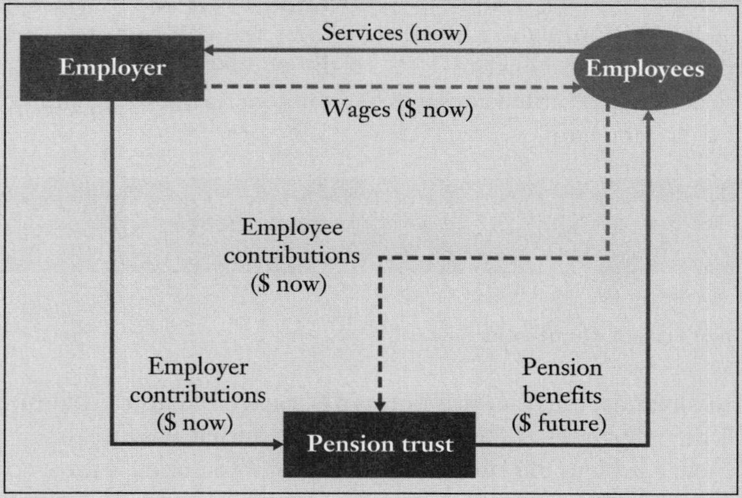

This diagram also helps to identify the two main types of pension plans. The two types reflect whether the pension plan specifies the *inflows* to the pension trust or the *outflows* from it.

1. Defined contribution plans

defined contribution plan A pension plan that specifies how much funds the employer needs to contribute.

A **defined contribution plan** specifies how much money the employer needs to contribute to the pension plan. For example, a plan may require the employer to contribute $10 per hour worked by an employee, or it may require the employer to contribute $1 for every $1 the employee contributes to the plan. These plans place investment risk on employees. That is, poor returns on the pension trust's investments correspondingly reduce the pension benefits that will be paid to employees (future retirees). On the other hand, high returns will result in higher benefit payments to the employees in the future.

2. Defined benefit plans

defined benefit plan A pension plan that specifies how much in pension payments employees will receive during their retirement.

A **defined benefit plan** specifies how much in pension payments employees will receive during their retirement. For example, a plan may require the employer to pay $200 per month for each year of service provided by the employee, so that someone who has worked 30 years for the employer would receive $6,000 per month. These plans place investment risk on employers since the eventual outflows from the pension trust to employees are pre-specified. Inadequate contributions by the pension plan sponsor (i.e., the employer) or poor investment returns will result in an underfunded pension where pension assets are insufficient to cover pension obligations. In this case, the sponsor needs to increase its contributions to the pension trust. In contrast, if the pension plan is overfunded, then the employer can reduce its contributions.[2]

C. ACCOUNTING FOR DEFINED CONTRIBUTION PLANS

L.O. 17-2. Apply the accounting standards for defined contribution pension plans.

When a company uses a defined contribution plan, its rights and obligations begin and end with making the specified contribution according to the contribution formula. The company faces neither the risks nor the benefits of low or high investment returns earned by the pension trust. Given the economics of this type of pension plan, the accounting is fairly straightforward: the company records compensation expense for the amount of contribution it owes according to the contribution formula.

For example, suppose Panorama Cameras provides its 300 employees with a defined contribution plan. The plan requires the company to contribute to the pension an amount equal to 10% of the employee's gross wages. During 2012, these employees earned a total of $15 million. As a result, Panorama would record the following entry:

Exhibit 17-2	Journal entry to record pension expense for Panorama Cameras' defined contribution plan
Dr. Pension expense ($15,000,000 × 10%) 1,500,000	
Cr. Cash or pension contribution payable 1,500,000	

Keep in mind that the pension cost could be capitalized instead of expensed. For example, if the employees are engaged in manufacturing products, then the debit would be capitalized into the labour component of inventories. This is no different from capitalizing the cost of production wages into inventories. Wages and pension cost incurred on employees engaged in constructing a building would be capitalized into property, plant, and equipment. For ease of exposition, this chapter will simply

2. In some instances, the employer may even be able to withdraw surpluses from the pension trust. However, the law in this area is complex and remains unsettled, so it is not clear whether surpluses can be withdrawn by the employer or whether such funds are stranded within the pension plan.

assume that the pension cost will be expensed with the understanding that, under the appropriate circumstances, that cost could be capitalized into various assets.

D. ACCOUNTING FOR DEFINED BENEFIT PLANS

In this type of plan, the employer guarantees to employees a certain amount of benefits in the future. Since pension benefit payments could be decades away from the services the company receives now, there is clearly a severe mismatch in the timing of the future cash payments to employees and when they earn those benefits. Thus, cash accounting is obviously inappropriate and accrual accounting is needed. However, the computations of the amounts to be accrued are complex due to the need to forecast decades into the future. In particular, we need to estimate (at least) the following:

> **L.O.** 17-3.   Analyze an array of pension plan data to determine the amount of pension expense for defined benefit pension plans.

  i. When will each employee be entitled to retire and receive pension payments?
 ii. For how long will each employee be entitled to pension payments? i.e., how long will employees live (how long is their life expectancy)?
iii. How much will be the periodic pension payments for each employee?
 iv. What part of the expected benefit payments relate to services provided in the current year?
  v. What is the value of the pension obligation at retirement?
 vi. How much in plan assets are required now in order to satisfy the pension obligation at retirement?

> **L.O.** 17-5.   Analyze the effect of actuarial assumptions on the financial statement assets, liabilities, and income, and evaluate the appropriateness of assumptions used to account for pensions.

Fortunately, accountants can rely on actuaries for these forecasts. An **actuary** is a professional who specializes in the estimation of risks and uncertainties. Nevertheless, accountants need to be familiar with the basics of the computations in order to assess the reasonability of the actuarial amounts, because these amounts will form the basis of the accounting for the pension plan.

> **actuary**   A professional who specializes in the estimation of risks and uncertainties.

To illustrate the actuarial computations, we focus on a single employee, Mabel Lam, who works for Peachland Canners. (The results for one person can be extrapolated to many people simply by multiplication.) Mabel has worked for Peachland for the past 25 years and she has just turned 55 at the end of 2011. Upon retirement at age 65, the pension specifies that Mabel will be entitled to receive pension payments of $2,000 per year for each year of service provided. Life expectancy tables indicate that a non-smoking female such as Mabel is expected to live until the age of 85. Peachland's management estimates that any assets invested in the pension plan will earn 8% on average, and this is the same rate used to discount her pension obligation.

Exhibit 17-3	Timeline of events for Mabel Lam

End of year:	1986		2011	2021		2041	
Age:	30		55	65		85	
	+		+	+		+	→ Time
Event:	Mabel begins working for Peachland		Now	Retirement		Expected end of pension payments (i.e., death)	

Ultimately, we need to determine the expense relating to the benefits Mabel has earned for the year 2011. To do this, we need to carry out the following steps:

1. Estimate the pension payments Mabel is entitled to receive during retirement for the services she provided during the current year (2011).

2. Estimate the amount of pension assets that will be required when Mabel turns 65 to fund these pension payments from age 65 to age 85, identified in Step 1.

3. Estimate the amount of pension assets required now (at the end of 2011) to obtain the amount of assets required at age 65, calculated in Step 2. This amount is the current service cost, which will be more precisely defined below.

The following diagram shows these three steps along with the calculations for Mabel Lam.

Exhibit 17-4 Calculations for estimating the current service cost for Mabel Lam

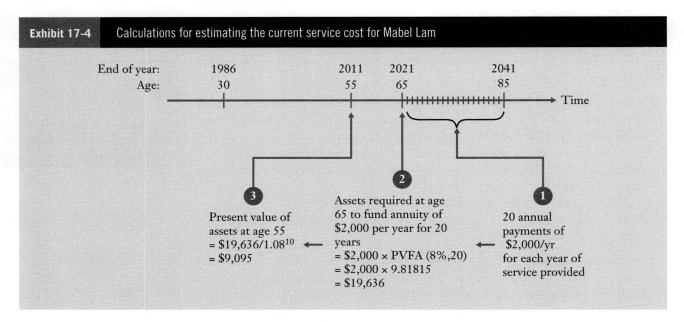

These calculations show that it will cost $9,095, in terms of 2011 dollars, to provide Mabel with pension payments of $2,000 per year over 20 years from 2021 to 2041. As these pension payments are what Mabel earns by working one year, in 2011, this is the amount of expense that Peachland Canners should record in that year. This expense is called the current service cost, which is technically defined in IAS 19 as follows:

current service cost The increase in the present value of pension obligations due to an employee's provision of services during the current period.

¶7. **current service cost** is the increase in the present value of a defined benefit obligation resulting from employee service in the current period.

For each additional year that Mabel works, she earns an additional $2,000 per year during her retirement, and Peachland would record an expense for the current service cost for that year of service received. In 2011, this amount was $9,095. In the following year, the amount would increase to $9,823 (= $19,636/$1.08^9$) because the number of years until retirement reduces by one, from ten years to nine years. Thus, the current service cost increases from year to year according to the discount rate; the amount for 2012 is 8% higher than the amount for 2011 ($9,095 × 1.08 = $9,823).

accrued benefit obligation The present value of pension benefits that employees have earned.

When we add together all of the benefits that Mabel has earned through all her years of employment with Peachland Canners, we obtain the **accrued benefit obligation** that Peachland has promised to Mabel. This obligation represents the present value of pension benefits that employees have earned.

Actual pension plans provide benefit formulas that are more complex than illustrated by this example. Plans will often specify that the pension payments depend on the highest salary earned over a number of years (e.g., highest three years). There can also be adjustments for inflation in the Consumer Price Index.

The current service cost is one of five components of the total pension expense in a period. We discuss all of these components next.[3]

1. What to account for in defined benefit plans

In terms of journal entries, the accounting required for a defined benefit plan is not very complicated. In fact, it typically will involve only three lines: cash, pension expense, and the defined benefit liability. For example, if computations show that the pension expense is $10 million, while the company contributes $8 million to the pension fund, then the journal entry would be as follows:

Exhibit 17-5	Example of a typical journal entry for a defined benefit plan	
Dr. Pension expense	10,000,000	
Cr. Defined benefit liability (difference between expense and cash contribution)		2,000,000
Cr. Cash		8,000,000

Given that the cash component can be readily identified, the important figure to determine is of course the amount of the pension expense. For defined benefit plans, there are five components of pension expense that are important and common across most plans (see IAS 19 ¶61):

a. current service cost,
b. interest cost on pension obligations,
c. income from plan assets,
d. amortization of past service cost, and
e. amortization of actuarial gains and losses.

We can relate these five components of pension expense directly to the three parties in a pension plan as shown in Exhibit 17-1. We repeat that diagram here with some additions:

Exhibit 17-6	The five components of pension expense in relation to the three parties in a defined benefit pension plan

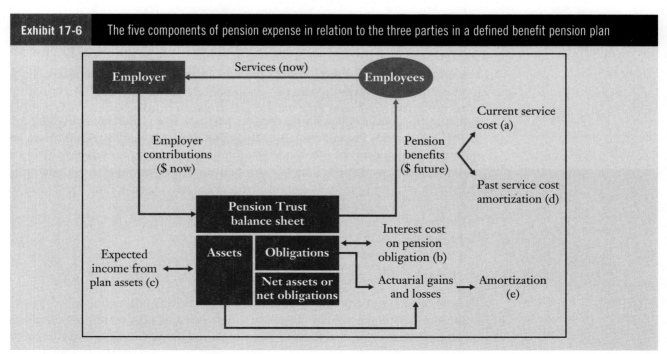

---

3. There are a number of other components that are less frequently encountered. Interested readers should consult the relevant standards (IAS 19 or ASPE Section 3461).

As shown in this diagram, components (a) and (d) relate to the benefits earned by employees, and such benefits arise from services they provided in the current period (current service cost) or in prior periods (past service cost). The other three components relate to the assets and liabilities held in the pension trust. The assets of the trust produce investment income (c), which in turn flows back into the trust to increase asset values. On the liability side, just as for most other debt, the pension obligations incur interest charges (b), which in turn increase the pension obligations. The last component, being the most unintuitive and most complicated, is the amortization of actuarial gains and losses, which are generated from both the assets and obligations of the pension plan. We now look at each of these five components in more detail.

a. Current service cost

As explained in the last section, this portion of the pension expense is the increase in the present value of the pension obligation that results from the employees' current services. In any active pension plan, this component will always be present. Information on current service cost is provided by the pension plan's actuary.

b. Interest cost

The interest cost component of the pension expense represents the increase in the pension obligation due to the passage of time (i.e., due to the pension payment dates becoming closer). IFRS specifies that enterprises should use the yields on high-quality corporate bonds. The term of the bonds should have a maturity that matches the term of the pension obligations. In particular, IAS 19 states:

> ¶77. Financial assumptions shall be based on market expectations, at the end of the reporting period, for the period over which the obligations are to be settled.

That is, generally, long-term rates are more appropriate to match the long-term nature of pension plans. If pension payments will be 20 years in the future for the average employee, then the yield on 20-year bonds would be most appropriate.

c. Expected income from plan assets

Assets in the pension plan earn investment income from interest, dividends, and capital gains. This income increases the value of plan assets. It is important to note that the amount of income used is the *expected* income rather than actual amounts, because over the long life of a pension plan it is the expected amounts that are relevant. For purposes of estimating expected income, long-term rates of return should be used rather than short-term rates. Deviations of actual investment results and the expected income accumulate in actuarial gains and losses (see item e).

d. Amortization of past service costs

past service cost The increase in the present value of pension obligations due to initiations or amendment of a pension plan that rewards employees with benefits for services provided in the past.

vesting date The date when an employee's entitlement to the pension benefits is no longer dependent on continued employment with the company.

Past service costs arise from plan initiations and amendments offered by the employer. A company could introduce a new pension plan or improve benefits on an existing plan, and give these new/improved benefits retroactively to cover several years of past service. These costs need to be amortized systematically. IFRS requires this amortization to be recorded on a straight-line basis over the period up to the vesting date. The **vesting date** is the date when an employee's entitlement to the pension benefits is no longer dependent on continued employment with the company. If the vesting date was prior to the plan initiation or amendment (i.e., the benefits have "vested"), the entire past service is expensed immediately.

e. Amortization of actuarial gains and losses—The corridor approach

Actuarial gains and losses can arise from either the assets or the obligations of a pension plan. On the asset side, these gains and losses come from the difference between the actual and the expected value of plan assets, which reflects an accumulation of differences between actual and expected investment earnings. On the obligation side, the gains and losses derive from differences between the actual and expected values of the obligation. Since these gains and losses are due to actual experience being different from expectations, actuarial gains and losses are also called "experience gains and losses."

The next step is to combine the gains and losses from the pension assets and obligations and determine the net gain or loss. The employer then evaluates whether this net gain or loss exceeds a **corridor** limit. If the amount of net gain or loss is within the corridor, no amortization is required. If the net gain or loss exceeds the corridor, the excess needs to be amortized.

The corridor limit at the end of a year is the greater of two amounts at that date:

- 10% of the pension plan assets, and
- 10% of the pension obligations.

The idea behind the corridor is that over short periods pension plan performance will deviate from expectations, but we expect these deviations to cancel out over time. To avoid temporary fluctuations in pension plan performance from affecting the amount of pension expense and ultimately the reported results of the sponsoring company (i.e., the employer), accounting standards allow deviations under a certain amount (the corridor limit) to not require amortization into income. Thus, the corridor acts as a shock absorber for temporary fluctuations in the pension plan's performance.

A second shock absorber is the treatment of the amount outside the corridor. If the amount of net gain or loss exceeds the corridor limit, then the excess needs to be amortized into income *beginning in the following year*. Third, the amortization of the amount outside the corridor occurs over a period of

actuarial gain   A favourable difference between actual and expected amounts for pension assets or obligations; also called an experience gain.

actuarial loss   An unfavourable difference between actual and expected amounts for pension assets or obligations; also called an experience loss.

corridor   The limit within which actuarial gains and losses need not be amortized into income.

WHY SHOCK ABSORBERS IN PENSION ACCOUNTING ARE ECONOMICALLY EFFICIENT

Without the corridor limit and amortization process acting as shock absorbers, companies would be less willing to use defined benefit pension plans because management generally dislikes volatile earnings. As noted in the introduction, the use of defined benefit plans is economically efficient from a risk-sharing point of view. In other words, these pension plans reduce risk for employees in general, but would increase risk for management if companies were required to record all actuarial gains and losses through income immediately.

time called the expected average remaining service lives (EARSL) of the active employee group. EARSL represents the number of years that the current employee cohort covered by the pension plan is expected to continue working for the company and earning pension benefits. The projected service life factors in expected retirements, employees voluntarily quitting, or termination by the employer.

To illustrate the corridor amortization, consider the following facts about Fogo Island Brewers, which has a December 31 fiscal year-end. The company has a small defined benefit pension plan for its executives. The EARSL for these executives is eight years.

Exhibit 17-7	Pension assets and liabilities for Fogo Island Brewers			
Balances at December 31	2011	2012	2013	2014
Pension assets	$14,000,000	$12,800,000	$13,500,000	$13,600,000
Pension obligations	13,200,000	13,500,000	13,800,000	14,200,000
Unamortized actuarial gains (losses)	(250,000)	(1,300,000)	120,000	(1,500,000)

Based on these values, the corridor limits for 2012 to 2015 would be as follows:

Exhibit 17-8	Corridor limits for Fogo Island Brewers			
Balances at December 31	2011	2012	2013	2014
10% of pension assets	$1,400,000	$ 1,280,000	$ 1,350,000	$ 1,360,000
10% of pension obligations	1,320,000	1,350,000	1,380,000	1,420,000
Corridor limit (greater of above)	$ 1,400,000	$ 1,350,000	$ 1,380,000	$ 1,430,000
Unamortized actuarial gains (losses)	$ (250,000)	$(1,300,000)	$ 120,000	$ (1,500,000)
Corridor limit	1,400,000	1,350,000	1,380,000	1,420,000
Amount outside corridor: gain (loss)	$ 0	$ 0	$ 0	$ (80,000)
EARSL				÷ 8 years
Amortization beginning following year				$ (10,000)

At the end of years 2011 to 2013, the amounts of actuarial gains or losses are within the corridor, so no amortization results. At the end of 2014, the amount outside the corridor is $80,000, which results in a minimum amortization of $10,000 per year *beginning in 2015*.

An important note about the amortization of actuarial gains and losses is that the amount determined using the corridor limit and EARSL is the *minimum* amortization. An enterprise may choose a faster amortizing policy, as long as it follows that policy consistently from period to period and for both gains and losses.

Immediate recognition alternative for actuarial gains and losses

The corridor amortization just described reduces the impact of changes in the pension plan value on a company's income in three ways. First, enterprises need not amortize actuarial gains or losses that are within the corridor. Second, any amortization of amounts in excess of the corridor limit begins in the year following the year-end in which the excess amount is identified. Third, the amortization takes place over many years (i.e., EARSL). However, IFRS also permits a company to forgo these three smoothing mechanisms and recognize all of the actuarial gains and losses in the periods in which they arise. The benefit of doing so is that the amount passes through other comprehensive income rather than through profit or loss. This option is available only if the enterprise applies this policy for all of its defined benefit plans and for all of its actuarial gains and losses.

2. Implementing pension accounting for defined benefit plans

As noted above, the major task in pension accounting is the determination of the pension expense, which has five components. This section explains how one goes about collecting the necessary information and synthesizing that information to compute these five components.

Two reports will contain much of the necessary information. The first is the Pension Trustee's Report on the pension plan assets. This report provides information about the changes in the assets of the pension plan. Among the information items are:

- expected income on plan assets;
- contribution to the plan;
- benefits paid out of the plan to retirees;
- actual value of the plan assets at end of year.

The second report is the Pension Actuary's Report on the pension plan obligations. This report provides information about the changes in the obligations of the pension plan. Among the items in this report are:

- interest cost on the obligation;
- current service cost;
- benefits paid out of the plan to retirees; and
- actual value of the pension obligation at end of year.

In addition to these two reports, enterprises will require two other pieces of information: the amount of past service cost that remains unamortized, and the balance of previous actuarial gains or losses that remain unamortized. This information is available from the enterprises' own accounting records.

Putting all this information together, we construct the five components of pension expense as illustrated in the following schematic. The bottom of the diagram also shows the other two elements in the three-line journal entry, namely the cash contribution to the pension plan and the amount of adjustment to the pension asset and liability accounts on the balance sheet.

| Exhibit 17-9 | Schematic showing the derivation of the five components of pension expense |

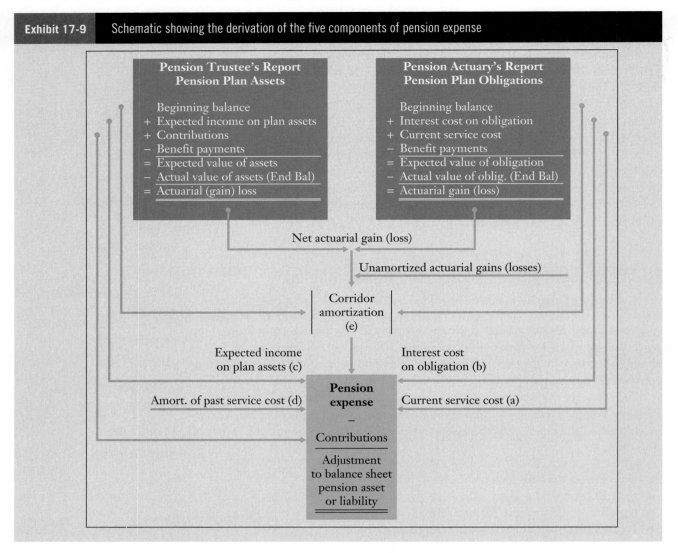

To illustrate the process of synthesizing the information shown in Exhibit 17-9, consider the following example of GB Corp. The example will proceed through two years, one at a time, to highlight different aspects of pension accounting.

| Exhibit 17-10 | Information compiled for GB Corp. to illustrate computation of pension expense |

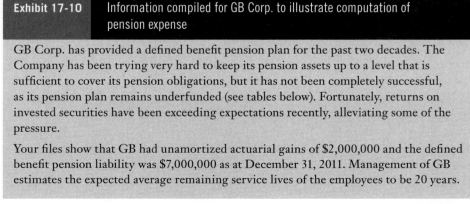

GB Corp. has provided a defined benefit pension plan for the past two decades. The Company has been trying very hard to keep its pension assets up to a level that is sufficient to cover its pension obligations, but it has not been completely successful, as its pension plan remains underfunded (see tables below). Fortunately, returns on invested securities have been exceeding expectations recently, alleviating some of the pressure.

Your files show that GB had unamortized actuarial gains of $2,000,000 and the defined benefit pension liability was $7,000,000 as at December 31, 2011. Management of GB estimates the expected average remaining service lives of the employees to be 20 years.

(Continued)

Exhibit 17-10	Continued

Table 1—Pension trustee's report on plan assets

	2012
Beginning balance, January 1, 2012	$50,000,000
Expected income on plan assets @8%*	4,000,000
Contributions	13,000,000
Benefit payments	(11,000,000)
Expected value of assets, December 31, 2012	56,000,000
Actual value of assets, December 31, 2012	60,000,000
Actuarial (gain) loss	$ (4,000,000)

*8% × beginning balance

Table 2—Actuary's report on pension obligations

	2012
Beginning balance	$55,000,000
Interest cost on obligation @8%†	4,400,000
Current service cost	15,900,000
Benefit payments	(11,000,000)
Expected value of obligation, December 31, 2012	64,300,000
Actual value of obligation, December 31, 2012	62,500,000
Actuarial gain (loss)	$ 1,800,000

†8% of beginning balance

Based on the above information, the computation of the pension expense and the journal entries would be as shown in the following exhibit.

Exhibit 17-11	Calculation of pension expense for GB Corp.

Calculation of the corridor and amortization of actuarial gain or loss

	2012
10% of beginning assets (Table 1)	$ 5,000,000
10% of beginning obligations (Table 2)	5,500,000
Greater of above = corridor	$ 5,500,000
Beginning unamortized actuarial gains (losses), Jan. 1, 2012 (given)	$ 2,000,000
Amount subject to amortization = gains or losses outside corridor	Nil
Beginning unamortized actuarial gains (losses), Jan. 1, 2012 (given)	$ 2,000,000
Current actuarial gain (loss) on assets (Table 1)	4,000,000
Current actuarial gain (loss) on obligations (Table 2)	1,800,000
Amortization of actuarial gains (losses) (above)	0
Ending unamortized actuarial gains (losses), December 31, 2012	$ 7,800,000

Calculation of pension expense

Dr (Cr)	2012
a. Current service cost (Table 2)	$ 15,900,000
b. Interest cost on obligation (Table 2)	4,400,000
c. Expected income on plan assets (Table 1)	(4,000,000)
d. Amortization of past service cost	0
e. Amortization of actuarial (gains) losses (above)	0
Pension expense	**$16,300,000**

Based on this amount of pension expense, GB Corp. would record the following journal entry for the defined benefit pension liability account.

Exhibit 17-12	GB Corp. example: Journal entries and balance of the defined benefit liability account		
Journal entry for pension expense in 2012			
Dr. Pension expense (Exhibit 17-11)		16,300,000	
Cr. Cash (Exhibit 17-10)			13,000,000
Cr. Defined benefit liability			3,300,000
Defined benefit liability account balances			
Balance, December 31, 2011 (given in Exhibit 17-10)			$ 7,000,000 Cr
2012 Adjustment (journal entry above)			3,300,000 Cr
Balance, December 31, 2012			$10,300,000 Cr

The example thus far demonstrates probably the simplest scenario in which a company has only three of the five components of pension expense. That is, GB did not have any past service cost (component d) nor did it have to record any corridor amortization (component e). We now illustrate these two additional components of the pension expense by following GB's pension plan through a second year.

Exhibit 17-13	Information compiled for GB Corp., second year

Effective Jan 1, 2013, the Company increased the future benefit payments for all existing employees. The actuarial cost of this plan amendment was $10 million and these additional benefits vest five years after the plan amendment

Management of GB believes that the estimate of 20 years for the expected average remaining service lives of the employees remains valid.

The following tables summarize information provided by the pension plan trustee and actuary.

Table 1—Pension trustee's report on plan assets

	2013
Beginning balance, January 1, 2013	$60,000,000
Expected income on plan assets @8%*	4,800,000
Contributions	15,000,000
Benefit payments	(12,000,000)
Expected value of assets, December 31, 2013	$67,800,000
Actual value of assets, December 31, 2013	72,000,000
Actuarial (gain) loss	$ (4,200,000)

*8% × beginning balance

Table 2—Actuary's report on pension obligations

	2013
Beginning balance, January 1, 2013	$62,500,000
Plan amendment, effective January 1, 2013	10,000,000
Beginning balance adjusted for plan amendment	$72,500,000
Interest cost on obligation @8%†	5,800,000
Current service cost	16,200,000
Benefit payments	(12,000,000)
Expected value of obligation, December 31, 2013	$82,500,000
Actual value of obligation, December 31, 2013	82,000,000
Actuarial gain (loss)	$ 500,000

†8% of beginning balance including plan amendment at beginning of year.

Based on the above information, the computation of the pension expense and the journal entries for 2013 would be as shown in the following exhibit.

Exhibit 17-14	Calculation of pension expense for GB Corp., second year

Calculation of the corridor and amortization of actuarial gain or loss

	2013
10% of beginning assets (Table 1)	$ 6,000,000
10% of beginning obligations (Table 2)	6,250,000
Greater of above = corridor	$ 6,250,000
Beginning unamortized actuarial gains (losses) (Exhibit 17-11)	7,800,000
Amount subject to amortization = gain or loss outside corridor	$ 1,550,000
EARSL	20 years
Minimum corridor amortization	$ 77,500
Beg. unamortized actuarial gains (losses) (Exhibit 17-11), Jan. 1, 2013	$ 7,800,000
Current actuarial gain (loss) on assets (Table 1)	4,200,000
Current actuarial gain (loss) on oblig. (Table 2)	500,000
Add (subtract): Amortization of actuarial (gains) losses (from above)	(77,500)
Ending unamortized actuarial gains (losses), December 31, 2013	$ 12,422,500

Calculation of pension expense

Dr (Cr)	2013
a. Current service cost (Table 2)	$ 16,200,000
b. Interest cost on obligation (Table 2)	5,800,000
c. Expected income on plan assets (Table 1)	(4,800,000)
d. Amortization of past service cost ($10,000,000/5 yrs)	2,000,000
e. Amortization of actuarial (gains) losses (from above)	(77,500)
Pension expense	**$ 19,122,500**

Based on this amount of pension expense, GB Corp. would record the following journal entry for the defined benefit pension liability account.

Exhibit 17-15	GB Corp. example: Journal entries and balance of the defined benefit liability, second year

Journal entry to record pension expense for 2013		
Dr. Pension expense (Exhibit 17-14)	19,122,500	
Cr. Cash (Exhibit 17-13)		15,000,000
Cr. Defined benefit liability		4,122,500
Defined benefit liability account balances		
Balance, December 31, 2012 (carry forward from Exhibit 17-12)		$10,300,000 Cr
2013 Adjustment (journal entry above)		4,122,500 Cr
Balance, December 31, 2013		$14,422,500 Cr

The above discussion and illustration of the accounting for pensions highlights the economic relationships among employers, employees, and pension plans. This approach emphasizes an understanding of the flows among the three parties. An equivalent approach that is sometimes used in practice standardizes the above analysis into a worksheet. We demonstrate this approach in the Appendix to this chapter.

3. Presentation and disclosure

The accounting for defined benefit pension plans affects only three accounts: cash, pension expense, and the defined benefit liability or asset. The latter two amounts, if they are not separately identified on the income statement or balance sheet, respectively, must be disclosed in the notes. In addition, enterprises need to disclose the components of pension expense.

When a company has more than one defined benefit plan, IFRS does not permit it to offset pension asset and pension liability amounts, in accordance with the general prohibition against offsetting assets and liabilities. If an enterprise has a pension plan with a defined benefit liability and another plan with a defined benefit asset, the two amounts would be shown separately in the balance sheet. (Exceptional cases in which offsetting would be permitted are rare; refer to IAS 19 for discussion of these conditions.) Two plans that both have net liability positions can be combined, and likewise if they both have net asset balances.

Note that the reporting on the employer's books does not fully reflect the assets and liabilities of the pension plan (i.e., due to the use of the corridor method and the presence of any unamortized past service cost). Consequently, information about the assets or liabilities of the pension plan would be useful to readers, so this information needs to be disclosed.

For GB Corp., the pension plan assets and liabilities would be as follows:

Exhibit 17-16	Pension plan assets, obligations, and net surplus or deficit for GB Corp.	
	2012	**2013**
Fair value of pension assets (from Pension Trustee's report)	$60,000,000	$ 72,000,000
Accrued pension obligation (from Pension Actuary's report)	62,500,000	82,000,000
Pension plan surplus (deficit)	$ (2,500,000)	$(10,000,000)

In addition to the above information, enterprises need to present a reconciliation between (i) the defined benefit asset or liability on the employer's books and (ii) the net pension surplus or deficit according to the pension plan. The reconciling items are those that enter into one set of financial statements but not the other. A careful analysis of Exhibit 17-9 reveals that there are two reconciling items: the unamortized portion of past service costs, and the unamortized portion of actuarial gains and losses. Being *unamortized*, these two amounts have not yet entered the financial statements of the reporting enterprise (the employer), but they are part of the pension plan's assets and liabilities. The reconciliation between the two amounts would have the following structure:

Exhibit 17-17	Structure of reconciliation between the reporting enterprise's books and those of the pension plan
Defined pension asset (dr) or liability (cr) on plan sponsor's books	
+ Unamortized past service cost (cr)	
+ Unamortized actuarial gains (dr) or losses (cr)	
= Net pension surplus (dr) or deficit (cr) in pension trust	

Unamortized past service costs are obligations of the employer to pay additional benefits to employees that have not yet been recorded on the company's financial statements; therefore, the reconciling item is a credit to reflect the off-balance-sheet liability. Unamortized actuarial gains are off-balance-sheet assets, while unamortized actuarial losses are off-balance-sheet liabilities, so they are debits and credits in the reconciliation, respectively. This reconciliation for GB Corp. would be as follows:

Exhibit 17-18	Reconciliation of defined benefit liability and pension deficit for GB Corp.	
Dr (Cr)	**2012**	**2013**
Defined benefit pension asset (liability) (from Exhibits 17-12 and 17-15)	$(10,300,000)	$ (14,422,500)
Add (subtract): Unamortized past service cost ($2 million of $10 million amortized; see Exhibit 17-14)	—	(8,000,000)
Add (subtract): Unamortized actuarial gains (losses) (see Exhibits 17-11 and 17-14)	7,800,000	12,422,500
Pension surplus (deficit) (from Exhibit 17-16)	$ (2,500,000)	$(10,000,000)

Depending on the magnitude of the reconciling items, it is possible for the sponsoring company to show a defined benefit asset while there is a deficit in the pension plan, or for the company to show a liability while the pension is in surplus.

In Exhibit 17-19, we use GB Corp. to illustrate the main note disclosures for defined benefit pension plans.

Exhibit 17-19	Note disclosures for GB Corp.	
The following components comprise the pension expense recorded through income:		
Dr (Cr)	**2012**	**2013**
Current service cost	$ 15,900,000	$ 16,200,000
Interest cost on obligation	4,400,000	5,800,000
Expected income on plan assets	(4,000,000)	(4,800,000)
Amortization of past service cost	0	2,000,000
Amortization of actuarial (gains) losses	0	(77,500)
Pension expense	$ 16,300,000	$ 19,122,500
The Company's pension plan had assets and liabilities as follows:		
	2012	**2013**
Fair value of pension assets	$ 60,000,000	$ 72,000,000
Accrued pension obligation	62,500,000	82,000,000
Pension plan surplus (deficit)	$ (2,500,000)	$(10,000,000)
The following reconciles the pension liability amounts reported on the balance sheet with surplus (deficit) in the pension plan:		
	2012	**2013**
Defined benefit pension asset (liability)	$(10,300,000)	$(14,422,500)
Add: Unamortized past service cost	—	(8,000,000)
Add: Unamortized actuarial gain (loss)	7,800,000	12,422,500
Pension plan surplus (deficit)	$ (2,500,000)	$(10,000,000)

E. OTHER ISSUES

1. Settlements and curtailments

settlement (of a pension) The extinguishment of all or part of an enterprise's pension obligations.

curtailment A reduction in the number of employees or the amount of benefits they will receive in the future.

A **settlement** occurs when an enterprise extinguishes all or part of its pension obligations. One way to do this is through a lump-sum cash payment in lieu of the future stream of payments. A **curtailment** is a reduction in the number of employees or the amount of benefits they will receive in the future. Upon settlement or curtailment, the pension obligations and asset values will change significantly, so these amounts need to be re-estimated. Any gains or losses from settlements and curtailments would flow through income.

2. Multi-employer plans

Pension plans typically have a single sponsor company. In some instances, a pension plan will have several sponsoring companies. This happens most commonly with small and medium-sized enterprises because each enterprise does not have a sufficiently large employee base to establish a pension plan on its own.

For *defined contribution* plans, a multi-employer plan adds no additional complexity because the risk relating to the performance of the pension plan rests with the employees. However, multi-employer *defined benefit* plans face an obvious problem: how do the different employers share the risk of the pension plan? If one company is unable to provide the funds necessary for the provision of the defined benefits, would the others have to make up the shortfall?

In general, IAS 19 requires a company participating in a multi-employer defined benefit plan to account for its proportionate share as a defined benefit plan. In exceptional circumstances where there is insufficient information available to apply defined benefit accounting, the company can account for the multi-employer plan as a *defined contribution* plan with accompanying disclosures regarding the plan as noted in IAS 19 paragraph 30.

3. Other long-term employee benefits

Some companies provide other employee benefits that are similar to pension benefits in that employees receive these benefits in the future rather than during their employment. For example, many companies in the U.S. continue to pay for health services used by former employees who have retired; similar benefits are less common and less significant in Canada given that basic health services are government-funded. Nevertheless, Air Canada, for example, (see the opening vignette) reported a liability of $1.1 billion for employee future benefits (other than pensions). This amount is double the amount reported for the defined pension liability of $540 million. The main reason that the number seems high is that these non–pension benefits are unfunded (meaning there are no assets set aside to pay for these benefits), whereas the pension plan obligation of $10.7 billion is almost fully funded by $9.7 billion in assets.

Following the logic of accounting for pension benefits, if an enterprise offers employees other future benefits, it should also account for those benefits in a way that is similar to defined benefit pension plans. That is, the company should accrue an expense for benefits earned by employees in the year they earn those benefits, and a liability for the provision of those benefits in the future.

While the basic idea is straightforward, the implementation requires many estimates that are even more subjective than for pension benefits.

- The benefits promised are often in terms of services (e.g., health care), not dollars as for pensions.
- Costs for promised services such as health care change considerably over time.
- Employees' use of those future services is irregular compared with periodic payments for pension plans.
- Whereas pension plans have formal and explicit contracts, there are usually no contractual obligations to pay for the promised services. The obligation is constructive rather than contractual, so the range and amount of services covered may be expanded or curtailed unilaterally by the company.

Due to all these factors, amounts reported for such future benefits should be interpreted with a considerable amount of caution.

F. SUBSTANTIVE DIFFERENCES BETWEEN RELEVANT IFRS AND ASPE

ISSUE	IFRS	ASPE
Past service cost	Enterprises shall amortize past service cost over the vesting period of the benefits.	Enterprises may choose one of two approaches: deferral and amortization over the vesting period, or immediate recognition in income.
Actuarial gains and losses	Enterprises may choose either the corridor method or the immediate recognition alternative. The effect of the latter passes through other comprehensive income (OCI).	Enterprises may choose either the corridor method or the immediate recognition alternative. The effect of the latter passes through income.

G. APPENDIX: WORKSHEET APPROACH FOR PENSION ACCOUNTING

The worksheet approach is frequently used in practice because it is a standardized way to keep track of the various transactions in a pension. The basic idea behind this worksheet is to systematically maintain a record of each transaction affecting the pension, regardless of whether it should be recognized in the books of the plan sponsor (i.e., employer). Each entry in the worksheet looks like a traditional journal entry in that each entry balances the debits and credits. However, it is important to note that the worksheet entries are not journal entries because they are not recorded in the sponsor's accounting system (i.e., general ledger).

To illustrate the worksheet approach, we repeat the example of GB Corp. that we used earlier in the chapter. For ease of reference, the following exhibit summarizes the facts for the two years.

| Exhibit 17-20 | Information on GB's pension plan for two years for illustrating worksheet approach |

GB Corp. has provided a defined benefit pension plan for the past two decades. Your files show that GB had unamortized actuarial gains of $2,000,000 and that the defined benefit pension liability was $7,000,000 as at December 31, 2011. Management of GB estimates the expected average remaining service lives of the employees to be 20 years.

Effective Jan. 1, 2013, the Company increased the future benefit payments for all existing employees. The actuarial cost of this plan amendment was $10 million and these additional benefits vest five years after the plan amendment.

Table 1—Pension trustee's report on plan assets

	2012	2013
Beginning balance, January 1	$50,000,000	$60,000,000
Expected income on plan assets @8%*	4,000,000	4,800,000
Contributions	13,000,000	15,000,000
Benefit payments	(11,000,000)	(12,000,000)
Expected value of assets, December 31	56,000,000	67,800,000
Actual value of assets, December 31	60,000,000	72,000,000
Actuarial (gain) loss	$ (4,000,000)	$ (4,200,000)

*8% × beginning balance

Table 2—Actuary's report on pension obligations

	2012	2013
Beginning balance, January 1	$55,000,000	$62,500,000
Plan amendment	n/a	10,000,000
Interest cost on obligation @8%[†]	4,400,000	5,800,000
Current service cost	15,900,000	16,200,000
Benefit payments	(11,000,000)	(12,000,000)
Expected value of obligation, December 31	64,300,000	82,500,000
Actual value of obligation, December 31	62,500,000	82,000,000
Actuarial gain (loss)	$ 1,800,000	$ 500,000

[†]8% of beginning balance including plan amendment at beginning of year.

The following tables are the two worksheets for the example of GB Corp., one for each year. Notice the top portion of each table shows the worksheet entries (not journal entries) for the pension. The net effect of these various transactions is then captured by the summary journal entry shown at the bottom portion of the table. The combination of the net effects of the transactions and the opening balances produces the balances at the end of the year, shown at the bottom of each table.

To understand this worksheet method, consider the current service cost of $15,900,000. The worksheet shows a debit for this amount in Column A for Annual Pension Expense because this is one of the five components of the expense. The credit for this entry is shown in Column E as an increase to the projected pension obligation (PBO). As noted before, the PBO account used for the credit portion of this entry is not an account on the books of the plan sponsor (GB Corp.). Similar to current service cost, the rows for the interest cost and the

| Exhibit 17-21 | Worksheet for GB Corp., first year |

	Accounts of plan sponsor			Other accounts			
Year 2012 Amounts in $000's	Annual pension expense	Cash	Defined benefit pension asset (dr) or liability (cr)	Plan assets	Projected benefit obligation (PBO)	Unrecognized past service cost (PSC)	Unrecognized actuarial gains (cr) or losses (dr)
Column reference	A	B	C	D	E	F	G
Transaction worksheet							
Current service cost	15,900 dr				15,900 cr		
Interest cost	4,400 dr				4,400 cr		
Expected income	4,000 cr			4,000 dr			
Amortization of PSC	0						
Amortization of actuarial gain/loss	0						
Contribution		13,000 cr		13,000 dr			
Benefit payments				11,000 cr	11,000 dr		
Actuarial gain on pension assets				4,000 dr			4,000 cr
Actuarial gain on pension obligation					1,800 dr		1,800 cr
Net amounts	16,300 dr	13,000 cr		10,000 dr	7,500 cr		5,800 cr
Summary journal entry	16,300 dr	13,000 cr	3,300 cr				
Balance, Jan. 1, 2012	n/a	n/a	7,000 cr	50,000 dr	55,000 cr	0	2,000 cr
Balance, Dec. 31, 2012	n/a	n/a	10,300 cr	60,000 dr	62,500 cr	0	7,800 cr

Note: The balances at the beginning and at the end of the period should be as follows: C = D + E + F + G.

expected income on the invested assets have only one side of the worksheet entry on GB's accounts. Cash contributions by GB into the pension plan decrease its cash and increase the cash assets in the pension trust.

The remaining three worksheet entries use accounts that are entirely outside of GB's books. First, the benefit payments to retirees reduce both pension plan assets and obligations. Second, the actuarial gain (loss) on the pension plan's assets increase (decrease) the pension assets relative to the expected amount. Third, the actuarial gain (loss) on the pension plan's obligations decrease (increase) the pension obligation relative to the expected amount. Under the corridor approach, actuarial gains (losses) on plan assets and obligations do not affect the plan sponsor (GB) until the amounts are amortized.

The bottom part of the worksheet brings together the worksheet entries above. The net amounts in Columns A and B are the amounts to be entered in the journal entry of the plan sponsor (GB). As discussed earlier in the chapter, the balancing amount is the adjustment to the defined benefit pension asset or liability. Columns C through G show the beginning balances, net adjustments for the year, and the ending balances.

Moving to the second year, the worksheet would be as follows:

| Exhibit 17-22 | Worksheet for GB Corp., second year |

	Accounts of plan sponsor			Other accounts			
Year 2013 **Amounts in $000's**	Annual pension expense	Cash	Defined benefit pension asset (dr) or liability (cr)	Plan assets	Projected benefit obligation (PBO)	Un-recognized past service cost (PSC)	Unrecognized actuarial gains (cr) or losses (dr)
Column reference	**A**	**B**	**C**	**D**	**E**	**F**	**G**
Transaction worksheet							
Plan amendment					10,000 cr	10,000 dr	
Current service cost	16,200 dr				16,200 cr		
Interest cost	5,800 dr				5,800 cr		
Expected income	4,800 cr			4,800 dr			
Amortization of PSC	2,000 dr					2,000 cr	
Amortization of actuarial gain/loss	77.5 cr						77.5 dr
Contribution		15,000 cr		15,000 dr			
Benefit payments				12,000 cr	12,000 dr		
Actuarial gain on pension assets				4,200 dr			4,200 cr
Actuarial gain on pension obligation					500 dr		500 cr
Net amounts	19,122.5 dr	15,000 cr		12,000 dr	19,500 cr	8,000 dr	4,622.5 cr
Summary journal entry	19,122.5 dr	15,000 cr	4,122.5 cr				
Balance, Jan. 1, 2013	n/a	n/a	10,300 cr	60,000 dr	62,500 cr	0	7,800 cr
Balance, Dec. 31, 2013	n/a	n/a	14,422.5 cr	72,000 dr	82,000 cr	8,000 dr	12,422.5 cr

Other than the specific amounts, the only difference between the worksheets of the two years is the addition of two items to the second worksheet that were not relevant to the first one: amortization of past service cost (PSC) and amortization of actuarial gain or loss. Just like the other three components of pension expense, one side of the worksheet entry uses GB's accounts and the other side uses accounts outside of GB.

H. SUMMARY

L.O. 17-1. Explain the nature of pension plans and distinguish between defined contribution and defined benefit plans.

■ Pension plans provide future cash flow benefits to employees in partial exchange for current services.
■ Defined contribution plans specify the inflow of funds that the sponsoring company needs to contribute to the plan, whereas defined benefit plans specify the outflows to retirees.

L.O. 17-2. Apply the accounting standards for defined contribution pension plans.

■ An enterprise should record an expense for the contribution it is required to make to the pension plan corresponding to the services provided by employees.

L.O. 17-3. Analyze an array of pension plan data to determine the amount of pension expense for defined benefit pension plans.

- There are five common components to the pension expense for a defined benefit plan: current service cost, interest on the obligation, income on plan assets, amortization of past service cost, and amortization of actuarial gains and losses.
- One can determine these five components of pension expense by using two reports from the pension trustee and the pension actuary, plus information on the opening balances of unamortized past service cost and actuarial gains and losses.

L.O. 17-4. Integrate pension plan information by preparing the note disclosures including the reconciliation of the pension asset or liability recorded on a company's accounts with the amount recorded by the pension plan.

- Enterprises need to provide information on the components of pension expense, pension plan assets and liabilities, and a reconciliation between the defined pension asset or liability reported and the surplus or deficit in the pension plan.
- The reconciling items are the unamortized balances of past service cost and actuarial gains and losses. These two items have not yet flowed through the financial statements of the employer/sponsor, but are nonetheless included in the pension plan's assets and obligations.

L.O. 17-5. Analyze the effect of actuarial assumptions on the financial statement assets, liabilities, and income, and evaluate the appropriateness of assumptions used to account for pensions.

- Pension accounting involves many estimates regarding uncertain future outcomes. These estimates can change significantly with small changes in assumptions about the rate of return on pension plan assets, the discount rate of pension obligations, life expectancy, employee turnover rates, inflation, and so on.

I. References

Authoritative standards:

IFRS	ASPE Section
IAS 19—Employee benefits	3461—Employee future benefits

J. Glossary

accrued benefit obligation: The present value of pension benefits that employees have earned.

actuarial gain: A favourable difference between actual and expected amounts for pension assets or obligations; also called an experience gain.

actuarial loss: An unfavourable difference between actual and expected amounts for pension assets or obligations; also called an experience loss.

actuary: A professional who specializes in the estimation of risks and uncertainties.

corridor: The limit within which actuarial gains and losses need not be amortized into income.

current service cost: The increase in the present value of pension obligations due to an employee's provision of services during the current period.

curtailment: A reduction in the number of employees or the amount of benefits they will receive in the future.

defined benefit plan: A pension plan that specifies how much in pension payments employees will receive during their retirement.

defined contribution plan: A pension plan that specifies how much funds the employer needs to contribute.

past service cost: The increase in the present value of pension obligations due to initiations or amendment of a pension plan that rewards employees with benefits for services provided in the past.

pension trust: The legal entity that holds the investments and discharges the obligations of a pension plan.

settlement (of a pension): The extinguishment of all or part of an enterprise's pension obligations.

vesting date: The date when an employee's entitlement to the pension benefits is no longer dependent on continued employment with the company.

K. PROBLEMS

MyAccountingLab ® Go to MyAccountingLab at **www.myaccountinglab.com**. You can practise the indicated exercises as often as you want, and guided solutions will help you find answers step by step. You'll find a personalized study plan available to you too!

P17-1. Nature of pension plans **(L.O.** 17-1) (Easy – 5 minutes)

Identify whether each of the following descriptions of pension plans describes defined contribution plans, defined benefit plans, or both.

		Defined contribution plans	Defined benefit plans
a.	Must use a pension trust to hold the plan's assets.		
b.	Transfers risk from retirees to plan sponsors.		
c.	Allows employees to contribute to pension plan.		
d.	Can be underfunded or overfunded.		
e.	Provides a guaranteed amount of retirement income.		
f.	Provides a guaranteed amount of plan funding.		

P17-2. Nature of pension plans **(L.O.** 17-1) (Easy – 3 minutes)

Peter is currently 30 years old and he plans to retire early, in 25 years' time. He would like to have an income of $50,000 per year during his retirement, which he anticipates will last for 30 years. Assume that Peter receives the retirement income at the end of each of the 30 years.

Required:

Determine the amount of money Peter will need to have accumulated by the time he starts his retirement. Assume a discount rate of 9%.

P17-3. Nature of pension plans **(L.O.** 17-1) (Easy – 5 minutes)

A pension plan promises to pay $30,000 at the end of each year for 25 years of the retirement period.

Required:

Compute the funds required to fund this pension plan at the start of the retirement period assuming:
a. a discount rate of 8%; or
b. a discount rate of 6%.

P17-4. Nature of pension plans **(L.O.** 17-1) (Easy – 10 minutes)

Hamilton Steel provides a defined benefit pension plan for its employees. One of its employees, Sue Cameron, who just turned 45 years old, expects to retire at age 65. At that time, the pension plan will pay Sue annual pension payments equal to 3% of her final year's salary for each year of services rendered by Sue. The pension payments will continue until Sue's death, which actuaries expect to be when she turns 80 years old. Sue is currently earning $50,000 per year, and this rate is not expected to increase due to the poor state of the steel industry. Hamilton Steel uses a 10% interest rate for its pension obligations.

Required:

Determine the current service cost for Sue Cameron's pension for the past year (the year just before she turned 45).

P17-5. Nature of pension plans (**L.O.** 17-1) (Medium – 10 minutes)

Sue Cameron (see P17-4) has a twin brother, Tom, who works for the Government of Alberta. Tom is covered by a defined benefit pension plan. Tom just turned 45 years old, and expects to retire at age 65. At that time, the pension plan will pay Tom annual pension payments equal to 3% of his final year's salary for each year of services rendered. The pension payments will continue until Tom's death, which actuaries expect to be when he turns 80 years old. For the current year, Tom will earn $50,000, and this rate is expected to increase by 8% per year. Assume that the Alberta Government uses a 10% interest rate for its pension obligations.

Required:

Determine the current service cost for Tom Cameron's pension for the past year (the year just before he turned 45).

P17-6. Accounting for defined contribution plans (**L.O.** 17-2) (Easy – 3 minutes)

Templeton Company sponsors a defined contribution pension plan for its employees. The plan specifies that the company will contribute $2 for every dollar that an employee contributes to the plan. Employees are eligible to contribute up to 5% of their salary to the pension plan.

During 2012, employees covered by the pension plan earned salaries totalling $40 million. Employee contributions to the pension totalled $1.8 million. Templeton contributed $3 million to the plan during the year.

Required:

Provide the summary journal entry for Templeton's pension plan for 2012.

P17-7. Accounting for defined contribution plans (**L.O.** 17-2) (Easy – 5 minutes)

Umbria Products has a defined contribution pension plan for its employees. The plan requires the company to contribute 15% of these employees' salaries to the pension. In 2013, total salary for employees covered by the pension plan totalled $60 million, of which 80% is attributable to employees involved in manufacturing while the remaining 20% of salaries relate to administrative staff. The company contributed $7 million to the pension during the year.

Required:

Provide the summary journal entry for Umbria's pension plan for 2013.

P17-8. Accounting for defined benefit plans (**L.O.** 17-2) (Easy – 3 minutes)[4]

A company reported $350,000 of pension expense in its income statement. The balance sheet showed that the pension liability increased by $20,000 over the year. How much cash was paid to the pension trustee during the period?

---

4. © 2009 CGA-Canada. Reproduced with permission.

P17-9. Accounting for defined benefit plans   (**L.O.** 17-3) (Easy – 5 minutes)

A company has a defined benefit pension liability of $600,000 at the beginning of the year. The company contributes $3,800,000 to the pension during the year and records a pension expense of $3,600,000. Determine the value of the defined benefit pension liability at year-end.

P17-10. Accounting for defined benefit plans   (**L.O.** 17-3) (Easy – 5 minutes)

A company's defined benefit pension plan incurs current service cost of $2,200,000. Expected income on the pension plan's assets amounted to $8,700,000, while actual income was $8,800,000. The interest on the pension obligation was $9,500,000, which matched the actuarial estimates. The pension plan has no past service costs, and unamortized actuarial gains or losses at the beginning of the year are within the corridor limit.

Required:

Compute the amount of pension expense for the year.

P17-11. Accounting for defined benefit plans   (**L.O.** 17-3) (Easy – 5 minutes)

Current service cost for a defined benefit pension plan amounted to $6,800,000. This pension plan's assets generated $5,500,000 of income, which exceeded expectations by $500,000. Pension obligations incurred interest cost of $4,800,000, which were above expectations by $200,000. Amortizations during the year included $300,000 for past service cost and $50,000 of corridor amortization relating to actuarial gains.

Required:

Compute the amount of pension expense for the year.

P17-12. Accounting for defined benefit plans—corridor amortization

(**L.O.** 17-3) (Easy – 5 minutes)

At the beginning of the current year, a pension has assets of $45,600,000 and accrued benefit obligation of $57,500,000. At this time, unamortized actuarial losses were $6,150,000 on plan assets and $3,800,000 on plan obligations. The expected average remaining service lives (EARSL) of current employees is 15 years.

Required:

Compute the minimum corridor amortization.

P17-13. Accounting for defined benefit plans—corridor amortization

(**L.O.** 17-3) (Easy – 10 minutes)

The following table provides information for a defined benefit pension plan at the end of each fiscal year. The expected average remaining service lives (EARSL) of current employees is 12 years and stable for the period described in the table.

End-of-year balances, in $000's	2010	2011	2012	2013
Pension assets	$60,000	$67,000	$71,000	$60,000
Pension obligations	56,000	60,000	65,000	75,000
Net pension surplus (deficit)	$ 4,000	$ 7,000	$ 6,000	$(15,000)
Unamortized actuarial gains (losses)	$ 5,500	$ 6,500	$ 7,400	$ (8,700)

Required:

Compute the minimum corridor amortization for 2011 to 2014.

P17-14.   Accounting for defined benefit plans   (L.O. 17-3) (Medium – 10 minutes)

Niagara Inns provides a modest defined benefit pension for its employees. At the end of fiscal year 2011, which ended on December 31, the pension plan supplied Niagara with information about the pension, which is summarized in the following tables.

Pension trustee report	
Opening assets, January 1	$2,100,000
+ Funding	400,000
+ Expected return on assets	168,000
− Payments to retirees	(40,000)
Expected value, December 31	$2,628,000
Actual market value, December 31	2,410,000
Actuarial gain (loss)	$ (218,000)

Pension actuary report	
Opening accrued benefit obligation, January 1	$3,000,000
+ Current service cost	225,000
+ Interest	240,000
− Payments to retirees	(40,000)
Expected value, December 31	$3,425,000
Actual obligation, December 31	2,964,000
Actuarial gain (loss)	$ 461,000

The company did not have any past service costs. Unamortized actuarial losses at December 31, 2010 were $800,000. The expected average remaining service lives of employees is 10 years.

Required:

Provide the summary journal entry for Niagara's pension plan for 2011.

P17-15.   Accounting for defined benefit plans   (L.O. 17-3) (Medium – 10 minutes)[5]

PEP Corporation has a defined benefit pension plan. As of January 1, 2010, the following balances exist:

Accrued benefit obligation	$2,400,000
Plan assets (at market value)	1,800,000
Unamortized past service cost from plan initiation	600,000
Unrecognized net loss from actuarial gains and losses	250,000
Interest rate on obligations	5%

For the year ended December 31, 2010, the current service cost as determined by an appropriate actuarial cost method was $330,000. A change in actuarial assumptions created a gain of $15,000 in 2010. The expected return on plan assets was $72,000; however, the actual return is $70,000. The expected period of full eligibility at January 1, 2010 (i.e., the vesting period) is 20 years, while the expected average remaining service life is 23 years. PEP paid $325,000 to the pension trustee in December 2010. The company recognizes only the minimum amount of corridor amortization.

---

5. © 2010 CGA-Canada. Reproduced with permission.

Required:

Prepare the journal entry to record pension expense for 2010.

P17-16. Accounting for defined benefit plans **(L.O. 17-3)** (Medium – 10 minutes)[6]

Koffee Corporation provides its employees with a defined benefit pension plan. As of January 1, 2011, the following balances exist:

Accrued benefit obligation	$8,000,000
Plan assets (at market value)	6,800,000
Unamortized past service cost from plan initiation	2,000,000
Unrecognized net loss from actuarial gains and losses	750,000
Interest rate on obligations	5%

For the year ended December 31, 2011, the current service cost, as determined by an appropriate actuarial cost method, was $570,000. A change in actuarial assumptions created a loss of $15,000 in 2011. The expected return on plan assets was $408,000. However, the actual return is $395,000. The expected period of full eligibility at January 1, 2011 (i.e., the vesting period) is 25 years, while the expected average remaining service life is 28 years. Koffee paid $730,000 to the pension trustee in December 2010. The company recognizes only the minimum amount of corridor amortization.

Required:

Calculate the pension expense for 2011 and determine the carryforward amount for unrecognized actuarial gains or losses at the end of 2011.

P17-17. Accounting for defined benefit plans—OCI alternative

(L.O. 17-3) (Medium – 15 minutes)

Muskoka Canoes has had a defined benefit pension plan for three decades. Two years ago, the company improved the benefits at a cost of $2,800,000. These benefits vest to employees four years after the plan amendment.

At the beginning of the current year, the company had unamortized actuarial gains of $10,200,000. Pension plan assets were $84,000,000 while pension obligations were $76,000,000 at the beginning of the year.

For the current year, Muskoka's pension plan incurred current service cost of $5,400,000 and interest of $7,600,000. The pension's assets earned $8,000,000, which is $400,000 below expectations. The expected average remaining service lives (EARSL) of current employees is 15 years.

Required:

Compute the pension expense assuming Muskoka treats unamortized actuarial gains and losses either (i) using the corridor approach or (ii) flowing the gains and losses through other comprehensive income (OCI).

P17-18. Accounting for defined benefit plans—OCI alternative

(L.O. 17-3) (Medium – 15 minutes)

The following tables are the reports of the pension trustee and pension actuary for Timmins Industries, which started the defined benefit pension plan at the beginning of 2011. The expected average remaining service life of the employee group is 20 years.

---

6. © 2009 CGA-Canada. Reproduced with permission.

Pension trustee report	2011	2012
Opening assets, January 1	$ 0	$ 476,000
+ Funding	500,000	545,000
− Payments to retirees	0	(20,000)
+ Expected return on assets	40,000	81,000
Expected value, December 31	$540,000	1,082,000
Actual market value, December 31	476,000	1,038,000
Actuarial gain (loss)	$ (64,000)	$ (44,000)

Pension actuary report	2011	2012
Opening accrued benefit obligation, January 1	$ 0	$ 520,000
+ Current service cost (accrued evenly during year)	500,000	580,000
− Payments to retirees (paid evenly through year)	0	(20,000)
+ Interest	22,000	64,000
Expected value, December 31	$522,000	$1,144,000
Actual obligation, December 31	520,000	1,150,000
Actuarial gain (loss)	$ 2,000	$ (6,000)

Required:

a. Using the corridor approach for actuarial gains and losses, compute the pension expense for the two years.
b. Flowing actuarial gains and losses through other comprehensive income (OCI), compute the pension expense and the amount of OCI for the two years.

P17-19. Presentation and disclosures for defined benefit plans
(**L.O.** 17-4) (Easy – 5 minutes)

Aegis Air Conditioning Company has three pension plans for three groups of employees: production, service, and administration. Information for the three plans is as follows:

	Production	Service	Administration	Total
Pension assets	$4,500,000	$3,000,000	$2,000,000	$9,500,000
Pension obligations	(5,000,000)	(3,200,000)	(1,400,000)	9,600,000
Net pension surplus (deficit)	$ (500,000)	$ (200,000)	$ 600,000	$ (100,000)
Defined benefit asset (liability)	$ (400,000)	$ 500,000	$ (700,000)	$ (600,000)

Required:

Provide an excerpt of Aegis's balance sheet showing the presentation of its pension plans.

P17-20. Note disclosures for defined benefit plans (**L.O.** 17-4) (Easy – 5 minutes)

Brockstone Masons' balance sheet shows a defined benefit liability of $790,000. Records show that there are $90,000 of past service costs and $620,000 of actuarial gains that remain unamortized.

Required:

Using the pension reconciliation required in Brockstone's note disclosures, determine the pension plan's surplus or deficit.

P17-21. Note disclosures for defined benefit plans (**L.O.** 17-4) (Medium – 10 minutes)

Cornwall has a defined benefit pension plan. The company's balance sheet shows a defined benefit asset of $670,000 at year-end. The company's records show that the company had amended the pension plan two years ago, giving rise to $500,000 of additional benefits to employees. These additional benefits vest 10 years after the plan amendment. The balance of unamortized actuarial losses at year-end is $350,000. The pension plan has $30,200,000 of assets at market value.

Required:

Determine the value of the accrued benefit obligation for Cornwall's pension plan.

P17-22. Note disclosures for defined benefit plans (**L.O.** 17-4) (Medium – 10 minutes)

Dovetail Furnishings produces quality household furniture. The company has only one defined benefit pension plan, which covers its 30 carpenters. The company has completed its accounting for the year and closed its books. The draft financial statements show a defined benefit liability of $250,000. Your review of the company's records shows that the pension plan has a deficit of $450,000. The company's working papers show that $120,000 of actuarial losses remain unamortized at year-end, and $20,000 of past service cost was amortized during the year.

Required:

Determine the number of years that remain until employees are entitled to receive the additional benefits related to the past service cost.

P17-23. Accounting for defined benefit plans and note disclosures
(**L.O.** 17-3, **L.O.** 17-4) (Medium – 20 minutes)

Microbyte Computer Company, as of January 1, 2011, began a defined benefit pension plan that covers all 300 of its employees. Employment levels have remained constant and are expected to remain so in the future. It is estimated that the expected average remaining service life of its employees is 25 years. Prior to 2011, rather than having a defined benefit plan, the company had a defined contribution plan that had accumulated assets of $2,100,000 at market value. All employees were retroactively grandparented as to the defined benefit entitlements they would receive under the new plan (i.e., the employees had been participating in the defined contribution plan and are now part of the defined benefit plan, so the new benefits vest to the employees immediately). The company's insurance company, which is administering the pension plan, determined the following values effective on January 1, 2011:

Plan assets at market value	$2,100,000
Accrued benefit obligation	3,000,000
Initial net asset (obligation)	$ (900,000)

The company's funding policy is to contribute annually on December 31 at a rate of 15% of covered employees' payroll. The annual payroll of employees covered by the pension plan amounted to $2,500,000 in 2011. Assume that all other cash flows as well as expense accruals occur on the last day of the year.

The insurance company provided the following information for 2011:

Plan assets at market value, December 31	$2,424,000
Accrued benefit obligation, December 31	2,964,000
Pension benefits earned by employees during year	125,000
Payments to retirees	40,000
Discount rate on actuarial obligations	10%
Expected return on plan assets	10%

Required:

a. Using the above information, complete the missing information in the reports of the pension trustee and the pension actuary for 2011.

Pension trustee report	
Opening assets, January 1	$2,100,000
+ Funding (occurs at end of year)	
+ Expected return on assets	
− Payments to retirees	
Expected value, December 31	
Actual market value, December 31	
Actuarial gain (loss)	

Pension trustee report	
Opening accrued benefit obligation, January 1	$3,000,000
+ Current service cost (accrued at end of year)	
+ Interest	
− Payments to retirees	
Expected value, December 31	
Actual obligation, December 31	
Actuarial gain (loss)	

b. Calculate the pension expense to be recognized in 2011 and show the individual components making up the pension expense.
c. Record the summary journal entry for Microbyte's pension in 2011.
d. Provide the note disclosure for the reconciliation of the net pension asset or liability position on Microbyte's books with the net asset or liability position in the pension plan.

P17-24. Accounting for defined benefit plans and note disclosures
(**L.O.** 17-3, **L.O.** 17-4) (Medium – 20 minutes)

DB Company operates a defined benefit pension plan. Until January 1, 2010, DB Company had a defined contribution plan that had been retroactively changed to a defined benefit plan. The plan was on this date underfunded by $1,000,000. This net obligation relates to the unrecognized amount of past service costs, which vest 10 years after the plan conversion date. DB Company has a December 31 year-end.

On January 1, 2012, valuations were completed with the following results:

Plan assets at market value	$1,750,000
Accrued benefit obligation	2,500,000
Net asset (obligation)	$ (750,000)

The company uses the following assumptions for its pension plan:

■ Expected average remaining service life: 15 years
■ Expected rate of investment return: 8%
■ Discount rate on obligations: 8%
■ All accruals and payments take place at mid-year.

DB's files show that it had a net unamortized actuarial gain of $300,000 on January 1, 2012. The balance of the defined pension liability on the balance sheet is $250,000 Cr on this date.

The following data are relevant for 2012:

Plan assets at market value, December 31	$2,075,000
Accrued benefit obligation, December 31	2,850,000
Pension benefits earned by employees during year	125,000
Funding contribution	150,000
Payments to retirees	50,000

Required:

a. Using the above information, complete the reports of the pension trustee and the pension actuary for 2012.

Pension trustee report
Opening assets, January 1
+ Funding (occurs mid-year)
− Payments to retirees (paid mid-year)
+ Expected return on assets
Expected value, December 31
Actual market value, December 31
Actuarial gain (loss)

Pension actuary report
Opening accrued benefit obligation, January 1
+ Current service cost (accrued mid-year)
− Payments to retirees (paid mid-year)
+ Interest
Expected value, December 31
Actual obligation, December 31
Actuarial gain (loss)

b. Calculate the pension expense to be recognized in 2012 and show the individual components making up the pension expense.
c. Record the summary journal entry for DB's pension in 2012.
d. Provide the note disclosure for the reconciliation of the net pension asset or liability position on DB's books with the net asset or liability position in the pension plan.

P17-25.   Accounting for defined benefit plans and note disclosures
(L.O. 17-3, L.O. 17-4) (Medium – 20 minutes)

Corus Manufacturing Ltd. has a defined benefit pension plan that covers its production employees. On September 1, 2001, Corus initiated this plan and had immediately contributed $12 million toward covering the costs of the plan because the plan provided for retroactive benefits. The actuary valued these retroactive benefits at $12 million. These benefits vest to the employees after 15 years.

You have the following information with respect to the plan as at August 31, 2011 (10 years after the plan initiation):

Plan assets at market value	$29,000,000
Accrued benefit obligation	25,800,000
Balance sheet defined benefit pension asset	3,400,000
Net unamortized actuarial gain	3,800,000

Information for fiscal year ended August 31, 2012:

Pension benefit obligation at year-end	$ 27,500,000
Market value of plan assets at year-end	33,000,000
Current service cost (accrued evenly through year)	2,700,000
Contributions to plan assets, made mid-year (February 28, 2012)	1,800,000
Benefit payments (paid evenly through year)	900,000
EARSL of employee group	12 years
Discount rate on pension obligation	7%
Expected earnings rate on plan assets	8%

Required:

a. Using the above information, complete the reports of the pension trustee and the pension actuary for the 2012 fiscal year.
b. Derive the pension expense for the fiscal year ended August 31, 2012.
c. Record the summary journal entry relating to the pension plan for the 2012 fiscal year.
d. Reconcile the August 31, 2012 closing balance sheet position of the defined benefit pension asset or liability to the net pension surplus or deficit.

P17-26.   Accounting for defined benefit plans and note disclosures
(L.O. 17-3, L.O. 17-4) (Difficult – 25 minutes)

Dayton Products Ltd. has a separate pension plan for management. This pension plan was put in place on January 1, 2001. The plan initiation created a pension obligation of $3 million. However, only $1 million was put into the plan initially. These benefits vest after five years. On January 1, 2011, the company improved the benefits for the plan, which increased the actuarial obligation by $750,000. These additional benefits also vest after five years.

The pension plan's trustee and actuary provided the following information for the fiscal year ended December 31, 2011:

Pension benefit obligation at year-end	$8,500,000
Market value of plan assets at year-end	6,600,000
Current service cost	240,000
Benefit payments (no employees have yet retired)	none
EARSL of employee group	16 years
Discount rate on pension obligation	9%
Expected earnings rate on plan assets	8%

Financial statements for the pension trust show that, as at December 31, 2010, plan assets were $5.4 million and the pension obligation was $7.2 million.

The accounting department provided the following information relevant to fiscal 2011:

Defined benefit pension liability, December 31, 2010	$3,500,000
Cash contributions to pension fund during 2011	$ 250,000

For purposes of interest calculations, management assumes that all accruals and cash flows occur at the beginning of the fiscal year.

Required:

a. Derive the pension expense for the fiscal year ended December 31, 2011. Please show your work. [*Hint:* be especially careful with the corridor amortization.]
b. Record the summary journal entry relating to the pension plan for the 2011 fiscal year.
c. Reconcile the December 31, 2011 closing balance sheet position of the defined benefit pension asset or liability to the net pension surplus or deficit.

P17-27. Accounting for defined benefit plans and note disclosures

(**L.O.** 17-3, **L.O.** 17-4) (Difficult – 30 minutes)

Generous Co. Ltd. (Gen) operates a defined benefit pension plan that offers its employees an annual retirement income based on years of service and average of the final five years' earnings prior to retirement.

On January 1, 2010, Gen improved the pension benefits by increasing the percentage of the last five years' earnings from 2.1% to 2.2%. This enhancement has been retroactively applied to all actively employed workers on January 1, 2010, and the additional benefits vest on January 1, 2020 (10 years after the plan amendment date). The amendment gave rise to an increase in the accrued benefit obligation of $100,000 on January 1, 2010.

On January 1, 2011, the balance of the accrued benefit obligation is $600,000 and the pension fund assets total $420,000. On this date, unamortized net actuarial losses were $93,500.

The following amounts relate to Gen's pension plan experience as determined by annual valuations in 2011 and 2012:

	2011	2012
Plan assets at market value, December 31	$591,250	$802,000
Accrued benefit obligation, December 31	724,500	865,000
Pension benefits earned by employees during year*	75,000	80,000
Payments to retirees*	15,000	20,000
Funding contribution (at end of year)	100,000	115,000
EARSL	15 years	14 years
Expected return on assets	10%	10%
Interest rate on pension obligations	10%	10%

*The company assumes that pension benefits are earned and paid evenly through the year.

Required:

a. Determine the balance of the defined benefit pension liability as at January 1, 2011.
b. Using the above information, complete the reports of the pension trustee and the pension actuary for 2011 and 2012.
c. Calculate the pension expense to be recognized in 2011 and 2012, and show the individual components making up the pension expense.
d. Record the summary journal entry for Gen's pension in 2011 and 2012.
e. Determine the balance of the defined benefit pension liability as at December 31, 2011 and 2012.
f. Provide the note disclosure for the reconciliation of the net pension asset or liability position on DB's books with the net asset or liability position in the pension plan as at December 31, 2012.

P17-28. Assumptions for defined benefit plans (**L.O.** 17-5) (Medium – 5 minutes)

The actuarial valuation and accounting for defined benefit pension plans involve a number of different estimates. For each of the following changes in assumptions, identify the likely effect on the amount of pension expense in the current period (increase, decrease, or no effect).

Change in assumption	Effect on pension expense
a. Increase expected return on assets	
b. Increase vesting period for past service costs	
c. Increase interest rate on pension obligations	
d. Increase EARSL when there are unamortized actuarial gains	

P17-29. Assumptions for defined benefit plans   (**L.O.** 17-5) (Medium – 10 minutes)

The actuarial valuation and accounting for defined benefit pension plans involves a number of different estimates. For each of the following changes in assumptions, identify the likely effect on the indicated items at the end of the current year (increase, decrease, or no effect). Assume that the pension has a surplus and the sponsor's balance sheet has a net defined benefit pension asset.

Change in assumption	Pension surplus	Defined benefit pension asset
a. Increase expected return on assets		
b. Increase vesting period for past service costs		
c. Increase interest rate on pension obligations		
d. Increase EARSL when there are unamortized actuarial gains		
e. Increase life expectancy of employees/retirees		
f. Increase age of retirement when employees become eligible for retirement benefits		
g. Increase rate of wage increase when pension benefits are specified relative to employees wages		

P17-30. Assumptions for defined benefit plans   (**L.O.** 17-5) (Medium – 20 minutes)

Changing Assumptions Ltd. has the following details related to its defined benefit pension plan as at December 31, 2013:

Pension fund assets	$800,000
Actuarial obligation	$790,264

The actuarial obligation represents the present value of a single benefit payment of $1,400,000 that is due on December 31, 2019, discounted at an interest rate of 10%; i.e., $1,400,000/1.10^6 = \$790,264$. The pension has no unamortized experience gains or losses, and no past service costs at the end of 2013.

Funding during 2014 was $65,000. The actual value of pension fund assets at the end of 2014 was $950,000. As a result of the current services received from employees, the single payment due on December 31, 2019 had increased from $1,400,000 to $1,500,000.

Required:

a. Compute the current service cost for 2014 and the amount of the accrued benefit obligation at December 31, 2014. Perform this computation for interest rates of 8%, 10%, and 12%.
b. Derive the pension expense for 2014 under various assumptions about (i) the expected return, and (ii) the discount rate, by completing the following table.

	Case 1	Case 2	Case 3	Case 4	Case 5	Case 6
Expected return assumption	8%	8%	10%	10%	12%	12%
Discount rate assumption	8%	10%	8%	10%	12%	8%
Current service cost						
Interest on obligation						
Expected return on assets						
Total pension expense						

c. Briefly comment on the different amounts of pension expense in relation to the assumptions for expected return and discount rate.
d. How does a change in the discount rate affect the accrued benefit obligation?

⚓ L. MINI-CASES

CASE 1
ESL Teachers Union
(30 minutes)

English as a second language (ESL) has been a significant part of the Canadian education landscape for several decades, and its importance continues to grow with the increasing amount of immigration from countries where English is not the mother tongue. In addition, many individuals visit Canada for the primary purpose of learning English. This demand has spawned a thriving industry of dozens of private ESL schools, which range in size from those that operate with a handful of teachers to those with several dozen teachers. A few of the larger schools have multiple locations in different cities. These ESL schools exist separately from the conventional educational system of primary, secondary, and post-secondary schools.

While practically all instructors in the conventional education system are covered by pension plans—be they defined benefit or defined contribution plans—the same cannot be said for teachers at ESL schools. While the number of ESL teachers is large and growing, there has been little coordination among teachers within and across schools.

Five years ago, a group of ESL teachers formed the ESL Teachers Union (ETU) at a school in Vancouver. The idea quickly spread and the union now represents a significant proportion of ESL teachers across the country. One of the key reasons for the formation of the union is to increase the bargaining position of its member teachers to improve working conditions and compensation. After five years solidifying its position, the union executive decided the time had come to push for pension benefits for its members.

So far, the ETU has had a good working relationship with the representatives of the ESL schools' management, and the two sides have been able to resolve issues amicably. For the current pension negotiations, the ETU and the affected ESL schools have jointly hired you to prepare a preliminary report that provides fair and independent advice that will aid them in their negotiations.

1. What amount should be contributed to the pension plan for each teacher? To be useful, this amount should be expressed as a percentage of a teacher's salary. For this purpose, the two parties have agreed that reasonable parameters for estimating this amount are for a teacher at the beginning of his/her career who will spend 30 years as a teacher, 20 years in retirement, and annual pension payments that equal 2% of the final year's salary for each year of service (i.e., a teacher who earns pension benefits for 30 years would expect to receive 60% of his/her final year's salary). The average salary of an ESL teacher at the beginning of the 30-year working period is $35,000 and increasing by 2% in real terms. Inflation can be ignored.

2. Should the pension be a defined benefit or defined contribution plan? How does this choice affect issue 1 above?

3. The representative of the ESL schools proposes that the teachers be provided with an "opt-in" clause, whereby the teachers would by default receive their full salary as they have in the past, but if they choose to be part of the pension plan then their salary payments would be reduced in exchange for the future pension benefits. On the other hand, the ETU has proposed an "opt-out" clause, whereby the teachers would by default be enrolled in the pension plan; if they choose to opt out, they can receive the full salary as they do currently.

Required:

Prepare the report requested by the ETU and the ESL schools. Assume an interest rate of 6% for both investment returns and discounting.

Syntax Inc., a public company, has undertaken to purchase Tubular Ltd., a manufacturer of home heating units and industrial heating systems. Your firm, Cox & Williams LLP, is the current auditor of Syntax and is advising the company on the acquisition of Tubular.

Tubular is a private corporation owned by Jason Kent and other members of the Kent family. The company's original business was casting and assembling wood stoves. Subsequently, Tubular improved its line to cast new energy-efficient wood and coal stoves. In the past decade, under the management of the eldest son, Allen, the company expanded its plant for the fabrication of industrial heating systems for installation in large industrial and commercial complexes. Because of recent high interest charges and rigorous competition, cash flow has been poor and the company is about to report the first large loss in its history, amounting to $500,000.

To become more competitive, Tubular will have to purchase new machinery and equipment and obtain additional financing. The Kent family considered the financing requirement too great and therefore decided to sell its common shares to Syntax. Syntax has sufficient cash to purchase the common shares and, if so desired, to extinguish the outstanding debt of Tubular.

Extracts from the share purchase agreement that Syntax and Tubular negotiated are provided below.

1. Tubular to provide financial statements for the year ending June 30, 2011. These financial statements are to be audited by the current auditors of Tubular (Robert & Rosberg LLP).
2. The closing date of the agreement is to be July 31, 2011, and a balance sheet at that date is to be prepared by Cox & Williams. This "closing balance sheet" will be used to determine the final purchase price.
3. The preliminary purchase price is $7 million, based on the audited financial statements of June 30, 2010. The price is to be adjusted upward or downward, dollar for dollar, based on the change in retained earnings during the 13-month period between June 30, 2010 and July 31, 2011.
4. The closing balance sheet will be prepared in accordance with generally accepted accounting principles applied on a basis consistent with the preceding period.

The partner on this engagement at Cox & Williams informed you, a staff member at Cox & Williams, that Robert & Rosberg had completed their field work on the June 30, 2011 audit of Tubular, but had not yet issued their report. Because of the time constraint, the partner has asked you to conduct a preliminary review of the audit working papers. Your notes are presented in Exhibit 1, and extracts from Tubular's balance sheet are given in Exhibit 2.

Exhibit 1	Notes on Tubular's audit file for the year ended June 30, 2011

1. Tubular started a pension plan for its employees in 1970. The last valuation report from the actuary, dated September 30, 2010, shows a surplus amounting to $97,000. This surplus occurred due to a better return on investment than anticipated. On June 30, 2011, Tubular recognized the surplus with a journal entry offsetting the amount against current-year service costs.

Management adopted this treatment because the surplus relates to the business prior to the date of sale. Furthermore, management said that, according to generally accepted accounting principles, actuarial revaluations can be immediately recognized in the current period instead of being amortized.

(Continued)

CASE 2
Tubular Ltd.
(60 minutes)[7]

---

7. Adapted with permission from The Canadian Institute of Chartered Accountants, Toronto, Canada. Any changes to the original material are the sole responsibility of the author and have not been reviewed or endorsed by the CICA.

Exhibit 1 Continued

2. In May 2010, the company paid a $60,000 deposit on a tube-bending machine costing $200,000. The machine was delivered in July 2010. The balance of the purchase price was to be paid by September 2010; however, before the final payment was made, the manufacturer of the tub-bending machine went into bankruptcy. The trustees of the bankrupt company have not made any claim.

Management feels that no additional liability should be set up since the manufacturer has breached the contract, which warranted that the manufacturer would service the machine for two years. Up to June 30, 2011, the company incurred and expensed $20,000 of service costs that should have been covered under the warranty. Management has determined that the machine has four years of service remaining as at June 30, 2011.

3. The deferred income taxes have resulted primarily from temporary differences in the recognition of capital cost allowance (CCA) claimed in excess of depreciation recorded. Management is reasonably certain that the tax benefits of the tax losses carried forward can be realized by claiming less CCA than depreciation. It has therefore reduced the current year's losses by recognizing the deferred income tax benefit. The average tax rate of the company is 30%.

When filing its income tax return for the past five years, the company reported no taxable income as a result of claiming enough CCA to offset its net income. This year, no CCA has been claimed because of the significant loss. Depreciation is calculated at 20% declining-balance.

Exhibit 2 Summarized balance sheet

$000's	2011 (unaudited)	2010 (audited)
Current assets		
Accounts receivable, net	$11,350,000	$10,000,000
Deferred income tax on losses carried forward	233,000	—
Other	9,300,000	5,600,000
Property, plant, and equipment (net)	320,000	400,000
Total assets	$21,203,000	$16,000,000
Current liabilities		
Bank indebtedness	$ 8,000,000	$ 7,000,000
Maintenance reserve	—	120,000
Other	6,241,000	3,544,000
Long-term debt	2,000,000	—
Deferred income taxes*	72,000	96,000
Common shares	1,000,000	1,000,000
Retained earnings	3,890,000	4,240,000
Total liabilities and equity	$21,203,000	$16,000,000

*Due to CCA in excess of depreciation.

Required:

Prepare a report to the partner analyzing the significant issues relating to the engagement.

CHAPTER 18

Accounting for Leases

Thinkstock

Sir David Tweedie, the former Chairman of the International Accounting Standards Board (IASB), has been known to say that he would like to one day fly on an aircraft that actually appears on its airline's balance sheet. Of course, there is no question that airlines use aircraft in their operations, so the implicit claim expressed by the IASB Chairman is that airlines and other companies are able to avoid recording certain assets (and liabilities) on their balance sheets.

Airlines are able to keep a considerable portion of their airline fleets off-balance-sheet by renting these aircraft under "operating leases." However, it is an exaggeration to say that *none* of the aircraft used by airlines shows up on their balance sheets. For example, British Airways reported £2.5 billion of aircraft that it owns and another £2 billion of aircraft under "finance lease" on its balance sheet for March 31, 2009. Similarly, Air Canada reported assets of $4.5 billion for owned aircraft and $1.3 billion for leased aircraft at the end of 2009.

What differentiates an operating lease from a finance lease? Why do accounting standards treat the two types of leases differently? What are the financial reporting implications for classifying a lease as operating or finance?

LEARNING OBJECTIVES

After studying this chapter, you should be able to:

L.O. 18-1. Evaluate the economic substance of a lease arrangement to determine the extent to which there is a transfer of risks and rewards.

L.O. 18-2. Apply the general and specific criteria for classifying leases as finance (capital) or operating leases and apply the accounting method appropriate for that classification.

L.O. 18-3. Analyze a lease to determine the present value of minimum lease payments, the interest rate implicit in a lease, the lease payments required by the lessor, and lease amortization schedules.

L.O. 18-4. Analyze the differences in financial reporting outcomes when a lease is treated as a finance lease as compared to an operating lease, and understand the consequent preferences for finance or operating lease treatment by the lessor or lessee.

L.O. 18-5. Apply the presentation and disclosure requirements applicable to leases.

L.O. 18-6. Describe the rationale for the deferral of gains or losses on sale-leaseback transactions and account for these transactions.

CONTENTS

A. INTRODUCTION

lease An agreement whereby the owner of an asset allows others the use of that asset in return for monetary or non-monetary consideration.

lessor The owner of the asset in a lease.

lessee The renter in a lease contract.

Whether we know it or not, all of us have used leases before. A **lease** is simply a contract (whether written or verbal) where the property owner allows another person the use of that property in exchange for something else (usually money). Most readers will be familiar with apartment leases. In that case, the landlord is the **lessor**, and the renter is the **lessee**. Other everyday transactions that involve leases include renting a movie for $5, paying 50¢ to use a payphone, and using a photocopier to make 20 copies at 10¢ per page. From your understanding of introductory accounting, you would most likely record the above transactions in the following way (assume $900 for the monthly apartment rent):

Dr. Rental expense	$900.00	
Dr. Entertainment expense	$ 5.00	
Dr. Communication expense	$ 0.50	
Dr. Administration expense	$ 2.00	
Cr. Cash		$907.50

This method of recording is known as the **operating lease** method, whereby the lessee/renter expenses the cost of the lease in the period in which the lessee receives the benefits. As we will see in this chapter, this method is justified by the fact that these lease arrangements involve only a small fraction of the total usefulness of the assets (i.e., the apartment building, the movie, the payphone, and the copier).

However, many businesses use leases that are much longer in duration. In the extreme, a lease can result in the lessee receiving *all* of the benefits (and risks) associated with the asset. In this situation, the operating lease approach does not reflect the economic substance of the transaction. Instead, a **finance lease** treatment becomes more appropriate: the lessee records an asset for the property being used, as well as a liability for the obligation to make future lease payments. ("Finance lease" is the term used in IFRS; the equivalent term in ASPE is "capital lease.")

In between these clear-cut extremes is a large grey area. As the duration of the lease increases, at which point does a lease become a finance lease to better reflect the economic substance of the transaction?

operating lease A type of lease that is not a finance lease.

finance lease (also **capital lease**) A type of lease that transfers substantially all of an asset's risks and rewards of ownership from the lessor to the lessee; for a lessor, a finance lease also has normal credit risk and no material unreimbursable costs.

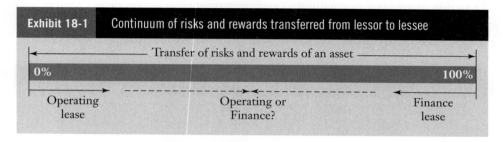

Exhibit 18-1 Continuum of risks and rewards transferred from lessor to lessee

The above discussion highlights the first and most crucial issue in accounting for leases, but there are several others that are also important. We can group these issues into three stages, as illustrated in the following diagram.

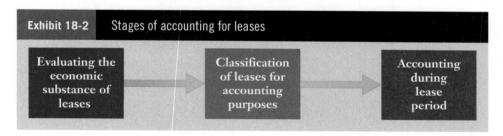

Exhibit 18-2 Stages of accounting for leases

This chapter first discusses the economics of leasing, which determines the characteristics of leases that are negotiated between lessors and lessees. The chapter then explains how these lease characteristics help accountants classify leases as operating or financing. Once that classification has been made, then the set of accounting procedures for that method follows.

B. ECONOMICS OF LEASING

Those who are in the leasing business often identify a number of advantages of leasing so as to attract customers (i.e., potential lessees), such as the following:

- "100%" financing of the asset's purchase price, which is often more than the amount that can be obtained from a loan.
- Payment schedules that are more flexible in comparison to loans.
- If the transaction qualifies for operating lease treatment, the enterprise obtains **off-balance-sheet financing**—obtaining financial funding without recognition of a liability in the balance sheet.

L.O. 18-1. Evaluate the economic substance of a lease arrangement to determine the extent to which there is a transfer of risks and rewards.

off-balance-sheet financing Obtaining financial funding without recognition of a liability in the balance sheet.

- After-tax costs are lower due to differences in tax rates for the lessor and lessee. (This is an advanced tax planning topic called "tax arbitrage," the details of which are beyond the scope of this text.)

Given these advantages, there must be some significant disadvantage to leasing; otherwise, everyone would lease and no one would own any assets that they use, which is clearly not descriptive of reality.

As mentioned above, a lease transfers usage/property rights from the lessor to the lessee for the duration of the lease. This type of contract creates an agency relationship, resulting in a moral hazard problem: the user who controls the asset during the lease (the lessee) is not the owner of the asset (because the lessor still owns it).[1] When the lessor relinquishes control of the leased property to the lessee, the lessor must bear a risk that the lessee will not take the utmost care of the leased property (or as much care as the lessor would). This reduced level of care due to separation of an asset's ownership and its control is the **agency cost of leasing**—see Exhibit 18-3 for a graphical illustration. As shown in this diagram, the value of an asset normally declines over time with usage, deterioration, and so on. However, the rate of decline depends on whether the asset is owned or leased, and to what extent the lease transfers risks and rewards of ownership.

agency cost of leasing
The reduced level of care due to the separation of an asset's ownership and its control.

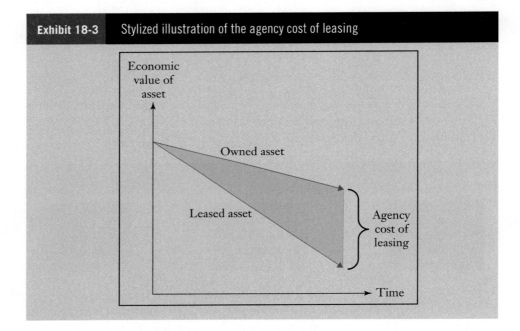

| Exhibit 18-3 | Stylized illustration of the agency cost of leasing |

If the lessor does not expect to regain control of the asset at the end of the lease, then the agency cost of leasing is nil because the lessee rather than the lessor bears the consequences of neglect. However, if the lease does transfer the property back to the lessor at the end of the lease, then the agency cost of leasing could be significant, and it must factor into the lessor's pricing decision. In other words, the lessor has to anticipate that the lease will lower the property's value at the end of the lease to an amount below what it would be without the lease. As a result, the lessor must raise the required rental payments accordingly to compensate for the agency cost of leasing.

The degree to which this agency cost matters depends on a number of factors:

1. *The inherent nature of the asset that is leased.* Assets that are robust and difficult to damage have lower agency costs and are better candidates for leasing.

---

1. Refer to Chapter 1 for a discussion of moral hazard and agency theory.

2. *The incentives of the lessee to maintain the condition of the leased asset.* Some types of lessees are more motivated to maintain the leased asset than others. For example, airlines are very keen to ensure that their leased aircraft are safe for their customers since the consequences of equipment failure are severe in terms of both the airlines' business and human lives.

3. *Regulations that require a high degree of care.* Airlines again are a good example here. Regulators have stringent requirements for maintaining commercial passenger aircraft.

4. *Conditions negotiated between the lessor and lessee.* Lease agreements often contain conditions that mitigate agency costs. For example, damage deposits for apartments deter renters from harming the property; long-term car leases often limit the amount of mileage that can be driven annually. A particularly important contract provision that reduces or even eliminates agency costs is a **bargain purchase option** that allows the lessee to purchase the asset at a price below the market value expected at the end of the lease. Also important is a **guaranteed residual value**, whereby the lessee must ensure that the leased asset retains a certain value at the end of the lease.

5. *The length of the lease contract.* As mentioned previously, if the lease transfers ownership to the lessee at the end of the lease, then no agency costs arise. Similarly, if the length of the lease contract covers substantially the entire useful life of the asset then agency costs will be minimal, since the lessee bears the cost of neglecting or abusing the property. As the duration of the lease shortens, agency costs increase.

> **bargain purchase option**
> An option given to the lessee to purchase the leased asset at a price that is below expected fair value at a future date; the assessment of whether a bargain exists is made at the time of entering the lease arrangement.

> **guaranteed residual value**
> A minimum value for the leased asset that is guaranteed to the lessor.

This last factor has important implications for the rental price. For example, suppose the rental rate for a lease that covers 100% of an asset's life is $400,000 in present value terms. In comparison, two consecutive lease terms each for 50% of the asset's life must have present value higher than $400,000 because the leases must compensate the lessor for the increased agency cost. Four consecutive leases, each for 25% of the asset's life, would cost even more.

Example 1—Lease pricing

Spyjet, a Canadian airline, is considering expanding its fleet of Boeing 737s. These planes cost $30 million each and are expected to last for 20 years. To finance this purchase, Spyjet would need to borrow at 10%/a (10% per year). Alternatively, Spyjet can lease the same aircraft from GE Capital. Assume that GE would expect a 10% pretax rate of return to lease this plane to Spyjet. For simplicity, ignore the effect of income taxes.[2]

Based on this information, GE determines that the *lowest* lease payment it can accept is $3.203m, received at the beginning of each of 20 years, computed as follows (LP = lease payment; PVFA = present value factor for an annuity; PVFAD = present value factor for an annuity due):

$$\text{Present value of lease payments} \geq \text{Aircraft purchase price}$$

$$\text{PVFAD}_{10\%,\,20} + \text{LP} \geq \$30\text{m}$$

$$(\text{PVFA}_{10\%,\,19} + 1) \times \text{LP} \geq \$30\text{m}$$

$$9.3649 \times \text{LP} \geq \$30\text{m}$$

$$\text{LP} \geq \$3.203\text{m}$$

---

2. For capital cost allowance purposes, aircraft are Class 9 assets with a 25% CCA rate.

Meanwhile, Spyjet computes the *highest* lease payment it is willing to pay:

$$\text{PV(lease payments)} \leq \text{Aircraft purchase price}$$
$$(\text{PVAF}_{10\%,19} + 1) \times \text{LP} \leq \$30m$$
$$9.3649 \times \text{LP} \leq \$30m$$
$$\text{LP} \leq \$3.203m$$

Therefore, lease payments must equal $3.203m for both parties to agree to the lease contract.

implicit interest rate The discount rate that is used, or implied to be used, by the lessor in the determination of the payments in a lease.

Suppose the lease payment negotiated between the two parties is in fact $3.203m. In this simple example, it is possible to use the payment schedule to infer the **interest rate implicit in the lease**, which is the discount rate at which the sum of discounted cash flows from the lease expected by the lessor (including any residual value) equals the fair value of the leased asset. In this example the implicit interest rate is 10%, computed as follows:

$$\text{PV(lease payments)} = \text{Aircraft purchase price}$$
$$(\text{PVAF}_{x,19} + 1) \times 3.203m = \$30m$$
$$(\text{PVAF}_{x,19} + 1) = \$30m/3.203m$$
$$\text{PVAF}_{x,19} = 8.3662$$
$$x = 10\%$$

Of course, the implicit interest rate need not be a whole number as in this example. Implicit interest rates can be computed using a financial calculator if payments are constant. A computer spreadsheet can solve for the implicit interest for any pattern of payments. In Excel, this can be done using the "solver" tool, illustrated below.

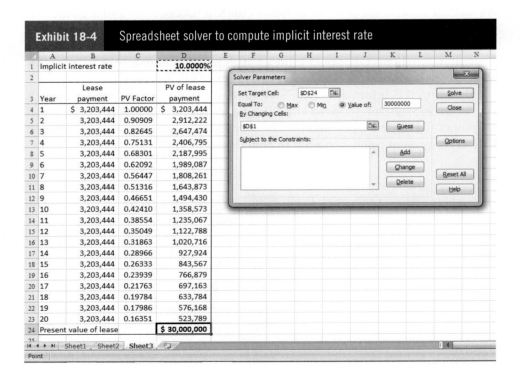

Exhibit 18-4 Spreadsheet solver to compute implicit interest rate

In this simple example, there are no economic gains (and no losses) from the leasing arrangement for either party. However, due to some of the advantages of leasing, the lessee (Spyjet) may be willing to pay more than the minimum amount that the lessor (GE) is willing to accept. For example, this would occur if GE requires a rate of return that is lower than Spyjet's borrowing rate, or if GE has a higher tax rate than Spyjet (and therefore GE values the tax shields more highly). These effects are clearly important as leases are so prevalent in the economy; however, further exploration of these additional effects of leases is beyond the scope of this text.

C. CLASSIFYING AND ACCOUNTING FOR OPERATING AND FINANCE LEASES

The above discussion highlights the important issue of who bears the risks and rewards of ownership, which is at the crux of lease accounting. The discussion below first explains how this criterion is applied to distinguish an operating lease from a finance/capital lease, and then describes the accounting procedures that follow the classification decision. The accounting consequences help explain why firms desire one lease classification over the other.

> **L.O. 18-2.** Apply the general and specific criteria for classifying leases as finance (capital) or operating leases and apply the accounting method appropriate for that classification.

1. Lease classification

International Financial Reporting Standards, as described in IAS 17 (and similarly described in ASPE Section 3065), recommend the following:

> **L.O. 18-3.** Analyze a lease to determine the present value of minimum lease payments, the interest rate implicit in a lease, the lease payments required by the lessor, and lease amortization schedules.

¶8. A lease is classified as a finance lease if it transfers substantially all the risks and rewards incidental to ownership. A lease is classified as an operating lease if it does not transfer substantially all the risks and rewards incidental to ownership.

Risks and rewards of ownership include but are not limited to the following:

- the risk of breakage and the reward of a longer-than-expected useful life;
- the risk of obsolescence and the reward of high resale value;
- the risks and rewards of changes in rental prices; and
- the risks and rewards of changes in demand for the usage of the property.

In the four examples presented in the introduction (apartment, movie, payphone, and photocopier rentals), the lessor retains the risks and rewards of ownership since the leases are for short durations relative to the items' useful lives. Therefore, we consider these leases to be operating leases for accounting purposes.

At the other extreme, some leases transfer almost all of the risks and rewards of ownership to the lessee. For example, suppose Spyjet, in the example from Section B, does sign a 20-year lease with GE Capital for payments of $3.203m at the beginning of each year. Since the lease term covers the entire expected useful life of 20 years, it is quite clear that the lessee (Spyjet) has incentives to maintain the aircraft to ensure that it operates well for the full 20 years. Therefore, Spyjet bears practically all the risks and rewards of ownership. (However, even in this case, the transfer of risks and rewards is not absolute: the useful life is just an estimate, so the actual useful life could turn out to be substantially more or less than 20 years.) Since the lease transfers substantially all the risks and rewards of ownership, the lease between GE and Spyjet would be considered a finance lease.

Reflecting the economic substance of the transaction, Spyjet would record the purchase of the asset (plane). In other words, this lease results in the lessee *capitalizing* an asset on its balance sheet, which explains the term "capital lease" used in ASPE. In addition to purchasing the plane in an economic sense (as opposed to legally), Spyjet also needs to pay for the purchase. From where does the company obtain the funds? We assume that Spyjet would have had to borrow to *finance* this purchase, which explains the term "finance lease" used in IFRS. Thus, upon the delivery of the plane, Spyjet would record:

Exhibit 18-5	Journal entry to record a finance lease for the lessee (Spyjet)	
Dr. Property, plant, and equipment (plane)	$30m	
Cr. Obligation under financing lease		$30m

From the perspective of GE Capital, the lessor, the company has sold a plane. As assumed previously, it would cost the company $30m to purchase this plane. After GE Capital orders the plane and Boeing delivers the plane to Spyjet, GE Capital will book the following entry:

Exhibit 18-6	Journal entry to record a finance lease for the lessor (GE Capital)[3]	
Dr. Lease payment receivable net of unearned interest[3]	$30m	
Cr. Cash (or accounts payable—Boeing)		$30m

As in this case, it is common for the lessor to not have the lease property in inventory, especially for high-value, low-volume items. Rather, the lessor orders the product from the manufacturer for direct delivery to the lessee. In such instances, the lessor would record neither the purchase of inventory nor the cost of goods sold.

2. Supporting indicators for lease classification

In addition to the general idea that a lease transferring substantially all of the risks and rewards of ownership should be treated as a finance lease, IFRS and ASPE provide additional guidance to help make this classification. Any one of the following indicators is sufficient to classify the lease as a finance lease.[4]

1. There is a transfer of ownership to the lessee or a bargain purchase option (BPO) at the end of the lease.
2. The lease term is a major part of the economic life of the asset. ASPE suggests that a lease with 75% or more of the asset's useful life constitutes "a major part."
3. The present value of the minimum lease payments comprises substantially all of the fair value of the leased asset. ASPE suggests "substantially all" means 90% or more. IAS 17 defines the **minimum lease payments (MLP)** as "the payments over the lease term that the lessee is or can be required to make. . . ."

minimum lease payments (MLP) The payments over the lease term that the lessee is or can be required to make.

3. This is the discounted value of the lease payments to be received. For bookkeeping purposes and for note disclosures, this amount is separated into the gross receivable and unearned interest. These amounts will be given later in the chapter as we further develop this example.

4. This is not an exhaustive list of indicators. IFRS–IAS 17, ¶10–11 provide other examples.

These indicators augment the general criterion and help to determine whether there is a transfer of the risks and rewards of ownership from the lessor to the lessee. Regarding the first indicator, if there is an automatic transfer of ownership then it is clear that the lessee bears the risks and rewards of ownership. Likewise, a bargain purchase option has the same effect: the lessee is almost certain to exercise the option given that the asset can be purchased at a price below market. We can think of a bargain purchase option as providing a future transfer of ownership, since the likelihood of eventual ownership transfer is very high (although not necessarily 100%).

The second and third indicators capture leases that do not have clear-cut transfers of ownership. As explained above, lessees have the incentive to avoid finance/capital lease treatment. Relying solely on an outright transfer of ownership or a bargain purchase would allow, for example, a lease for the entire useful life of an asset to be classified as an operating lease. Thus, the second and third indicators identify cases when there is, in substance, transfers of economic risks and rewards.

For the third indicator, and for lease accounting in general, it is important for the payments to distinguish and exclude any **executory costs**, which are incidental costs in a lease that would be incurred by the lessee independent of whether the lessee had purchased or leased the asset. For example, a lease contract can require the lessee to pay some amount to the lessor on a regular basis to repair and maintain the leased property. Such maintenance costs would be incurred whether the lessee bought or leased the property. Payments for executory costs are normally expensed in the period incurred.

executory costs Incidental costs in a lease that would be incurred by the lessee independent of whether the lessee had purchased or leased the asset.

For leases of land, only the first criterion is applicable. Why? The second criterion based on time is irrelevant because land has an indefinite life. Arguably, the third criterion is relevant because, as for any other type of property, the present value of the MLP could exceed 90% of the land's fair value if the lease term is long enough and if the residual value at the end of the lease is small enough. For land, however, the residual value tends not to diminish with the length of the lease, as it does for other types of assets; indeed, land values sometimes increase substantially over time. For long land leases (some are 99 years, for example), these residual values are impossible to predict with any degree of accuracy. In other words, this is an issue of reliability: the accounting standard for land leases excludes the minimum lease payment criterion because to include it would require the use of unreliable estimates of land values many years into the future.

3. Accounting for finance and operating leases

The journal entries covered so far occur at the beginning of a finance lease. Other journal entries will naturally follow in subsequent periods. For a finance lease, the lessee records entries relating to both the leased asset as well as the lease obligation.

- For the leased asset, the lessee accounts for depreciation/amortization.
- For the lease liability, the lessee accounts for interest expense and the loan payments.

The lessor accounts for interest income and cash collected on the lease receivable. The following summarizes the accounting required for both lease classifications.

Exhibit 18-7	Summary of journal entries for lessee and lessor for finance and operating leases			
	Financing/capital lease		**Operating lease**	
	For the lessee	**For the lessor**	**For the lessee**	**For the lessor**
At start of lease	An asset purchase	An asset sale	—	—
	Borrowing for that purchase	Loan receivable	—	—
During lease	Depreciation/ amortization	—	—	Depreciation/ amortization
	Interest expense, loan payments	Interest income, cash collected	Lease payments	Lease payments received
At end of lease	Depends on terms of lease	Depends on terms of lease	—	—

Note that the treatment is often but not always symmetric for both parties. It is possible for the two parties to record different amounts because they use different assumptions to classify and to record the lease, as we will see below.

4. Preference for finance or operating lease treatment

Contrast the accounting under the operating and finance lease methods. If you were the lessee, which method would you prefer if you had a choice that is unrestricted by accounting rules? Why? If you were the lessor, which classification would you prefer and why?

Generally, lessees prefer operating lease treatment while lessors prefer finance lease treatment. Consider the lessee first. A lessee would rather not record the asset and liability of a finance lease, even though they are equal in amount at the inception of the lease, as doing so adversely affects solvency ratios such as debt-to-assets or debt-to-equity. (In general, when equity is positive, adding equal amounts of assets and liabilities increases the debt-to-assets ratio toward one and the debt-to-equity ratio toward infinity.) In other words, a lessee prefers operating lease treatment because it provides off-balance-sheet financing (discussed previously in Chapter 12).

In addition, the operating lease treatment is more favourable toward the income statement in the short term: the lease expense under operating lease treatment will be lower than the combined expense of depreciation and interest expense under finance lease treatment in the early years of the lease. (This effect reverses later in the lease; over the life of the lease, the total expense under either lease treatment is exactly the same.)

Using the Spyjet example given earlier, operating lease treatment would result in lease expense of $3.203 million per year. Under finance lease treatment, the expenses in the first year add up to $4.180 million, derived as follows:

Exhibit 18-8	Computation of total expenses under finance lease treatment for lessee (Spyjet)	
Depreciation ($30 million cost straight-line over 20 years)		$1.500 million
Interest expense (($30 million − $3.203 million) × 10%)		2.680 million
Total expense under finance lease treatment		$4.180 million

The total expense would be even higher with declining balance depreciation rather than straight-line.

For lessors, the opposite is true—a lessor generally prefers the finance lease treatment. On the balance sheet, a non-monetary item (inventory or capital asset) is converted to a monetary item (loan receivable), which appears more liquid. On the income statement, any profit from the asset sale is recognized immediately. During the life of the lease, interest income is recorded. Under operating lease treatment, the lessor shows a leased asset and must depreciate the asset. Lease payments are recognized as revenue when earned (which is usually close to its receipt). In the early years of a lease, interest income under finance lease treatment will usually exceed lease revenue net of depreciation under operating lease treatment.

Again using the Spyjet example, the interest income is $2.680 million in the first year under finance lease treatment. In comparison, operating lease treatment results in the following revenue and expense:

Exhibit 18-9	Computation of revenues net of expenses under operating lease for the lessor (GE Capital)
Lease revenue	$3.203 million
Depreciation ($30 million cost straight-line over 20 years)	1.500 million
Revenue net of expense under operating lease treatment	$1.703 million

It is also important to note that this effect reverses later in the lease for the lessor (as it also does for the lessee, as mentioned above). The amount of interest income decreases over time as the loan balance is partially repaid each year; over the life of the lease, the cumulative net income under either lease treatment is exactly the same.

5. Rationale for supporting indicators relating to lease term and present value

At this point, it is worthwhile to pause and consider the rationale underlying the lease classification indicators relating to the lease term and present value of the lease payments. Whether in subjective terms under IFRS or in quantitative terms under ASPE, the wording seems to be too broad, classifying too many leases as finance leases. Why do the rules say a "major part" of the economic life instead of the "entire" economic life, and "substantially all" rather than "all" of the asset's fair value? Does the lessor not face significant risks and rewards of ownership if the lessor retains ownership of the used but not fully depleted asset at the end of the lease term?

Part of the answer to these questions can be found in the discussion earlier in Section B of this chapter on the economics of leasing arrangements. The length of time covered by a lease is not arbitrary—it is part and parcel of the pricing negotiated between the lessor and lessee. Shorter leases imply higher lease payments because the lessee must compensate the lessor for higher agency costs. Thus, a lessee who reduces the lease term to the point where it would qualify for operating lease treatment must bear the cost of higher payments. This additional cost makes it more likely that the lease term is chosen to meet the lessee's business needs rather than for accounting reasons.

Another part of the reason for the second and third indicators for finance lease treatment can be found in the discussion in Chapter 1. Positive accounting theory predicts that management has incentives to use its discretion to manage earnings and the balance sheet. In response, accounting standards need to anticipate the potential for manipulation. In the process of assessing whether a lease covers a major part of the economic life of the leased asset, there is no subjectivity about the length of the lease term, but there is considerable subjectivity about the estimated useful life. The wording of the accounting standards anticipates that subjectivity and the application of management discretion to make estimates in its favour. For instance, using the quantitative guidance in ASPE, suppose a lease actually covers the entire six-year useful life of an asset; to escape capital lease treatment the lessee would need to increase the estimated useful life to more than eight years, which is expected to be beyond the amount of discretion available to management.

For the third indicator, there is potential for subjectivity in both the calculation of present value and the estimate of fair value. In the present value calculation, the cash flow stream is set according to the lease contract; however, when there is a range of interest rates for discounting those cash flows, the lessee has incentives to choose the highest rate available to minimize the discounted present value. For the fair value side of the comparison, fair value can be overestimated if, for example, the property's "list price" is used rather than a lower negotiated price that would prevail in an actual purchase.

6. Basic numerical example

Continuing with the example started in Section B, assume that Spyjet agrees to lease a new Boeing 737 from GE on January 1, 2011, for $3.603m per year, paid in advance (i.e., at the beginning of the year). These payments include $400,000 per year for GE to maintain the aircraft to conform to federal aviation regulations. GE orders the plane from Boeing, which delivers it directly to Spyjet. Assume that Spyjet uses the straight-line method to depreciate aircraft. The following demonstrates the accounting for this lease on Spyjet's books and on GE's books.

a. Lease classification

This lease would be classified as a finance lease for either of two reasons:

- the lease term is 100% of the aircraft's useful life of 20 years; or
- the present value of lease payments is $3.203m \times (PVAF_{10\%,19} + 1) = \$30m$, or 100% of the fair value of the aircraft.

Note that the $400,000 maintenance cost should not be included in the lease payments. These executory costs are not part of the lease; Spyjet would incur these maintenance costs regardless of whether it purchased or leased the asset.

b. Recording the lease at inception

On January 1, 2011, the two companies would record the finance lease as follows:

Exhibit 18-10	Illustration of journal entries at the inception of a finance lease				
	Lessee—Spyjet	**$ millions**	**Lessor—GE Capital**	**$ millions**	
Jan. 1, 2011	Dr. PPE—leased aircraft*	30	Dr. Lease payments receivable (net of unearned finance income)	30	
	Cr. Obligation for finance lease	30	Cr. Cash (paid to Boeing)		30

*PPE = property, plant, and equipment

c. Recording the lease during the lease term

The entries during the lease term are facilitated by completing an amortization table for the lease obligation (for Spyjet) and lease receivable (for GE Capital).

Exhibit 18-11	Lease amortization schedule for Spyjet and GE Capital				
Period	Year	Lease payments on Jan. 1	Interest for year @ 10%	Reduction in principal	Principal after payments and interest
					$30,000,000
1	2011	$3,203,444	$2,679,656*	$523,788	29,476,212
2	2012	3,203,444	2,627,277	576,167	28,900,045
3	2013	3,203,444	2,569,660	633,784	28,266,261
⋮	⋮	⋮	⋮	⋮	⋮
18	2028	3,203,444	555,971	2,647,473	6,115,682
19	2029	3,203,444	291,224	2,912,220	3,203,462
20	2030	3,203,462†	—	3,203,462	—
Total		$64,068,898	$34,068,898		

*10% × ($30,000,000 − $3,203,444) = $2,679,656

†Last payment adjusted to make up rounding error

As an exercise, you could reproduce this amortization schedule using a spreadsheet so that you can see the omitted rows in years 4 to 17.

This schedule shows two totals at the bottom of the table: $64,068,898 for gross lease receivable and $34,068,898 of interest. From a finance perspective, these two numbers are not meaningful, since they are sums of amounts at different points in time without adjusting for the time value of money. However, for practical reasons, the lessor uses them in its accounting procedures. The gross lease receivable is the amount that is useful to the accounts receivable department to keep track of the payments due (i.e., $3,203,444 each year for 20 years = $64,068,898), whereas the interest income would be separately computed and recorded by a financial accountant. In addition, these two totals are necessary for note disclosures (discussed later in the chapter).

Using information from this amortization table, Spyjet and GE Capital would record the following entries in 2011 and 2012:

Exhibit 18-12	Illustration of journal entries during a finance lease, first year			
	Lessee—Spyjet	$ millions	Lessor—GE Capital	$ millions
Jan. 1, 2011	Dr. Obligation for finance lease	3.203	Dr. Cash	3.603
	Dr. Prepaid maintenance expense	0.400	Cr. Unearned maintenance revenue	0.400
	Cr. Cash	3.603	Cr. Lease receivable	3.203
Dec. 31, 2011	Dr. Interest expense	2.680	Dr. Lease receivable	2.680
	Cr. Oblig. for finance lease	2.680	Cr. Interest revenue	2.680
	Dr. Maintenance expense	0.400	Dr. Unearned maintenance revenue	0.400
	Cr. Prepaid maint. expense	0.400	Cr. Maintenance service revenue	0.400
	Dr. Depreciation expense	1.500		
	Cr. Accumulated depreciation	1.500		

Exhibit 18-13	Illustration of journal entries during a finance lease, second year				
	Lessee—Spyjet	**$ millions**	**Lessor—GE Capital**	**$ millions**	
Jan. 1, 2012	Dr. Obligation for finance lease	3.203	Dr. Cash	3.603	
	Dr. Prepaid maintenance expense	0.400	Cr. Unearned maintenance revenue		0.400
	Cr. Cash		3.603	Cr. Lease receivable		3.203
Dec. 31, 2012	Dr. Interest expense	2.627	Dr. Lease receivable	2.627	
	Cr. Oblig. for finance lease		2.627	Cr. Interest revenue		2.627
	Dr. Maintenance expense	0.400	Dr. Unearned maintenance revenue	0.400	
	Cr. Prepaid maint. expense		0.400	Cr. Maintenance service revenue		0.400
	Dr. Depreciation expense	1.500			
	Cr. Accumulated depreciation		1.500			

d. Accounting at the end of the lease

Since there is no transfer of title at the end of this lease, Spyjet must return the aircraft to GE at the end of 20 years. Therefore, Spyjet would record the following entry at the end of 2030 to remove the plane from its books, while GE would record an aircraft acquisition at zero cost:

Exhibit 18-14	Illustration of journal entry for the end of a lease			
	Lessee—Spyjet	**$ millions**	**Lessor—GE Capital**	**$ millions**
Dec. 31, 2030	Dr. Accum. depreciation—leased aircraft	30	Dr. Aircraft inventory	memo
	Cr. PPE—leased aircraft	30		

The meaning of "memo" is to reflect the fact that there is nothing to record in GE's general ledger because the amount is nil. However, GE would record the aircraft in the sub-ledger for property, plant, and equipment at zero cost. If GE is able to sell the aircraft later, it would then record a gain equal to the proceeds.

7. Additional considerations for lease classification on lessor's books under ASPE

For a lessor, ASPE provides two additional indicators to determine whether a lease is a finance or operating lease:

- *The lessee's credit risk is normal:* This indicator asks whether the particular lessee under consideration has a risk of default that is materially different from the lessor's other customers. Unusually high credit risk suggests a higher than normal chance that the lessor will repossess the leased property and the retention of significant risk of ownership.
- *Any unreimbursable costs arising from the lease are reasonably estimable:* This indicator is consistent with the general recognition criterion regarding measurability. For instance, one of the revenue recognition criteria is that the amount ultimately collectible needs to be reasonably measurable; otherwise, the revenue would be deferred to a later date when collection occurs (see Chapter 4). Likewise, the lessor needs to be able to estimate

costs to fulfill the lease in order to record the lease as a finance lease (i.e., as a sale of an asset).

Both of these indicators must be satisfied for a lease to be considered a finance lease. These indicators are consistent with the general idea that the lessor must have assurance that the risks (and rewards) of ownership have indeed been transferred.

These two indicators apply to lessors but not to lessees for two reasons. First, the nature of the indicators is that they relate to lessors only, because the indicators relate to risks faced by the lessor. Second, recall that lessors generally prefer finance lease treatment over operating lease treatment (opposite the preferences of lessees); these additional hurdles make it more difficult for lessors to obtain finance lease treatment.

ASPE (but not IFRS) further sub-classifies a finance lease into two types. Since a finance lease for a lessor is treated as a sale of the asset, there is potentially a profit margin on that sale. When there is such a profit, the lease is a **sales-type lease**. If the sale price is equal to the cost of the asset to the lessor, then the lease is a **direct-financing lease**. For example, a car dealership offering a long-term lease arrangement would have a profit margin on the sale. In contrast, a finance company such as GE Capital that acts solely as a financial intermediary and does not take possession of the leased property (such as an aircraft) would usually not have a profit margin. In other words, the profit margin is usually associated with the seller bearing some risk of holding inventory.

The following diagram helps to summarize the classification of leases from the lessor's perspective under ASPE.

sales-type lease A type of finance lease in which the lessor obtains a profit margin on the sale of the leased asset (used in Canadian ASPE).

direct-financing lease A type of finance lease in which the sale price is equal to the cost of the asset to the lessor (used in Canadian ASPE).

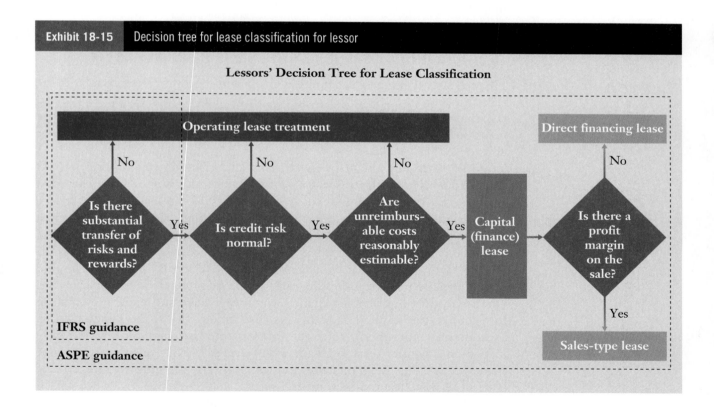

| Exhibit 18-15 | Decision tree for lease classification for lessor |

Lessors' Decision Tree for Lease Classification

Under IFRS, the classification decision is much simpler, involving only the first question on the far left. In other words, the IFRS classification criteria are the same for lessor and lessee.

D. COMPLICATING FACTORS IN LEASES

1. Residual values—Guaranteed and unguaranteed

L.O. 18-3. Analyze a lease to determine the present value of minimum lease payments, the interest rate implicit in a lease, the lease payments required by the lessor, and lease amortization schedules.

Section B discussed the economics behind leasing arrangements, with an emphasis on the agency costs of leasing. Among the various tools that can be used to mitigate moral hazard is the use of a *guaranteed residual value*. By agreeing to provide a guarantee that the leased property will be worth at least a certain amount, the lessee assures the lessor that the property will be treated with due care, since the lessee bears the risk and cost of the property falling below the specified value of the guarantee.

Since the lessor is assured of receiving the guaranteed amount (or more), the guaranteed residual value forms part of the minimum lease payment, along with all the other payments due from the lessee to the lessor. In contrast, residual values that are not guaranteed are not part of the minimum lease payment since the lessee has no obligation for any additional payments regardless of the eventual value of the leased property.

2. Inclusion of bargain purchase options in minimum lease payments

By its nature, a bargain purchase option (BPO) is almost certain to be exercised. As a result, the cost of exercising the option is another cash flow that the lessor expects to receive from the lessee, and therefore the BPO is a part of the minimum lease payment.

3. Interest rate used in present value calculations

Finance theory suggests that the appropriate discount/interest rate is the risk-adjusted rate. However, there is some uncertainty as to the type of risk that should be factored into this rate: the risk associated with the asset being leased, or the risk of the lessee? Ideally, both types of risk should be considered.

How does one quantify these risks and risk-adjusted interest rates? First, note that a rational lessor should factor in risks of both the asset and the risk of the lessee in setting the terms of the lease, especially the lease payments. Thus, we can infer the appropriate risk-adjusted interest rate from the cash flow stream expected by the lessor and the fair value of the leased property; this is called the *interest rate implicit in the lease*, or simply the "implicit rate," as first mentioned in Section B. The lessor should always be able to determine this rate, so *the lessor must use the implicit rate*. The *lessee*, on the other hand, may not always have sufficient information to calculate the implicit rate. In this case, under IFRS, the lessee uses its **incremental borrowing rate**, the interest rate that the lessee would have to pay on a similar lease or loan. Thus, under IFRS, the interest rate for the lessee is determined on a hierarchical basis: use the implicit rate if available; otherwise, use the incremental rate.

incremental borrowing rate   The interest rate that the lessee would have to pay on a similar lease or loan.

Relating to lessees, ASPE takes a somewhat different approach. While ASPE also refers to the implicit interest rate and the incremental borrowing rate, it recommends that the lessee use the *lower* of the two rates when both are known. What is the rationale for this rule? The reason is related to the lessee's preference for operating lease treatment: the lessee wants to use the highest interest rate justifiable so as to minimize the present value of minimum lease payments, which is one of the quantitative criteria for lease classification. Recognizing the lessee's tendency to have this bias, ASPE requires the use of the lower of the two interest rates so as to maximize the present value of minimum lease payments, making it more difficult for the lessee to escape finance lease treatment.

When the lessee does use its incremental borrowing rate, it is possible for the lessee's present value of minimum lease payments to exceed the fair value of the leased property. However, recording such a finance lease using the present value amount would result in an overvalued asset on the books. In such a circumstance, the lease is recorded at the fair value of the leased property, and the lessee must recompute the interest rate in the lease using the fair value.

Example—Interest rate for computing the present value of a lease

Precision Computing enters into a lease agreement for 100 servers at the beginning of 2011. Lease conditions include the following:

- down payment of $50,067; and
- annual payments of $30,000 at the end of each of five years, which equals the useful life of the servers.

The fair value is $1,700 per server, while the estimated residual value is $100 per server, which is not guaranteed by the lessee. Precision Computing has received a government loan guarantee that allows it to borrow at a low interest rate of 5%.

Using a spreadsheet (employing the "solver" tool), we can determine the interest rate implicit in this lease to be 10%. Under IFRS, if Precision Computing is able to determine this rate, it would use this implicit rate to account for the lease, regardless of its incremental borrowing rate. Doing so results in the following amortization schedule:

Exhibit 18-16		Lease amortization schedule for Precision Computing using implicit rate of 10%			
Period	Year	Interest for year @ 10%	Payments	Reduction in principal	Principal after interest and payments
					$170,000
0			$50,067	$50,067	119,933
1	2011	$11,993*	30,000	18,007	101,926
2	2012	10,193	30,000	19,807	82,119
3	2013	8,212	30,000	21,788	60,331
4	2014	6,033	30,000	23,967	36,364
5	2015	3,636	30,000	26,364	10,000

*10% × $119,933 = 11,993

Now, suppose Precision Computing does not have the information on the residual value and is thus unable to compute the implicit rate. It must then use the incremental borrowing rate of 5%. This rate would also be appropriate if the company were private and it applied ASPE standards. The company's incremental borrowing rate of 5% is clearly lower than the rate implicit in the lease. Using 5% as the interest rate, the resulting present value of lease payments would be $179,952.[5] This value exceeds the fair value of $170,000, so the present value of minimum lease payments is capped at $170,000. Accordingly, Precision Computing must use this $170,000 to recompute the implicit interest rate. Using

5. The present value is computed as $50,067 + $30,000 × (PVAF$_{5\%,5}$) = $50,067 + $30,000 × 4.3295 = $179,952.

a spreadsheet, we can solve for this rate, which turns out to be 7.952%, resulting in the following amortization schedule for Precision Computing:

Exhibit 18-17		Lease amortization schedule for Precision Computing after applying fair value cap			
Period	Year	Interest for year @ 7.952%	Payments	Reduction in principal	Principal after interest and payments
					$170,000
0			$50,067	$50,067	119,933
1	2011	9,537*	30,000	20,463	99,470
2	2012	7,910	30,000	22,090	77,380
3	2013	6,153	30,000	23,847	53,533
4	2014	4,257	30,000	25,743	27,790
5	2015	2,210	30,000	27,790	0

*7.952% × $119,933 = $9,537.

4. Cash flows to be included in present value calculations

All three stages of a lease, as outlined in the diagram in Section A, require the use of present values and related interest calculations. In the simplest case, when the lease covers 100% of the useful life of the property and there is no residual value—as was the case for the Boeing 737 example used above—the calculations are the same in all three stages. However, confusion sometimes arises because these calculations can involve different amounts depending on the circumstance. To the unwary, the inclusions and exclusions could seem arbitrary. The following helps to explain why different amounts or calculations are used in each of the three stages.

a. Determining lease pricing

When a lessor and lessee negotiate the conditions of a lease, particularly the lease payments, the lessor takes into account all expected cash flows derived from the property. These cash flows may come from the lessee, but may also come from other sources. Take an extreme case for example: a hotel rents a room for a night to a tourist. In this scenario, the lessor (hotel) cannot expect to recover the entire cost of the room from this one lessee (tourist). Instead, the hotel recovers the cost from many different rentals. Clearly, for pricing purposes the hotel takes into account both the one night of rent as well as any residual value at the end of the lease, even if it is unguaranteed.

b. Classifying a lease as finance or operating

One of the indicators to determine whether there is a transfer of risks and rewards involves calculating the present value of the minimum lease payments (MLP). In this instance, only amounts included in MLP (i.e., those amounts required by the lessee or assured to the lessor) are included in the calculation. Using the hotel room example again, the present value of the MLP would be only a small fraction of the value of the room, so the one-night rental contract would not constitute a finance lease. Thus, any unguaranteed residual value would be excluded from this calculation.

c. Determining amounts in lease amortization schedules

If the lessee or lessor classifies a lease as a finance lease, then amortization schedules will be required to determine the amounts to record in each period. The amortization tables of the lessee and lessor will not necessarily be the same. Differences will arise if the lessor and lessee use different interest rates, as discussed above. The amortization tables will also differ due to unguaranteed residual values.

For the lessee, the amortization schedule includes only the minimum lease payments (which, as noted above, include any guaranteed residual value or bargain purchase option). For the lessor, the amortization schedule includes the minimum lease payments *plus* any unguaranteed residual value. The following illustrates amortization schedules for Mitchell Co. (the lessor) and Nobel Corp. (the lessee) for a four-year lease for equipment having fair value of $50,000 and estimated useful life of five years. The estimated residual value is $10,000 at the end of the lease and $2,000 at the end of five years. The annual payments (in advance) are $12,830, and the implicit interest rate is 12%. This is classified as a finance lease as there is a substantial transfer of the risks and rewards of ownership to the lessee. In particular, the lease term is a substantial majority (four-fifths) of the estimated useful life of the equipment.

Notice that the lessor's amortization has a balance of $10,000 at the end of the lease, which equals the expected residual value.

Exhibit 18-18	Illustration of lease amortization schedules for a lease with an unguaranteed residual value

Lease receivable/obligation amortization schedules

	Lessor—Mitchell Co.			Lessee—Nobel Corp.		
Year	Annual lease payment	Interest income @ 12%	Ending balance of net lease receivable	Annual lease payment	Interest expense @ 12%	Ending balance of lease obligation
0			$50,000			$43,645*
1	$12,830	$4,460[†]	41,631	$12,830	$3,698[‡]	34,513
2	12,830	3,456	32,257	12,830	2,602	24,285
3	12,830	2,331	21,758	12,830	1,375	12,830
4	12,830	1,071	**10,000**	12,830	0	0

*$12,830 \times (\text{PVAF}_{12\%,\ 3\ \text{years}} + 1) = \$12,830 \times 3.40183 = \$43,645$

[†]$12\% \times (\$50,000 - 12,830) = \$4,460$

[‡]$12\% \times (\$43,645 - 12,830) = \$3,698$

5. Third-party guarantees: An example of rules avoidance

Because lessees generally prefer operating lease treatment to improve the appearance of the financial statements, they try very hard to avoid capital lease treatment. Accounting standards attempt to curtail the use of leases as a method of off-balance-sheet financing by requiring capitalization (i.e., finance lease treatment) when there is a substantial transfer of risks and rewards of ownership. However, the rules are not water-tight. For example, an industry has developed to provide "third-party guarantees" of the residual value of leased assets.

Exhibit 18-19	Schematic of a lease with a third-party guarantee

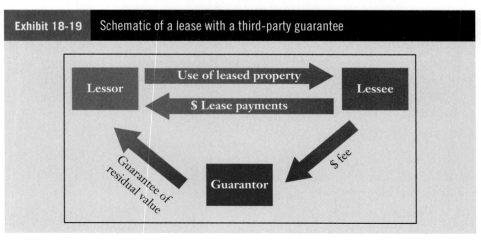

In such arrangements, the lessee does not directly guarantee the residual value, but rather pays a fee to the third-party guarantor. As a result, the residual value is considered unguaranteed and not counted as part of the lessee's MLP. To the lessor, however, the residual value is guaranteed—by the third-party guarantor. If the residual value is large enough, both the lessee and the lessor obtain their preferred accounting method: the lessee can use operating lease treatment, while the lessor can treat it as a finance lease.

E. PRESENTATION AND DISCLOSURE

1. Current/non-current classification of lease liability or lease receivables

L.O. 18-5. Apply the presentation and disclosure requirements applicable to leases.

As with any type of borrowing, it is necessary for the lessee to separate the liability for a finance lease into current and non-current components. Likewise, the lessor needs to separate its lease receivable between current and non-current portions. The simplest way to make this classification is to understand that the lease obligation or receivable reflects the financing component of the lease, so the lease obligation is like a mortgage. For a mortgage, the amount that is current is the amount of principal due within a year, plus any interest that has been accrued up to the year-end (but not any interest to be incurred in the future). This will be the same amount as the lease payment **only if** the lease payment date falls on the first day of the next fiscal year. This is the case for the example given in Exhibit 18-18 and repeated in the following exhibit. The bottom of this exhibit shows what the lessor and lessee should present in their balance sheets at the end of Year 1:

Exhibit 18-20	Separating current and non-current portion of lease receivables

Lease receivable/obligation amortization schedules from Exhibit 18-18

	Lessor—Mitchell Co.			Lessee—Nobel Corp.		
Year	Annual lease payment	Interest income @ 12%	Ending balance of net lease receivable	Annual lease payment	Interest expense @ 12%	Ending balance of lease obligation
0			$50,000			$43,645*
1	$12,830	$4,460†	**41,631**	$12,830	$3,698‡	**34,513**
2	**12,830**	3,456	32,257	**12,830**	2,602	24,285
3	12,830	2,331	21,758	12,830	1,375	12,830
4	12,830	1,071	10,000	12,830	0	0

Presentation by Mitchell Co.—end of Year 1

Current lease receivable (for payment due in Year 2)	$12,830
Long-term lease receivable*	28,801
Total lease receivable	$41,631

Presentation by Nobel Corp.—end of Year 1

Lease obligation—current portion (for payment due in Year 2)	$12,830
Lease obligation—long-term*	21,683
Total lease obligation	$34,513

*Long-term amounts are computed as the total − current portion

This example has payments occurring immediately following the fiscal year-end. In all other instances, the amount in current receivables will be smaller. In the extreme case where the next lease payment occurs at the end of the next fiscal year, then the current portion of the lease is just the amount of principal portion of the payment in the following year (which excludes the interest portion of that payment).

2. Disclosures

Leases potentially bind lessors and lessees for many years. Consequently, accounting standards require significant disclosures so that users are able to understand whether, to what extent, and how a company has used leases. The following table summarizes some of the more important disclosures. (For a complete list of disclosures, the reader should refer to IAS 17 and *CICA Handbook* 3065.)

Exhibit 18-21	Summary of disclosure requirements for leases	
	Lessee	**Lessor**
Finance lease	■ The net carrying amount of each class of leased asset	■ The allowance for uncollectible amounts relating to lease receivables.
	■ A reconciliation between the total of future minimum lease payments and their present value at the balance sheet date (i.e., how much of future minimum lease payments is represented by interest cost)	■ A reconciliation between the gross lease receivable and their present value at the balance sheet date (i.e., how much of future minimum lease payments is represented by interest revenue)
	■ Future minimum lease payments over the following terms: – within the next fiscal year; – between the second and fifth years in the future, inclusive; – after the fifth year in the future.	■ Future minimum lease payments over the following terms: – within the next fiscal year; – between the second and fifth years in the future, inclusive; – after the fifth year in the future.
	■ A description of leases that are material, including information such as that pertaining to contingent rents, renewal options, purchase options, and restrictions on the company's activities.	■ A description of leases that are material.
Operating lease	■ Future minimum lease payments over the following terms: – within the next fiscal year; – between the second and fifth years in the future, inclusive; – after the fifth year in the future.	■ Future minimum lease payments over the following terms: – within the next fiscal year; – between the second and fifth years in the future, inclusive; – after the fifth year in the future.
	■ A description of leases that are material, including information such as that pertaining to contingent rents, renewal options, purchase options, and restrictions on the company's activities.	■ A description of leases that are material.

F. SALE-LEASEBACKS

A company that is short of cash but that has substantial fixed assets can obtain financing through sale-leaseback arrangements without affecting its operating capabilities. As the label suggests, a sale-leaseback involves the sale of an asset and immediate leasing of that asset from the new owner. The prior owner of the asset becomes the lessee, and the buyer is the lessor. The following diagram illustrates these relationships.

Exhibit 18-22	Schematic of a sale-leaseback transaction

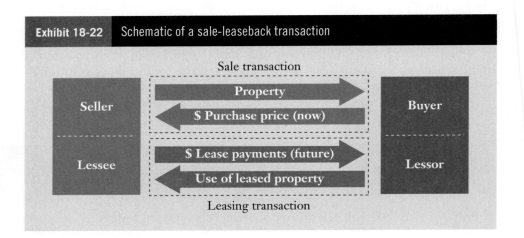

If the sale transaction were separate from the leasing transaction, there would be no additional accounting issues. That is, first record the asset sale transaction and its consequent gains/losses, then record the lease transaction. The problem in a sale-leaseback is that the two transactions are bundled, with the same two parties involved in both transactions. As a result, the sale price could be quite arbitrary because the buyer-lessor can recover the sale price through future lease payments from the seller-lessee. As a result, any gains or losses on the sale would be correspondingly arbitrary. To prevent manipulation of gains and losses through sale-leasebacks, the accounting treatment defers any gains or losses over the term of the lease.

What method should be used to amortize these gains or losses? If the lease is classified as a finance lease, the seller-lessee amortizes any gain or loss in proportion to the depreciation of the leased asset. If the lease is classified as an operating lease, the seller-lessee amortizes the gain or loss in proportion to the lease payments.

Example of a sale-leaseback Graydon Hunnicutt LLP is a law firm that purchased its office building many years ago. On January 1, 2011, the firm decided to enter into a sale-leaseback arrangement on the building in order to secure funds required to buy out two retiring partners. The transaction generated $16 million, and the firm committed to rent the space for the remaining 20 years of its useful life for $1,508,922 per year due in advance. These payments imply an interest rate of 8% implicit in the lease. Before the sale-leaseback, Graydon Hunnicutt's books showed cost of $5 million and accumulated depreciation of $3 million for the building. The firm uses the straight-line method of depreciation for buildings. Since the lease is for the entire remaining useful life of the building, this is a finance lease.

Graydon Hunnicutt and the counterparty would record the following entries to reflect this sale-leaseback:

Exhibit 18-23	Journal entries for a sale-leaseback transaction			
	Seller-lessee—Graydon Hunnicutt	**$ thousands**	**Buyer-lessor**	**$ thousands**
Jan. 1, 2011	Dr. Cash	16,000	Dr. Building	16,000
	Dr. Accum. depreciation—building	3,000	Cr. Cash	16,000
	Cr. Building	5,000		
	Cr. Deferred gain on sale-leaseback	14,000		
	Dr. Leased building	16,000	Dr. Leased receivable (net)	16,000
	Cr. Oblig. under finance lease	16,000	Cr. Building	16,000
	Dr. Obligation under finance lease	1,509	Dr. Cash	1,509
	Cr. Cash	1,509	Cr. Lease receivable	1,509
Dec. 31, 2011	Dr. Interest expense	1,159*	Dr. Lease receivable	1,159*
	Cr. Oblig. for finance lease	1,159	Cr. Interest revenue	1,159
	Dr. Depreciation expense	800†		
	Cr. Accumulated depreciation	800		
	Dr. Deferred gain on sale-leaseback	700‡		
	Cr. Depreciation expense	700		

*8% × ($16,000,000 − $1,508,922) = $1,159,286
†$16,000,000/20 years = $800,000/year
‡$14,000,000/20 years = $700,000/year

The effects of these entries are twofold. First, they nullify the effect of the sale-leaseback on the income statement. The seller-lessee (Graydon Hunnicutt) does not record any gain for the sale of the building, and the amortization of the deferred gain reduces future depreciation expense. As you can see from above, the net amount of depreciation for the year 2011 is $100,000 (= $800,000 − $700,000), which is exactly equal to the depreciation that would be recorded had the building not been sold ($2,000,000/20 years = $100,000/year). Second, the substance of a sale-leaseback boils down to a financing transaction, much like mortgaging a property to a bank. The above accounting reflects this economic substance: Graydon Hunnicutt obtained a loan for $16 million which is to be repaid over 20 years with annual installments of $1,508,922.

G. SUBSTANTIVE DIFFERENCES BETWEEN RELEVANT IFRS AND ASPE

ISSUE	IFRS	ASPE
Lease capitalization criteria—lessee	Based on qualitative considerations of whether the lease transfers substantially all the risks and rewards of ownership.	Based on both qualitative and quantitative considerations of whether the lease transfers substantially all the risks and rewards of ownership.
Lease capitalization criteria—lessor	Use the same criteria as for lessee.	In addition to the criteria for the lessee, the lessor must also consider the credit risk of the lessee and whether unreimbursable costs are reasonably estimable.

(Continued)

ISSUE	IFRS	ASPE
Lessor's classification of finance (capital) leases	No sub-classification of finance leases.	Capital leases are further sub-classified into sales-type and direct-financing leases depending on whether there is a profit margin on the sale.
Lessee's discount rate for present value calculations	Use implicit rate if it is known to lessee. Otherwise, use the incremental borrowing rate.	If the implicit rate is known to lessee, use the lower of the implicit rate and the incremental borrowing rate. Otherwise, use the incremental borrowing rate.

H. STANDARDS IN TRANSITION

In August 2010, the International Accounting Standards Board (IASB) issued an exposure draft (ED) to replace IAS 17. The ED proposes a radically different approach to accounting for leases based on the concept of "right-to-use." Specifically, the proposal would require lessees to capitalize assets and liabilities for essentially all leased property, without considering any characteristics of the property involved (such as useful life). As discussed earlier in this chapter, capitalization of what are currently operating leases would have substantially negative effects on the financial statements of many enterprises in the form of higher leverage and lower income. At time of writing, it is unclear whether this proposal will withstand the significant resistance that is expected for such a dramatic revision.

I. SUMMARY

L.O. 18-1. Evaluate the economic substance of a lease arrangement to determine the extent to which there is a transfer of risks and rewards.

■ The economic substance of a lease depends on the transfer of risks and rewards because the extent of transfer determines the size of the agency cost of leasing.
■ A lease that substantially transfers all the risks and rewards of ownership to the lessee has low agency cost.
■ If the lessor retains the risks and rewards of ownership, then the agency cost will tend to be high.
■ Lease pricing takes into consideration the agency cost of leasing: those leases that transfer risks and rewards to the lessee will tend to be more economical, while leases without such transfers will be relatively more costly on a per-unit-of-service basis.

L.O. 18-2. Apply the general and specific criteria for classifying leases as finance (capital) or operating leases and apply the accounting method appropriate for that classification.

■ The general criterion for classifying a lease as finance or operating reflects the economic substance of the transaction: is there a transfer of risks and rewards of ownership?
■ There are a number of indicators to help assess whether there is a transfer of risks and rewards.
■ Clear-cut indicators are an outright transfer of ownership or a bargain purchase option in the lease agreement.
■ Other indicators are the fraction of the property's useful life covered by the lease and the proportion of the property's fair value represented by the lease payments. While ASPE (though not IFRS) provides quantitative guidelines with respect to lease term and present value, it is difficult to argue that a lease term or present value of one percent less automatically changes a lease from a finance lease into an operating

lease. So, assessing these two quantitative indicators requires accountants to exercise professional judgment that takes into account all the lease's characteristics.

L.O. 18-3.   Analyze a lease to determine the present value of minimum lease payments, the interest rate implicit in a lease, the lease payments required by the lessor, and lease amortization schedules.

- Accounting for leases requires numerous figures and computations.
- Pay particular attention to residual values that are unguaranteed, payments to exercise bargain purchase options, and the interest rate that should be used to discount the cash flows that flow from the lease or that flow from the property outside of the lease term. Due to the long duration of many leases, it is also necessary to distinguish the portion of the lease that is current versus the portion that is long-term for presentation in the balance sheet.

L.O. 18-4.   Analyze the differences in financial reporting outcomes when a lease is treated as a finance lease as compared to an operating lease, and understand the consequent preferences for finance or operating lease treatment by the lessor or lessee.

- Accounting standards for leases attempt to have enterprises reflect the substance of the transaction rather than their legal form.
- The resulting differences in accounting outcomes from finance versus operating lease treatments provide strong incentives for management to try to obtain the treatment that is most favourable for it.
- To counteract earning management incentives, the classification rules make it difficult and costly for lessees to escape finance lease treatment if that is the method that reflects the substance of the transaction. Nevertheless, some firms are willing to bear that cost, for example by using third-party guarantees to obtain operating lease treatment.

L.O. 18-5.   Apply the presentation and disclosure requirements applicable to leases.

- Lessees and lessors need to separately present the current and non-current portions of lease obligations or receivables.
- Disclosures should provide descriptions of material leases, future minimum lease payments, and other information that would be useful to understanding the enterprise's lease commitments or receivables.

L.O. 18-6.   Describe the rationale for the deferral of gains or losses on sale-leaseback transactions and account for these transactions.

- Gains or losses on sale-leaseback transactions are potentially artificial; standards require the deferral and amortization of gains or losses on sale-leasebacks.

J. References
Authoritative standards:

IFRS	ASPE Section
IAS 17—Leases	3065—Leases

K. Glossary

agency cost of leasing: The reduced level of care due to the separation of an asset's ownership and its control.

bargain purchase option: An option given to the lessee to purchase the leased asset at a price that is below expected fair value at a future date; the assessment of whether a bargain exists is made at the time of entering the lease arrangement.

direct-financing lease: A type of finance lease in which the sale price is equal to the cost of the asset to the lessor (used in Canadian ASPE).

executory costs: Incidental costs in a lease that would be incurred by the lessee independent of whether the lessee had purchased or leased the asset.

finance lease (also **capital lease**): A type of lease that transfers substantially all of an asset's risks and rewards of ownership from the lessor to the lessee; for a lessor, a finance lease also has normal credit risk and no material unreimbursable costs.

guaranteed residual value: A minimum value for the leased asset that is guaranteed to the lessor.

implicit interest rate: The discount rate that is used, or implied to be used, by the lessor in the determination of the payments in a lease.

incremental borrowing rate: The interest rate that the lessee would have to pay on a similar lease or loan.

lease: An agreement whereby the owner of an asset allows others the use of that asset in return for monetary or non-monetary consideration.

lessee: The renter in a lease contract.

lessor: The owner of the asset in a lease.

minimum lease payments (MLP): The payments over the lease term that the lessee is or can be required to make.

off-balance-sheet financing: Obtaining financial funding without recognition of a liability in the balance sheet.

operating lease: A type of lease that is not a finance lease.

sales-type lease: A type of finance lease in which the lessor obtains a profit margin on the sale of the leased asset (used in Canadian ASPE).

L. PROBLEMS

 Go to MyAccountingLab at **www.myaccountinglab.com**. You can practise the indicated exercises as often as you want, and guided solutions will help you find answers step by step. You'll find a personalized study plan available to you too!

P18-1. Substance of lease arrangements and classification

(**L.O.** 18-1) (Easy – 5 minutes)

Identify whether the following are lease characteristics relevant to the classification of a lease as a finance (capital) lease.

	Yes/No
a. Lease transfers title to the lessee at the end of the lease.	
b. Lease payments include executory costs.	
c. Lease transfers substantially all risks and rewards of ownership.	
d. Lease is for tangible property.	
e. Lease is for intangible property.	
f. Lease is considered long-term.	

P18-2. Substance of lease arrangements and classification—lessee

(**L.O.** 18-1) (Easy – 5 minutes)

Identify whether the following are characteristics relevant to the classification of a lease as a finance (capital) lease.

	Yes/No
a. Minimum lease payments comprise at least 75% of the fair value of the leased asset (under ASPE).	
b. Minimum lease payments comprise substantially all of the fair value of the lease asset.	
c. The lease is a lease on land.	
d. The lease contains a bargain purchase option.	
e. The lease term comprises a major part of the economic life of the asset.	
f. The lease term comprises at least 75% of the economic life of the asset (under ASPE).	

P18-3. Substance of lease arrangements and classification—lessee

(**L.O.** 18-1) (Easy – 5 minutes)

Accounting standards for leases require an assessment of whether the lease transfers substantially all the risks and rewards of ownership.

Required:

Discuss how these standards relate to the definition of assets in the IFRS framework.

P18-4. Substance of lease arrangements and classification—lessee

(**L.O.** 18-1) (Medium – 10 minutes)

Accounting standards for leases require an assessment of whether the lease transfers substantially all the risks and rewards of ownership.

Required:

Discuss how these standards relate to the concept of information asymmetry in financial accounting theory.

P18-5. Substance of lease arrangements and classification

(**L.O.** 18-1) (Easy – 5 minutes)

The following are the characteristics of a lease:

Fair value of leased asset	$100,000
Lease payments	$26,380
Lease term	5 years
Payment frequency	Annual
Payment timing	End of year
Guaranteed residual value	None
Interest rate implicit in the lease (known to lessee)	10%

Required:

Determine the present value of minimum lease payments (MLP) and the appropriate classification of this lease for the lessee.

P18-6. Substance of lease arrangement and classification

(**L.O.** 18-1) (Easy – 5 minutes)

The following are the characteristics of a lease:

Fair value of leased asset	$600,000
Lease payments	$80,000
Lease term	5 years
Payment frequency	Annual
Payment timing	End of year
Guaranteed residual value	None
Interest rate implicit in the lease (known to lessee)	8%

Required:

Determine the present value of minimum lease payments (MLP) and the appropriate classification of this lease for the lessee.

P18-7. Substance of lease arrangement   **L.O.** 18-1) (Medium – 10 minutes)

The following are characteristics of a lease:

Fair value of leased asset	$500,000
Lease payments	$90,000
Lease term	7 years
Payment frequency	Annual
Payment timing	End of year
Guaranteed residual value at end of lease term	$60,000
Interest rate implicit in the lease (known to lessee)	9%

Required:

Determine the present value of minimum lease payments (MLP) and the appropriate classification for this lease for the lessee.

P18-8. Lease classification and accounting—lessee   (**L.O.** 18-2) (Easy – 5 minutes)

On January 1, 2011, Hanover Company entered a lease to rent office space. The lease requires Hanover to pay $200,000 per year, at the beginning of each year, for 10 years. The lease is non-cancellable and non-renewable. The building's estimated useful life is 30 years, and its current fair value is estimated to be $5 million. Hanover's incremental borrowing rate is 10%.

Required:

Classify this lease for Hanover Company and record the journal entries for the first year of the lease.

P18-9. Lease classification and accounting—lessee

            (**L.O.** 8-2, **L.O.** 18-3) (Medium – 10 minutes)[6]

On February 1, 2010, Star Company leased equipment to Planet Company. The terms of the lease are as follows:

Lease term	6 years
Economic life of equipment	8 years
Fair market value of equipment	$80,000
Guaranteed residual value	$5,000
Annual lease payment, due each February 1	$16,000
Lessee's incremental borrowing rate	10%

Planet uses straight-line depreciation for its property, plant, and equipment, and its year-end is December 31.

Required:

Prepare the journal entries for the lease from February 1 through December 31, 2010.

---

6. © 2010 CGA-Canada. Reproduced with permission.

P18-10. Lease classification and accounting—lessee

(**L.O.** 18-2, **L.O.** 18-3) (Medium – 15 minutes)[7]

Cappy leased equipment to Swew Company on July 1, 2010. The terms of the lease are as follows:

Lease term	8 years
Economic life of equipment	10 years
Fair market value of equipment	$120,000
Guaranteed residual value	$15,000
Annual lease payment, due each July 1	$16,000
Lessee's incremental borrowing rate (implicit rate unknown)	6%

Swew uses straight-line depreciation for its property, plant, and equipment.

Required:

a. Prepare the journal entries for the lease from July 1 through December 31, 2010.
b. You are the director of finance for Swew Company. You are concerned about the impact the lease will have on your key performance indicator, the total debt to total assets ratio. Discuss the impact the lease will have on this performance indicator.

P18-11. Lease classification and accounting—lessor

(**L.O.** 18-2) (Medium – 10 minutes)

The following are characteristics of a lease:

Price of leased asset from manufacturer	$500,000
Lease payments	$92,823
Lease term	7 years
Payment frequency	Annual
Payment timing	End of year
Guaranteed residual value at end of lease term	$60,000
Interest rate implicit in the lease	9%

Required:

Determine the appropriate classification for this lease for the lessor (who is not the manufacturer) and record the journal entries for the lessor for the first year of the lease.

P18-12. Analysis of leases—MLP, implicit rate, lease payments, amortization

(**L.O.** 18-3) (Easy – 10 minutes)

The following are some of the characteristics of an asset available for lease.

Fair value of asset	$100,000
Lease term	5 years
Payment frequency	Annual
Payment timing	End of year
Guaranteed residual value	None
Interest rate implicit in the lease (known to lessee)	10%
Lessee's incremental borrowing rate	10%

Required:

a. Determine the amount of lease payment that the lessor would require to lease the asset.
b. Compute the present value of minimum lease payments for the lessee.
c. Compute the present value of minimum lease payments for the lessor.
d. Evaluate whether the lessee should classify the lease as operating or finance.

---

7. © 2010 CGA-Canada. Reproduced with permission.

P18-13. Analysis of leases—MLP, implicit rate, lease payments, amortization

(**L.O.** 18-3) (Medium – 10 minutes)

The following are some of the characteristics of an asset available for lease:

Fair value of leased asset	$100,000
Lease term	5 years
Payment frequency	Annual
Payment timing	End of year
Guaranteed residual value	$20,000
Interest rate implicit in the lease (known to lessee)	10%
Lessee's incremental borrowing rate	11%

Required:

a. Determine the amount of lease payment that the lessor would require to lease the asset.
b. Compute the present value of minimum lease payments for the lessee.
c. Compute the present value of minimum lease payments for the lessor.
d. Evaluate whether the lessee should classify the lease as operating or finance.

P18-14. Analysis of leases—MLP, implicit rate, lease payments, amortization

(**L.O.** 18-3) (Medium – 10 minutes)

The following are some of the characteristics of an asset available for lease:

Fair value of leased asset	$100,000
Lease term	5 years
Payment frequency	Annual
Payment timing	Beginning of year
Guaranteed residual value	$20,000
Interest rate implicit in the lease (not known to lessee)	10%
Lessee's incremental borrowing rate	8%

Required:

a. Determine the amount of lease payment that the lessor would require to lease the asset.
b. Compute the present value of minimum lease payments for the lessee.
c. Compute the present value of minimum lease payments for the lessor.
d. Evaluate whether the lessee should classify the lease as operating or finance.

P18-15. Analysis of leases—MLP, implicit rate, lease payments, amortization

(**L.O.** 18-3) (Medium – 15 minutes)

The following are some of the characteristics of an asset available for lease.

Fair value of leased asset	$100,000
Useful life	8 years
Lease term	5 years
Payment frequency	Annual
Payment timing	Beginning of year
Residual value (unguaranteed)	$20,000
Interest rate implicit in the lease (not known to lessee)	10%
Lessee's incremental borrowing rate	8%

Required:

a. Determine the amount of lease payment that the lessor would require to lease the asset.
b. Compute the present value of minimum lease payments for the lessee.

c. Compute the present value of minimum lease payments for the lessor.

d. Evaluate whether the lessee should classify the lease as operating or capital lease using the quantitative guidelines in ASPE.

e. Evaluate whether the lessor should classify the lease as operating or capital lease using the quantitative guidelines in ASPE.

P18-16. Analysis of leases—MLP, implicit rate, lease payments, amortization
(**L.O.** 18-3) (Medium – 15 minutes)

LaSalle Leasing Company agrees on January 1, 2012 to rent Rockwood Winery the equipment that Rockwood requires to expand its production capacity to meet customers' demands for its products. The lease agreement calls for five annual lease payments of $200,000 at the end of each year. Rockwood has identified this as a finance lease. Furthermore, the company has determined that the present value of the lease payments, discounted at 15%, is $670,431. The leased equipment has an estimated useful life of five years and no residual value. Rockwood uses the straight-line method for depreciating similar equipment that it owns.

Required:

a. Prepare a lease amortization schedule for this lease.

b. Prepare the necessary journal entries for the first year of the lease.

P18-17. Comprehensive lease question (**L.O.** 18-2, **L.O.** 18-3) (Medium – 25 minutes)

Salem Creamery leases its ice cream making equipment from Big City Finance Company under the following lease terms:

- The lease term is five years, non-cancellable, and requires equal rental payments of $46,498 due at the beginning of each year starting January 1, 2011.
- Upon inception of the lease on January 1, 2011, Big City purchased the equipment at its fair value of $200,100 and immediately transferred it to Salem Creamery. The equipment has an estimated economic life of five years, and a $10,000 residual value that is guaranteed by Salem Creamery.
- The lease contains no renewal options, and the equipment reverts to Big City Finance Company upon termination of the lease.
- Salem's incremental borrowing rate is 10%; the rate implicit in the lease is also 10%.
- Salem depreciates similar equipment that it owns on a straight-line basis.
- Both companies have December 31 year-ends.

Required:

a. Evaluate how the lessee should account for the lease transaction.

b. Evaluate how the lessor should account for the lease transaction.

c. Prepare the lessee's amortization schedule for this lease.

d. Prepare the journal entries on January 1, 2011 for both parties.

e. Prepare the journal entries on December 31, 2011 and January 1, 2012 for both parties.

f. On December 31, 2015, the actual residual value of the equipment is $4,000. Salem returns the equipment to Big City and pays for the guaranteed residual value as promised. Prepare the journal entry for this final transaction on Salem's books.

P18-18. Comprehensive lease question (**L.O.** 18-2, **L.O.** 18-3) (Difficult – 30 minutes)

A lessor agrees to rent a truck with fair value and carrying value of $130,000 for a period of four years at an annual rental of $34,478 payable at the beginning of each year. The truck's residual value is estimated to be $20,000. The interest rate implicit in the lease is 12%, and the lessee is aware of this rate. Previous analysis has already concluded that this is a finance lease to both the lessor and lessee.

Required:

For parts a through d, assume that the lessee has guaranteed the residual value.

   a. Compute the present value (PV) of the minimum lease payments (MLP). Round your answer to the nearest $100.
   b. Prepare a lease amortization table for the lessee (and the lessor will use the same schedule).
   c. Record all journal entries for both parties for the first year of the lease.
   d. Record all journal entries required for both parties at the end of the lease term assuming that the truck's actual residual value is (i) $20,000; (ii) $4,000; or (iii) $35,000.

     For part e, assume that the residual value is not guaranteed.

   e. Record all the journal entries for both parties for the first year of the lease.

P18-19. Comprehensive lease question—Thornhill/Vanier companies Part 1
(**L.O.** 18-2, **L.O.** 18-3) (Difficult – 30 minutes)

Thornhill Equipment leased a construction crane to Vanier Construction on January 1, 2011. The following information relates to the leased asset and the lease agreement.

Cost of crane to lessor	$100,000
Thornhill's normal selling price for crane	$146,913
Useful life	10 years
Estimated value at end of useful life	$4,000
Lease provisions	
Lease term	7 years
Payment frequency	Annual
Payment timing	December 31
Amount of each lease payment	$31,200
Estimated residual value at end of lease (unguaranteed)	$10,000
Other: Crane will revert back to lessor at end of lease term, title does not transfer to lessee at any time, and there are no bargain purchase options.	
Interest rate implicit in the lease (known to lessee)	12%
Lessee's incremental borrowing rate	13%

Both companies use the straight-line depreciation method for cranes, and they both have December 31 year-ends.

Required:

   a. Classify this lease from the perspective of the lessee, Vanier Construction.
   b. Classify this lease for the lessor, Thornhill Equipment.
   c. Provide the lease amortization schedule for the lessee.
   d. Provide the lease amortization schedule for the lessor.
   e. Record the lease-related journal entries for both companies from the year 2011.

P18-20. Comprehensive lease question—Thornhill/Vanier companies Part 2
(**L.O.** 18-2, **L.O.** 18-3) (Difficult – 15 minutes)

Refer to the facts presented in P18-19 for Thornhill Equipment and Vanier Construction. Consider the following four independent variations on the scenario.

   i. The original fact pattern as presented in P18-19.
   ii. The $10,000 residual value is guaranteed by Vanier. When the lease ended on December 31, 2017, the crane was worth $8,000.
   iii. The unguaranteed residual value is $20,000, and Vanier has the option to purchase the crane at the end of the lease at a bargain price of $10,000. The actual value of the crane at the end of the lease was $20,000, so Vanier exercised its option to purchase.
   iv. The unguaranteed residual value is $20,000, and Vanier has the option to purchase the crane at the end of the lease at a bargain price of $10,000. The actual value of the crane at the end of the lease was $1,000, so Vanier did not exercise its option to purchase.

Required:

a. For each of the four scenarios, compute the interest revenue for the lessor (Thornhill) for 2011.

b. For each of the four scenarios, provide the journal entries for the lessor (Thornhill) at the end of the lease on December 31, 2017. Assume that the journal entry for the final lease payment of $31,200 has already been made.

P18-21. Comprehensive lease question—Thornhill/Vanier companies Part 3

(**L.O.** 18-2, **L.O.** 18-3) (Difficult – 20 minutes)

Refer to the facts presented in P18-19 for Thornhill Equipment and Vanier Construction. Consider the following four independent variations on the scenario.

i. The original fact pattern as presented in P18-19.

ii. The $10,000 residual value is guaranteed by Vanier. When the lease ended on December 31, 2017, the crane was worth $8,000.

iii. The unguaranteed residual value is $20,000, and Vanier has the option to purchase the crane at the end of the lease at a bargain price of $10,000. The actual value of the crane at the end of the lease was $20,000, so Vanier exercised its option to purchase.

iv. The unguaranteed residual value is $20,000, and Vanier has the option to purchase the crane at the end of the lease at a bargain price of $10,000. The actual value of the crane at the end of the lease was $1,000, so Vanier did not exercise its option to purchase.

Required:

a. For each of the four scenarios, compute the annual depreciation expense for the lessee using the straight-line method.

b. For each of the four scenarios, provide the journal entries for the lessee (Vanier) at the end of the lease on December 31, 2017. Assume that the journal entry for the final lease payment of $31,200 has already been made.

P18-22. Reporting consequences of operating versus finance leases

(**L.O.** 18-4) (Easy – 5 minutes)

Company A and Company B operate in the same industry, where leasing assets is common practice. Company A engages in more finance leases than Company B. Company B's leases are classified as operating leases, but they are essentially a form of financing as well. Both companies disclose information with respect to their leases. Which of the two companies will tend to appear stronger financially according to the balance sheet and income statement?

P18-23. Reporting consequences of finance leases (**L.O.** 18-4) (Medium – 20 minutes)[8]

Longview Corporation started operations on March 1, 2009. It needs to acquire a special piece of equipment for its manufacturing operations. It is evaluating two options as follows.

Option 1: Lease the equipment for 8 years. Lease payments would be $11,950 per year, due at the beginning of each fiscal year (March 1). Longview's incremental borrowing rate is 6%. There is no bargain purchase or renewal option. Longview is responsible for all executory costs of operating the equipment.

Option 2: Purchase the equipment for $78,900 by borrowing the full purchase amount at 6% over 8 years. This price is considered the fair value of the equipment. Payments are due at the end of each fiscal year (February 28).

The equipment has a useful life of 8 years and would be depreciated on a straight-line basis. No residual value is expected to exist at the end of 8 years.

Required:

a. Calculate the present value of the lease payments (Option 1).

b. Calculate the payment that would be required under the purchase option (Option 2).

---

8. © 2009 CGA-Canada. Reproduced with permission.

c. Calculate and briefly discuss the financial impact of each option on the non-current assets, total liabilities, and net income of Longview for the first year of operations. Assume all payments were made when due. Show your calculations.

d. Indicate which option you would recommend for Longview. Provide one explanation to support your recommendation.

P18-24. Lease classification, accounting, and presentation

(**L.O.** 18-2, **L.O.** 18-5) (Medium – 15 minutes)[9]

On April 1, 2012, Hedf Company entered into a five-year lease for equipment. Annual lease payments are $25,000, payable at the beginning of each lease year (April 1). At the end of the lease, possession of the equipment will revert to the lessor. The equipment has an expected useful life of 5 years.

Similar equipment could be purchased for $170,000 cash. Hedf's incremental borrowing rate is 6%. The company has a March 31 year-end, and it uses straight-line depreciation for its property, plant, and equipment.

Required:

a. Prepare the journal entries relating to the lease and leased asset for Hedf's fiscal year ending March 31, 2013.

b. State the amounts related to the lease that would be reported on the March 31, 2013 balance sheet, indicating the balance sheet classifications, account names, and amounts.

P18-25. Presentation and disclosure of leases   (**L.O.** 18-5) (Easy – 10 minutes)

A lessee has the following amortization schedule for a particular lease:

Period	Year	Payments at beginning of year	Balance after payment	Interest for year @ 12%	Reduction in principal	Principal after interest and payments
1	2011	$34,478	$95,522	$11,463	$23,015	106,985
2	2012	34,478	72,507	8,701	25,777	81,207
3	2013	34,478	46,729	5,608	28,870	52,337
4	2014	34,478	17,859	2,141*	32,337	20,000

*Adjusted by $2 for rounding

The company entered into the lease at the beginning of its fiscal year, on January 1, 2011. Depreciation follows the straight-line method.

Required:

Provide the appropriate presentation of this lease in the lessee's balance sheet for December 31, 2012, distinguishing amounts that are current from those that are non-current.

P18-26. Presentation and disclosure of leases   (**L.O.** 18-5) (Medium – 10 minutes)

A lessee has the following amortization schedule for a particular lease:

Period	Year	Interest for year @ 12%	Payments at end of year	Reduction in principal	Principal after interest and payments
					$142,389
1	2011	$17,087	31,200	14,113	128,276
2	2012	15,393	31,200	15,807	112,469
3	2013	13,496	31,200	17,704	94,765
4	2014	11,372	31,200	19,828	74,937
5	2015	8,992	31,200	22,208	52,729
5	2016	6,328	31,200	24,872	27,857
7	2017	3,343	31,200	27,857	0

9. © 2009 CGA-Canada. Reproduced with permission.

The company entered into the lease at the beginning of its fiscal year, on January 1, 2011. Depreciation follows the straight-line method.

Required:

Provide the appropriate presentation of this lease in the lessee's balance sheet for December 31, 2013, distinguishing amounts that are current from those that are non-current.

P18-27. Accounting and presentation of leases
(**L.O.** 18-2, **L.O.** 18-3, **L.O.** 18-5) (Medium – 20 minutes)

Prairie Railroad and Loco-Motive Corporation enter into an agreement that requires Loco-Motive to build three diesel-electric engines to Prairie's specifications. Upon completion of the engines, Prairie has agreed to lease them for a period of 12 years and to assume all costs and risks of ownership. The lease is non-cancellable, becomes effective on January 1, 2011, and requires annual rental payments of $280,000 due each January 1 beginning in 2011.

Prairie's incremental borrowing rate is 13%, and the implicit interest rate used by Loco-Motive and known to Prairie is 12%. The total cost of building the three engines is $1,550,000. The economic life of the engines is estimated to be 12 years with residual value set at zero. The railroad depreciates similar equipment on a straight-line basis. At the end of the lease, the railroad obtains title to the engines.

Required:

a. Classify the lease for both the lessee and lessor.
b. Prepare the journal entries for both parties to record the inception of the lease and the first rental payment.
c. Prepare a lease amortization schedule for the lessee for the first 3 years.
d. Prepare the journal entries for both parties to record interest at December 31, 2011.
e. Show the items and amounts that would be reported for both parties as at December 31, 2011. Clearly distinguish current from non-current items.

P18-28. Sale-leaseback
(**L.O.** 18-6) (Medium – 15 minutes)

On January 1, 2011, Devlin Company sold a building to Bancroft Bank for $64,000,000 and immediately leased it back under a 20-year non-cancellable lease at $7,650,000 per year, payable at the beginning of each year. Bancroft used an implicit rate of 12% to determine the lease payments, and this rate is known to Devlin. The building had a carrying value of $40,000,000 on Devlin's books.

Required:

Assume that the lease is a finance lease for both the lessee and lessor, and there is no profit margin for the lessor. Prepare all necessary journal entries for 2011 for Devlin (the seller-lessee) and Bancroft (the buyer-lessor). Devlin will continue to depreciate the building on a straight-line basis over the lease term.

P18-29. Sale-leaseback
(**L.O.** 18-6) (Medium – 10 minutes)

Refer to the facts in P18-28 for the sale-leaseback of Devlin Company and Bancroft Bank.

Required:

Assume that the lease is an operating lease for both the lessee and lessor. Prepare all necessary journal entries for 2011 for Devlin (the seller-lessee) and Bancroft (the buyer-lessor). Bancroft will depreciate the building on a straight-line basis over the remaining useful life of 20 years.

P18-30. Sale-leaseback

(**L.O.** 18-6) (Difficult – 25 minutes)[10]

Sportco Ltd. is a sports equipment manufacturer. In 2012, because of poor economic conditions in the United States, the company's main market, it suffered temporary cash-flow difficulties. In order to raise sufficient capital to allow operations to continue until economic conditions improve, Sportco entered into an agreement with a major leasing organization, Leaseco Ltd.

On January 1, 2012, Sportco sold its largest manufacturing property (having a carrying amount of $250,000) to Leaseco for $1,750,000.

Sportco, in turn, leased back the property from Leaseco for 15 years with an annual rental payment of $175,000 due January 1 of each year. It can purchase the property at the end of the 15 years for $2,500,000, which is the estimated fair value at that time. The land is estimated to be 40% of the total fair value of the property, while the building represents the other 60%. Sportco depreciates its buildings at a rate of 10% using the declining balance method.

Sportco's incremental borrowing rate is 7%. Its financial statements are prepared in accordance with IFRS.

Required:

How should Sportco account for the above transaction in its financial statements for the year ending December 31, 2012? Provide support. Ignore any income-tax implications and disclosure issues.

---

10. Adapted with permission from The Canadian Institute of Chartered Accountants, Toronto, Canada. Any changes to the original material are the sole responsibility of the author and have not been reviewed or endorsed by the CICA.

M. MINI-CASES

It is January, and Ms. Deb. T. Laiden, President of Debt Laiden Inc. (Debt Laiden), has just returned from an annual visit with the company's banker, Mr. Green, to present Debt Laiden's December financial statements. Mr. Green expressed concern over Debt Laiden's profitability and debt level. In an effort to alleviate Mr. Green's concerns, Ms. Laiden proposed to sell a major piece of production equipment to a local finance company, provided Debt Laiden is able to lease it back. The equipment was purchased two years ago from a Japanese manufacturer for $1,000,000 and is being depreciated at 15% per year on a declining balance basis. Due to the rise in the value of the Japanese yen relative to the Canadian dollar, Ms. Laiden estimates that the machinery is currently worth $1,500,000.

She has approached Mr. Fin, President of Sharky's Financial Services Ltd. (Sharky's), who indicated that he would be willing to purchase the equipment for $1,500,000 and lease it back to Debt Laiden for $274,252 per year for the next 10 years, payable at the end of each year. Debt Laiden would have the option to repurchase the asset at the end of the lease term at its estimated fair value of $500,000, as it would be usable for at least another five years. Ms. Laiden thinks Sharky's is getting a pretty good deal, as she estimates Debt Laiden's cost of capital to be 12%. However, Mr. Fin indicated over lunch, "Hey, I gotta earn 15% or I just don't make no money on this lease!"

Ms. Laiden is eager to complete the transaction in an effort to improve the company's profitability (by recording the gain on the sale of the equipment), and to concurrently reduce the company's debt level (by using the sale proceeds to pay down a loan of $1,500,000 with a 12% interest rate).

CASE 1
Debt Laiden Inc.
(45 minutes)

Required:

Analyze the above information and provide your recommendation to Ms. Laiden as to whether she should undertake the proposed transaction.

Parcels Delivered Quickly (PDQ) is a public company that provides shipping and delivery services for household and commercial parcels ranging from a few grams to several hundred kilograms. The company uses a fleet of 800 trucks and vans to pick up and deliver parcels. For inter-city shipping, the company has an arrangement with commercial airlines to ship parcels using airlines' cargo capacity.

The volume of parcel shipments has been increasing steadily since the birth of online shopping in the late 1990s, as consumers search for the best deals regardless of physical location. As a result, PDQ needs to expand its fleet capacity by 200 vehicles to meet the increasing demand. In addition, 200 of the existing vehicles will need to be replaced over the next two years as they come to the end of their service lives.

Management is concerned about the potential for adverse reactions from investors should the company's leverage become too high or if profitability suffers as a result of this program to replace and expand the vehicle fleet. As a result, instead of borrowing and buying the needed vehicles outright, PDQ's management is considering two other alternatives.

Option 1: Lease the trucks and vans with short-term leases, one year at a time. For a truck with a cost of $80,000, the annual lease payment would amount to $15,000, due in advance.

Option 2: Lease the vehicles with long-term leases that last for the 10 years of the expected useful life. For a truck with a cost of $80,000, the annual payments would be $11,000. These leases would transfer title to PDQ at the end of the lease.

CASE 2
PDQ Leasing Options
(30 minutes)

With either option, PDQ would be responsible for maintenance and repairs on the vehicles.

PDQ currently has about $32 million in total assets and $19 million in liabilities. Debt on the balance sheet carries an average interest rate of 7%. The company's bank has quoted a 9% interest rate for additional borrowing.

Required:

Analyze the alternatives relevant to the fleet replacement and expansion and provide your recommendation to management for the best course of action. Assume that PDQ depreciates vehicles using the declining balance method at a 20% rate.

CHAPTER **19** # Statement of Cash Flows

The Canadian Imperial Bank of Commerce (CIBC) is one of the largest banks in Canada, with assets of more than $335 billion as at October 31, 2009.

In 2008, at the height of the global liquidity crisis and credit meltdown, CIBC reported a net loss for the year of $2.060 billion. These dismal results bore little resemblance to the $3.296 billion profit earned in 2007. Despite the recorded loss, however, CIBC's statement of cash flows disclosed a $101 million net *increase* in cash during the year. How are these seemingly inconsistent results possible?

The statement of cash flows showed that this net increase of $101 million was due to cash inflows of $434 million from operating activities offset by $333 million of outflows from investing and financing activities. Furthermore, CIBC presented operating cash flows using the indirect method in contrast to the direct method used for investing and financing cash flows. Why does the company categorize cash flows as arising from operating, investing, or financing activities? What is the difference between the direct and indirect methods of reporting cash flows from operating activities? Why does CIBC produce a statement of cash flows? What information does this statement provide?

LEARNING OBJECTIVES

After studying this chapter, you should be able to:

L.O. 19-1. Describe the purpose of the statement of cash flows and the information it conveys.

L.O. 19-2. Define cash and cash equivalents.

L.O. 19-3. Differentiate among cash flows from operating activities, investing activities, and financing activities.

L.O. 19-4. Describe the difference between the direct and indirect methods of calculating cash flows from operating activities.

L.O. 19-5. Prepare a statement of cash flows using both the direct and indirect methods.

CONTENTS

A. INTRODUCTION

L.O. 19-1. Describe the purpose of the statement of cash flows and the information it conveys.

Net income is an important metric as it measures the financial performance of the company. Equally important is the firm's ability to generate cash—because it is ultimately cash, not income, that pays employees, suppliers, creditors, investors, and governments. Income statements are prepared on an accrual basis, and consequently net income seldom equals the change in cash during the period.

In the opening vignette, CIBC's cash increased $101 million in fiscal 2008 despite the reported loss. While CIBC's affairs are very complex, their financial statements do give some insight into sources of the noted gap between the increase in cash and the net loss. For example, CIBC recorded $773 million in credit losses and amortization of $245 million. These expenses increased the reported loss but did not result in an outflow of cash.

Investors, creditors, and managers are interested in how entities generate and use cash. Responding to this demand, IAS 1, Presentation of Financial Statements, requires all companies to present both an income statement and a statement of cash flows (SCF). The statement of cash flows speaks to the capacity of a business to generate cash and the business's need for cash resources. Managing cash flow to ensure that the company has sufficient monies to pay bills when due is an essential function. Larger companies will have a treasury department dedicated to managing cash resources.

To provide information useful to decision makers, IAS 1 requires companies to report cash inflows and outflows using standardized categories such as operations, investments, and financing. Second, the SCF provides information on why the change in cash for a period differs from its reported income. Moreover, comparative SCFs provide a historical record of both the firm's ability to generate cash and its ongoing need for funds. The statement of cash flows thus provides very useful information that is not available in other financial statements (i.e., the balance sheet, income statement, and so on).

The SCF is useful for evaluating a company's liquidity—its ability to generate sufficient cash to meet its obligations when due. Users can also glean valuable information about the timing and uncertainty of cash flows by analyzing past relationships between items like sales and cash flow from operations. Utilizing these facts facilitates more accurate forecasts of future cash flows than relying solely on the income statement. Lastly, the SCF can also be used to ascertain the firm's quality of earnings. As discussed in Chapter 3, the quality of earnings refers to how closely reported earnings correspond to earnings that would be reported in the absence of managerial bias. One way to evaluate earnings quality is to compare the company's net income with cash from operating activities, because cash flows are less subject to managerial bias compared with accrual income. If the reported net income is consistently close to or less than cash from operating activities, the company's net income or earnings are said to be of a "high quality." If net income is consistently more than cash from operating activities, further investigation is needed to ascertain why the reported net income is not matched by an increase in cash.

For all of the reasons above, the statement of cash flows is a useful and important component of an enterprise's financial report. The next section discusses *what* should appear on the statement of cash flows. Section C will then describe the procedures for *how* one goes about compiling the figures that appear in the SCF.

B. PRESENTATION OF THE STATEMENT OF CASH FLOWS

The general standards for the presentation of the SCF appear in IAS 1, Presentation of Financial Statements, with more specific standards provided by IAS 7, Statement of Cash Flows. To properly specify the reporting requirements for the statement of cash flows, it is necessary to identify what is a "cash flow." To do so, we need to review what are considered to be cash and cash equivalents (see also Chapter 5).

1. Cash and cash equivalents defined

In IAS 7, "cash and cash equivalents" is an important concept. The standard defines the two components separately as follows:

L.O. 19-2. Define cash and cash equivalents.

> ¶6. . . . *Cash* comprises cash on hand and demand deposits.
> **Cash equivalents** are short-term, highly liquid investments that are readily convertible to known amounts of cash and which are subject to an insignificant risk of changes in value.

cash equivalents Short-term, highly liquid investments that are readily convertible to known amounts of cash and which are subject to an insignificant risk of changes in value.

The reference to "demand deposits" means funds in accounts with financial institutions that can be withdrawn without notice or penalty; for example, a chequing account.

To qualify as a cash equivalent, an item must meet both requirements of *convertibility* and *insignificant risk*. Many items meet one but not both criteria. For example, an investment in widely traded stock is readily convertible to cash because it can be sold on a stock exchange, but its price is subject to significant risk of change. A non-redeemable term deposit is not subject to significant risk of change in value, but cannot be readily converted to cash if the maturity date is far in the future. Neither the stock investment nor the term deposit would be considered cash equivalents. In contrast, treasury bills (which are government bonds with maturity under a year) that mature within the next ninety days could be considered a cash equivalent because they can be readily sold in a public market and their value does not fluctuate significantly. Likewise, a term deposit with a short enough maturity also meets the criteria of convertibility and insignificant risk; IAS 7 paragraph 7 suggests that three months or less would be a short enough duration.

Note that a security holding that satisfies the criteria for cash equivalent need not be classified as such. An enterprise has a choice to classify such securities either as cash equivalents or as held-for-trading financial assets. Whichever choice is made, the enterprise needs to disclose this accounting policy in the notes to the financial statements.

Cash is an idle asset that does not earn income. Consequently, most enterprises try to keep cash holdings close to zero, so it is common for bank balances to be in overdraft (i.e., to be negative). IAS 7 also considers bank overdrafts as part of cash and cash equivalents:

¶8. . . . bank overdrafts which are repayable on demand form an integral part of an entity's cash management. In these circumstances, bank overdrafts are included as a component of cash and cash equivalents. A characteristic of such banking arrangements is that the bank balance often fluctuates from being positive to overdrawn.

The reason for considering the details of "cash" and "cash equivalents" above is that the two are considered together in the definition of cash flows. IAS 7 indicates the following:

¶9. Cash flows exclude movements between items that constitute cash or cash equivalents because these components are part of the cash management of an entity rather than part of its operating, investing and financing activities. Cash management includes the investment of excess cash in cash equivalents.

Thus, for purposes of the cash flow statement, we do not look at cash versus cash equivalents as two separate items but rather as a single unit of "cash and cash equivalents." For brevity, the remainder of this chapter will simply use "cash" to mean "cash and cash equivalents."

2. Classifying cash flows

L.O. 19-3. Differentiate among cash flows from operating activities, investing activities, and financing activities.

As discussed in Chapter 3, there are three distinct cash cycles. The shortest cash cycle relates to operations, followed by investments, with the financial cycle being the longest. Consistent with these cash cycles, IAS 7 classifies cash flows into three categories: operating activities, investing activities, and financing activities.

a. Operating activities

Cash flows from operating activities arise from the day-to-day running of the business. Technically, IAS 7 defines operating activities as follows:

> ¶ 6. **Operating activities** are the principal revenue-producing activities of the entity and other activities that are not investing or financing activities.

operating activities The principal revenue-producing activities of the entity and other activities that are not investing or financing activities.

Cash flows from operating activities give considerable insight into a firm's ability to generate sufficient cash to maintain its business operations, repay loans, and make new investments without having to arrange external financing.

b. Investing activities

IAS 7 defines investing activities as follows:

> ¶6. **Investing activities** are the acquisition and disposal of long-term assets and other investments not included in cash equivalents.

investing activities The acquisition and disposal of long-term assets and other investments not included in cash equivalents.

Cash flows related to investing summarize net expenditures for assets meant to generate future income. There are two distinct components to investing activities. The first is the acquisition and disposal of fixed assets, the second is investing in financial assets. To establish and maintain the infrastructure necessary to run their businesses, companies purchase and sell assets such as property, plant, and equipment. Investing in the more traditional sense involves buying and selling debt and equity securities. However, as discussed above, buying and selling investments that are classified as cash equivalents are not reported as cash flows. In addition, purchases and sales of investments classified as held for trading are reported as operating activities because these transactions are primarily driven by cash management considerations.

c. Financing activities

Companies raise money by issuing debt and selling equity, using the proceeds to acquire fixed assets or for operating purposes. Financing activities record the cash flows associated with the issuance and retirement of debt and equity. Technically, IAS 7 defines financing activities as follows:

> ¶6. **Financing activities** are activities that result in changes in the size and composition of the contributed equity and borrowings of the entity.

financing activities Activities that result in changes in the size and composition of the contributed equity and borrowings of the entity.

For purposes of the statement of cash flows, financing activities do not include financing resulting from ordinary operations. For example, supplier financing through accounts payable is an operating rather than a financing activity.

To illustrate these three classes of cash flows, consider an electronics retail store. Some of the operating activities include cash received from customers, payments for inventories, wages of the sales staff, and taxes to the government. Investing activities include purchasing cash registers and computer systems, buying a long-term bond issued by another entity, and selling a delivery vehicle. Financing activities include issuing bonds, repurchasing preferred shares, and reducing the principal on an outstanding finance lease.

d. Cash flows with classification options

For most transactions, the classification of a cash flow is unambiguous. However, there are two situations where the standards allow a choice of classification (IAS 7 paragraphs 31–34).

■ *Interest and dividends received*: An enterprise may classify the receipt of interest and dividends as either an operating or an investing activity. The ambiguity here is because it is not clear-cut whether this type of income is part of an enterprise's normal operations or part of its investments.

■ *Interest and dividends paid*: An enterprise may choose to report the payment of interest and dividends as either an operating or a financing activity. The ambiguity arises because interest and dividend payments arise from financing activities (issuance of debt and equity); interest is recorded through income, while dividends are not.

Regardless of the choice for this accounting policy, the enterprise must apply it consistently to all similar transactions.

Accounting Standards for Private Enterprises (ASPE) does not provide options.[1] Rather, the receipt of interest and dividends and the payment of interest are operating activities; the payment of dividends is a financing activity.

Exhibit 19-1 categorizes common cash inflows and outflows.

e. Non-cash transactions

When a company borrows money from the bank and then uses the funds to purchase a vehicle, the loan is recorded as a cash inflow from financing activities, and the automobile purchase as a cash outflow from investing activities. However, if the company leases this vehicle from the automobile dealer, the transaction is not recorded on the statement of cash flows as this is a non-cash transaction. **Non-cash transactions** are activities that do not involve cash. Investing and financing activities that involve non-cash transactions are not recorded on the SCF because the SCF reports only the cash effect of a company's activities. Common non-cash transactions include:

non-cash transactions Activities that do not involve cash.

■ exchanging assets such as parcels of land with another company
■ converting bonds or preferred shares into common shares
■ stock dividends
■ finance leases

Certain transactions are only partially settled in cash; for example, a company acquires a building for $1,000,000 by paying $200,000 in cash and signing an $800,000 note payable. The SCF records only the $200,000 cash paid as an outflow in the investing activities section. Significant non-cash transactions are disclosed in the notes to the financial statements.

3. Format of the statement of cash flows

a. Illustrative example

L.O. 19-4. Describe the difference between the direct and indirect methods of calculating cash flows from operating activities.

Exhibit 19-2 reproduces the 2009 cash flow statement for British Airways (BA). Preliminary comments about the structure and format of the statement are provided as a prelude to a full discussion of these points later in the chapter.

■ The cash flows are grouped by type of activity: operating, investing, and financing.
■ Cash inflows and outflows are not netted against each other. Rather they are presented separately; for example, BA reports "purchase of property, plant, and equipment" and "proceeds from the sale of property, plant, and equipment."
■ The amount of interest and dividends received and paid and income taxes paid was presented on the face of the statement.

---

1. Accounting Standards for Private Enterprises requirements are not illustrated as all examples in this chapter are based on IFRS.

| Exhibit 19-1 | Common examples of cash flows by type of activity |

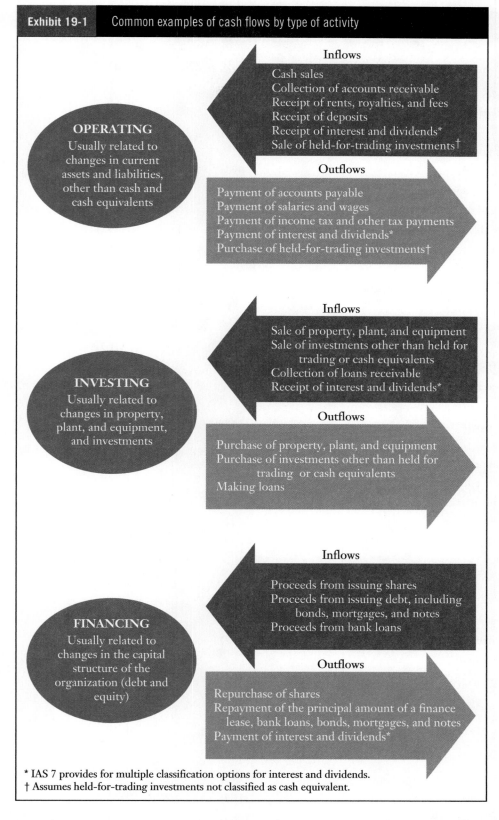

OPERATING
Usually related to changes in current assets and liabilities, other than cash and cash equivalents

Inflows
Cash sales
Collection of accounts receivable
Receipt of rents, royalties, and fees
Receipt of deposits
Receipt of interest and dividends*
Sale of held-for-trading investments†

Outflows
Payment of accounts payable
Payment of salaries and wages
Payment of income tax and other tax payments
Payment of interest and dividends*
Purchase of held-for-trading investments†

INVESTING
Usually related to changes in property, plant, and equipment, and investments

Inflows
Sale of property, plant, and equipment
Sale of investments other than held for trading or cash equivalents
Collection of loans receivable
Receipt of interest and dividends*

Outflows
Purchase of property, plant, and equipment
Purchase of investments other than held for trading or cash equivalents
Making loans

FINANCING
Usually related to changes in the capital structure of the organization (debt and equity)

Inflows
Proceeds from issuing shares
Proceeds from issuing debt, including bonds, mortgages, and notes
Proceeds from bank loans

Outflows
Repurchase of shares
Repayment of the principal amount of a finance lease, bank loans, bonds, mortgages, and notes
Payment of interest and dividends*

* IAS 7 provides for multiple classification options for interest and dividends.
† Assumes held-for-trading investments not classified as cash equivalent.

■ The opening and closing cash and cash equivalents balance at the bottom of the SCF match those presented on the accompanying balance sheet. Remember that the SCF explains the change between the opening and closing cash.

■ BA used the "indirect method" to present its cash flows from operating activities. The company could have also used the "direct method." We discuss these two methods next.

Exhibit 19-2	Cash flow statements for 2009, British Airways

£ million	Note	Group 2009	Group 2008 Restated	Company 2009	Company 2008 Restated
Cash flow from operating activities					
Operating (loss)/profit		(220)	878	(165)	862
Operating loss from discontinued operations			(2)		
Depreciation, amortisation and impairment		694	692	670	672
Operating cash flow before working capital changes		474	1,568	505	1,534
Movement in inventories, trade and other receivables		32	96	(28)	89
Movement in trade and other payables and provisions		(136)	(325)	(132)	(276)
Payments in respect of restructuring		(64)	(32)	(62)	(30)
Cash payment to NAPS pension scheme	36		(610)		(610)
Payment to DOJ in settlement of competition investigation			(149)		(149)
Other non-cash movement		1	3	7	(32)
Cash generated from operations		307	551	290	526
Interest paid		(177)	(182)	(163)	(169)
Taxation		3	(66)	26	(108)
Net cash flow from operating activities		133	303	153	249
Cash flow from investing activities					
Purchase of property, plant, and equipment	15	(547)	(596)	(528)	(592)
Purchase of intangible assets	18	(24)	(33)	(24)	(32)
Purchase of shares in associated undertakings	20		(54)		
Proceeds from sale of other investments		7		7	
Proceeds from sale of property, plant, and equipment		5	11	10	11
Insurance recoveries for write-off of Boeing 777 aircraft		12	51	12	51
Purchase of subsidiary (net of cash acquired)		(34)		(144)	(1,016)
Cash inflow from disposal of subsidiary company			1		
Interest received		105	117	53	123
Dividends received		17	3	6	4
Decrease in other current interest-bearing deposits		202	458	356	1,238
Net cash used in investing activities		(257)	(42)	(252)	(213)
Cash flows from financing activities					
Proceeds from long-term borrowings		377	172	377	172
Repayments of borrowings		(66)	(68)	(55)	(57)
Payment of finance lease liabilities		(402)	(356)	(411)	(355)
Exercise of share options		1	4	1	4
Dividends paid		(58)		(58)	
Distributions made to holders of perpetual securities		(17)	(14)		
Net cash used in financing activities		(165)	(262)	(146)	(236)
Net decrease in cash and cash equivalents		(289)	(1)	(245)	(200)
Net foreign exchange differences		8	(29)	31	(29)
Cash and cash equivalents at April 1		683	713	433	662
Cash and cash equivalents at March 31	25	402	683	219	433

b. Direct and indirect methods of reporting cash flows from operating activities

Cash flows from operations can be reported using either the direct or indirect method. IAS 7 states the following:

¶18. An entity shall report cash flows from operating activities using either:

(a) the **direct method**, whereby major classes of gross cash receipts and gross cash payments are disclosed; or

(b) the **indirect method**, whereby profit or loss is adjusted for the effects of transactions of a non-cash nature, any deferrals or accruals of past or future operating cash receipts or payments, and items of income or expense associated with investing or financing cash flows.

Although the net amount of operating cash flows remains the same, the direct and indirect methods involve different line items within cash flow from operating activities. Moreover, the choice of the direct or indirect method does not affect the reporting of cash flows from investing and financing activities. Cash flows from investing and financing are presented using the direct method.

The International Accounting Standards Board (IASB) and the Accounting Standards Board in Canada (AcSB) have long favoured the direct method of reporting because, they argue, this method provides more useful information than the indirect method. Indeed, the first sentence of IAS 7 paragraph 19 reads "Entities are encouraged to report cash flows from operating activities using the direct method." Notwithstanding this support, the vast majority of companies choose to use the indirect method of presentation. While hard statistics are not readily available, it is estimated that less than one percent of entities use the direct method of presentation in Canada. To reflect common practice, we focus on the indirect method in this chapter.

To increase usage of the direct approach, standard setters may at some point make the direct method mandatory. In this respect, the IASB is working on a project to establish standards for the organization and presentation of financial statements. One proposal being considered requires all entities to report cash flows from operations using the direct method.

As IAS 7 provides only general guidance on the format of the statement of cash flows, users will observe that entities do present their results in different ways. The two exhibits that follow illustrate the general form of presentation. (Ignore the "Reference" column for now; these references will be used later in the chapter.)

Some observations about these two exhibits:

■ Notice that net cash from operating activities of $590 is the same under both the direct and indirect methods.

■ The format employed of separately disclosing related items together (e.g., income tax expense and income taxes paid) facilitates disclosure requirements discussed elsewhere in this chapter.

■ The starting point for the indirect method is profit or loss according to IAS 7 paragraph 18 (see above). IAS 7 does not specify what this includes, however, leading to observed differences in practice. This exhibit begins with net income as a starting point, which is consistent with past practice in Canada. The illustrative example in appendix A to IAS 7 uses profit and losses before tax as a starting point. In Exhibit 19-2, the first line of British Airways' SCF is its pre-tax operating loss that excluded financing costs and income and other non-core revenue and expenses.

direct method A method of presenting the statement of cash flows by showing major classes of gross cash receipts and gross cash payments.

indirect method A method of presenting the statement of cash flows by adjusting profit or loss for the effects of transactions of a non-cash nature, any deferrals or accruals of past or future operating cash receipts or payments, and items of income or expense associated with investing or financing cash flows.

Exhibit 19-3	Sample operating section of statement of cash flows using the indirect method

Illustrative Company
(Partial) Statement of Cash Flows
Year Ended December 31, 2013

Cash flow from operating activities		Reference
Net income	$3,050	(i)
Adjustments for:		
Depreciation	450	(ii)
Gain on sale	(50)	
Investment income	(400)	
Interest expense	400	(iii)
Income tax expense	300	
Subtotal	3,750	
Increase in trade and other receivables	(500)	
Decrease in inventories	1,050	(iv)
Decrease in trade payables	(1,740)	
Cash generated from operating activities	2,560	
Dividends received*	200	
Interest received*	200	
Dividends paid[†]	(1,200)	(v)
Interest paid[†]	(270)	
Income taxes paid	(900)	
Net cash from operating activities	$ 590	(vi)

*Can also be shown as cash flows from investment
[†]Can also be shown as cash outflows for financing

Exhibit 19-4	Sample operating section of statement of cash flows using the direct method

Illustrative Company
(Partial) Statement of Cash Flows
Year Ended December 31, 2013

Cash flow from operating activities	
Cash receipts from customers	$30,360
Cash paid to suppliers and employees	(27,800)
Cash generated from operating activities	2,560
Dividends received*	200
Interest received*	200
Dividends paid[†]	(1,200)
Interest paid[†]	(270)
Income taxes paid	(900)
Net cash from operating activities	$ 590

*Can also be shown as cash flows from investment
[†]Can also be shown as cash outflows for financing

The above discussion reveals some flexibility in the presentation of the statement of cash flows. For the sake of consistency, unless specifically stated otherwise the remainder of this chapter assumes that the company has adopted the following conventions:

- Net income is the starting point for determining cash flow from operating activities using the indirect method.
- Interest paid, interest received, dividends paid, and dividends received are all classified as operating activities.

Having discussed what should be presented in the statement of cash flows, we now turn to the procedures for how one goes about preparing this financial statement. Whereas standards specify the required presentation, there are not any formal standards for the preparation of the statement of cash flows.

C. PREPARING THE STATEMENT OF CASH FLOWS

The statement of cash flows explains the change in cash and cash equivalents during the year, categorizing the cash flows by activity: operating, investing, or financing. The general format of the SCF is:

L.O. 19-5. Prepare a statement of cash flows using both the direct and indirect methods.

Exhibit 19-5	General format of the statement of cash flows

Company Name Statement of Cash Flows Period Ended	
Cash flow from operating activities	
Details of the adjustments to profit or loss by category (indirect method)	
Details of cash inflows and outflows by category (direct method)	
Net cash from (used in) operating activities	xx
Cash flow from investing activities	
Details of cash inflows and outflows by category	
Net cash from (used in) investing activities	xx
Cash flow from financing activities	
Details of cash inflows and outflows by category	
Net cash from (used in) financing activities	xx
Net increase (decrease) in cash and cash equivalents	xx
Cash and cash equivalents at beginning of period	xx
Cash and cash equivalents at end of period	xx

Observe how the net increase (decrease) in cash and cash equivalents explains the difference between the opening and ending balance of cash and cash equivalents.

1. Sources of information

The balance sheet and income statement are prepared directly from the adjusted trial balance, as they each present select components of the general ledger. In contrast, preparing the statement of cash flows requires additional information outside of the trial balance, which only contains information about the ending cash balance but not changes in that balance. The required information comes from three primary sources:

- *Comparative balance sheets:* The change in cash for the year can be explained by the net change of all the other accounts on the balance sheet.
- *The income statement for the period:* The income statement is a necessary starting point to determine cash from operating activities under the indirect method. It also provides information about the change in retained earnings.
- *Select transaction data:* The income statement and comparative balance sheets provide aggregated information that is insufficient for identifying some cash flows. For example, the purchase of furniture for $50,000 and the sale of computers originally costing $20,000 would result in a net change of $30,000 in property, plant, and equipment (gross of depreciation) on the balance sheet. The $30,000 net figure is inadequate for SCF purposes because cash flows arising from the purchase and sale of assets must be presented separately rather than netted against each other. Furthermore, the cost of assets sold do not directly correspond to the proceeds from their sale.

2. The process—Indirect method

a. When are adjustments required?

When preparing the statement of cash flows, we consider the net change in each balance sheet account during the year. Nevertheless, it is instructive to contemplate individual transactions so as to gain greater insight into the underlying mechanics of preparing the SCF. There are four types of straightforward transactions to be considered, depending on whether each half of the transaction involves income/expenses or cash inflows/outflows:

Exhibit 19-6	Types of transactions according to impact on income/expense and cash inflows/outflows			
One-half of transaction involves **income or expenses**	Yes	No	Yes	No
One-half of transaction involves **cash inflows or outflows**	No	Yes	Yes	No
Label for convenience	**Transaction type 1**	**Transaction type 2**	**Transaction type 3**	**Transaction type 4**
Example transaction	Sale to a customer on credit	Purchase of equipment using cash	Cash sale	Purchase of equipment using note payable
Example journal entry	Dr. Accounts receivable Cr. Sales revenue	Dr. Equipment Cr. Cash	Dr. Cash Cr. Sales revenue	Dr. Equipment Cr. Notes payable
Adjustment required in indirect method	Yes	Yes	No	No
Reason	Income or expense recorded but not received/paid in cash	Cash received or paid but not reflected in income or expenses	Cash flow equals income or expense	No cash involved

As shown in the table, whenever the amount reflected in the income statement differs from the amount of cash flow for a transaction, there needs to be an adjustment in the SCF using the indirect method (transaction types 1 and 2). When the effect is the same on the income statement and on cash flows, then an adjustment would not be required (transaction types 3 and 4).

b. The indirect method described

The indirect method of compiling the statement of cash flows involves converting the company's accrual-based income statement to a cash-based statement. Net income, rather than comprehensive income, is the starting point as items that are included in other comprehensive income do not affect cash flows.[2] The opening balance of cash plus (or minus) cash generated from (used in) operating, investing, and financing activities results in the closing balance, which should match the amount on the balance sheet. The process of preparing the statement of cash flows follows:[3]

Step 1: Determine the change in cash that needs to be explained. This is a simple matter of comparing this year's closing cash and cash equivalents balance to the prior year's balance.

Step 2: Adjust net income as necessary to determine net cash from operating activities (i to vi refer to the numbers noted in Exhibit 19-3):

   i. The starting point is the company's recorded profit or loss.

   ii. Adjust net income for all non-cash items including depreciation and gains and losses on the sale of assets or the settlement of debt.

   iii. Add back interest and income tax expense and subtract investment income from interest and dividends.

   iv. Adjust for the unexplained changes in working capital accounts representing operating activities, for example trade receivables, inventory, trade payables, and prepaid expenses, amongst others. (Note that changes in interest and dividends receivable, interest and dividends payable, and income taxes payable accounts are adjusted for in (iii) and (v).)

   v. Add dividends and interest received and subtract dividends, interest, and income taxes paid. Separately itemizing these cash flows meets the disclosure requirements set out in paragraphs 31 and 35 of IAS 7.

   vi. The total of items (i) to (v) equals net cash from operating activities for the year.

Step 3: Account for the changes in remaining balance sheet accounts. The reconciling items are recorded in the financing or investing activities section according to their nature.

Step 4: Calculate subtotals for operating, investing, and financing activities and ensure the net change in cash and cash equivalents thus determined is equal to the actual change for the period computed from Step 1.

c. The indirect method illustrated—Example 1

The process of preparing a relatively straightforward statement of cash flows using the steps outlined above is set out in the three exhibits that follow. Exhibit 19-7 shows the information necessary for compiling the SCF for Kimzoo Fireworks for the year 2013; Exhibit 19-8 illustrates the process to prepare the SCF; and Exhibit 19-9 presents the results.

---

2. Alternatively, we can use comprehensive income as a starting point, reversing the components of other comprehensive income. However, this would be redundant and uninformative.

3. The procedure discussed relates to the example of the indirect method statement of cash flows set out in Exhibit 19-9. The process will vary slightly for companies that present their SCF differently.

| Exhibit 19-7 | Information necessary for indirect method, example 1 |

Kimzoo Fireworks Ltd.
Income Statement
Year Ended December 31, 2013

Sales	$660,000
Cost of sales	363,000
Gross profit	297,000
Operating expenses	160,000
Interest expense	5,000
Amortization and depreciation expense	32,000
Income before income taxes	100,000
Income tax expense	33,000
Net income	$ 67,000

Balance Sheets with Change in Balances Computed
As at December 31

	2013	2012	Change
Assets			
Cash and cash equivalents	$ 99,000	$ 51,000	$ 48,000
Accounts receivable	53,000	39,000	14,000
Inventory	50,000	60,000	(10,000)
Prepaid expenses	6,000	9,000	(3,000)
Property, plant, and equipment at cost	420,000	350,000	70,000
Accumulated depreciation	(150,000)	(125,000)	(25,000)
Patents	51,000	58,000	(7,000)
Total assets	$529,000	$442,000	
Liabilities			
Dividends payable	$ 2,000	$ 2,000	$ 0
Trade payables	69,000	68,000	1,000
Mortgage payable	0	150,000	(150,000)
Total liabilities	71,000	220,000	
Shareholders' Equity			
Preferred shares	215,000	-0-	215,000
Common shares	200,000	200,000	0
Retained earnings	43,000	22,000	21,000
Total shareholders' equity	458,000	222,000	
Total liabilities and shareholders' equity	$529,000	$442,000	

Supplemental information: The company's policy is to report interest and dividends paid as cash outflows from operating activities.

Exhibit 19-8	Applying process for preparing a statement of cash flows using the indirect method, example 1

Step 1: Determine the change in cash that needs to be explained.

From the comparative balance sheet, the company's closing C&CE balance was $99,000, an increase of $48,000 over the opening balance of $51,000.

Step 2: Adjust net income as necessary to determine net cash from operating activities.

i.   Start with the company's net income.

The income statement shows net income of $67,000.

ii. Adjust for all non-cash items.

Depreciation and amortization expense reported on the income statement totalled $32,000. This amount is added to net income as the expense did not involve a cash outflow.

iii. Add back interest and income tax expense and subtract investment income.

The income statement reports interest expense of $5,000 and income tax expense of $33,000.

iv. Adjust for the unexplained changes in working capital accounts representing operating activities.

The working capital accounts included on the balance sheet requiring adjustment are accounts receivable, inventory, prepaid expenses, and trade payables.

Accounts receivable *increased* $14,000 during the year as the cash collected was *less* than the revenue recognized. While the $14,000 increase was the aggregate change for the year, to help visualize the required adjustment it is sometimes instructive to think of events that could have caused the noted difference in terms of an originating journal entry.

Dr. Accounts receivable	14,000	
Cr. Sales revenue		14,000

Revenue and income *exceeds* the amount of cash collected by $14,000 so, starting with net income, we need to deduct this $14,000 difference.

Once you understand this, you can apply a more straightforward way to determine the amount and direction of adjustment: think of what the cash balance must do in response to a change in a non-cash account on the balance sheet. If a non-cash asset increases, holding all else constant, the cash account must decline to keep the balance sheet in balance. Likewise, an increase in a liability results in an increase in cash. The increase in accounts receivable requires a −$14,000 adjustment in the SCF.

Inventory *decreased* $10,000 during the year. A decrease in a non-cash asset is accompanied by an increase in cash, so this requires a +$10,000 adjustment in the SCF.

Prepaid expenses *decreased* $3,000 during the year. A decrease in a non-cash asset is accompanied by an increase in cash, so this requires a +$3,000 adjustment in the SCF.

Trade payables *increased* $1,000 during the year. An increase in a liability is accompanied by an increase in cash, so this requires a +$1,000 adjustment in the SCF.

v.   Add dividends and interest received and subtract dividends, interest, and income taxes paid.

Interest paid = interest expense − change in interest payable. Interest payable for both years was $0, so interest paid equals interest expense, which was $5,000 as shown in the income statement.

Income taxes paid = income tax expense − change in income taxes payable. Income taxes payable for both years was $0, so income taxes paid equals income taxes expense, which was $33,000 as shown on the income statement.

Dividends paid = dividends declared − change in dividends payable. The balance in the dividends payable account remains unchanged so dividends payable equals dividends declared. However, the amount of dividends declared is not directly apparent from the balance sheet and income statement. In the absence of capital transactions that directly affect retained earnings (see Chapters 13 and 14), changes in retained earnings are due to net income and dividends declared.

Retained earnings, beginning of year (from balance sheet)	$22,000
Plus: net income (from income statement)	67,000
Less: dividends declared (solve)	(46,000)
Retained earnings, end of year (from balance sheet)	$43,000

In practice, the amount of dividends declared can be determined from the general ledger. We show this analysis here to demonstrate the relationship between income, dividends, and retained earnings.

In all three of the above formulas, "change" is a positive number for increases and a negative number for decreases.

vi. The total of items (i)−(v) equals net cash from operating activities.

$67,000 + $32,000 + $5,000 + $33,000 − $14,000 + $10,000 + $3,000 + $1,000 − $5,000 − $33,000 − $46,000 = $53,000. From a practical perspective, this step is fulfilled by completing the cash flows from operating activities section of the statement of cash flows.

(Continued)

Exhibit 19-8	Continued

Step 3: Account for the changes in remaining balance sheet accounts. The reconciling items are recorded in the financing or investing activities section according to their nature.

The remaining account balances requiring adjustment are: property, plant, and equipment at cost (PPE); mortgage payable; and preferred shares. From the comparative balance sheet the respective changes are a $70,000 increase, a $150,000 decrease, and a $215,000 increase. Note that the change in accumulated depreciation and patents was dealt with when depreciation and amortization was added back in the operating activities section. Similarly, the change in retained earnings was explained by net income and dividends declared, both of which were allowed for in cash flow from operating activities. Unless provided with specific information to the contrary, assume that these transactions are all cash-based.

- The company paid $70,000 to acquire the PPE, so record a $70,000 cash outflow in the investing activities section.
- To reflect the $150,000 paid to extinguish the mortgage obligation, record a $150,000 cash outflow in the financing activities section.
- The sale of preferred shares raised $215,000, so record a $215,000 cash inflow in the financing activities section.

Step 4: Calculate subtotals for operating, investing, and financing activities and ensure the net change in cash and cash equivalents thus determined is equal to the actual change for the period computed from Step 1.

The completed statement of cash flows follows. Note how the $48,000 increase in cash corresponds to the amount from Step 1.

Exhibit 19-9	Result of applying procedures for statement of cash flows, example 1

Kimzoo Fireworks Ltd.
Statement of Cash Flows
Year Ended December 31, 2013

Cash flows from operating activities		
Net income	$ 67,000	
Adjustments for:		
Depreciation and amortization	32,000	
Interest expense	5,000	
Income tax expense	33,000	
Subtotal	137,000	
Increase in trade and other receivables	(14,000)	
Decrease in inventory	10,000	
Decrease in prepaid expenses	3,000	
Increase in trade payables	1,000	
Cash generated from operating activities	137,000	
Dividends paid	(46,000)	
Interest paid	(5,000)	
Income taxes paid	(33,000)	
Net cash from operating activities		$53,000
Cash flows from investing activities		
Purchase of plant assets	(70,000)	
Net cash used in investing activities		(70,000)
Cash flows from financing activities		
Retirement of mortgage payable	(150,000)	
Sale of preferred shares	215,000	
Net cash from financing activities		65,000
Net increase in cash		48,000
Cash and cash equivalents, January 1, 2013		51,000
Cash and cash equivalents, December 31, 2013		$ 99,000

d. The indirect method illustrated—Example 2

To help you master the process for preparing a statement of cash flows, we use the same steps to work through a more complex example, Fred's Fajitas Ltd (FFL).

Exhibit 19-10	Information necessary for indirect method, example 2

Fred's Fajitas Ltd.
Income Statement
Year Ended December 31, 2015

Sales	$1,000,000
Cost of sales	400,000
Gross profit	600,000
General and administrative expenses	175,000
Interest expense	10,000
Depreciation expense	110,000
Operating income	305,000
Loss on sale of available-for-sale investments	2,000
Loss on sale of land	50,000
Income before income taxes	253,000
Income tax expense	107,000
Net income	$ 146,000

Balance Sheets with Change in Balances Computed
As at December 31

Assets	2015	2014	Change
Cash and cash equivalents	$ 17,000	$ 43,000	$ (26,000)
Accounts receivable	104,000	90,000	14,000
Inventory	80,000	65,000	15,000
Prepaid expenses	48,000	45,000	3,000
Current assets	249,000	243,000	
Land	551,000	310,000	241,000
Buildings at cost	860,000	810,000	50,000
Accumulated depreciation	(250,000)	(220,000)	(30,000)
Investments (available for sale)	84,000	90,000	(6,000)
Total assets	$ 1,494,000	$1,233,000	
Liabilities			
Trade payables	$ 52,000	$ 65,000	(13,000)
Dividends payable	7,000	12,000	(5,000)
Income tax payable	9,000	4,000	5,000
Notes payable	129,000	116,000	13,000
Current liabilities	197,000	197,000	
Bank loan	620,000	410,000	210,000
Total liabilities	817,000	607,000	

(Continued)

Exhibit 19-10   Continued

Shareholders' Equity

Preferred shares	0	100,000	(100,000)
Common shares	265,000	210,000	55,000
Retained earnings	412,000	316,000	96,000
Total shareholders' equity	677,000	626,000	
Total liabilities and shareholders' equity	$1,494,000	$1,233,000	

Supplemental information:

- FFL's policy is to report interest and dividends paid as cash outflows from operating activities.
- During the year, FFL bought and sold land. The historical cost of the land sold was $250,000.
- FFL sold a building originally costing $250,000 for proceeds equal to its carrying value.
- The available-for-sale (AFS) investments did not have unrealized gains or losses recognized in other comprehensive income.

Exhibit 19-11   Applying process for preparing a statement of cash flows using the indirect method, example 2

Step 1: Determine the change in cash that needs to be explained:

From the comparative balance sheet, the company's closing cash balance was $17,000, a decrease of $26,000 from the opening balance of $43,000.

Step 2: Adjust net income as necessary to determine net cash from operating activities:

i. Record the company's net income:

The income statement reported net income for the year of $146,000.

ii. Adjust for all non-cash items:

Depreciation expense reported on the income statement was $110,000. This amount is added back on the SCF because the expense did not involve a cash outflow.

The income statement recorded a loss *on the sale of investments* of $2,000 and *a loss on the sale of land* of $50,000. These losses are the difference between the sales price of the assets and their respective carrying values. It may be instructive to consider one of the underlying transactions to help visualize the required adjustments.

Dr. Cash	200,000	
Dr. Loss on sale of land	50,000	
Cr. Land		250,000

The $200,000 cash received is a cash inflow from investing activities. Since this $200,000 fully reflects the cash flow from this transaction, we need to add back $50,000 to cash flow from operating activities for the loss included in income.

iii. Add back interest and income tax expense and subtract investment income:

The income statement reports interest expense of $10,000 and income tax expense of $107,000.

iv. Adjust for the unexplained changes in working capital accounts representing operating activities:

The working capital accounts included on the balance sheet requiring adjustment are accounts receivable, inventory, prepaid expenses, trade payables, and notes payable.

Accounts receivable increased $14,000 during the year. Cash collected was less than the revenue recognized on the income statement, so this is a cash outflow from operating activities.

Inventory increased $15,000 during the year. The cash outflow was more than the related expense (cost of goods sold), so this is a cash outflow from operating activities.

Prepaid expenses increased $3,000. The cash outflow was more than the related expense, so this is a cash outflow from operating activities.

Trade payables decreased $13,000. The cash outflow was more than the related expense, so this is a cash outflow from operating activities.

(Continued)

Exhibit 19-11   Continued

v. Add dividends and interest received and subtract dividends, interest, and income taxes paid.

Interest paid = interest expense − change in interest payable. Interest payable for both years was $0, so interest paid equals interest expense of $10,000.

Income taxes paid = income tax expense − change in income taxes payable. The balance of the income taxes payable account increased $5,000. Therefore, income taxes paid equals $107,000 − $5,000 = $102,000.

Dividends paid = dividends declared − change in dividends payable. First, the amount of dividends declared can be determined from the change in retained earnings and net income.

Retained earnings, beginning of year (from balance sheet)	$316,000
Plus: net income (from income statement)	146,000
Less: dividends declared (solve)	(50,000)
Retained earnings, end of year (from balance sheet)	$412,000

Second, the balance of the dividends payable account decreased $5,000 during the year. Dividends paid were thus $50,000 − −$5,000 = $55,000.

vi. The total of items (i)–(v) equals net cash from operating activities for the year:

Cash flow from operating activities totalled $213,000 as set out on the statement of cash flows in the next exhibit.

Step 3: Account for the changes in remaining balance sheet accounts. The reconciling items are recorded in the financing or investing activities section according to their nature.

The remaining account balances requiring adjustment are: land, building at cost, accumulated depreciation, investments, bank loan, preferred shares, and common shares. Note that the change in accumulated depreciation was only partially explained when depreciation was added back in the operating activities section. The change in retained earnings was fully explained by net income and dividends declared, both of which were allowed for in cash flow from operating activities.

We first deal with transactions that do not require supplemental calculations.

Notes payable increased $13,000 during the year and is recorded as a cash inflow from financing.

The *increased bank loan* is recorded as a cash inflow of $210,000 in the financing section.

The *retirement of preferred shares* is recorded as a cash outflow of $100,000 in the financing section.

The *issuance of common shares* is recorded as a cash inflow of $55,000 in the financing section.

Sale of investments: There was a $2,000 *loss on the sale of investments* costing $6,000 (from the comparative balance sheet). Therefore the sales proceeds were $4,000, which is recorded as a cash inflow from investing.

Dr. Cash	4,000	
Dr. Loss on sale of investments	2,000	
Cr. Investments (available for sale)		6,000

Land: There were two transactions involving land. The historical cost of the land sold is known ($250,000 from the supplemental information section) as is the loss on sale ($50,000 from the income statement). Therefore, as already established in point 2(ii) above, the sales proceeds were $200,000. This amount is recorded as a cash inflow from investing.

A T-account can be used to solve for the cost of the land purchased. The $491,000 purchase price (from the T-account) is recorded as a cash outflow from investing.

Land

Jan. 1 balance	310,000		
		250,000	Cost of land sold
Cost of land purchased	**491,000**		
Dec. 31 balance	551,000		

Buildings: There were two transactions involving buildings, a sale and a purchase. For the building sold, the historical cost is known ($250,000 from the supplemental information section), but the related accumulated depreciation must be found by analyzing the T-account for accumulated depreciation. The T-account below shows that the building sold had accumulated depreciation of $80,000, so the carrying value of the building sold was $250,000 − $80,000 = $170,000. This is also the amount of the sale proceeds since there was no gain or loss on the sale. This amount is recorded as a cash inflow from investing.

(Continued)

Exhibit 19-11	Continued

For the building purchased in the year, analysis of the T-account for buildings shows that the purchase price was $300,000. This amount is recorded as a cash outflow from investing.

	Building					Accumulated depreciation	
Jan. 1 balance (given)	810,000					220,000	Jan. 1 balance (given)
Cost of building purchased	**300,000**					110,000	Depr. expense (given)
		250,000	Cost of building sold (given)	Accumulated depreciation of building sold	**80,000**		
Dec. 31 balance (given)	860,000					250,000	Dec. 31 balance (given)

Step 4: Calculate subtotals for operating, investing, and financing activities and ensure the net change in cash and cash equivalents thus determined is equal to the actual change for the period computed from Step 1. The completed statement of cash flows follows. Note how the $26,000 decrease in cash from step one has been explained.

Exhibit 19-12	Applying procedures for statement of cash flow, example 2

Fred's Fajitas Ltd.
Statement of Cash Flows
Year Ended December 31, 2015

Cash flows from operating activities		
Net income	$ 146,000	
Adjustments for:		
Loss on sale of investment	2,000	
Loss on sale of land	50,000	
Depreciation and amortization	110,000	
Interest expense	10,000	
Income tax expense	107,000	
Subtotal	425,000	
Increase in accounts receivable	(14,000)	
Increase in inventory	(15,000)	
Increase in prepaid expenses	(3,000)	
Decrease in trade payables	(13,000)	
Cash generated from operating activities	380,000	
Dividends paid	(55,000)	
Interest paid	(10,000)	
Income taxes paid	(102,000)	
Net cash from operating activities		$213,000
Cash flows from investing activities		
Purchase of land	$(491,000)	
Sale of land	200,000	

(*Continued*)

Exhibit 19-12	Continued		
Purchase of building		(300,000)	
Sale of building		170,000	
Sale of available-for-sale investment		4,000	
Net cash used in investing activities			(417,000)
Cash flows from financing activities			
Issuance of notes payable		13,000	
Proceeds of bank loan		210,000	
Redeem preferred shares		(100,000)	
Issue ordinary shares		55,000	
Net cash from financing activities			178,000
Net increase in cash			(26,000)
Cash and cash equivalents, January 1, 2015			43,000
Cash and cash equivalents, December 31, 2015			$ 17,000

3. The process—Direct method

The indirect method just described and illustrated refers only to cash flows from operating activities. Cash flows from investing and financing activities are always presented using the direct method. We now apply the direct method also to operating activities. Moreover, the method of determining dividends and interest received and dividends, interest, and income taxes paid is the same for both methods. Therefore, discussion is confined to how to ascertain cash receipts from customers and cash paid to suppliers and employees.

a. The direct method described

The direct method differs from the indirect method as it does not directly consider net income; rather, it focuses on cash received from sales and cash paid to suppliers and employees to generate those sales.

The general format for presenting cash flows from operating activities as first presented in Exhibit 19-4 is partially reproduced below.

Exhibit 19-13	Sample of operating section of cash flow statement	
Illustrative Company **Statement of Cash Flows (Partial)** **Year Ended December 31, 2013**		
Cash flow from operating activities		
Cash receipts from customers	$ 30,360	Described below
Cash paid to suppliers and employees	(27,800)	Described below
Cash generated from operating activities	2,560	
Dividends received	200	These amounts are determined in the same manner whether the direct or indirect method is used.
Interest received	200	
Dividends paid	(1,200)	
Interest paid	(270)	
Income taxes paid	$ (900)	
Net cash from operating activities	590	

This example shows only two lines other than those involving dividends, interest, and taxes. This presentation is the minimum required since inflows should not be netted against outflows. Enterprises can choose to provide more details by using additional lines. For example, "cash paid to suppliers and employees" could be divided into "cash paid to suppliers," "cash paid to employees," and "other operating expenses." There is no concrete guidance as to what level of detail should be provided, so professional judgment is required. In the discussion and illustrations below, we will use this two-line presentation.

Cash receipts from customers   The starting point for determining cash receipts from customers is sales. This accrual-based number is transformed to a cash-based figure by adjusting for the net change in accounts receivable (AR) during the period. If AR increased during the year, sales exceeded cash collections; if AR decreased during the year, sales were less than cash collections. Thus, cash receipts from customers = sales − change in accounts receivable. In this formula, "change" can be an increase or decrease, with increases being positive amounts and decreases being negative.

It may be instructive to consider the underlying summary journal entry of a simple example and compare with the formula solution.

Exhibit 19-14	Illustration for computing cash receipts from customers

Facts

- Zil Baguettes Ltd. sales for the year totalled $1,000,000.
- Zil's receivables increased $10,000 during the year.

Summary journal entry

Dr. Cash	$990,000	
Dr. Accounts receivable	$10,000	
Cr. Sales		$1,000,000

Direct computation

Cash receipts from customers = Sales − change in accounts receivable
= $1,000,000 − $10,000 = $990,000

Cash paid to suppliers and employees   Cash paid to suppliers and employees is the sum of the cash paid for inventory and cash paid for operating expenses.

Cash paid for inventory is determined in two steps: i) establishing the cost of inventory purchased; and ii) ascertaining the cash paid for the purchases. We first compute cost of inventory purchased (or produced) using the formula:

purchases = cost of goods sold + change in inventory.

Second, cash paid for purchases is:

cash paid for inventory = purchases − change in accounts payable.

We can then combine these into one calculation (COGS denotes cost of goods sold):

cash paid for inventory = COGS + change in inventory
− change in accounts payable.

Cash paid for operating expenses is determined in much the same manner as just illustrated for inventories; that is, adjust the accrual-based income statement number to determine the cash outflow for the year:

cash paid for operating expenses = operating expenses
+ change in prepaid expenses.

In all of the above formulas, "change" is a positive number for increases and a negative number for decreases. The foregoing points are summarized in Exhibit 19-15.

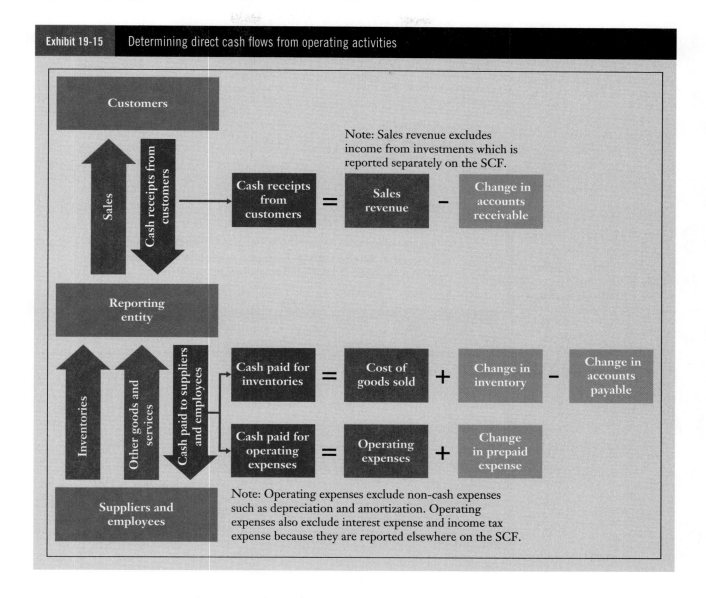

Exhibit 19-15   Determining direct cash flows from operating activities

Note: Sales revenue excludes income from investments which is reported separately on the SCF.

Cash receipts from customers = Sales revenue − Change in accounts receivable

Cash paid for inventories = Cost of goods sold + Change in inventory − Change in accounts payable

Cash paid for operating expenses = Operating expenses + Change in prepaid expense

Note: Operating expenses exclude non-cash expenses such as depreciation and amortization. Operating expenses also exclude interest expense and income tax expense because they are reported elsewhere on the SCF.

b. Schedule of cash provided by operating activities using the direct method—Example 1

The schedule of cash provided by operating activities set out below is based on the information for Kimzoo Fireworks in Exhibit 19-7. Observe that the $53,000 net cash from operating activities derived using the direct method is the same as that previously determined using the indirect method in Exhibit 19-9.

c. Schedule of cash provided by operating activities using the direct method—Example 2

The schedule of cash provided by operating activities set out below is based on the information for Fred's Fajitas Ltd. in Exhibit 19-10. Observe that the $213,000 net cash from operating activities derived using the direct method is the same as that previously determined using the indirect method in Exhibit 19-12.

Exhibit 19-16	Schedule of cash provided by operating activities using direct method, Example 1

Kimzoo Fireworks Ltd.
Schedule of Cash Provided by Operating Activities
Year Ended December 31, 2013

Cash flows from operating activities	
Cash receipts from customers*	$646,000
Cash paid to suppliers and employees†	(509,000)
Cash generated from operating activities	137,000
Dividends paid	(46,000)
Interest paid	(5,000)
Income taxes paid	(33,000)
Net cash from operating activities	$53,000

Supporting computations
*Sales − Change in accounts receivable = $660,000 − $14,000 = $646,000
†COGS + Change in inventory − Change in accounts payable + Operating expenses + Change in prepaid expenses = $363,000 − $10,000 − $1,000 + $160,000 − $3,000 = $509,000.

Exhibit 19-17	Schedule of cash provided by operating activities using the direct method, Example 2

Fred's Fajitas Ltd.
Schedule of Cash Provided by Operating Activities
Year Ended December 31, 2015

Cash flows from operating activities	
Cash receipts from customers*	$986,000
Cash paid to suppliers and employees†	(606,000)
Cash generated from operating activities	380,000
Dividends paid	(55,000)
Interest paid	(10,000)
Income taxes paid	(102,000)
Net cash from operating activities	$213,000

Supporting computations
*Sales − Change in accounts receivable = $1,000,000 − $14,000 = $986,000
†COGS + Change in inventory − Change in accounts payable + Operating expenses + Change in prepaid expenses = $400,000 + $15,000 + $13,000 + $175,000 + $3,000 = $606,000

4. Effects of specific items on the statement of cash flows

The process for preparing the statement of cash flows as described above provides general guidance on how to deal with common situations. The list that follows provides additional direction on select items not already addressed.

a. Accounts receivable—Allowance for bad debts

Companies often report receivables at the gross amount less an allowance. To obtain the amount of operating cash flow, the indirect method simply adjusts for the change in the net receivables. For the direct method of presentation, the two elements are dealt with separately. Specifically, cash from sales is adjusted for the change in the gross amount of the receivables, and cash paid to suppliers and employees is adjusted for the change in the allowance account.

b. Discontinued operations

Cash flows from discontinued operations are shown separately in the operating, investing, and financing activities of the SCF according to their nature. Alternatively, as per paragraph 33(c) of IFRS 5 Non-current Assets Held for Sale and Discontinued Operations, this information may be disclosed in the notes to the financial statements.

c. Discounts and premiums on bonds and other financial instruments

IAS 7 does not address the classification of the amortization of discounts and premiums on financial instruments. Interest payments may be classified as cash outflows from operating activities or cash outflows from financing activities. However, it makes practical sense to use the same category to record both the payment and related amortization. This is easily accomplished by following the format set out in the preceding examples. Specifically, interest expense is added back and interest paid is deducted collectively in the same section. IFRS differs from past Canadian practice, whereby the amortization of discounts was recorded in the operating activities section and the amortization of premiums was reported as a financing activity.

d. Held-for-trading investments not designated as cash equivalents—Unrealized gains and losses

Unrealized profit or loss on trading investments is recorded in the income statement. When the indirect method of presentation is used, the unrealized profit or loss must be reversed in the cash flow from operating activities section of the SCF.

e. Income taxes—Classification

IAS 7 paragraph 35 require that "taxes on income. . . shall be classified as cash flows from operating activities unless they can be specifically identified with financing and investing activities." In this text, all cash flows arising from income taxes are classified as operating activities.

f. Income taxes—Current and deferred

There are two components of income tax on both the balance sheet and the income statement—current and deferred. We compute cash paid for income taxes using the formula:

income taxes paid = income tax expense – change in income taxes payable

This equation still holds providing you recognize that income tax expense includes both current and deferred tax expense and that taxes payable encompasses the current and deferred portions.

g. Investments in associates

Investments in associates are typically accounted for using the equity method. The SCF is concerned only with the cash received or advanced, rather than investment income. The required adjustment for the indirect method of presentation entails deducting income from investments in the operating section and recording dividends received in either the operating or investing section.

h. Other comprehensive income

Other comprehensive income (OCI) is not normally reported on the SCF. OCI does not affect cash since it records only unrealized gains and losses on select items. If companies use comprehensive income as a starting point in the indirect method, the components of other comprehensive income are shown as reversing items in the cash flows arising from operating activities.

i. Stock splits and dividends

Stock splits and dividends are non-cash transactions. They are not recorded on the SCF.

j. Treasury shares

Cash flows from the purchase and sale of treasury shares are reported as a financing activity.

5. Putting it all together—A comprehensive example

This section has described the process for preparing the statement of cash flows using both the direct and indirect methods. You now have an opportunity to work through a comprehensive example to confirm your knowledge of the topic. Many aspects of this example are more involved than the previous two examples provided above. To solve, you will need to supplement the material in this chapter with your general knowledge of accounting. When complete, compare your answer to the solution that follows.

Exhibit 19-18	Comprehensive example to illustrate preparation of cash flow statement

You have been provided with the income statement and comparative balance sheets of Zippo Hosiery Inc. along with supplemental information.

Zippo Hosiery Inc.
Income Statement
Year Ended December 31, 2015

Sales	$1,432,000
Cost of sales	756,000
Gross profit	676,000
Other expenses	256,600
Interest expense	75,000
Depreciation expense	334,400
Income before income taxes	10,000
Income tax expense	4,000
Net income before discontinued operations	6,000
Discontinued operations, net of taxes ($100,000)	283,100
Net income	$ 289,100

(Continued)

Exhibit 19-18	Continued

Zippo Hosiery Inc.
Comparative Balance Sheet
As at December 31, 2015 and 2014

	2015	2014	Change
Assets			
Cash and cash equivalents	$ 172,000	$ 210,000	$ (38,000)
Accounts receivable	150,000	170,000	(20,000)
Inventory	575,000	498,000	77,000
Investments—held for trading	140,000	190,000	(50,000)
Current assets	1,037,000	1,068,000	
Property, plant, and equipment at cost	1,984,000	1,396,000	588,000
Accumulated depreciation	(650,400)	(487,000)	(163,400)
Patents	690,000	552,000	138,000
Total assets	$3,060,600	$2,529,000	
Liabilities			
Trade payables	$ 93,000	$ 86,000	$ 7,000
Current liabilities	93,000	86,000	
Bank loan	-0-	100,000	(100,000)
Bonds payable	659,500	674,000	(14,500)
Total liabilities	752,500	860,000	
Shareholders' Equity			
Ordinary shares	1,150,000	700,000	450,000
Retained earnings	1,158,100	969,000	189,100
Total shareholders' equity	2,308,100	1,669,000	
Total liabilities and shareholders' equity	$3,060,600	$2,529,000	

Supplemental information:

- The decrease in bonds payable is due entirely to the the amortization of the related premium.
- Zippo's policy is to report interest and dividends paid as a cash outflow from operating activities.
- The held-for-trading investments do not meet the criteria for cash equivalents.
- $10,000 of held-for-trading investments were purchased during the year; none were sold.
- Property, plant, and equipment costing $570,000 was sold for $422,000.
- 100,000 ordinary shares were issued to acquire $450,000 of property, plant, and equipment.
- The $212,000 cost of successfully suing a competitor for patent infringement was capitalized during the year.
- "Other Expenses" includes gains and losses on asset sales, holding losses, and patent amortization.
- Cash was received or paid for all revenues and expenses other than those relating to inventories, sales, depreciation, and amortization.
- Income from discontinued operations represents the operating profits of a plant that is in the process of being decommissioned. The recorded profit was received in cash.

Required:
1. Prepare Zippo Hosiery Inc.'s cash flow statement for the year ended December 31, 2015 using the indirect method, including disclosure of non-cash activities.
2. Prepare a schedule of Zippo's cash provided by operating activities for the year ended December 31, 2015 using the direct method.

Solution to the comprehensive example

For the year ended December 31, 2015, Zippo Hosiery Inc. cash inflows from operating activities totalled $560,000. Zippo's investing and financing activities for the year resulted in cash outflows of $498,000 and $100,000, respectively. These amounts were determined using the procedures illustrated in the chapter. Note that both the direct and indirect methods established that the aggregate cash inflows from operating activities were $560,000.

| Exhibit 19-19 | Solution for comprehensive example | |

Zippo Hosiery Inc.
Statement of Cash Flows
Year Ended December 31, 2015

Cash flows from operating activities	References		
Net income from continuing operations		$ 6,000	
Net income from discontinued operations	1	283,100	
Adjustments for:			
Holding loss on held for trading investment	6	60,000	
Gain on sale of property, plant, and equipment	4, 9	(23,000)	
Depreciation and amortization expense	3, 8	408,400	
Interest expense		75,000	
Income tax expense—continuing operations		100,000	
Income tax expense—discontinued operations		4,000	
Subtotal		913,500	
Purchase of held-for-trading investment		(10,000)	
Decrease in accounts receivable		20,000	
Increase in inventory		(77,000)	
Increase in trade payables		7,000	
Cash generated from operating activities		853,500	
Dividends paid	7	(100,000)	
Interest paid	5	(89,500)	
Income taxes paid—continuing operations		(4,000)	
Income taxes paid—discontinued operations	1	(100,000)	
Net cash from operating activities			$560,000
Cash flows from investing activities			
Purchase of property, plant, and equipment	9	(708,000)	
Sale of property, plant, and equipment		422,000	
Patent		(212,000)	
Net cash used in investing activities			(498,000)
Cash flows from financing activities			
Retire bank loan		(100,000)	
Net cash from financing activities			(100,000)
Net increase (decrease) in cash			(38,000)
Cash, January 1, 2015			210,000
Cash, December 31, 2015			$ 172,000

Required disclosure—Notes to financial statement (reference 2)
Note: During the year the company issued $450,000 of ordinary shares in exchange for property, plant, and equipment having a fair market value of $450,000

Supporting comments and calculations as per the references in SCF

1. Income and income taxes pertaining to discontinued operations must be separately disclosed.

2. Non-cash transactions relating to financing and investing activities must be disclosed.

(Continued)

Exhibit 19-19   Continued

3. $334,400 depreciation (PPE) + $74,000 amortization (patent) = $408,400. Depreciation is reported on the income statement, while amortization is determined using a T-account—see #8 below.

4. Sales proceeds − net book value = gain on sale = $422,000 − ($570,000 − $171,000) = $23,000. The accumulated depreciation on the PPE sold is determined using a T-account—see #9 below.

5. Interest paid = interest expense + amortization of the bond premium = $75,000 + $14,500 = $89,500. Amortization of the bond premium is the change in the bonds payable balance from the comparative balance sheet.

6.

Investment (HFT)			
Jan. 1 balance	190,000		
Cost of investments purchased	10,000		
		60,000	Unrealized holding loss
Dec. 31 balance	140,000		

7.

Retained earnings			
		969,000	Jan. 1 balance
		289,100	Net income
Dividends declared	100,000		
		1,158,100	Dec. 31 balance

8.

Patent			
Jan. 1 balance	552,000		
Legal defence costs	212,000		
		74,000	Patent amortization
Dec. 31 balance	690,000		

9.

PPE			Accumulated depreciation	
Jan. 1 balance	1,396,000		487,000	Jan. 1 balance
Cost of PPE purchased for shares	450,000		334,400	Depr. expense
		Cost of PPE sold 570,000	Accumulated depreciation of PPE sold 171,000	
PPE purchased for cash	708,000			
Dec. 31 balance	1,984,000		650,400	Dec. 31 balance

Zippo Hosiery Inc.
Schedule of Cash Provided by Operating Activities
Year Ended December 31, 2015

Cash flows from operating activities	
Cash receipts from customers (1)	$1,452,000
Cash receipts from discontinued operations (2)	383,100
Cash paid to suppliers and employees (3)	(971,600)
Cash paid to acquire HFT investment	(10,000)
Cash generated from operating activities	853,500
Dividends paid	(100,000)
Interest paid	(89,500)
Income taxes paid—continuing operations	(4,000)
Income taxes paid—discontinued operations	(100,000)
Net cash from operating activities	$560,000

(Continued)

Supporting computations
1. $1,432,000 (sales) + $20,000 (decrease in accounts receivable) = $1,452,000
2. $283,100 (income net of tax from discontinued operations) + $100,000 (income tax paid—discontinued operations)
3. $756,000 (COGS) + $256,600 (other expenses) + $77,000 (increase in inventory) − $7,000 (increase in trade payables) − $74,000 (amortization included in other expenses) − $60,000 (holding loss included in other expenses) + $23,000 (gain on sale included in other expenses) = $971,600

D. PRESENTATION AND DISCLOSURE

The previous sections of this chapter have described the presentation and disclosure requirements regarding the statement of cash flows. These requirements are primarily contained in IAS 1 and IAS 7. The following table provides a summary of the principal requirements:

Exhibit 19-20	Summary of presentation and disclosure requirements relating to the statement of cash flows

Presentation

■ The change in cash and cash equivalents must be explained.

■ Cash flows must be classified as arising from operating, investing, or financing activities.

■ Cash flows from operating activities may be reported using either the direct or indirect method.

■ Major classes of cash inflows and outflows for both investing and financing activities must be separately reported.

■ Cash flows from interest paid and received, dividends paid and received, and income taxes paid must be individually disclosed. This information may be included directly on the statement of cash flows or discussed in the supporting notes to the financial statements.

Disclosure

■ The components of cash and cash equivalents must be disclosed.

■ The policy adopted to determine the composition of cash and cash equivalents must be disclosed.

■ Non-cash transactions are not reported on the statement of cash flows, but must be disclosed elsewhere in the financial statements.

E. SUBSTANTIVE DIFFERENCES BETWEEN IFRS AND ASPE

ISSUE	IFRS	ASPE
Interest and dividends earned	Enterprises may classify cash inflows arising from the receipt of interest and dividends as either an operating or an investing activity.	Cash inflows arising from the receipt of interest and dividends must be classified as an operating activity.
Interest paid	Enterprises may classify cash outflows arising from the payment of interest as either an operating or a financing activity.	Cash outflows arising from the payment of interest must be classified as an operating activity.
Dividends paid	Enterprises may classify cash outflows arising from the payment of dividends as either an operating or a financing activity.	Cash outflows arising from the payment of dividends must be classified as a financing activity.
Income taxes paid	IFRS requires disclosure of the amount of income taxes paid.	ASPE does not require disclosure of the amount of income taxes paid.

L.O. 19-1. Describe the purpose of the statement of cash flows and the information it conveys.

- The statement of cash flows helps users determine the entity's ability to make payments when due and to pay dividends.
- The statement of cash flows helps users assess the company's quality of earnings.

L.O. 19-2. Define cash and cash equivalents.

- Cash is cash on hand and demand deposits.
- Cash equivalents are short-term, highly liquid investments that are easily convertible to a known amount of cash and which are subject to an insignificant risk of changes in value.

L.O. 19-3. Differentiate among cash flows from operating activities, investing activities, and financing activities.

- Operating cash flows arise from the day-to-day running of the business.
- Cash flows from investing result from the acquisition and disposal of non-current assets and other investments.
- Cash flows from financing activities stem from issuing and retiring debt and equity.

L.O. 19-4. Describe the difference between the direct and indirect methods of calculating cash flows from operating activities.

- Net income is the starting point for the indirect method of presenting cash flows from operating activities. Profit and loss is adjusted for non-cash transactions, deferrals and accruals, and income or expense items related to investing and financing activities.
- The direct method of presenting cash flows from operating activities discloses the gross amount of cash receipts and cash payments by category.

L.O. 19-5. Prepare a statement of cash flows using both the direct and indirect methods.

- The statement of cash flows is prepared in accordance with the methodology outlined in this chapter.

G. References

Authoritative standards:

IFRS	ASPE Section
IAS 1—Presentation of Financial Statements	1400—General Standards of Financial Statement Presentation
IAS 7—Statement of Cash Flows	1540—Cash Flow Statement
IFRS 5—Non-current Assets Held for Sale and Discontinued Operations	3475—Disposal of Long-lived Assets and Discontinued Operations

H. Glossary

cash equivalents: Short-term, highly liquid investments that are readily convertible to known amounts of cash and which are subject to an insignificant risk of changes in value.

direct method: A method of presenting the statement of cash flows by showing major classes of gross cash receipts and gross cash payments.

financing activities: Activities that result in changes in the size and composition of the contributed equity and borrowings of the entity.

indirect method: A method of presenting the statement of cash flows by adjusting profit or loss for the effects of transactions of a non-cash nature, any deferrals or accruals of past or future operating cash receipts or payments, and items of income or expense associated with investing or financing cash flows.

investing activities: The acquisition and disposal of long-term assets and other investments not included in cash equivalents.

non-cash transactions: Activities that do not involve cash.

operating activities: The principal revenue-producing activities of the entity and other activities that are not investing or financing activities.

I. PROBLEMS

MyAccountingLab ® Go to MyAccountingLab at **www.myaccountinglab.com**. You can practise the indicated exercises as often as you want, and guided solutions will help you find answers step by step. You'll find a personalized study plan available to you too!

P19-1. **Describe the purpose of the statement of cash flows**
(L.O. 19-1) (Easy – 5 minutes)

Describe in a general way the purpose of the statement of cash flows and the information that it conveys.

P19-2. **Usefulness of the statement of cash flows** **(L.O.** 19-1) (Easy – 5 minutes)

The statement of cash flows provides information relative to the entity's cash inflows and outflows for the period. List three ways that stakeholders may use this information.

P19-3. **Cash and cash equivalents** **(L.O.** 19-2) (Easy – 10 minutes)

a. Describe cash equivalents.
b. Describe the options available for reporting held-for-trading investments on the statement of cash flows when these securities meet the definition of a cash equivalent.
c. What guidance does IFRS provide with respect to reporting bank overdrafts on the statement of cash flows?

P19-4. **Classifying cash flows** **(L.O.** 19-3) (Medium – 10 minutes)

a. Describe operating activities, investing activities, and financing activities and provide three examples of each.
b. Describe in a general way what information each category of cash flows provides.
c. Describe the options available with respect to classifying the receipt and payment of interest and dividends.

P19-5. **Classifying cash flows—indirect method** **(L.O.** 19-3) (Medium – 15 minutes)

A list of items that may affect the statement of cash flows prepared using the **indirect** method follows. Assume that the transactions are for cash unless stated otherwise. For each item, indicate by using the associated letter whether it is:

A—a cash receipt reported as an operating activity or an amount added to net income in the cash flows from operating activities section
B—a cash outflow reported as an operating activity or an amount deducted from net income in the cash flows from operating activities section
C—a cash receipt in the cash flows from investments section

D—a cash outflow in the cash flows from investments section
E—a cash receipt in the cash flows from financing section
F—a cash outflow in the cash flows from financing section
G—not reported on the statement of cash flows
H—an item for which there is more than one alternative for reporting this item

Item	Transaction	Categorization on the statement of cash flows
1.	Receipt of dividends	
2.	Increase in accounts receivable	
3.	Decrease in deferred income taxes payable	
4.	Sale of a held-for-trading investment not designated as a cash equivalent	
5.	Issuing (selling) shares	
6.	Depreciation expense	
7.	Loss on the sale of a held-to-maturity investment	
8.	Payment of interest	
9.	Goodwill impairment loss	
10.	Purchase of an available-for-sale investment	
11.	Decrease in accounts payable	
12.	Conversion of bonds to ordinary shares	
13.	Borrowing money from the bank	
14.	Sale of a computer at book value	
15.	Retirement of bonds	

P19-6.   Classifying cash flows—direct method   (**L.O.** 19-3) (Easy – 10 minutes)

A list of items that may affect the statement of cash flows prepared using the **direct** method follows. Assume that the transactions are for cash unless stated otherwise. For each item indicate by using the associated letter whether it is:

A—a cash receipt in the cash flows from operations section
B—a cash outflow in the cash flows from operations section
C—a cash receipt in the cash flows from investments section
D—a cash outflow in the cash flows from investments section
E—a cash receipt in the cash flows from financing section
F—a cash outflow in the cash flows from financing section
G—not reported on the statement of cash flows
H—an item for which there is more than one alternative for reporting this item
I—none of the above

Item	Transaction	Categorization on the statement of cash flows
1.	Sale of land at a loss	
2.	Gain on the sale of equipment	
3.	Repurchasing own shares	
4.	Receipt of interest	
5.	Purchase of a held-for-trading investment designated as a cash equivalent	
6.	Depreciation expense	
7.	Equipment acquired under a finance lease	
8.	Payment of dividends	
9.	Other comprehensive income	
10.	Impairment loss on a patent	

P19-7. Classifying cash flows—Other comprehensive income and non-cash transactions **(L.O.** 19-3) (Medium – 5 minutes)

a. Describe how other comprehensive income is reported on the statement of cash flows prepared using the direct method of presenting cash flows from operating activities.
b. Describe how other comprehensive income is reported on the statement of cash flows prepared using the indirect method of presenting cash flows from operating activities.
c. Describe how the statement of cash flows reports significant non-cash investing and financing transactions.
d. Provide three examples of non-cash investing or financing transactions.

P19-8. Identifying and determining cash flows from operating activities—indirect method **(L.O.** 19-3, **L.O.** 19-5) (Medium – 10 minutes)

Hobnob Corp.'s policy is to report all cash flows arising from interest and dividends in the operating activities section. Hobnob's activities for the year ended December 31, 2018 included the following:

- 2018's net income after taxes totalled $125,000.
- Declared and issued a stock dividend valued at $50,000.
- Accounts receivable decreased $32,000 in 2018.
- Sold a held-for-trading investment for $12,000. The book value was $10,000.
- Interest revenue for the period was $12,000. The interest receivable account decreased $3,000.
- Declared a $20,000 dividend payable. The dividends payable account decreased $12,000 in 2018.
- Sold an available-for-sale investment for $8,000. The book value was $9,000.
- Hobnob recorded a $10,000 goodwill impairment loss during the year
- Depreciation expense for the year was $8,000.

Required:

a. Prepare the cash flows from operating activities section of the statement of cash flows using the indirect method.
b. Identify how the activities listed above that are not operating activities would be reported in the statement of cash flows.

P19-9. Cash flows from operating activities—direct method **(L.O.** 19-3, **L.O.** 19-5) (Medium – 10 minutes)

Jill K. Ltd.'s policy is to report all cash flows arising from interest and dividends in the operating section. Jill's activities for the year ended December 31, 2018 included the following:

- Income tax expense for the year was $30,000.
- Sales for the year were $650,000.
- Accounts payable decreased $10,000 in 2018.
- Selling and administration expenses for the year totalled $200,000.
- Accounts receivable increased $20,000 in 2018.
- Jill's cost of goods sold in 2018 was $325,000.
- Jill's inventory decreased $15,000 during the year.
- Interest expense for the period was $12,000. The interest payable account increased $1,000.
- Dividends were not declared during the year; however, the dividends payable account decreased $10,000.
- Sold an available-for-sale investment for $8,000. The book value was $9,000.
- Depreciation expense for the year was $13,000.

Required:

a. Prepare the cash flows from operating activities section of the statement of cash flows using the direct method.

b. Identify how the activities listed above that are not operating activities would be reported in the statement of cash flows.

P19-10. Identifying and determining cash flows from investing

(**L.O.** 19-3) (Medium – 10 minutes)

Recon Cile Ltd.'s policy is to report all cash flows arising from interest and dividends in the operating section. Recon Cile's activities for the year ended December 31, 2018 included the following:

- Sold a held-for-trading investment for $11,000. The book value of this investment, which was not designated as a cash equivalent, was $10,000.
- Purchased an available-for-sale investment for $16,000.
- Borrowed $50,000 from the bank for investment purposes.
- Sold equipment for $20,000 that originally cost $30,000. The net book value of this item at time of sale was $25,000.
- Purchased inventory costing $45,000 for cash.
- Received $10,000 in interest and $5,000 in dividends on sundry investments.
- Acquired a forklift costing $24,000 under a finance lease.
- Acquired land and buildings valued at $300,000 by issuing ordinary shares.
- Bought $100,000 in bonds at a discount, paying $95,000 cash.

Required:

a. Prepare the cash flows from investing activities section of the statement of cash flows.

b. Identify how the activities listed above that are not investing activities would be reported in the statement of cash flows assuming that the statement is prepared using the indirect method.

P19-11. Identifying and determining cash flows from investing

(**L.O.** 19-3, 19-5) (Medium – 10 minutes)

Jamie Bleay Law Ltd.'s policy is to report all cash inflows from interest and dividends in the investing section and cash outflows arising from interest and dividends in the financing section. Jamie Bleay Law's activities for the year ended December 31, 2016 included the following:

- Sold a held-for-trading investment for $11,000. The book value of this investment, which was designated as a cash equivalent, was $11,000.
- Sold an available-for-sale investment for $12,000. The book value of the investment was $12,000.
- Borrowed $40,000 from the bank for investment purposes.
- Sold equipment for $30,000 that originally cost $50,000. The net book value of this item at time of sale was $20,000.
- Received $8,000 in interest and $9,000 in dividends on sundry investments.
- Paid $2,000 interest on the investment loan.
- Acquired land and buildings valued at $500,000 by paying $300,000 cash and issuing ordinary shares for the balance.
- Bought $100,000 in bonds at a premium, paying $105,000 cash.

Required:

a. Prepare the cash flows from investing activities section of the statement of cash flows.

b. Identify how the activities listed above that are not investing activities would be reported in the statement of cash flows assuming that the statement is prepared using the indirect method.

P19-12. Identifying and determining cash flows from financing
(**L.O.** 19-3, 19-5) (Medium – 10 minutes)

Angela's Angels Corp.'s policy is to report all cash inflows from interest and dividends in the investing section and cash outflows arising from interest and dividends in the financing section. Angela's activities for the year ended December 31, 2016 included the following:

- Declared and issued a stock dividend valued at $50,000.
- Issued $500,000 in ordinary shares.
- Accounts payable decreased $28,000 during the year.
- Paid $985,000 to repurchase bonds. The book value of the bonds was $1,000,000.
- Made a $10,000 principal payment on a bank loan.
- Interest expense for the period was $18,000. The interest payable account increased $2,000.
- Declared a $10,000 cash dividend payable on January 15, 2017.
- Acquired an automobile costing $40,000 under a finance lease.

Required:

a. Prepare the cash flows from financing activities section of the statement of cash flows.
b. Identify how the activities listed above that are not financing activities would be reported in the statement of cash flows assuming that the statement is prepared using the indirect method.

P19-13. Identifying and determining cash flows from financing
(**L.O.** 19-3) (Medium – 10 minutes)

Boboto Inc.'s policy is to report all cash flows arising from interest and dividends in the operating section. Boboto's activities for the year ended December 31, 2018 included the following:

- Declared and issued a stock dividend valued at $100,000.
- Paid $40,000 to repurchase ordinary shares and cancelled them. The book value was $30,000.
- Accounts payable increased $32,000 during the year.
- Issued $1,000,000 in bonds. The cash proceeds were $985,000.
- Interest expense for the period was $15,000. The interest payable account decreased $2,000.
- Made a $20,000 principal payment on a bank loan.
- Declared a $20,000 cash dividend payable on January 15, 2019.

Required:

a. Prepare the cash flows from financing activities section of the statement of cash flows.
b. Identify how the activities listed above that are not financing activities would be reported in the statement of cash flows assuming that the statement is prepared using the indirect method.

P19-14. Statement of Cash Flows—indirect method—classification of transactions (**L.O.** 19-3) (Medium – 30 minutes)

Select transactions of Jack Lin Accounting Inc. (JLAI) are listed below. JLAI uses the indirect method to determine cash flows from operating activities.

1. JLAI purchases a $100,000, 60-day treasury bill held-for-trading investment.
2. JLAI amortizes $30,000 of the discount on bonds payable.
3. At year-end JLAI increases its allowance for bad debts by $50,000.

4. JLAI's income tax expense totalled $40,000. Its income tax payable account increased $7,000, while its deferred income tax liability account decreased $10,000.
5. JLAI acquires equipment valued at $100,000 under a finance lease.
6. JLAI makes payments of $20,000 on an operating lease.
7. JLAI declares and distributes a stock dividend valued at $30,000.
8. JLAI declares a cash dividend of $20,000. The dividends payable account increases $15,000.
9. JLAI's comprehensive income for the year totalled $200,000 consisting of $150,000 net income and $50,000 other comprehensive income.
10. JLAI sells a held-to-maturity investment for $12,000. The investment's amortized cost is $10,000.

Required:

Discuss how the activities listed above would be reported in the statement of cash flows. For items with multiple reporting options, identify all available options. For items not reported on the statement of cash flows, indicate the disclosure requirements, if any.

P19-15. Analysis of changes in account balances—effects of specific transactions   (**L.O.** 19-3) (Difficult – 30 minutes)

Information pertaining to select activities of Rosamelia Corp. during 2017 is set out below:

1. On January 1, 2017, Rosamelia acquired equipment under a finance lease. The lease calls for five annual payments of $20,000 due at the beginning of the year. Rosamelia must return the equipment to the lessor at the end of the lease. The January 1, 2017 payment was made as agreed. The implicit rate in the lease is 4%; the present value of the lease payments is $92,598.
2. The opening balance in the computer account was $70,000; the closing balance was $80,000. The corresponding balances in the accumulated depreciation accounts were $42,000 and $53,000. During the year Rosamelia scrapped a computer originally costing $10,000 having a remaining net book value of $2,000 and purchased a replacement machine for cash.
3. The opening balance in the land account was $250,000; the closing balance was $300,000. During the year land costing $40,000 was given to a creditor in full settlement of a $50,000 loan. The fair value of the land at the time of the exchange was $50,000. The company also purchased a separate parcel of land for cash during the year.

Required:

a. Prepare the underlying journal entries to record the foregoing transactions and record events stemming from the transactions (e.g., the accrual of interest at year-end).
b. For each entry identify the cash flow effects, if any, under both the direct and indirect methods of presentation and classify the cash flow according to its nature.
c. Why does the IASB require that companies classify cash flows as arising from operations, investing, or financing activities?

P19-16. Contrast the direct and indirect methods of preparing the statement of cash flows   (**L.O.** 19-4) (Easy – 5 minutes)

a. What are the similarities and differences between the direct and indirect methods of preparing the statement of cash flows?
b. In practice, do more companies use the direct or indirect method of preparation?
c. Does the IASB encourage the use of the direct or indirect method of presenting the statement of cash flows?

P19-17. Presentation and disclosure of cash flows   (**L.O.** 19-5) (Easy – 5 minutes)

Summarize the principal presentation, reporting, and disclosure requirements for the statement of cash flows.

P19-18. Preparing a statement of cash flows   (**L.O.** 19-5) (Easy – 10 minutes)

a. Briefly discuss how unrealized gains and losses arising from held-for-trading investments that are not designated as cash equivalents are reported on the statement of cash flows.
b. Briefly discuss how cash flows arising from income taxes are reported on the statement of cash flows.
c. Briefly discuss how stock splits and stock dividends are reported on the statement of cash flows.
d. Briefly discuss how cash flows arising from the purchase and sale of treasury shares are reported on the statement of cash flows.

P19-19. Preparing a statement of cash flows   (**L.O.** 19-5) (Medium – 15 minutes)

a. Briefly discuss how the amortization of discounts and premiums on financial instruments are classified in the statement of cash flows.
b. Briefly discuss how other comprehensive income is reported on the statement of cash flows.
c. Briefly discuss how cash flows arising from investments in associates are reported on the statement of cash flows.

P19-20. Preparing a statement of cash flows   (**L.O.** 19-5) (Easy – 10 minutes)

a. List the three primary sources of information required to prepare a statement of cash flows.
b. A company may report its accounts receivable at the gross amount less an allowance for bad debts. Contrast the direct and indirect methods of adjusting for accounts receivable reported at the gross amount.
c. Briefly discuss the alternatives for reporting discontinued operations in the statement of cash flows.

P19-21. Cash flows from operating activities—indirect method
    (**L.O.** 19-3, **L.O.** 19-5) (Medium – 10 minutes)

Coastal Cares Inc.'s (CCI) policy is to report all cash flows arising from interest and dividends in the operating section. The company's activities for the year ended December 31, 2016 included the following:

- Comprehensive income totalled $350,000 including $50,000 in other comprehensive income.
- Paid a cash dividend of $50,000 that was declared in 2015.
- Interest expense for the year was $30,000; the opening and closing balances in the interest payable account were $25,000 and $10,000, respectively.
- Accounts receivable increased $24,000 and accounts payable decreased $18,000 during the year.
- CCI paid $47,000 cash for equipment.
- CCI sold held-to-maturity investments for $18,000. The book value of the investment was $20,000.
- Depreciation expense for the year totalled $37,000.
- Suffered an impairment loss on patents of $12,000.
- Declared and issued a 2-for-1 stock split. There were 10,000 ordinary shares outstanding before the split with a collective market value of $2,500,000.

Required:

a. Prepare the cash flows from operating activities section of the statement of cash flows using the indirect method.
b. Identify how the activities detailed above that are not operating activities would be reported in the statement of cash flows.

P19-22. Cash flows from operating activities—indirect method

(L.O. 19-5) (Medium – 5 minutes)

Refer to the information set out in P19-21 above.

Required:

Prepare the cash flows from operating activities section of the statement of cash flows using the indirect method assuming that Coastal Cares Inc.'s policy is to report interest and dividends received as an investing activity and interest and dividends paid as a financing activity.

P19-23. Statement of cash flows—indirect method—comprehensive

(L.O. 19-3, L.O. 19-5) (Difficult – 60 minutes)

Brigitte's Bathrooms Ltd. balance sheet for the year ended December 31, 2013 follows:

Brigitte's Bathrooms Ltd.
Comparative Balance Sheet
As at Ended December 31, 2013

	2013	2012
Assets		
Cash	$ 17,000	$ 43,000
Accounts receivable	104,000	90,000
Inventory	80,000	65,000
Prepaid expenses	48,000	45,000
Current Assets	249,000	243,000
Land	551,000	310,000
Buildings	860,000	810,000
Accumulated depreciation	(250,000)	(220,000)
Long-term investment (equity)	84,000	90,000
Total assets	$1,494,000	$1,233,000
Liabilities and shareholders' equity		
Accounts payable	$ 50,000	$ 60,000
Accrued interest payable	2,000	5,000
Notes payable	145,000	132,000
Current liabilities	197,000	197,000
Long-term bank loan	600,000	400,000
Deferred income taxes payable	20,000	10,000
Total liabilities	817,000	607,000
Preferred shares	0	100,000
Ordinary shares	285,000	210,000
Retained earnings	392,000	316,000
Total equity	677,000	626,000
Total liabilities and shareholders' equity	$1,494,000	$1,233,000

Other information includes the following:

■ Brigitte uses the equity method to account for investments.
■ During the year, Brigitte declared and paid cash dividends of $50,000. They also declared and distributed stock dividends valued at $20,000.
■ Brigitte bought and sold land during the year. The land that was sold for $200,000 originally cost $250,000.
■ Brigitte's long-term investment consists of holding ordinary shares in one company (GFF Services Inc.). For most of the year, Brigitte owned 50,000 of the 200,000 ordinary shares outstanding. GFF's net income for the year (which ended December 15) was $40,000. GFF's income from December 16 to December 31 was not material. The company paid dividends of $100,000 on December 15. Brigitte bought additional shares in GFF on December 31.

■ A gain of $25,000 was realized on the sale of a building that cost $200,000. Accumulated depreciation at time of sale was $150,000.
■ Brigitte borrowed money from a finance company, which accounted for the increase in notes payable.
■ The company's expenses for the year included $40,000 for income tax and $30,000 for interest.
■ Brigitte's policy is to report investment income and interest paid in the cash flows from operating activities section, while dividends paid are classified as a cash outflow from financing activities.

Required:

a. Prepare a statement of cash flows for Brigitte's Bathrooms Ltd. for 2013 using the indirect method
b. Identify what supplemental disclosure, if any, is required

P19-24. Prepare statement of cash flows from transactions
(**L.O.** 19-3, **L.O.** 19-5) (Difficult – 30 minutes)

Golf Is Great Corp.'s condensed balance sheet for the year ended December 31, 2017 follows:

Golf Is Great Corp. Balance Sheet As at December 31, 2017			
Cash	$ 30,000	Accounts payable	$ 20,000
Inventory	50,000	Other current liabilities	60,000
Other current assets	60,000	Bank loans	50,000
Investments—available for sale	40,000	Bonds payable	100,000
Plant and equipment (net)	100,000	Share capital	10,000
Land	80,000	Retained earnings	120,000
	$360,000		$360,000

Golf Is Great's 2018 transactions are set out below:

1. Net income for the year was $27,000 after recording $20,000 in depreciation expense on the plant and equipment.
2. Received cash proceeds of $20,000 from the issuance of preferred shares.
3. Purchased $10,000 inventory on account.
4. Received $19,000 cash from the sale of available-for-sale investments. The book value of the securities sold was $22,000.
5. Issued $100,000 in bonds to acquire land having a fair value of $100,000.
6. Declared and paid dividends totalling $25,000. Golf has a policy of including dividends paid in the financing section.
7. Made a $10,000 principal payment on the bank loan.

Required:

a. Prepare a statement of cash flows for 2018 using the indirect method.
b. Discuss how the transaction(s) above that are not reported on the statement of cash flows are reported in the financial statements.
c. Prepare a balance sheet as at December 31, 2018. Assume that other current assets and other current liabilities remain unchanged.
d. Golf's policy is to report dividends paid as a cash outflow from financing activity. What are its alternatives in this respect? How would the statement of cash flows that you prepared in part a differ if Golf had adopted the alternative presentation method?

P19-25. Statement of cash flows—operating activities—direct method
(**L.O.** 19-3, **L.O.** 19-5) (Medium – 15 minutes)

Quitzau's Supplies Inc.'s income statement for the year ended December 31, 2014 follows:

Quitzau's Supplies Inc. Income Statement Year Ended December 31, 2014		
Sales		$1,000,000
Cost of goods sold		
Beginning inventory	$500,000	
Purchases	400,000	
Cost of goods available for sale	900,000	
Ending inventory	300,000	
Cost of goods sold		600,000
Gross profit		400,000
Operating expenses		200,000
Interest expense		10,000
Amortization and depreciation expense		30,000
Income before income taxes		160,000
Income tax expense		40,000
Net income		$ 120,000

Additional information:

- Accounts receivable decreased $20,000 during the year.
- Accounts payable increased $15,000 during the year.
- Prepaid expenses increased $5,000 during the year.
- Income taxes payable decreased $3,000 during the year.
- Accrued interest payable increased $2,000 during the year.
- Quitzau has adopted a policy of reporting the cash flows arising from the receipt and payment of dividends and interest as an operating activity.

Required:

Prepare the operating section of Quitzau's statement of cash flows for the year ended December 31, 2014 using the direct method.

P19-26. Statement of cash flows—indirect method
(**L.O.** 19-3, **L.O.** 19-5) (Difficult – 40 minutes)

Financial information for Solnickova Inc. follows:

Solnickova Inc. Balance Sheets As at December 31, 2013 and 2014		
Assets	**2014**	**2013**
Cash	$ 150,000	$ 500,000
Accounts receivable	1,400,000	1,500,000
Inventory	600,000	400,000
Investments—held for trading	100,000	—
Investments—held to maturity	200,000	—
Property, plant, and equipment	3,250,000	3,250,000
Accumulated depreciation	(1,950,000)	(1,700,000)
Total	$ 3,750,000	$ 3,950,000

(*Continued*)

Liabilities and shareholders' equity		
Accounts payable	$ 320,000	$ 100,000
Bank loans	1,967,200	2,550,000
Bonds payable	382,800	380,000
Preferred shares	—	10,000
Ordinary shares	600,000	500,000
Retained earnings	480,000	410,000
Total	$ 3,750,000	$ 3,950,000

Additional information:

1. Preferred shares were converted to common shares during the year at their book value.
2. The face value of the bonds is $400,000; they pay a coupon rate of 5% per annum. The effective interest rate of interest is 6% per annum.
3. Net income was $80,000.
4. There was an ordinary stock dividend valued at $4,000 and cash dividends were also paid.
5. Interest expense for the year was $125,000. Income tax expense was $20,000.
6. Solnickova arranged for a $250,000 bank loan to finance the purchase of the held-to-maturity investments.
7. Solnickova has adopted a policy of reporting cash flows arising from the payment of interest and dividends as operating and financing activities, respectively.
8. The held-for-trading investments are not cash equivalents.

Required:

a. Prepare a statement of cash flows for the year ended December 31, 2014 using the indirect method.
b. Discuss how the transaction(s) above that are not reported on the statement of cash flows are reported in the financial statements
c. Independent of part a, assume that Solnickova designates the held-for-trading investment as a cash equivalent. Summarize the impact of this change on the company's statement of cash flows for the year ended December 31, 2014.

P19-27. Statement of cash flows—operating activities—direct method

(**L.O.** 19-5) (Medium – 20 minutes)

Refer to the information set out in P19-26 above and the supplemental information below:

Sales	$1,600,000
Cost of goods sold	$ 600,000
Sales and admin expenses	$ 525,000

Required:

a. Prepare the cash flows from operating activities section of the statement of cash flows using the direct method.
b. Compare and contrast the cash flows from operating activities prepared in this question using the direct method with that prepared in P19-26 part a using the indirect method. Which statement do you feel provides investors and other users of the financial statements with more useful information? Why?

P19-28. Statement of cash flows—indirect method—comprehensive

(**L.O.** 19-5) (Difficult – 60 minutes)

Zippo's financial statements as at December 31, 2016 appear below (PPE denotes property, plant, and equipment):

Zippo Ltd.
Balance Sheet
As at December 31, 2016

	2016	2015
Cash	$ 160,000	100,000
Held-for-trading investments	12,000	10,000
Accounts receivable	300,000	375,000
Less allowance for bad accounts	(10,000)	(15,000)
Inventory	575,000	498,000
Property, plant, and equipment	1,984,000	1,396,000
Less accumulated depreciation	(650,400)	(487,000)
Intangibles, net	126,000	135,000
Deferred product development costs	564,000	417,000
	$3,060,600	$2,429,000
Accounts payable	81,000	84,000
Income taxes payable	12,000	2,000
Bonds payable	659,500	674,000
Ordinary shares	1,150,000	700,000
Retained earnings	1,158,100	969,000
	$3,060,600	$2,429,000

Zippo Ltd.
Income Statement
For the Year Ended December 31, 2016

Sales	$2,511,100
Cost of goods sold	1,256,000
Gross profit	1,255,100
Depreciation of PPE	334,400
Interest expense	75,000
Other expenses	256,600
Income before income taxes	589,100
Income taxes	300,000
Net income	$ 289,100

Other information follows:

- PPE costing $570,000 was sold for $422,000.
- 100,000 ordinary shares were issued to acquire $450,000 of PPE.
- $212,000 of deferred development costs were capitalized during the year.
- The company nets many items to "Other Expenses," for example gains and losses on fixed assets sales and some amortization.
- The deferred product development expenditures were all paid in cash.
- The decrease in the bonds payable account was due to the amortization of the premium.
- Zippo has elected to designate its held-for-trading investments as cash equivalents.
- Zippo has adopted a policy of classifying cash outflows from interest and dividends as financing activities.

Required:
a. Prepare a statement of cash flows for Zippo Ltd. for 2016 using the indirect method
b. Identify what supplemental disclosure, if any, is required
c. Based on your analysis of Zippo's cash flow activities during the year, do you think that you should consider investing in the company? Why or why not?

P19-29. Statement of cash flows—operating activities—direct method
(**L.O.** 19-5) (Medium – 15 minutes)

Based on the information set out in P19-28 above, prepare the cash flows from operating activities section of the statement of cash flows using the direct method.

P19-30. Statement of cash flows—indirect and direct methods—comprehensive income (**L.O.** 19-5) (Difficult – 75 minutes)

Valli Ltd.'s financial statements as at December 31, 2016 appear below:

Valli Ltd.
Comparative Balance Sheet
As at December 31, 2016

	2016	2015
Cash	$ 69,000	$ 21,000
Investments—held for trading	25,000	22,000
Investments—available for sale	30,000	25,000
Accounts receivable	53,000	39,000
Inventory	50,000	60,000
Prepaid expenses	6,000	9,000
Plant assets	540,000	380,000
Accumulated depreciation	(140,000)	(125,000)
Goodwill	51,000	58,000
	$684,000	$489,000
Accounts payable	$ 41,000	$ 46,000
Accrued liabilities	33,000	24,000
Cash dividends payable	8,000	6,000
Bonds payable	50,000	47,000
Mortgage payable	—	136,000
Deferred income tax liability	5,000	8,000
Preferred shares	201,000	—
Ordinary shares	320,000	200,000
Retained earnings	21,000	22,000
Reserves	5,000	—
	$684,000	$489,000

Valli Ltd.
Statement of Comprehensive Income
For the Year Ended December 31, 2016

Sales	$660,000
Cost of sales	359,000
Gross profit	301,000
Interest expense, long-term	(6,000)
Depreciation expense	(25,000)
Operating expenses	(160,000)
Other gains and losses	(4,000)
Income before income tax	106,000
Income tax expense	39,000
Net income	67,000
Other comprehensive income: Holding gain on available-for-sale securities	5,000
Comprehensive income	$ 72,000

Supplemental information:

- During the year Valli exchanged 5,000 ordinary shares for plant assets having a fair value of $100,000.
- During the year Valli declared and issued a stock dividend of 1,000 ordinary shares. The transaction was valued at $20,000.
- During the year goodwill was written down $7,000 to reflect a permanent impairment of the asset.
- The deferred income tax liability represents temporary differences relating to the use of capital cost allowance for income tax reporting and straight-line depreciation for financial statement reporting.
- Valli did not buy or sell any held-for-trading or available-for-sale securities during the year. The held-for-trading securities have not been designated as cash equivalents.
- The recorded increase in the bonds payable account was due to the amortization of the discount.
- Valli elects to record interest paid as an operating activity and dividends paid as a financing activity.
- During the year Valli sold equipment (plant assets) that originally cost $40,000 for $30,000 cash.

Required:

a. From the information above, prepare Valli's statement of cash flows for the year ended December 31, 2016 using the indirect method.
b. Prepare Valli's cash flows from operating activities for the year ended December 31, 2016 using the direct method.
c. Prepare note disclosure(s) for non-cash transactions.

⚓ J. MINI-CASES

CASE 1
CompuCo Ltd.
(45 minutes)[4]

You have been asked to prepare a statement of cash flows using the balance sheet provided in Exhibit I, the income statement in Exhibit II, and the extracts from the notes provided in Exhibit III. Assume that the term deposits are cash equivalents. Further assume that CompuCo elects to report both the payment and collection of interest as operating activities.

Required:

1. Use the indirect method to prepare a statement of cash flows for 2012 on a non-comparative basis in good form from the information provided.
2. Use the direct method to prepare the cash flow from operations section of the statement of cash flows for 2012.
3. What are the objectives of a statement of cash flows prepared in accordance with generally accepted accounting principles?

Exhibit I		

CompuCo Ltd.
Extracts from Consolidated Balance Sheet
As at December 31

	2012	2011
	(in thousands of dollars)	
Assets		
Current		
Cash and term deposits	$ 3,265	$ 3,739
Accounts receivable	23,744	18,399
Inventories	26,083	21,561
Income taxes recoverable	145	0
Prepaid expenses	1,402	1,613
	54,639	45,312
Investments (note 1)	5,960	6,962
Property, plant, and equipment (note 2)	37,332	45,700
Deferred income taxes	4,875	2,245
Goodwill	0	12,737
Development costs (note 3)	4,391	1,911
	$107,197	$114,867
Liabilities		
Current		
Bank indebtedness	$ 6,844	$ 6,280
Accounts payable	3,243	4,712
Current portion of long-term debt	1,800	1,200
	11,887	12,192
Long-term debt (note 4)	14,900	14,500
Total liabilities	26,787	26,692
Shareholders' equity		
Share capital (Note 5)	79,257	62,965
Retained earnings	1,153	25,210
Total shareholders' equity	80,410	88,175
	$107,197	$114,867

4. Adapted with permission from the Uniform Final Examination (1993), The Canadian Institute of Chartered Accountants, Toronto, Canada. Any changes to the original material are the sole responsibility of the author and have not been reviewed or endorsed by the CICA.

Exhibit II

CompuCo Ltd.
Extracts from the Consolidated Income Statement
For the Years Ended December 31

	2012	2011
	(in thousands of dollars)	
Revenue		
Operating	$ 89,821	$ 68,820
Interest	1,310	446
	91,131	69,266
Expenses		
Operating	76,766	62,355
General and administrative	13,039	12,482
Depreciation and amortization	10,220	11,709
Goodwill write-off	12,737	0
Interest	1,289	1,521
Loss on sale of property, plant, and equipment	394	0
	114,445	88,067
Income (loss) before income from associates and income taxes	(23,314)	(18,801)
Income (loss) from associates (Note 1)	(2,518)	0
Income (loss) before income taxes	(25,832)	(18,801)
Recovery of income taxes	2,775	5,161
Net loss	$(23,057)	$(13,640)

Exhibit III

CompuCo Ltd.
Extracts from Notes to Financial Statements
For the Year Ended December 31

1. Investments

The company's investments at December 31 are as follows:

	2012	2011
	(in thousands of dollars)	
XYZ Inc. (market value 2012, $8.3 million)		
Shares	$5,962	$5,962
Income (loss) from associates	(2,518)	—
	3,444	$5,962
Other investments (held-to-maturity)	2,516	1,000
	$5,960	$6,962

2. Property, plant, and equipment (PPE)

Additions to PPE for the current year amounted to $2.29 million and proceeds from the disposal of PPE amounted to $250,000.

3. Development costs

Development costs for a product are amortized once the product is ready for market. The rate depends on the expected life of the product.

(Continued)

Exhibit III   Continued

4. Long-term debt

	2012	2011
	(in thousands of dollars)	
Debentures	$12,500	$12,500
Bank term loans, due December 31, 2019; principal repayable $150,000 a month (2011 $100,000 a month)	4,200	3,200
	16,700	15,700
Current maturities	(1,800)	(1,200)
	$14,900	$14,500

Debentures bear interest at 12% per annum and are due in 2015. Bank term loans bear interest at 8% and the bank advanced $2.2 million during the year.

5. Share capital

On May 14, 2012, CompuCo Ltd. issued 3.8 million shares with special warrants. Net proceeds from issuing 3.8 million shares amounted to $14.393 million. Net proceeds from issuing 3.8 million warrants amounted to $899,000. On December 31, 2012, a stock dividend of $1 million was issued.

CASE 2
Big City Gymnastics
(60 minutes)[5]

Big City Gymnastics (BCG or the Club) is a not-for-profit organization that operates a gymnastics club. BCG was incorporated in May 1983 and has operated the Club at the same facility since that time. BCG was started with a generous donation of equipment after a gymnastics competition that was held in April 1983.

BCG is governed by an elected Board of Directors of 10 members, all of whom are parents of athletes who train at the Club.

BCG trains both male and female athletes, from preschool to young adult. Its programs are preschool gymnastics, recreational gymnastics, and competitive gymnastics. BCG's athletes have qualified for national and international gymnastics meets, with some even going on to full scholarships at Canadian and American universities. BCG's coaches and programs are recognized by the Canadian gymnastics community as being of high quality.

Like most gymnastics clubs, BCG has paid coaching staff. Salaried staff, paid in total $20,000 a month including all required government remittances, include an office manager, a program director who coaches and also oversees the program and staffing, and three head coaches who oversee respectively the women's competitive, men's competitive, and recreational/preschool programs.

You, CA, are the parent of a gymnast. You were appointed to the Board of BCG as treasurer three and a half weeks ago. During your short time as treasurer, you have interviewed the office manager (Exhibit I) to become familiar with the workings of BCG, and gathered some historical financial information (Exhibit II).

Today, July 23, 2015, the president of BCG, Jim Taylor, approached you while you were watching your daughter train at BCG's facility. He informed you that the treasurer is responsible for preparing and presenting a financial report to the BCG Board of Directors at each monthly Board meeting. Jim mentioned that, in the past, the report usually consisted of a quick update on the cash balance in the Club's bank account. At the May 2015 Board meeting, the report stated a cash balance of $19,823. At the June 30, 2015 Board meeting, the cash balance was $4,324. The Board was concerned about the deteriorating cash situation and wondered how it would look at the end of the fiscal year.

---

5. Adapted with permission from The Canadian Institute of Chartered Accountants, Toronto, Canada. Any changes to the original material are the sole responsibility of the author and have not been reviewed or endorsed by the CICA.

At previous Board meetings, members often asked for more financial information but the previous treasurer was unable to provide it. Jim let you know that the lack of information caused some frustration among the Board members and asks you to recommend reporting improvements to the Board.

As you think about Jim's comments, you remember that, as a parent of a BCG athlete, you had your own questions about the financial situation of BCG, the success of the various programs and of the fundraisers, and so on. You tell Jim that your report will be different. You will report to the Board the findings from your recent discussions and recommendations for improvement, and you will provide some insights into BCG's current financial situation.

Required:

Prepare the report, paying specific attention to i) BCG's cash flow and ii) the sufficiency of the financial reports currently being produced.

Exhibit I	Notes from interview with office manager

The office manager is Joan Epp. She was hired three weeks ago to replace the outgoing office manager, Tom Dickens, who quit after only 11 months on the job.

Joan's role as office manager:

- Receive payments from athletes' families for their gymnastics fees. These fees are paid monthly in advance. BCG accepts cash, cheques, and credit card payments. Receipts are issued upon request.

- Tally the cash received and credit card slips on a deposit sheet and enter the amounts monthly into the accounting records. Deposits are made on an occasional basis at the nearby bank branch, once sufficient cash has been accumulated to warrant making a deposit.

- Receive and pay suppliers' invoices. One signature is required for all cheques. Signing officers are the office manager, the treasurer, and the president.

Joan reviewed the records on her first day. She had examined the paid invoices, stored in a filing cabinet, to become familiar with BCG's operations. Joan mentioned that there were several small cheques, most of which were posted as debits to the revenue accounts, that did not have corresponding invoices. Most of those cheques were made out to Tom Dickens. Also, one large cheque for $5,617 had a note that it was to reimburse Tom for the purchase of a trampoline, but no supporting invoice was attached. Joan also noted there were several cheques to suppliers, totalling $820, that are still outstanding.

As far as Joan is aware, there is no formal policy established for approval of spending. Joan can order what she needs for her job. Coaches can order the equipment or other gymnastics materials that they believe are needed for BCG's various programs.

BCG has a chocolate fundraiser where athletes sell chocolate bars for $3 apiece. An envelope marked Chocolate Fundraiser was in Joan's desk. It had $3,750 cash in it, with various notes on who had paid for chocolate bars. The drawer is locked when Joan is out of the office. Joan will deposit the money as soon as all the chocolate bars are sold, so that she will know the exact amount raised. The chocolate supplier shipped 1,500 chocolate bars. Joan received an invoice for $3,300, dated July 20, from the chocolate supplier. The terms on the invoice are that any unsold chocolate bars cannot be returned and, if payment is made within 30 days, the supplier's discount is 20%.

Exhibit II	CA's notes on BCG's historical financial information

The fiscal year-end of the Club is August 31.

Revenues are seasonal. The fall and winter recreational sessions are busy. The competitive season starts in September and runs through June. The spring recreational session appears to have one-third less revenue than the other two sessions due to the start of competing outdoor sports in the spring (baseball, football, soccer, etc.). The two summer months provide approximately 10% of BCG's annual revenue because of school summer holidays. Some weekly gymnastics camps are run, but attendance is muted due to athletes being away or taking time off. In addition to the chocolate fundraiser, BCG holds two other fundraisers during the year.

BCG receives a grant of $1,200 per month from the city-wide gymnastics organization.

General and administrative costs include building rent and utilities, which combined are approximately $2,000 per month.

The net book value of BCG's equipment was $54,563 as of August 31, 2014.

BCG does not have any bank loans or lines of credit because it has never needed credit.

Exhibit III	BCG financial data produced by the system

	10 months ended June 30, 2015	12 months ended August 31, 2014
Cash Receipts		
Donations/grants	$ 20,549	$ 22,547
Facility rentals	9,094	12,402
Fundraising activities	68,685	73,158
Fees, recreational and competitive	201,864	209,402
	300,192	317,509
Cash Disbursements		
General and administrative	45,301	45,465
Repairs and maintenance	50,281	50,419
Salaries, benefits, and travel	220,603	217,056
Fundraising activities	6,635	9,219
	322,820	322,159
Net change in cash	(22,628)	(4,650)
Beginning cash	26,952	31,602
Ending cash	$ 4,324	$26,952

CASE 3
Community Care Services
(60 minutes)[6]

Community Care Services (CCS) is a not-for-profit organization formed in January 2013 and is located in a rural community of Thomas County. CCS is dedicated to serving the needs of seniors. CCS's informational literature and website contain the following statement:

> "Our mission is to provide a secure retirement community in a carefully selected location in the heart of our beloved Thomas County. Our organization provides a warm, attractive setting as the surroundings for a vibrant, healthy living space—one that our residents deserve. Our vision is to serve the community, and it encompasses accommodation and leisure as well as the provision of health care."

---

6. Adapted with permission from The Canadian Institute of Chartered Accountants, Toronto, Canada. Any changes to the original material are the sole responsibility of the author and have not been reviewed or endorsed by the CICA.

Background information on CCS is provided in Exhibit I, and some details of CCS's operations are included in Exhibit II. The executive director, Janet Admer, joined the organization in the last month and was recruited from a nearby city. Janet has extensive experience in managing the construction and operations of a major hotel. It was the board of directors' view that, even though Janet's salary of $120,000 seemed high, her hospitality-industry skills would be a good contribution to the operation of CCS.

It is now November 15, 2013. You, CA, have known Janet Admer for many years, and she has approached you for advice. Janet has asked your firm, Yelt and Rerdan, Chartered Accountants, to advise her and the board on the issues facing CCS as it moves from the construction phase to the operating phase. Janet has prepared a cash budget, included in Exhibit III, and she is very pleased that her estimate indicates that a surplus will exist in the first year of full operation. Because the board members would like to make sure that CCS will have sufficient cash to meet its obligations as it starts to operate the residences, Janet wants you to look at her budget. The board had approved obtaining a bank loan to complete the construction phase but is still concerned that there is a risk that CCS will run out of cash by the end of the year.

CCS has already appointed KZY, Chartered Accountants, as the auditor, and KZY will be reporting on the first fiscal year-end of December 31, 2013. Janet has deliberately not assigned the engagement to you and your firm so that the functions of auditor and adviser will be independent.

The board is made up of highly respected individuals in the community; however, the members have very little experience in running an operation such as CCS. Janet would like you to help her determine the kind of information, financial and otherwise, that would be useful to them to evaluate the performance of CCS in meeting its goals.

You are pleased at the prospect of bringing in a client to the firm, and you have discussed the engagement with a partner at Yelt and Rerdan. The partner has agreed to accept the engagement and has asked you to prepare a draft report addressing Janet's requests.

Required:

Prepare the the draft report addressing Janet's requests, including a comprehensive analysis of CCS's cash flow situation and an analysis of CCS's information needs.

Exhibit I	Background information

In the last decade, foreign investors who believed that land was a bargain as a result of the weak Canadian dollar have purchased many of the farms in Thomas County. The community was concerned that there were no residential alternatives in the county for older farmers who left their farms as a result of a sale or retirement.

Mr. MacDougall, an advocate for the local farmers and seniors, started with the idea of providing residential options to the families. He was instrumental in setting up CCS and was appointed the chairman of the board. He donated 10 acres of land from his farm for the facility. He also donated $1 million for the construction of the residential units. The conditions of the donations were as follows:

1. The land can never be sold.
2. At least one-third of all residential units must be provided to low-income seniors who must meet an annual income test, and the rent charged cannot generate a surplus on the operational costs of these units. (These units have been designated as Building C.)
3. At least one-third of all residential units must provide full health care services. (These units have been designated as Building A, commonly referred to as the "Nursing Home.")
4. One-half of the sales proceeds from the retirement home sales units must be maintained in a separate account to be used for the maintenance and capital repairs of the complex.

If these terms are not met the land reverts to Mr. MacDougall, or to a special MacDougall trust if the breach occurs after the death of Mr. MacDougall.

Exhibit I   Continued

The layout of the complex is as follows:

	Retirement Home Units for Sale Building B	
Nursing Home Building A	Common Area (Outdoors)	Retirement Home Rental Units Building C
	Recreation Facility Building D	

Construction began in February 2013 and is almost complete. The nursing home and both retirement homes are completed. The recreation facility is scheduled to be completed by December 31. All of the units in the nursing home and the rental retirement home have been assigned to residents. Sales contracts have been signed for all of the units in the other retirement home. These sales are expected to close in January 2014. The complex is expected to be fully operational in early January 2014.

The costs of construction and the budget are as follows:

	Original budget	Estimate to December 2013*
Land improvements	$ 170,000	$168,000
Buildings		
Building A—Nursing Home	300,000	421,000
Equipment and furniture	150,000	150,000
Building B—Retirement Homes for Sale	250,000	250,000
Building C—Retirement Homes for Rent	275,000	270,000
Building D—Recreation Facility	150,000	100,000
	$1,295,000	$1,359,000

*Total actual costs incurred plus revised estimate to complete.

Source of funds	
Mr. MacDougall	$1,000,000
Thomas County Grant	200,000
Bank loan—no interest until January 1, 2014, then payments of $20,000 per month, plus annual interest of 5%	200,000
	$1,400,000

Exhibit II

Additional information

Building A—Nursing Home

This building has 20 beds and its operations will be funded by the provincial government's Ministry of Community and Social Services (the Ministry). The funding formula is $130/day/bed, and any surplus from operations must be returned to the Ministry. To determine the surplus the Ministry will allow direct costs plus a reasonable allocation of overheads. The Ministry, which provides some funding, has requested the audit of the annual financial statements as part of the funding requirement.

Building B—Retirement Home, Units for Sale

There are 10 unfurnished units and the residents will have a "life-lease" on the land, which means that the residents will have the right to use the portion of the land on which the building is located but they will not own it, and the right will expire at either the death of the resident or sooner if mutually agreed to. In addition to the purchase price, the

(Continued)

Exhibit II	Continued

residents will also pay $550 per month to cover the occupancy costs, and this amount could be adjusted to meet actual costs if necessary. There are two types of "sales" and there are five units of each type:

Type I—The units are "sold" for fair market value. At the end of the lease (i.e., death or resident moves out), CCS must pay back the full price paid.

Type II—The units are "sold" for 120% of fair market value. At the end of the lease (i.e., death or resident moves out), CCS must pay back the fair market value at the date the resident purchased the unit plus 50% of any increase in value.

For both types, CCS has the right to select the next occupant, and the price to be charged for the unit is to be based on fair market value and must be supported by an independent opinion. The fair market value for all the initial sales was determined to be $100,000. The board is confident that the value of these units will increase. These units are designed to appeal to those who want a "premium" unit and can afford to pay for it.

Building C—Retirement Home, Rental Units

There are 15 unfurnished units. The rent will be approximately $400 per month per unit and includes all utilities, cable, etc. To be eligible for these units, the applicants must prove that the combined annual income available to them is not more than $20,000. CCS will receive an annual operating grant of $200,000 from the Ministry.

Building D—Recreation Facility

When it is completed, Building D will hold the administration offices and a recreation facility to be used for social activities. The residents of all buildings can use the common area and recreation facility.

Other

Each of the four buildings has a staff member employed as the "Program Director." Each program director has an annual salary of $60,000. The total administrative costs incurred in 2013 are expected to be limited to $115,000.

Exhibit III	

Budgeted operating cash flows
For the Year Ending December 31, 2014
(in thousands of dollars)

Cash inflows	
Government funding—Nursing Home (20 beds × $130 × 365 days)	$ 949
Government funding—Retirement Home rental units	200
Sales proceeds—Retirement Home sales units	1,100
Occupancy fees—Retirement Home sales units (10 units × $550 × 12 months)	66
Rent—Retirement Home rental units (15 units × $400 × 12 months)	72
Interest (same amount as earned in 2013)	29
	2,416

Cash outflows	
Salaries and benefits (including medical staff costs of $260)	850
Medical supplies	55
Furniture and equipment (Nursing Home and Administration)	44
Food costs—Nursing Home	160
Staff training (one-time cost)	34
Repairs and maintenance	23
Communications, office, etc.	15
Utilities and property taxes	23
Insurance	10
	1,214
Excess of cash inflows over cash outflows	$1,202

CASE 4
Enviro Ltd.
(60 minutes)[7]

You, CA, are employed by McDowell and Partners, Chartered Accountants (M&P). A new client, Community Finance Corporation (CFC), approached M&P for assistance. Enviro Ltd. (Enviro) has asked CFC for a loan of $10 million in the form of long-term debt to fund capital expenditures and other operating requirements. CFC has already conducted a general assessment of Enviro but now needs an accounting firm to look closely at the financial aspects, including the areas of financial risk. In particular, CFC needs to be assured that it will receive the payments of principal and interest over the term of the loan. M&P has accepted the engagement and is responsible for preparing a report to CFC.

It is now August 2012. Enviro's board of directors have provided both CFC and M&P with recent financial statements (Exhibit I) and extracts from the working papers of Enviro's auditors, Y&Z, for the most recent year-end (Exhibit II). The engagement partner wants you to prepare a memo addressing CFC's concerns.

Required:
Prepare the memo requested by the engagement partner.

Exhibit I			

Extracts from the Financial Statements of Enviro Ltd.
Consolidated Balance Sheet
As at June 30
(audited, in thousands of dollars)

	2012	2011	2010
Assets			
Current assets			
Cash	$ 15	$ 105	$ 655
Marketable securities	0	870	1,495
Accounts receivable	3,870	3,705	3,580
Inventory			
Metals and scrap	7,775	5,260	4,005
Other	610	585	570
Prepaid expenses	130	120	110
	12,400	10,645	10,415
Land	910	1,160	1,160
Building and equipment	8,985	8,720	8,570
Accumulated depreciation	(2,880)	(2,290)	(1,720)
Waste disposal equipment, net of depreciation	2,060	1,435	1,410
Development cost, net of depreciation	330	240	390
Goodwill	640	700	770
Investment in Klens & Breeth	4,990	3,730	3,160
	$27,435	$24,340	$24,155

7. Adapted with permission from The Canadian Institute of Chartered Accountants, Toronto, Canada. Any changes to the original material are the sole responsibility of the author and have not been reviewed or endorsed by the CICA.

Exhibit I	Continued			
		2012	**2011**	**2010**
Liabilities				
Current liabilities				
Bank demand loan, secured		$ 3,000	$ 2,000	$ 2,200
Accounts payable and accrued liabilities		3,815	1,880	1,185
Other liabilities		790	580	315
		7,605	4,460	3,700
Mortgage payable, 12%, due 2013		2,310	2,490	2,670
Notes payable, 13%, due 2013		4,000	4,000	4,000
Bank term loan, 12%, due 2014		2,500	2,200	2,400
		16,415	13,150	12,770
Shareholders' equity				
Ordinary shares		5,000	5,000	5,000
Preferred shares, 11% cumulative dividend		4,000	4,000	4,000
Retained earnings		2,020	2,190	2,385
		11,020	11,190	11,385
		$27,435	$24,340	$24,155

Enviro Ltd.
Extracts from the Financial Statements
Consolidated Income Statements
For the Year Ended June 30
(audited, in thousands of dollars)

	2012	**2011**	**2010**
Revenues	$9,660	$10,450	$8,795
Expenses			
Cost of goods sold	3,180	3,360	2,265
Wages and benefits	3,420	3,210	2,370
Depreciation	950	790	615
Maintenance and insurance	1,440	1,470	1,305
General and administrative	1,335	1,165	865
Gain on disposal of securities	(360)	(910)	0
Gain on sale of land	(1,105)	0	0
	8,860	9,085	7,420
Income before income from associates	800	1,365	1,375
Income from associate—Klens & Breeth	1,260	570	490
Income before interest and income tax expenses	2,060	1,935	1,865
Interest expense	1,670	1,590	1,005
Income tax expense	120	100	320
Net income	$ 270	$ 245	$ 540

Exhibit II

Extracts from Y&Z's Working Papers
For the Year Ended June 30, 2012

Enviro

1. Enviro is a holding company that was incorporated under federal legislation several years ago as an investment company for a small group of investors. Enviro owns the following:
   – 100% of the voting shares of Waste Disposal Corporation (WDC), which collects and disposes of environmentally hazardous chemicals.
   – 50% of a partnership that specializes in designing advertisements for organizations that promote improvements to the environment. The partnership is called Klens & Breeth (KB). KB in turn owns all the voting shares of two corporations involved in advertising design and development.
   – 100% of the voting shares of Scrap Metal Enterprises Ltd. (SMEL), which deals in the collection and sale of non-precious metals (copper, iron, and others).
2. Enviro's existing bank loans are secured by a first charge on receivables. The mortgage payable is secured by a first mortgage on the land and building. The notes payable are secured by inventory and are due in August 2013. The notes payable cannot be renewed because payment in full has been demanded.
3. Enviro is insured for liability and accidents but not for theft and fire.
4. Enviro paid dividends on preferred shares of $440,000 in each of 2010, 2011, and 2012. In additition, the company paid $100,000 of dividends on common shares in 2010.

WDC

1. To meet government requirements, WDC's disposal equipment has to be upgraded by October 1, 2013; otherwise, large segments of the operations will have to be suspended and other safe disposal methods will have to be found—an unlikely prospect. Upgrading is really the only alternative if WDC is to avoid having to cancel contracts and incur significant cancellation penalties. Approximately $7 million is needed as soon as possible.
2. Using its own waste disposal technology, WDC builds some of the equipment that it needs to process certain wastes. During fiscal 2012, the following expenditures were capitalized:

Components and parts	$ 322,100
Wages and benefits	208,220
Overhead costs	208,000
Interest on borrowings	12,680
	$751,000

The overhead costs are allocated based on roughly 100% of wages and benefits.

KB

1. We do not audit KB but have reviewed the audit working papers and have had discussions with KB's auditors. KB's income for the year ended March 31, 2012, was $2,520,000, and Enviro has appropriately accounted for its share using the equity method of accounting. Enviro is a silent partner. However, Enviro provides major assistance in developing new client contracts for KB. The other partner needs the partnership form of ownership for various purposes. Among the more significant transactions during fiscal 2012 were the following:
   a. KB accounts for its investments on an equity basis; its subsidiaries paid cash dividends in fiscal 2012 of $1,200,000. KB retained these funds to develop new technology.

KB

b. KB earned $1,875,000 from a federal government contract that has expired this month. Most of the fee was recognized in income in 2012 because the ideas had already been generated for another project and few additional costs were necessary.

c. The other partner of KB operates an advertising firm for non-environmental promotion. KB paid this firm $895,000 for a variety of services.

SMEL

1. SMEL's scrap metal piles are large, and it is difficult to estimate the quantity of metal in the piles. To satisfy ourselves, we photographed the piles, compared them geometrically to photographs of previous years, and discussed important issues with management. We also conducted extra checks of the perpetual inventory system against arrival and departure weights of trucks. The system was operating satisfactorily, but estimates were necessary for wastage.

2. The scrap metal is recorded at cost because resale prices of scrap vary considerably. If prices are low, SMEL stores the metals until selling prices improve. Management believes there is no need to sell at a loss.

3. The government requires a soil test of SMEL's scrap yard every five years. The most recent soil test was conducted four years ago.

A Time Value of Money and Simple Valuation Techniques

This appendix reviews several aspects of the time value of money, which is covered in introductory finance. The first section looks at the basic relationships and formulas for future and present values. The second section goes through the practical approaches (formulas, calculators, and spreadsheets) to make computations frequently encountered in accounting applications. The third section briefly discusses simple valuation techniques used to estimate the value of assets and enterprises. The end of the chapter includes a present value table for an annuity.

A. FUTURE VALUES AND PRESENT VALUES

The time value of money is a concept that will be useful for many parts of this book. It is simply the idea that people value a dollar received today more than a dollar received tomorrow, next week, or next year. We can ask the question, "In order to be as satisfied as being paid a dollar now, how much would you need to be paid in one year's time?" If the answer is $1.10, then the interest rate you demand is 10% (i.e., 10% more than a dollar). We usually use "r" to denote the interest rate, also called the discount rate. Once we have an interest rate, we can express the value of money at any point in time, at the present time or in the future, giving rise to the concepts of present value and future value.

1. Future value of a single sum received now

In the example just given, $1.10 is the future value in one year's time of a dollar today. Changing the example slightly, if you invest a hundred dollars now, you expect to obtain $110 in a year's time because you would earn 10% interest. If you invest for two years, you would have $100 \times 1.10 \times 1.10 = \$100 \times 1.10^2 = \$121$. Formally, we can express this relationship by the following equation:

Exhibit A-1	Future value of a single sum

$$FV_t = PV_0 \times (1 + r)^t$$

In this equation, FV_t denotes future value at time t (a dollar amount), PV_0 denotes present value (a dollar amount) at time 0, and r is the interest rate per period. Time is usually measured in years, but it could be any length of time, as long as the interest rate is defined accordingly.

2. Present value of a single sum to be received in the future

We can rearrange the equation in Exhibit A-1 to isolate PV_0, the present value at time 0, as follows:

Exhibit A-2   Present value of a single sum

$$PV_0 = \frac{FV_t}{(1 + r)^t}$$

Thus, the present value of $121 to be received in two years' time when the interest rate is 10% per year is $PV_0 = \$121/1.10^2 = \$121/1.21 = \$100$. The following diagram summarizes the relationship between the present and future values just calculated.

Exhibit A-3   Timeline illustrating the relationship between present and future values

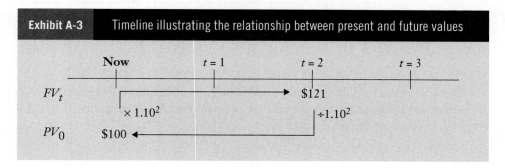

One reason for computing future and present values is to allow us to add together cash flows that occur at different times. For example, if you were to receive $100 next year, $100 in two years, and $100 three years from now, how much are you really receiving? Simply adding together the three cash flows is not appropriate because the cash flows occur at different times and each cash flow has a different time value of money. Instead, all the cash flows need to be expressed in terms of one particular point in time. In most instances, it is most convenient to choose the present time as the point of reference. If the interest rate is 10%, we can compute the present value of each of the three cash flows and then they can be summed up, as follows:

Exhibit A-4   Computation of present value of three cash flows of $100 each

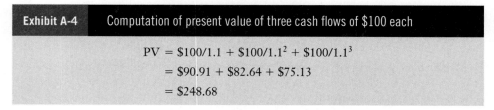

As you can see, the present value ($248.68) is considerably less than the simple sum of the three cash flows ($300). The following diagram illustrates this computation:

Exhibit A-5   Timeline showing the computation of present value of three cash flows

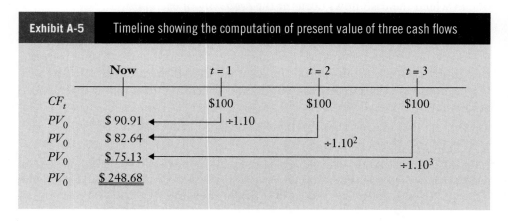

3. Present value of a perpetuity

perpetuity A series of cash flows in equal amounts occurring at regular intervals for an infinite number of periods.

A **perpetuity** is a series of cash flows in equal amounts occurring at regular intervals for an infinite number of periods. The present value of a perpetuity is not infinite, even though the cash flows occur for an infinite number of periods. In fact, we can compute the value of a perpetuity using the following formula, where each cash flow occurs at the end of period t:

Exhibit A-6	Present value of a perpetuity[1]

$$PV_0 = \frac{CF_t}{r}$$

For example, if each cash flow, denoted CF in the formula, is $100 and received at the end of each year forever into the future, and the discount rate is 10%, then PV = $100/0.10 = $1,000.

4. Present value of a perpetuity with growth

perpetuity with growth A series of cash flows occurring at regular intervals for an infinite number of periods with cash flows that grow at a constant rate.

Instead of the same cash flow every period, a **perpetuity with growth** is one in which the cash flows grow at a constant rate. The present value of a perpetuity with the cash flow CF_1 occurring at the end of one year and growing at rate g, discounted at rate r, is given by the following formula:

Exhibit A-7	Present value of a perpetuity with growth

$$PV_0 = \frac{CF_1}{r - g}$$

5. Present value of an ordinary annuity

annuity A series of cash flows in equal amounts occurring at regular intervals. An **ordinary annuity** has cash flows at the *end* of each period. In comparison, an **annuity due** has cash flows at the *beginning* of each period.

The pattern of cash flows illustrated by the computation in Exhibit A-5 is an example of an **annuity,** which is a series of cash flows in equal amounts occurring at regular intervals (i.e., $CF1 = CF2 = \ldots$). In this example, $100 is received at the end of each of three years. In addition, this is an **ordinary annuity** because the cash flows occur at the *end* of each period. In comparison, an **annuity due** is one in which the cash flows occur at the *beginning* of each period.

In cases where there are a small number of cash flows, as in the example illustrated in Exhibit A-5, we can compute the present value by computing the present value of each individual cash flow and then adding them up. However, this approach is laborious even using a spreadsheet if the number of cash flows in the annuity is large. Instead, using the following formula is often more efficient.

---

1. For those curious as to the source of this formula, it is an application of the general formula for the sum of an infinite series from high school algebra: $\sum_{t=1}^{\infty}(1/a^t) = 1/(a-1)$. For example, if $a = 2$, then $\frac{1}{2} + \frac{1}{4} + \ldots = 1$ which is $1/(a - 1) = 1/(2 - 1)$. If $a = 10$, then $0.1 + 0.01 + 0.001 + \ldots = 0.111 \ldots = 1/9$. If $a = 1 + r$, then $1/(1 + r) + 1/(1 + r)^2 + \ldots = 1/(1 + r - 1) = 1/r$.

| Exhibit A-8 | Present value of an ordinary annuity[2] |

$$PV_0 = CF_1 \times \left(\frac{1}{r} - \frac{1}{r(1+r)^t}\right)$$

$$= CF_1 \times \left(\frac{1-(1+r)^{-t}}{r}\right)$$

$$= CF_1 \times PVFA(r, t)$$

The term in parentheses is known as the *present value factor for an annuity* at discount rate r for t periods. For convenience of reference, we denote this factor as $PVFA(r, t)$.

For example, if you were to receive \$100 at the end of each of the next three years, the present value of those three payments is \$248.69, calculated as follows:

| Exhibit A-9 | Computation of present value of three cash flows of \$100 each |

$$PV_0 = \$100 \times \left(\frac{1}{0.10} - \frac{1}{0.10(1.10)^3}\right)$$

$$= \$100 \times 2.48685$$

$$= \$248.69$$

Of course, this is the same answer as obtained using the calculations in Exhibit A-5.

6. Present value of an annuity due

As mentioned above, the cash flows for an annuity due occur at the beginning of the period. The simplest way to deal with such annuities is to recognize that, setting aside the first cash flow, the remainder is just an ordinary annuity with one less period. Thus, we can write the present value factor for an annuity due (*PVFAD*) as follows:

| Exhibit A-10 | Present value factor for an annuity due *(PVFAD)* |

$$PVFAD(r, t) = 1 + PVFA(r, t-1)$$

$$= 1 + \left(\frac{1}{r} - \frac{1}{r(1+r)^{t-1}}\right)$$

For example, if you receive three cash flows of \$100 each at the beginning of each of three years, and the discount rate is 10%, then:

| Exhibit A-11 | Present value of \$100 received at the beginning of each of three years |

$$PV_0 = CF_0 \times PVFAD(10\%, 3)$$

$$= \$100 \times \left(1 + \frac{1}{0.10} - \frac{1}{0.10(1.10)^2}\right)$$

$$= \$100 \times 2.73554$$

$$= \$273.55$$

2. This formula is derived from the perpetuity formula. A \$1 annuity of t periods is equivalent to a \$1 perpetuity minus a \$1 perpetuity that starts at the end of period t. The first perpetuity has value $1/r$. The second perpetuity starts after t periods, so it has value $1/r \times 1/(1+r)^t = 1/r(1+r)^t$. Thus, PVAF = $1/r - 1/r(1+r)^t$.

Notice that this present value of $273.55 is 10% more than $248.69, the value of the ordinary annuity ($248.69 × 1.1 = $273.55). So another way to think of an annuity due is to imagine that it is like an ordinary annuity with every payment shifted by one period closer to the present time. Thus, we can also express the present value annuity factor for an annuity due as follows:

Exhibit A-12	Alternate formula for present value factor for an annuity due

$$PVFAD(r, t) = PVFA(r, t) \times (1 + r)$$

$$= \left(\frac{1}{r} - \frac{1}{r(1 + r)^t} \right) \times (1 + r)$$

B. COMPUTATION TECHNIQUES

The previous section reviewed the fundamentals of present and future values, as well as the formulas for computing these values. The following table summarizes techniques to make these computations using formulas, a financial calculator (Texas Instruments BA II Plus), or a spreadsheet (Microsoft Excel). Notation is as follows:

- FV = future value
- PV = present value
- CF = cash flow
- r = interest rate per period
- t = number of periods
- g = growth rate
- $PVFA$ = present value factor for an annuity
- subscripts denote the timing of a variable (e.g., 0 is the present, 1 is one period in the future)
- for the calculator entries, keystrokes are either numbers or function keys denoted by ⬚; items in [square brackets] are informational and not for keying.

Exhibit A-13	Basic computation techniques for future and present values

Objective	Example	Formula calculation	Texas Instruments BA II Plus	Microsoft Excel
FV of a single sum	A $100 investment earns 5% interest compounded annually. Compute the future value of this investment at the end of 10 years.	$FV_t = PV_0 \times (1 + r)^t$ $FV_{10} = 100 (1.05)^{10}$ $= \$162.89$	−100 [PV] 5 [I/Y] 10 [N] [CPT] [FV] [Output] 162.89	Input: =FV(5%, 10, , −100) Output: 162.89
PV of a single sum	You agree to pay $162.89 at the end of 10 years. If the interest rate is 5%, how much would you need to set aside today to fund that future payment?	$PV_0 = \dfrac{FV_t}{(1 + r)^t}$ $PV_0 = \dfrac{162.89}{(1.05)^{10}}$ $= 100.00$	−162.89 [FV] 5 [I/Y] 10 [N] [CPT] [PV] [Output] 100.00	Input: =PV(5%, 10, , −162.89) Output: −100.00

Exhibit A-13	*(Continued)*			
PV of a perpetuity	An investment promises to pay $100 at the end of each year indefinitely. If the discount rate is 5%, how much would it cost to buy the investment?	$PV_0 = \dfrac{CF_t}{r}$ $PV_0 = \dfrac{100}{0.05}$ $= 2{,}000$	No special financial functions. Use normal arithmetic functions.	No special financial function. Input according to formula.
PV of a perpetuity with growth	An investment promises to make a stream of payments indefinitely, with payments starting at $100 at the end of the first year and growing at 1% each year. If the interest rate is 5%, how much would it cost to buy the investment?	$PV_0 = \dfrac{CF_1}{r - g}$ $PV_0 = \dfrac{100}{0.05 - 0.01}$ $= 2{,}500$	No special financial functions. Use normal arithmetic functions.	No special financial function. Input according to formula.
PV of an ordinary annuity	You promise to pay $100 at the end of each year for 10 years. If the interest rate is 5%, how much would you need to set aside now to fund these 10 payments?	$PV_0 = CF_1 \times PVFA(r,\ t)$ $= CF_1 \times \left(\dfrac{1}{r} - \dfrac{1}{r(1+r)^t}\right)$ $PV_0 = 100 \times PVFA(5\%,\ 10)$ $= 100 \times \left(\dfrac{1}{0.05} - \dfrac{1}{0.05(1.05)^{10}}\right)$ $= 100 \times 7.7217$ $= 772.17$	−100 [PMT] 5 [I/Y] 10 [N] [CPT] [PV] [Output] 772.17	Input: = PV(5%, 10, −100) Output: −772.17
PV of an annuity due	You promise to pay $100 at the beginning of each year for 10 years. If the interest rate is 5%, how much would you need to set aside now to fund these 10 payments?	$PV_0 = CF_1 \times [1 + PVFA(r,\ t-1)]$ $= CF_1 \times \left(1 + \dfrac{1}{r} - \dfrac{1}{r(1+r)^{t-1}}\right)$ $PV_0 = 100 \times [1 + PVFA(5\%,\ 9)]$ $= 100 \times \left(1 + \dfrac{1}{0.05} - \dfrac{1}{0.05(1.05)^{9}}\right)$ $= 100 \times 8.1078$ $= 810.78$	[2ND] [BGN] [2ND] [SET] [2ND] [QUIT] −100 [PMT] 5 [I/Y] 10 [N] [CPT] [PV] [Output] 810.78	Input: = PV(5%, 10, −100, , 1) Output: 810.78

In addition to the above future and present value computations, it is sometimes necessary to determine the interest rate or yield of an annuity or a bond. It is not generally possible to calculate yields using algebraic formulas. Instead a financial calculator or a spreadsheet is necessary.

Exhibit A-14	Techniques for computing yields on annuities and bonds			
Objective	**Example**	**Formula**	**Texas Instruments BA II Plus**	**Microsoft Excel**
Interest rate or yield of an annuity	An ordinary annuity has annual cash payments of $100 for 10 periods. The present value of the annuity is $772.17. Compute the interest rate of the annuity.	No formula	−100 [PMT] 10 [N] 772.17 [PV] [CPT] [I/Y] [Output] 5.00	Input: =RATE(10, −100, 772.17) Output: 5.00%

Exhibit A-14	(Continued)				

Objective	Example	Formula	Texas Instruments BA II Plus		Microsoft Excel
Annual yield of a bond	You purchase a bond on Jan. 1, 2011. The bond has an annual coupon rate of 6% and semi-annual coupon payments until maturity on Dec. 31, 2020, at which time it will repay the principal of $1,000. You paid $900 for this bond.	No formula	[Start bond functions] 2ND BOND		Input cell A1: Jan 1, 2011
			[Purchase date] 1.0111	ENTER ↓	Input cell A2: Dec 31, 2020
			[Coupon rate] 6	ENTER ↓	Input cell A3: = YIELD(A1, A2, 6%, 900, 1000, 2, 0)
			[Maturity date] 12.3120	ENTER ↓	Output cell A3: 7.44%
			[Maturity payment per $100 face value] 100	ENTER ↓	
			[Display shows ACT]	↓	
			[Display shows 2/Y]	↓	
			[Display shows YLD]	↓	
			[Price per $100 face value] 90	ENTER ↑	
			[Display shows YLD]	CPT	
			[Output] 7.44		

The above table shows an example of a bond with standard characteristics, but the number of steps in the calculator is already becoming unwieldy. For more complex bonds, it is advisable to use a spreadsheet that identifies the timing and amount of all cash flows, and then sum the present value of each cash flow.

C. SIMPLE VALUATION METHODS

As noted in Chapter 1, the demand for accounting information arises from uncertainty about the future. Due to this uncertainty, equity investors are only able to make imperfect forecasts about the future prices of shares, which influence whether and in which companies they invest. Given the importance of this topic, it is the subject of many books in finance and investments. The following discussion touches on the basic approaches to equity valuation using accounting information. This will provide a basis for understanding why accounting information is important in equity markets.

In all the methods discussed below, our goal is to estimate a fundamental value (V). If prevailing stock price (P) in the market is below V, then the valuation suggests that the stock is underpriced. In contrast, $P > V$ suggests that the stock is overpriced. However, it is important to recognize that these estimates of V are just that: estimates. Each estimation approach has its limitations because of the assumptions required. Below, we will discuss approaches using book value, dividends, and earnings.

1. Valuation using book value

The simplest method of share valuation is to use a company's book value per share $(BVPS)$. "Book value" in this context refers to the amount for common shares, retained earnings, and any other amounts in equity on the balance sheet that pertain to the common shareholders. We divide book value by the number of shares outstanding[3] to obtain a value comparable to the company's stock price, which is naturally expressed on a per share basis.

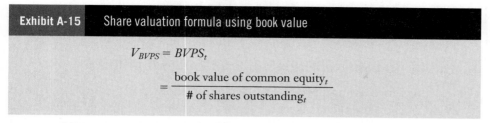

Exhibit A-15	Share valuation formula using book value

$$V_{BVPS} = BVPS_t$$

$$= \frac{\text{book value of common equity}_t}{\text{\# of shares outstanding}_t}$$

While this method is simple, it is useful in very limited circumstances. Specifically, this valuation approach requires the following assumptions to be approximately correct.

- *Completeness:* The company's balance sheet has recorded all significant assets and liabilities. That is, the company cannot have unrecorded assets such as patents, or unrecorded liabilities such as pending lawsuits.
- *Neutrality:* Accounting policies are neutral such that the recorded values of assets and liabilities on the balance sheet approximate their current values. In other words, the accounting can be neither conservative nor aggressive.
- *Stability:* The company's operations are stable rather than growing (or declining). Usually, this also requires that the company's industry be mature and stable.

Using the book value method, the estimate V will usually be substantially below stock price P because (1) the balance sheet does not show all economic assets such as valuable patents and internally generated goodwill; (2) accounting tends to be conservative; and (3) firms tend to grow over time along with growth in the overall economy. Despite these limitations, the book value method often provides a reliable lower bound estimate of fundamental value, and it is a good starting point to gauge the reasonability of the other methods discussed below. For instance, if another valuation method produces a value estimate that is four times book value, is the 300% difference reasonably explained by incomplete accounting of assets, conservative accounting, or future growth?

2. Valuation using dividends

Finance theory suggests that the value of common equity is equal to the present value of expected future dividends. This idea is summarized by the following formula:

Exhibit A-16	Valuation formula using expected dividends

$$V_{Div} = \sum_{t=1}^{\infty} \frac{E(DPS_t)}{(1 + r)^t}$$

$E(DPS_t)$ is the expected dividends per share in period t. This formula is just an application of basic discounted cash flow analysis. However, the difficulty with applying this approach is that dividends are hard to predict: they are at

---

3. There are some complexities relating to the number of shares that should be used in the denominator. These issues are addressed in Chapter 15 on earnings per share. For simplicity, we use the number of shares outstanding.

the discretion of companies' boards of directors, and some companies have no history of dividends to help forecast future dividends. One way to overcome these difficulties is to replace expected dividends with another measure of expected cash flow, such as cash flow from operations. Another approach is to use earnings forecasts in place of expected dividends, because earnings eventually result in cash inflows, from which the firm pays dividends.

3. Valuation using earnings and earnings multiples

The earnings forecasting process can be quite elaborate and complex. A good starting point is to use the most recent reported earnings per share. For valuation purposes, it is useful to "normalize" the earnings per share: adjusting the actual earnings for temporary fluctuations so as to obtain a better forecast of permanent earnings. We can then use this normalized earnings per share (EPS_0) as an indicator for future dividend-paying capacity, and apply the perpetuity with growth formula (see Exhibit A-7) to obtain the following formula:

Exhibit A-17	Valuation formula using expected earnings

$$V_{Earn} = \frac{E(EPS_1)}{r - g}$$

$$= \frac{EPS_0 \times (1 + g)}{r - g}$$

In this equation, $E(EPS1)$ is the expected earnings per share next year. If growth is zero ($g = 0$), then the formula is particularly simple: $V_{Earn} = EPS_0/r$.

To illustrate this approach and the related computations below, assume the following for Alpha Corporation:

Exhibit A-18	Assumptions about Alpha Corporation		
Item description		**Notation**	**Amount**
Current stock price		P_0	$39.00
Most recent year's earnings per share		EPS_0	$1.50
Discount rate		r	9%
Growth rate in earnings per share		g	4%

Applying the equation in Exhibit A-16, we obtain V_{Earn} = $1.50 × 1.04/ (0.09 − 0.04) = $1.56/0.05 = $31.20 as the estimated value per share for Alpha Corporation.

It is also useful to write the formula for V_{Earn} from Exhibit A-16 in a slightly different way to emphasize what is commonly known as an **earnings multiple.**

earnings multiple   A number that, when multiplied with earnings, provides an estimate of a share's value. When earnings are expected to grow at rate g and the discount rate is r, the earnings multiple is equal to $(1 + g)/(r − g)$.

Exhibit A-19	Valuation formulas using earnings multiples

$$V_{Earn} = EPS_0 \times \frac{1 + g}{r - g}$$

$$= EPS_0 \times \text{earnings multiple}$$

Using the assumptions for Alpha Corporation shown above in Exhibit A-17, we have the following results:

Exhibit A-20	Valuation of Alpha Corporation using multiples
Earnings multiple	**Value estimate**
Earnings multiple $= \dfrac{1+g}{r-g} = \dfrac{1.04}{0.09-0.04} = 20.8$	$V_{Earn} = EPS_0 \times$ earnings multiple $= \$1.50 \times 20.8$ $= \$31.20$

Of course, the estimated value of $31.20 is the same as computing the value using the perpetuity with growth formula in Exhibit A-16.

One of the reasons for isolating the multiple in the earnings valuation method is that it allows for comparisons among different firms. Along the same line, instead of making predictions about r and g directly to calculate the multiple, one can also use the average multiple for a set of firms that is comparable to the firm being analyzed.[4] Thus, if the set of comparable firms has an average earnings multiple of 23, and $EPS_0 = \$1.50$, then $V_{Earn} = 23 \times \$1.50 = \$34.50$.

Another way to use an earnings multiple is to compare it against the price–earnings ratio, or P/E ratio, which is simply the share price divided by earnings per share:

Exhibit A-21	The price–earnings (P/E) ratio
	P/E ratio $= \dfrac{P_0}{EPS_0}$

If the prevailing stock price (P_0) is $39, then the P/E ratio is $39/$1.50 = 26. This ratio exceeds the earnings multiple of 20.8, as well as the average multiple of 23 for comparable firms. This analysis suggests that the stock is overpriced. The same inference of overpricing would be drawn by comparing the actual price of $39 with the estimated value of $31.20.

Exhibit A-22	Summary of earnings valuation for Alpha Corporation	
Earnings multiple for the firm (estimated):	$\dfrac{1+g}{r-g} = 20.8$	The actual P/E ratio of 26 exceeds the earnings multiple corresponding to the discount rate and growth rate estimated for the firm. The P/E ratio also exceeds the earnings multiple for comparable firms.
Earnings multiple for comparable firms (given): 23		
Actual P/E ratio:	$\dfrac{P_0}{EPS_0} = \dfrac{\$39}{\$1.50} = 26$	
Value estimate:	$V_{Earn} = \$31.20$	The actual market price for the shares at $39 exceeds estimated value of $31.20. Therefore, this analysis suggests that the shares are overvalued.
Actual price:	$P_0 = \$39$	

---

4. This method of using earnings multiples of comparable firms is one application of an approach called the method of comparable multiples. This method involves using multiples of earnings, sales, book value, cash flow, or any other measure that helps to predict share price.

D. TABLE OF PRESENT VALUE FACTORS FOR AN ORDINARY ANNUITY OF $1 (PVFA)

Periods (t)	Interest rate per period (r)											
	2%	3%	4%	5%	6%	7%	8%	9%	10%	11%	12%	15%
1	0.9804	0.9709	0.9615	0.9524	0.9434	0.9346	0.9259	0.9174	0.9091	0.9009	0.8929	0.8696
2	1.9416	1.9135	1.8861	1.8594	1.8334	1.8080	1.7833	1.7591	1.7355	1.7125	1.6901	1.6257
3	2.8839	2.8286	2.7751	2.7232	2.6730	2.6243	2.5771	2.5313	2.4869	2.4437	2.4018	2.2832
4	3.8077	3.7171	3.6299	3.5460	3.4651	3.3872	3.3121	3.2397	3.1699	3.1024	3.0373	2.8550
5	4.7135	4.5797	4.4518	4.3295	4.2124	4.1002	3.9927	3.8897	3.7908	3.6959	3.6048	3.3522
6	5.6014	5.4172	5.2421	5.0757	4.9173	4.7665	4.6229	4.4859	4.3553	4.2305	4.1114	3.7845
7	6.4720	6.2303	6.0021	5.7864	5.5824	5.3893	5.2064	5.0330	4.8684	4.7122	4.5638	4.1604
8	7.3255	7.0197	6.7327	6.4632	6.2098	5.9713	5.7466	5.5348	5.3349	5.1461	4.9676	4.4873
9	8.1622	7.7861	7.4353	7.1078	6.8017	6.5152	6.2469	5.9952	5.7590	5.5370	5.3282	4.7716
10	8.9826	8.5302	8.1109	7.7217	7.3601	7.0236	6.7101	6.4177	6.1446	5.8892	5.6502	5.0188
11	9.7868	9.2526	8.7605	8.3064	7.8869	7.4987	7.1390	6.8052	6.4951	6.2065	5.9377	5.2337
12	10.5753	9.9540	9.3851	8.8633	8.3838	7.9427	7.5361	7.1607	6.8137	6.4924	6.1944	5.4206
13	11.3484	10.6350	9.9856	9.3936	8.8527	8.3577	7.9038	7.4869	7.1034	6.7499	6.4235	5.5831
14	12.1062	11.2961	10.5631	9.8986	9.2950	8.7455	8.2442	7.7862	7.3667	6.9819	6.6282	5.7245
15	12.8493	11.9379	11.1184	10.3797	9.7122	9.1079	8.5595	8.0607	7.6061	7.1909	6.8109	5.8474
16	13.5777	12.5611	11.6523	10.8378	10.1059	9.4466	8.8514	8.3126	7.8237	7.3792	6.9740	5.9542
17	14.2919	13.1661	12.1657	11.2741	10.4773	9.7632	9.1216	8.5436	8.0216	7.5488	7.1196	6.0472
18	14.9920	13.7535	12.6593	11.6896	10.8276	10.0591	9.3719	8.7556	8.2014	7.7016	7.2497	6.1280
19	15.6785	14.3238	13.1339	12.0853	11.1581	10.3356	9.6036	8.9501	8.3649	7.8393	7.3658	6.1982
20	16.3514	14.8775	13.5903	12.4622	11.4699	10.5940	9.8181	9.1285	8.5136	7.9633	7.4694	6.2593
21	17.0112	15.4150	14.0292	12.8212	11.7641	10.8355	10.0168	9.2922	8.6487	8.0751	7.5620	6.3125
22	17.6580	15.9369	14.4511	13.1630	12.0416	11.0612	10.2007	9.4424	8.7715	8.1757	7.6446	6.3587
23	18.2922	16.4436	14.8568	13.4886	12.3034	11.2722	10.3711	9.5802	8.8832	8.2664	7.7184	6.3988
24	18.9139	16.9355	15.2470	13.7986	12.5504	11.4693	10.5288	9.7066	8.9847	8.3481	7.7843	6.4338
25	19.5235	17.4131	15.6221	14.0939	12.7834	11.6536	10.6748	9.8226	9.0770	8.4217	7.8431	6.4641
26	20.1210	17.8768	15.9828	14.3752	13.0032	11.8258	10.8100	9.9290	9.1609	8.4881	7.8957	6.4906
27	20.7069	18.3270	16.3296	14.6430	13.2105	11.9867	10.9352	10.0266	9.2372	8.5478	7.9426	6.5135
28	21.2813	18.7641	16.6631	14.8981	13.4062	12.1371	11.0511	10.1161	9.3066	8.6016	7.9844	6.5335
29	21.8444	19.1885	16.9837	15.1411	13.5907	12.2777	11.1584	10.1983	9.3696	8.6501	8.0218	6.5509
30	22.3965	19.6004	17.2920	15.3725	13.7648	12.4090	11.2578	10.2737	9.4269	8.6938	8.0552	6.5660
31	22.9377	20.0004	17.5885	15.5928	13.9291	12.5318	11.3498	10.3428	9.4790	8.7331	8.0850	6.5791
32	23.4683	20.3888	17.8736	15.8027	14.0840	12.6466	11.4350	10.4062	9.5264	8.7686	8.1116	6.5905
33	23.9886	20.7658	18.1476	16.0025	14.2302	12.7538	11.5139	10.4644	9.5694	8.8005	8.1354	6.6005
34	24.4986	21.1318	18.4112	16.1929	14.3681	12.8540	11.5869	10.5178	9.6086	8.8293	8.1566	6.6091
35	24.9986	21.4872	18.6646	16.3742	14.4982	12.9477	11.6546	10.5668	9.6442	8.8552	8.1755	6.6166
36	25.4888	21.8323	18.9083	16.5469	14.6210	13.0352	11.7172	10.6118	9.6765	8.8786	8.1924	6.6231
37	25.9695	22.1672	19.1426	16.7113	14.7368	13.1170	11.7752	10.6530	9.7059	8.8996	8.2075	6.6288
38	26.4406	22.4925	19.3679	16.8679	14.8460	13.1935	11.8289	10.6908	9.7327	8.9186	8.2210	6.6338
39	26.9026	22.8082	19.5845	17.0170	14.9491	13.2649	11.8786	10.7255	9.7570	8.9357	8.2330	6.6380
40	27.3555	23.1148	19.7928	17.1591	15.0463	13.3317	11.9246	10.7574	9.7791	8.9511	8.2438	6.6418
45	29.4902	24.5187	20.7200	17.7741	15.4558	13.6055	12.1084	10.8812	9.8628	9.0079	8.2825	6.6543
50	31.4236	25.7298	21.4822	18.2559	15.7619	13.8007	12.2335	10.9617	9.9148	9.0417	8.3045	6.6605

E. Glossary

annuity: A series of cash flows in equal amounts occurring at regular intervals. An **ordinary annuity** has cash flows at the *end* of each period. In comparison, an **annuity due** has cash flows at the *beginning* of each period.

earnings multiple: A number that, when multiplied with earnings, provides an estimate of a share's value. When earnings are expected to grow at rate g and the discount rate is r, the earnings multiple is equal to $(1 + g)/(r - g)$.

perpetuity: A series of cash flows in equal amounts occurring at regular intervals for an infinite number of periods.

perpetuity with growth: A series of cash flows occurring at regular intervals for an infinite number of periods with cash flows that grow at a constant rate.

British Airways 2008/09 Annual Financial Statements

Financial statements

Independent auditor's report to the members of British Airways Plc

We have audited the Group and Parent Company financial statements (the 'financial statements') of British Airways Plc for the year ended March 31, 2009, which comprise the Group consolidated income statement, the Group and Parent Company balance sheets, the Group and Parent Company cash flow statements, the Group and Parent Company statements of changes in equity and the related notes 1 to 39. These financial statements have been prepared under the accounting policies set out therein. We have also audited the information in the directors' remuneration report that is described as having been audited.

This report is made solely to the Company's members, as a body, in accordance with Section 235 of the Companies Act 1985. Our audit work has been undertaken so that we might state to the Company's members those matters we are required to state to them in an auditor's report and for no other purpose. To the fullest extent permitted by law, we do not accept or assume responsibility to anyone other than the Company and the Company's members as a body, for our audit work, for this report, or for the opinions we have formed.

Respective responsibilities of directors and auditors

The directors' responsibilities for preparing the annual report, the directors' remuneration report and the financial statements in accordance with applicable United Kingdom law and International Financial Reporting Standards (IFRS) as adopted by the European Union are set out in the statement of directors' responsibilities.

Our responsibility is to audit the financial statements and the part of the directors' remuneration report to be audited in accordance with relevant legal and regulatory requirements and International Standards on Auditing (UK and Ireland).

We report to you our opinion as to whether the financial statements give a true and fair view and whether the financial statements and the part of the directors' remuneration report to be audited have been properly prepared in accordance with the Companies Act 1985 and, as regards the Group financial statements, Article 4 of the IAS Regulation. We also report to you whether in our opinion the information given in the directors' report and business review is consistent with the financial statements.

In addition, we report to you if, in our opinion, the Company has not kept proper accounting records, if we have not received all the information and explanations we require for our audit, or if information specified by law regarding directors' remuneration and other transactions is not disclosed.

We review whether the corporate governance statement reflects the Company's compliance with the nine provisions of the 2006 Combined Code specified for our review by the Listing Rules of the Financial Services Authority, and we report if it does not. We are not required to consider whether the Board's statements on internal control cover all risks and controls, or form an opinion on the effectiveness of the Group's corporate governance procedures or its risk and control procedures.

We read other information contained in the annual report and consider whether it is consistent with the audited financial statements. The other information comprises only the directors' report and business review, the unaudited part of the report of the Remuneration Committee, the Chairman's statement, the Chief Executive's review, the Chief Financial Officer's report and the corporate governance statement. We consider the implications for our report if we become aware of any apparent misstatements or material inconsistencies with the financial statements. Our responsibilities do not extend to any other information.

Basis of audit opinion

We conducted our audit in accordance with International Standards on Auditing (UK and Ireland) issued by the Auditing Practices Board. An audit includes examination, on a test basis, of evidence relevant to the amounts and disclosures in the financial statements and the part of the directors' remuneration report to be audited. It also includes an assessment of the significant estimates and judgements made by the directors in the preparation of the financial statements, and of whether the accounting policies are appropriate to the Group's and Company's circumstances, consistently applied and adequately disclosed.

We planned and performed our audit so as to obtain all the information and explanations which we considered necessary in order to provide us with sufficient evidence to give reasonable assurance that the financial statements and the part of the directors' remuneration report to be audited are free from material misstatement, whether caused by fraud or other irregularity or error. In forming our opinion we also evaluated the overall adequacy of the presentation of information in the financial statements and the part of the report of the Remuneration Committee to be audited.

Opinion

In our opinion:

- The Group financial statements give a true and fair view, in accordance with IFRS as adopted by the European Union, of the state of the Group's affairs as at March 31, 2009, and of its loss for the year then ended;

- The Parent Company financial statements give a true and fair view, in accordance with IFRS as adopted by the European Union as applied in accordance with the provisions of the Companies Act 1985, of the state of the Parent Company's affairs as at March 31, 2009;

- The financial statements and the part of the report of the Remuneration Committee to be audited have been properly prepared in accordance with the Companies Act 1985 and, as regards the Group financial statements, Article 4 of the IAS Regulation; and

- The information given in the directors' report and business review is consistent with the financial statements.

Ernst & Young LLP
Registered auditor
London
May 21, 2009

Group consolidated income statement

For the year ended March 31, 2009

£ million	Note	Group 2009	Group 2008 Restated
Traffic revenue			
Passenger		**7,836**	*7,600*
Cargo		**673**	*615*
		8,509	*8,215*
Other revenue		**483**	*543*
Revenue	3	**8,992**	*8,758*
Employee costs (excluding restructuring)	8	**2,193**	*2,165*
Restructuring	4	**78**	*1*
Depreciation, amortisation and impairment	4	**694**	*692*
Aircraft operating lease costs		**73**	*68*
Fuel and oil costs		**2,969**	*2,055*
Engineering and other aircraft costs		**510**	*451*
Landing fees and en route charges		**603**	*528*
Handling charges, catering and other operating costs		**1,021**	*977*
Selling costs		**369**	*361*
Currency differences		**117**	*6*
Accommodation, ground equipment and IT costs		**585**	*576*
Total expenditure on operations		**9,212**	*7,880*
Operating (loss)/profit	4	**(220)**	*878*
Fuel derivative (losses)/gains		**(18)**	*12*
Finance costs	9	**(182)**	*(175)*
Finance income	9	**95**	*111*
Net financing (expense)/income relating to pensions	9	**(17)**	*70*
Retranslation charges on currency borrowings	9	**(59)**	*(11)*
Profit on sale of property, plant and equipment and investments	10	**8**	*14*
Share of post-tax profits in associates accounted for using the equity method	20	**4**	*26*
Net charge relating to available-for-sale financial assets	11	**(12)**	*(3)*
(Loss)/profit before tax		**(401)**	*922*
Tax	12	**43**	*(194)*
(Loss)/profit after tax from continuing operations		**(358)**	*728*
Loss from discontinued operations (after tax)	5	**–**	*(2)*
(Loss)/profit after tax		**(358)**	*726*
Attributable to:			
Equity holders of the parent		**(375)**	*712*
Minority interest		**17**	*14*
		(358)	*726*
Earnings/(loss) per share			
Continuing operations:			
Basic	13	**(32.6)p**	*62.1p*
Diluted	13	**(32.6)p**	*61.6p*
Discontinued operations:			
Basic	13		*(0.2)p*
Diluted	13		*(0.2)p*
Total:			
Basic	13	**(32.6)p**	*61.9p*
Diluted	13	**(32.6)p**	*61.4p*

Balance sheets

At March 31, 2009

£ million	Note	Group 2009	Group 2008 Restated	Company 2009	Company 2008 Restated
Non-current assets					
Property, plant and equipment:					
Fleet	15	**5,996**	5,976	**5,805**	5,794
Property	15	**971**	977	**920**	924
Equipment	15	**266**	310	**258**	301
		7,233	7,263	**6,983**	7,019
Intangibles:					
Goodwill	18	**40**	40		
Landing rights	18	**205**	159	**163**	159
Software	18	**22**	22	**22**	22
		267	221	**185**	181
Investments in subsidiaries	20			**2,356**	2,207
Investments in associates	20	**209**	227		
Available-for-sale financial assets	21	**65**	80	**27**	24
Employee benefit assets	36	**340**	320	**340**	320
Derivative financial instruments	32	**3**	51	**3**	51
Prepayments and accrued income		**25**	19	**9**	9
Total non-current assets		**8,142**	8,181	**9,903**	9,811
Current assets and receivables					
Inventories	22	**127**	112	**125**	109
Trade receivables	23	**530**	586	**517**	574
Other current assets	24	**268**	308	**382**	371
Derivative financial instruments	32	**40**	241	**40**	241
Other current interest-bearing deposits	25	**979**	1,181	**43**	399
Cash and cash equivalents	25	**402**	683	**219**	433
		1,381	1,864	**262**	832
Total current assets and receivables		**2,346**	3,111	**1,326**	2,127
Total assets		**10,488**	11,292	**11,229**	11,938
Shareholders' equity					
Issued share capital	33	**288**	288	**288**	288
Share premium		**937**	937	**937**	937
Investment in own shares		**(9)**	(10)	**(9)**	(10)
Other reserves	35	**430**	1,847	**10**	1,444
Total shareholders' equity		**1,646**	3,062	**1,226**	2,659
Minority interest	35	**200**	200		
Total equity		**1,846**	3,262	**1,226**	2,659
Non-current liabilities					
Interest-bearing long-term borrowings	28	**3,074**	2,751	**3,333**	2,971
Employee benefit obligations	36	**191**	330	**182**	322
Provisions for deferred tax	12	**652**	1,075	**592**	1,017
Other provisions	30	**256**	210	**215**	185
Derivative financial instruments	32	**123**	4	**123**	4
Other long-term liabilities	27	**204**	168	**169**	132
Total non-current liabilities		**4,500**	4,538	**4,614**	4,631
Current liabilities					
Current portion of long-term borrowings	28	**689**	423	**689**	421
Trade and other payables	26	**2,796**	2,875	**4,045**	4,036
Derivative financial instruments	32	**471**	20	**471**	20
Current tax payable		**4**	4	**4**	3
Short-term provisions	30	**182**	170	**180**	168
Total current liabilities		**4,142**	3,492	**5,389**	4,648
Total equity and liabilities		**10,488**	11,292	**11,229**	11,938

Willie Walsh
Keith Williams
May 21, 2009

Cash flow statements

For the year ended March 31, 2009

£ million	Note	Group 2009	Group 2008 Restated	Company 2009	Company 2008 Restated
Cash flow from operating activities					
Operating (loss)/profit		**(220)**	878	**(165)**	862
Operating loss from discontinued operations			(2)		
Depreciation, amortisation and impairment		**694**	692	**670**	672
Operating cash flow before working capital changes		**474**	1,568	**505**	1,534
Movement in inventories, trade and other receivables		**32**	96	**(28)**	89
Movement in trade and other payables and provisions		**(136)**	(325)	**(132)**	(276)
Payments in respect of restructuring		**(64)**	(32)	**(62)**	(30)
Cash payment to NAPS pension scheme	36		(610)		(610)
Payment to DOJ in settlement of competition investigation			(149)		(149)
Other non-cash movement		**1**	3	**7**	(32)
Cash generated from operations		**307**	551	**290**	526
Interest paid		**(177)**	(182)	**(163)**	(169)
Taxation		**3**	(66)	**26**	(108)
Net cash flow from operating activities		**133**	303	**153**	249
Cash flow from investing activities					
Purchase of property, plant and equipment	15	**(547)**	(596)	**(528)**	(592)
Purchase of intangible assets	18	**(24)**	(33)	**(24)**	(32)
Purchase of shares in associated undertakings	20		(54)		
Proceeds from sale of other investments		**7**		**7**	
Proceeds from sale of property, plant and equipment		**5**	11	**10**	11
Insurance recoveries for write-off of Boeing 777 aircraft		**12**	51	**12**	51
Purchase of subsidiary (net of cash acquired)		**(34)**		**(144)**	(1,016)
Cash inflow from disposal of subsidiary company			1		
Interest received		**105**	117	**53**	123
Dividends received		**17**	3	**6**	4
Decrease in other current interest-bearing deposits		**202**	458	**356**	1,238
Net cash used in investing activities		**(257)**	(42)	**(252)**	(213)
Cash flows from financing activities					
Proceeds from long-term borrowings		**377**	172	**377**	172
Repayments of borrowings		**(66)**	(68)	**(55)**	(57)
Payment of finance lease liabilities		**(402)**	(356)	**(411)**	(355)
Exercise of share options		**1**	4	**1**	4
Dividends paid		**(58)**		**(58)**	
Distributions made to holders of perpetual securities		**(17)**	(14)		
Net cash used in financing activities		**(165)**	(262)	**(146)**	(236)
Net decrease in cash and cash equivalents		**(289)**	(1)	**(245)**	(200)
Net foreign exchange differences		**8**	(29)	**31**	(29)
Cash and cash equivalents at April 1		**683**	713	**433**	662
Cash and cash equivalents at March 31	25	**402**	683	**219**	433

Statements of changes in equity

For the year ended March 31, 2009

£ million	Issued capital	Share premium	Investment in own shares	Other reserves (note 35)	Total shareholders' equity	Minority interest	Group Total equity
At April 1, 2008	288	937	(10)	1,818	**3,033**	200	**3,233**
Adoption of IFRIC 13				(206)	**(206)**		**(206)**
Adoption of IFRIC 14				235	**235**		**235**
At April 1, 2008 (Restated)	288	937	(10)	1,847	**3,062**	200	**3,262**
Loss for the year				(375)	**(375)**	17	**(358)**
Exchange differences and other movements				38	**38**		**38**
Net movement on cash flow hedges				(988)	**(988)**		**(988)**
Exercise of share options			2	(2)			
Cost of share-based payment				1	**1**		**1**
Purchase of own shares			(1)		**(1)**		**(1)**
Share of other movements in reserves of associates				(26)	**(26)**		**(26)**
Held-to-maturity investments marked-to-market				(5)	**(5)**		**(5)**
Available-for-sale financial assets – gains recycled to the income statement				(4)	**(4)**		**(4)**
Total income and expense for the year			1	(1,361)	**(1,360)**	17	**(1,343)**
Net dividends (note 14)				(56)	**(56)**		**(56)**
Distributions made to holders of perpetual securities						(17)	**(17)**
At March 31, 2009	**288**	**937**	**(9)**	**430**	**1,646**	**200**	**1,846**

For the year ended March 31, 2008

£ million	Issued capital	Share premium	Investment in own shares	Other reserves (note 35)	Total shareholders' equity	Minority interest	Group Total equity
At April 1, 2007	288	933	(10)	1,000	2,211	200	2,411
Adoption of IFRIC 13				(202)	(202)		(202)
Adoption of IFRIC 14				199	199		199
At April 1, 2007 (Restated)	288	933	(10)	997	2,208	200	2,408
Profit for the year				712	712	14	726
Exchange differences and other movements				24	24		24
Net movement on cash flow hedges				119	119		119
Cost of share-based payment				3	3		3
Tax effect of share-based payment				(7)	(7)		(7)
Deferred tax – rate change adjustment				6	6		6
Share of other movements in reserves of associates				(2)	(2)		(2)
Net fair value adjustment on available-for-sale financial assets				(5)	(5)		(5)
Total income and expense for the year				850	850	14	864
Issue of shares		4			4		4
Distributions made to holders of perpetual securities						(14)	(14)
At March 31, 2008 (Restated)	288	937	(10)	1,847	3,062	200	3,262

£ million	Issued capital	Share premium	Investment in own shares	Other reserves (note 35)	Company Total equity
At April 1, 2008	288	937	(10)	1,344	**2,559**
Adoption of IFRIC 13				(135)	**(135)**
Adoption of IFRIC 14				235	**235**
At April 1, 2008 (Restated)	288	937	(10)	1,444	**2,659**
Profit for the year				(389)	**(389)**
Exercise of share options			2	(2)	
Cost of share-based payment				1	**1**
Purchase of own shares			(1)		**(1)**
Net movement on cash flow hedges				(988)	**(988)**
Total income and expense for the year			1	(1,378)	**(1,377)**
Net dividends (note 14)				(56)	**(56)**
At March 31, 2009	**288**	**937**	**(9)**	**10**	**1,226**

For the year ended March 31, 2008

£ million	Issued capital	Share premium	Investment in own shares	Other reserves (note 35)	Company Total equity
At April 1, 2007	288	933	(10)	683	1,894
Adoption of IFRIC 13				(136)	(136)
Adoption of IFRIC 14				199	199
At April 1, 2007 (Restated)	288	933	(10)	746	1,957
Profit for the year				577	577
Cost of share-based payment				3	3
Tax effect of share-based payments				(7)	(7)
Deferred tax – rate change adjustment				6	6
Net movement on cash flow hedges				119	119
Total income and expense for the year				698	698
Issue of shares		4			4
At March 31, 2008 (Restated)	288	937	(10)	1,444	2,659

Notes to the accounts

1 Authorisation of financial statements and compliance with IFRSs

The Group's and Company's financial statements for the year ended March 31, 2009, were authorised for issue by the Board of Directors on May 21, 2009, and the balance sheets were signed on the Board's behalf by Willie Walsh and Keith Williams. British Airways Plc is a public limited company incorporated and domiciled in England and Wales. The Company's ordinary shares are traded on the London Stock Exchange.

The Group has prepared its consolidated financial statements in accordance with International Financial Reporting Standards (IFRSs)* as adopted by the EU. IFRSs as adopted by the EU differ in certain respects from IFRSs as issued by the International Accounting Standards Board (IASB). However, the consolidated financial statements for the periods presented would be no different had the Group applied IFRSs as issued by the IASB. References to 'IFRS' hereafter should be construed as references to IFRSs as adopted by the EU. The principal accounting policies adopted by the Group and by the Company are set out in note 2.

The Company has taken advantage of the exemption provided under Section 230 of the Companies Act 1985 not to publish its individual income statement and related notes.

* For the purposes of these statements, IFRS also includes International Accounting Standards (IASs).

2 Summary of significant accounting policies

Basis of preparation
The basis of preparation and accounting policies set out in this Report and Accounts have been prepared in accordance with the recognition and measurement criteria of IFRS as issued by the IASB and with those of the Standing Interpretations issued by the International Financial Reporting Interpretations Committee (IFRIC) of the IASB.

The financial statements for the prior period include reclassifications that were made to conform to the current period presentation. The amendments have no material impact on the financial statements.

These financial statements have been prepared on a historical cost convention except for certain financial assets and liabilities, including derivative financial instruments and available-for-sale financial assets that are measured at fair value. The carrying value of recognised assets and liabilities that are subject to fair value hedges are adjusted to record changes in the fair values attributable to the risks that are being hedged.

The Group's and Company's financial statements are presented in pounds sterling and all values are rounded to the nearest million pounds (£ million), except where indicated otherwise.

Basis of consolidation
The Group accounts include the accounts of the Company and its subsidiaries, each made up to March 31, together with the attributable share of results and reserves of associates, adjusted where appropriate to conform with the Group's accounting policies.

Subsidiaries are entities controlled by the Group. Control exists when the Group has the power either directly or indirectly to govern the financial and operating policies of the entity so as to obtain benefit from its activities. Subsidiaries are consolidated from the date of their acquisition, which is the date on which the Group obtains control, and continue to be consolidated until the date that such control ceases.

All intra-group account balances, including intra-group profits, have been eliminated in preparing the consolidated financial statements. Minority interests represent the portion of profit or loss and net assets in subsidiaries that are not held by the Group and are presented separately within equity in the consolidated balance sheet.

Revenue
Passenger and cargo revenue is recognised when the transportation service is provided. Passenger tickets net of discounts are recorded as current liabilities in the 'sales in advance of carriage' account until recognised as revenue. Unused tickets are recognised as revenue using estimates regarding the timing of recognition based on the terms and conditions of the ticket and historical trends.

Other revenue is recognised at the time the service is provided. Commission costs are recognised at the same time as the revenue to which they relate and are charged to operating expenditure.

Revenue recognition – mileage programmes
The Group operates two principal loyalty programmes. The airline's frequent flyer programme operates through the airline's 'Executive Club' and allows frequent travellers to accumulate 'BA Miles' mileage credits that entitle them to a choice of various awards, primarily free travel. The fair value attributed to the awarded mileage credits is deferred as a liability and recognised as revenue on redemption of the miles by the participants to whom the miles are issued. The accounting policy for mileage revenue recognition was amended during the year in line with the adoption of IFRIC 13. Refer to 'Impact of new International Financial Reporting Standards' note in this section for impact of the change in policy.

In addition, 'BA Miles' are sold to commercial partners to use in promotional activity. The fair value of the miles sold is deferred and recognised as revenue on redemption of the miles by the participants to whom the miles are issued. The cost of the redemption of the miles is recognised when the miles are redeemed.

The Group also operates the AIRMILES scheme, operated by the Company's wholly-owned subsidiary Air Miles Travel Promotions Limited. The scheme allows companies to purchase miles for use in their own promotional activities. Miles can be redeemed for a range of benefits, including flights on British Airways and other carriers. The fair value of the miles sold is deferred and recognised as revenue on redemption of the miles by the participants to whom the miles are issued. The cost of providing redemption services is recognised when the miles are redeemed.

Segmental reporting
Operating segments are reported in a manner consistent with the internal reporting provided to the chief operating decision-maker. The chief operating decision-maker, who is responsible for resource allocation and assessing performance of the operating segments, has been identified as the Management Board as detailed on page 35. The nature of the operating segments is set out in note 3.

Intangible assets

Intangible assets are held at cost and are either amortised on a straight-line basis over their economic life, or they are deemed to have an indefinite economic life and are not amortised, but tested annually for impairment.

a Goodwill

Where the cost of a business combination exceeds the fair value attributable to the net assets acquired, the resulting goodwill is capitalised and tested for impairment annually and whenever indicators exist that the carrying value may not be recoverable. Any goodwill arising on the acquisition of equity accounted entities is included within the cost of those entities.

Goodwill is allocated to cash-generating units for the purpose of impairment testing.

b Landing rights

Landing rights acquired from other airlines are capitalised at cost or at fair value, less any accumulated impairment losses. Capitalised landing rights based outside the EU are amortised on a straight-line basis over a period not exceeding 20 years. In October 2008 the Group revised the economic life for landing rights acquired within the EU to that of an indefinite economic life, due to regulation changes in the EU regarding the ability to trade landing rights. Landing rights with indefinite economic lives are reviewed annually for impairment. Had the Group not revised the economic life for landing rights, the amortisation charge for the year would have been £5 million greater than is currently reported.

c Software

The cost of purchase or development of computer software that is separable from an item of related hardware is capitalised separately and amortised over a period not exceeding four years on a straight-line basis.

The carrying value of intangibles is reviewed for impairment if events or changes in circumstances indicate the carrying value may not be recoverable.

Property, plant and equipment

Property, plant and equipment is held at cost. The Group has a policy of not revaluing property, plant and equipment. Depreciation is calculated to write off the cost less estimated residual value on a straight-line basis, over the useful life of the asset. Residual values, where applicable, are reviewed annually against prevailing market values for equivalently aged assets and depreciation rates adjusted accordingly on a prospective basis.

The carrying value is reviewed for impairment when events or changes in circumstances indicate the carrying value may not be recoverable and the cumulative impairment losses are shown as a reduction in the carrying value of property, plant and equipment.

a Capitalisation of interest on progress payments

Interest attributed to progress payments, and related exchange movements on foreign currency amounts, made on account of aircraft and other significant assets under construction is capitalised and added to the cost of the asset concerned.

b Fleet

All aircraft are stated at the fair value of the consideration given after taking account of manufacturers' credits. Fleet assets owned, or held on finance lease or hire purchase arrangements, are depreciated at rates calculated to write down the cost to the estimated residual value at the end of their planned operational lives on a straight-line basis.

Cabin interior modifications, including those required for brand changes and relaunches, are depreciated over the lower of five years and the remaining life of the aircraft.

Aircraft and engine spares acquired on the introduction or expansion of a fleet, as well as rotable spares purchased separately, are carried as property, plant and equipment and generally depreciated in line with the fleet to which they relate.

Major overhaul expenditure, including replacement spares and labour costs, is capitalised and amortised over the average expected life between major overhauls. All other replacement spares and other costs relating to maintenance of fleet assets (including maintenance provided under 'pay-as-you-go' contracts) are charged to the income statement on consumption or as incurred respectively.

c Property and equipment

Provision is made for the depreciation of all property and equipment, apart from freehold land, based upon expected useful lives, or in the case of leasehold properties over the duration of the leases if shorter, on a straight-line basis.

d Leased and hire purchase assets

Where assets are financed through finance leases or hire purchase arrangements, under which substantially all the risks and rewards of ownership are transferred to the Group, the assets are treated as if they had been purchased outright. The amount included in the cost of property, plant and equipment represents the aggregate of the capital elements payable during the lease or hire purchase term. The corresponding obligation, reduced by the appropriate proportion of lease or hire purchase payments made, is included in borrowings.

The amount included in the cost of property, plant and equipment is depreciated on the basis described in the preceding paragraphs and the interest element of lease or hire purchase payments made is included in interest payable in the income statement.

Total minimum payments, measured at inception, under all other lease arrangements, known as operating leases, are charged to the income statement in equal annual amounts over the period of the lease. In respect of aircraft, certain operating lease arrangements allow the Group to terminate the leases after a limited initial period (normally 10 years), without further material financial obligations. In certain cases the Group is entitled to extend the initial lease period on predetermined terms; such leases are described as extendable operating leases.

Inventories

Inventories, including aircraft expendables, are valued at the lower of cost and net realisable value. Such cost is determined by the weighted average cost method.

Notes to the accounts continued

2 Summary of significant accounting policies continued

Interests in associates

An associate is an undertaking in which the Group has a long-term equity interest and over which it has the power to exercise significant influence. The Group's interest in the net assets of associates is included in investment in associates in the consolidated balance sheet and its interest in their results is included in the income statement, below operating profit. Certain associates make up their annual audited accounts to dates other than March 31. In the case of Iberia, published results up to the year ended December 31 are included. In other cases, results disclosed by subsequent unaudited management accounts are included. The attributable results of those companies acquired or disposed of during the year are included for the periods of ownership.

Cash and cash equivalents

Cash and cash equivalents includes cash in hand and deposits with any qualifying financial institution repayable on demand or maturing within three months of the date of acquisition and which are subject to an insignificant risk of change in value.

Other current interest-bearing deposits

Other current interest-bearing deposits, principally comprising funds held with banks and other financial institutions, are carried at amortised cost using the effective interest method. Such financial assets are classified as held-to-maturity when the Group has the positive intention and ability to hold to maturity. Gains and losses are recognised in income when the deposits are derecognised or impaired, as well as through the amortisation process.

Trade and other receivables

Trade and other receivables are stated at cost less allowances made for doubtful receivables, which approximates fair value given the short dated nature of these assets. A provision for impairment of trade receivables (allowance for doubtful receivables) is established when there is objective evidence that the Group will not be able to collect all amounts due according to the original terms of the receivable.

Available-for-sale financial assets

Available-for-sale financial assets are those non-derivative financial assets that are not classified as loans and receivables. After initial recognition, available-for-sale financial assets are measured at fair value, with gains or losses recognised as a separate component of equity until the investment is derecognised or until the investment is determined to be impaired, at which time the cumulative gain or loss previously reported in equity is included in the income statement.

The fair value of quoted investments is determined by reference to bid prices at the close of business on the balance sheet date. Where there is no active market, fair value is determined using valuation techniques. Where fair value cannot be reliably estimated, assets are carried at cost.

Employee benefits

a Pension obligations

Employee benefits, including pensions and other post-retirement benefits (principally post-retirement healthcare benefits) are presented in these financial statements in accordance with IAS 19 'Employee Benefits'. The Group has both defined benefit and defined contribution plans. A defined contribution plan is a pension plan under which the Group pays fixed contributions into a separate entity. The Group has no legal or constructive obligations to pay further contributions if the fund does not hold sufficient assets to pay all employees the benefits relating to employee service in the current and prior periods. A defined benefit plan is a pension plan that is not a defined contribution plan. Typically, benefit plans define an amount of pension benefit that an employee will receive on retirement, usually dependent on one or more factors such as age, years of service and compensation.

The asset or liability recognised in the balance sheet in respect of defined benefit pension plans is the present value of the defined benefit obligation at the balance sheet date, less the fair value of plan assets, together with adjustments for unrecognised past service costs. Where plan assets exceed the defined benefit obligation, an asset is recognised to the extent that an economic benefit is available to the Group, in accordance with the terms of the plan and applicable statutory requirements. The benefit should be realisable during the life of the plan or on the settlement of the plan liabilities. Refer to the 'Impact of new International Financial Reporting Standards' note in this section for the impact of the adoption of IFRIC 14.

Past service costs are recognised when the benefit has been given. The financing cost and expected return on plan assets are recognised within financing costs in the periods in which they arise. The accumulated effect of changes in estimates, changes in assumptions and deviations from actuarial assumptions (actuarial gains and losses) that are less than 10 per cent of the higher of pension benefit obligations and pension plan assets at the beginning of the year are not recorded. When the accumulated effect is above 10 per cent the excess amount is recognised on a straight-line basis in the income statement over the estimated average remaining service period.

b Termination benefits

Termination benefits are payable when employment is terminated by the Group before the normal retirement date, or whenever an employee accepts voluntary redundancy in exchange for these benefits. The Group recognises termination benefits when it is demonstrably committed to either terminating the employment of current employees according to a detailed formal plan without possibility of withdrawal, or providing termination benefits as a result of an offer made to encourage voluntary redundancy.

Other employee benefits are recognised when the obligation exists for the future liability.

Share-based payments

The fair value of employee share option plans is measured at the date of grant of the option using an appropriate valuation model. The resulting cost, as adjusted for the expected and actual level of vesting of the options, is charged to income over the period in which the options vest. At each balance sheet date before vesting, the cumulative expense is calculated, representing the extent to which the vesting period has expired and management's best estimate of the achievement or otherwise of non-market conditions, of the number of equity instruments that will ultimately vest.

The movement in the cumulative expense since the previous balance sheet date is recognised in the income statement with a corresponding entry in equity.

Taxation

Current tax assets and liabilities are measured at the amount expected to be recovered from or paid to the taxation authorities, based on tax rates and laws that are enacted or substantively enacted at the balance sheet date.

Deferred income tax is recognised on all temporary differences arising between the tax bases of assets and liabilities and their carrying amounts in the financial statements, with the following exceptions:

• Where the temporary difference arises from the initial recognition of goodwill or of an asset or liability in a transaction that is not a business combination that at the time of the transaction affects neither accounting nor taxable profit or loss;

• In respect of taxable temporary differences associated with investments in subsidiaries or associates, where the timing of the reversal of the temporary differences can be controlled and it is probable that the temporary differences will not reverse in the foreseeable future; and

• Deferred income tax assets are recognised only to the extent that it is probable that taxable profit will be available against which the deductible temporary differences, carried forward tax credits or tax losses can be utilised.

Deferred income tax assets and liabilities are measured on an undiscounted basis at the tax rates that are expected to apply when the related asset is realised or liability is settled, based on tax rates and laws enacted or substantively enacted at the balance sheet date.

Income tax is charged or credited directly to equity if it relates to items that are credited or charged to equity. Otherwise income tax is recognised in the income statement.

Provisions

Provisions are made when an obligation exists for a future liability in respect of a past event and where the amount of the obligation can be reliably estimated. Restructuring provisions are made for direct expenditures of a business reorganisation where the plans are sufficiently detailed and well advanced and where appropriate communication to those affected has been undertaken at the balance sheet date. If the effect is material, expected future cash flows are discounted using a rate that reflects, where appropriate, the risks specific to the liability. Where discounting is used, the increase in the provision due to unwinding the discount is recognised as a finance cost.

Foreign currency translation

Transactions in foreign currencies are initially recorded in the Group's functional currency, sterling, by applying the spot exchange rate ruling at the date of the transaction. Monetary foreign currency balances are translated into sterling at the rates ruling at the balance sheet date. All other profits or losses arising on translation are dealt with through the income statement except where hedge accounting is applied.

The net assets of foreign operations are translated into sterling at the rate of exchange ruling at the balance sheet date. Profits and losses of such operations are translated into sterling at average rates of exchange during the year. The resulting exchange differences are taken directly to a separate component of equity until all or part of the interest is sold, when the relevant portion of the cumulative exchange is recognised in the income statement.

Derivatives and financial instruments

Under IAS 39 'Financial Instruments – Recognition and Measurement', financial instruments are recorded initially at fair value. Subsequent measurement of those instruments at the balance sheet date reflects the designation of the financial instrument. The Group determines the classification at initial recognition and re-evaluates this designation at each year end except for those financial instruments measured at fair value through the income statement.

Other investments (other than interests in associates) are designated as available-for-sale financial assets and are recorded at fair value. Any change in the fair value is reported in equity until the investment is sold, when the cumulative amount recognised in equity is recognised in the income statement. In the case of equity securities classified as available-for-sale investments, a significant or prolonged decline in the fair value of the security below its cost is considered as an indicator that the security is impaired. If any such evidence exists for available-for-sale financial assets, the cumulative gain or loss previously reported in equity is included in the income statement.

Exchange gains and losses on monetary items are taken to the income statement unless the item has been designated and is assessed as an effective hedging instrument in accordance with the requirement of IAS 39. Exchange gains and losses on non-monetary investments are reflected in equity until the investment is sold when the cumulative amount recognised in equity is recognised in the income statement.

Long-term borrowings are recorded at amortised cost. Certain leases contain interest rate swaps that are closely related to the underlying financing and, as such, are not accounted for as an embedded derivative.

Derivative financial instruments, comprising interest rate swap agreements, foreign exchange derivatives and fuel hedging derivatives (including options, swaps and futures), are measured at fair value on the Group balance sheet.

Cash flow hedges

Changes in the fair value of derivative financial instruments are reported through operating income or financing according to the nature of the instrument, unless the derivative financial instrument has been designated as a hedge of a highly probable expected future cash flow. Gains and losses on derivative financial instruments designated as cash flow hedges and assessed as effective for the period, are taken to equity in accordance with the requirements of IAS 39. Gains and losses taken to equity are reflected in the income statement when either the hedged cash flow impacts income or its occurrence ceases to be probable.

Notes to the accounts continued

2 Summary of significant accounting policies continued

Certain loan repayment instalments denominated in US dollars, euro and Japanese yen are designated as cash flow hedges of highly probable future foreign currency revenues. Exchange differences arising from the translation of these loan repayment instalments are taken to equity in accordance with IAS 39 requirements and subsequently reflected in the income statement when either the future revenue impacts income or its occurrence ceases to be highly probable.

Impairment in financial assets
The Group assesses at each balance sheet date whether a financial asset or group of financial assets is impaired.

Investment in own shares
Shares in the Company held by the Group are classified as 'Investments in own shares' and shown as deductions from shareholders' equity at cost. Consideration received for the sale of such shares is also recognised in equity, with any difference between the proceeds from the sale and the original cost being taken to reserves.

No gain or loss is recognised in the income statement on the purchase, sale, issue or cancellation of equity shares.

Derecognition of financial assets and liabilities
A financial asset or liability is generally derecognised when the contract that gives rise to it has been settled, sold, cancelled or has expired.

Where an existing financial liability is replaced by another from the same lender on substantially different terms, or the terms of an existing liability are substantially modified, such an exchange or modification is treated as a derecognition of the original liability and the recognition of a new liability, such that the difference in the respective carrying amounts together with any costs or fees incurred are recognised in the income statement.

Exceptional items
Exceptional items are those that in management's view need to be disclosed by virtue of their size or incidence. Such items are included on the income statement under a caption to which they relate, and are separately disclosed in the notes to the consolidated financial statements.

Discontinued operations
Disposal groups are classified as discontinued operations where they represent a major line of business or geographical area of operations.

Key accounting estimates and judgements
The preparation of financial statements requires management to make judgements, estimates and assumptions that affect the application of policies and reported amounts of assets and liabilities, income and expenses. These estimates and associated assumptions are based on historical experience and various other factors believed to be reasonable under the circumstances. Actual results could differ from these estimates. These underlying

assumptions are reviewed on an ongoing basis. Revisions to accounting estimates are recognised in the period in which the estimate is revised if the revision affects only that period, or in the period of the revision and future periods if these are also affected. The estimates and assumptions that have a significant risk of causing a material adjustment to the carrying amounts of assets and liabilities within the next financial year are discussed below.

a Impairment of non-financial assets
The Group assesses whether there are any indicators of impairment for all non-financial assets at each reporting date. Goodwill is tested for impairment annually and at other times when such indicators exist. The recoverable amounts of cash-generating units have been determined based on value-in-use calculations. These calculations require the use of estimates (note 19).

Other non-financial assets are tested for impairment when there are indicators that the carrying amounts may not be recoverable.

b Share-based payments
The Group measures the cost of equity-settled transactions with employees by reference to the fair value of the equity instruments at the date at which they are granted. Estimating fair value requires determining the most appropriate valuation model for a grant of equity instruments, which is dependent on the terms and conditions of the grant.

This also requires determining the most appropriate inputs to the valuation model including the expected life of the option and volatility and making assumptions about them. The assumptions and models used are disclosed in note 34.

c Pensions and other post-retirement benefits
The cost of defined benefit pension plans and other post-employment medical benefits is determined using actuarial valuations. The actuarial valuation involves making assumptions about discount rates, expected rates of return on assets, future salary increases, mortality rates and future pension increases. Due to the long-term nature of these schemes, such estimates are subject to significant uncertainty and are disclosed in note 36.

d Impairment of available-for-sale financial assets
The Group classifies certain financial assets as available-for-sale and recognises movements in their fair value in shareholders' equity. When the fair value declines, management makes assumptions about the decline in value to determine whether it is an impairment that should be recognised in the income statement. Impairment losses recognised in the income statement are disclosed in note 11.

e Passenger revenue recognition
Passenger revenue is recognised when the transportation is provided. Ticket sales that are not expected to be used for transportation ('unused tickets') are recognised as revenue using estimates regarding the timing of recognition based on the terms and conditions of the ticket and historical trends.

During the current year, changes in estimates regarding the timing of revenue recognition primarily for unused flexible tickets were made, resulting in increased revenue in the current year of £109 million.

During the prior year, changes in estimates regarding the timing of revenue recognition for unused restricted tickets were made, resulting in increased revenue in the prior year of £36 million.

Both the above changes reflect more accurate and timely data obtained through the increased use of electronic tickets.

Impact of new International Financial Reporting Standards

The accounting policies adopted are consistent with those of the previous financial year except as follows:

IFRIC 13 'Customer Loyalty Programmes'; effective for periods beginning on or after July 1, 2008, which addresses accounting by entities that operate or otherwise participate in customer loyalty programmes for their customers. IFRIC 13 applies to sales transactions in which the entities grant their customers award credits that, subject to meeting further qualifying conditions, the customers can redeem in the future for free or discounted goods or services. The interpretation requires that an entity recognises credits that it awards to customers as a separately identifiable component of revenue, which would be deferred at the date of the initial sale. The Group has chosen to 'early adopt' this interpretation, the results for the year ended March 31, 2008, have been restated accordingly. The net impact on the income statement for the year ended March 31, 2008, is a £5 million increase in total revenue, a £2 million increase in expenditure on operations and a £7 million increase to the taxation charge for the year. The net impact to the balance sheet as at March 31, 2008, is a £206 million decrease in shareholders' equity, a £285 million increase in trade and other payables and a £79 million decrease in the provision for deferred tax.

IFRIC 14 'Limit on a Defined Benefit Asset, Minimum Funding Requirements and Their Interaction' is effective for periods beginning on or after January 1, 2008, and provides guidance on assessing the limit in IAS 19 'Employee Benefits', on the amount of the surplus that can be recognised as an asset. It also provides guidance on how the pension asset or liability may be affected by a statutory or contractual minimum-funding requirement. The results for the year ended March 31, 2008, have been restated accordingly. The net impact on the income statement for the year ended March 31, 2008, is a £36 million increase in finance income. The net impact on the balance sheet as at March 31, 2008, is a £235 million increase to shareholders' equity and a £235 million increase in employee benefit assets.

IFRS 8 'Operating Segments' is effective for annual periods beginning on or after January 1, 2009. IFRS 8 requires a 'management approach', under which segment information is presented on the same basis as that used for internal reporting purposes. The Group has chosen to early adopt IFRS 8. All disclosures relating to segment information including all comparative information have been updated to reflect the new requirements. The composition of the Group's business segments has not changed as a result of the adoption of IFRS 8.

New standards, amendments and interpretations not yet effective

The IASB and IFRIC issued the following standards, amendments and interpretations with an effective date after the date of these financial statements which management believe could impact the Group in future periods. Management has not yet determined the potential effect of the amendments.

IFRS 2 (Amendment) 'Share Based Payments – Vesting Conditions and Cancellations'; effective for periods beginning on or after January 1, 2009, clarifies that only service and performance conditions are vesting conditions, and other features of a share-based payment are not vesting conditions. In addition, it specifies that all cancellations, whether by the entity or by other parties, should receive the same accounting treatment. The Group will apply this amendment from April 1, 2009.

IAS 28 (Amendment) 'Investments in Associates'; effective for periods beginning on or after January 1, 2009, subject to EU endorsement, requires an investment in an associate to be treated as a single asset for the purposes of impairment testing. Any impairment loss is not allocated to specific assets included within the investment. The Group will apply this amendment from April 1, 2009.

IAS 36 (Amendment) 'Impairment of Assets'; effective for periods beginning on or after January 1, 2009, subject to EU endorsement, requires that where the fair value less costs to sell is calculated on the basis of discounted cash flows, disclosures equivalent to those for value-in-use calculations should be made. The Group will apply this amendment from April 1, 2009.

IAS 38 (Amendment) 'Intangible Assets'; effective for periods beginning on or after January 1, 2009, subject to EU endorsement, requires that expenditure on advertising and promotional activities be recognised as an expense as soon as the entity has the 'right to access' the goods or has received the services. Advertising and promotional goods now specifically include mail order catalogues. The Group will apply this amendment from April 1, 2009.

IAS 39 (Amendment) 'Financial Instruments: Recognition and Measurement'; effective for periods beginning on or after January 1, 2009, allows the reclassification of derivative instruments into or out of the classification of 'at fair value through profit or loss'. Furthermore, the amendment offers guidance on the designation and documentation of hedges at the segment level and the applicable interest rate on cessation of fair value hedge accounting. The Group will apply this amendment from April 1, 2009.

IFRS 7 (Amendment) 'Financial Instruments: Disclosure'; effective for periods beginning on or after January 1, 2009, subject to EU endorsement. The amendment requires enhanced disclosure about fair value measurements and liquidity risks relating to financial instruments. The Group will apply this amendment from April 1, 2009.

There are no other standards and interpretations in issue but not yet adopted that the directors anticipate will have a material effect on the reported income or net assets of the Group.

Notes to the accounts continued

3 Segment information

a Business segments

The Group's network passenger and cargo operations are managed as a single business unit. The Management Board makes resource allocation decisions based on route profitability, which considers aircraft type and route economics, with only limited reference to the strength of the cargo business. The objective in making resource allocation decisions is to optimise consolidated financial results. While the operations of OpenSkies and CityFlyer are considered to be separate operating segments, their activities are considered to be sufficiently similar in nature to aggregate the two segments and report them together with the network passenger and cargo operations. Therefore, based on the way the Group treats the network passenger and cargo operations, and the manner in which resource allocation decisions are made, the Group has only one reportable operating segment for financial reporting purposes, reported as the 'airline business'.

Financial results from other operating segments are below the quantitative threshold for determining reportable operating segments and consist primarily of Air Miles Travel Promotions Limited, British Airways Holidays Limited and Speedbird Insurance Company Limited.

For the year ended March 31, 2009

£ million	Airline business	All other segments	Unallocated	Total
Revenue				
Sales to external customers	8,840	152		**8,992**
Inter-segment sales	18			**18**
Segment revenue	8,858	152		**9,010**
Segment result	(240)	20		**(220)**
Other non-operating expense	(30)			**(30)**
(Loss)/profit before tax and finance costs	(270)	20		**(250)**
Net finance costs	78	(59)	(182)	**(163)**
Profit on sale of assets	8			**8**
Share of associates' profit	4			**4**
Tax			43	**43**
Loss after tax	(180)	(39)	(139)	**(358)**
Assets and liabilities				
Segment assets	10,164	115		**10,279**
Investment in associates	209			**209**
Total assets	10,373	115		**10,488**
Segment liabilities	3,842	381		**4,223**
Unallocated liabilities*			4,419	**4,419**
Total liabilities	3,842	381	4,419	**8,642**
Other segment information				
Property, plant and equipment – additions (note 15d)	643	2		**645**
Intangible assets – additions (excluding L'Avion – note 18c)	21			**21**
Purchase of subsidiary (net of cash acquired – note 6c)	34			**34**
Depreciation, amortisation and impairment (note 4a)	693	1		**694**
Impairment of available-for-sale financial asset – Flybe (note 21)	13			**13**
Exceptional items (note 4b):				
Restructuring	78			**78**
Unused tickets (note 2)	(109)			**(109)**
Impairment of OpenSkies goodwill	5			**5**

* Unallocated liabilities primarily include deferred taxes of £652 million and borrowings of £3,763 million which are managed on a Group basis.

3 Segment information continued

For the year ended March 31, 2008, Restated

£ million	Airline business	All other segments	Unallocated	Total	Discontinued operations*	Total
			Continuing operations			
Revenue						
Sales to external customers	8,570	188		8,758		8,758
Inter-segment sales	31			31		31
Segment revenue	8,601	188		8,789		8,789
Segment result	857	21		878	(2)	876
Other non-operating income	9			9		9
Profit/(loss) before tax and finance costs	866	21		887	(2)	885
Net finance income/(costs)	181	(11)	(175)	(5)		(5)
Profit/(loss) on sale of assets	16	(2)		14		14
Share of associates' profit	26			26		26
Tax			(194)	(194)		(194)
Profit/(loss) after tax	1,089	8	(369)	728	(2)	726
Assets and liabilities						
Segment assets	10,966	99		11,065		11,065
Investment in associates	227			227		227
Total assets	11,193	99		11,292		11,292
Segment liabilities	3,479	298		3,777		3,777
Unallocated liabilities**			4,253	4,253		4,253
Total liabilities	3,479	298	4,253	8,030		8,030
Other segment information						
Property, plant and equipment – additions (note 15d)	636	1		637		637
Intangible assets – additions (note 18c)	40			40		40
Depreciation, amortisation and impairment (note 4a)	690	2		692		692
Impairment of available-for-sale financial asset – Flybe (note 21)	6			6		6
Exceptional items (note 4b):						
Restructuring	1			1		1
Unused tickets (note 2)	(36)			(36)		(36)

* As disclosed in note 5, BA Connect, which previously comprised the majority of the 'Regional airline business' segment, was disposed of in March 2007.

** Unallocated liabilities primarily include deferred taxes of £1,075 million and borrowings of £3,174 million which are managed on a Group basis.

b Geographical segments – by area of original sale

£ million	2009	2008 Restated
		Group
Europe:	**5,617**	*5,581*
UK	**4,197**	*4,362*
Continental Europe	**1,420**	*1,219*
The Americas	**1,719**	*1,697*
Africa, Middle East and Indian sub-continent	**875**	*821*
Far East and Australasia	**781**	*659*
Revenue	**8,992**	*8,758*

Total of non-current assets excluding available-for-sale financial assets, employee benefit assets, derivative financial instruments and prepayments and accrued income located in the UK is £7,337 million (2008: £7,336 million) and the total of these non-current assets located in other countries is £372 million (2008: £375 million).

Notes to the accounts continued

---

4 Operating (loss)/profit

a Operating (loss)/profit is arrived at after charging/(crediting)
Depreciation, amortisation and impairment of fixed assets:

£ million	Group 2009	2008
Owned assets	381	362
Finance leased aircraft	131	119
Hire purchased aircraft	110	118
Other leasehold interests	50	62
Impairment charge on goodwill	5	
Amortisation of intangible assets	17	31
Total depreciation, amortisation and impairment	**694**	*692*

Operating lease costs:

£ million	Group 2009	2008
Minimum lease rentals – aircraft	82	80
– property	106	119
Sub-lease rentals received	(10)	(16)
Net onerous lease provision release	(1)	(9)
	177	174

Cost of inventories:

£ million	Group 2009	2008
Cost of inventories recognised as an expense, mainly fuel and other	2,078	2,128
Includes: write-down of inventories to net realisable value	2	5

b Exceptional items

£ million	Group 2009	2008
Recognised in operating (loss)/profit:		
Employee costs – restructuring (note 8)	78	1
Unused tickets (note 2)	(109)	(36)
Impairment of goodwill (note 19)	5	
	(26)	(35)

During the year the Group incurred restructuring costs in relation to the reduction in employees announced during the year.

5 Discontinued operations

On November 3, 2006, the Group announced that it had reached an agreement in principle to sell the regional operation of its subsidiary airline BA Connect to the Flybe Group Limited (Flybe). The acquisition of BA Connect by Flybe excluded the London City airport routes and the BA Connect-operated service from Manchester to New York. The disposal was completed on March 5, 2007. The business sold comprised the majority of the 'Regional airline business' segment as disclosed in the financial statements for the year ended March 31, 2006.

The £2 million loss from discontinued operations for the year ended March 31, 2008, is attributed to the resolution of uncertainties that arose from the terms of the disposal transaction, primarily adjustments to the restructuring provision previously reported within discontinued operations.

5 Discontinued operations continued

Reconciliation of the tax charge relating to discontinued operations

The tax credit for the year on the loss from discontinued operations is less than the notional tax credit on those losses calculated at the UK corporation tax rate of 28 per cent (2008: 30 per cent). The differences are explained below:

	Group	
£ million	**2009**	*2008*
Accounting loss before income tax from discontinued operations	–	*(2)*
Accounting loss multiplied by standard rate of corporation tax in the UK of 28 per cent (2008: 30 per cent)		*(1)*
Effects of:		
Non-deductible expenses		*1*
Total tax credit on discontinued operations for the year	–	–

6 Business combinations

In July 2008, the Group subsidiary, OpenSkies, acquired the entire issued share capital of the French airline L'Avion, for a cash consideration of €68 million (£54 million). Additional consideration of €10 million (£9 million, retranslated as at March 31, 2009) is payable in July 2009, based on the terms of the Purchase Agreement. The retranslation difference of £1 million has been charged to currency differences in the income statement. L'Avion was a privately owned business class airline that operated two Boeing 757s between Paris (Orly) and New York (Newark) airports. The operations of OpenSkies and L'Avion were merged in April 2009.

Details of the fair value of the net assets acquired and goodwill arising on the acquisition of L'Avion are as follows:

a Purchase consideration

£ million	
Cash consideration	54
Transaction costs directly associated with the acquisition	2
Contingent consideration	8
Total purchase consideration	**64**
Fair value of net assets acquired	59
Goodwill arising on acquisition	**5**

The goodwill is attributable to the workforce of the acquired business and synergies expected to arise after OpenSkies' acquisition of L'Avion. As a result of the goodwill impairment review performed as at March 31, 2009, goodwill associated with the acquisition was considered to be impaired, and accordingly an impairment charge of £5 million has been recognised in the consolidated income statement (note 19).

b The assets and liabilities arising from the acquisition are as follows

£ million	Carrying amount	Fair value
Property, plant and equipment	6	6
Landing rights		35
Prepayments and accrued income	3	3
Other current assets	4	4
Cash and cash equivalents	22	22
Trade and other payables	(11)	(11)
Net assets acquired	**24**	**59**

c Net cash flow in respect of the acquisition comprises

£ million	
Cash consideration	54
Transaction costs directly associated with the acquisition	2
Cash and cash equivalents in subsidiary acquired	(22)
Cash outflow on acquisition included in the cash flow statement	**34**

Notes to the accounts continued

6 Business combinations continued

d Contribution to Group results

The acquired airline contributed revenues of £23 million and a net loss of £7 million to the Group for the period from the date of acquisition to March 31, 2009. If the acquisition occurred on April 1, 2008, Group revenues would have been £9,012 million and loss after tax would have been £363 million. These amounts have been calculated using the Group's accounting policies and by adjusting the results of the airline to reflect the additional amortisation that would have been charged assuming the fair value adjustment to intangible assets had been applied from April 1, 2008, together with the consequential tax effects. The amounts calculated are not affected by the Group's decision to change the economic life of landing rights acquired within the EU to that of an indefinite economic life as this prospective change took place in the post-acquisition period, on September 30, 2008 (note 18).

7 Auditor's remuneration

£'000	Group 2009	Group 2008	Company 2009	Company 2008
Group auditor				
Fees payable to the Group's auditor for the audit of the Group's accounts	1,882	1,985	1,882	1,985
Audit of the Group's subsidiaries pursuant to legislation	352	271		
Other services pursuant to legislation	59	57	43	43
Other services relating to taxation	360	308	360	308
Services relating to corporate finance transactions	1,654	286	1,654	286
All other services	10	113	6	113
	4,317	3,020	3,945	2,735

Of the Group fees, £3,933,000 relates to the UK (2008: £2,788,000) and £384,000 relates to overseas (2008: £232,000).

Of the Company fees, £3,585,000 relates to the UK (2008: £2,527,000) and £360,000 relates to overseas (2008: £208,000).

The audit fees payable to Ernst & Young LLP are approved by the Audit Committee having been reviewed in the context of other companies for cost effectiveness.

The Committee also reviews and approves the nature and extent of non-audit services to ensure that independence is maintained.

8 Employee costs and numbers

a Staff costs

The average number of persons employed during the year was as follows:

Number	Group 2009	Group 2008	Company 2009	Company 2008
UK	39,137	39,193	37,041	36,962
Overseas	5,850	5,947	5,057	5,159
	44,987	45,140	42,098	42,121

£ million	Group 2009	Group 2008	Company 2009	Company 2008
Wages and salaries	1,466	1,432	1,389	1,361
Social security costs	158	150	147	142
Costs related to pension scheme benefits	175	216	169	211
Other post-retirement benefit costs	4	4	3	3
Other employee costs	390	363	372	352
Total employee costs excluding restructuring	2,193	2,165	2,080	2,069
Restructuring	78	1	78	1
Total employee costs	2,271	2,166	2,158	2,070
Employee costs relating to continuing operations	2,271	2,166	2,158	2,072
Employee income relating to discontinued operations				(2)

8 Employee costs and numbers continued

In addition, included in 'Wages and salaries' is a total expense for share-based payments of £1 million (2008: £3 million) that arises from transactions accounted for as equity-settled share-based payment transactions.

Other employee costs include allowances and accommodation for crew.

b Directors' emoluments

£'000	Group	
	2009	*2008*
Fees	**748**	*732*
Salary and benefits	**1,189**	*1,123*
Performance-related bonuses		*134*
	1,937	*1,989*

During the year, one director accrued benefits under a defined benefit pension scheme and one director accrued benefits under a defined contribution pension scheme.

The report of the Remuneration Committee discloses full details of directors' emoluments and can be found on pages 65 to 73.

9 Finance costs and income

£ million	Group	
	2009	*2008*
a Finance costs		
On bank loans*	**34**	*36*
On finance leases	**75**	*70*
On hire purchase arrangements	**22**	*31*
On other loans*	**38**	*39*
Interest expense	**169**	*176*
Unwinding of discounting on provisions**	**12**	*10*
Capitalised interest	**(4)**	*(15)*
Change in fair value of cross currency swaps	**5**	*4*
	182	*175*

* Total interest expense for financial liabilities not at fair value through the income statement is £72 million (2008: £75 million).

** Unwinding of discount on the competition investigation provision and restoration and handback provisions (note 30).

Interest costs on progress payments are capitalised at a rate based on London Interbank Offered Rate (LIBOR) plus 0.5 per cent to reflect the average cost of borrowing to the Group unless specific borrowings are used to meet the payments in which case the actual rate is used.

£ million	Group	
	2009	*2008*
b Finance income		
Bank interest receivable (total interest income for financial assets not at fair value through the income statement)	**95**	*111*
	95	*111*
c Financing income and expense relating to pensions		
Net financing (expense)/income relating to pensions	**(34)**	*70*
Amortisation of actuarial gains on pensions	**17**	
	(17)	*70*
d Retranslation charges on currency borrowings	**59**	*11*

Notes to the accounts continued

10 Profit on sale of property, plant and equipment and investments

		Group
£ million	**2009**	*2008*
Net profit on sale of property, plant and equipment	**2**	*12*
Write-off of Boeing 777 aircraft		*(60)*
Insurance recoveries on Boeing 777 aircraft		*63*
Net profit/(loss) on the disposal of investments	**6**	*(1)*
	8	*14*

11 Net charge relating to available-for-sale financial assets

		Group
£ million	**2009**	*2008*
Income from available-for-sale financial assets*	**3**	*5*
Amounts written off investments**	**(15)**	*(8)*
	(12)	*(3)*

* Includes £3 million (2008: £4 million) attributable to interest earned on loans to The Airline Group Limited, an available-for-sale financial asset.

** Includes £13 million (2008: £6 million) attributable to impairment of the Group's investment in Flybe (note 21) and £2 million (2008: £2 million) impairment of its investment in Inter-Capital and Regional Rail Ltd, a loss making entity that manages Eurostar (UK) Limited until 2010.

12 Tax

a Tax on (loss)/profit on ordinary activities
Tax (credit)/charge in the income statement

		Group
	2009	*2008*
£ million		*Restated*
Current income tax		
UK corporation tax	**(37)**	*72*
Relief for foreign tax paid	**(3)**	*(2)*
Advance corporation tax reversal	**26**	*(47)*
UK tax	**(14)**	*23*
Foreign tax	**2**	*1*
Adjustments in respect of prior years – UK corporation tax	**(18)**	*(8)*
Adjustments in respect of prior years – advance corporation tax	**21**	
Total current income tax (credit)/charge	**(9)**	*16*
Deferred tax		
Effect of the change in the rate of UK corporation tax on opening balances		*(70)*
Property, plant and equipment related temporary differences	**(65)**	*(57)*
Effect of abolition of industrial buildings allowances	**79**	
Pensions	**41**	*237*
Unremitted earnings of associate companies	**11**	*5*
Advance corporation tax	**(26)**	*47*
Tax losses carried forward	**(56)**	
Exchange differences	**(3)**	
Share option deductions written back	**1**	*5*
Other temporary differences	**(3)**	*(1)*
Adjustments in respect of prior years – deferred tax	**8**	*12*
Adjustments in respect of prior years – advance corporation tax	**(21)**	
Total deferred tax (credit)/charge	**(34)**	*178*
Total tax (credit)/charge in the income statement	**(43)**	*194*

12 Tax continued

Tax (credit)/charge directly to equity

£ million	2009	Group 2008
Deferred tax		
Deferred tax on net movement on revaluation of cash flow hedges	**(251)**	67
Deferred tax on foreign exchange in reserves	**(133)**	(21)
Deferred tax on share options in issue		7
Corporation tax rate change for items credited directly to reserves		(6)
Deferred tax on Iberia unremitted earnings	**(6)**	
Tax (credit)/charge taken directly to equity	**(390)**	47

b Reconciliation of the total tax (credit)/charge

The tax (credit)/charge for the year on the (loss)/profit from continuing operations is less than the notional tax credit on those (losses)/profits calculated at the UK corporation tax rate of 28 per cent (2008: 30 per cent). The differences are explained below:

£ million	2009	Group 2008 Restated
Accounting (loss)/profit before tax	**(401)**	922
Accounting (loss)/profit multiplied by standard rate of corporation tax in the UK of 28 per cent (2008: 30 per cent)	**(112)**	277
Effects of:		
Non-deductible expenses	**7**	7
Foreign exchange and unwind of discount on competition investigation provisions	**9**	2
Share option deductions written back	**1**	5
Deductions available on aircraft refinancing surpluses	**(4)**	(5)
Disposals and write-down of investments	**3**	(1)
Tax on associates' profits and dividends		(5)
Tax on subsidiary unremitted earnings	**(2)**	
Overseas tax in relation to branches	**(1)**	
Euro preferred securities accounted for as minority interest	**(5)**	(4)
Tax on revaluation of intra-group foreign currency loans	**(4)**	(5)
Effect of pension fund accounting under IFRIC 14	**(5)**	(11)
Effect of abolition of industrial buildings allowances	**79**	
Unrecognised deferred tax asset on pension deficit	**2**	
Other permanent differences		(2)
Current year losses not recognised	**2**	
Adjustments in respect of prior years	**(10)**	4
Rate benefit of trading loss carry back	**(3)**	
Effect of UK corporation tax rate reduction from 30 per cent to 28 per cent		(68)
Tax (credit)/charge in the income statement (note 12a)	**(43)**	194

c Deferred tax

The deferred tax included in the balance sheet is as follows:

£ million	Group 2009	2008 Restated	Company 2009	2008 Restated
Fixed asset related temporary differences	**1,121**	1,105	**1,034**	1,019
Pensions related temporary differences	**(16)**	(56)	**(13)**	(54)
Exchange differences on funding liabilities	**(69)**	68	**(69)**	67
Advance corporation tax	**(94)**	(47)	**(94)**	(47)
Tax losses carried forward arising from the implementation of IFRIC 13	**(52)**		**(52)**	
Tax losses carried forward arising from loss per income statement	**(57)**	(1)	**(57)**	
Subsidiary and associate unremitted earnings	**27**	18	**17**	4
Fair value (losses)/profits recognised on cash flow hedges	**(174)**	78	**(174)**	78
Share options related temporary differences	**(1)**	(3)	**(1)**	(3)
Deferred revenue in relation to loyalty reward programmes	**(35)**	(93)		(52)
Other temporary differences	**2**	6	**1**	5
At March 31	**652**	1,075	**592**	1,017

Notes to the accounts continued

12 Tax continued

c Deferred tax continued

Movement in provision

£ million	Group 2009	Group 2008 Restated	Company 2009	Company 2008 Restated
Balance at April 1	**1,154**	930	**1,069**	855
Restatement of balances arising from implementation of IFRIC 13	**(79)**	(86)	**(52)**	(58)
Restated balance at April 1	**1,075**	844	**1,017**	797
Deferred tax (credit)/charge relating to profit (note 12a)	**(34)**	178	**(41)**	173
Deferred tax (credit)/charge taken directly in reserves (note 12a)	**(390)**	47	**(384)**	47
Deferred tax arising on acquisition of equity in Iberia		3		
Revaluation of foreign currency balances and other movements	**1**	3		
At March 31	**652**	1,075	**592**	1,017

d Other taxes

The Group also contributed tax revenues through payment of transaction and payroll related taxes. A breakdown of these other taxes payable during 2009 was as follows:

£ million	Group 2009	Group 2008
UK Air Passenger Duty	**319**	365
Other ticket taxes	**155**	144
Payroll related taxes	**158**	150
Total	**632**	659

The UK Government has proposed substantial increases in the rates of Air Passenger Duty from November 1, 2009, and further increases are proposed to take effect from November 1, 2010.

e Factors that may affect future tax charges

The Group has UK capital losses carried forward of £141 million (2008: £158 million). These losses are available for offset against future UK chargeable gains. No deferred tax asset has been recognised in respect of these capital losses as no further utilisation is currently anticipated. The Group has deferred taxation arising on chargeable gains by roll-over and hold-over relief claims that have reduced the tax basis of fixed assets by £69 million (2008: £69 million). No deferred tax liability has been recognised in respect of the crystallisation of these chargeable gains as they could be offset against the UK capital losses carried forward. The Group also has unrecognised temporary differences representing future capital losses of £281 million (2008: £nil) if properties which previously qualified for industrial buildings allowances were realised at their residual value.

The Group has overseas net operating losses of £8 million (2008: £nil) that are carried forward for offset against suitable future taxable profits. No deferred tax asset has been recognised in respect of these losses as their utilisation is not currently anticipated.

The Group has an unrecognised temporary difference of £8 million (2008: £nil) arising from contributions to pension funds that are not expected to create a reduction in the Group's future tax liabilities.

Deferred tax has been provided on the Group's share of the unremitted earnings of associate companies and on the unremitted earnings of subsidiary companies that are expected to be paid as dividends to the parent company within the foreseeable future. Were the retained earnings of other overseas subsidiary companies to be remitted to the parent company as a dividend, the temporary differences upon which the Group has not provided for deferred tax are £26 million (2008: £19 million).

13 Earnings per share

	2009 £ million	2008 £ million Restated	2009 Pence	2008 Pence Restated
		Profit		Earnings per share
(Loss)/profit for the year attributable to shareholders and basic earnings per share	(375)	712	(32.6)	61.9
Represented by:				
Continuing operations	(375)	714	(32.6)	62.1
Discontinued operations		(2)		(0.2)
Diluted (loss)/profit for the year attributable to shareholders and diluted earnings per share	(375)	712	(32.6)	61.4
Represented by:				
Continuing operations	(375)	714	(32.6)	61.6
Discontinued operations		(2)		(0.2)
Weighted average number of shares for basic EPS ('000)			1,151,230	1,150,537
Dilutive potential ordinary shares:				
Employee share options ('000)			2,702	8,093
Weighted average number of shares for diluted EPS ('000)			1,153,932	1,158,630

Basic earnings per share are calculated on a weighted average number of ordinary shares in issue after deducting shares held for the purposes of Employee Share Ownership Plans including the Long Term Incentive Plan.

The Group has granted additional options over shares to employees that were not dilutive during the year but which may be dilutive in the future. Details of the Group's share options can be found in note 34.

14 Dividends

The directors recommended not to declare a dividend for the year ended March 31, 2009. The Company declared a dividend of 5 pence per share (totalling £58 million) for the year ended March 31, 2008. The dividend was paid in July 2008 and was accounted for as a reduction in shareholders' equity for the year ended March 31, 2009.

The Group reversed £2 million of previously declared dividends, relating to historic unclaimed dividends that are no longer expected to be collected.

Equity dividends

£ million	2009	2008
		Group
Prior year 5 pence dividend per ordinary share paid during the year	58	
Unclaimed dividends	(2)	
	56	–

Notes to the accounts continued

15 Property, plant and equipment

a Group

£ million	Fleet	Property	Equipment	Group total
Cost				
Balance at April 1, 2007	11,223	1,398	753	13,374
Additions (note 15d)	428	122	87	637
Disposals	(262)	(12)	(36)	(310)
Balance at March 31, 2008	11,389	1,508	804	13,701
Additions (note 15d)	584	54	13	651
Disposals	(118)	(45)	(30)	(193)
Reclassifications	(19)	1	(1)	(19)
Exchange movements		(2)	(3)	(5)
At March 31, 2009	**11,836**	**1,516**	**783**	**14,135**
Depreciation and impairment				
Balance at April 1, 2007	5,070	466	481	6,017
Charge for the year	542	72	47	661
Disposals	(199)	(7)	(34)	(240)
Balance at March 31, 2008	5,413	531	494	6,438
Charge for the year	561	59	52	672
Disposals	(116)	(45)	(29)	(190)
Reclassifications	(18)			(18)
At March 31, 2009	**5,840**	**545**	**517**	**6,902**
Net book amounts				
March 31, 2009	**5,996**	**971**	**266**	**7,233**
March 31, 2008	5,976	977	310	7,263
Analysis at March 31, 2009				
Owned	2,535	950	260	**3,745**
Finance leased	2,004			**2,004**
Hire purchase arrangements	1,342			**1,342**
Progress payments	85	21	6	**112**
Assets not in current use*	30			**30**
	5,996	**971**	**266**	**7,233**
Analysis at March 31, 2008				
Owned	2,572	952	300	3,824
Finance leased	1,728			1,728
Hire purchase arrangements	1,549			1,549
Progress payments	127	25	10	162
	5,976	977	310	7,263

	Group	
£ million	**2009**	*2008*
The net book amount of property comprises:		
Freehold	**267**	274
Long leasehold improvements	**260**	256
Short leasehold improvements**	**444**	447
At March 31	**971**	977

*   During the year, two Boeing 747-400 aircraft were temporarily stood down. The net book value of the two aircraft as at March 31, 2009, amounts to £30 million. These aircraft are expected to return to the operating fleet and, as such, the Group continues to depreciate the aircraft.

** Short leasehold improvements relate to leasehold interests with a duration of less than 50 years.

15 Property, plant and equipment continued

As at March 31, 2009, bank and other loans of the Group are secured on fleet assets with a cost of £624 million (2008: £477 million) and letters of credit of £330 million in favour of the British Airways Pension Trustees are secured on certain aircraft (2008: £330 million).

Included in the cost of tangible assets for the Group is £349 million (2008: £345 million) of capitalised interest.

Property, plant and equipment with a net book value of £3 million was disposed of by the Group during the year ended March 31, 2009 (2008: £70 million) resulting in a net gain on disposal of £2 million (2008: £15 million).

b Company

£ million	Fleet	Property	Equipment	Company total
Cost				
Balance at April 1, 2007	*10,875*	*1,310*	*688*	*12,873*
Additions	*427*	*121*	*81*	*629*
Disposals	*(260)*	*(10)*	*(33)*	*(303)*
Balance at March 31, 2008	*11,042*	*1,421*	*736*	*13,199*
Additions	559	54	8	**621**
Disposals	(118)	(45)	(30)	**(193)**
Reclassifications	(19)			**(19)**
At March 31, 2009	**11,464**	**1,430**	**714**	**13,608**
Depreciation and impairment				
Balance at April 1, 2007	*4,918*	*434*	*422*	*5,774*
Charge for the year	*527*	*70*	*45*	*642*
Disposals	*(197)*	*(7)*	*(32)*	*(236)*
Balance at March 31, 2008	*5,248*	*497*	*435*	*6,180*
Charge for the year	545	58	50	**653**
Disposals	(116)	(45)	(29)	**(190)**
Reclassifications	(18)			**(18)**
At March 31, 2009	**5,659**	**510**	**456**	**6,625**
Net book amounts				
March 31, 2009	**5,805**	**920**	**258**	**6,983**
March 31, 2008	*5,794*	*924*	*301*	*7,019*
Analysis at March 31, 2009				
Owned	2,356	899	252	**3,507**
Finance leased	2,004			**2,004**
Hire purchase arrangements	1,342			**1,342**
Progress payments	73	21	6	**100**
Assets not in current use*	30			**30**
	5,805	**920**	**258**	**6,983**
Analysis at March 31, 2008				
Owned	*2,394*	*899*	*292*	*3,585*
Finance leased	*1,728*			*1,728*
Hire purchase arrangements	*1,549*			*1,549*
Progress payments	*123*	*25*	*9*	*157*
	5,794	*924*	*301*	*7,019*

Notes to the accounts continued

15 Property, plant and equipment continued

£ million	Company total	
	2009	*2008*
The net book amount of property comprises:		
Freehold	**220**	*226*
Long leasehold improvements	**256**	*256*
Short leasehold improvements**	**444**	*442*
At March 31	**920**	*924*

* During the year, two Boeing 747-400 aircraft were temporarily stood down. The net book value of the two aircraft as at March 31, 2009, amounts to £30 million. These aircraft are expected to return to the operating fleet and, as such, the Company continues to depreciate the aircraft.

** Short leasehold improvements relate to leasehold interests with a duration of less than 50 years.

As at March 31, 2009, bank and other loans of the Company are secured on fleet assets with a cost of £551 million (2008: £404 million).

Included in the cost of tangible assets for the Company is £347 million (2008: £343 million) of capitalised interest.

Property, plant and equipment with a net book value of £3 million was disposed of by the Company during the year ended March 31, 2009 (2008: £67 million) resulting in a net gain on disposal of £2 million (2008: £15 million).

c Depreciation

Fleet is generally depreciated over periods ranging from 18 to 25 years after making allowance for estimated residual values. Effective annual depreciation rates resulting from those methods are shown in the following table:

Per cent	Group	
	2009	*2008*
Boeing 747-400 and 777-200	**3.7**	*3.7*
Boeing 767-300	**4.8**	*4.8*
Boeing 757-200	**4.4**	*4.4*
Boeing 737-400	**4.8**	*4.9*
Airbus A319, A320, A321	**4.9**	*4.9*

For engines maintained under 'pay-as-you-go' contracts, the depreciation lives and residual values are the same as the aircraft to which the engines relate. For all other engines, the engine core is depreciated to residual value over the average remaining life of the related fleet.

Major overhaul expenditure is depreciated over periods ranging from 54 to 78 months, according to engine type. During the prior year, the Group changed the depreciation period for the RB211 engine, used on Boeing 747 and 767 fleets, from 54 months to 78 months. The change resulted in a £33 million decrease in the annual depreciation charge for this engine type.

The economic lives of the Boeing 737-400 aircraft were reviewed and extended during the year in accordance with the planned usage of the aircraft. The net impact to the income statement is a £1 million decrease to the depreciation charge for the year ended March 31, 2009.

Property, with the exception of freehold land, is depreciated over its expected useful life subject to a maximum of 50 years. Equipment is depreciated over periods ranging from four to 20 years, according to the type of equipment.

d Analysis of Group property, plant and equipment additions

£ million	Fleet	Property	Equipment	Group total	
				2009	*2008*
Cash paid	438	66	43	**547**	*596*
Capitalised interest	4			**4**	*15*
Acquired through business combinations	6			**6**	
Reclassification of operating leases to finance leases	122			**122**	
Accrual movements	14	(12)	(30)	**(28)**	*26*
At March 31	**584**	**54**	**13**	**651**	*637*

During the year ended March 31, 2009, the Group acquired property, plant and equipment with a cost of £651 million (2008: £637 million), including £6 million of additions arising from the acquisition of L'Avion (note 6). Included in the acquisition of these assets is £122 million relating to the reclassification of 10 Airbus A319 aircraft from operating leases to finance leases, where the Group waived the right to return the aircraft to the lessor.

16 Capital expenditure commitments

Capital expenditure authorised and contracted for but not provided for in the accounts amounts to £4,805 million for the Group commitments (2008: £3,306 million) and £4,617 million for the Company commitments (2008: £3,301 million). The majority of capital expenditure commitments are denominated in US dollars, as such the commitments are subject to exchange movements.

The outstanding commitments include £4,793 million for the acquisition of five Boeing 777s (from 2009 to 2012), 24 Boeing 787s (from 2012 to 2016), two Airbus A318s (2009), 10 Airbus A320s (from 2009 to 2012), 12 Airbus A380s (from 2012 to 2014) and 11 Embraer E-Jets (from 2009 to 2010).

17 Assets held for sale

Assets held for sale comprise non-current assets and disposal groups that are held for sale rather than for continuing use within the business. The carrying value represents the estimated sale proceeds less costs to sell.

During the year ended March 31, 2009, no assets were sold (2008: £3 million aircraft and £5 million property).

At March 31, 2009, there were no assets held for sale (2008: £nil).

In April 2009, the Group agreed to the sale of 11 Boeing 757 aircraft, these aircraft will exit the business over a two-year period beginning June 2010. The economic lives and residual values of the aircraft were adjusted in April 2009 to reflect the terms of the sale agreement.

18 Intangible assets

a Group

£ million	Goodwill	Landing rights	Software	Group total
Cost				
Balance at April 1, 2007	40	175	143	358
Additions		28	12	40
Disposals			(2)	(2)
Balance at March 31, 2008	40	203	153	396
Additions	5	44	12	**61**
Disposals			(15)	**(15)**
Impairment (note 19)	(5)			**(5)**
Exchange movements*		7		**7**
At March 31, 2009	40	254	150	444
Amortisation				
Balance at April 1, 2007	–	36	110	146
Disposals			(2)	(2)
Charge for the year		8	23	31
Balance at March 31, 2008	–	44	131	175
Disposals			(15)	**(15)**
Charge for the year		5	12	**17**
At March 31, 2009	–	49	128	177
Net book amounts				
March 31, 2009	40	205	22	267
March 31, 2008	40	159	22	221

* Goodwill and landing rights with a carrying value of £5 million and £42 million respectively are associated with the acquisition of L'Avion, an airline operating services between Paris (Orly) and New York (Newark) airports. The functional currency of L'Avion is euros, as such, these assets are subject to exchange movements.

Notes to the accounts continued

---

18 Intangible assets continued

b Company

£ million	Landing rights	Software	Company total
Cost			
Balance at April 1, 2007	175	143	318
Additions	28	11	39
Disposals		(1)	(1)
Balance at March 31, 2008	203	153	356
Additions	9	12	21
Disposals		(15)	(15)
At March 31, 2009	212	150	362
Amortisation			
Balance at April 1, 2007	36	109	145
Charge for the year	8	23	31
Disposals		(1)	(1)
Balance at March 31, 2008	44	131	175
Charge for the year	5	12	17
Disposals		(15)	(15)
At March 31, 2009	49	128	177
Net book amounts			
March 31, 2009	163	22	185
March 31, 2008	159	22	181

c Analysis of Group intangible asset additions (excluding goodwill)

£ million	Landing rights	Software	Group 2009	Group 2008
Cash paid	12	12	24	33
Acquired through business combinations	35		35	
Accrual movements	(3)		(3)	7
Total additions	44	12	56	40

d Allocation of indefinite-life intangibles to cash-generating units

Landing rights based within the EU, considered to have an indefinite useful life, are assigned to 'cash-generating units' for the purposes of impairment review. An impairment review has been conducted on the network airline operations, including passenger operations, cargo operations and related ancillary operations. A separate review has been conducted on the operations of OpenSkies and the landing rights acquired as a result of the acquisition of L'Avion in July 2008.

The allocation of indefinite-life landing rights to cash-generating units is as follows:

£ million	Group 2009	Group 2008
Network airline operations	163	
OpenSkies	30	
Total indefinite-life landing rights	193	–

19 Impairment of goodwill

Goodwill impairment review is carried out at the level of a 'cash-generating unit', defined as the smallest identifiable group of assets, liabilities and associated goodwill that generates cash inflows that are largely independent of the Group's other cash flows from other assets or groups of assets. On this basis, the impairment review has been conducted on two cash-generating units identified as containing an element of goodwill. An impairment review was performed on the goodwill associated with the network airline operations, including passenger and cargo operations out of all operated airports as well as all related ancillary operations. A separate impairment review has been conducted on the operations of OpenSkies, for the additional goodwill arising on the acquisition of L'Avion in July 2008 (note 6).

Goodwill is reviewed for impairment annually by comparison of the carrying value of the cash-generating unit to the recoverable amount. If the carrying value exceeds the recoverable amount, goodwill is considered impaired. The amount of impairment loss is measured as the difference between the carrying value and the recoverable amount.

a Goodwill analysed by cash-generating units

		Group
£ million	2009	2008
Network airline operations	40	40
OpenSkies	5	
Carrying value of goodwill before impairment charges	45	40
Impairment of OpenSkies goodwill	(5)	
Carrying value of goodwill	40	40

Network airline operations

The recoverable amount of the network airline operations has been measured based on its value in use, based on the discounted cash flow model; cash flow projections are based on the business plan approved by the Board covering a five-year period. Cash flows beyond the five-year period are projected to increase in line with UK long-term growth assumptions. This growth rate reflects the planned expansion of the Group as a result of the introduction into service of committed aircraft such as the Airbus A380 and Boeing 787. The pre-tax discount rate applied to the cash flow projections are derived from the Group's post-tax weighted average cost of capital, adjusted for the risks specific to the market.

No impairment charge has arisen as a result of the impairment review performed on the network airline operations.

OpenSkies

The recoverable amount of the OpenSkies cash-generating unit has been measured on its value-in-use, based on the discounted cash flow model; cash flow projections are based on the business plan approved by the Board covering a five-year period. Cash flows beyond the five-year period are projected to increase in line with EU long-term growth assumption. The pre-tax discount rate applied to the cash flow projections are derived from OpenSkies' post-tax weighted average cost of capital, adjusted for the risks specific to the market.

The operating margins of both cash-generating units are based on the estimated effects of planned business efficiency and business change programmes, approved and enacted at the balance sheet date. These are adjusted for the volatile trading conditions that have impacted the airline over the past three years. The trading environment is subject to both regulatory and competitive pressures that can have a material effect on the operating performance of the business.

An impairment charge of £5 million has been recognised in the consolidated income statement against the goodwill of OpenSkies as a result of the impairment review performed.

The key assumptions used in the value-in-use calculations for both the network airline operations and OpenSkies are:

	2009	2008
Pre-tax discount rate (derived from the long-term weighted average cost of capital)	8.90%	8.90%
Long-term growth rate	2.50%	2.50%
Operating margin range	(6.6)% – 10.0%	7%
Fuel price range per barrel	$60 – $75	$85

Notes to the accounts continued

19 Impairment of goodwill continued

b Key assumptions used in goodwill impairment review
Sensitivity of cash-generating units' recoverable amounts to changes in key assumptions.

The following table demonstrates the excess of the recoverable amount over the carrying amount of each cash-generating unit.

		2009
£ million	Network airline	Total
Goodwill	40	**40**
Excess of recoverable amount over carrying amount	400	**400**

		2008
£ million	Network airline	Total
Goodwill	40	40
Excess of recoverable amount over carrying amount	600	600

Network airline operations
The network airline unit's recoverable amount exceeds its carrying amount by £400 million. Based on sensitivity analysis, it is estimated that if there were an adverse change in the long-term operating margin by 2 per cent, the recoverable amount of the network airline unit would equal its carrying amount. An increase in the discount rate of 0.9 per cent would result in the value-in-use of the network airline unit being equal to its carrying amount.

20 Investments

a Group

Investment in associates

	Group	
£ million	2009	2008
Balance at April 1	227	125
Exchange movements	27	24
Additions*		57
Share of attributable results	4	23
Share of movements on other reserves	(32)	(2)
Dividends received	(17)	
At March 31	209	227

* £3 million of the 2008 additions are non-cash, attributed to deferred tax liabilities recognised on Iberia's unremitted earnings.

Market value of listed associates

	Group	
£ million	2009	2008
At March 31	**184**	275

Details of the investments that the Group accounts for as associates using the equity method are set out below:

	Percentage of equity owned	Principal activities	Holding	Country of incorporation and principal operations
Iberia, Lineas Aéreas de España, S.A. (Iberia)*	13.15	Airline operations	Ordinary shares	Spain

* Held by a subsidiary company.

The Group accounts for its investment in Iberia as an associate although the Group holds less than 20 per cent of the issued share capital as the Group has the ability to exercise significant influence over the investment due to the Group's voting power (both through its equity holding and its representation on key decision-making committees) and the nature of its commercial relationships with Iberia.

In February 2008, the Group purchased 28.7 million additional shares in Iberia at an average price of €2.34 per share (£54 million), taking its holding from 9.95 per cent at March 31, 2007, to 13.15 per cent. The acquisition of these additional shares in Iberia resulted in goodwill of £9 million, which was reflected in investment in associates.

20 Investments continued

The following summarised financial information of the Group's investment in associates is shown based on the Group's share of results and net assets:

£ million	2009	2008
		Group
Non-current assets	300	*218*
Current assets	392	*414*
Current liabilities	(284)	*(234)*
Non-current liabilities	(216)	*(188)*
Share of net assets	192	*210*
Goodwill attributable to investments in associates	17	*17*
Revenues	574	*556*
Net profit after tax	4	*26*

b Company

£ million	Cost	Provisions	2009	2008
				Company
Balance at April 1	3,219	(1,012)	2,207	*1,185*
Exchange movements	23		23	*17*
Additions	144		144	*1,016*
Intra-group transfer				*(5)*
Provision		(18)	(18)	*(6)*
At March 31	3,386	(1,030)	2,356	*2,207*

The provision of £18 million at March 31, 2009, relates to the £5 million impairment of the Company's investment in OpenSkies, associated with goodwill arising on the acquisition of L'Avion and the £13 million impairment of the Group's investment in The Plimsoll Line, which holds the investment in Flybe (2008: £6 million).

The Company accounts for its investments in subsidiaries and associates using the cost method.

The Group's and Company's principal investments in subsidiaries, associates and other investments are listed in principal investments on page 134.

During the prior year, the Company invested £999 million in a subsidiary whose primary purpose is to invest the Company's excess cash. In addition, the Company invested £17 million in a subsidiary relating to the launch of a new airline, OpenSkies.

During the year, the Company invested £40 million in the subsidiary OpenSkies in order to fund the acquisition of L'Avion and £104 million in the subsidiary CityFlyer in order to fund operations.

21 Available-for-sale financial assets

£ million	Group 2009	2008	Company 2009	2008
Available-for-sale financial assets	65	*80*	27	*24*

Available-for-sale financial assets are measured at fair value. For listed investments the fair value comprises the market price at the balance sheet date. For unlisted investments the fair value is estimated by reference to an earnings multiple model or by reference to other valuation methods. On March 5, 2007, the Group acquired a 15 per cent investment in Flybe in connection with the disposal of the regional business of BA Connect. The investment in Flybe was valued at £49 million at acquisition.

In the prior year, the Group performed a review of its investment in Flybe and due to an expected significant and prolonged decline in fair value associated with fuel price increases, the Group recognised a £6 million impairment of the investment. The impairment charge was reflected in the income statement within amounts relating to available-for-sale financial assets.

Notes to the accounts continued

21 Available-for-sale financial assets continued

The Group performed a review of its investment in Flybe at March 31, 2009. Despite a growth in Flybe's revenue and an expected reporting of profit for the year ended March 31, 2009, the review showed a further decline in fair value, associated with lower rate of forecast revenue and earnings growth than previously expected. Accordingly, the Group recognised a £13 million impairment of the investment. The impairment charge has been recognised in the income statement relating to available-for-sale financial assets. The investment is now valued at £30 million.

Available-for-sale investments include investments in listed ordinary shares, which by their nature have no fixed maturity date or coupon rate.

The table below shows total listed and unlisted available-for-sale investments.

	Group		Company	
£ million	2009	2008	2009	2008
Listed	8	13		
Unlisted	57	67	27	24
At March 31	65	80	27	24

22 Inventories

	Group		Company	
£ million	2009	2008	2009	2008
Expendables and consumables	127	112	125	109

23 Trade receivables

	Group		Company	
£ million	2009	2008	2009	2008
Trade receivables	543	598	530	586
Less: provision for doubtful receivables	13	12	13	12
Net trade receivables	530	586	517	574

Movements in the provision for doubtful trade receivables were as follows:

£ million	Group	Company
At April 1, 2007	16	16
Provision for doubtful receivables	7	7
Receivables written off during the year	(7)	(7)
Unused amounts reversed	(4)	(4)
At March 31, 2008	12	12
Provision for doubtful receivables	3	3
Exchange movement on revaluation	2	2
Receivables written off during the year	(2)	(2)
Unused amounts reversed	(2)	(2)
At March 31, 2009	13	13

As at March 31, the ageing analysis of trade receivables is as follows:

		Neither past due	Past due but not impaired		
£ million	Total	nor impaired	< 30 days	30-60 days	> 60 days
Group					
2009	530	510	14	2	4
2008	586	578	1	1	6
Company					
2009	517	510	2	1	4
2008	574	567	1	1	5

Trade receivables are generally non-interest-bearing and on 30 days' terms.

24 Other current assets

£ million	Group		Company	
	2009	*2008*	**2009**	*2008*
Amounts owed by subsidiaries			**169**	*116*
Other debtors	**88**	*103*	**88**	*102*
Prepayments and accrued income	**180**	*205*	**125**	*153*
At March 31	**268**	*308*	**382**	*371*

25 Cash, cash equivalents and other current interest-bearing deposits

a Cash and cash equivalents

£ million	Group		Company	
	2009	*2008*	**2009**	*2008*
Cash at bank and in hand	**247**	*180*	**219**	*175*
Short-term deposits falling due within three months	**155**	*503*		*258*
Cash and cash equivalents	**402**	*683*	**219**	*433*
Other current interest-bearing deposits maturing after three months	**979**	*1,181*	**43**	*399*

Cash at bank earns interest at floating rates based on daily bank deposit rates. Short-term deposits are made for periods up to three months depending on the cash requirements of the Group and earn interest based on the floating deposit rates. The fair value of cash and cash equivalents is £402 million for the Group (2008: £683 million) and for the Company £219 million (2008: £433 million).

At March 31, 2009, the Group and Company had no outstanding bank overdrafts (2008: £nil).

Other current interest-bearing deposits are made for periods in excess of three months with maturity typically within 12 months and earn interest based on the market rates available at the time the deposit was made.

b Reconciliation of net cash flow to movement in net debt

£ million	Group	
	2009	*2008*
Decrease in cash and cash equivalents during the period	**(289)**	*(1)*
Net cash outflow from decrease in debt and lease financing	**468**	*424*
Decrease in other current interest-bearing deposits	**(202)**	*(458)*
New loans and finance leases taken out and hire purchase arrangements made	**(377)**	*(172)*
Increase in net debt resulting from cash flow	**(400)**	*(207)*
Exchange movements and other non-cash movements	**(672)**	*(112)*
Increase in net debt during the period	**(1,072)**	*(319)*
Net debt at April 1	**(1,310)**	*(991)*
Net debt at March 31	**(2,382)**	*(1,310)*

Notes to the accounts continued

25 Cash, cash equivalents and other current interest-bearing deposits continued

c Analysis of net debt

£ million	Balance at April 1	Net cash flow	Other non-cash	Exchange	Group Balance at March 31
Cash and cash equivalents	713	(1)		(29)	683
Current interest-bearing deposits maturing after three months	1,642	(458)		(3)	1,181
Bank and other loans	(946)	68		2	(876)
Finance leases and hire purchase arrangements	(2,400)	184	(7)	(75)	(2,298)
Year to March 31, 2008	(991)	(207)	(7)	(105)	(1,310)
Cash and cash equivalents	683	(289)		8	**402**
Current interest-bearing deposits maturing after three months	1,181	(202)			**979**
Bank and other loans	(876)	66		(38)	**(848)**
Finance leases and hire purchase arrangements	(2,298)	25	(126)	(516)	**(2,915)**
Year to March 31, 2009	**(1,310)**	**(400)**	**(126)**	**(546)**	**(2,382)**

Net debt comprises the current and non-current portions of long-term borrowings less cash, cash equivalents and other current interest-bearing deposits.

26 Trade and other payables

£ million	Group 2009	Group 2008 Restated	Company 2009	Company 2008 Restated
Trade creditors	666	648	624	621
Unredeemed frequent flyer liabilities	1	1	1	1
Amounts owed to subsidiary companies			1,639	1,543
Other creditors:				
Other creditors	669	577	661	572
Other taxation and social security	39	40	37	40
	708	617	698	612
Accruals and deferred income:				
Sales in advance of carriage	769	911	743	892
Accruals and deferred income	652	698	340	367
	1,421	1,609	1,083	1,259
At March 31	**2,796**	2,875	**4,045**	4,036

27 Other long-term liabilities

£ million	Group 2009	Group 2008	Company 2009	Company 2008
Other creditors	11	13	4	7
Accruals and deferred income	193	155	165	125
At March 31	**204**	168	**169**	132

28 Long-term borrowings

£ million	Group		Company	
	2009	*2008*	**2009**	*2008*
a Current				
Loans, finance leases and hire purchase arrangements:				
Bank and other loans*	**69**	*113*	**57**	*102*
Finance leases**	**103**	*64*	**115**	*73*
Hire purchase arrangements	**517**	*246*	**517**	*246*
At March 31	**689**	*423*	**689**	*421*
b Non-current				
Loans, finance leases and hire purchase arrangements:				
Bank and other loans*	**779**	*764*	**582**	*554*
Finance leases**	**1,979**	*1,376*	**2,156**	*1,567*
Hire purchase arrangements	**316**	*611*	**316**	*611*
Loans from subsidiaries			**279**	*239*
At March 31	**3,074**	*2,751*	**3,333**	*2,971*

* Bank and other loans are repayable up to the year 2019. Bank and other loans of the Group amounting to US$108 million (2008: US$132 million), £382 million (2008: £410 million) and ¥6,915 million (2008: ¥nil) and bank loans of the Company amounting to US$108 million (2008: US$132 million) and £172 million (2008: £189 million) and ¥6,915 million (2008: ¥nil) are secured on aircraft. Euro-sterling notes, other loans and loans from subsidiary undertakings are not secured. Finance leases and hire purchase arrangements are all secured on aircraft or property assets.

** Included in finance leases for the Company is £188 million (2008: £200 million) of finance leases with other subsidiaries of the Group, of which £11 million (2008: £9 million) is classified as current.

c Bank and other loans
Bank and other loans comprise the following:

£ million	Group		Company	
	2009	*2008*	**2009**	*2008*
£250 million fixed rate 8.75 per cent eurobonds 2016 [i]	**248**	*248*	**248**	*248*
£100 million fixed rate 10.875 per cent eurobonds 2008		*61*		*61*
Floating rate sterling mortgage loans secured on aircraft [ii]	**187**	*201*	**143**	*153*
Floating rate US dollar mortgage loans secured on aircraft [iii]	**76**	*67*	**76**	*67*
Fixed rate sterling mortgage loans secured on aircraft [iv]	**194**	*209*	**29**	*36*
Floating rate Japanese yen mortgage loans secured on aircraft [v]	**49**		**49**	
Floating rate US dollar mortgage loans not secured on aircraft [vi]	**49**	*40*	**49**	*40*
European Investment Bank loans [vii]	**45**	*51*	**45**	*51*
	848	*877*	**639**	*656*
Less: current instalments due on bank loans	**69**	*113*	**57**	*102*
At March 31	**779**	*764*	**582**	*554*

(i)   £250 million fixed rate 8.75 per cent unsecured eurobonds 2016 are repayable in one instalment on August 23, 2016.

(ii)   Floating rate sterling mortgage loans are secured on specific aircraft assets of the Group and bear interest of between 0.53 per cent and 0.59 per cent above LIBOR. The loans are repayable between 2015 and 2019.

(iii) Floating rate US dollar mortgage loans are secured on specific aircraft assets of the Group and bear interest of between 0.40 per cent and 0.99 per cent above LIBOR. The loans are repayable between 2009 and 2016.

(iv) Fixed rate sterling mortgage loans are secured on specific aircraft assets of the Group and bear interest at 6.14 per cent to 7.35 per cent. The loans are repayable between 2012 and 2018.

(v)   Floating rate Japanese yen mortgage loans are secured on specific aircraft assets of the Group and bear interest of 0.55 per cent above LIBOR. The loans are repayable in March 2014.

(vi) Floating rate US dollar mortgage loans are not secured on aircraft and bear interest of 0.75 per cent above LIBOR. The loans are repayable in 2014.

(vii) European Investment Bank loans are secured on certain property assets of the Group and bear interest of between 0.20 per cent below LIBOR and LIBOR. The loans are repayable between 2014 and 2017.

Notes to the accounts continued

28 Long-term borrowings continued

d Total loans, finance leases and hire purchase arrangements

million	Group 2009	Group 2008	Company 2009	Company 2008
Bank and other loans:				
Bank:				
US dollar	$178	$211	$178	$211
Japanese yen	¥6,915		¥6,915	
Sterling	£427	£461	£217	£240
	£600	£568	£391	£347
Euro-sterling notes:				
Sterling	£248	£309	£248	£309
Loans from subsidiary undertakings:				
Euro			€300	€300
			£279	£239
Finance leases:				
US dollar	$1,518	$1,205	$1,518	$1,205
Euro	€77		€77	
Sterling	£948	£834	£1,136	£1,034
	£2,082	£1,440	£2,271	£1,640
Hire purchase arrangements:				
US dollar	$72	$89	$72	$89
Japanese yen	¥101,350	¥112,442	¥101,350	¥112,442
Sterling	£62	£244	£62	£244
	£833	£857	£833	£857
At March 31	£3,763	£3,174	£4,022	£3,392

e Obligations under finance leases and hire purchase contracts

The Group uses finance leases and hire purchase contracts principally to acquire aircraft. These leases have both renewal options and purchase options. These are at the option of the Group. Future minimum lease payments under finance leases and hire purchase contracts are as follows:

£ million	Group 2009	Group 2008	Company 2009	Company 2008
Future minimum payments due:				
Within one year	687	389	707	407
After more than one year but within five years	1,163	1,218	1,252	1,303
In five years or more	1,672	1,268	1,811	1,431
	3,522	2,875	3,770	3,141
Less: Finance charges	607	578	666	644
Present value of minimum lease payments	2,915	2,297	3,104	2,497
The present value of minimum lease payments is analysed as follows:				
Within one year	620	310	632	319
After more than one year but within five years	926	989	981	1,040
In five years or more	1,369	998	1,491	1,138
At March 31	2,915	2,297	3,104	2,497

29 Operating lease commitments

The Group has entered into commercial leases on certain properties, equipment and aircraft. These leases have durations ranging from five years for aircraft to 150 years for ground leases. Certain leases contain options for renewal.

a Fleet
The aggregate payments, for which there are commitments under operating leases as at March 31, fall due as follows:

£ million	Group		Company	
	2009	*2008*	**2009**	*2008*
Within one year	**84**	*77*	**60**	*62*
Between one and five years	**334**	*169*	**309**	*143*
Over five years	**444**	*17*	**444**	*17*
At March 31	**862**	*263*	**813**	*222*

b Property and equipment
The aggregate payments, for which there are commitments under operating leases as at March 31, fall due as follows:

£ million	Group		Company	
	2009	*2008*	**2009**	*2008*
Within one year	**84**	*86*	**80**	*82*
Between one and five years	**249**	*244*	**238**	*229*
Over five years, ranging up to the year 2145	**1,562**	*1,612*	**1,557**	*1,603*
At March 31	**1,895**	*1,942*	**1,875**	*1,914*

The Group and Company sub-lease surplus rental properties and aircraft assets held under non-cancellable leases to third parties and subsidiary companies. These leases have remaining terms of one to seven years and the assets are surplus to the Group's requirements.

Future minimum rentals receivable under non-cancellable operating leases are as follows:

£ million	Group		Company	
	2009	*2008*	**2009**	*2008*
Fleet				
Within one year	**6**	*6*	**4**	*1*
Between one and five years	**8**	*13*	**9**	*2*
At March 31	**14**	*19*	**13**	*3*
Property and equipment				
Within one year	**6**	*5*	**6**	*5*
Between one and five years	**24**	*19*	**24**	*19*
Over five years	**10**	*1*	**10**	*1*
At March 31	**40**	*25*	**40**	*25*

Notes to the accounts continued

30 Provisions for liabilities and charges

Group

£ million	Insurance provisions	Onerous lease contracts	Restoration and handback provisions	Restructuring	Litigation	Other	Total
At April 1, 2008:							
Current			29	7	134		170
Non-current	22	11	83		84	10	210
	22	11	112	7	218	10	380
Arising during the year	10		15	81	(9)	35	132
Utilised		(3)	(29)	(64)	(10)	(32)	(138)
Release of unused amounts		(1)	(7)	(3)			(11)
Exchange		2	19		42		63
Unwinding of discount			1		11		12
At March 31, 2009	**32**	**9**	**111**	**21**	**252**	**13**	**438**
Analysis:							
Current			24	21	137		182
Non-current	32	9	87		115	13	256
	32	**9**	**111**	**21**	**252**	**13**	**438**

Company

£ million	Onerous lease contracts	Restoration and handback provisions	Restructuring	Litigation	Other	Total
At April 1, 2008:						
Current		29	5	134		168
Non-current	11	80		84	10	185
	11	109	5	218	10	353
Arising during the year		12	81	(9)	35	119
Utilised	(3)	(29)	(62)	(10)	(32)	(136)
Release of unused amounts	(1)	(7)	(3)			(11)
Exchange	2	19		42		63
Other movements	(5)					(5)
Unwinding of discount		1		11		12
At March 31, 2009	**4**	**105**	**21**	**252**	**13**	**395**
Analysis:						
Current		22	21	137		180
Non-current	4	83		115	13	215
	4	**105**	**21**	**252**	**13**	**395**

Insurance provisions relate to provisions held by the Group's captive insurer, Speedbird Insurance Company Limited, for incurred but not reported losses. Such provisions are held until utilised or such time as further claims are considered unlikely under the respective insurance policies.

The onerous lease provision relates partly to the sub-lease of one Jetstream 41 aircraft to Eastern Airways and six Avro RJ100 aircraft to Swiss International Air Lines. This provision will be fully utilised by October 2011. In addition, the provision includes amounts relating to properties leased by the Group that are either sub-leased to third parties or are vacant with no immediate intention to utilise the property. This provision will be fully utilised by April 2037.

30 Provisions for liabilities and charges continued

Restoration and handback costs include provision for the costs to meet the contractual return conditions on aircraft held under operating leases. The provision also includes amounts relating to leased land and buildings where restoration costs are contractually required at the end of the lease. Where such costs arise as a result of capital expenditure on the leased asset, the restoration costs are also capitalised. This provision will be utilised by March 2051.

The balance remaining on the Group restructuring provision was £21 million at March 31, 2009, mainly relating to targeted voluntary severance costs expected to be paid during the next financial year.

There are ongoing investigations into the Group's passenger and cargo surcharges by the European Commission and other jurisdictions. These investigations are likely to continue for some time. The Company is also subject to related class action claims. The final amount required to pay the remaining claims and fines is subject to uncertainty. A detailed breakdown of the remaining provision is not presented as it may seriously prejudice the position of the Company in these regulatory investigations and potential litigation.

Included in the amount arising during the year for litigation is a £22 million reduction in the competition provision relating to a change in the net present value of the provision arising from changes to the expected payment profile, offset by a £12 million increase in the provision as a result of the accrual of legal fees.

Other provisions include staff leaving indemnities relating to amounts due to staff under various overseas contractual arrangements.

31 Financial risk management objectives and policies

The Group is exposed to a variety of financial risks: market risk (including foreign currency risk, interest rate risk and fuel price risk), credit risk, capital risk and liquidity risk. The Group's overall risk management programme focuses on the unpredictability of financial markets and seeks to minimise potential adverse effects on the Group's financial performance.

Group treasury carries out financial risk management under governance approved by the Board. Group treasury identifies, evaluates and hedges financial risks. The Board provides written principles for overall risk management, as well as written policies covering specific areas, such as foreign exchange risk, interest rate risk, credit risk, capital risk and the use of derivative financial instruments and investment of excess liquidity.

a Fuel price risk
The Group is exposed to fuel price risk. The Group's fuel price risk management strategy aims to provide the airline with protection against sudden and significant increases in oil prices while ensuring that the airline is not competitively disadvantaged in a serious way in the event of a substantial fall in the price of fuel.

In meeting these objectives, the fuel risk management programme allows for the judicious use of a number of derivatives available on the over-the-counter (OTC) markets with approved counterparties and within approved limits.

The following table demonstrates the sensitivity of financial instruments to a reasonably possible change in fuel prices, with all other variables held constant, on (loss)/profit before tax and equity:

					Group						Company
	2009				2008		2009				2008
Increase/ (decrease) in fuel price per cent	Effect on loss before tax £ million	Effect on equity £ million	Increase/ (decrease) in fuel price per cent	Effect on profit before tax £ million	Effect on equity £ million	Increase/ (decrease) in fuel price per cent	Effect on loss before tax £ million	Effect on equity £ million	Increase/ (decrease) in fuel price per cent	Effect on profit before tax £ million	Effect on equity £ million
30	**15**	**301**	*10*	*14*	*166*	**30**	**15**	**301**	*10*	*14*	*166*
(30)	**(4)**	**(337)**	*(10)*	*(11)*	*(163)*	**(30)**	**(4)**	**(337)**	*(10)*	*(11)*	*(163)*

b Foreign currency risk
The Group is exposed to currency risk on revenue, purchases and borrowings that are denominated in a currency other than sterling. The currencies in which these transactions are primarily denominated are euro, US dollar and Japanese yen. The Group generates a surplus in most currencies in which it does business. The US dollar can be an exception as capital expenditure, debt repayments and fuel payments denominated in US dollars can create a deficit.

Notes to the accounts continued

31 Financial risk management objectives and policies continued

The Group can experience adverse or beneficial effects arising from foreign exchange rate movements. The Group seeks to reduce foreign exchange exposures arising from transactions in various currencies through a policy of matching, as far as possible, receipts and payments in each individual currency. Surpluses of convertible currencies are sold, either spot or forward, for US dollars or sterling.

The Group has substantial liabilities denominated in euro, US dollars and Japanese yen.

The Group utilises its euro, US dollar and Japanese yen debt repayments as a hedge of future euro, US dollar and Japanese yen revenues.

Forward foreign exchange contracts and currency options are used to cover near-term future revenues and operating payments in a variety of currencies.

The following table demonstrates the sensitivity of financial instruments to a reasonably possible change in the euro, US dollar and Japanese yen exchange rates, with all other variables held constant, on (loss)/profit before tax and equity.

Group	Strengthening/ (weakening) in euro rate per cent	Effect on (loss)/profit before tax £ million	Effect on equity £ million	Strengthening/ (weakening) in US dollar rate per cent	Effect on (loss)/profit before tax £ million	Effect on equity £ million	Strengthening/ (weakening) in Japanese yen rate per cent	Effect on (loss)/profit before tax £ million	Effect on equity £ million
2009	**20**	**(7)**	**(33)**	**20**	**(52)**	**(162)**	**20**	**(8)**	**(138)**
	(20)	**6**	**32**	**(20)**	**52**	**162**	**(20)**	**8**	**138**
2008	*10*	*(2)*	*(26)*	*10*	*(4)*	*(42)*	*10*	*(7)*	*(57)*
	(10)	*2*	*22*	*(10)*	*3*	*32*	*(10)*	*5*	*47*
Company									
2009	**20**	**(7)**	**(33)**	**20**	**(52)**	**(162)**	**20**	**(8)**	**(138)**
	(20)	**6**	**32**	**(20)**	**52**	**162**	**(20)**	**8**	**138**
2008	*10*	*(2)*	*(26)*	*10*	*(6)*	*(42)*	*10*	*(7)*	*(57)*
	(10)	*2*	*22*	*(10)*	*5*	*32*	*(10)*	*5*	*47*

c Interest rate risk
The Group is exposed to changes in interest rates on floating debt and cash deposits.

The following table illustrates the sensitivity of financial instruments on (loss)/profit before tax for the year to a reasonably possible change in interest rates, with effect from the beginning of the year. There was no impact on shareholders' equity. These changes are considered to be reasonably possible based on observation of current market conditions. The calculations are based on financial instruments held at each balance sheet date. All other variables were held constant.

	2009	
	Effect on loss before tax	
£ million	100 basis points increase	50 basis points decrease
Group		
Variable rate instruments	**(2)**	1
Company		
Variable rate instruments	**(10)**	5

	2008	
	Effect on profit before tax	
£ million	100 basis points increase	100 basis points decrease
Group		
Variable rate instruments	*3*	*(3)*
Company		
Variable rate instruments	*(3)*	*3*

31 Financial risk management objectives and policies continued

d Credit risk

The Group is exposed to credit risk to the extent of non-performance by its counterparties in respect of financial assets receivable. However, the Group has policies and procedures in place to ensure credit risk is limited by placing credit limits on each counterparty. The Group continuously monitors counterparty credit limits and defaults of counterparties, incorporating this information into credit risk controls. Treasury activities which include placing money market deposits, fuel hedging and foreign currency transactions could lead to a concentration of different credit risks on the same counterparty. This risk is managed by the allocation of an overall exposure limit for the counterparty that is then allocated down to specific treasury activities for that party. Exposures at the activity level are monitored on a daily basis and the overall exposure limit for the counterparty is reviewed at least monthly in the light of available market information such as credit ratings and credit default swap levels. It is the Group's policy that all counterparties who wish to trade on credit terms are subject to credit verification procedures.

The maximum exposure to credit risk is limited to the carrying value of each class of asset as summarised in note 32.

The Group does not hold any collateral to mitigate this exposure. Credit risks arising from acting as guarantor are disclosed in note 37.

e Liquidity risk

Prudent liquidity risk management includes maintaining sufficient cash and interest-bearing deposits, the availability of funding from an adequate amount of credit facilities and the ability to close out market positions. Due to the dynamic nature of the underlying business, Group treasury maintains flexibility in funding by maintaining availability under committed credit lines.

The Company's long-term corporate debt ratings at March 31, 2009, assigned by Moody's and Standard & Poor's respectively were Ba1 and BB+. The Moody's rating was reduced from Baa3 in February 2009 and the Company is on credit watch for a further downgrade. The Standard & Poor's rating was reduced to BB with a stable outlook in May 2009. The downgrades were due to adverse trading conditions. The downgrades have had no impact on debt covenants or liquidity since the Group has committed borrowing facilities through to 2016, and adequate cash reserves to meet operating requirements for the next 12 months.

At March 31, 2009, the Group and Company had unused overdraft facilities of £20 million (2008: £20 million) and €4 million (£4 million) (2008: €20 million (£16 million) respectively).

The Group and Company held undrawn uncommitted money market lines of £25 million as at March 31, 2009 (2008: £45 million).

The Group and Company had the following undrawn general and committed aircraft financing facilities:

| | 2009 | |
million	Currency	£ equivalent
US dollar facility expiring June 2013	$1,301	911
US dollar facility expiring March 2014	$940	658
US dollar facility expiring June 2010	$228	160
US dollar facility expiring September 2016	$509	356
US dollar facility expiring December 2012	$270	189
US dollar facility expiring June 2012	$269	189
Japanese yen facility expiring January 2011	¥68,085	485

| | 2008 | |
million	Currency	£ equivalent
US dollar facility expiring June 2010	$266	134
US dollar facility expiring June 2012	$115	58
US dollar facility expiring December 2015	$509	256
US dollar facility expiring March 2014	$940	472
US dollar facility expiring December 2012	$1,615	812
Japanese yen facility expiring January 2011	¥75,000	381

Notes to the accounts continued

31 Financial risk management objectives and policies continued

e Liquidity risk continued
The table below analyses the Group's financial assets and liabilities into relevant maturity groupings based on the remaining period at the balance sheet date to the contractual maturity date. The amounts disclosed in the table are the contractual undiscounted cash flows and include interest.

Group

£ million	Within 6 months	6-12 months	1-2 years	2-5 years	More than 5 years	Total 2009
Cash and cash equivalents	402					**402**
Other current interest-bearing deposits	740	248				**988**
Trade receivables	530					**530**
Interest-bearing loans and borrowings:						
Finance lease and hire purchase obligations	(447)	(240)	(474)	(689)	(1,672)	**(3,522)**
Fixed rate borrowings	(31)	(21)	(51)	(141)	(425)	**(669)**
Floating rate borrowings	(20)	(40)	(60)	(171)	(156)	**(447)**
Trade and other payables	(1,374)					**(1,374)**
Derivative financial instruments:						
Cross currency swaps			(1)	(2)	(4)	**(7)**
Forward currency contracts	(13)	(2)	(3)			**(18)**
Fuel derivatives	(252)	(204)	(111)	(2)		**(569)**
Forward currency contracts	31	9	3			**43**
At March 31	**(434)**	**(250)**	**(697)**	**(1,005)**	**(2,257)**	**(4,643)**

Group

£ million	Within 6 months	6-12 months	1-2 years	2-5 years	More than 5 years	Total 2008
Cash and cash equivalents	683					683
Other current interest-bearing deposits	861	360				1,221
Trade receivables	586					586
Interest-bearing loans and borrowings:						
Finance lease and hire purchase obligations	(169)	(220)	(523)	(695)	(1,268)	(2,875)
Fixed rate borrowings	(98)	(21)	(51)	(150)	(468)	(788)
Floating rate borrowings	(20)	(37)	(56)	(143)	(211)	(467)
Trade and other payables	(1,265)					(1,265)
Derivative financial instruments:						
Cross currency swaps				(1)	(1)	(2)
Forward currency contracts	(15)	(5)	(1)			(21)
Fuel derivatives				(1)		(1)
Forward currency contracts	5	3				8
Fuel derivatives	151	82	50	1		284
At March 31	719	162	(581)	(989)	(1,948)	(2,637)

Company

£ million	Within 6 months	6-12 months	1-2 years	2-5 years	More than 5 years	Total 2009
Cash and cash equivalents	219					**219**
Other current interest-bearing deposits	20	24				**44**
Trade receivables	517					**517**
Interest-bearing loans and borrowings:						
Finance lease and hire purchase obligations	(461)	(246)	(495)	(757)	(1,811)	**(3,770)**
Fixed rate borrowings	(25)	(25)	(50)	(137)	(1,058)	**(1,295)**
Floating rate borrowings	(20)	(36)	(56)	(157)	(125)	**(394)**
Trade and other payables	(2,961)					**(2,961)**
Derivative financial instruments:						
Cross currency swaps			(1)	(2)	(4)	**(7)**
Forward currency contracts	(13)	(2)	(3)			**(18)**
Fuel derivatives	(252)	(204)	(111)	(2)		**(569)**
Forward currency contracts	31	9	3			**43**
At March 31	**(2,945)**	**(480)**	**(713)**	**(1,055)**	**(2,998)**	**(8,191)**

31 Financial risk management objectives and policies continued

e Liquidity risk continued

£ million	Within 6 months	6-12 months	1-2 years	2-5 years	More than 5 years	Company Total 2008
Cash and cash equivalents	433					433
Other current interest-bearing deposits	414					414
Trade receivables	574					574
Interest-bearing loans and borrowings:						
Finance lease and hire purchase obligations	(182)	(225)	(543)	(760)	(1,431)	(3,141)
Fixed rate borrowings	(92)	(24)	(47)	(138)	(986)	(1,287)
Floating rate borrowings	(18)	(33)	(51)	(126)	(172)	(400)
Trade and other payables	(2,776)					(2,776)
Derivative financial instruments:						
Cross currency swaps				(1)	(1)	(2)
Forward currency contracts	(15)	(5)	(1)			(21)
Fuel derivatives				(1)		(1)
Forward currency contracts	5	3				8
Fuel derivatives	151	82	50	1		284
At March 31	(1,506)	(202)	(592)	(1,025)	(2,590)	(5,915)

f Capital risk management

The Group's objectives when managing capital are to safeguard the Group's ability to continue as a going concern in order to provide returns for shareholders and benefits for other stakeholders and to maintain an optimal capital structure to reduce the cost of capital.

Consistent with others in the industry, the Group monitors capital on the basis of the gearing ratio, net debt as a percentage of total capital. Net debt is defined as the total borrowings, finance leases and hire purchase liabilities, net interest-bearing deposits and cash and cash equivalents less overdrafts. See note 25 for details of the calculation of net debt. Total capital is defined as the total of capital, reserves, minority interests and net debt.

The gearing ratios at March 31, 2009 and 2008 were as follows:

£ million (except ratios)	2009	Group 2008 Restated
Capital reserves	1,646	3,062
Add minority interests	200	200
Total equity	1,846	3,262
Net debt (a)	2,382	1,310
Total capital (b)	4,228	4,572
Gearing ratio (a)/(b)	56.3	28.7

The increase in the gearing ratio during 2009 resulted primarily from decreased equity due to adverse marked-to-market adjustments on fuel derivatives and foreign currency borrowings, as well as the operating loss reported. The gearing ratio was further impacted by increased borrowings relating to the delivery of nine Airbus A320s and one Boeing 777 aircraft. The carrying value of foreign currency borrowings has increased as a result of the weakening of sterling during 2009.

Notes to the accounts continued

32 Financial instruments

a Fair values of financial assets and financial liabilities
The carrying amounts and fair values of the Group's financial assets and liabilities at March 31, 2009, are set out below:

£ million	Group		Company	
	Carrying value	Fair value	Carrying value	Fair value
Financial assets:				
Cash and cash equivalents	402	402	219	219
Other liquid deposits maturing over three months	979	979	43	43
Trade receivables	530	530	517	517
Available-for-sale financial assets	65	65	27	27
Forward currency contracts*	43	43	43	43
Financial liabilities:				
Trade and other payables	1,374	1,374	2,961	2,961
Interest-bearing loans and borrowings:				
Finance lease and hire purchase obligations	2,915	3,030	3,104	3,239
Fixed rate borrowings	442	386	556	490
Floating rate borrowings	406	406	362	362
Cross currency swaps**	7	7	7	7
Forward currency contracts**	18	18	18	18
Fuel derivatives**	569	569	569	569

* Current portion of derivative financial assets is £40 million.

** Current portion of derivative financial liabilities is £471 million.

The fair values of the Group's financial assets and liabilities at March 31, 2008, are set out below:

£ million	Group		Company	
	Carrying value	Fair value	Carrying value	Fair value
Financial assets:				
Cash and cash equivalents	683	683	433	433
Other liquid deposits maturing over 3 months	1,181	1,181	399	399
Trade receivables	586	586	574	574
Available-for-sale financial assets	80	80	24	24
Forward currency contracts*	8	8	8	8
Fuel derivatives*	284	284	284	284
Financial liabilities:				
Trade and other payables	1,265	1,265	2,776	2,776
Interest-bearing loans and borrowings:				
Finance lease and hire purchase obligations	2,297	2,324	2,497	2,526
Fixed rate borrowings	518	526	584	586
Floating rate borrowings	359	359	311	311
Cross currency swaps**	2	2	2	2
Forward currency contracts**	21	21	21	21
Fuel derivatives**	1	1	1	1

* Current portion of derivative financial assets is £241 million.

** Current portion of derivative financial liabilities is £20 million.

The following methods and assumptions were used by the Group in estimating its fair value disclosures for financial instruments:

Available-for-sale financial assets and loan notes
Listed fixed asset investments are stated at market value as at March 31, 2009. For other investments the fair value is estimated by reference to a discounted cash flow that is not expected to reverse.

Bank and other loans, finance leases, hire purchase arrangements and the non-Japanese yen denominated portions of hire purchase arrangements carrying fixed rates of interest
The repayments which the Group is committed to make have been discounted at the relevant interest rates applicable at March 31, 2009.

32 Financial instruments continued

Japanese yen denominated portions of hire purchase arrangements carrying fixed rates of interest
These amounts relate to the tax equity portions of Japanese leveraged leases which are personal to the Group, cannot be assigned and could not be refinanced or replaced in the same cross border market on a marked-to-market basis and accordingly, a fair value cannot be determined. The carrying value of £722 million (2008: £569 million) has therefore been included as the fair value above.

Euro-sterling notes and Euro-sterling bond 2016
These are stated at quoted market value.

b Fair values of financial assets and financial liabilities

Forward currency transactions
These are stated at the marked-to-market value of the instruments.

Over-the-counter (OTC) fuel derivatives
These are stated at the marked-to-market value of the instruments.

c Hedges

i Cash flow hedges
At March 31, 2009, the Group and Company held four principal risk management activities that were designated as hedges of future forecast transactions. These were:

• A hedge of a proportion of future long-term revenue receipts by future debt repayments in foreign currency hedging future foreign exchange risk;

• A hedge of certain short-term revenue receipts by foreign exchange contracts hedging future foreign exchange risk;

• A hedge of certain short-term foreign currency operational payments by forward exchange contracts hedging future foreign exchange risk; and

• A hedge of future jet fuel purchases by forward crude, gas oil and jet kerosene derivative contracts hedging future fuel price risk.

To the extent that the hedges were assessed as highly effective, a summary of the amounts included in equity and the periods in which the related cash flows are expected to occur are summarised below:

£ million	Within 6 months	6-12 months	1-2 years	2-5 years	More than 5 years	Group Total 2009
Debt repayments to hedge future revenue	30	30	69	178	150	**457**
Forward contracts to hedge future payments	(10)	(6)	(1)			**(17)**
Hedges of future fuel purchases	361	178	97	2		**638**
	381	202	165	180	150	**1,078**
Related deferred tax charge						**(301)**
Total amount included within equity						**777**

Notional value of financial instruments used as cash flow hedging instruments:

million	Group Notional amount	Company Notional amount
To hedge future currency revenues against US dollars	$118	$118
To hedge future currency revenues against sterling	£60	£60
To hedge future operating payments in US dollars	$365	$365
To hedge future Brazilian real capital payments against US dollars	$67	$67
Hedges of future fuel purchases	$2,612	$2,612
Debt repayments to hedge future revenue – Euro	€77	€77
– US dollars	$1,570	$1,570
– Japanese yen	¥95,358	¥95,358

Notes to the accounts continued

---

32 Financial instruments continued

c Hedges continued

i Cash flow hedges continued

£ million	Within 6 months	6-12 months	1-2 years	2-5 years	More than 5 years	Group Total 2008
Debt repayments to hedge future revenue	(1)	(1)		(5)	(10)	(17)
Forward contracts to hedge future payments	10	1	1			12
Hedges of future fuel purchases	(148)	(94)	(45)	(2)		(289)
	(139)	(94)	(44)	(7)	(10)	(294)
Related deferred tax charge						83
Total amount included within equity						(211)

Notional value of financial instruments used as cash flow hedging instruments:

million	Group Notional amount	Company Notional amount
To hedge future currency revenues against US dollars	$143	$143
To hedge future currency revenues against sterling	£235	£235
To hedge future operating payments against US dollars	$440	$440
Hedges of future fuel purchases	$4,143	$4,143
Debt repayments to hedge future revenue – US dollars	$1,307	$1,307
– Japanese yen	¥100,798	¥100,798

The ineffective portion recognised in the income statement that arose from hedges of future fuel purchases amounts to a loss of £7 million (2008: £12 million gain). There was no ineffective portion of cash flow hedges other than hedges of future fuel purchases. In the current year, £5 million of cash flow hedging losses previously recognised in equity were transferred to the income statement, relating to forecast transactions (future revenue) that are no longer expected to occur.

ii Fair value hedges
The Group has no hedges designated as fair value hedges.

iii Net investments in foreign operations
The Group has no hedges designated as hedges of net investments in foreign operations.

Company
The Company undertakes hedging activities on behalf of other companies within the Group and performs the treasury activities of the Group centrally. As a result, the disclosures above apply to the Company as for the Group.

33 Share capital

Ordinary shares of 25 pence each	2009 Number of shares 000s	2009 £ million	2008 Number of shares 000s	2008 £ million
Authorised				
At April 1 and March 31	1,512,000	378	1,512,000	378
Allotted, called up and fully paid				
At April 1	1,153,105	288	1,151,575	288
Exercise of options under Employee Share Option Schemes	523		1,530	
At March 31	1,153,628	288	1,153,105	288

34 Share options

The Group operates share-based payment schemes as part of the total remuneration package provided to employees – these schemes comprise both share option schemes where employees acquire shares at a grant price and share award plans whereby shares are issued to employees at no cost, subject to the achievement by the Group of specified performance targets. Details of the performance criteria to be met for each of the schemes, and details of the awards to the directors, are set out in the report of the Remuneration Committee on pages 67 to 73.

a Share Option Plan 1999

The British Airways Share Option Plan granted options to qualifying employees based on performance at an option price which was not less than the market price of the share at the date of the grant (or the nominal value if shares are to be subscribed and this value is greater than the market value). The options are subject to a three-year vesting period. Upon vesting, options may be exercised at any time until the 10th anniversary of the date of grant with the exception of grants made during the year ending March 31, 2005, when there will be a single re-test after a further year which will measure performance of the Group over the four-year period from the date of grant. No further grants of options under the Share Option Plan will be made other than those during the year ending March 31, 2006, in relation to performance during the year ending March 31, 2005 (for which there will be no re-testing).

b Long Term Incentive Plan

The Long Term Incentive Plan (LTIP) awarded options to senior executives conditional upon the Company's achievement of a performance condition measured over three financial years. If granted, all options are immediately exercisable for seven years and no payment is due upon exercise of the options. No further awards under the LTIP have been made since June 16, 2004.

c Performance Share Plan

In 2005 the Group introduced a Performance Share Plan (PSP) for senior executives. Options over shares are awarded conditional on the achievement of a variety of performance conditions and will vest after three years subject to the executive remaining employed by the Group. A further award will be made that will vest based 100 per cent on meeting Total Shareholder Return (TSR) performance conditions over the following three financial years (pages 67 and 68). No payment is due upon exercise of the options. Executives awarded shares under the PSP will be expected to retain no fewer than 50 per cent of the shares (net of tax) which vest from the new schemes until they have built up a shareholding equivalent to 100 per cent of basic salary.

d Deferred Share Plan

In 2006 the Group introduced a Deferred Share Plan (DSP) granted to qualifying employees based on performance and service tests. It will be awarded when a bonus is triggered subject to the employee remaining in employment with the Group for three years after the grant date. The relevant management population will receive a percentage of their bonus in cash and the remaining percentage in shares through the DSP. The maximum deferral is 50 per cent.

e Share options summary

Group and Company

	Deferred Share Plan		Performance Share Plan		Long Term Incentive Plan		Share Option Plan		
	Number of shares 000s	Weighted average fair value £	Number of shares 000s	Weighted average fair value £	Number of shares 000s	Weighted average fair value £	Number of shares 000s	Weighted average exercise price £	Weighted average fair value £
Outstanding at April 1, 2007*	830		2,643		1,483		19,340	2.74	
Granted in the year			1,444	2.61					
Exercised during the year**/***					(157)		(1,530)	2.71	
Expired/cancelled	(43)		(191)		(44)		(896)	2.73	
Outstanding at April 1, 2008*	787		3,896		1,282		16,914	2.75	
Granted in the year	710	2.74	2,573	2.15					
Exercised during the year**/***	(269)		(454)		(183)		(69)	1.64	
Expired/cancelled	(187)		(1,476)				(2,765)	2.83	
Outstanding at April 1, 2009	**1,041**		**4,539**		**1,099**		**14,080**	**2.74**	
Options exercisable:									
At March 31, 2009					**1,099**		**14,080**	**2.74**	
At March 31, 2008	7	4.84			1,282		11,413	2.74	

*   Included within this balance are options over 3,875,252 (2008: 5,235,228) shares that have not been recognised in accordance with IFRS 2 as the options were granted on or before November 7, 2002. These options have not been subsequently modified and therefore do not need to be accounted for in accordance with IFRS 2.

**   The weighted average share price at the date of exercise for the Share Option Plan exercised is £2.36 (2008: £4.19).

*** Part of the exercise of share options during the year was met through shares previously held by British Airways Employees Benefits Trust (Jersey) Limited.

Notes to the accounts continued

34 Share options continued

e Share options summary continued
Range of exercise prices 2009 for Share Option Plan

	Options outstanding			Options exercisable	
Range of exercise prices	Number of shares 000s	Weighted average remaining life (years)	Weighted average exercise price £	Number of shares 000s	Weighted average exercise price £
£1.57 – £2.61	2,168	3.88	1.66	2,168	1.66
£2.62 – £3.20	8,830	5.78	2.70	8,830	2.70
£3.21 – £3.94	3,082	1.41	3.61	3,082	3.61
At March 31, 2009	**14,080**	**4.53**	**2.74**	**14,080**	**2.74**

Range of exercise prices 2008 for Share Option Plan

	Options outstanding			Options exercisable	
Range of exercise prices	Number of shares 000s	Weighted average remaining life (years)	Weighted average exercise price £	Number of shares 000s	Weighted average exercise price £
£1.57 – £2.61	2,784	4.82	1.67	2,784	1.67
£2.62 – £3.20	10,073	6.79	2.70	4,572	2.62
£3.21 – £3.94	4,057	2.40	3.61	4,057	3.61
At March 31, 2008	16,914	5.41	2.75	11,413	2.74

For all outstanding share option schemes as at March 31, 2009, the weighted average remaining contractual life is four years (2008: five years). For options granted during the year the weighted average option life was three years (2008: three years).

The fair value of equity-settled share options granted is estimated as at the date of grant using a binomial lattice or Monte-Carlo model, taking into account the term and conditions upon which the options were granted. The following table lists the inputs to the models for the PSP options granted in the year:

	2009	2008
Expected share price volatility (per cent)	24	24
Historical volatility (per cent)	35	24
Expected comparator group volatility (per cent)	21-98	19-96
Expected comparator correlation (per cent)	41	28
Expected life of options (years)	3	3
Weighted average share price (£)	1.88	3.82

The expected life of the options is based on historical data and is not necessarily indicative of exercise patterns that may occur. Volatility was calculated with reference to the Group's weekly share price volatility. The expected volatility reflects the assumption that the historical volatility is indicative of future trends, which may also not necessarily be the actual outcome. The fair value of the PSP also takes into account a market condition of total shareholder returns as compared to strategic competitors. No other features of options granted were incorporated into the measurement of fair value.

The share-based payments charge has been recorded in the income statement as follows:

	2009	2008
Employee costs	1	3

35 Other reserves and minority interests

a Group

£ million	Retained earnings	Unrealised gains and losses	Currency translation	Total	Group Minority interests*
Balance at April 1, 2007	903	99	(2)	1,000	200
Profit for the year attributable to shareholders	680			680	
Exchange differences and other movements			24	24	
Fair value of cash flow hedges transferred to passenger revenue		(5)		(5)	
Fair value of cash flow hedges transferred to fuel and oil costs		(136)		(136)	
Fair value of cash flow hedges transferred to currency differences		15		15	
Net change in fair value of cash flow hedges		245		245	
Cost of share-based payment	3			3	
Tax effect of share-based payment	(7)			(7)	
Deferred tax – rate change adjustment	6			6	
Share of other movements in reserves of associates	(2)			(2)	
Net fair value adjustment on available-for-sale financial assets		(5)		(5)	
Total income and expense for the year	680	114	24	818	
Balance at March 31, 2008:	1,583	213	22	1,818	200
Adoption of IFRIC 13	(206)			(206)	
Adoption of IFRIC 14	235			235	
At March 31, 2008 (Restated)	1,612	213	22	1,847	200
Loss for the year attributable to shareholders	(375)			**(375)**	
Exchange differences and other movements			38	**38**	
Fair value of cash flow hedges transferred to passenger revenue		13		**13**	
Fair value of cash flow hedges transferred to fuel and oil costs		(78)		**(78)**	
Fair value of cash flow hedges transferred to currency differences		(46)		**(46)**	
Net change in fair value of cash flow hedges		(877)		**(877)**	
Exercise of share options	(2)			**(2)**	
Cost of share-based payment	1			**1**	
Share of other movements in reserves of associates	(26)			**(26)**	
Held-to-maturity investments marked-to-market		(5)		**(5)**	
Available-for-sale financial assets – gains recycled to the income statement		(4)		**(4)**	
Net dividends	(56)			**(56)**	
Total income and expense for the year	(458)	(997)	38	**(1,417)**	
At March 31, 2009	**1,154**	**(784)**	**60**	**430**	**200**

* Minority Interests comprise €300 million of 6.75 per cent fixed coupon euro perpetual preferred securities issued by British Airways Finance (Jersey) L.P. in which the general partner is British Airways Holdings Limited, a wholly-owned subsidiary of the Company. The holders of these securities have no rights against Group undertakings other than the issuing entity and, to the extent prescribed by the subordinated guarantee, the Company. The effect of the securities on the Group as a whole, taking into account the subordinate guarantee and other surrounding arrangements, is that the obligations to transfer economic benefits in connection with the securities do not go beyond those that would normally attach to preference shares issued by a UK company.

Notes to the accounts continued

35 Other reserves and minority interests continued

b Company

£ million	Retained earnings	Unrealised gains and losses	Company Total
Balance at April 1, 2007	591	92	683
Profit for the year attributable to shareholders	540		540
Cost of share-based payment	3		3
Tax effect of share-based payment	(7)		(7)
Deferred tax – rate change adjustment	6		6
Fair value of cash flow hedges transferred to passenger revenue		(5)	(5)
Fair value of cash flow hedges transferred to fuel and oil costs		(136)	(136)
Fair value of cash flow hedges transferred to currency differences		15	15
Net change in fair value of cash flow hedges		245	245
Total income and expense for the year	542	119	661
Balance at March 31, 2008:	1,133	211	1,344
Adoption of IFRIC 13	(135)		(135)
Adoption of IFRIC 14	235		235
At April 1, 2008 (Restated)	1,233	211	1,444
Loss for the year attributable to shareholders	(389)		(389)
Cost of share-based payment	(2)		(2)
Deferred tax – rate change adjustment	1		1
Fair value of cash flow hedges transferred to passenger revenue		13	13
Fair value of cash flow hedges transferred to fuel and oil costs		(78)	(78)
Fair value of cash flow hedges transferred to currency differences		(46)	(46)
Net change in fair value of cash flow hedges		(877)	(877)
Net dividends	(56)		(56)
Total income and expense for the year	(446)	(988)	(1,434)
At March 31, 2009	**787**	**(777)**	**10**

The unrealised gains and losses reserve records fair value changes on available-for-sale investments and the portion of the gain or loss on a hedging instrument in a cash flow hedge that is determined to be an effective hedge.

The currency translation reserve is used to record exchange differences arising from the translation of the financial statements of foreign subsidiaries and associates.

Total shareholders' equity also includes the balance classified as share capital that includes the total net proceeds (both nominal value and share premium) on issue of the Company's equity share capital, comprising 25 pence ordinary shares. Investment in own shares consists of shares held by British Airways Employee Benefits Trust (Jersey) Limited, a wholly-owned subsidiary, for the purposes of the Employee Share Ownership plans including the Long Term Incentive Plan (LTIP). At March 31, 2009, the Group and Company held 2,134,461 shares for the LTIP and other employee share schemes (2008: 2,087,147 shares). The purchase of shares was financed by the Company granting a loan to British Airways Employee Benefits Trust (Jersey) Limited.

36 Pension costs

The Company operates two funded principal defined benefit pension schemes in the UK, the Airways Pension Scheme (APS) and the New Airways Pension Scheme (NAPS) both of which are closed to new members. APS has been closed to new members since March 31, 1984, and NAPS closed to new members on March 31, 2003. From April 1, 2003, the Company commenced a new defined contribution scheme, the British Airways Retirement Plan (BARP), of which all new permanent employees over the age of 18 employed by the Company and certain subsidiary undertakings in the UK may become members. The assets of the scheme are held in separate trustee-administered funds.

Benefits provided under APS are based on final average pensionable pay and, for the majority of members, are subject to increases in payment in line with the Retail Price Index (RPI). Those provided under NAPS are based on final average pensionable pay reduced by an amount (the 'abatement') not exceeding one and a half times the government's lower earnings limit. NAPS benefits are subject to RPI increases in payment up to a maximum of five per cent in any one year.

In February 2007, following consultation with members and agreement with the Trustees, the Group amended NAPS for future service to restrict future increases in pensionable pay to RPI and increase the normal retirement age to 65. In addition, the Group agreed to make a one-off cash injection of £800 million into NAPS, of which £240 million was paid in February 2007, with the remaining balance of £560 million paid in April 2007 and an additional £50 million was paid in March 2008. The Group also agreed to make annual contributions of approximately £280 million a year for the next 10 years. Additionally, guarantees are issued in respect of APS, £230 million and NAPS, £100 million.

Most employees engaged outside the UK are covered by appropriate local arrangements. The Company provides certain additional post-retirement healthcare benefits to eligible employees in the US. The Company participates in a multi-employer defined benefit plan operated in the US by the International Association of Machinists (IAM) and presents the plan in the financial statements as if it were a defined contribution plan as it is not possible to allocate the assets and liabilities of the scheme due to the nature of the scheme. Contributions to the IAM plan were £2.1 million (2008: £1.9 million).

Pension contributions for APS and NAPS were determined by actuarial valuations made as at March 31, 2006, using assumptions and methodologies agreed between the Company and the Trustees of each scheme. At the date of the actuarial valuation, the market values of the assets of APS and NAPS amounted to £6,650 million and £5,832 million respectively. The value of the assets represented 100 per cent (APS) and 74 per cent (NAPS) of the value of the benefits that had accrued to members after allowing for assumed increases in earnings. These valuations determined employer contribution rates of an average of 34.6 per cent of pensionable pay for APS and 20.7 per cent of pensionable pay for NAPS. For NAPS, the contribution rate to be paid by the employer depends on the normal retirement age chosen by members.

Employer contributions in respect of overseas employees have been determined in accordance with best local practice.

Total employer contributions to defined contribution pension plans both in the UK and overseas for the year ended March 31, 2009, were £25 million (2008: £17 million). The Company's contributions to APS and NAPS in the next year as determined by the actuarial review completed in March 2006 are expected to be approximately £320 million.

a Employee benefit schemes recognised on the balance sheet

£ million	Employee benefit obligations 2009	2008	Employee benefit assets 2009	2008
Arising under defined benefit pension plans and post-retirement benefits	57	204	340	320
Arising under post-retirement medical benefit plans	123	116		
Total arising under post-retirement benefits	180	320	340	320
Other employee benefit obligations	11	10		
At March 31	191	330	340	320

At March 31, 2009, NAPS was recognised on the balance sheet as an asset. However, due to the level of unrecognised losses it holds, its net position is a liability and therefore on all future tables within this note, it is included as an employee benefit obligation.

Employee benefit assets refer to the Group and Company in all instances. Employee benefit obligations include £9 million (2008: £8 million) relating to British Airways Holidays Limited with the remainder relating to the Company.

Notes to the accounts continued

36 Pension costs continued

b Scheme assets and liabilities

| | Employee benefit obligations | | | Employee benefit assets | | 2009 |
	NAPS	Other schemes	Total	APS	Other schemes	Total
£ million						
Scheme assets at fair value:						
Equities	3,780	122	**3,902**	898	16	**914**
Bonds	1,665	76	**1,741**	4,679	12	**4,691**
Others	604	5	**609**	348		**348**
Fair value of scheme assets	6,049	203	**6,252**	5,925	28	**5,953**
Present value of scheme liabilities	7,216	497	**7,713**	5,065	28	**5,093**
Net pension (liability)/asset	**(1,167)**	**(294)**	**(1,461)**	**860**	**–**	**860**
Net pension asset/(liability) represented by:						
Net pension asset/(liability) recognised	26	(180)	**(154)**	304	10	**314**
Tax effect of APS surplus recognised				135		**135**
Cumulative actuarial (losses)/gains not recognised	(1,193)	(114)	**(1,307)**	421	(10)	**411**
	(1,167)	**(294)**	**(1,461)**	**860**	**–**	**860**

| | Employee benefit obligations | | | Employee benefit assets | | 2008 Restated |
	NAPS	Other schemes	Total	APS	Other schemes	Total
£ million						
Scheme assets at fair value:						
Equities	4,488	147	4,635	1,033	20	1,053
Bonds	1,882	68	1,950	5,079	15	5,094
Others	978	6	984	556		556
Fair value of scheme assets	7,348	221	7,569	6,668	35	6,703
Present value of scheme liabilities	7,705	384	8,089	5,432	29	5,461
Net pension (liability)/asset	(357)	(163)	(520)	1,236	6	1,242
Net pension (liability)/asset represented by:						
Net pension (liability)/asset recognised	(148)	(172)	(320)	312	8	320
Tax effect of APS surplus recognised				126		126
Cumulative actuarial (losses)/gains not recognised	(209)	9	(200)	798	(2)	796
	(357)	(163)	(520)	1,236	6	1,242

The pension plans have not invested in any of the Group's own financial instruments nor in properties or other assets used by the Group.

36 Pension costs continued

c Amounts recognised in the income statement

	Employee benefit obligations			Employee benefit assets		2009
£ million	NAPS	Other schemes	**Total**	APS	Other schemes	**Total**
Current service cost	129	7	**136**	14		**14**
Past service cost	3		**3**	1		**1**
Recognised in arriving at operating loss	**132**	**7**	**139**	**15**	**–**	**15**
Expected return on scheme assets	(502)	(19)	**(521)**	(338)	(3)	**(341)**
Interest costs on scheme liabilities	502	26	**528**	367	1	**368**
Amortisation of APS surplus (net of tax)				(17)		**(17)**
Other finance cost	**–**	**7**	**7**	**12**	**(2)**	**10**

	Employee benefit obligations			Employee benefit assets		2008 Restated
£ million	NAPS	Other schemes	Total	APS	Other schemes	Total
Current service cost	170	7	177	20		20
Past service cost	1		1	1		1
Recognised in arriving at operating profit	171	7	178	21	–	21
Expected return on scheme assets	(495)	(18)	(513)	(341)	(2)	(343)
Immediate recognition of losses and the effect of the asset ceiling				19		19
Interest costs on scheme liabilities	425	23	448	318	1	319
Other finance cost	(70)	5	(65)	(4)	(1)	(5)

d Unrecognised cumulative actuarial gains and losses

	Employee benefit obligations			Employee benefit assets		
£ million	NAPS	Other schemes	Total	APS	Other schemes	Total
Amount of unrecognised actuarial losses at April 1, 2007 (Restated)	(593)	7	(586)			
Actual return on scheme assets	6	(8)	(2)	523	3	526
Less: Expected return on scheme assets	(495)	(18)	(513)	(341)	(2)	(343)
	(489)	(26)	(515)	182	1	183
Other actuarial gains/(losses)	873	28	901	616	(3)	613
Cumulative unrecognised actuarial (losses)/gains at March 31, 2008	(209)	9	(200)	798	(2)	796
Actual return on scheme assets	(1,462)	(6)	**(1,468)**	(385)	(6)	**(391)**
Less: Expected return on scheme assets	(502)	(19)	**(521)**	(338)	(3)	**(341)**
	(1,964)	(25)	**(1,989)**	(723)	(9)	**(732)**
Other actuarial gains/(losses)	980	(98)	**882**	372	1	**373**
Amortisation of APS surplus (gross of tax)				(26)		**(26)**
Cumulative unrecognised actuarial (losses)/gains at March 31, 2009	**(1,193)**	**(114)**	**(1,307)**	**421**	**(10)**	**411**

The actuarial assumptions made for the expected rates of return on assets were derived by considering best estimates for the expected long-term real rates of return from the main asset classes and combining these in proportions for each scheme. These assumed rates of return are net of investment expenses.

Notes to the accounts continued

36 Pension costs continued

e Actuarial assumptions

At March 31

Per cent per annum	2009 NAPS	2009 APS*	2009 Other schemes	2008 NAPS	2008 APS*	2008 Other schemes
Inflation	3.0	2.7	2.5-3.0	3.5	3.5	3.0-5.0
Rate of increase in salaries	3.0	2.7	2.8-8.5	3.5	4.0	1.5-5.5
Rate of increase of pensions in payment	2.9	2.7	1.5-10.0	3.4	3.5	1.5-11.0
Discount rate	6.9	7.1	1.9-7.6	6.6	7.0	2.0-6.6
Expected rate of return on scheme assets	7.1	4.7	5.5-8.5	6.9	5.2	4.0-7.6

* Rate of increase in salaries is assumed to be in line with inflation (2008: 4.0 per cent per annum for three years, 1.0 per cent in excess of RPI to March 2016 and 1.5 per cent in excess of RPI thereafter).

Rate of increase in healthcare costs are based on medical trend rates of 10 per cent grading down to 5 per cent over five years (2008: 11 per cent grading down to 5 per cent over six years).

In the UK, mortality rates are calculated using the 00-series standard mortality tables for APS and the PA80 standard mortality tables for NAPS (the two largest Group and Company schemes). The standard mortality tables were selected based on the actual recent mortality experience of members and were adjusted to allow for future mortality changes. In the US, mortality rates were based on the 1994 GAM Static tables. If the post-retirement mortality tables used for APS and NAPS were to be changed such that the life expectancy of members was increased by one year, the defined benefit obligations would increase by approximately £110 million in APS and approximately £140 million in NAPS.

If the discount rate were to be decreased by 0.1 per cent without changing any other assumptions, the defined benefit obligations would increase by approximately £50 million in APS and £120 million in NAPS.

A one percentage point change in the assumed rate of increase in healthcare costs would have the following effects:

£ million	Increase	Decrease
Effect on aggregate service cost and interest cost	(3)	2
Effect on defined benefit obligation	(26)	21

f Present value of scheme liabilities

£ million	Employee benefit obligations NAPS	Employee benefit obligations Other schemes	Employee benefit obligations Total	Employee benefit assets APS	Employee benefit assets Other schemes	Employee benefit assets Total
As at April 1, 2007	8,110	397	8,507	6,076	27	6,103
Current service cost	170	7	177	20		20
Past service cost	1		1	1		1
Interest cost	425	23	448	318	1	319
Benefits paid	(202)	(15)	(217)	(375)	(2)	(377)
Employee contributions	74		74	8		8
Actuarial (gains)/losses	(873)	(28)	(901)	(616)	3	(613)
As at March 31, 2008	7,705	384	8,089	5,432	29	5,461
Current service cost	129	7	**136**	14		**14**
Past service cost	3		**3**	1		**1**
Interest cost	502	26	**528**	367	1	**368**
Benefits paid	(221)	(18)	**(239)**	(385)	(1)	**(386)**
Employee contributions	78		**78**	8		**8**
Actuarial (gains)/losses	(980)	98	**(882)**	(372)	(1)	**(373)**
At March 31, 2009	**7,216**	**497**	**7,713**	**5,065**	**28**	**5,093**

The defined benefit obligation comprises £169 million (2008: £134 million) arising from unfunded plans and £7,544 million (2008: £7,955 million) from plans that are wholly or partly funded.

36 Pension costs continued

g Fair value of scheme assets

£ million	Employee benefit obligations			Employee benefit assets		
	NAPS	Other schemes	Total	APS	Other schemes	Total
As at April 1, 2007	6,553	238	6,791	6,491	34	6,525
Expected return on plan assets	495	18	513	341	2	343
Employer contributions	917	6	923	21		21
Contributions by employees	74		74	8		8
Benefits paid	(202)	(15)	(217)	(375)	(2)	(377)
Actuarial (losses)/gains	(489)	(26)	(515)	182	1	183
As at March 31, 2008	7,348	221	7,569	6,668	35	6,703
Expected return on plan assets	502	19	**521**	338	3	**341**
Employer contributions	306	6	**312**	19		**19**
Contributions by employees	78		**78**	8		**8**
Benefits paid	(221)	(18)	**(239)**	(385)	(1)	**(386)**
Actuarial losses	(1,964)	(25)	**(1,989)**	(723)	(9)	**(732)**
At March 31, 2009	**6,049**	**203**	**6,252**	**5,925**	**28**	**5,953**

h History of experience gains and losses

£ million	Employee benefit obligations			Employee benefit assets		
	NAPS	Other schemes	**Total**	APS	Other schemes	**Total**
As at March 31, 2009						
Fair value of scheme assets	6,049	203	**6,252**	5,925	28	**5,953**
Present value of defined benefit obligation	(7,216)	(497)	**(7,713)**	(5,065)	(28)	**(5,093)**
(Deficit)/surplus in the scheme	(1,167)	(294)	**(1,461)**	860		**860**
Experience adjustments arising on plan liabilities	(980)	98	**(882)**	(372)	(1)	**(373)**
Experience adjustments arising on plan assets	(1,964)	(25)	**(1,989)**	(723)	(9)	**(732)**
As at March 31, 2008 (Restated)						
Fair value of scheme assets	7,348	221	7,569	6,668	35	6,703
Present value of defined benefit obligation	(7,705)	(384)	(8,089)	(5,432)	(29)	(5,461)
(Deficit)/surplus in the scheme	(357)	(163)	(520)	1,236	6	1,242
Experience adjustments arising on plan liabilities	(873)	(28)	(901)	(616)	3	(613)
Experience adjustments arising on plan assets	(489)	(26)	(515)	182	1	183
As at March 31, 2007						
Fair value of scheme assets	6,553	238	6,791	6,491	34	6,525
Present value of defined benefit obligation	(8,110)	(397)	(8,507)	(6,076)	(27)	(6,103)
APS irrecoverable surplus				(306)		(306)
(Deficit)/surplus in the scheme	(1,557)	(159)	(1,716)	109	7	116
Experience adjustments arising on plan liabilities	(113)	52	(61)	(272)	3	(269)
Experience adjustments arising on plan assets	(27)	(21)	(48)	(138)	(3)	(141)
As at March 31, 2006						
Fair value of scheme assets	5,832	318	6,150	6,650	36	6,686
Present value of defined benefit obligation	(7,902)	(538)	(8,440)	(5,867)	(30)	(5,897)
APS irrecoverable surplus				(652)		(652)
(Deficit)/surplus in the scheme	(2,070)	(220)	(2,290)	131	6	137
Experience adjustments arising on plan liabilities	(920)	(25)	(945)	(285)	(5)	(290)
Experience adjustments arising on plan assets	794	35	829	581	5	586
As at March 31, 2005						
Fair value of scheme assets	4,554	266	4,820	6,031	29	6,060
Present value of defined benefit obligation	(6,523)	(488)	(7,011)	(5,603)	(24)	(5,627)
APS irrecoverable surplus				(296)		(296)
(Deficit)/surplus in the scheme	(1,969)	(222)	(2,191)	132	5	137

The directors are unable to determine how much of the pension scheme surplus or deficit recognised on transition to IFRS and taken directly to equity is attributable to actuarial gains and losses since inception of those pension schemes.

Notes to the accounts continued

37 Contingent liabilities

There were contingent liabilities at March 31, 2009, in respect of guarantees and indemnities entered into as part of the ordinary course of the Group's business. No material losses are likely to arise from such contingent liabilities. A number of other lawsuits and regulatory proceedings are pending, the outcome of which in the aggregate is not expected to have a material effect on the Group's financial position or results of operations.

The Group and the Company have guaranteed certain borrowings, liabilities and commitments, which at March 31, 2009, amounted to £185 million (2008: £173 million) and £498 million (2008: £448 million) respectively. For the Company these included guarantees given in respect of the fixed perpetual preferred securities issued by subsidiary undertakings.

The Group is involved in certain claims and litigation related to its operations. In the opinion of management, liabilities, if any, arising from these claims and litigation will not have a material adverse effect on the Group's consolidated financial position or results of operations. The Group files income tax returns in many jurisdictions throughout the world. Various tax authorities are currently examining the Group's income tax returns. Tax returns contain matters that could be subject to differing interpretations of applicable tax laws and regulations and the resolution of tax positions through negotiations with relevant tax authorities, or through litigation, can take several years to complete. While it is difficult to predict the ultimate outcome in some cases, the Group does not anticipate that there will be any material impact on the Group's financial position or results of operations.

38 Related party transactions

The Group and Company had transactions in the ordinary course of business during the year under review with related parties.

£ million	Group		Company	
	2009	*2008*	**2009**	*2008*
Associates:				
Sales to associates	**41**	*43*	**41**	*43*
Purchases from associates	**53**	*54*	**53**	*54*
Amounts owed by associates	**1**	*4*	**1**	*4*
Amounts owed to associates	**2**		**2**	
Subsidiaries:				
Sales to subsidiaries			**26**	*36*
Purchases from subsidiaries			**131**	*126*
Amounts owed by subsidiaries			**169**	*116*
Amounts owed to subsidiaries			**2,106**	*1,982*

In addition, the Company meets certain costs of administering the Group's retirement benefit plans, including the provision of support services to the Trustees. Costs borne on behalf of the retirement benefit plans amounted to £3.8 million in relation to the costs of the Pension Protection Fund levy (2008: £3.6 million).

Associates

a Iberia, Lineas Aéreas de España, S.A. (Iberia)
The Group has a 13.15 per cent investment in Iberia. Areas of opportunity for cooperation have been identified and work continues to pursue and implement these. Sales and purchases between related parties are made at normal market prices and outstanding balances are unsecured and interest free. Cash settlement is expected within the standard settlement terms specified by the IATA Clearing House.

As at March 31, 2009, the net trading balance owed to Iberia by the Group amounted to £1 million (2008: £3 million owed by Iberia).

b Other associates
The remaining net trading balance of £1 million as at March 31, 2009, was due to transactions between the Group and Dunwoody Airline Services (Holdings) Limited.

38 Related party transactions continued

Subsidiaries

Transactions with subsidiaries are carried out on an arm's length basis. Outstanding balances that relate to trading balances are placed on inter-company accounts with no specified credit period. Long-term loans owed to and from the Company by subsidiary undertakings bear market rates of interest in accordance with the inter-company loan agreements.

Directors' and officers' loans and transactions

No loans or credit transactions were outstanding with directors or officers of the Company at March 31, 2009, or arose during the year that need to be disclosed in accordance with the requirements of Schedule 6 to the Companies Act 1985.

In addition to the above, the Group and Company also have transactions with related parties that are conducted in the normal course of airline business. These include the provision of airline and related services.

Neither the Group nor Company have provided or benefited from any guarantees for any related party receivables or payables. During the year ended March 31, 2009, the Group has not made any provision for doubtful debts relating to amounts owed by related parties (2008: £nil).

Compensation of key management personnel (including directors):

£ million	Group		Company	
	2009	*2008*	**2009**	*2008*
Short-term employee benefits	**4**	*4*	**4**	*4*
Share-based payments	**1**	*2*	**1**	*2*
Termination benefits	**1**		**1**	
At March 31	**6**	*6*	**6**	*6*

39 Foreign currency translation rates

£1 equals	At March 31		Annual average	
	2009	*2008*	**2009**	*2008*
Euro	**1.07**	*1.26*	**1.21**	*1.43*
US dollar	**1.43**	*1.99*	**1.75**	*2.01*
Japanese yen	**140**	*197*	**177**	*231*

Operating and financial statistics

For the five years ended March 31, 2009

Total Group operations (note 1)

		2009	2008*	2007	2006**	2005***
Traffic and capacity						
Revenue passenger km (RPK)	m	114,346	118,395	112,851	109,713	107,892
Available seat km (ASK)	m	148,504	149,576	148,321	144,194	144,189
Passenger load factor	%	77.0	79.1	76.1	76.1	74.8
Cargo tonne km (CTK)	m	4,638	4,892	4,695	4,929	4,954
Total revenue tonne km (RTK)	m	16,054	16,797	16,112	15,909	15,731
Total available tonne km (ATK)	m	22,293	22,872	22,882	22,719	22,565
Overall load factor	%	72.0	73.4	70.4	70.0	69.7
Passengers carried	'000	33,117	34,613	33,068	32,432	35,717
Tonnes of cargo carried	'000	777	805	762	795	877
Revenue aircraft km	m	644	644	637	614	661
Revenue flights	'000	279	281	276	280	378
Operations						
Average manpower equivalent (MPE)		41,473	41,745	42,683	43,814	47,472
RTKs per MPE		387.1	402.4	377.5	363.1	331.4
ATKs per MPE		537.5	547.9	536.1	518.5	475.3
Aircraft in service at year end		245	245	242	284	290
Aircraft utilisation (average hours per aircraft per day)		10.68	10.91	10.82	10.29	9.83
Unduplicated route km	'000	621	629	589	574	623
Punctuality – within 15 minutes	%	77	63	67	75	76
Regularity	%	98.6	98.2	98.5	98.8	98.8
Financial						
Passenger revenue per RPK	p	6.85	6.42	6.44	6.31	6.02
Passenger revenue per ASK	p	5.28	5.08	4.90	4.80	4.51
Cargo revenue per CTK	p	14.51	12.57	12.74	12.94	9.73
Average fuel price before hedging (US cents/US gallon)		284.06	245.26	209.60	188.22	136.44
Interest cover (note 2)	times	(3.6)	15.4	16.7	6.0	3.8
Dividend cover	times	(5.2)	n/a	n/a	n/a	n/a
Operating margin (note 3)	%	(2.4)	10.0	7.1	8.5	7.2
Earnings before interest, tax, depreciation, amortisation and rentals (EBITDAR)	m	645	1,780	1,549	1,666	1,552
Net debt/total capital ratio (note 4)	%	56.3	28.7	29.1	44.2	67.7
Net debt/total capital ratio including operating leases	%	62.8	38.2	39.6	53.0	72.4
Total traffic revenue per RTK	p	53.00	48.91	48.79	47.53	44.4
Total traffic revenue per ATK	p	38.17	35.92	34.35	33.28	30.94
Total operating expenditure per RTK (note 5)	p	57.38	46.91	49.26	47.26	40.85
Total operating expenditure per ATK (note 5)	p	41.32	34.45	34.68	33.10	28.48

* Restated for the adoption of IFRIC 13 and 14 and to include frequent flyer passenger numbers.

** Restated for the disposal of the regional business of BA Connect.

*** Restated for the adoption of IFRS.

n/a = not applicable

Notes:

1. Operating statistics do not include those of associate undertakings and franchisees.

2. Interest cover is defined as the number of times (loss)/profit before tax excluding net interest payable covers the net interest payable. Interest cover is not a financial measure under IFRS. However, management believes this measure is useful to investors when analysing the Group's ability to meet its interest commitments from current earnings. The following table shows a reconciliation of net interest payable for each of the two most recent financial years:

	Year ended March 31	
£ million (except ratios)	2009	2008*
(Loss)/profit before tax	(401)	922
Net interest payable (a)	(87)	(64)
(Loss)/profit adjusted for interest payable (b)	(3.14)	986
Interest cover (b)/(a)	(3.6)	15.4

* Restated for the adoption of IFRIC 13 and 14 and to include frequent flyer passenger numbers.

3. Operating margin is defined as operating (loss)/profit as a percentage of revenue. Revenue comprises: passenger revenue (scheduled services and non-scheduled services), cargo services and other revenue.

4. Net debt as a percentage of total capital. Net debt is defined as the total of loans, finance leases and hire purchase liabilities, net of short-term loans and deposits and cash less overdrafts. See note 25 to the financial statements for details of the calculation of net debt. Total capital is defined as the total of capital, reserves, minority interests, and net debt. Total capital and the net debt/total capital ratio are not financial measures under IFRS. Similarly, net debt adjusted to include obligations under operating leases is not a financial measure under IFRS. However, management believes these measures are useful to investors when analysing the extent to which the Group is funded by debt rather than by shareholders' funds. The following table shows a reconciliation of total capital to total shareholders' funds and the net debt/capital ratio for each of the two most recent financial years:

	Year ended March 31	
£ million (except ratios)	2009	2008*
Capital and reserves	1,646	3,062
Add minority interests	200	200
Total shareholders' equity	1,846	3,262
Net debt (a)	2,382	1,310
Total capital (b)	4,228	4,572
Net debt/total capital percentage (a)/(b)	56.3	28.7

* Restated for the adoption of IFRIC 13 and 14 and to include frequent flyer passenger numbers.

5. Total expenditure on operations, total expenditure on operations per RTK and total expenditure on operations per ATK are not financial measures under IFRS. However, management believes these measures are useful to investors as they provide further analysis of the performance of the Group's main business activity, namely airline operations. The Board of directors reviews these measures internally on a monthly basis as an indication of management's performance in reducing costs. The following table shows a reconciliation of total expenditure on operations per RTK and total expenditure on operations per ATK for each of the two most recent financial years:

	Year ended March 31	
£ million (except ratios)	2009	2008*
Total expenditure on operations	9,212	7,880
RTKs	16,054	16,797
ATKs	22,293	22,872
Total expenditure on operations per RTK (p)	57.38	46.91
Total expenditure on operations per ATK (p)	41.32	34.45

* Restated for the adoption of IFRIC 13 and 14 and to include frequent flyer passenger numbers.

Principal investments

At March 31, 2009

Investments in subsidiaries

The following table includes those principal investments which significantly impact the results or assets of the Group.

These subsidiaries are wholly-owned except where indicated.

	Principal activities	Country of incorporation and registration and principal operations
Air Miles Travel Promotions Limited (from April 1, 2009, The Mileage Company Limited)	Airline marketing	England
BA & AA Holdings Limited	Holding Company	England
BA Cash Management Limited Partnership	Investment	England
BA Cityflyer Limited (referred to as CityFlyer)	Airline operations	England
BA European Limited (trading as OpenSkies)	Airline operations	England
BritAir Holdings Limited	Holding Company	England
British Airways 777 Leasing Limited	Aircraft financing	England
British Airways Avionic Engineering Limited	Aircraft maintenance	England
British Airways Holdings Limited	Airline finance	Jersey
British Airways Holidays Limited	Package holidays	England
British Airways Interior Engineering Limited	Aircraft maintenance	England
British Airways Leasing Limited	Aircraft financing	England
British Airways Maintenance Cardiff Limited	Aircraft maintenance	England
Speedbird Cash Management Limited	Investment	Bermuda
Speedbird Insurance Company Limited	Insurance	Bermuda
The Plimsoll Line Limited	Holding Company	England

Investments in associates

	Percentage of equity owned	Principal activities	Country of incorporation and principal operations
Iberia, Lineas Aéreas de España, S.A. (Iberia)*	13.15	Airline operations	Spain

Available for sale and other investments

	Percentage of equity owned	Principal activities	Country of incorporation and principal operations
Comair Limited*	10.9	Airline operations	South Africa
Flybe Group Limited*	15.0	Airline operations	England
The Airline Group Limited	16.7	Air traffic control holding company	England

*   Not owned directly by British Airways Plc.

Shareholder information

General Information

Financial calendar

Financial year end	March 31, 2009
Annual general meeting	July 14, 2009

Announcement of 2009/10 results

Three-month results to June 30, 2009	July 31, 2009
Six-month results to September 30, 2009	November 6, 2009
Nine-month results to December 31, 2009	February 5, 2010
Preliminary announcement	May 21, 2010
Report and Accounts	June 2010

Registered Office

Waterside, PO Box 365, Harmondsworth, UB7 0GB

Registered number – 1777777

Outside advisers

Company Registrars: Computershare Investor Services Plc,
PO Box 82, The Pavilions, Bridgewater Road, Bristol, BS99 7NH

ADR Depositary: Citibank Shareholder Services, PO Box 43077,
Providence, RI 02940-3077, USA

Unsolicited mail

The Company is obliged by law to make its share register available
on request to other organisations which may then use it as a
mailing list. This may result in receiving unsolicited mail. If you wish
to limit the receipt of unsolicited mail you may do so by writing
to the Mailing Preference Service, an independent organisation
whose services are free to you. Once your name and address have
been added to its records, it will advise the companies and other
bodies which support the service that you no longer wish to
receive unsolicited mail.

If you would like more details please write to: The Mailing
Preference Service, FREEPOST 22, London, W1E 7EZ.

The Company asks organisations which obtain its register
to support this service.

ShareGift

Shareholders with small numbers of shares may like to consider
donating their shares to charity under ShareGift, administered by
the Orr Mackintosh Foundation. Details are available from the
Company Registrars.

Glossary

Airline operations	This includes British Airways Plc, CityFlyer, Flyline Tele Sales & Services GmbH and OpenSkies.
Available seat kilometres (ASK)	The number of seats available for sale multiplied by the distance flown.
Available tonne kilometres (ATK)	The number of tonnes of capacity available for the carriage of revenue load (passenger and cargo) multiplied by the distance flown.
Revenue passenger kilometres (RPK)	The number of revenue passengers carried multiplied by the distance flown.
Cargo tonne kilometres (CTK)	The number of revenue tonnes of cargo (freight and mail) carried multiplied by the distance flown.
Revenue tonne kilometres (RTK)	The revenue load in tonnes multiplied by the distance flown.
Passenger load factor	RPK expressed as a percentage of ASK.
Overall load factor	RTK expressed as a percentage of ATK.
Revenue per RPK	Passenger revenue from airline scheduled operations divided by airline scheduled RPK.
Total traffic revenue per RTK	Revenue from total traffic (scheduled and non-scheduled) divided by RTK.
Total traffic revenue per ATK	Revenue from total traffic (scheduled and non-scheduled) divided by ATK.
Punctuality	The industry's standard, measured as the percentage of flights departing within 15 minutes of schedule.
Regularity	The percentage of flights completed to flights scheduled, excluding flights cancelled for commercial reasons.
Shortlanded baggage performance	Ratio of number of mislaid or misdirected bags to every 1,000 passengers flown.
Unduplicated route kilometres	All scheduled flight stages counted once, regardless of frequency or direction.
Interest cover	The number of times (loss)/profit before taxation and net interest expense and interest income covers the net interest expense and interest income.
Dividend cover	The number of times (loss)/profit for the year covers the dividends paid and proposed.
Operating margin	Operating (loss)/profit as a percentage of revenue.
Net debt	Loans, finance leases and hire purchase arrangements net of other current interest-bearing deposits and cash and cash equivalents less overdrafts.
Net debt/total capital ratio (including operating leases)	Net debt as a ratio of total capital, adjusted to include the discounted value of future operating lease commitments.
Total capital	Total equity plus net debt.
Net debt/total capital ratio	Net debt as a ratio of total capital.
Manpower equivalent	Number of employees adjusted for part-time workers, overtime and contractors.
EBITDAR	Earnings before interest, tax, depreciation, amortisation and rentals.
n/a	Not applicable.

GLOSSARY

accounting income The amount of income (before subtracting income tax) recognized for financial reporting purposes. Contrast with **taxable income**. *579*

accrual method (of accounting for income tax) Focuses on obtaining the balance sheet value for the income tax liability (or asset) that best reflects the assets and liabilities recognized on the balance sheet. *579*

accrued benefit obligation The present value of pension benefits that employees have earned. *618*

actuarial gain A favourable difference between actual and expected amounts for pension assets or obligations; also called an experience gain. *621*

actuarial loss An unfavourable difference between actual and expected amounts for pension assets or obligations; also called an experience loss. *621*

actuary A professional who specializes in the estimation of risks and uncertainties. *617*

agency cost of leasing The reduced level of care due to the separation of an asset's ownership and its control. *654*

amortized cost (of debt) The amount initially recognized for the debt adjusted by subsequent amortization of premium or discount. *447*

annuity A series of cash flows in equal amounts occurring at regular intervals. An **ordinary annuity** has cash flows at the *end* of each period. In comparison, an **annuity due** has cash flows at the *beginning* of each period. *A3*

appropriation The process that allocates a portion of retained earnings to a reserve. *479*

at-the-money An option is at the money if the market price of the share equals the exercise price. Compare with **in-the-money** and **out-of-the-money**. *549*

bargain purchase option An option given to the lessee to purchase the leased asset at a price that is below expected fair value at a future date; the assessment of whether a bargain exists is made at the time of entering the lease arrangement. *655*

basic EPS An indicator of profitability that measures how much of the company's earnings are attributable (belong) to each ordinary share. *539*

best efforts approach Occurs where the broker simply agrees to try to sell as much of the (debt) issue as possible to investors. *442*

bond indenture Contract that outlines the terms of the bond, including the maturity date; rate of interest and interest payment dates; security pledged; and financial covenants. *442*

call option See **option**. *512*

call premium The excess over par value paid to the bondholders when the security is called. *443*

callable bonds Bonds that permit the issuing company to "call" for the bonds to be redeemed before maturity. *443*

capital cost allowance (CCA) Depreciation for tax purposes. *588*

capital lease See **finance lease** *653*

cash equivalents Short-term, highly liquid investments that are readily convertible to known amounts of cash and which are subject to an insignificant risk of changes in value. *692*

cash flow hedge A financial instrument that reduces the exposure to changes in future cash flows. *522*

common share An equity interest that has the lowest priority and represents the residual ownership interest in the company. *476*

complex capital structure A capital structure that includes potentially dilutive securities. Contrast with **simple capital structure**. *539*

compound financial instruments Those financial instruments with more than one financial instrument component. *515*

contingency An existing condition that depends on the outcome of one or more future events. *410*

contingent asset A possible asset that arises from past events and whose existence will be confirmed only by the occurrence or non-occurrence of one or more future events. *413*

contingent liability Is (a) a possible obligation that arises from past events and whose existence depends on one or more future events; or (b) a present obligation that arises from past events that is not recognized as a liability because: (i) it is not probable that an outflow of economic resources will be required to settle the obligation; or (ii) the amount of the obligation cannot be measured with sufficient reliability. *411*

contributed capital The component of equity that reflects amounts received by the reporting entity from transactions with its owners, net of any repayments from capital. *476*

contributed surplus The component of contributed capital other than par value. *477*

convertible bonds Bonds that allow the holder to exchange or "convert" the bond into other securities in the corporation, usually common shares. *443*

corridor The limit within which actuarial gains and losses need not be amortized into income. *621*

coupon (stated) rate The interest rate specified in the bond indenture. *445*

covenant The borrower's promise to restrict certain activities. *442*

current assets Assets that are expected to be consumed or sold within one year of the balance sheet date or the business' normal operating cycle, whichever is longer. Also includes assets held primarily for trading purposes. *397*

current liabilities Obligations that are expected to be settled within one year of the balance sheet date or the business' normal operating cycle, whichever is longer. Also includes held-for-trading liabilities. *395*

current service cost The increase in the present value of pension obligations due to an employee's provision of services during the current period. *618*

curtailment A reduction in the number of employees or the amount of benefits they will receive in the future. *630*

debentures Unsecured bonds. *443*

deductible temporary difference A temporary difference that results in *future taxable* income being less than accounting income; contrast with **taxable temporary difference**. *586*

deferral method (of accounting for income tax) Focuses on obtaining the income statement value for income tax expense that best matches the amount of income recognized for the year. *579*

deferred revenue A non-financial obligation arising from the collection of revenue that has not yet been earned. *405*

deferred tax asset The amount of income tax recoverable in future periods as a result of deductible temporary differences, losses carried forward, or tax credits carried forward. *586*

deferred tax liability The amount of income tax payable in future periods as a result of taxable temporary differences. *586*

defined benefit plan A pension plan that specifies how much in pension payments employees will receive during their retirement. *616*

defined contribution plan A pension plan that specifies how much funds the employer needs to contribute. *616*

derivative A financial instrument that is derived from some other underlying quantity. *511*

diluted EPS Measures the amount of the company's earnings attributable to each ordinary shareholder in a hypothetical scenario in which all dilutive securities are converted to ordinary shares. *546*

dilutive potential ordinary shares Potential ordinary shares whose conversion to ordinary shares would decrease EPS or increase loss per share from continuing operations. *546*

direct-financing lease A type of finance lease in which the sale price is equal to the cost of the asset to the lessor (used in Canadian ASPE). *665*

direct method A method of presenting the statement of cash flows by showing major classes of gross cash receipts and gross cash payments. *697*

earnings multiple A number that, when multiplied with earnings, provides an estimate of a share's value. When earnings are expected to grow at rate g and the discount rate is r, the earnings multiple is equal to $(1 + g)(r - g)$ *A9*

earnings per share (EPS) Measures each ordinary share's interest in a company's earnings. *538*

effective interest rate The **yield** on the date of issuance of a debt security. *445*

employee stock option An option a company issues to its employees, giving them the right to buy shares in their employer at a pre-specified price. *513*

executory costs Incidental costs in a lease that would be incurred by the lessee independent of whether the lessee had purchased or leased the asset. *659*

expected value The value determined by weighting possible outcomes by their associated probabilities. *404*

fair value hedge Reduces the exposure to changes in fair value. *522*

fair value The amount for which an asset could be exchanged, or a liability settled, between knowledgeable, willing parties in an arm's-length transaction. *396*

finance lease (also capital lease) A type of lease that transfers substantially all of an asset's risks and rewards of ownership from the lessor to the lessee; for a lessor, a finance lease also has normal credit risk and no material unreimbursable costs. *653*

financial guarantee contract A contract that requires the issuer to make specified payments to reimburse the holder for a loss it incurs because a specified debtor fails to make payment when due. *416*

financial leverage Quantifies the relationship between the relative level of a firm's debt and its equity base. *439*

financial liability A contractual obligation to deliver cash or other financial assets to another party. *395, 441*

financing activities Activities that result in changes in the size and composition of the contributed equity and borrowings of the equity. *693*

firm commitment underwriting Occurs where the investment bank guarantees the borrower a price for the bonds. *442*

forward A contract in which one party commits upfront to buy or sell something at a defined price at a defined future date. *513*

future Similar to a forward but contract is written in more standardized terms (e.g., prices, maturity dates) and involves commonly traded items (e.g., commodities, currencies). *514*

guaranteed residual value A minimum value for the leased asset that is guaranteed to the lessor. *655*

if-converted method Assumes: i) that the security was converted into ordinary shares at the beginning of the period; and ii) interest and/or dividends were not paid on the security during the year. *548*

implicit interest rate The discount rate that is used, or implied to be used, by the lessor in the determination of the payments in a lease. *656*

income effect Indicates the incremental after-tax income available to ordinary shareholders if a category of potential ordinary shares had been converted into ordinary shares. *547*

incremental borrowing rate The interest rate that the lessee would have to pay on a similar lease or loan. *666*

incremental EPS Quantifies the relationship between the income effect and the share effect for each class of potential ordinary share. *547*

indirect method A method of presenting the statement of cash flows by adjusting profit or loss for the effects of transactions of a non-cash nature, any deferrals or accruals of past or future operating cash receipts or payments, and items of income or expense associated with investing or financing cash flows. *697*

inflation-linked (real-return) bonds A bond that provides protection against inflation. *443*

in-substance defeasance An arrangement where funds sufficient to satisfy a liability are placed in trust with a third party to pay directly to the creditor at maturity. *455*

in-the-money When the value of the underlying instrument in an option contract is favourable to the holder exercising the option compared with letting the option expire. In the case of a call option, this occurs when the underlying price exceeds the strike price; for a put option, it is when the underlying price is below the strike price. *512*

in-the-money (options or warrants) Describes the condition of an option when the market price is favourable for exercising the option; a call option or warrant is in-the-money if the market price of the share exceeds the exercise price. Contrast with **out-of-the-money**. *549*

intrinsic value of an option In a call option, the greater of zero and $(S - K)$, the difference between the market price and the strike price. *512*

investing activities The acquisition and disposal of long-term assets and other investments not included in cash equivalents. *693*

lease An agreement whereby the owner of an asset allows others the use of that asset in return for monetary or non-monetary consideration. *652*

lessee The renter in a lease contract. *652*

lessor The owner of the asset in a lease. *652*

leveraged buyout A purchase where a significant part of the purchase price is raised by borrowing against the acquired assets. *440*

liability A present obligation of the entity arising from past events, the settlement of which is expected to result in an outflow of resources. *394*

market rate See **yield**. *445*

minimum lease payments (MLP) The payments over the lease term that the lessee is or can be required to make. *658*

net income available to ordinary shareholders The company's net income less dividends on preferred shares. *540*

non-cash transactions Activities that do not involve cash. *694*

non-current liabilities Obligations that are expected to be settled more than one year after the balance sheet date or the business' normal operating cycle, whichever is longer. *438*

off-balance-sheet financing Obtaining financial funding without recognition of a liability in the balance sheet. *653*

onerous contract A contract in which the unavoidable costs of fulfilling it exceed the benefits expected to be received. *415*

operating activities The principal revenue-producing activities of the entity and other activities that are not investing or financing activities. *693*

operating lease A type of lease that is not a finance lease. *653*

option A derivative contract that gives the holder the right, but not the obligation, to buy or sell an underlying financial instrument at a specified price. A call option gives the right to buy, whereas a put option provides the right to sell. *512*

ordinary share See **common share**. *476*

originating difference A temporary difference that widens the gap between accounting and tax values of an asset or liability; contrast with **reversing difference**. *589*

out-of-the-money When the value of the underlying instrument in an option contract is unfavourable to the holder exercising the option compared with letting the option expire. In the case of a call option, this is when the underlying price is lower than the strike price; for a put option, it is when the underlying price is higher than the strike price. *512*

out-of-the-money (options or warrants) The condition of an option when the market price is unfavourable for exercising the option; a call option or warrant is out-of-the-money if the market price of the share is less than the exercise price. Contrast with **in-the-money**. *549*

par value shares Shares with a dollar value stated in the articles of incorporation; for preferred shares, the dividend rate may be stated as a percentage of the par value. *477*

par value The amount to be repaid to the investor at maturity. *445*

past service cost The increase in the present value of pension obligations due to initiations or amendment of a pension plan that rewards employees with benefits for services provided in the past. *620*

pension trust The legal entity that holds the investments and discharges the obligations of a pension plan. *615*

permanent difference Arises from a transaction or event that affects accounting income but never taxable income, or vice versa; contrast with **temporary difference**. *584*

perpetual bonds Bonds that never mature. *443*

perpetuity A series of cash flows in equal amounts occurring at regular intervals for an infinite number of periods. *A3*

perpetuity with growth A series of cash flows occurring at regular intervals for an infinite number of periods with cash flows that grow at a constant rate. *A3*

possible A probability of 50% or less. *410*

potential ordinary share A financial instrument or other contract that may **entitle** its holder to ordinary shares. *546*

preferred shares Any shares that are not common shares. *477*

priority The rank of a liability or equity claim when a company liquidates, where higher priority confers preferential payout before other claimants of lower priority. *475*

probable The probability of occurrence is greater than 50%. *410*

provision A liability in which there is some uncertainty as to the timing or amount of payment. *395*

put option See **option**. *512*

recaptured depreciation The taxable income recorded for the reversal of previous capital cost allowance when the sale proceeds of an asset exceed its undepreciated capital cost. Applies to assets separately identified for tax purposes. *590*

retained earnings A component of equity that reflects the cumulative net income (profit or loss) minus dividends paid. *479*

reversing difference A temporary difference that narrows that gap between accounting and tax values of an asset or liability; contrast with **originating difference**. *589*

sales-type lease A type of finance lease in which the lessor obtains a profit margin on the sale of the leased asset (used in Canadian ASPE). *665*

secured bonds Bonds backed by specific collateral such as a mortgage on real estate. *443*

serial bonds A set of bonds issued at the same time but that mature at regularly scheduled dates rather than all on the same date. *443*

settlement (of a pension) The extinguishment of all or part of an enterprise's pension obligations. *630*

share effect Indicates the incremental number of ordinary shares outstanding if a category of potential ordinary shares had been converted into ordinary shares. *547*

shares authorized The number of shares that are allowed to be issued by a company's articles of incorporation. *478*

shares issued The number of shares issued by the corporation, whether held by outsiders or by the corporation itself. *478*

shares outstanding Those shares held by outsiders. *478*

simple capital structure A capital structure that does not include potentially dilutive securities. Contrast with **complex capital structure**. *539*

stock split An increase in the number of shares issued without the issuing company receiving any consideration in return. *481*

stripped (zero-coupon) bonds Bonds that do not pay interest; stripped bonds are sold at a discount and mature at face value. *443*

swap A derivative contract in which two parties agree to exchange cash flows. *514*

taxable income The amount of income recognized for tax purposes used to compute taxes payable; contrast with **accounting income**. *579*

taxable temporary difference A temporary difference that results in future taxable income being higher than accounting income; contrast with **deductible temporary difference**. *586*

taxes payable method A method that records an amount for income tax expense equal to the tax payments for the current period. *578*

temporary difference Arises from a transaction or event that affects both accounting income and taxable income but in different reporting periods. *586*

terminal loss The tax loss arising from the sale of an asset for proceeds below its undepreciated capital cost. Applies to assets separately identified for tax purposes. *590*

time value of an option The portion of an option's value that reflects the probability that the future market price of the underlying instrument will exceed the strike price. *512*

trade payables Obligations to pay for goods received or services used. *397*

treasury shares Shares issued but held by the issuing corporation; treasury shares are not outstanding. *478*

treasury stock method The process used to determine the share effect for call options and warrants. *549*

undepreciated capital cost (UCC) The net carrying amount of an asset or asset class for tax purposes. *589*

underlying quantity or underlying The value of an asset, an index value, or an event that helps determine the value of a derivative. *511*

vesting date The date when an employee's entitlement to the pension benefits is no longer dependent on continued employment with the company. *620*

warrant A right but not the obligation to buy a share at a specified price over a specified period of time. Can be considered a type of **call option**. *513*

warranty A guarantee that a product will be free from defects for a specified period. *404*

yield The rate of return (on a bond) actually earned by the investor at a particular time. *445*

INDEX

Note: Entries for figures, tables, and footnotes are followed by "*f*," "*t*," and "*n*" respectively.